RECENT RESEARCH ON LADAKH

4 & 5

RECENT RESEARCH ON LADAKH 4 & 5

Proceedings of the Fourth and Fifth International Colloquia on Ladakh

Henry Osmaston & Philip Denwood

(Editors)

MOTILAL BANARSIDASS PUBLISHERS
PRIVATE LIMITED • DELHI

First Asian Edition: 1995

ISBN: 81-208-1404-5

Also available at:
MOTILAL BANARSIDASS
41 U.A. Bungalow Road, Jawahar Nagar, Delhi 110 007
120 Royapettah High Road, Mylapore, Madras 600 004
16 St. Mark's Road, Bangalore 560 001
8 Camac Street, Calcutta 700 017
Ashok Rajpath, Patna 800 004
Chowk, Varanasi 221 001

Typeset in CGTimes by
P. Denwood & H.A. Osmaston

PRINTED IN INDIA
BY JAINENDRA PRAKASH JAIN AT SHRI JAINENDRA PRESS,
A-45 NARAINA, PHASE I, NEW DELHI 110 028
AND PUBLISHED BY NARENDRA PRAKASH JAIN FOR
MOTILAL BANARSIDASS PUBLISHERS PRIVATE LIMITED,
BUNGALOW ROAD, DELHI 110 007

PREFACE

The proceedings of the first international colloquium on Ladakh at Konstanz were published under the title of *Recent Research on Ladakh,* but those of the next two colloquia were published under quite different titles (see next page) which did not make it clear that they constituted a continuing series. Indeed this was not assured until the formation of the International Association for Ladakh Studies in 1987.

To clarify this point and for the convenience of readers and libraries we have decided to revert to the original title of *"Recent Research on Ladakh"* for this volume , and to number it *"4 & 5"* to correspond with the colloquium numbers. Thus there is no volume entitled *Recent Research in Ladakh 2* or *3*.

In view of the wide range of styles and approaches of the authors, and the diversity of secondary sources used, we have not standardised spellings or the transliteration of Tibetan between papers, although in general it follows Wylie.

We are grateful to the School of Oriental & African Studies for providing the majority of the funds for publication, the balance coming from the IALS.

Henry Osmaston & Philip Denwood

THE INTERNATIONAL ASSOCIATION FOR LADAKH STUDIES

PATRON

H.E.The Ven.Kushok Bakula Rinpoche

PERMANENT COMMITTEE

John Bray (U.K.)
John Crook (U.K.)
Studies,
Claude Dendaletche (France)
Philip Denwood (U.K.)
Uwe Gielen (U.S.A.)
Kim Gutschow (U.S.A.)
Patrick Kaplanian (France)
Gudrun Meier (Germany)
Tashi Rabgias (India)
Dieter Schuh (Germany)
Harjit Singh (India)
Manfred Taube (Germany)
Nawang Tsering Shakspo (India)

LEH COMMITTEE

Dr.Nawang Tsering (Chairman),
Central Institute for Buddhist

Leh, Ladakh 194101, INDIA
Sonam Dawa
Dr.Mohamed Din
Rev. E.S.Gergan
Jamyang Gyaltsen
Thubstan Palden
Nawang Tsering Shakspo
Abdul Ghani Sheik
Sonam Wangchuk

Editor & Hon. Sec.: Dr.Henry Osmaston, Finsthwaite Cottage, Finsthwaite, Ulverston, Cumbria LA12 8BN U.K. Tel. & Fax: (-44)-15395-31070

Only in the last decade has Ladakh (northwest India, once known as Little Tibet) been readily accessible for study, but in that short time it has been the focus of much attention by students in many disciplines. These have been attracted by the interest of its physical situation at high altitude in the rain-shadow of the geologically active Himalaya; by the natural ecology of this rugged desert and the skilful adaptations of pastoralism and agriculture; by the sociology, history and cultural tradition, especially as a surviving example of Tibetan Buddhism; and by the problems presented by modern development and conservation. Informal study groups organised international colloquia on Ladakh in 1981 at Konstanz (Federal Republic of Germany), in 1985 at Pau (France) and in 1987 at Herrnhut near Dresden (German Democratic Republic). The proceedings of these have been published*. The 4th IALS Colloquium was at Bristol (UK) in 1989; the 5th at SOAS in London in 1992; the 6th in Ladakh in August 1993. The 7th will be at Bonn in June 1995.

At Herrnhut the International Association for Ladakh Studies (IALS) was formed with an international committee of distinguished scholars. The functions of the IALS are to provide contacts between all who are interested in the study of Ladakh, and to disseminate information about proposed and completed research and publications. To do this the IALS organises colloquia, arranges publication of the proceedings, and publishes an occasional newsletter, "Ladakh Studies". This includes information about conferences, planned and current studies, requests for specific information and help, short reports, publications and general information about Ladakh. The close integration of resources, culture and religion in Ladakh demands a holistic approach, and members of the IALS are concerned with a wide variety of topics. Membership is open to all who are interested in Ladakh; for further information apply to the Hon.Sec.

***D.KANTOWSKI & R.SANDER** (eds) 1983 *Recent Research on Ladakh: history, culture, sociology, ecology.* Weltforum Verlag,Munich.
***C.DENDALETCHE** (ed) 1985 *Ladakh, Himalaya Occidental: ethnologie, ecologie. Recent Research No.2.* Acta Biologica Montana 5, Pau.
***L.ICKE-SCHWALBE & G.MEIER** (eds) 1990 *Wissenschaftsgesichte und gegenwärtige Forschungen in Nordwest-indien.* Dresden Museum of Ethnology.

N.B. The first two are out of print. The third is nearly so; copies are available from:-

Dr.Gudrun Meier, Staatliches Museum fur Volkerkunde,
Japanisches Palais, Karl-Marx-Platz, 8060 Dresden, GERMANY

or from:-

John Bray, 8 Glendall St., Brixton, London SW9 8AJ U.K..

Publication of the 6th is in hand.

The Fourth International Colloquium on Ladakh

Bristol 1989

4TH. COLLOQUIUM

CONTENTS

Introduction

The International Association for Ladakh Studies held its Fourth Colloquium at Bristol University on 31 March - 3 April, attended by over 60 participants, of whom eleven were Indians, including seven from Ladakh itself.

In order to give participants an introduction to the main centres and resources for Ladakhi and Tibetan studies in Britain, a preliminary day was spent in London based on SOAS, where Dr.Philip Denwood described the work of the School and recounted the results of his own research into the strange tale of William Moorcroft's apparent reincarnation in Lhasa. We then visited three sites of special interest to Ladakhi scholars in London.

The first was the British Library Oriental collection where our hosts were Dr.Albertine Gaur and Michael O'Keefe. Several Tibetan and Ladakhi items from their collection were on display, including edicts by the Fifth Dalai Lama, a 19th century register showing levels of taxation in Zangskar, and a set of the *La dvags kyi ag bar*, the newspaper produced by Moravian missionaries in the early years of the twentieth century.

A team of specialists led by Graham Shaw of the India Office Library and Records (now part of the British Library) then showed us a a selection from their collection in Blackfrars Road. Their exhibits included Wlliam Moorcroft's manuscript accounts of his travels in Ladakh in the early 19th century; a lithograph of Hemis Monastery made by the Schlagintweit brothers in the early 19th century; and A.H.Francke's draft typescript for a third projected volume of the *Antiquities of Indian Tibet* which was never published. The portfolio of "*Wise Drawings*" was perhaps the most impressive item at the India Office. These large maps with pictorial embellishments illustrate the routes from Leh to Lhasa and along the Zangskar valley with drawings and paintings of the main monasteries and other features on the way. They are the work of an unknown Tibetan or Ladakhi artist, but are named after their reputed collector, probably James Fownes Norton Wise who was in India from 1856.

Finally, at the Victoria & Albert Museum, John Clarke arranged a special showing of the whole collection of Ladakhi and Tibetan metalwork and thangkas not normally on view. It was a great privilege to see behind the scenes at the Museum and to gain an appreciation of the breadth of its collection, only a small part of which is put on display at any one time.

At Bristol twenty-five papers and audio-visual presentations were given and discussed, starting with the more factual topics of history, archaeology and artefacts, and moving on through social studies, nutrition and health to the more philosophical or debatable fields of development and religion. Nineteen of these are published here.

Prof. Robert Roaf (Liverpool) gave us a fascinating glimpse of what Ladakh was like half a century ago when he travelled to Leh, then still functioning in its traditional role as a major *entrepot* for international trade, and preparing what was to be nearly the last of the triennial Lapchak missions to Lhasa, bearing trade and tribute. Mr.Tim Malyon (UK) described the Sumda Gogpo (Maitreya), a wooden statue thought to be over 1000 years old, still deeply revered and feared but in urgent need of conservation.

The economic background to these activities was then illustrated with detailed trade statistics by Dr.Warikoo (Delhi), who emphasised the close links between Ladakh and Baltistan; Mr.John Bray (London) complemented this with an entertaining account of the Indian Government's ambivalent attitude to the Lapchak and relations between Leh and Lhasa[1]. Mr. and Mrs. Howard (UK) described their surveys and dating of Zangskar forts, mostly now in ruinous condition, and of Ladakhi chortens of which there are many fine examples. Mr.John Clarke (V & A) complemented our visit to the V & A by a detailed account of traditional copper- and silver-smithing, and Mr.Tim Malyon (UK) described the Sumda Gogpo (Maitreya), a wooden statue thought to be over 1000 years old, still deeeply revered and feared but in urgent need of conservation.

The interlinked subjects of health, nutrition and agricultural production were next discussed. Prof.Roaf and Dr.Keith Ball (London) described some of the types of chronic illness, especially those associated with the local environmental conditions of smoke and dust such as silicosis and tuberculosis; Dr.Nigel Padfield (UK) recounted the results of nutritional surveys sponsored by the Save the Children Fund in eight villages, which indicated that deficiences existed among certain groups, such as some women and especially young children at the time of weaning. Mr.Tim Malyon showed a video that he had produced in Ladakh to assist in the training of S.C.F. field-workers involved in projects to improve child health and nutrition. There was considerable discussion as to the validity of different criteria for the assessment of nutritional status, illustrated by the way in which FAO standard dietary requirements have been

---

1. see Tib.J. 15, 75-96, 1990

progressively reduced over the last few decades. Another aspect of uncertainty was represented by two contributions on agriculture: one by Dr.Harjit Singh (Delhi) emphasising the severe environmental constraints on production; the other by Dr.Henry Osmaston (Bristol) showing that on the limited areas of good irrigated land the productivity of staple crops much exceeded official estimates, and compared favourably with western world agriculture. However he showed that medical statistics on child growth and adult size indicate that Ladakhis are significantly slighter and shorter than other ethnic groups world-wide, even compared with Tibetans and lowland Chinese. The causes and significance of this are debatable.

Dr.Gudrun Meier from Dresden was especially welcome as she had organised the 3rd colloquium there in 1987; her contribution on social structures in Hunza villages related these to the influences of political relationships, especially with China and with local chiefships such as Gilgit. Mr.Abdul Ghani Sheik recounted the history of the Muslim community in Ladakh, starting with the arrival of Mir Syed Ali Hamdani in 1384 AD and describing how, even within the same family, some brothers might have been Muslim and others Buddhist, sharing a common pot of stew, but with individual morsels distinguished by different coloured strings to show meat conforming to the requirements of different faiths. Mr.Nawang Tsering Shakspo described similar co-existence of Shia Muslims and Buddhists in the village of Kushko, where all the villagers used to join in common dances and offerings to the village deity. Ms. Helena Norberg-Hodge (Bristol) brought us firmly face to face with the social and economic problems which are now posed by various aspects of "Development" in Ladakh, and Mr.Sonam Wangchuk emphasised the particular difficulties facing the younger generation, torn between respect for tradition and the attractions of western style life. Naturally this provoked considerable discussion, but in view of the constraints of environment and communications it was agreed that development must be cautious and "appropriate", such as the technology promoted by the Ladakh Ecological Development Group.

This led naturally into the last session on religion, ritual and myth, launched by Dr.Nawang Tsering's discussion of the fate of traditional Buddhist education in present-day Ladakh, and the measures which are in hand to maintain it, spearheaded by the Central Institute of Buddhist Studies and the Ladakh Academy of Arts & Culture, and using such channels as All India Radio transmitting from Leh. Mr.Jamyang Gyaltsen described the practice of Buddhist tantra in Ladakh's gompas, showing that even quite young people take part, and Ms.Amelie Schenk (W.Germany) described and illustrated with a dramatic video the training and testing of Ladakhi oracles[2]. Mrs.Abby Ripley (USA) discussed the importance of food as a ritual, since it plays a major part in so many occasions of social exchange or spiritual entreaty in Ladakh. Mr.Patrick Kaplanian (Paris) explained the classification of the traditional Ladakhi spirits into the categories of *lha, tsan* and *lhu*, and finally Dr.John Crook (Bristol) analysed in terms of social psychology the interactions of both individuals and groups in modern Ladakh, emphasising the stresses arising from monetization, inflation and competition.

Other activities included a reception at Bristol City Museum to mark the opening of a special exhibition of Ladakhi and Tibetan artefacts; photographic exhibitions by Mr.Lofquist (Sweden) and Mr.Malyon (UK); and botanical displays by Mr.Chadwell (UK) who undertakes seed-collecting expeditions in Ladakh. Our foreign visitors were introduced to some aspects of the British cultural heritage during visits to Bath & Wells.

I thank Philip Denwood and John Bray for organising the London activities; the British Library, the Victoria & Albert Museum and the Bristol City Museum for their displays; and John Crook for help at Bristol.

We are very grateful for generous support from the Spalding Trust, the Nuffield Foundation, the British Academy, the British Council, Dr.Keith Ball, Exodus Travel, Mr.John Randall, Himalayan Kingdoms, Bristol University, Wycliffe College and the Ladakh Project.

Finsthwaite Cottage,
Finsthwaite, Ulverston,
Cumbria LA12 8BN U.K.

Henry Osmaston
Research Fellow
University of Bristol

2. *Schamanen auf den Dach der Welt*. Graz, Akad. Druck- u. Verlag. 1993

A SURVEY OF METALWORKING IN LADAKH

*John Clarke**

The metalworkers of contemporary Ladakh may be classified within either of two predominant categories, the *gSer-gar* or goldsmiths and *mGar-pa* or blacksmiths. In general terms there is some differentiation between the materials used and the type of work undertaken by these groups.

The goldsmiths of Ladakh traditionally work the noble metals in addition to brass and copper but never use iron or steel. The name *gSer-gar* also has the meaning of jeweller though there are very few *gSer-gar* who produce only jewellery. The blacksmiths by contrast, though specialising in the making of iron tools and steel stoves, also sometimes produce objects in silver and gold, including jewellery. They also work in copper and brass. Although there is thus considerable overlap, both in the type of objects produced and the metals worked, the blacksmiths spend a much smaller percentage of their time working the noble metals than the goldsmiths.

Blacksmiths produce the hanging waist ornament called *dor-chas,* the vanity set (*son-dus*), *ga'u,* rings, silver teacups, offering bowls and butterlamps. These are all traditionally goldsmith's work. Several blacksmith informants in the Leh area commented that although they had the necessary skills to work gold or silver they were seldom asked to do so. Some attributed this to the ready availability of jewellery in Leh while others believed it was the result of a lack of raw material.

Evidence suggests that the former reason is closer to the truth and that where possible people tend to order fine quality products from the more specialised goldsmiths. Domestic vessels such as beer jugs,teapots and ladles are also sometimes ordered, though again goldsmiths produce more of this type of object.

Both blacksmiths and goldsmiths work for monasteries in addition to secular patrons and those blacksmiths who find themselves carrying out substantial amounts of traditional goldsmith's work may try to call themselves goldsmiths. By this means they hope to change

* .....Indian Department, Victoria & Albert Museum, Cromwell Gardens, London SW7, U.K.

their status and escape the social stigma that is attached to the role of blacksmith, traditionally the lowest class in Ladakhi society, together with the Mon and Bedha. An example of this recent phenomenon, which has probably only started occurring since the early 1980's, is furnished by two blacksmiths working at Spituk. The 54 year old *Shes-rab gTsang-po* and his brother *bSod-nams Thub-bstan* have begun to call themselves goldsmiths on the basis of the large amounts of work undertaken for the monasteries of Matro and Spituk. Together they fabricate ritual objects, musical instruments such as shawms (*rgya-gling*) and the long trumpets, (*dung-chen*), roof ornaments and *mchod-rten* of various sizes. They also recently set stones into new statues at Spituk monastery. Despite this prestigious work, in the spring, when the demand is greatest, they continue to forge and repair iron agricultural tools. Goldsmith's work is only undertaken during the rest of the year. It is also common for blacksmiths to be small-time farmers themselves which allows them to generate extra income.

One of the specialities of the Ladakhi blacksmith is the production of stoves or *thabs* made from sheet steel. A prime source for this production are the steel oil drums imported into the area by the Indian army. Patrons normally bring blacksmiths steel sheets from oil drums or other pieces of corrugated iron. These are beaten roughly into shape over a large stone, usually without the application of heat. Surfaces are decorated with auspicious motifs such as lotus petals, dragons and monster masks in openwork brass or blackened steel which contrast strikingly with the bare metal. Most construction takes place at the home of the craftsman but a final fitting is carried out at the patron's house. A small - roughly 1 metre by 1.5 metre - stove takes on average 20 days to construct. *Gur-phug-pa Don-grub rNam-rgyal* from Stok said that he produced on average 3 such small sized stoves a year. The most elaborate stoves such as the large "range" made by *Shes-rab gTsang-po* and his brother for a family in Spituk in 1987 can take up to 3 months to complete.

Craftsmen and patrons commented that today's stoves are much more elaborate than those of former decades and have only been made since the mid 1960's. They attributed this trend to a general increase of wealth amongst the population. In fact the making of steel stoves in any form appears to be a 20th century phenomenon and may be a unique example of a new Ladakhi craft.

The creation of the stove in its present form is generally credited to Moravian missionaries, who carried their own stoves up to Ladakh at the end of the last century and particularly to the Reverend Joseph Gergan. These new stoves had the advantage of smoke pipes and ovens. It may be that as late as the 1930's even plain steel stoves were rare. This is suggested by Giotto Dainelli who recounts in *Buddhists and Glaciers of Western Tibet* a journey through Ladakh in 1930. At that time he noted that fireplaces in the kitchens of rich men were made of a compacted mud with mouldings and ornamentations in relief.

Blacksmiths also produce large mani or prayerwheels up to 2 metres in height from sheet steel while *mChod-rten* and other ritual objects such as butterlamps are made in brass or copper. In these cases the objects are usually produced in base metals, undecorated and often larger than normal size. Where the order is for a number of objects or the items are themselves large a team of colleagues is gathered by the leading craftsman and travels to the patron to produce the order. This traditional pattern is also followed by the goldsmiths and the patron provides food and lodging in addition to a daily wage. Raw materials are also often provided by the patron. A 60 cm-high brass and copper butterlamp beneath the large clay statue of Guru Rinpoche at Hemis monastery is typical of the plain but competent work of a team of blacksmiths. In this instance it also illustrates the co-operation possible between blacksmiths and goldsmiths. The piece was made by two blacksmiths, *bSod-nams Tshe-ring* from Sabu and *Gur-phug-pa rNam-rgyal* from Stok and the goldsmith *Ngag-dbang Khus-grub* from Timosgang. Most blacksmiths carry out much repair work and sometimes repair categories of object that they do not themselves make.

The techniques used by goldsmiths and blacksmiths are mostly identical in nature and are described by Friedl (1983) and Rauber-Schweizer (1976).

Most goldsmiths work copper and brass in addition to the noble metals and only in a few instances are they solely jewellers, as their name implies. Leh itself is home to the Moslem jeweller Gulam Sultam Chunka who was a trader until the age of 30 and then trained for three years as a goldsmith. After an abortive attempt at making a living in Nubra he set up in the Leh bazaar in 1965 with his brother. The most frequent article he makes is the ornamental women's charmbox or *ga'u* of star or Maltese cross shape decorated with gold filigree and turquoises. Today turquoises and other imitation stones are imported from Jaipur. Before the cessation of the Central Asian and Tibetan trade in the early 1950's turquoise was brought mainly from Iran via Turkestan. This craftsman commented that the designs and finish of such *ga'u* had grown considerably more elaborate in the last two decades with many more gold pieces being commissioned. He also makes the hanging waist ornament called *dod-chas* and the head ornament vanity sets called *son-dus.* The largest market for these is from people living in the Zangskar and Nubra valleys though he also sells rings to the Moslem population of Kargil.

By far the most significant group of goldsmiths are the farmer/craftsmen of Chiling (*Phyi-gling*) in the lower Zangskar valley. This is the only village in Ladakh where the whole male population works metal. It also maintains a unique oral tradition related to its founding at the end of the 16th century by a group of Nepalese craftsmen.

A full discussion of these legends can be found in Rigal (1983). The name of the village which means "place of the foreigner" probably refers to the original group of skilled craftsmen although Rigal suggests it may relate to an earlier settlement by Moslems who have left a small cemetery. Nevertheless the link between the village and Nepalese metalworkers seems secure, both from an examination of contemporary documents and an inscription on the *mchod-rten* outside the Buddha temple at Shey. These metalworkers were evidently invited by the Ladakhi king for the purpose of fabricating images and religious objects. Rigal has examined a number of 17th and 18th century documents which are copies of royal grants of land and other gifts given by the kings of Ladakh in exchange for the building of statues and *mchod-rten.* The unusually high and privileged status of these metalworkers is apparent from these documents and included a tax exemption. It may be contrasted with the position of goldsmiths in Central and Southern Tibet who were regarded as being of an inferior social status despite working the noble metals. The higher social standing of the Ladakhi goldsmith has persisted down to the present day.

Rigal says that the documents referred to state that the 8 metre high copper-gilt statue of the Buddha at Shey monastery was built by 5 Chiling craftsmen under a Nepalese master during the reign of *bDe-ldan rNam-rgyal* (1624-42). Similarly the 12 metre high Maitreya at Basgo was also built by Chiling craftsmen, though during the reign of *Seng-ge rNam-rgyal* (1590-1624). It would also seem likely that they constructed the large *mchod-rtens* in the *Tshogs-khang* of Hemis monastery which date from the 17th and 18th centuries. Outside the Shey Buddha temple there is a *mchod-rten* bearing a brass plate with an inscription stating that it was built by a Nepalese master and two craftsmen from Chiling during the reign of *Seng-ge* r*Nam-rgyal.*

The village of Chiling lies nearly 40 Km up the Zangskar river from the point at which it joins the Indus. Up until 1989 when the road from Nimu was finished raw material in the form of sheet metal and all other goods had to be carried in on the backs of men along narrow and sometimes dangerous paths. The situation was somewhat easier in the winter when the frozen *Chadar* was used, the traditional route along the frozen Zangskar river.

According to the oldest inhabitant (Memele at 80 years in 1987) sheet copper and brass has been brought from Srinagar since at least the start of the present century. The Zangskar river has also been a source of copper and gold in the past. The Chiling craftsmen commented that it was regularly used up until 70 years ago but has been exploited infrequently since then. Pieces of virgin copper up to 2kg in weight were formerly recovered from the river bed and on heating yielded nearly pure copper. Informants said that "river copper" can be detected by the whistle that it emits from under water.

The source for the Chiling craftsmen was the Zangskar river upstream from the village to Zangla. The presence of alluvial copper, wood for the charcoal forges and fertile farmland are reasons given in oral legend for the siting of the village at its present location.

Silver was formerly obtained from ingots of Chinese origin (*yambu*) which passed through Yarkand to Leh. Today's silver is Indian though the further traditional source of broken jewellery, objects and old rupees is also used. Charcoal is obtained from poplar and thorn growing in the nearby villages of Skiu and Kaya while borax for the flux comes from the uplands of Rupshu.

Estimates of the numbers of fully competent craftsmen who might be described as "master craftsmen" fall between 8 and 13 depending on the opinion of different informants. There are also a further 12 who could be described as trainees and who are younger sons or grandsons of the experienced men. The total village population is about 60. Work is carried out mainly at times when there are few agricultural demands as farming forms the basic subsistence economy of the village. In practice this means that most work occurs in the winter or between planting and harvesting during the summer.

The arrangement of the hearth and anvils is typical of those used by both goldsmiths and blacksmiths throughout Ladakh. In front of the worker is the mud-brick hearth with an inner aperture of approximately 20cms containing charcoal. The goatskin bellows or *phud-pa* to one side has an iron nozzle protruding through the hearth wall and is used to fan the charcoal to a red heat for soldering together joints or annealing metal after working. No casting of objects is done except for the simple re-melting of scrap or sheet metal to produce the correct thickness of ingot needed for making handles, vessel rims and the bowls of ladles. All other operations involve the raising and decorating of sheet metal objects using a wide variety of differently weighted and shaped hammers and punches.

Hammers are used in conjunction with either the flat-ended anvil fixed into a wooden beam directly in front of the worker or with the movable anvil based on an A-frame, called "chak-ber". The flat anvil is used for making flat or gently curving surfaces while the chak-ber has two differently shaped removable ends which can produce a corresponding range of curved surfaces. A more detailed description of the tools and anvils used may be found in Friedl (1983).

Craftsmen use their trained eyes when raising vessels or when producing the fine embossed surface decoration. The circles needed for basic shapes are however laid out with a set of dividers before raising starts. Repetitive decoration on some cheaper objects is made by means of striking a strip of metal over bronze or iron dies. These are traded up from Bombay and obtainable in the Leh market. Any fine chasing or embossing is effected by laying the piece on a bed of pitch spread over a wooden board. This arrangement gives support to the metal while absorbing any excess shocks from the hammer blows. Metal can only be worked for 2 to 3 minutes before it becomes necessary to heat it to a red heat to prevent "work hardening" and cracking.

By far the most commonly produced objects are brass spoons and ladles, plain teapots and beer (chang) jugs. During his work at Chiling in the late 1970's Tsetan Bangbol told J.P.Rigal that he made 40 to 50 ladles in a year and the same number of chang and teapots combined. By 1987 the same informant gave the figure of 25 ladles and the same (combined number) of chang and teapots. Sodnams Rinchen stated that he produced 20 tea and chang pots per year while Phuntsog Spalzang said that he made a total of 30 of these objects. It is at present difficult to gauge whether the discrepancy between the earlier and later figures represents a real drop in demand or merely a fluctuation.

Ladles (*thum-bu*) are found in three main sizes ranging from approximately 8cm diameter up to 14 cm and are used for serving any liquid, but especially tea. The man's spoon (*pho-thur*) has the type of round bowl found in other Tibetan areas, the woman's (*mo-thur*) is distinguishable by its narrow ovoid bowl and shorter length. The cheapest form of teapot or "ta-gu" consists of a flat bottomed, round bodied vessel with plain spout and strap handle. Die-hammered repeating decoration is also sometimes found on these functional objects. The most elaborately decorated teapots with dragon handles and spouts called *'brug-lung* are essentially display pieces used at festivals, weddings, or during the visit of an honoured guest. They take on average a month to produce, in contrast to the plain pots which take just over a week. They can cost from 3,000 to 10,000 rupees wheras the plain vessels cost around 500 rupees. The most highly decorated teapots make use of the full range of motifs found throughout the Tibetan world. These include the monster mask or zhi-pa-tra, garuda, kinnara or heavenly musicians, the wish granting jewel and dragons. Such decoration is added to the bodies of vessels in the form of openwork or *repoussé* plaques often in contrasting coloured metals to the main body of the piece. William Moorcroft noticed these teapots in 1820 though the type may be considerably older. When in use teapots are placed on braziers ("mes-lang") filled with smouldering charcoal to keep the contents warm; when not in use they line the shelves of local kitchens. Several interesting examples of these teapots are held by *Rig-'dzin rNam-rgyal bKa'-blon,* a former prominent patron of the village who lives at Changspa on the outskirts of Leh. These include a copper teapot decorated with silver which was made in about 1910 by *mGon-po bKra-shis*, the teacher of *Phun-tshogs dPal-bzang*. This craftsman was described by Marco Pallis in *Peaks and Lamas,* 1940 as "the foremost metalworker of Ladakh" when he met him in 1936. The same patron also keeps an equally fine copy of this teapot made in silver by *Phun-tshogs dPal-bzang* around 1950. The copying of older pieces by a new generation of craftsmen, found throughout the Tibetan world, is one of the mechanisms by which such conservative tradition maintains itself. Other vessels made for the domestic market include silver cups ("sol-car") stands ("sol-tak") and covers ("jhal-chod"), brass beer pots ("chabs-rkyan") and round-bottomed copper cooking pots up to 60cm in diameter.

Although the Chiling craftsmen still make several trips a year to Leh to sell their products, by far the greatest number are ordered on the traditional commission basis. Similarly to the blacksmiths, the village goldsmiths travel to their secular or monastic patrons where they set up their forge and produce the order on the spot. They receive wages of between 60 and 70 rupees per day (1987) together with food and lodging. The family of *Rig-'dzin rNam-rgyal bKa'-blon* who were formerly prominent landholders in the Leh area have patronised leading craftsmen from the village since at least the start of this century. In particular the present *bKa'-blon's* father and grandfather would invite *Phun-tshogs dPal-bzang* and in earlier days his master *mGon-po bKra-shis,* on an almost annual basis to the family home outside Leh.

There they would produce teapots, cups and sometimes ritual objects which would often be held as future gifts or payments to local monasteries for their officiation at family ceremonies. The royal family also patronised the village and several of the fine teapots at the

Stok palace were made by *Phun-tshogs dPal-bzang's* grandfather.

When craftsmen travel to a distant monastery it is often to produce a number of items. In 1981 for example, *Phun-tshogs dPal-bzang* was commissioned to set with precious stones the hat of the large Padmasambhava statue at Chemre monastery. During the same period he made a pair of *rgya-gling* and a pair of long telescopic trumpets or *dung-chen* for the same monastery. Together with his son Ishe Namgyal and his son in law Tsetan Bangbol, *Phun-tshogs dPal-bzang* has constructed *mchod-rten* for many of the more important monasteries in Ladakh. These have included Spituk, Stakna, Chemre, Hemis and Likhir. *mChod-rten,* musical instruments and ritual objects are also made for the chapels of secular patrons. Both production for monasteries and for private individuals continues today. As Chiling is en route from the main areas of settlement in Zangs-dkar to Leh the Zangskar people are able to leave orders on their outward journey to the capital which they collect on their return. Alternatively they are sometimes able to buy finished products which the craftsmen happen to have at the time. *Phun-tshogs dPal-bzang* remembered making three *mchod-rten* during the 1970's for a monastery in Zangskar which he thinks may have been Bardan. In this case monks from the monastery visited the village to collect the pieces of *mchod-rten* which they presumably re-erected with help from their local blacksmiths. Although the Chiling craftsmen do not, as their ancestors did, build statues, they have in the past repaired them. The Buddha image in the main temple in the centre of Leh for example was brought from Tibet in several pieces in the 1950's. *Phun-tshogs dPal-bzang* repaired and regilded it. In addition to the production of ritual and domestic objects the goldsmith of Chiling also make traditional jewellery, charmboxes or *ga'u,* rings, earrings and the hanging waist ornament (*dod-chas*). Lastly it must be mentioned that other goldsmiths have for several generations existed in the villages surrounding Chiling. At present there are two families of craftsmen at Skiu Kaya, and around 6 craftsmen at Sumda Chenpo.

Bibliography

FRIEDL, W., 1983 *Gesellschaft, Wirtschaft und Materielle Kultur in Zanskar.* Sankt Augustin, Konstanz.

RIGAL, J.P., 1983 "Chiling, un village du Ladakh" in D.Kantowski & R.Sander (eds.) *Recent Research in Ladakh* (Schriftenreihe Internationales Asienforum, Band 1), Weltforum Verlag, Munich. .

SCHWEIZER, H.R., 1976 *Der Schmied und sein Handwerk in traditionellen Tibet.* Zurich.

Plates

Clarke Pl.1. Steel stove decorated with brass, early 1980's, kitchen of Standzin Bangmo, Leh.

Clarke Pl.2. *mChod-rten* made in 1981 for the Langto family in Changspa by *Phun-tshogs dPal-bzang* . 1 metre high, copper gilt.

Clarke Pl.3. *Phun-tshogs dPal-bzang* in his winter workshop at Chiling, in 1987.

Clarke Pl.4. Teapot (*'Brug-lung-ma*) by *mGon-po bKra-shis* c.1910. Copper from the Zangskar river and silver, 34 cm. high. Property of *Rig-'dzin rNam-rgyal bKa'-blon,* Leh.

Clarke Pl.5. Detail from no.4, silver plaque with kinnara figure.

Clarke Pl.6. Cup cover, embossed silver by *mGon-po bKra-shis* , 10.5 cm. diameter. Property of *Rig-'dzin rNam-rgyal bKa'-blon,* Leh.

ECOLOGY AND CULTURE in the Adaptive Radiation of Tibetan Speaking Peoples in the Himalayas[1]

John H. Crook[2]

Socioecological study of Tibetan peoples in the Himalayas

All along the Himalayan range from Ladakh to Assam there are scattered groups of people known to Indian anthropologists as Bhotias. These peoples, often to varying degrees acculturated to Indian or Nepalese ways of life and religion, are in fact groups of Tibetan speakers who found themselves to the south of the border when the frontiers were drawn up along the Himalayan range. Their close relationship and origins have often been ignored due largely to the nationalist pressures of the polities wherein they now live, where regionalism in any form has commonly been perceived as a threat rather than as a matter of cultural interest. Since I have spent the last fourteen years making repeated visits to the western Himalayas, especially Ladakh, studying the village culture of the Tibetan speaking Buddhists[3], it seemed of interest to observe in what ways the Ladakhi village culture was similar to or differed from that of other Himalayan Tibetan groups who still retained their basic Buddhist affiliations. A comparative study of this kind suggests two questions: what may the common origins of these similar peoples have been and what produces the contrasts between them?

The patterning of socio-ecological correlations shows the extent to which groups resemble one another and can indicate whether this may be due to convergence from contrasting origins, parallelism or adaptive radiation. Research in which sets of correlations are compared cannot however yield direct evidence for causal arguments and it then becomes important to investigate the causal process that

---

1. The lecture upon which this paper is based was delivered to the Primate Society of Great Britain and the Association for the Study of Animal Behaviour at their joint meeting at the Zoological Society of London Dec 3rd 1992 on the occasion of the award of the Osman Hill Medal to the author.

2. Department of Psychology, University of Bristol, Bristol BS8 1TH, U.K.

3. Crook, J.H and H.A.Osmaston (eds) 1994, *Himalayan Buddhist Villages*. Bristol University, Bristol, and Motilal Banarsidass, Delhi.

underlies such changes.[4]

In the cases studied in this paper there is strong linguistic evidence that the people in question had a common origin on the Tibetan plateau. It is reasonable then to suppose that they also originally lived within a common culture which has changed in divergent ways when migration brought them into environments demanding contrasting ways of exploitation.

As a socio-ecologist with a strong awareness of sociobiological interpretations of social organisations in animals I was naturally especially interested to see how far some predictions of this origin could be confirmed with this selected human population. Animal socioecology is concerned with the comparison of social organisation and life ways of populations living in contrasting ecologies. The differences found in inter-species or intra-species comparisons are often found to be correlated with contrasts in their environment and the populations shown to have undergone an adaptive radiation in relation to differing ecological circumstances or niches. Biologists have developed a sophisticated analysis of the natural selection of the genetic basis for the evolution of social characteristics which may emerge in this process and which may also result from social selection within contrasting demographic regimes.[5]

Primatologists focussing on intraspecies comparisons have emphasised the additional fact that acquired behavioural traits based in social learning are also responsible for contrasts in monkey and ape social organisation and that such proto-cultural traits arise during adaptation to changing ecological and demographic conditions. It has been but a short step to the interpretation of contrasts between human groups in a similar manner thus resurrecting earlier functionalist approaches within social anthropology; based however now upon the sophistication of contemporary socioecological theory.[6]

Some social anthropologists have not responded at all

---

4. Krebs, J. and N. Davies. 1978. *Behavioural Ecology: an Evolutionary Approach*. Blackwell, Oxford.

5. Crook, J.H. 1989. "Socioecological paradigms, evolution and history: perspectives for the 1990s." In : V. Standen and R.A. Foley. *Comparative Socioecology. The behavioural ecology of Humans and other mammals. British Ecological Society Special Publication No 8*. Blackwell, Oxford.

6. See: Alexander, R.D. 1980 *Darwinism and Human Affairs*. Pitman, London. Borgerhoff Mulder, M.B. 1981 "Adaptation and evolutionary approaches to Anthropology." *Man (NS)* 22, 25-41. Boyd, R and P.J. Richerson 1985.*Culture and the Evolutionary Process*. University of Chicago Press, Chicago. Dunbar, R.I.M. 1988. "Darwinising man: a commentary." In: L.Betzig et al. *Human Reproducative Behaviour*. Cambridge University Press, Cambridge.

favourably to the sociobiological revolution in Ethology and its attempt to generalise to human problems. Sahlins[7], Hallpike[8] and Leach[9] have all contributed critical if not disparaging comments on the biologists' endeavour. For many years[10] there has been a prevailing fear among anthropologists of some sort of biological takeover and of a genetic reductionism in the interpretation of culture which might deny validity to analyses of cultural expression based on structuralist approaches. Certainly Ed Wilson's influential book[11] overstated the case for biology but the attempt to rubbish sociobiologiocal studies within anthropology has not been particularly successful. We need to understand the biasses, often of a quite narrowly scholastic nature, which restrict the focus of the questions that are being asked in these contrasting and unhappily competitive investigations.

Disregarding older functionalist and evolutionary argument, social anthropologists have tended to focus on *emic* questions: that is, analyses of what peoples say about their existence and social organisation. This is important for the inherent subjectivity here is a vital aspect of human experience. Yet such an approach offers little in the way of causal interpretation, so-called *etic* analysis.[12] Etic interpretation in this field has had two aspects. In the first, functionalist interpretation asks in what way social form is adapted to environment. The second aspect is the sociobiological one: how far does individual human behaviour influence genetic transmission of inheritable traits? Are strategies for optimising personal genetic fitness observable here?

Now the sorting out of these questions is important for my study because while my work has followed the perspectives of Melvyn Goldstein[13] in offering socioecological and sociobiological perspectives on the lives of Himalayan villagers, Nancy Levine in a very important

---

7. Sahlins, M.D. 1977 *The use and abuse of biology: an anthropological critique of sociobiology*. Tavistock, London.
8. Hallpike,.C.R. 1988. *The principles of social evolution*. Clarendon, Oxford.
9. Leach,E.1991. "The social anthropology of marriage and mating." In: V.Reynolds and J Kellett (eds*) Mating and Marriage*. Biosocial Society Series 3. Oxford University Press, Oxford.
10. For example see Kroeber's early discussions of these issues: Kroeber, A.L. 1952. "The Superorganic." In: *The Nature of Culture* (A.L. Kroeber ed) Chicago University Press, Chicago.
11. Wilson.E.1975. *Sociobiology: the new synthesis*. Belknap, Harvard, Mass.
12. Harris.M. 1968. *The Rise of Anthropological Theory*. Crowell. New York.
13. For example Goldstein, M.1971 "Stratification, polyandry and family structure in central Tibet." *J. Anthropol.* 27, 64-74 and numerous other contributions.

book[14] argues potently that such "materialist approaches not only oversimplify but take attention away from critical facts of historical experience and neglect to focus on social and demographic change that 'cultural' analysis provides." Her approach links emic analysis with studies of social and family organisation in a manner she calls socio-cultural and which she wishes to demarcate sharply from the socio-ecological perspective.

Yet, when I look closely at the fascinating information she provides on a population only a few mountain ranges away from my own, I am struck by the way in which her description provides evidence for both a sociobiological and a socio-ecological perspective in addition to her own. And indeed in a recent paper in preparation co-authored with Joan Silk[15], Nancy Levine seems to be moving towards a less dogmatic stance.

My own approach does not accept the distinction between socio-ecological and socio-cultural approaches stressed in Levine's work. To make this clear I would like to outline the propositions that form the metanarrative to my account and within which hypotheses are framed. The view adopted here, of which my first formulation dates from 1980[16], is closely comparable with William Durham's "coevolutionary" perspective based on a very thorough analysis of some of the same materials.[17]

1) Unless obscured by other factors I would expect individuals to behave in ways that reflect sociobiological principles; that is persons are expected to attempt marital relations which will optimise the transmission of their genes to future generations through reproductive success. While individuals are not likely to have a conscious rationalisation of such a strategy, optimisation is not considered here to be a consequence of genetically determined programmes of behaviour but rather to arise through the expression of personal preferences for certain cultural traits over others which therefore undergo a process of selection analogous to the traditional Darwinian paradigm.

2) People inhabiting differing environments of exploitation are likely to prefer household systems which allow

14. Levine, N.1988 *The dynamics of polyandry: Kinship, Domesticity and Population on the Tibetan border*. Chicago University Press, Chicago.

15. Levine,.N. and J.Silk. In preparation. "When polyandry fails: tests of the causes of dissolutions of polyandrous marriages." MSS. May 1992.

16. Crook, J.H. 1980.*The Evolution of Human Consciousness*. Oxford University Press. See Chapters 8 and 14.

17. Durham, W. 1991. *Co-evolution: Genes, Culture and Human diversity*. Stanford University Press, Stanford.

optimisation of their reproductive success in ways related to the carrying capacity of the environment and their means of exploitation. Observation of the results of living in contrasting household structures over many generations is assumed to be the basis of preference here and to form the roots of value judgements in local cultures.

3) Household circumstances vary with intergenerational contrasts in family size, sex ratio, sexual relations, health, personal longevity and other factors all of which influence the viability of the unit and the reproductive success of its members. Within these circumstances I expect individuals to adopt tactics that attempt to relate to circumstance in such a way as to optimise their genetic advantage in procreation.

4) Human environments are more than situationally given; they are also ideologically constructed. It is not therefore so much the environment itself as the mental representations of it which will determine behavioural preferences. Where these allow effective exploitation and reproduction they may then be described as adaptive. However, if these representations become influenced by ideals that fail to relate functionally to environmental circumstances then the community in question may be described as maladapted[18]. The people then live within a conceptual "ecology of meaning" which constrains individuals to behave in ways that may fail to sustain their reproductive success.[19]

5) These points imply that the involvement of psychological processes in cultural evolution means that adaptation to the environment has not occurred exclusively in the same way as in non-human examples and that individual behavioural adjustment to cultural norms may produce maladaptive rather than adaptive social practices. The partial autonomy of culture from the physical environment will thus always be a potential factor in analyses of the type attempted here.

---

18. Rappoport, R.A. 1982 "Maladaptation in Social systems." In: J.Friedman & M.J.Rowlands (eds). *The Evolution of Social Systems*. Duckworth.

19. See Crook, J.H.1991. "Consciousness and the ecology of meaning: new findings and old philosophies." In: M.H.Robinson and L.Tiger.(Eds). *Man and Beast Revisited*. Smithsonian Institution, Washington. Also *ibid*. 1995. "Psychological processes in cultural and genetic co-evolution." In V.Reynolds & E. Jones.(Eds) *Religion and Survival, biological evolution and cultural change*. Wiley.

Comparisons between Tibetan peoples of the Himalayas

My research team of 1980, backed up by further visits throughout the decade, worked primarily in the Zangskar valley, a remote region of Ladakh in the Indian state of Jammu & Kashmir. The Ladakhi people are ethnically Tibetans and speak a dialect of the Tibetan language. As we have seen similar peoples occupy remote areas all along the northern and central areas of the Himalayan chain penetrating to varying degrees southwards towards the plains.

It seems clear that the Tibetans pushed south and west into the Himalayan region over many centuries and that the origin of the Bhotias therefore lies on the high montane desert region of the Tibetan plateau. Of these peoples particularly detailed studies have been made on Sherpas, Nyinba, and Ladakhis of both the Zangskar and the Indus valleys as well as plateau Tibetans themselves, nomads and agriculturists. In this paper I have have compared the results of our study of social life in Zangskar with that described for certain other areas occupied by related peoples in several ways in order to see in what ways the Tibetans have altered their social form in regions of differing ecology. In this paper I offer four types of comparison:

Intrapopulation comparisons focusing on contrasts in behaviour and tradition between peoples of the same area but who have contrasting occupations and family economy;

Between-time comparisons of social structure of the same populations to detect the nature of change with time and the way these changes are environmentally and culturally influenced;

Interpopulation comparisons focussing on contrasts in behaviour and tradition between peoples with differing ecologies of exploitation and economic resources;

Demographic analysis of the family to see whether individual behaviour in these societies can be described as sociobiologically strategic.

Intrapopulation comparisons

The origin of the Bhotias in Tibet implies that the original form of their society was adapted to the Tibetan plateau where cereal growing on restricted valley farmland was associated with semi-nomadic yak and sheep/goat herding on surrounding pasture. Available accounts of the state of this society prior to the Chinese invasion of 1959 and the consequent cultural holocaust have been prepared mainly from refugee studies in India. However direct field evidence comes from certain populations living in similar ecology in northern Nepal and India.

The prime feature in all these studies is what Goldstein calls the Monomarital family. In brief this term designates the way in which an agricultural estate is socially organised around a single marriage which, depending upon sex ratio and family size, is commonly polyandrous, several brothers co-marrying a single wife. The marriage system is characterised by the following features:

1) Farming estates are located in montane desert on restricted areas where irrigation is possible and where irrigation works are laboriously maintained. In Ladakh such areas of land are relatively small and can accomodate villages of up to thirty houses.

2) Each estate in Zangskar is owned by a single family consisting of several co-married brothers with their single wife and other relatives. In traditional Tibet such estates were leased to such families by large landowners.

3) On the marriage of an eldest son, usually together with brothers, the estate passes into his ownership. In Zangskar this co-marrying group lives in a main house on the estate, the parents and other relatives being accommodated elsewhere on the estate. The marriage in the main house is the only official marriage in each generation. Some sexual liaisons are however established from time to time in other estate dwellings but the offspring of these are not treated as estate inheritors.

4) If there are no sons the estate is inherited by daughters of the main house family who, singly or in a pair, may marry an incoming husband, a *magpa*, commonly a young son from another non-kin estate. He has no rights to the estate but it passes to his sons in the next generation which thus maintains the patriline of the sisters.

5) Informants over a wide area invariably say that this arrangement is to maintain the estate of a family intact from one generation to another. It is argued that a set of brothers is required because much male labour is needed to meet the heavy physical demands of such agriculture. It also implies that the number of mouths, i.e. children, on the estate and within the community is kept low.

We found this system in its basic form in our study area at Stongde in Zangskar where the class structure had been simplified due to the elimination of aristocratic influences following the take-over of the region by the Dogras in the last century. In Tibet proper, however, a class hierarchy imposed complexities. Reconstructions of the traditional village household of Tibet have been made by Goldstein, Aziz and Dargyay based on interviews with refugees in

India.[20]

After 1751 when the system of theocracy under the Dalai Lama was established, the Tibetan polity provided both aristocrats and monasteries with vast estates each of which was farmed by tied serfs on residential units or estates. These supported the families of whom we have spoken. Not only did they have to maintain themselves but in addition there were various forms of taxation imposed on them by landowners and the government. Further, their land had to be cultivated, if not by them as the holders, then by substitutes employed for the purpose.

These Tibetan households could only maintain themselves by employing labour additional to that of the family. This was obtained from a population of landless people known as the "small smoke". Now while the estate holders married polyandrously with great attention paid to marriage appropriateness and lineage, the small smoke married monogamously and by individual choice. The aristocrats could marry in any style they liked but monogamy was common.

In our study area of Zangskar, the aristocrats today are no more than ordinary farmers but the large monasteries own land which is leased out to the estates for cultivation. Polyandry has remained a prime traditional characteristic even in this less pressurising context. However, it is characteristic only of farming families. Relatives in small towns living as merchants, traders or shopkeepers, or employed in government marry monogamously and the inheritance is split per capita among their offspring. Relatives may thus marry and inherit property in different ways depending on the type of household economy within which they find their subsistence.

It is clear then that polyandry is closely associated with a particular pattern of farming subsistence. When individuals move either into other patterns of living or from others into subsistence farming the appropriate marital pattern is assumed.

Polyandry raises a number of questions. Where only one wife marries into a family what happens to other unmarried women? Again, where there are large families, what happens to supernumerary brothers?

The facts from Zangskar are stark. Many women fail to marry at all. They remain in their natal households as additional labour. Some have a lowly status as simple religious. In this culture these women are the prime altruists. Illegitimacy occurs but is rare.

---

20. See review in Durham (Note 17 above) and Crook and Osmaston (Note 3 above).

Brothers that do not co-marry are mainly monks, a few end up as *magpa* husbands. In fact some thirty percent of brothers in Zangskar are monks: a remarkable figure. Since the religious order to which most of them belong favours celibacy we can assume that these men too are reproductive altruists here.

Between-time comparisons

i) **Ladakh**. Statistical data on social organisation in the Himalayas is understandably meagre but in Ladakh I was fortunate to have the genealogical family surveys made by Prince Peter of Greece in 1938[21] in the course of his study of polyandry. We were able to contact these households and bring the genealogies up to date. We found the structural changes between 1938 and 1980 to have been as follows.[22]

Firstly, there has been a change in the physical location of family members. In the traditional household only the co-marrying brothers live with their wife and offspring in the Big House (*khang.chen*). Parents, grandparents, uncles, aunts and non-co-marrying brothers all live in one or several small houses (*khang.chung*). On the marriage of the next generation of brothers there is a musical chairs situation as the family settles in changed accomodation. Often the *khang.chung* are quite far removed from the *khang.chen* and have a limited degree of autonomy. In law the eldest brother in the reproductive generation is considered to be head of household.

By 1981 this system had substantially altered. Due to fresh opportunities for employment in the Leh area, uncles, brothers and even a few of the women could find employment off the farm in the military, tourism, hotels, transportation, trekking and other services apart from some professional careers in medicine, agriculture or administration with the government. All this meant that a cash economy was replacing agricultural subsistence and that wage earners were increasingly independent of the farming life. Brothers could now aford to live separately and, although the farm was maintained, land could be rented for building and cash inflows could be used collectively. The use of the *khang.chung* changed. It became the home of the more or less independent wage earning males who now proceeded to marry monogamously in them. The old elder brother

---

21. Peter, Prince of Greece and Denmark. 1938.*A study of polyandry*. Mouton, The Hague.
22. Crook, J.H. & T.Shakya. see note 27 and chap.23 in Crook & Osmaston, Note 3.

remained in the Big House and his influence thus lasted longer, while cooperation between brothers was reduced. The *khang.chen*, if large, now held families of perhaps two generations. The estate was not so much broken up as reorganised through a diversification of economic activities.

As ecologists will note, one could say that the old system where the farm is limited by carrying capacity has given way to a situation with multiple financial inflows (i.e. a contrast between a *K* and an *r* situation) to individual participants who become potential competitors for control and influence.

These changes have also been influenced by cultural factors. Ladakhis now favour an increase in population which numerous monogamous marriages promotes. This is to increase demographic competition with the local Muslims whose rate of increase may allow them soon to dominate the Ladakhis in local and regional elections. Changes in values are also influenced by the monetization of the economy and the availability of employment producing a new middle class. There is a move away from a stress on collective reciprocality to an individualistic entrepreneurial style in which maximisation of individual wealth rather than that of a subsistence group is becoming the norm.

In the short term these changes mark an adaptation to the increased economic activity in a modernising region. However as the population reaches the economic carrying capacity of an area weak in opportunities for urban employment some positive reassesment of the value of the old farming system may arise. What has been demonstrated here is the manner in which family and estate structure changes in response to economic opportunities breaking the hold of old ecologically based limitations.

ii) **Western Tibet: Purang**. A recent visit to Purang in Western Tibet has given Nancy Levine an opportunity to exame the way in which the imposition of a Chinese communist ideology has affected Tibetan family structure and marriage since 1959.[23] Her brief study reveals a contrasting sequence of changes from those noted from Ladakh.

In Purang, as elsewhere in Tibet, the traditional taxpaying monomarital family was typical but there were also landless peasants who leased land and worked on the estates of others. Formal marriage whether polyandrous polygynous or monogamous was typical for land

23. Levine, N. 1994 "The Demise of Marriage in Tibet:1959-1990." in: *Tibetan Studies, Proc. 6th Sem. IATS*; Oslo, Inst. Comp. Res. Human Cult., Occas. Paper..

holders. Landless people, however, often had no formal marriage of this type but "became involved in consensual relations which did not involve co-residence of spouses." These were however often socially recognised relationships which had given rise to the loose label "monogamy" in previous studies.

Among the land holders marriage was "inevitably" polyandrous where more than one brother was available; although the satisfaction with this arrangement varied greatly between brothers, some of whom established other relations outside the family.

There were three phases of Chinese communist influence. In the first, small collective farms based on existing land holdings were created. Newly linked households were often close kin or associated because some had certain tools and equipment and others different ones. In the second phase communal agriculture was introduced on a wide scale. All land and animals fell under collective ownership and mutual criticism of each person's labour was instituted. Production was shared according to various systems of awarding work points. In the third phase communes were eliminated and both lands and animals redistributed to members of former communes on a per capita basis. The new owners could either farm or lease their holdings but were not entitled to sell them. They could also engage in trade.

Family arrangements responded differentially to these changes in agricultural practice. The first reforms caused the partitioning of the old land holding families and especially the refusal of many women to remain together under traditional conditions. Co-residential marriage became rare. This was assisted by new legal, political and economic reforms associated with the agricultural changes. Basically the changes shifted rights over resources from the original family to the individual who, through scoring high work points, could earn considerable personal reward even within the collective commune system.

In the current post-communal phase households are tending to reform but upon a different principle from the old "monomarital" structure. Households of varying size form around core sets of male and female siblings each of whom has equal rights in the resources they produce and utilise. Children of polyandrous or monogamous liaisons have no greater rights to domestic property than the children of an unmarried sibling.

It is notable that both during the commune period and under the current dispensation parents and sibling still tended to stay together in spite of the break up of the traditional family economy. Groups of relatives in communes could benefit from the work points gained by kin. At the present time when family members stay together the household can retain control over a relatively larger parcel of grouped shares. Although individuals have the right to take shares away or to live separately this is discouraged within a group of relatives. It is clear too that co-residential marriages incorporating childrens' spouses and their land shares could also be mutually beneficial.

In the past the solidarity of polyandrously marrying brothers was stressed whereas today it is the solidarity of all siblings male and female which is emphasised. As in the past consensual out-of-house relations occur but, as before, these are economically of less relevance than the solidarity of the group. Children inherit from a custodial parent wherever that person may live. In conclusion, the old multigenerational polyandrous households have become sibling households each member of which has more of less equal right to the resources of the whole.

From the sociobiological perspective what is of interest here is the extent to which biological kinship still plays a crucial role in these household arrangements. The welfare of an individual's offspring is increased through such collaboration; as is that of the children of close relatives. Kin selection is evidently as important under these changed conditions of rights over resources as it was under the traditional regime.

Interpopulation comparisons

When we look at populations of Tibetan speakers in the Himalayas outside Ladakh we can trace forms of restructuring comparable to the Ladakhi one. The Sherpa moved into eastern Nepal some centuries ago. They farmed an environment characterised by vast slopes of mountains in which the areas for terraced agriculture and grazing were often far apart. Along the huge valleys where they live trade routes wind their way. The economy diversified into trading and transportation and latterly into tourism and mountaineering from which high incomes can be made. According to Haimendorf[24] polyandrous households were originally common, with women arguing in their favour since it meant that at least one husband would be in the household while others were distributed about the far flung fields and grazing areas. Such households were also considered richer than monogamous ones. However, under the dual influence of moralistic notions against polyandry coming from India and Hindu Katmandu and changed economic opportunities, polyandry has almost disappeared amongst Sherpas.

The main factor here seems again to have been the appearance

24. Fürer Haimendorf, C.von 1964. *The Sherpas of Nepal*. Murray, London.

of fresh economic opportunities breaking the need for subsistence on the land alone. One aspect of the change is that the system of inheritance has changed from the passing of the estate intact from one generation to another to a partitioning of estates on the death of the main owner. This has had the sad consequence that old people are often left in poverty instead of being sustained by the family cooperative. In Nepal, there are few large monasteries so that the syphoning off of non-co-husbanding brothers into monastic life was, less pronounced than in Ladakh. The increased competition between brothers in the family may have played a role in promoting a per capita splitting of inherited wealth between generations and hence the deterioration of the old monomarital family.

Other Tibetan speakers in the lower Himalayas continue the Sherpa trend, tending to live monogamously on farms of small size which split between generations. Because of their poor viability as units these estates frequently change hands as farmers try to build up functional estates while their unemployed relatives move to the cities. Soil erosion and agricultural deterioration is widespread.[25]

An entirely different trend is found among the Nyinba however. These people live in high land near the NW frontier of Nepal with Tibet. Due to pressure from people living adjacently at lower altitudes the Nyinba are losing their lower lands and are forced to farm at higher altitudes. Here the agricultural limitations are extreme, approaching those of Ladakh or Tibet proper. The Nyinba remain vigorously polyandrous but their social system has subtle and fascinating differences from that in Zangskar. Levine's outstanding work describes it well.[26]

The Nyinba live in large households in which complex marital arrangements are found. Polyandry may be extreme with many brothers co-marrying. However, unlike Ladakh, a strict tally of relationships and offspring is maintained and wives form favoured liaisons with particular brothers. The household tends to allocate particular quarters to these subgroups. Yet these households do not practice a regular inter-generational subdivision into units inhabiting separate dwellings so that they tend to become pressure cookers with little opportunity for reduction in social stress. Household splitting through partitioning is often an inevitable consequence and provides the anthropologist with an excellent natural experiment which we will

---

25. See review by J.H. Crook, "Explaining Tibetan polyandry: sociocultural, demographic and biologiocal perspectives." Chap.24 in:Crook, J.H and H.A.Osmaston. (Eds), 1994, *Himalayan Buddhist Villages*. Bristol University, Bristol, and Motilal Banarsidass, Delhi.

26. Levine: Note 14 above.

discuss below.

Another peculiarity of the Nyinba is that each household in the past owned a number of slaves who inhabited small houses on the estate. It is fascinating that these slaves, functionally the equivalent of the landless in Tibet, married monogamously, yet, since their emancipation in the twenties, a number of them have taken over abandoned estates and proceeded to farm them while at the same time marrying polyandrously. This is a nice example of a trend reversing the more frequent move from polyandry to monogamy.

A final contrast with Ladakh is due to the absence of large monasteries. Relatively few brothers become monks so that the in-house tensions cannot be relieved by their departure to a reclusive life.

Demographic analysis of the family and sociobiology

We now turn to the question as to whether individuals who marry polyandrously under the traditional regime may be said to be optimising their reproductive potential under the low carrying capacity of montane desert agriculture.

Goldstein's demographic analysis of a population in E. Nepal leaves little doubt that under polyandry population growth in both family and community is restrained. We confirmed this in our demographic analysis of three Zanskari villages. In general, were the frequency of polyandry to fall in such a population and monogamy increase, a very considerable increase in births would be expected. Computer modelling then suggests that where the enviromental carrying capacity is unlimiting (i.e. *r* circumstances) the frequency of monogamy will rise and the reverse obtain as the carrying capacity is in one way or another approached (K circumstances). Field studies tend to confirm this idea as we have seen.

The sociobiological question is whether individuals who marry polyandrously are optimising their reproductive fitness under the circumstances prevailing. Clearly women who do not marry are reproductive altruists here while we would predict co-marrying brothers with a single wife to have a lower fitness than that of monogamous ones each with his own wife.

We have asked two major questions of our Ladakhi data (our data is derived from the genealogical material updated since Prince Peter's research):[27]

a) How do polyandrous marriages compare reproductively with monogamous ones? - i.e. does the parity of the wife differ

---

27. See Crook, J.H. and T. Shakya 1983. "Six families of Leh." In Kantowsky and R. Sander (Eds) *Recent research on Ladakh*. Weltforum Verlag, München.

under these two conditions?

b) Do grandmothers show greater fitness with respect to the number of grandchildren if their own daughters marry polyandrously or monogamously?

Our findings show that :

i) Completed monogamous and polyandrous families on estates differed significantly in size, the mean for polyandrous families being the larger.

ii) A comparison of family sizes in *khang.chen* and *khang.chung* also showed a significant difference.

It follows from these findings that if the strategy is to maximise her reproductive fitness a traditional family wishing to place a daughter in a marital alliance should therefore choose for her a polyandrous unit in a *khang.chen* over any other.

It is of further interest here that *khang.chen* marriages in Zangskar[28] are made by arrangements negotiated by the phaspun, a group of relatives of households of close kin relations. These family groups constitute a clan so that the marriages have significance to the whole lineage and not just for individual family estates. By contrast any monogamous liaisons in the *khang.chung* which are as it were unofficial and in contradiction to the monomarital principle, are not negotiated by the phaspun and are matters of personal choice.

We also found that grandmothers whose daughters married polyandrously have more grandchildren than those whose daughters married monogamously. Grandmothers with polyandrous daughters are thus fitter than those with monogamous daughters.

Turning to the males; men marrying polyandrously are predicted to have a lower fitness than monogamous brothers due to their sharing a common wife. In a recent paper my son and I modelled this situation to demonstrate the numbers of additional children a polyandrous family would have to produce in order for the brothers concerned to have a fitness equal to a monogamous one. Working the figures through our formulation[29] we demonstrated that the family size of polyandrous families could be large enough to eliminate any loss of fitness due to polyandry - but only so long as each brother had equal

---

28. The nature of phaspun in the Indus valley of Ladakh differs in that these relations are not based in kinship. Economic contrasts between Zangskar and Leh seem to be responsible, with the Zangskar situation being the more ancestral one. See Dollfus, P. 1989. *Lieu de neige et de genévriers : organisation sociale et religieuse des communautés bouddhistes du Ladakh*. CNRS, Paris.

29. Crook, J.H. and S. Crook. 1989. "Tibetan polyandry: problems of adaptation and fitness." In: L.Betzig *et al* (eds) *Human reproductive behaviour*. Cambridge University Press, Cambridge.

access to the wife.

In fact equality of access is very unlikely. Both among Zangskaris and the Nyinba younger brothers do less well reproductively. Most children are probably sired by the elder brother. Indeed in Zangskar the potential competition between the eldest and second brother is strikingly reduced by the common practice of sending second brothers into the monkhood. It is as if parents strongly favour the reproductive success of their eldest son.

The age of the wife in both Ladakh and among Nyinba is often such that the younger sons are married to women considerably older than they[30]. Their reproductive opportunities are thus correspondingly reduced further. It is not surprising then that in both Zangskar and among the Nyinba younger brothers commonly opt out of the polyandrous unit either by seeking to become a *magpa* husband or by setting up a separate domus. The question is whether such a move improves their reproductive prospects.

The best evidence comes from data on the partitioning of households. In Zangskar partitioning whereby a brother tries to set up a farming estate on his own is rare. The few farms where this had occured were on poor land and barely viable. Furthermore several important features of Zanskari life favour sustaining the monomarital estate without partition:

i) The intergenerational separation of the household into separate accomodation units around the estate must greatly reduce social tension.

ii) The allocation of many second sons to the large monastic communities further reduces in-house competition between brothers.

iii) The process whereby the inheritance of the intact estate goes from one group of co-marrying brothers to the next favours an attitude of collaboration. It is noticeable that fathers do not know which children are theirs and mothers do not discuss which child has been sired by which father. This seems to be a social device revealing an attitude of mind favouring peace in the house.

By comparison Nancy Levine's data shows partitioning to be common among the Nyinba. This is associated with the following features that contrast strongly with those in Zangskar:

i) The family as a whole occupies a single dwelling and is not spaced out in a variety of accomodations on the estate.

30. The same contrast is found in reports from Tibetan plateau inhabitants at Ding.ri. Aziz. B. 1978. *Tibetan frontier families*. Vikas, New Delhi.

ii) There are few large monasteries in the area to which sons could go.

iii) The inheritance system is more complex. If partition is contemplated the inheritance is divided per stirpes and not according to the more usual Tibetan per capita. This means that if one brother has three sons and another only one the single son gets half the estate while the others get one third of a half each. Clearly in such a context brothers are likely to be concerned about which child is theirs; and this is indeed the case.

Within the packed Nyinba household favouritisms between particular brothers and wife or wives generates tensions which are commonly only resolved through household partition. The question is whether individual tactics tend to sustain fitness during this process.

Levine found that the largest sibling groups were the most liable to partition. A sociobiological prediction is that men will leave polyandrous households if they have been unsuccesful in producing children of their own and if opportunities to improve their reproductive success arise. They may perhaps also leave if the average degree of relatednes among the co-husbands is low.

Levine and Silk[31] show:

i) Prior to partition the most senior husbands are the main genitors of the children

ii) The birth order of co-marrying brothers is a good predictor of partitioning. Younger brothers are more likely to split. Typically while the eldest brother is older than the wife in common the younger brothers are often younger. On average active partitioners are 6 years younger than the wife.

iii) On remarriage partitioners marry women younger than themselves and they do increase their reproductive success. However their lifetime reproductive success remains lower than that of men who remain in polyandrous marriage.

iv) The farms created by partitioning brothers are commonly barely viable and often fail, the property being reabsorbed into the estate of a more successful relative. Some such estates have been purchased by emancipated slaves who apparently make a success of them by marrying polyandrously and making use of the higher labour input available.

Levine and Silk did not find that the relatedness of brothers was related to the probability of partitioning. Nor was there an increase in relatedness when new polyandrous associations were created by partition.

---

31. See Note 15.

Our comparison between Zangskaris and the Nyinba are striking. They show that the social arrangements in Zangskar seem to facilitate the maintenance of the monomarital estate more effectively than among the Nyinba. It seems likely that both ecological and cultural factors may be involved here. Thus one might suspect a more difficult agricultural situation in Zangskar than in the lands of the Nyinba. This could be so but the work has not been done to test it. Historical happenstance and cultural factors are however certainly playing determining roles here. In particular the comparative absence of the cultural and eco-demographic influences of large monasteries in the Himalayas of Nepal may be critical. The presence or absence of these institutions are largely the results of differing historical circumstance determining overall polity and attitudes in these contrasted areas of the Himalayas.[32]

Summary

These studies demonstrate the complexity of the relations between agricultural economics and culture as determinants of the social organisations within which Himalayan peoples live.

It is clear that the form of the household not only relates to the base of exploitation by which the family sustains itself but that as this changes so does the form of the household. Socio-ecological and socio-economic approaches are thus well supported.

We have evidence from at least certain populations that in the traditional farming communities individuals tend to form marital liaisons in ways that sustain their reproductive fitness. Preferences for marital structures are strategic both in the context of individual lives and from the viewpoint of the kinship clan. The traditional polyandrous household does however entail sustaining an uneasy balance between cooperative and competitive behaviours of brothers if socio-economic success in a subsistence economy of low carrying capacity is to be secured. Where opportunities arise brothers faced with low reproductive success will tend to split off and create their own small estates. These have low viability but in the short term do increase the individuals' reproductive success.

It is clear however that in addition to these environmental and demographic factors the broad historical context of life in these households has had a strong, often limiting influence on the expression of both socio-ecological and socio-biological strategy. In particular historical processes of invasion, conquest and political pressure have

32. See further: Ortner, S. 1992 *High Religion: a cultural and political history of Sherpa Buddhism*, Banarsidass, Delhi.

determined the degree to which socially significant ideological institutions, whether Buddhist or Communist, are present. The influence of resulting contrasts in law and custom has effects on patterns of inheritance which in turn influence social struture and individual choice.

We may also argue that while individuals adapt to prevailing cultural constraints, since these are conventions commonly owing more to ideologically based customs than to economic functions, it can and indeed does happen that people may come to behave in ways that are ecologically dysfunctional. Culture may or may not therefore assist ecological adaptation and can be severely maladaptive from a sociobiological perspective. In this context one of the striking features of this account is the way in which the importance of biological kinship reaffirms itself as significant to personal welfare and reproductive fitness under a wide range of sociocultural conditions. This appears to be a stabilising factor reducing the possibility of social chaos and acting as a constraint on the expression of social form

We have in our examples a strong case for attempting to integrate explanatory viewpoints previously isolated under the banners of competing academic perspectives. Each field of enquiry discussed here has a role to play in understanding the lives of these remote villagers. We need to move away from the prejudices of the academy to a wiser consideration of the type of holistic analysis that is needed if we are to a achieve a balanced understanding of the facts before us

Robert Hinde has argued: "any attempt to apply evolutionary theory to human behaviour must come to terms with two issues. First, whilst some human behaviour is primarily influenced by basic propensities of one sort or another, virtually all is influenced by social forces and some is primarily determined by the values and norms attendant upon roles in institutions. The second issue [is to] understand the genesis of the sociocultural structure in all its complexity before attempting to assess the relation between behaviour determined by that structure and inclusive fitness."[33]

This account of the remote village life of the Himalayas is a small move in this direction.

I thank the Harry Frank Guggenheim Foundation and the Nuffield Foundation for support with these field studies.

---

33. Hinde, R.A. 1987. *Individuals, relationships and culture. Links between Ethology and the Social Sciences*. Cambridge University Press, Cambridge (p172).

WILLIAM MOORCROFT AN ASSESSMENT

Philip Denwood*

But for William Moorcroft, Alexander Csoma de Kôrös might well never have taken up the study of Tibetan. The whole cult of Csoma (if I may be forgiven for referring to it as such) might never have arisen in its present form, and the Western study of Tibetan and Mahayana Buddhism would certainly not have got off to such a flying start.

I shall begin by quoting a passage from the writings of another remarkable Hungarian traveller, Arminius Vambery. In the year 1863, heavily disguised as, in his own words, "a genuine Turk and Effendi from Constantinople", he passed through the town of Andkhuy in Afghanistan. Here, he writes,

"An old Özbeg remarked to me that 'even the Feringhi [English] (God pardon him his sins!) would be better than the present Musselman Government'. he added that he still remembered a Hekim Bashi (Moorcroft) who died in his uncle's house in the time of Emir Haydar; that he was a clever magician and good physician; that he might have become rich as he pleased; but with all these advantages he remained unassuming and condescending towards every one, even towards women. I made many enquiries respecting the death of this traveller, and all agreed in their accounts, that he had died of fever; which is indeed far more probable than the story of his having been poisoned."

Well, that is what Vambery thought! But the ghost of William Moorcroft has had some fun with his biographers over the last 150 years. For Moorcroft was one of those people who refuse to die. As such he conforms to a mythic and literary stereotype which, incidentally, is known in Tibetan culture as well as our own.

To Moorcroft's intriguing "life after death" I shall return later. While preparing this paper I soon came to see that it was entirely in keeping with his life before death. Let me then go back to the beginning.

---

* School of Oriental & African Studies, University of London, Thornhaugh Street, Russell Square, London WC1H 0XG, U.K.

Moorcroft in England

The early part of Moorcroft's life is conveniently summarised in the Dictionary of National Biography, from which I quote with some condensation:

"Moorcroft, William, 1765(?)-1825. A native of Lancashire, was educated in Liverpool for the medical profession. While he was a pupil under Dr.Lyon at the Liverpool Infirmary, it was agreed to depute a student to investigate a serious epidemic among the cattle of the district. The choice fell on Moorcroft. Encouraged by the anatomist John Hunter, Moorcroft spent some years in France studying veterinary science. He afterwards settled in London and for some years had a very lucrative veterinary practice. In Kelly's Directory for 1800 his name appears at 224 Oxford Street. He seems to have realised an ample fortune, but he lost largely over patents which he took out for the manufacture of horseshoes by machinery. He therefore readily accepted the offer in 1808 of an appointment as veterinary surgeon to the Bengal army and superintendent of the East India Company's stud at Pusa, near Cawnpore. He advocated the improvement of the native cavalry horse by the introduction of English or Turcoman bone and muscle."

Up to that time Moorcroft had published the following works: English translation of Valli's *Experiments in Animal Electricity*, London 1793; *Directions for using the Portable Horse-medicine Chest adopted for service in India*, London 1795; and *Cursory account of the various methods of shoeing horses hitherto in use*, London 1800.

On his arrival in India, then, Moorcroft had made his mark as veterinary surgeon, professional man and author, and was a would-be businessman and inventor. In the remainder of his life he was to appear in the guises of Government servant, explorer, merchant and commercial agent, diarist and topographer, freelance diplomat, military strategist, intelligence agent and spymaster, and sponsor of linguistic and literary research: a kind of one-man colonial government on the move. Put like that it sounds absurd, but as I shall try to show, Moorcroft in his peculiar way actually managed to carry it off, at least for a time.

Moorcroft's private life is shadowy, probably because of the fragmentary nature of our sources rather than any attempts at concealment. His daughter, born in India in perhaps 1816, was brought up in France by a Mary Moorcroft. On Mary's death in 1820 the girl was sent to England. Meanwhile Moorcroft had a son by another woman at Pusa. The exact status of these two women is unclear to me.

Early interest in the Himalayas

Soon after his arrival in India, Moorcroft was looking towards Central Asia. In 1810 he attended the fair at Janakpur in the Nepal Terai on the lookout for horses and for intelligence of horse-breeding areas beyond the Himalayas. In 1812 he made his first Himalayan journey, in company with Captain Hearsey. Apparently the main aim on this occasion, apart from general exploration, was to investigate sources of high-quality wool in the western Himalayas. Disguised as Hindu pilgrims the pair travelled through Kumaon, then held by the Gurkhas, and crossed the Niti pass to Daba and Gartok in western Tibet. Their disguise was soon penetrated by the Tibetans, who sent them back via Lake Manasarowar. In Kumaon they were again arrested on orders from Kathmandu and escorted back to British territory.

Soon after returning, Moorcroft wrote to the Government in Bengal setting out his views on Franco-Russian ambitions in Central Asia, based on information gleaned in Western Tibet. Starting from the assumption that France and Russia were planning to attack British India, he offered a well-argued, detailed plan of campaign whereby the Franco-Russian armies might march from Yarkand to Kashmir, and thence to Ladakh and Western Tibet, where they would be well-placed to seize the hill states of the Western Himalayas, then controlled by the Sikhs and the Gurkhas. The whole argument, though entirely speculative, was sparked off by Moorcroft's discovery that Russian traders in the guise of Muslims or in concert with Armenians, were building up markets in Kashmir and Western Tibet, and that Russians and Armenians were in the service of the Sikh leader Ranjit Singh.

From this point onwards the subjects of horses, British trade and the Russian threat were closely intertwined in Moorcroft's thinking, and he could not pursue them separately. Suspicion of Russia was to become an obsession, and Moorcroft was one of the early proponents of the so-called "great game" between Russia and Britain in Central Asia. The kingdom of Ladakh, Tibetan in culture but politically either independent or part of the Indo-Afghan sphere, he saw as a pivotal strategic area in any coming struggle.

Moorcroft's main expedition

In 1819 Moorcroft set out on his main journey towards the horse-breeding areas of Central Asia, an expedition from which he was never to return. Accompanying him were a young German, George Trebeck, two Indians, Mir Izzat Ullah and Ghulan Hyder Khan (all three of whom kept journals of their travels), and an Anglo-Indian hindu physician named Guthrie, together wih servants, transport staff, guards and others who swelled the numbers of the expedition to a total of about sixty. The venture was made entirely on Moorcroft's own initiative and largely financed by him, though he was granted leave of absence on full pay. It was in no sense an official mission.

The chronology and itinerary of this journey is briefly as follows:

October 1819: the expedition leaves Bareilly for the Indian Hill States. February 1820: leaves Srinagar (Garhwal). March-August: Moorcroft makes two trips to Lahore and visits Ranjit Singh, the Sikh ruler. 1821-22: arrives in Ladakh, based at Leh, and travels around. Unsuccessful in attempts to get permission to visit Yarkand in Chinese Turkestan. September 1822: gives up attempt to travel to Yarkand. Leaves Leh for Kashmir, arriving in November. September 1823: leaves Kashmir, arriving at Peshawar in December. May 1823: leaves Peshawar for Afghanistan, arriving at Kabul in June. August 1823: leaves Kabul for Balkh and Bokhara. September-December: is obliged to make two detours from Tash Kurghan to Qunduz. Mir Izzat Ullah returns to India. January 1825: arrives at Balkh. February: travels from Balkh to Bokhara. July: makes an excursion from Bokhara to Katta Kurghan and back. Leaves Bokhara and moves south. August: having crossed the Oxus, Moorcroft branches off at Aqchah for Maimana: Trebeck and Guthrie continue to Balkh. Moorcroft reported dead of fever at Andkhuy. September: a body purported to be Moorcroft's is brought to Balkh and buried. Guthrie's death reported a few days later. December: Trebeck reported to have died at Mazar. Ghulam Hyder Khan heads back for India,

The sources

The principal sources for Moorcroft's main journey are his own journals - 28 closely written volumes - 150 letters to Moorcroft and over 200 written by him; numerous notes, drawings and memoranda; as well as journals, notes, drawings and letters of George Trebeck; all amounting to some 10,000 pages and assembled as the "Moorcroft Collection" at the India Office Library and Records, London, where they have been listed and bound in as good order as possible considering their heterogeneous nature. The exact provenance of these materials is discussed in detail by Kaye, and it was mainly from them that H.H.Wilson produced the major work on Moorcroft, entitled *Travels in the Himalayan Provinces of Hindustan and the Punjab, in Ladakh and Kashmir, in Peshawar, Kabul, Kunduz and Bokhara*, published in 1841. Another eight manuscript items, listed by Kaye, are now missing, and since some of them were used by Wilson, the Travels may now be an original source for a few points concerning Moorcroft's journey.

There is also some information available to us which was not used by Wilson. Extracts from the journals of three members of the exedition - Mir Izzat Ullah, Ghulam Hyder Khan and Trebeck - were printed in the *Asiatic Journal*, and letters and news from the expedition appeared from time to time in that periodical and the *Journal of the Royal Geographical Society*. In the Life and Works of Alexander Csoma de Kôrös, by Duka, Csoma's relations with Moorcroft are described, and letters from Csoma and Moorcroft are reproduced. The Bengal Government secret and political records at the India Office Library contain many of Moorcroft's lengthy letters, some of them not duplicated in the main Moorcroft collection.

These sources amount to a vast corpus of material, difficult to use because of its disorganised nature and Moorcroft's bad handwriting, which yet leaves a number of gaps. Moorcroft seems to have kept his journal only when on the move, and unfortunately let it lapse when staying in, for instance, Ladakh, Kashmir, Kabul and Bokhara. These gaps may be partly filled by his letters and notes, but the day-to-day narrative is broken. Nevertheless there is an enormous amount of information occurring in a haphazard manner throughout the manuscripts.

As a straight topographer Moorcroft is not outstanding (though Trebeck is good); nor was he knowledgable about cultural or religious matters; but he had a very keen eye for political and strategic situations, trade movements and frontiers, for people of all classes and their material conditions, and for natural and manufactured products of all kinds. The agricultural and industrial revolutions were in full swing in Britain, and Moorcroft was always on the lookout for unexploited potential.

Anything approaching a complete edition of Moorcroft's papers would be too long to be manageable. Wilson has been forced to cut out large masses of material in order to concentrate on the narrative of the journey, excising especially passages dealing with politics and strategy, and long disquisitions on everything from local architecture to rhubarb-growing and the feasibility of domesticating the Tibetan wild ass for the use of small farmers in Britain. What remains undoubtedly gives an accurate summary of the journey. Errors do creep in - for instance the remark about Englishmen coming as traders in order to take over kingdoms (p. 274) was actually made by the Rajah of Giah and not by the Kalon of Ladakh as stated - but they are rare. What is missing is the richness of the journals and letters - the anecdotes, observations and verbatim conversations which colour in the personalities of Moorcroft and Mir Izzat Ullah particularly.

Moorcroft and his expedition

Wilson had a high opinion of Moorcroft's sincerity and honesty, but he at least partly subscribed to the often-expressed view of Moorcroft as an opinionated, obstinate man leading a wild goose chase amid hostile populations, loaded down with an embarrassingly large quantity of unsaleable trade goods. Moorcroft certainly had his detractors in Government circles; Sir David Ochterlony, British Resident at Delhi for one had no time for him. Trebeck too, according to Sandberg, was under something of a cloud, though I have been unable to verify this aspersion.The whole enterprise bristled with risks - physical, financial and political - and in one of his own letters Moorcroft admits that to fail would cost him his post at the Pusa stud: "To return, *re infecta*, would even now be fatal to my fortunes, and I must push the adventure to its end".

Against these doubts one may range plenty of evidence of the expedition's success. It is obvious from his journals that Moorcroft was endowed with a subtle and resourceful personality. He was an inspirer of warm friendships and great loyalty, and had a genuine feeling for people of many types and classes. Dr.P.B.Lord, who retrieved many of Moorcroft's papers from Afghanistan, writes:

"it is but justice to add that the impression everywhere left by this enterprizing, but ill-fated party has been in a high degree favorable to our national character."

and again

"...on the authority of several Bokhara merchants, who were on terms of intimacy with him during his stay in that city, ... his character was highly appreciated by the king, who frequently sent for him to enjoy the pleasure of his conversation, and conferred on him the privilege, never before granted to a Christian, of riding through the city, and even to the gate of the king's palace on horseback."

and again:

"... it is impossible to hear the warm terms in which poor Trebeck is still mentioned by the rude natives amongst whom he died, without feeling the deepest sympathy in the fate of one who fell 'So young, and yet so full of promise'."

The testimony of Vambery's "Old Özbeg" may be mentioned again in this connection.

Moorcroft's effect is remarkable on Asian rulers, most of whom were far more impressed with him than were his own superiors. He travelled equipped with testimonials and introductions from the appropriate quarters, and often with escorts and friendly intermediates provided by the ruler of the state he had just left. According to a report in the Calcutta Gazette, quoted in the *Asiatic Journal*:

"A very extensive feeling of interest in his adventures seems to have been excited among the different chiefs in that part of Asia. Mir Kammer-ad-din sent a mullah to accompany him through Badakshan ... and forwarded letters from the hill chiefs and heads of the Yusefzais, offering every aid in their power, and assurances of the most friendly welcome. The brother princes of Peshawar wrote singly to the same effect; and Mehr Del Khan and Pir Mohammed Khan engaged to send persons of trust in their employ to meet him on his return, with sufficient escorts to ensure him against all danger on the road."

Naturally most of these potentates were highly suspicious of the expedition to begin with, and no doubt their help was partly given with a view to keeping it under surveillance and speeding its onward journey, but Moorcroft undoubtedly did win over most of the rulers he encountered. Appoaching a ruler with due deference and forwarding presents - usually guns, swords or textiles - he would quickly try to strike up a personal relationship with him. As this developed he would use impressive resources of friendly conversation, offers of medical assistance, reasoned argument, skilful persuasion and where necessary sarcasm and even heavily veiled threats in order to achieve his aims: the furtherance of British trade and access towards the horse-breeding areas of Central Asia.

The approach usually succeeded, even with such unlikely candidates as the king of Bokhara who was intrigued enough with Moorcroft's personality to give him fairly free rein. Ranjit Singh, the Sikh ruler, perhaps sensed a fellow spirit in Moorcroft and regarded him with good humour even when they were at cross purposes; while Moorcroft seems almost to have hypnotised the Kalon (Prime Minister) of Ladakh. He managed to extricate himself from some very awkward situations by his shrewd judgement of people, and was in fact more than a match for many of what he called the "needy and unprincipled adventurers" he met in Central Asia. A ready means of ingratiating himself with any local population as well as its ruler was the offer of medical services, particularly immediate operations for cataract, a disease endemic in those parts.

Moorcroft in Ladakh

An examination of Moorcroft's diplomatic activities in Ladakh will serve to show how Wilson's *Travels* may be filled out by material from the India Office collections, and to set the background for his involvement with Alexander Csoma de Kôrös.

The Ladakhi authorities were naturally suspicious of the sixty-man expedition when it arrived in their country. The verbatim accounts of the first interview between the two parties show them sizing one another up. The Kalon (Prime Minister) at first parried Moorcroft's suggestions of increased trade, vaccination schemes and so forth by saying that they would all have to be referred to Lhasa and to China -"We are tributaries of China". He did in fact write to the Tibetan Government telling them of Moorcroft's arrival and asking advice. A copy of the Tibetan reply exists among Moorcroft's papers. The gambit was the same: the Tibetans reminded the Kalon that they had no authority in Ladakh and that they very much doubted whether the Chinese, if asked, would allow Moorcroft to proceed into Tibet or Chinese Turkestan. This invoking of China in order to put off foreign approaches was a convenient evasive tactic used by Himalayan states which were quite outside the Chinese orbit, including both Ladakh and Bhutan.

Meanwhile Moorcroft and his assistant Mir Izzat Ullah worked hard to improve their position, and they were soon in the confidence of the Kalon, despite several plots against them. Moorcroft was determined to put Ladakh's relations with the British Government onto some formal basis and from the first interview had impressed upon the Kalon the advantages of British "protection". He had a good grasp of the political situation.

When visiting Ranjit Singh in 1820 he had naturally mentioned that he hoped to pass through Ladakh. Ranjit Singh immediately asked to whom that country belonged, and was told by a minister that it came under Kashmir, which Ranjit Singh himself had taken fom the Afghans the year before. Mir Izzat Ullah had the presence of mind to interject that any tributes being paid by Ladakh to Kashmir were actually in respect of rent for some lands owned by Ladakh in Kashmir. Ranjit Singh's question had been proof enough to Moorcroft that Ladakh could not be regarded as part of the Sikh empire in any real sense.

From the Kalon of Ladakh Moorcroft obtained letters from Aurangzeb which he forwarded to Calcutta, claiming that they showed Ladakh's real allegiance was to Delhi. Eventually, after long negotiation, he managed to get the Ladakh authorities to sign a "trade agreement" and finally an offer of allegiance to the British Govenment. These seem to have been genuine documents: copies of the Tibetan-language versions are still available. Presumably the Ladakhi Government saw their offer of allegiance as a hedge against the Sikhs or some other aggressor, demanding nothing in return but the payment of the sort of nominal tribute which they were already paying, in theory at least, to both Lhasa and Srinagar.

According to Moorcroft, Ranjit Singh meanwhile made some inconclusive moves to attack Ladakh, inspired by his (Moorcroft's) calling attention to the country in his interview of 1820. He wrote to Ranjit Singh advising him of Ladakh's independence from the Sikhs. Ranjit Singh promptly forwarded the letter to Sir David Ochterlony, Resident at Delhi, and the wrath of the British Government was naturally aroused. It is interesting that Ranjit Singh remained on the best of personal terms with Moorcroft, who believed that the former was under a powerful obligation to him, perhaps because of medical services rendered. The Sikh leader made a point of commissioning Moorcroft to seek some good horses for him in Central Asia, and made every effort to ease his onward journey.

At the same time as all this freelance diplomacy was going on, Moorcroft was gathering intelligence on Russian activities. The story of his interception of a Russian letter to Ranjit Singh is told in the *Travels*. It was this letter, from Count Nesselrod, that he got Alexander Csoma de Kôrös to translate. He also saw letters from Russia to the Ladakhi Government, proposing that a road be built through Ladakh, and he got wind of Russian diplomatic moves in Central Asia. According to his information, the Tsar had sent a mission in March 1821 to Bokhara, asking permission for his armies to cross Bokharan territory to attack Choresmia and possibly Kabul. The Tsar was also stirring up trouble in Chinese Turkestan and had offered a Russian army to the ruler of Kashgar. This information was enough to prompt Moorcroft to devise a new version of the enemy's master plan. According to this, the Russians would establish themselves in Kabul and ally themselves with the Sikhs and with Ladakh. They would then make a two-pronged attack on Chinese Turkestan, one army attacking Kashgar, Yarkand and Khotan direct and the other outflanking the Chinese by striking through Kashmir and Ladakh. This would leave the Russians in possession of Central Asia and put themselves within striking distance of British India. To counter the plan, Moorcroft suggested a British protection of Ladakh and an alliance with Kabul. He supported his arguments with detailed studies of the terrain involved.

Had Moorcroft been active ten or fifteen years later, his Government might have taken some notice of his proposals. As it was, his ideas were too forward-looking and far-ranging to catch their imagination, and his schemes were dismissed as wild theorisings and absurd projects: which, to be fair, is what they often were. At any rate it was Moorcroft's vision of a Central Asia dominated by British influence and trade that gave him the driving force for his expedition. It is doubtful if the simple quest for horses, genuine though it was, would have sustained him in his long and hazardous travels.

Moorcroft and Alexander Csoma de Kôrös

Such is the background to Moorcroft's interest in the Tibetan language. Already in 1816 he was making extensive enquiries in order to try and obtain samples of Tibetan writings from contacts and local rulers in the Himalayas. He acquired a copy of Giorgi's *Alphabetum Tibetanum* but evidently realised that much of the material therein as inadequate and unreliable. In 1823 he wrote a letter to the Asiatic Society in Calcutta from Kashmir, listing the various Tibetan scripts, giving a sketch of the language, and enclosing some specimens of Tibetan drawings and blockprinted pictures. Various pieces of information on the country were included, the report of the letter stating "Mr.Moorcroft has been led to believe, from what he has seen, that the libraries of Lassa abound with matter, which, considering the insulated situation of that country, would surprise the learned in Europe, were they accessible to European research". This letter must have been written after Moorcroft had met Csoma, but before the latter had started work on Tibetan.

At least three factors contributed to Moorcroft's interest in Tibetan. The first was the difficulty of conducting relations with Tibet caused by the policy of rigid exclusion of Europeans, of which Moorcroft had first-hand experience. The second was the immense strategic importance, real or imagined, of both Tibet and Ladakh in the three-cornered game between Britain, Russia and China. The third was the almost unexplored possibility of trade, never far from his mind.

Moorcroft himself had no pretensions to scholarship. He had a good knowledge of French and evidently an adequate working grasp of Persian, though he twice remarks in his journals that his knowledge of Persian leaves something to be desired. At any rate he certainly had a fair estimation of the state of Tibetan studies at the time and an idea of what needed to be done. It is in no way surprising that he saw the possibilities presented by Alexander Csoma de Kôrös when he met him in the Dras valley in July 1822. Here was an accomplished scholar and collector of languages who had just been frustrated in his goal of reaching Chinese Central Asia. Practically penniless, he was in need of support. As a result of past favours received from British institutions and individuals in Hungary and Teheran, he was likely to be favourably disposed to the British interest. Both Moorcroft and Trebeck helped Csoma by showing him the *Alphabetum Tibetanum* and engaging a Tibetan tutor. According to Csoma it was his own idea to devote himself to the serious study of Tibetan: "I communicated my ideas respecting this matter to Mr.Moorcroft who, after a mature consideration, gave me his approbation, favoured me with money for my necessary subsistence, and permitted me to return to Ladak; nay, he recommended me to the chief officer at Leh, and to the Lama of Yangla, in Zanskar".

Moorcroft further recommended Csoma to the British Government and the Asiatic Society in Calcutta, whom he asked for more materials to aid Csoma's studies into Tibetan. From early in 1823 at the latest until at least January 1825, Csoma lived solely off funds provided by Moorcroft out of his own pocket. Csoma always refers warmly to Moorcroft, and altogether it is not difficult to agree with Duka's description of Moorcroft as "his best and first friend".

The end of the expedition

An estimation of the overall success of Moorcroft's expedition is interesting both for its own sake and for its bearing on his subsequent fate. An expedition of up to sixty men had been maintained in good order throughout, and detailed and accurate records and accounts kept. Large quantities of useful information had been gathered, and friendly relations established with many rulers. Moorcroft had kept himself financially above water, having supported the expedition mainly from his own pocket without selling his property or prejudicing the education of his children. According to Lord, who retrieved Moorcroft's last account books, the amount of goods he was carrying, often supposed to be a great embarrassment to him, had been much exaggerated by his critics and had mostly been sold. Although far less than their real value had been obtained, Moorcroft had never intended to make a profit on them but merely to use them as samples of British merchandise.

As to whether he had succeeded in his aim of getting horses, his letter of 17th August 1825, reported in the *Asiatic Journal*, would suggest not. However, this is contradicted by his own journal in which he records sending Trebeck from Bokhara to Balkh "with the stallions"; by Lord who heard that he had obtained up to 100 excellent horses; by Gurudas Sinh's letter stating that valuable horses were acquired at Bokhara and Andkhuy; and by a report in the *Delhi Ukhbar* stating that he had left Bokhara with twelve very fine horses.

Moorcroft's relations with the Government are also of interest. He always knew he had enemies and detractors there, but he could usually count upon support for the genuine gathering of information on his travels. His trip to Western Tibet in 1812 was undertaken without official permission. He was told afterwards that had he asked for permission, it would not have been granted because of the personal hazards involved and the danger of offending the Nepalese Government, but the tone of the letter is friendly and thanks are expressed to Moorcroft for the information he collected. He was not officially rebuked, and the Government continued to supply him with goods intended as presents for various rulers and dignitaries.

His correspondence with Ranjit Singh about Ladakh's independence in 1821 was clearly a mistake and aroused the annoyance of the Government (although Ranjit Singh did not take it too seriously), but they continued to forward him trade goods when asked. Incidentally, if his merchandise had really proved an embarrassment to him, it is hard to see why he several times asked to be sent more. Eventually the Government suspended his salary and asked him to return, but with the proviso that if he had reached Kabul, he was free to continue.

Altogether there seems no reason why Moocroft should have felt that he faced disaster on his return to India, as some have suggested. Given his determination and powers of persuasion, he would have been able to put up a powerful case that the expedition had been a great success.

There are ten apparently independent pieces of evidence suggesting that Moorcroft died, probably of fever, at Andkhuy, and/or that Trebeck died at Mazar. (Andkhuy is now just inside the northen border of Afghanistan; Mazar or Shah Murdan as it was sometimes known is modern Mazar-i-Sharif.)

1. A report of a letter from Aga Hussain, dated Amritsar, 4.11.1825, referring to another letter from Kabul. This stated that Moorcroft had died near "Ankho", and his companion had gone to Balkh, where he had fallen ill.

2. A report of a letter from Trebeck to Wade, dated 6.9.1825, stating that Moorcroft had died at "Andkho" on August 25th. Additional information in the report said that Trebeck was recovering from his illness.

3. A report of a letter from "a respectable native residing at Cabul", evidently the Gurudas Sinh of Wilson's preface, stating that Moorcroft died at "Andkho"; that the body was taken to Balkh where "the second gentleman was", and buried; that Guthrie died a few days later; and that Trebeck went to Mazar and died in December.

4. In 1834, Burnes, visiting Mazar, remarks, "One of our companions, a Hajee, attended him (Trebeck) on his death-bed, and conducted us to the spot where he is laid ..." Burnes evidently spoke to many local people about the fate of the expedition, and supports the "official version" of the story.

5. In 1838, Lord and Wood found at Mazar most of Moorcroft's printed books and some papers. These included a map completed by Moorcroft to within one stage of Andkhuy, and a sketch

of the whole detour via Maimana; also a note of Trebeck's saying "Mr.M.died August 27th". Lord and Wood met a man who was at Trebeck's deathbed and who recalled Trebeck's grief at the loss of Moorcroft.

6. The Reverend Joseph Wolff visited Bokhara in 1832-3. Told in Meshed that Moorcroft had been publicly executed in Bokhara, he made enquiries on his arrival and was told the Moorcroft had died of fever at "Ankhoy", Guthrie and Trebeck at Mazar.

7. Arminius Vambery, the Hungarian traveller, visited Andkhuy in 1863 and met the "old Özbeg" whose remarks I have already quoted. His story was confirmed as a result of many local enquiries.

8. It would appear from the introductory remarks to the pblished extracts of Ghulam Hyder Khan's journal that these were to contain an account of Moorcroft's death, and that this would conform to the generally accepted version. The final extracts were however never actually published.

9. Trebeck's death at Mazar was separately reported in the *Asiatic Journal*.

10. G.T.Vigne met one of Moorcroft's servants at Ghazni in 1836: "I could collect nothing from him but what is already known, respecting that much-regretted traveller, whose name is never mentioned without the greatest respect."

These accounts of Moorcroft's death and other secondary sources are not without inconsistencies and doubts. Different dates, places and modes of death are given. Some of the evidence is provided by Trebeck, "whose *bona fides* we have reason to distrust", according to Sandberg. The doubt is echoed by Holdich, who claims "This story was always regarded with suspicion in India." But these criticisms of Trebeck are unsupported by evidence and are at variance with the picture which emerges from his own and Moorcroft's papers. It is difficult to demolish the accepted version of Moorcroft's death at Andkhuy.

Moorcroft 's "second life"

But, it seems, we ought to try. Our story now moves to Lhasa, the capital of Tibet. In 1846 two French Lazarist missionaries, Father Huc and Father Gabet, arrived in Lhasa from Pekin. They were soon suspected of being spies, and the job of interrogating them was entrusted by the Tibetan authorities to the governor of the Tibetan muslim community, who were descended from Kashmiri traders and still carrying on an active trade with Kashmir via Ladakh. The governor, evidently chosen for the task because of his knowledge of the ways of foreigners, was soon satisfied of their bona fides, but cited in justification for Tibetan suspicions the case of an Englishman named Moorcroft. This man, he said, had arrived in Lhasa where he lived in the disguise of a Kashmiri. After having stayed there twelve years he left, but was murdered en route for Ladakh. Among his effects were found a large number of drawings and maps. This made the Chinese authorities very suspicious.

The missionaries further write:

"One day the muslim governor took us to one of his compatriots, called Nisan, who had long served as a servant of Moorcroft's in Lhasa. He spoke at length of his former master, and the particulars he gave confirmed everything which had already been told to us. Moorcroft arrived in Lhasa from Ladakh in 1826, dressed as a muslim and speaking such excellent Farsi that the Kashmiris of Lhasa took him for one of themselves. He rented a house in the town and lived there for twelve years with his servant Nisan, whom he had brought from Ladakh. He bought several flocks of goats and yaks which he farmed out to Tibetan shepherds in the valleys around Lhasa. Under pretext of visiting these, he travelled freely in order to make his drawings and maps. He never learned to speak Tibetan and had little contact with the people of the country. Finally he was killed by bandits in Western Tibet while returning to Ladakh. The bandits were pursued and caught by the Tibetan Government who recovered a part of his effects, including many drawings and maps. Only then did the Tibetan Government realise that Moorcroft was an Englishman. Moorcroft had given his servant Nisan a letter of recommendation to the British Government in Calcutta, but in the alarm occasioned by the recovery of Moorcroft's papers, he destroyed it."

Huc and Gabet continue:

"These facts were confirmed by the Regent of Tibet, the muslim governor, and several other inhabitants of Lhasa. Before arriving in that city, we had never heard of Moorcroft; it was there that we first heard his name."

The two French missionaries were later disposed to retain their belief in this story despite the official version of Moorcroft's death, as after their eventual return from Tibet to Macao, they had read in a journal from Calcutta a detailed and circumstantial account of their own deaths!

We are asked to believe, then, that Moorcroft, at the age of sixty, presumably faced with the failure of his expedition and disgrace on his return to India, and possibly by the danger of arrest or murder, faked his own death. He then made his own way to Lhasa over a period of some sixteen months, crossing the Himalayas presumably in winter, acquiring on the way a new facility for assuming the guise of a Kashmiri merchant. There he lived till the age of about seventy-two. Is it possible? Substitute most other human names for that of Moorcroft, and the answer must be: just possible, maybe, but highly improbable. Robert Fazy has examined the whole question and concluded that the official version of Moorcroft's death in Afghanistan cannot be demolished, and that the Tibetans, on finding the papers of some undoubted British agent, or of someone who had stolen some of Moorcroft's papers, were mixing the man up with Moorcroft, who had made his incursion into Tibet in 1812. Another possibility is that the man was a Kashmiri, and an agent commissioned by Moorcroft some time between 1820 and 1823, either in Ladakh or Kashmir. Letters or papers bearing Moorcroft's name might have led the Tibetans to assume that the man who had been murdered was Moorcroft himself.

To my mind, the weakest part of the Tibetan version is Moorcroft's assumption of the guise of a Kashmiri. His attempts at disguise in 1812 had been a pathetic failure, and on his own evidence his command of Farsi was not very good before 1825. On the other hand, we know he was willing to try such subterfuges, and in facial appearance many Europeans could pass themselves off as Kashmiris. Another doubt is cast by the evidence suggesting that his expedition had been, not a disastrous failure, but more like a roaring success.

Tibetans are fond of such stories, and have produced some of their own. The sixth Dalai Lama is alleged in a long biography to have survived a bogus death at the hands of the Chinese to live for many years in Mongolia. Having perused Moorcroft's personal papers at length, I am convinced he was perfectly capable of conceiving such an after-life and of attempting to live it out. Whether even he could have actually carried it off, I am not so sure.

MONKS OF MANGTRO GOMPA

*Jamyang Gyaltsen**

In Ladakh, people first settled in valleys along the banks of the Indus river. Buddhism had yet to be established. Misfortune, illness and death were attributed to the anger of spirits, and people tried to appease them. Mountains, trees, rocks and unseen gods were worshipped; animals even were sacrificed. Incense and medicinal ingredients were burnt at sources of water to appease water-dwelling spirits, or *klu*. Misfortune, at this time, was attributed to spirits rather than *karma*.

In the 7th century, Buddhism first entered Tibet from India. In the 8th century, during the reign of king *Khri-srong lde-brtsan*, Indian pandits like Santaraksita and Padmasambhava visited Tibet and Ladakh. Guru Padmasambhava began building the monastery of Samye in Tibet, modelled on Odantapuri Vihara in India. In the night, harmful spirits undid all the work done by humans on the construction of the monastery. Guru Padmasambhava then turned all the spirits into friendly deities of Buddhism in Tibet. From then on, the deities built on in the night from the work humans had accomplished during the day. In this way, the building of the monastery was quickly completed.

At that time, Bon, the original religion of Tibet, was popular. In this religion gods and water spirits, the *lha* and *klu,* were worshipped. Instead of doing away with Bonpo beliefs, Mahayana Buddhism assimilated them and therefore spread easily in Tibet. Many centuries ago Buddhism spread throughout Asian countries. Now, in the 20th century, it is spreading in the west. One of the most important features of Buddhism is that wherever it goes, local beliefs are respected.

In Ladakh and Tibet, Buddhism contains both Hinayana and Mahayana elements. Moreover, the vehicle of Vajrayana helps the individual striving for Buddhahood. Several local traditions were also integrated within the Buddhist tradition. The spirit deities of Mangtro Gonpa do not belong to the Indian pantheon of protective and meditation deities. Because of their skilful means, deities like *Rong-btsan Pe-har rgyal-po,* or *Tshe-ring che-nya,* are considered protective

---

* Professor Jamyang Gyaltsen, Central Institute of Buddhist Studies, Choglamsar, Leh 194101, Ladakh.

deities (*chos-skyong srung-ma*), although they are not **main** protective deities. This paper concerns the origin of the great *Rong-btsan* deities of Mangtro Gonpa.

Mangtro Gonpa is the only monastery in Ladakh belonging to the Sakya tradition of Tibetan Buddhism. The so called *Rong-btsan dkar-dmar* are renowned for the prophecies they make during the religious ceremony of Mangtro Nagrang.

The *Rong-btsan dkar-dmar* first came to Mangtro as protective deities. As they were in intimate contact with the founder of Mangtro gonpa, *bla-ma Drung-pa rdo-rje,* the community of monks here subsequently came to relate themselves to these two deities. They take possession of two monks specially selected for this purpose. Even after the appearance of the deities in the physical form of the monks, the ritual for the presence of *Kye rdo-rje* (Hevajra) continues. They are, moreover, blessed by the Vajramaster (*rdo-rje slob-dpon*) of the gonpa. The appearance of the *Rong-btsan dkar-dmar* in borrowed bodies is a sign of the greatness of Buddhism in Ladakh. The event also links the public with the monastery. Thousands of worshippers throng to Mangtro during the festival of Nagrang. They come with personal problems concerning finance, family well being, and state matters. They consult the *Rong-btsan dkar-dmar* deities, who help to remove all problems and protect worshippers from evil.

The oracle tradition has existed here since the establishment of the monastery. Originally, the two protectors were brothers who lived at a place called Khawa Karpo in Kham (in eastern Tibet). Having become local deities of that area, they became attached to the Sakya scholar *rDo-rje dpal-bzang*. He propitiated them with sacrificial cakes, and when he came to Ladakh, they followed him. The two protectors were violent and strong, and could only be settled in the upper part of the valley.

Every five years, on the 15th day of the 10th month, the two oracles are chosen from among the senior monks. The monks' names are put in a bowl which is slowly whirled around, until two names fall out. If after this is done three times, an individual's name does not fall out, he is never chosen as an oracle. While the selection process is going on, the monks gather and perform Mahakala puja.

Those who are chosen as oracles must undergo proper training. First they must accomplish a one year meditation retreat, propitiate Shri Hevajra, perform sacrificial cake offerings to the Dharma protectors, and various other activities. Then they remain in strict retreat, beginning on Sakya Pandita's Mahaparanirvana Day on the 14th of the 11th month, until the 6th of the 1st month. During the retreat they meditate, mostly on Hevajra. The meditation session is concluded with the offering of sacrifical cakes, *gtor-ma,* to the Dharma protectors in general, and the *Rong-btsan dkar-dmar* in particular. During the retreat the two monks keep very clean and bathe with scented water. Each year they conclude the retreat on the 10th day of the 1st month. As they end the retreat, the *Rong-btsan dkar-dmar* protectors enter their bodies, and they each go into trance. In this trance state they first visit the monastery temple, followed by the shrinerooms of Mahakala. People are then allowed to meet and question them. Next, they go to another Mahakala shrineroom, Chisa, and having been seated on the balcony in front of the shrineroom they meet the Ladakhi public and predict the events of the following year. They choose four men from the crowd to bring piles of juniper from the village of Skyurbuchan, in the lower Indus valley. The juniper is used to remake their own shrines. The four men are given blessings and protective cords, and then sent off. After the selection of the four men, the oracles come out of trance for the day.

On the following day, the 11th, they again go into trance in their rooms. In trance state they leave their rooms, go to the temple and Mahakala shrinerooms, and then give audiences to high lamas and officials. The oracles bestow their old clothes and other articles on these officials, who accept them as talismans. In exchange the oracles are given new clothing and other objects.

On the 12th and 13th, they go into trance again. They meet visitors and make predictions in response to individual questions. On the 14th they enter into trance as before, and in the monastery courtyard they perform religious dances with the other monks who are dressed as Mahakala and surrounding deities, as well as two deer. The individual dressed as Mahakala then performs a rite which the two oracles watch over and assist. From the 11th to the 14th, the oracles come out of trance in the courtyard where they perform religious dances.

On the 15th, the oracles bathe, and then a wrathful face is drawn on their chests and backs. They are clothed in tiger-skin skirts. They are adorned with ornaments of bone and many small relic boxes worn as bracelets and given many years ago by a Ladakhi. A cloth mask with a small opening at the nose, and much hair on the top, is placed over their faces. In their hands they hold a small drum and a wooden rod (struck to call monks together). It is said that on this day the *Rong-btsan dkar-dmar* enter into the men in the form of the transcendant knowledge of Mahakala. The monks and the Vajramaster then perform a special ceremony.

When this is completed, the two oracles enter the temple,

holding above their heads the upper robe of *rDo-rje dpal-bzang*. In ancient times it was said that the oracles would fly into the temple by holding this robe aloft. In the temple they receive a blessing from the Vajramaster and then visit many places; the inner part of the temple, the upper Mahakala shrine, the ancient king's palace ruins, the Mahakala shrine in the lower part of the temple, known as Kalon gonkhang. While visiting these places they meet people and give predictions in reponse to their questions. Returning to the temple courtyard, they take roasted barley flour and throw it in every direction. The amount which falls in any particular direction, indicates which part of the country will have good or bad crops. Finally, the oracles pray for the preservation and increase of lord Buddha's dharma, and for the prosperity of the country. The trance then ends.

Each day, from the 10th onwards, the oracles do their normal daily prayers, make offerings at the various shrines, receive scented water from the Vajramaster. When they are in trance they sometimes run very fast along the edge of the outer walls of the courtyard and the monastery roof, without ever falling. Sometimes they cut their mouth and hands with sharp knives and bleed heavily. The following day, however, no trace of scars or wounds can be found on their bodies.

On the 15th, the oracles go about with blindfolds. It is said that they are able to see through the eyes of the wrathful deities drawn on their chests and backs. This tradition was begun by an ancient Ladakhi queen who wanted to test the oracles' superhuman powers. It is an event which produces great faith.

The two deities predict the future welfare of Ladakhi society. The public receive blessings from the *Rong-btsan dkar-dmar* through the physical medium of the two monks. Those afflicted with problems of body and mind feel relieved.

The ultimate goal of each individual is the removal of suffering. The *Rong-btsan dkar-dmar* of Mangtro help people achieve happiness. They are consulted for help when something is beyond human effort. This has deepened the relations between the monastery and the lay population. According to the teachings of Mahayana Buddhism all religious activities lead to enlightenment. The *Rong-btsan dkar-dmar* deities help in the removal of obstacles on the path to Buddhahood.

The Mangtro *lha* also prophesy coming national political events, and politicians in Ladakh have faith in them. If the *Rong-btsan* deities appear with red ribbons attached to their headgear, this warns the public of impending national disasters; war, plague or famine.

The *Rong-btsan dkar-dmar* deities ensure that no harm comes to the Buddhadharma and to high religious personages. In particular, they ensure the preservation of the Sakya religious tradition, and long life to its head lamas.

The seventh and final day on which the oracles go into trance, is the 8th day of the 2nd month. Early in the morning, servants and horses arrive from the monastery of Hemis and from the king of Ladakh. After bathing and performing morning prayers, they leave the monastery. At a certain place on the way to the upper part of the valley, they go into trance. In trance state they ride on the horses until they reach the regional shrines of *Rong-btsan dkar-dmar,* made of juniper branches. Upon reaching the shrine, they examine the grains contained in a vase inside the shrine itself. This again foretells whether or not the crops will be good in the coming year. Finally, the protectors leave the bodies of the oracles, and are absorbed into the recently changed juniper. This brings to a close the oracles' annual appearance.

ARCHAEOLOGICAL NOTES ON CHORTEN *(mChod-rten)* types in Ladakh and Zanskar from the 11th - 15th Centuries

Kath Howard[1]

Preliminary field work in 1987 indicates that the period from the 11th to the 15th century provided some distinctive and interesting *mChod-rten* shapes which have not been built in more recent times. These have been tentatively classified into five types, the last of which is an assortment of oddities which may, after further fieldwork be capable of being assigned to as-yet unexamined categories.

mChod-rten associated with *Rin-chen-bzang-po*

There are several types of *mChod-rten* which seem to be of an early date and appear to have strong connections with the period of the Second Diffusion (10th-11th centuries).

Rin-chen-bzang-po type

This type is so named on account of local attribution and by Francke. Two good examples of this type are known. One, now considerably more decayed and encroached upon than it appears in the photograph by Francke[2], is at Saspola, where it was referred to by the name of its builder quite spontaneously by the people of the village. The remains of this structure are of mudbrick (400 mm x 260/275 mm x 70/75 mm).

Much better preserved, so that its form may be ascertained clearly, is that at Basgo, called Rag-po (Pl. 1). This is a tall structure consisting of a hemispherical dome placed on a high drum. Both are of mudbrick (300mm x 200mm x 80mm). There are four niches in the drum which itself is hollow. This drum stands upon a square base of three tiers of mortared stone with a prominent ramp up the centre of each side so that the ground plan is like a cross on a square (Fig. 1). The ramps were, no doubt, finished in stucco to give the familiar ladder pattern. The east side is now collapsing into a swampy patch of

---

1. Mrs.K.R.Howard, 27 Clarendon Road, Birmingham B19 9SD, U.K.

2. A.H.Francke: *Antiquities of Indian Tibet*, vol. 1, p.88 & pl. XXXVIb.

ground, revealing the rubble core, but the rest of its structural outline is in reasonable condition. The general shape of drum and dome is clearly like that of ancient stupas in Buddhist Western Himalaya as described by Stein[3]. Originally, of course, this *mChod-rten* would have been surmounted by a harmika and 13 rings or a srog-shing and the whole edifice would have been plastered over and whitewashed. A few traces of mud-plaster still remain. It is possible that relics were placed within the hollow drum beneath the dome.

There is possibly another *mChod-rten* of this type, with stone ladders, at Stok; but it is in such a ruinous condition that little can be seen but the cruciform plan; if it had a drum and dome of brick they have vanished without trace (Pl. 2).

Lotsava *mChod-rten* type

It is remarkable that the *mChod-rten* type associated with the name of *Rin-chen-bzang-po* is not found at Nyarma, the great monastery built by him in the 11th century and possibly destroyed in the 14th century, according to Snellgrove and Skorupski[4]. Here instead we have another type, stated by Ladakhi scholars[5] to be called a "Lotsava *mChod-rten*". This consists of a tall plinth of square or rectangular plan up to six metres in length and 3 metres high, made of mortared stone or river-cobbles. On this large base is set a disproportionately small *mChod-rten* (Pl. 3), or more than one in some cases, which may be of a variety of shapes: *Lha-'bab*, or ladder *mChod-rten* are not uncommon; some have five steps and a dome, others may be a series of square or circular tiers, some have multiple or facetted corners and there may be combinations of different elements. A number have traces of lotus pattern moulding around the upper edge of the plinth. It is in a *mChod-rten* of this type that the frescoes and statue fragments described by Panglung are to be found[6]. He omits to mention the corbels supporting the dome of this *mChod-rten* which are painted to resemble lions, rather like those carved on the temple porches at Wanla, Alchi and elsewhere.

---

3. M.A.Stein: *On Alexander's Track to the Indus*, frontispiece & passim
4. D.L.Snellgrove & T.Skorupski: *The Cultural Heritage of Ladakh*, vol. 1, p.106.
5. I am grateful to Gelong Thupstan Paldan of the Jammu and Kashmir Academy for the information that this type of *mChod-rten* is known to Ladakhi scholars by this name and is considered by them to be of great age and in a style no longer built.
6. J.L.Panglung: "Die Überreste des Klosters Ñar Ma in Ladakh." *Wiener Studien zur Tibetologie und Buddhismuskunde*, Heft 10, Csoma de Körös Symposium.1981.

Nyarma

The sketch-plan of the Nyarma monastery ruins was made by taking compass-bearings and pacing (Fig. 2). It shows all the surviving structures within the enclosure wall. The main concentration of buildings lies by the lake. Buildings A and B were full of the rubble of collapsed walls, but the structure marked Chaitya Hall is clear and is used in the annual winter festival of the modern temple which adjoins it. C was a large separate building with a porch, and E a small apsidal building of the type very common for this period. F, another porticoed temple, has an apse containing a small ruined *mChod-rten*. LS is the vandalised *mChod-rten* shrine with mural paintings. At the centre of the Chaitya Hall stands what appears to be a throne or statue base having lotus patterns about its lower edge and on either side of the entrance the walls hold traces of medallions, such as are found at Tabo[7], another *Rin-chen-bzang-po* foundation, where they contained figures modelled in high relief. The buildings, all of which are of mudbrick (Appendix), stand to a height of about 4 metres and holes for the roofbeams are discernible in some.

Other, but smaller, enclosures are found in Ladakh - according to Ladakhi scholars there were many[8]. The most famous is of course *Alchi Chos-'khor*. Another is at Mundig, of which there remains only a part of of a temple and fragments of the enclosure wall which Francke took to be a degraded *mChod-rten*[9] row. It does indeed look very like at a distance, but close examination shows that it is just weathered bricks (410mm x 260mm x 90/110mm) of the enclosure wall.

Within the settlement at Basgo, at the foot of the approach to the castle there are traces to be seen amongst the houses of what may possibly have been a temple of the type associated with *Rin-chen-bzang*-po and therefore datable to the period of the second diffusion and certainly there are two very decrepit passage *mChod-rten* whose upper parts resemble the *Rin-chen-bzang-po mChod-rten* in shape, though constructed entirely of mud with many niches in the sides, ladders and domes (Pl.4). These are extremely similar in appearance to one at Man-gyu, which is stated by Khosla[10] to have *Rin-chen-bzang-po* associations.

Very fine examples of Lotsava *mChod-rten* are to be seen at

---

7. Francke: *op.cit.* p.38.
8. Information from Gelong Thupstan Paldan.
9. Francke: *op.cit.* p.99.
10. R.Khosla: *Buddhist Monasteries in the Western Himalaya*,. p.71

Stok (Pl.2). They have plinths of large river pebbles set in mud-mortar, or of mud-brick. The brick domes are very badly weathered and the original shape is hard to decipher. One edifice has a larger central *mChod-rten* of brick layered with stone, which may explain why it has kept its shape better than the others, and this is surrounded by eight little brick *mChod-rten* (Fig.3). To the right stand the remains of some kind of ladder *mChod-rten* which may have been of the Basgo *Rin-chen-bzang-po* type, as I have already suggested.

It is worth noting in passing that the *mChod-rten* to which the name *Rin-chen-bzang-po* attaches at Alchi is, in fact of the Lotsava type - a huge plinth, hollow and decorated within like the one described at Nyarma, with a stepped central structure surrounded by four smaller ones.

On the road beyond Stok that leads to the gonpa is a cremation ground with four large and numerous small *mChod-rten* exhibiting a variety of shapes. Some consist of several circular tiers, or alternate square and circular steps. There are several Lotsava type structures, one double.

Although the Gelugpa monastery at Stok was established in the 15th century, tsatsa depicting ladder *mChod-rten* have been found there which Tucci dates to the 10th and 11th centuries.[11]

Although at Sabu the most striking *mChod-rten* is the great passage *mChod-rten, sKu-'dun-bkra-shis-'od-'bar*, there are many interesting structures of other types and greater antiquity. To the north is an area of old houses, many in ruins, and stockpens and threshing floors. Here is to be seen a square pyramid of five levels made of large stones crudely set together except at the corners, where they have been relatively carefully shaped. Below this is another roughly set stone base with squared corners held together by mud-mortar on which stands a brick dome resting on a mortared stone plinth, with a rounded upper dome or possibly a harmika of stone with a layer of mud plaster over it.

It seems to me to be possible that this is in fact the true *Rin-chen-bzang-po*, and the other type was given the name simply because it was old and unusual and nothing was known of its origin. It may be the case that the tall dome on a cruciform base, reminiscent of the stupas of the first millenium described by Aurel Stein, is of a more ancient origin; it is to be found in rock-drawings of the 1st to 9th centuries .

lHa-'bab

---

11. G.Tucci: Indo-Tibetica, vol. 1, p.75.

The *lha-'bab* or ladder *mChod-rten* symbolising the descent of the Buddha from heaven after preaching there to his mother, is a very common form at ancient sites in Greater Ladakh, and occurs as petroglyphs in many parts of the region.

Many are to be found at Nyarma, inside and outside the enclosure wall, erected on the characteristic Lotsava plinth.

At Shey they are also numerous and they are of a distinctive appearance. Tucci speaks[12] of them as being found in association with *Rin-chen-bzang-po* and the *bKa'-gdams-pa*, nowhere else, and describes them as being one of the most interesting things in the region, being co-eval with the second diffusion.

The photographs (Pl.5a & 5b) show the two types found at Shey. Pl.5a shows the more common ladder on a plinth - with rather sketchy ladders, rising over five steps to a shallow dome. Occasionally I came across ones with a band of lotus decoration at the upper edge of the plinth. This example serves to illustrate the method of construction which was a hollow edifice of mudbrick (410/420mm x 270mm x 100mm) with the dome as an integral part, not a separate element. The other type illustrated (Pl. 5b) is constructed in the same way but the steps rise straight out of the desert floor and the ladders are moulded as part of the steps, not stuck on as a debased ornament.

Mani Gsermo

Another *mChod-rten* said to have been built by *Rin-chen-bzang-po* is the Mani Gsermo at Leh. In plan (Fig.4) it has a base which is a square of mortared stone on which is superimposed a circle (A) whose diameter equals the length of the sides of the square. Above this a slope rises to two square tiers and a shallow dome with a *srog-shing* and umbrella of cloth. All except the base is constructed of brick (400mm x 210mm x 100mm) with stone ledges. On each side there are projections; those of the lower tier (B) are embellished with ridges which may represent ladders or pillars. On the upper tier (C), the west side displays a niche containing a seated figure with blue hair and elongated earlobes. The trefoil arched niche and the style of the figure certainly suggest an early date for this structure.

It has a number of other interesting features including the fact that it is painted yellow. It stands at the end of a small ridge below the palace, at the edge of the old town. In front of it is a row of five small *mChod-rten* of the common pattern and which are probably of more recent date flanked by two structures not quite in the same

11. G.Tucci: *op.cit.* p.51.

alignment; one is quite ruined and was described by Francke[13] as a depository for rubbish from which he obtained manuscripts and cremation tablets; the other, of similar pattern, is complete, rectangular rather than square and has two tiers and a dome.

sGo-mang type

A large and elaborate structure which is certainly of great age is the *bkra-shis-sgo-mang* the "many gates" *mChod-rten* at Chanspa (Pl.6). It is built entirely of stone on six levels, on each side of which there are three small doorways or niches, of which the central ones are doorways into narrow courtyards (Fig.5). Behind the wall on each of the two lower levels is a pathway; above this the platforms are solid. The dome is much newer than the rest of the structure; from the photographic evidence of Francke and de Filippi[14], it has certainly been renewed twice this century. The *mChod- rten* is enclosed by a wall of 108 smal*l mChod-rten* .

Francke records a legend that this *mChod-rten* was built by invading Turks or Mongols, an attribution which he noted was spuriously attached to a number of structures of great age and unknown origin. He also points out that *mChod-rten* rows were not built much later than the fifteenth century, a tradition still current among Ladakhi scholars.

The great stepped *mChod-rten* at Shey seems to me to have features in common with Chanspa *bkra-shis-sgo-mang* (Fig.6). It stands by the roadside below Shey castle, west of the ridge (Pl.7). It has three deep steps on which it is possible to walk and a very narrow fourth step. These are all built of brick (300mm x 170mm x 120mm) and paved with random stone slabs and mani stones. On the bottom platform there is only one set of steps, parallel to the edge of the platform. The other three have four sets of steps rising at rightangles to the dome. The steps and niches of the lower platform are flanked by projections with small *mChod-rten* on them and there are larger ones of the same pattern at each corner. The dome is a shallow hemisphere set on a short drum (similar to the one shown in Francke's photograph) joined to the top platform by a moulded ring. Above this rises a the Harmika and 13 square terracotta "rings". There are remains of a mud-brick enclosure wall (brick dimensions as above) and gateway on two sides of the *mChod-rten*. Here, as with Chanspa *bkra-shis-sgo-mang* there is a legend concerning Mongol invaders who, in

13. Francke: *op.cit.* p.75.

13. Francke: *op.cit.* p.80 & pl.XXXI; F.de Filippi: *Himalaya, Karakoram and East Turkestan 1913-1914*, p.200.

this case, are said to have built it to prevent local warriors renewing their strength in a magic spring which rose at this spot. I think it is possible to speculate that there was a wall of 108 small *mChod-rten* here as there is at Chanspa.

The one ancient *mChod-rten* which can be firmly dated is the great *mChod-rten* of Tisseru (Pl.8), which stands in the oasis 2km above Leh and was built by *Grags-'bum-lde* who ruled from 1410 to 1435[15]. It was erected to incapacitate a troublesome demon who lived in a crack in the rock at that point. It is of the *sgo-mang* type and had 108 temples or shrines in it according to the Chronicles of Ladakh[16]. It has a circular stone base on which is a circular stone plinth, stuccoed and decorated with geometric designs and small fragments what may be parts of winged figures. Above rise two square platforms; the first is of mortared stone for half its height above which there are double walls of brick (400mm x 200mm x 100mm) with a narrow passage between. The second tier is all of brick, again with a narrow passageway, and above this is another square tier twice the height of the others, within which there are niches or doorways with timber lintels. There appear to be internal diagonal walls presumably to brace the whole structure which has a rubble core. The fragment remaining at the top may be part of the dome or of a drum.

A mound with the appearance of a miniature Tisseru is to be seen at Shey, in the large concentration of *mChod-rten* and *mChod-rten* rows which lie to the north-east of the village. This mound stands in a hollow and is a much-decayed mass of mudbricks with buttresses inside. There are traces of stone facings and it is just possible to make out the squared sides of a base. It is about 10 metres in length along each side and 7-10 metres high.

Others

At a number of ancient sites other distinctive styles of *mChod-rten* are to be found. For example, the *mgo-chen mChod-rten* at Khalsi are also examples of structures of an ancient form whose construction is laid at the door of the Mongols, an untenable attribution, but one which suggests at least an early date for their erection. There were also *mChod-rten* rows nearby.

At Karsha by the path between the fort and old village, there is a ruined temple of the 11th century type called *lang-thra'o*[17] and above it stands a large and interesting passage *mChod-rten*, which has a

---

15. L. Petech: *The Kingdom of Ladakh C.950-1842*. p.22.
16. Francke: *op.cit*. vol.2, p. 99.
17. According to a monk of Karsha.

tiered structure (Pl.9). Inside it is decorated to the height of the first upper tier and contains lifesize clay busts in recesses.[18] Skorupski states that the architecture and style of painting are practically identical with that of *mChod-rten* at Alchi, which gives this one an early date of approximately 11th century. There is a similar passage *mChod-rten* on the path to the old palace at Zangla, but this is not decorated.

Also in the neighbourhood there are several rows of eight *mChod-rten*, an arrangement I have only found in Zanskar, including one row in a shelter, whose date is not known.

mChod-rten rows or walls have been mentioned in connection with several sites and there are numerous others to be found, for example at Shey where there are rows of 108 and 216 quite close to the mound referred to above. Others are to be found at Taru, and at Ranbirpur, between a point opposite Stakna monastery and Nyarma, and some at Alchi fort, which dates from the 11th century[19]. Rows seem to have been in fashion until the beginning of the fifteenth century: *Khri-gstug-lde* built one at Leh and two at Sabu, perhaps round about 1400[20], of which no traces seem to have survived. Interestingly, his successor, *Grags-'bum-lde* is not said to have built any although he did a lot of religious building.

Another feature at Shey which I have not seen anywhere else is the small stupa mandala close to the large mound (seen in the foreground of Pl.6b). It consists of 108 small mudbrick chortens arranged in a square of 10 x 10, with 2 in the centre of each side. The best-preserved of these much-decayed objects were about 30 centimetres high.

Quite close to the main agglomeration of *mChod-rten* at Shey, but on the south side of the road near the gonpa stands a curious hybrid *mChod-rten*. It rises in tiers, has niches, and rests on a large plinth which is stepped on two sides (Pl.10). It is built entirely of brick (420mm x 230mm x 70mm) like the *lha-'bab* and its upper structure is a large square base then a circular tier with a niche, with another square tier and a dome with a niche. As the photograph shows there are blind arches inside, presumably for lightness of mass, or to economise on bricks. It was possibly intended to have the plinth to the same height on the south side with a third arch; perhaps it collapsed .

At this place I met an old woman who told me an interesting story: it was the custom in her girlhood - very early this century - for village women to go out into the desert amongst the *mChod-rten* to

18. Snellgrove & Skorupski: *op.cit.* vol 2, p.41.

19. Snellgrove & Skorupski: *op.cit.* vol 1, p.30.

20. Francke: *op.cit.* vol 2, p.99.

give birth[21]. This seems to me to have a possible link with the custom of the Ladakhi queens coming to Shey castle when the heir was due to be born.

Decoration

There are recurring decorative motifs to be found on a number of old *mChod-rten* which are not found in the same form, if at all, on edifices of a later date. An interesting form of decoration on a Lotsava *mChod-rten* below the ruins of an old settlement between Takthak and Sakti fort is a little pilaster (Fig.7) which appears to show a design basically similar to that of early column capitals such as those in the Sum-tsek temple at Alchi, which presumably date from the 11th-12th centuries as do the murals[22]. This is the only example of such a column capital used as *mChod-rten* decoration that I have come across.

Lotus decoration has already been mentioned in connection with Shey where it is much in evidence, but examples are to be found at Nyarma and elsewhere. There is a good specimen on an old *mChod-rten* above Tashi Gephel gonpa at Sabu (Pl.11) and some to be seen at Taru on the plinth of a *lha-'bab mChod-rten* near the castle (Pl.12). This *mChod-rten* is one of a very interesting group which appear to be of considerable antiquity. One is of the form - *lha-'bab* on a circular plinth - which Francke found at Gya where he was told it was Mon; in other words it was too old for its provenance to be remembered[23]. The Gya *mChod-rten* also has the lotus motif in the same elongated form. Lotuses are often depicted on rock drawings of *mChod-rten* and one variant of the eight *mChod-rten* types is a cone of lotuses.

mChod-rten at Taru, Sabu (Fig.8), Shey, Nyarma and elsewhere display facetted corners suggestive of the plan of the *sGo-mang*. This design element is certainly not modern and may be derived from the cruciform stepped *mChod-rten*, or may possibly relate to the facetting used in India in Hindu shikaras.

---

21. Ghani Sheikh translated for me, as he did on other occasions, which I acknowledge with gratitude for all his help and friendship.
22. Snellgrove & Skorupski: *op.cit.* vol 1, p.79.
23. Francke: *op.cit.* vol.1,p.62.

Appendix
Brick sizes at Nyarma.
See Fig.2 for location of buildings

Building A	(1)	370mm x 230mm x 90mm
,,	(2)	390mm x 230mm x 90mm
,,	(3)	400mm x 260mm x 90mm
Building B		390mm x 230mm x 90mm
Building C		420mm x 250mm x 100mm
Building E		400mm x 250mm x 100mm
Building F		380/390mm x 230mm x 100mm
Enclosure wall		390mm x 250mm x 90mm

Plates

K.Howard Pl.1: Basgo: *Rag-po.*

K.Howard Pl.2: Stok: Lotsava *mChod-rten* (chorten) with cruciform type at right.

K.Howard Pl.3: Nyarma: Lotsava *mChod-rten.*

K.Howard Pl.4: Basgo: Ancient *mChod-rten*, similar to that at Man-gyu.

K.Howard Pl.5a: *lha-'bab mChod-rten* - plinth type.

K.Howard Pl.5b: Shey: *lha-'bab mChod-rten* (lhaba chorten) - without plinth; stupa mandala in foreground.

K.Howard Pl.6: Chanspa: *bKra-shis-sgo-mang* (tashi goma).

K.Howard Pl.7: Shey: stepped *mChod-rten.*

K.Howard Pl.8: Tisseru.

K.Howard Pl.9: Karsha: passage *mChod-rten.*

K.Howard Pl.10: Shey: hollow *mChod-rten* near gonpa.

K.Howard Pl.11: Sabu: lotus decoration.

K.Howard Pl.12: Taru: *mChod-rten* types: circular plinth (2nd left); *lha-'bab* with lotus pattern (4th from right).

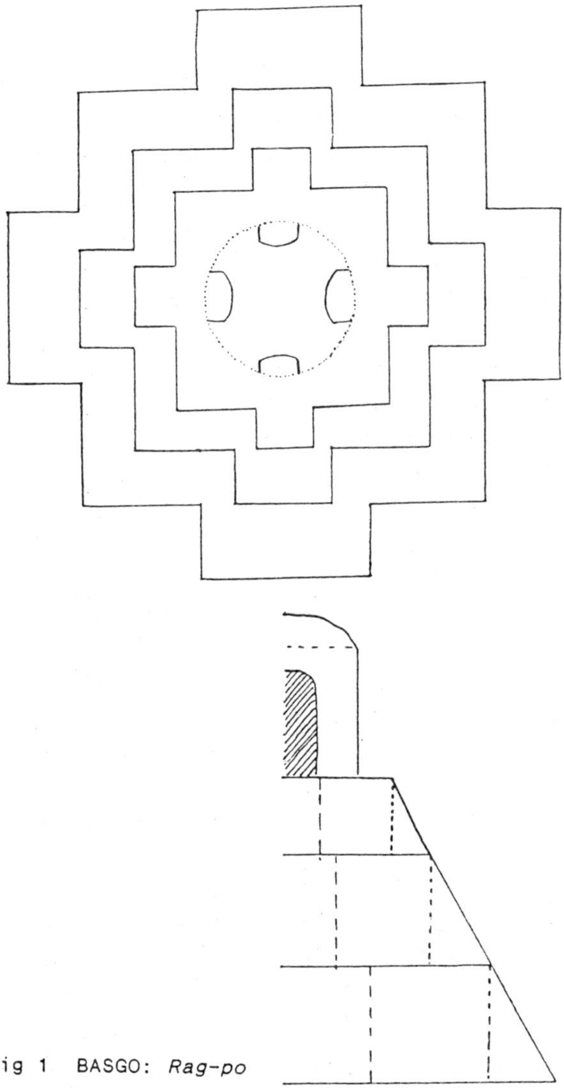

Fig 1 BASGO: *Rag-po*

K.Howard Fig.1: Basgo - *rag-po*.

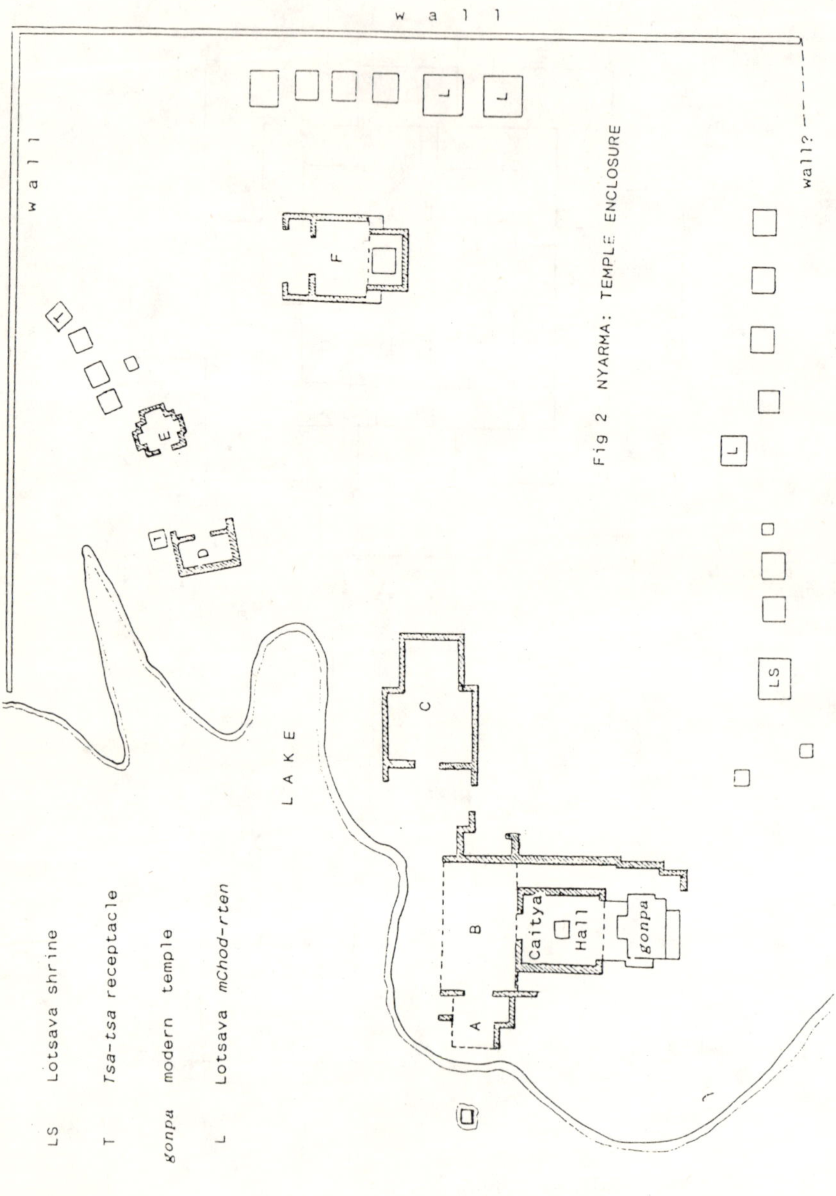

K.Howard Fig.2: Nyarma - temple enclosure.

Fig 3 STOK: LOTSAVA *mChod-rten*

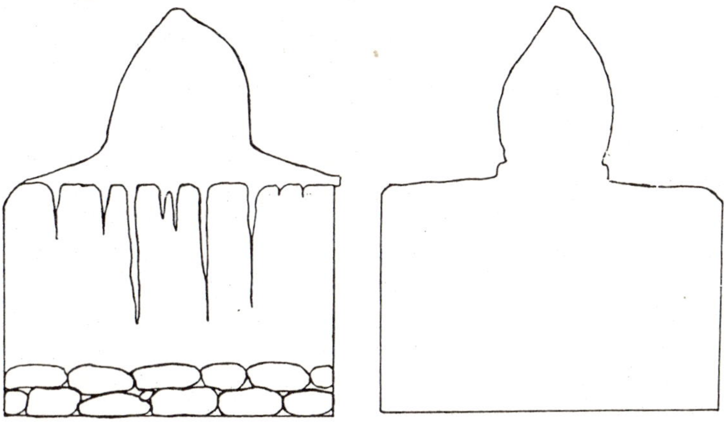

a) mud-brick base on plinth of large pebbles, two dome variations

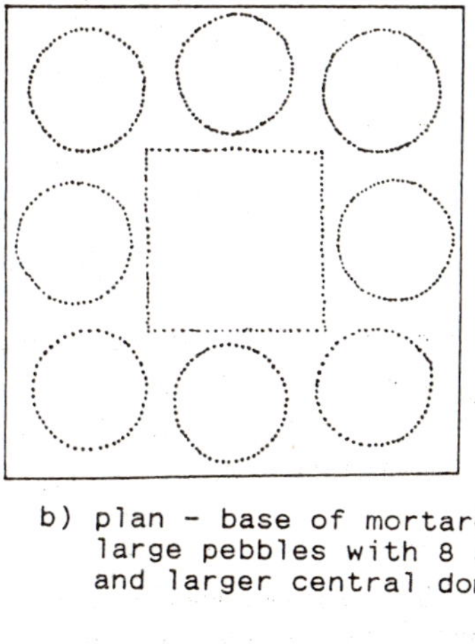

b) plan - base of mortared stone and large pebbles with 8 small domes and larger central dome

K.Howard Fig.3: Stok - lotsava *mChod-rten*

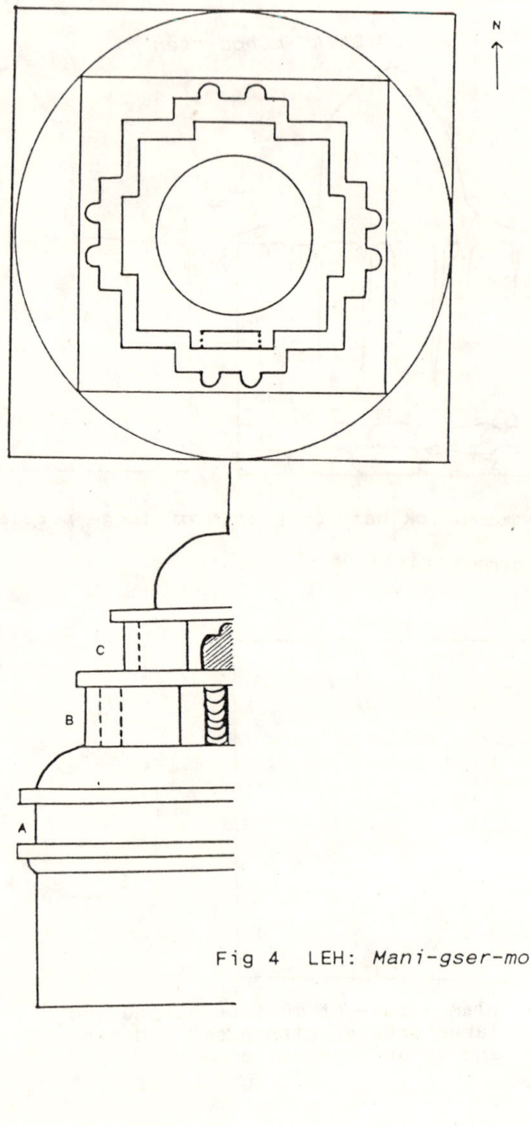

K.Howard Fig.4: Leh - *mani-gser-mo.*

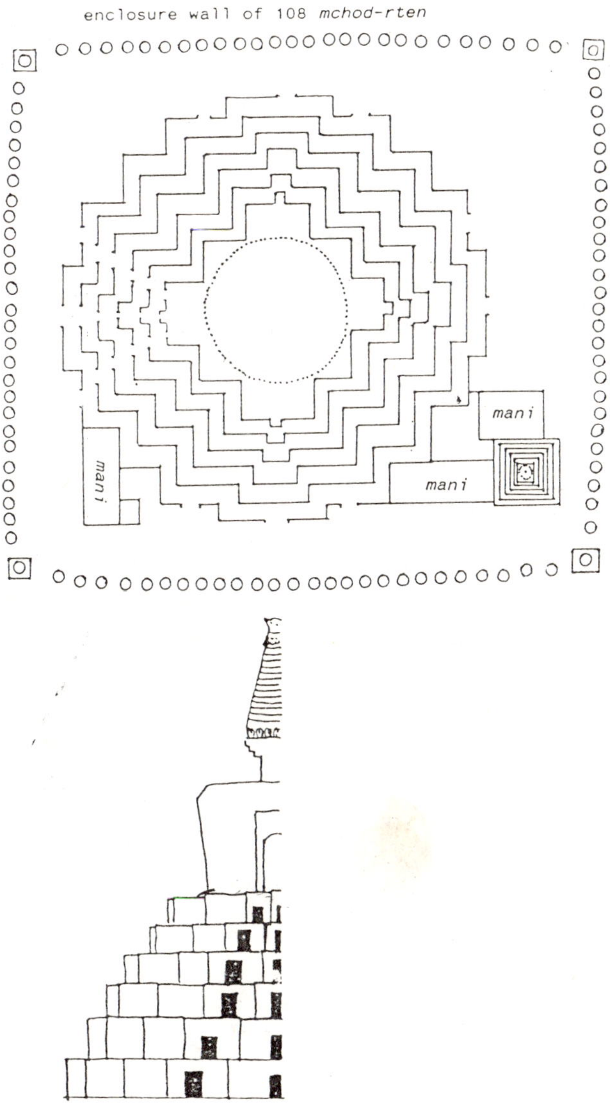

Fig 5 CHANSPA: *bKra-śis-sgo-mang*

K.Howard Fig.5: Chanspa - bKra-shis-sgo-mang.

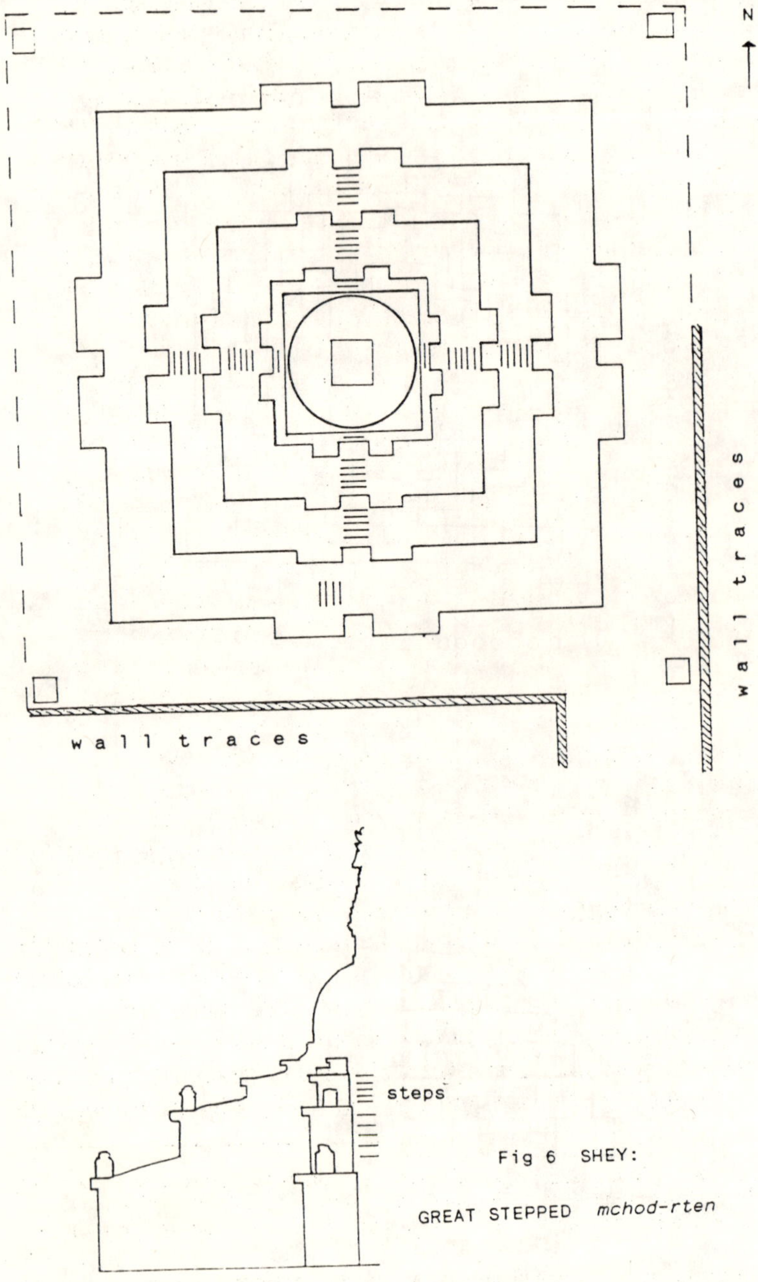

K.Howard Fig.6: Shey - great stepped *mChod-rten*.

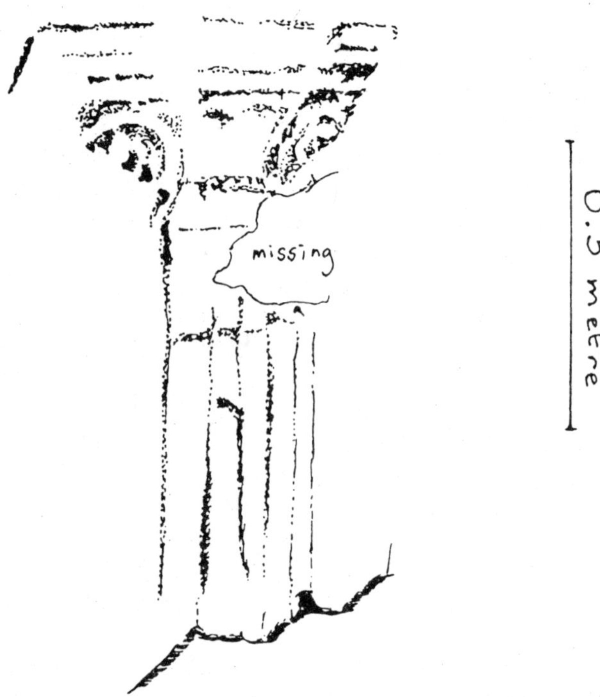

Fig 7 DECORATIVE MOTIF : *mchoc-'rten*

between SAG-TI AND THAK-TAK

K.Howard Fig.7: Between Sag-ti and Tak-thak - decorative motif on *mChod-rten*.

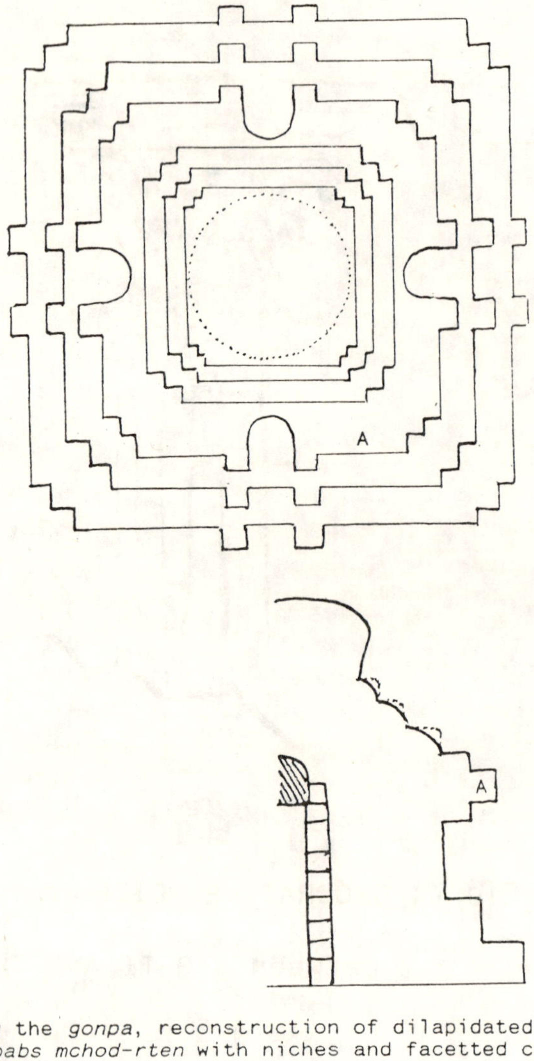

Fig 8 SABU: below the *gonpa*, reconstruction of dilapidated *lha-babs mchod-rten* with niches and facetted corners

K.Howard Fig.8: Sabu: below the gonpa, reconstruction of dilapidated *lha-babs mChod-rten*, with niches and facetted corners.

THE FORTIFIED PLACES OF ZANSKAR[1]

Neil Howard[2]

Introduction

I have suggested elsewhere (Howard 1987, 1991) that archaeological evidence from the fortifications of Ladakh suggests that in different periods the Ladakhis built with distinctly different masonry techniques and employed distinctly different fortification principles; and that each different period has a characteristic combination of masonry techniques and elements of fortification. These may be summarised as follows:

- random-texture mud-mortared stone (Pl.11): occurs at all times up to the early 16th century; but in important buildings the masonry texture is much neater from the 15th century onwards;

- shuttered mud: buildings of mud, moulded *in situ* between wooden formers, or shuttering, are the characteristic royal style of the reigns of *bKra-shis-rnam-rgyal* and *Ts'e-dbang-rnam-rgyal,* roughly the second half of 16th century (Pl.11);

- banded-texture mud-mortared stone (Pl.17): buildings using this technique seem all to be datable from the reigns of *Seng-ge-rnam-rgyal* and *bDe-ldan-rnam-rgyal,* approximately the last three-quarters of 17th century; again, I suggest they are the characteristic royal style of this period;

- random-texture mud-mortared stone again becomes the style of all important buildings (including royal, eg. Stok palace) from the 18th to the 20th centuries;

- timber lacing of stonework (Pl.11): used in important buildings at all periods after the early 15th century, except in shuttered mud buildings;

- defensible settlements (Pl.10, Fig.8): occur in all periods, except perhaps at royal seats of power from the early 15th century;

- curtain walls enclosing whole hill-sides (eg. Shey) seem to have been the method of fortifying royal places from the early 15th century; they do not appear to occur in Zanskar, presumably that country could not afford the expense;

---

1. The Dogra fortification at Upti is excluded; this paper is concerned with fortifications built, apparently, by the Zanskaris themselves. Place-name spellings are given as they are found in the sources (chiefly Francke 1926); no unified system of transliteration from Tibetan has been attempted.

2. N.F.Howard, 27 Clarendon Road, Birmingham, B16 9SD, U.K.

- defensive towers: are round, D-shaped or rectangular in plan at all times, except where the building method is shuttered mud in which case they are always rectangular;

- loopholes: are rectangular or triangular; in shuttered mud they are always triangular.

Where possible this evidence will be used, in conjunction with documentary evidence and field evidence from Zanskar, in the discussion of the ages of Zanskari fortresses.

The south-east

The first five places discussed below have, or had, fortifications according to Francke, quoting a report in 1908 by his colleague George Hettasch who had travelled amongst them (Francke 1926, p. 152).

Kurgiak *(dKar-rgyags)*

Francke states that here there were the remains of an ancient castle with very well-built walls. On three separate occasions I have been assured by the villagers that there is no castle and there never was. Perhaps Hettasch was confused by the fortress-like appearance of the little monastery above the village.

Tanze *(Tang-tse/Drang-rtse/Grang-tse)*

According to Francke above the present village is situated an ancient monastery, if not a whole town. A.F.Peter (1975, p. 11) adds the information that it was taken by the Tibetans in the 10th century and in retaliation destroyed by the Kashmiris who had previously occupied Zanskar. Dieter Schuh, in his extremely illuminating study of the chronicle fragments from Phugtal monastery (1983, p. 22) suggests that its position near the borders of Lahul-Spiti may have given it a boundary function. I am not personally acquainted with these ruins. If they are of such great antiquity they should be expected to show features distinct from the usual style of Ladakhi-Zanskari architecture, which dates from after the 10th century conquest by the Tibetan line of rulers and the Second Diffusion of Buddhism.

Cha *(Bcah-ba/Bya)*

Francke and Peter (*ibid.*) report castle ruins below the village. Again I have no personal knowledge to add; I could see no such ruins, unless they were refering to those across the Tsarap river, on the river bank below Purni, which, being low, is not a normal site for a Zanskari fortification.

Spang

Hettasch reported to Francke otherwise unknown castle ruins and deserted fields here above the stone bridge.

Ichar *(Gyi-char)*

In the same publication Francke reports a square tower above the village which stands on top of a rock. From a distance this village appears to be a typical defensible settlement (see below).

Bardan Monastery

Since this fortress is a monastery rather than a castle it also lies outside the terms of reference of this paper. But it is worth mentioning briefly because it is, in fact, the best surviving example of a fortification in all Zanskar. The buildings on the tallest part of the rock are inherently defensible, having their outer walls contiguous and, with the exception of a building which may be later than the rest, with no doors or windows low down; the result is as effective for defence as a tall curtain wall. This is the principle of the defensible settlement. On the easier side of the rock there is a short length of curtain wall, enclosing a yard, which incorporates a gate house. From here the approach path descends behind what must have been another wall (or possibly on top of high revetting) to an outer gate house. The outer wall of the path and the general steepness of the ground secured the main gate from attack. The remains of another wall can be seen running directly down the rock below the outer gate; it was built to hinder flanking or encircling movements by an attacker (Pl.1). Such simple, effective defensive structures were to be found widely throughout the Himalaya (and beyond) but are rarely in such a complete state in greater Ladakh.

Trakkar *(Brag-mkhar)*

All that remains today is a good deal of rubble, mud from mortar and a few unconnected wall-footings on a rock above the southern bank of the river (the new motor road passes beneath it). Some of the wall-footings might have been from a rounded tower of approximately 7 m diameter and I was told a local tradition that the fort was a tower - presumably with out-buildings. As we shall see, tower fortifications are common in Zanskar.

The function of Trakkar was, one may guess, to command the south-western entrance to central Zanskar. For Francke this was one of his four Mon fortresses (1907, p. 24) but unfortunately he provided no archaeological evidence to support this attribution. It may have been disused for a long time, since it is so decayed, but there is no need to postulate an origin before the 10th century. We may, however, speculate that its function as the guardian of the door to central Zanskar was taken over in the 17th century by Bardan monastery.

The north-west

Tarungtse *(Dar-khung-rtse/Turkun)*

Turkun is the name used on the Quarter-Inch Survry of India map and Dar-khung-rtse is the name given by Francke (1926, map p. 162); Tarungtse is the local pronunciation, I was told. These ruins may prove to have been a large droksa (*'brog-sa*) but I do not think so, because they were apparently designed as a fortification as will be shown below and in my experience a droksa is never fortified. However some parts of the ruins do appear to have been rebuilt for use as a droksa.

The ruins (Fig.1, Pl.2) stand along a ridge of moraine and outwash in the mouth of the first significant south-side tributary of the Doda or Changpo river (Francke's *Dpon-rtse-chu*) a mile or two to the north-west of Sani; very slightly east of a point directly opposite Tungri village.

At the upper, western end of the site there is a large pile of rubble with wall-footings which may have been a tower commanding the enclosure below it. The remains of the enclosure wall are often of very large boulders. The zig-zag course of the wall is not dictated by the ground surface and must therefore be intentional with the purpose of providing a flanking angle of counter attack against a storming party. If the south side of the enclosure was originally walled, its wall must have fallen down the steep slope to the stream.

Below the enclosure there are no building remains until the ruins at A are reached. A short relic of wall west of A has no known purpose but the space between it and A could have been a door or gate. The rubble at A contains the footings of a rectangular building 3.5 x 6 m in floor area and still standing 1.5 m high. It is surrounded by other rooms or buildings which together may have formed the principal strong point or chief's house.

From B to the gate in the east wall there is a long narrow open space or street with the ruins of rectangular houses on either side. On the north side it is clear that their unbroken outer walls provided the defence here (Pl.3); on the south side the remains, and therefore the defences, are much less distinct and may have been lost down the steep slope. Some of the buildings east of B seem to have been roughly rebuilt for use as temporary shelters. The curtain wall at the east end of the site is quite distinct and in the area of the carefully constructed gate, at least, is free-standing. Beyond the gate there are traces of a slightly-built enclosure of unknown purpose.

I found no pottery or other relics of human occupation on the ground surface except the feature at F which may have been a fireplace - but if it is, it is of unusual construction for these parts, being like neither the fireplaces constructed inside houses nor the three-stone arrangements of temporary camping places.

The masonry throughout uses the flaky rock of the hill-side as it naturally occurs, without dressing. The stones used are enormous in the enclosure wall and large in building A, up to 0.75 m across; elsewhere they are of a more convenient size. The masonry is carefully done and the evidence suggests that mud mortar was perhaps not used, except in the buildings A to A1 - none is to be seen elsewhere and a large number of packing stones have been used which would not have been necessary if mud mortar had been used.

These ruins are important because the only historical reference that I know of to Tarungtse is Francke's, that it was a Mon castle; but again he does not give his evidence. I could discover no clear evidence that it dates from before the 10th century, but it is certainly well designed for defence. However some features of the ruins suggest that they may be very old, even if we cannot be more precise than that. The building technique: dry-stone, without mud mortar, is not found in either Zanskar or Ladakh in permanently inhabited settlements known to date from after the 10th century. And the stones have not been dressed.

The two fortifications immediately to the west of Tarungtse (see below) are built of the same naturally occuring stone of the hill-side, but the stones have been dressed and mud mortar has been used; Tarungtse may therefore possibly be the product of an older culture and people. Also Tarungtse is considerably more ruined, although in a similar geographical environment, which may indicate a longer process of decay. Finally, the curtain wall at the east end of the settlement and the clear central street are unlike the plan of defended settlements elsewhere in Zanskar and Ladakh, which may also indicate a different, and older, culture. Francke's other three Mon castles, though undoubtedly old, and very likely their origins forgotten, can all be explained within a post-10th century context, but Tarungtse presents different problems of interpretation which may, perhaps, only be solved by excavation.

House (?) - opposite Tungri (*Dung-ring*)

The ruin on the near shoulder of the next tributary nullah to the west is, according to an a-mchi gathering plants by the road below, a "*mkhar-gog*" - a ruined fort (fig.2). It looks more like a house, but very strongly built; the walls which survive to 2.5/3.0 m high show no specifically defensive features. The walls are of a similar stone, and laid in a similar manner, to the two following, clearly defensive, structures.

Tower - opposite Tungri

On the farther, western, shoulder of the same tributary, and even higher, the ruins of a tower and some associated buildings cling to the steep smooth surface of outcropping slabs (Fig.3, Pl.4). The tower is at the highest point, overlooking a lower ridge which joins the slabs to the hill-side - the strongest defence at the weakest point. Overlooking the nullah there is a revetted platform and on the slabs in front of the tower there are the ruins of some small buildings. Little survives, and the tower ruins stand only to some 2 m or so. The building material has already been referred to: lightly dressed, mud-mortared stone in random texture.

Apparently we have here a watch tower with accommodation for a small garrison but it is impossible to say to whom it belonged or what its strategic function was.

Castle (?) - opposite Tungri

Above the eastern bank of the next tributary to the west, and directly opposite Tungri bridge, a ruined fortification stands on an outcrop which is similar to the one above but has gentler surfaces, better suited to habitation (Fig.4). Remains of the walls of rectangular rooms or houses are to be found on the oval-shaped upper surface of the outcrop which is bounded by cliffs, in some cases reinforced by revetting. At the highest point, and overlooking the saddle which joins the outcrop to the hillside, there is a tall defensive wall. In the saddle there are possible traces of more masonry and indications that some ditching or scarping may have taken place to improve the defences on that side (Pl.5).

The wall, well-built of lightly dressed, mud-mortared stone from the hillside has a striking facetted trace; the function of the facets, if any, is not immediately apparent. Its maximum height today is approximately 4 m but was clearly originally more. Rubble is piled against the inside but two loopholes can be identified; they are flared laterally on the inside and one, at least, was originally triangular outside (i.e. to the field of attack) (P.6). They are typical of Greater Ladakh.

The size and solidity of the defences, and the number of building ruins behind them, suggest that this was more than a watch-tower - perhaps a castle in its own right. The ruins are much too small in extent for a town and the defences too massive for a village. As in the previous case, it is not known when this fortification was built or for what purpose; but the extensive decay suggests long abandonment and the masonry style and the loopholes would, in the context of local fortification practice, be at least appropriate to a building date in the 15th or early 16th centuries.

Rimala

There are two small square towers here, each on its outcrop on either side of the mouth of a tributary nullah on the north bank of the Doda or Chankpo river. There are probably more such towers waiting to be discovered in in many places in Zanskar.

Jyagam

Also spelled Shagam (Quarter-Inch map of the Survey of India), this village is roughly half way between Rimala and Hemaling. Above the village there is a high rocky shoulder on which stand the ruins of a large stone building which the local people referred to as a *"mkhar"*. I did not have time to examine it but Peissel reports massive walls, 5 chambers and few openings (1984, p. 50). From a distance it did not resemble any of the usual types of Zanskari or Ladakhi fortification.

Hemaling (also pronounced Hamilang)

On an isolated knoll by the hillside at the back of the village are some rubble and low wall ruins with a number of chortens and other devotional structures. I did not examine this site but Peissel (ibid.) states that the entire village used to be on this hillock and that it was destroyed by an invading army from Mandi .

If true, this is probably the raid referred to in The Chronicle of Ladakh "....a Mande and Waran army came and devastated Upper Zanskar up to Dung-ring (Tungri)" (Francke 1926, p. 126) which Petech implies must have been in about 1825 (Petech 1977, pp. 131-132). Unfortunately, both Peissel and Petech have identified an unknown Mande as the well-known Mandi, away to the south-east, beyond Kulu. The Mande army was operating with one from Waran which, Francke says, is Wardwan, a district north of Kishtwar, in Kashmir. This army would, of course, have been a raiding party. The identification of Mande must be sought close to Wardwan, in the territory west of Zanskar, which is the only explanation of a raid through Upper Zanskar, through Hemaling, up to Dung-ring. Interestingly, The Chronicle states that the Dogras began their conquest of Ladakh from *Man-ldra-ba'i*" which Francke translates as Mandre and Waran (1926, p. 127); they entered Ladakh by way of southern Suru, as we know.

Umatanche tower

This small stone tower stands a few hundred feet above the valley floor and the road, opposite the mouth of the Sumche Tokpo (which comes from the Hagshu glacier) and above the point where it joins the Pholokiow stream, the two then forming the Doda or Chankpo river (refer Trekking Route Map of Jummu and Kashmir) (local name Stod. *Ed.*). The tower was, clearly, built to guard the western door of Zanskar. To the north it commands a view of several miles towards the Pensi La and to the south as far as Phe (Pl.7).

The tower consists of a single building, without surrounding accommodation. Its highest point today may be only a little less than the original height. Its plan is a fairly regular D-shape with a rectangular projection at the back (Pl.8, Fig.5). Maximum outside diameter across the D is approximately 6.5 m and the walls are roughly 1m thick at ground level. The construction is of quite neat mud-mortared stone in random texture. The door was presumably high up in the back. There are two triangular loopholes in the east side, commanding the easiest approach from the hillside above, which have been made in one of the characteristic ways of Greater Ladakh: the sides of the triangle are made by leaning two long, flat stones together as mullions. There are also two rectangular openings, which are not flared on the inside and overlook the sheer cliff, which may be presumed to be windows.

The random-texture stonework, the shape of the loopholes and the rounded plan of the tower would all be appropriate to a building date in the 15th century - compare with a similar tower at Temisgam in Ladakh which has been encased in a 16th century rectangular mud tower (Howard 1991). There is, however, no direct evidence of date at Umatanche nor any reference to it in the sources.

The central area

Padum *(dPal-'dum/dPah-gtum/Spa-dum)*

According to Francke (1907, p. 25) the fortifications at Padum consisted of a castle on the Padum hill connected to the fortified village of Ghor-ghor by a long rampart. Since both settlements extended to the top of the precipitous river bank, in military terms they defended the flanks and the rampart closed the centre. Such rampart defences are well-known in the Tibetan world and their function is to bar a road - in this case the junction of three roads: from the north, the south-east and the north-west (Fig.7). These are the three easiest routes and, before the building of the motor road and the Pibiting bridge, to go from the first to either of the others (or vice versa) it would have been necessary to pass through the town and cross by the old bridge which stood on the prominent triangular rock in the river just below Padum town (near the site of the foot bridge under construction in 1985). By prohibiting other bridges within their territory, rulers could check on, and tax, all travellers.

Unfortunately a degree of speculation has to be recognised in this reconstruction, and in my belief that Padum and Ghor-ghor were probably defensible settlements rather than towns with separate defensive curtain walls, because the palace and the defences of Padum have entirely disappeared since their destruction by the Dogras (Francke 1906, p. 650). Of the village of Ghor-ghor only some traces of rubble remain, all the rest having been quarried for building material. The rampart, however, can still be traced although it is half buried under the new police buildings and carries a water channel along its top. Also on its top, by the police station, there is an ancient carved stele, noted by Francke, which has been recently re-erected. The rampart was originally built of river cobbles, set in mud mortar, and in its collapsed state it varies in width between 1 and 2 metres.

Francke includes Padum in his list of Mon fortifications. The site is clearly of ancient importance, as the carvings on the stele and the Buddha rock on the river bank below Ghor-ghor indicate, but the first mention of Padum which implies it is a capital (of the southern kingdom), and which can be dated, does not occur in the known chronicles until the reference to king "*Tshang-rgyal-po* of *Dpah-gtum*" (Francke 1926, p. 158), who probably reigned about the middle of the 15th century (Schuh 1983, p.34). There are other references to Padum which may imply that it was a capital earlier than the 15th century but these references are not capable of sufficiently close analysis (eg. Dargay 1987, p. 24; Francke 1926, p. 164). We cannot guess when the surviving fortifications were built. The more recent dominance of Padum as the chief town of all Zanskar presumably dates from 1638 when the last of the southern kingdom's rulers was deposed by *Seng-ge-rnam-rgyal* of Ladakh (Petech 1977, p.48); his youngest son, *bDe-mc'og-rnam-rgyal* became king of Zanskar (ibid., p. 58). In passing, I suggest that it was during the reign of *bDe-mc'og-rnam-rgyal* or an immediate successor that the northwestern side of the topmost little temple on the hill of Padum was rebuilt. In contrast to the other three walls, it is built in the banded masonry texture which came into use in royal Ladakhi buildings in the early 17th century (Pl.17).

sTong-sde

A small sub-kingdom was founded here, roughly half way between Padum and Zangla, about the middle of the 15th century (Francke 1926, p. 157) and there was a castle to be seen recently, immediately behind *sTong-sde* monastery. However in the last few years it has been almost entirely quarried away - to provide building material for repairs and extensions to the monastery, as I was told. Only heaps of dug-over rubble and one short length of wall were to be seen in 1985. Interestingly, this wall, but not necessarily the whole castle, was built of shuttered mud which indicates a building date in the second half of the 16th century.

Ts'a-zar (*Cha-zar*, and various other spellings)

Due east of the southern end of Tshazar village, along the crest of a bank of outwash between two small nullahs, stand some ruins referred to by the villagers as a *"mkhar-gog"* (Pl.9, Fig.6). They are very decayed but seem to have comprised a number of useful-sized, rectangular buildings with a terrace at their western end. Down the north slope of the ridge there are traces of an enclosure (a pen for horses, hidden from an attack from the south?) and on the easier slopes down the ridge to the west there are traces of further buildings. The walls are constructed of rough lumps of stone from the hill-side, mortared in mud; a few lengths only survive and no doors, windows, etc.

This was the fourth of Francke's Mon fortifications but it is probably not so ancient. The great decay of these buildings may result from their having been long abandoned but it may also have been caused by the instability of the earth ridge on which they were built. The random texture of the masonry would be appropriate to a building date before the middle of the 16th century; however in Zanskar such rough building styles may have been common throughout history. The appearance and site of the ruins suggest that originally they were a small fort or a large watch tower. Their location is probably the chief indication of their function and date of building: as Schuh has demonstrated (1983, p. 26), Tshazar was close to the southern boundary of the northern kingdom Zangla - and we may guess therefore that this was a defence against *sTong-sde* and Padum. Zangla rose to prominence, as far as we know, in the first half of the 15th century but Tshazar fort would have become redundant in 1638 following the conquest of Zanskar.

Zangla *(bZang-la)*

The ruins of old Zangla, on a high rock above the Zamlung nullah, where it debouches into the valley of the Zanskar river, provide the best surviving example of a defensible settlement (Pl.10). Its defences consist of the houses themselves: their outer walls form a continuous barrier round the top of the rock without the addition of a separate curtain. Today the houses are very ruined but there appears to have been only one entrance to the town, through a space between the houses at the top of the approach path. This path must follow the line of the original path because it comes up through a large group of ancient chortens - groups of chortens typically adorn the way into royal palaces in Greater Ladakh. The buildings of the town are constructed almost exclusively of mud-mortared stone in random texture.

In the middle of the town stands a white painted palace of four storeys. Its lower parts are also built of random-texture, mud-mortared stone and incorporate a good deal of light timber reinforcement - which has done its job well since the building still stands despite the many cracks, particularly in the south-west face. Mud brick has been used for the upper parts and also in places where the stone-work has been repaired or replaced with brick; and there is a large stone buttress on the north-west front.

On the north-east side there are some extensions to the original structure in shuttered mud and some outlying buildings are made of the same material. On this side there is also a blocked-up window with a balcony in the third storey which has a column capital in a very similar style to that used in buildings in Ladakh which are associated with kings *bKra-shis-rnam-rgyal* and *Ts'e-dbang-rnam-rgyal*, who are also the kings associated with shuttered mud building (Pl.11). We appear therefore to have evidence for a substantial remodelling of the palace in the second half of the 16th century. The relative positions of shuttered mud and random-textured stone work suggest that the stone work is earlier, from which we may conclude that that represents the original structure. On the Ladakhi model such stone-work is typical of the 15th century which, in turn, appears to be the century of the founding of the Zangla kingdom (see below). There is a capital in a balcony on the fourth storey which may be in a later style but the general appearance of the building suggests that no major construction work was undertaken after the 16th century.

Karsha monastery towers *(dKar-sha)*

High above the monastery at Karsha are some ruined structures which are clearly of a defensive type. The upper tower (Pl.12) is a rounded rectangle in plan, approximately 6 x 5 m overall; its top is missing. It is built of random-textured mud-mortared stone. On the up-hill side, the easiest for attack, seven loopholes can be seen today; they are triangular, well flared on the inside, typically 550 mm high and 120 mm wide at the bottom on the outside of the building and some of them have their apertures defined by long thin mullions leaning together. The whole structure is typical of defensive towers in Ladakh which seem to come from the 15th century.

The lower tower, circular and also of random-texture mud-mortared stone, has tall rectangular loopholes with good flaring inside (Pl.13). From it, two walls run outward (in V plan) down the rocky spur of the hill-side. The interior space is filled with dangerously loose rubble and therefore could not be examined. Parts of the eastern wall are built of shuttered mud. In Ladakh, shuttered mud towers are always built on a rectangular plan, so here we seem to have work of two periods, presumably 15th and 16th century.

The monks in the monastery in 1985 seemed to know nothing about the towers but they told me they called them *rgyal-po mts'ams-phug*. One of my porter guides - Puntsok Stobden of Pibiting village - told me that Karsha was built by a king Indrabodhi (perhaps significantly? he did not use the Tibetan, *dBang-po'i-byan-c'ub).* It is difficult to know whether anything can be made of these pieces of information. *Seng-ge-rnam-rgyal's* second son became a monk under that name and later he ruled Guge, when he was also referred to as *Indra-rnam-rgyal* (Petech 1977, pp. 56-58). But he was a follower of the Drukpa school whereas Karsha was Gelugpa. During the Tibeto-Mongol invasion of Ladakh 1680-4 Indrabodhi was in charge of the defence of Zanskar but how that can be related to building at Karsha when it was apparently some Karsha monks who invited the Mongols into Zanskar in the first place (Petech 1977, p. 73) I cannot say. It is intriguing to think, however, that the answer to this problem might explain the small piece of banded texture masonry above the monastery but below the towers (Pl.14) - this was the royal masonry style in Ladakh in Indrabodhi's time, if this is the Indrabodhi referred to.

Karsha old castle

Across the nullah, westwards from the monastery, some ruins occupying the shoulder of the hill are said to have been an ancient castle (Snellgrove and Skorupski 1980, p. 48). They appear, in fact, to have been a defensible settlement occupying the rocky outcrops of the ridge (Fig.8). Along the north side, the outer walls of houses and, possibly, some lengths of parapet wall occupy the cliff top. Half way along, a small salient may have been intended to give defenders the ability to deliver flanking fire against attackers. Towards the eastern end a small triangular tower must have been for that purpose and in the middle of the three small salients beyond that there is a triangular loophole commanding the face of the tower. Further east, a double wall of compartmented construction, or a line of small square buildings, extended the defences to the end of the outcrop. The remains of fairly substantial buildings are to be found along the cliff, along the southern side, and the rubble indicates that there were more between them.

At the north-western apex of the site - the easiest point to attack overlooking the saddle joining the site to the rest of the hill-side, there are the remains of a strong tower. Like almost all the other buildings in these ruins it was built of random-textured mud-mortared stone but at a later date it was reinforced with a cladding of shuttered mud, mud brick and stone revetting (Pl.15). On the western side of the stone part of the tower, there are the remains of a window.

Half way down the slope below the tower are two fragments of shuttered mud on a different alignment which may have been part of an outer defensive wall; perhaps it joined up with the angle of shuttered mud which stands by the complex of buildings and the hollow way, nearby.

The whole site is so extremely ruined that is not possible to be sure of the function of any of its structures except on the basis of general principles. Near the highest point, at A, there is a substantial piece of wall which is plastered on both sides and was clearly part of an important building; outside it, to the west, there appears to have been a yard. Perhaps this was a temple or part of the ruler's dwelling. The gate into the settlement may have been at the top of the hollow way, near the shuttered mud angle. It would have been an appropriate place for it, the path from there going out to the passage chorten which contains paintings in an 11-12th century style (Snellgrove and Skorupski *ibid.*) then on past the little roofless temple T (called *lang-thra'o,* according to a monk of Karsha; Hirschberg reports lhakang tao, the Keilhauers lhakang khrabo) which has an 11th century appearance. The path would then have descended to the group of inhabited buildings below the ruins, as it does today, among which is the temple dedicated to 11-headed Avalokiteshvara dated to approximately the late 11th century by Snellgrove and Skorupski (*ibid.*, p. 41).

We have therefore plenty of evidence for this settlement having been in existence in some form in the 11th century. Its stone building techniques fit the Ladakhi model for continuous use up to the early 16th century. The shuttered mud structures are so placed that they may be additional buildings: perhaps a strengthening of fortification in the later 16th century; however the chronicles of Ladakh and Zanskar give no clue who their builder might have been.

There is no masonry in these ruins of the characteristic 17th century type and they are extremely decayed, with no evidence of quarrying, so perhaps the site ceased to be a major settlement soon after the end of the 16th century.

Old Karsha may present a more complex problem. Its ruins have about the same area as old Zangla and, probably, Padum before its modern development took place. These two have, apparently, been the chief places of the northern and southern kingdoms since the early 15th century, according to the generally accepted evidence. However, in the available, fragmentary, documentary evidence there are a number of references to Zanskar having been divided into northern and southern kingdoms before the 15th century; in fact, if the positioning of the evidence within the documents is a true indicator of its historical significance, this division stretches back to a time before the conquest by the Tibetan line of kings (Francke 1926, p. 156; Schuh 1983, p. 21). The important places of these first two divisions are: *Rang-thag-sha* and *Ri-nam* in the north, but not Karsha, and *Bib-ca* and *Ku-mi* in the south, but not Padum.

We have seen that at both Padum and Old Karsha there are relics of the art of a time long anterior to the 15th century. How important Padum may have been before the 15th century cannot be pursued at present for lack of sufficient evidence. In the case of Karsha we can make a tentative suggestion, but first we must return briefly to the question of the age of Zangla, the known chief place of the northern kingdom in more recent times. The Chronicle of Zanskar tells us that *Khri-nam-dpal-lde,* the uncle of *Ts'ang-rgyal-po* of Padum (one of the second generation rulers of the southern kingdom) received the region to the north of the water, and in addion to it *Ts'a-zar, Bzang-la,* and the region down to the brook of *Me-ltse* (Francke 1926, p. 157; Schuh 1983, p. 26). The implication seems clear: for *Khri-nam-dpal-lde, Ts'a-zar* and *bZang-la* were added to the pre-existing northern kingdom, although whose that kingdom had been we do not know. *Ts'a-zar* and *bZang-la* are spoken of here merely as villages; neither is stated to be of special importance. Importance came to *Ts'a-zar* in the next reign when it became the site of a monastery founded by *sTod Shes-rab bzang-po,* ie "*Byang-sems*" (Francke *ibid.*, Schuh *ibid.*, p. 31), a disciple of *Tsong-kha-pa. Khri-nam-dpal-lde's* reign may be dated to approximately the first quarter of the 15th century, therefore, and the archaeological remains at old Zangla are quite consistent with the hypothesis that it was built then. Perhaps at that time it became the royal seat of the northern kingdom.

To return to old Karsha. Since it is not mentioned along with *Ri-nam* and *Rang-thag-sha* it is difficult to conclude that it was the chief place of the earlier northern kingdom which, in any case, must have existed before the conquest of Zanskar by the Tibetan line of kings (and therefore before the presumed foundation of the earliest religious structures there) if the sources are to be believed. But at least 400 years lie between the conquest by the Tibetan kings and the foundation of Zangla, and perhaps we have hints of a much larger kingdom when the Chronicle tells us that *Khri-nam-dpal-lde's* father, *Seng-ge-ldor,* ruled Kishtwar, left it to his eldest son, and then, in some unknown way (the sources differ in detail on this) his two younger sons inherited Zanskar between them as northern and southern kingdoms. For this to have happened, *Seng-ge-ldor* may, in some way, have ruled all Zanskar. Was Old Karsha a capital of a much larger and older kingdom, perhaps including Kishtwar, of which we have no knowledge? If so we must seek the reason why Karsha was omitted from the Chronicle's account of the two sons' inheritance. This is, of course, wild speculation - we need more sources.

Phima Ralakung

In the middle of the upland pastures east of Phe there is a settlement of three houses and a tower on a rock above them (Pl.16). The defensive concept resembles those of Tshazar and the tower opposite Tungri. There are indications of at least two floors and there are the footings of two or three other buildings on top of the cliff next to the tower. It is built of mud-mortared stone in random texture and seems to have had some timber lacing. There are well-made triangular loopholes with leaning mullions commanding the neck of land joining the tower's rock to the hill-side.

The villagers referred to these ruins as a *"mkhar"* but apparently knew nothing of their history.

Postscript

Tanze

In August 1993 I visited this place, the Drang-rtse of Francke and Hettasch. The ruins above the present village (called Mosoma Dangze by Hasmatullah Khan) proved to consist of a temple whose main room was locked (and no lama available) but which otherwise showed no architectural details which need be older than the 17th century. It is surrounded by a few, mostly ruined, houses of lamas; there are far too few ruins to have once been a town. A little higher, on a steep-sided rock shoulder, are the ruins of a small fort, consisting of very rough mud-mortared random stone built into small rooms, and there is a good deal of building rubble on the slopes below. On a higher shoulder there is a small watch tower. There is no evidence to suggest that the ruins are of any great antiquity and they cannot be identified with the *Drang-rtse* mentioned in the text of Francke's Chronicles of Zanskar which was captured by the Tibetans in (presumably) the 10th century.

Tsarap river

On the same trek I noticed two small forts, or watch towers with associated buildings, on the brink of the gravel cliffs of the west bank of the Tsarap river (unfortunately I was on the east bank). Both were about half an hour from Satok village, one upstream and the other downstream, and neither has been recorded previously. The former consisted in part of a round tower. In general terms they are the same sort of small fort as can be found in all the valleys leading into Zanskar and the function of these was, presumably, to bar the way of an attacker using the west bank.

Bibliography

DARGYAY, Eva K. 1987. "The Dynasty of Bzang-La (Zanskar, West-Tibet) and its Chronology - A Reconsideration." in *Silver on Lapis,* ed. by C.I. Beckwith, Bloomington, 13-32.

FRANCKE, A.H. 1906. "Kleine archaologische Ertrage einer Missions-reise nach Zangskar in Westtibet." *Zeitschrift der Deutschen Morgenlandischen Gesellschaft* 60, 645-661.

FRANCKE, A.H. 1907. *A History of Western Tibet.* London.

FRANCKE, A.H. 1926. *Antiquities of Indian Tibet* Vol.2, Calcutta.

HIRSCHBERG, H. 1978. *Ladakh, das andere Tibet.* Munich.

HOWARD, N.F. 1987. "Royal Fortresses of Ladakh." *Archaeology Today* 8, no 4, Frome.

HOWARD, N F. 1991 "The development of the Fortresses of Ladakh" *East and West* 39, 217-288.

KEILHAUER, A. and P. 1980. *Ladakh und Zanskar: Lamaistische Klosterkulture Zwischen Indien und Tibet.* Cologne.

PEISSEL, M. 1984. *Ant's Gold,* London.

PETECH, L. 1977. *The Kingdom of Ladakh (c.950-1842).* Rome.

PETER, F.A. 1975. "A Glossary of Place Names in Western Tibet." *Ethnologische Zeitschrift* 2, 5-29.

SCHUH, D. 1983. *Historiographische Dokumenta aus Zans-dkar* (Archiv fur Zentralasiatische Geschichts-forschung heft 6), Sankt Augustin.

SNELLGROVE, D L and SKORUPSKI T, 1980. *The Cultural Heritage of Ladakh,* Vol 2. Warminster.

PLATES

N.Howard Pl.1: Bardan Monastery, the gate-house is on the right; the revetting/wall and the outer gate below it; the flank wall runs down the edge of the hill, bottom right.

N.Howard Pl.2: Tarungtse, view from the north, ruins along the ridge of moraine; the tower (?) and the enclosure wall are to the right; the buildings at A-A1 to the left.

N.Howard Pl.3: Tarungtse, unbroken outer wall of buildings around A1 (north side looking west); note the stones are not dressed and little, if any, mud mortar has been used.

N.Howard Pl.4: Tower, opposite **Tungri**, view of tower from the north; the ruins of the lesser buildings run down the ridge to the left.

N.Howard Pl.5: Castle (?) opposite **Tungri**, view from south-east; from left: the ditched (?) saddle, massive wall with facetted trace and the gentler slope with remains of dwellings.

N.Howard Pl.6: Castle (?) opposite **Tungri**, loophole from inside, note : the stones appear to have been somewhat dressed and much of the mud mortar has weathered out.

N.Howard Pl.7: Umatanche tower, view from north, note loopholes and remaining mud mortar on left, windows on right.

N.Howard Pl.8: Umatanche tower, back view.

N.Howard Pl.9: Tsha-zar, view from north.

N.Howard Pl.10: Zangla, view from west; chortens and approach path centre and left; the white building on the rock is the palace; the outer walls of the buildings of the town (the defensible settlement) are before it to right.

N.Howard Pl.11: Zangla palace, shuttered mud extensions on right; the blocked window with balcony and column capital is to left of flag pole; timber lacing can be seen in the near corner on left.

N.Howard Pl.12: Karsha monastery, upper tower, and triangular loopholes.

N.Howard Pl.13: Karsha monastery, lower tower, mud wall on left; the other wall of the V plan runs down the edge of the rock towards bottom right.

N.Howard Pl.14: Karsha monastery, banded texture masonry below towers.

N.Howard Pl.15: Karsha old castle, north-western apex tower, from north-east (ie. inside); window on left; the mud and brick cladding is the lighter material on the right.

N.Howard Pl.16: Phima Ralagung tower, the outbuildings were beyond the tower, where the rock is hidden.

N.Howard Pl.17: Padum hill-top temple, banded texture masonry.

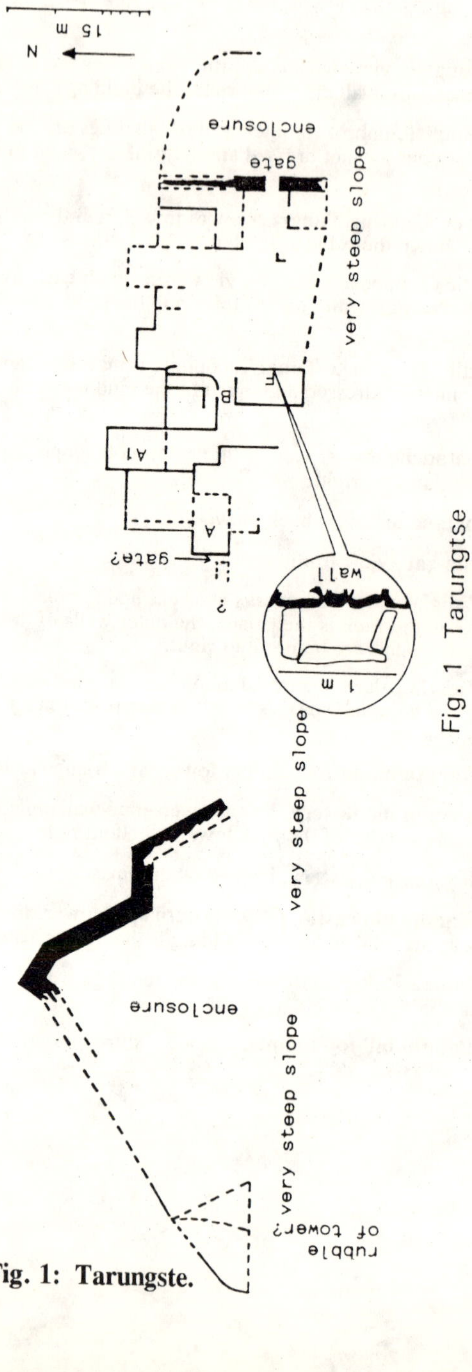

N.Howard Fig. 1: Tarungste.

Fig. 5 Umatanche tower

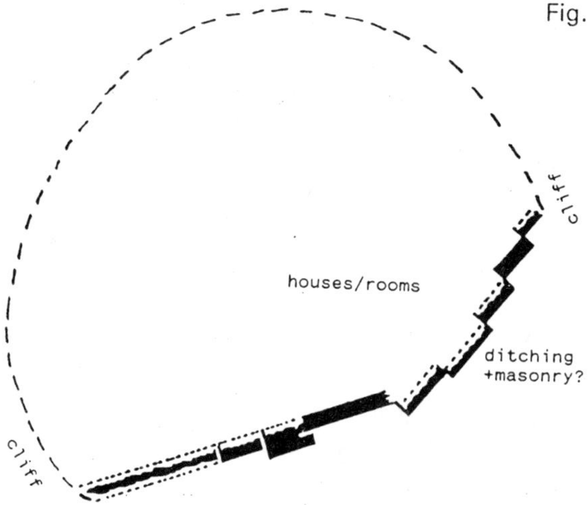

Fig. 4 Tungri, castle ?

Fig. 6 Tsha-zar

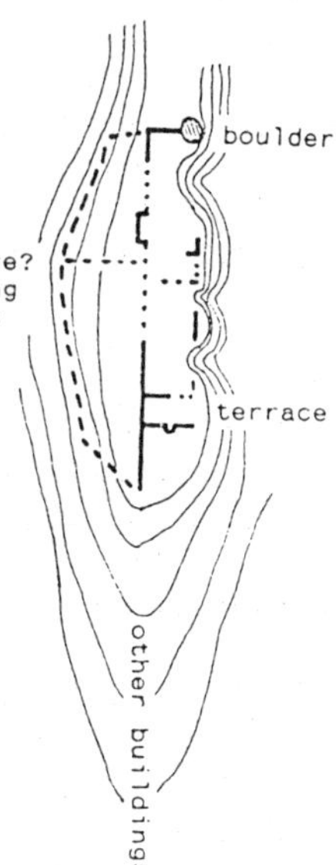

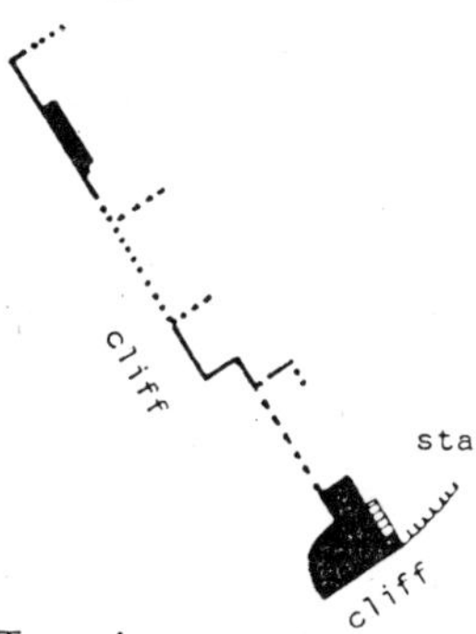

Fig. 3 Tungri, tower

Fig. 2 Tungri, house ?

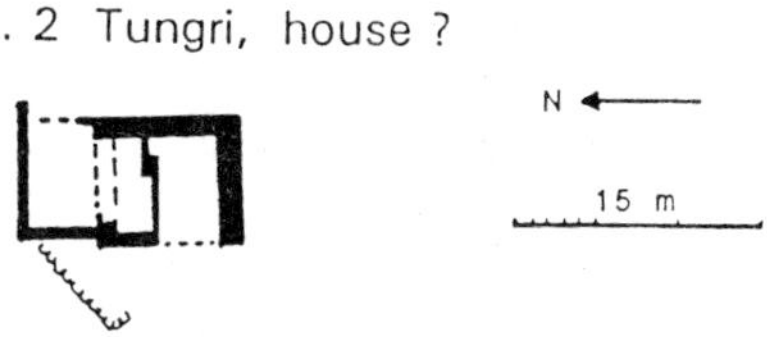

N.Howard Figs. 2, 3, 4: Tungri. Fig. 5: Umatanche. Fig.6 Tsha-zar.

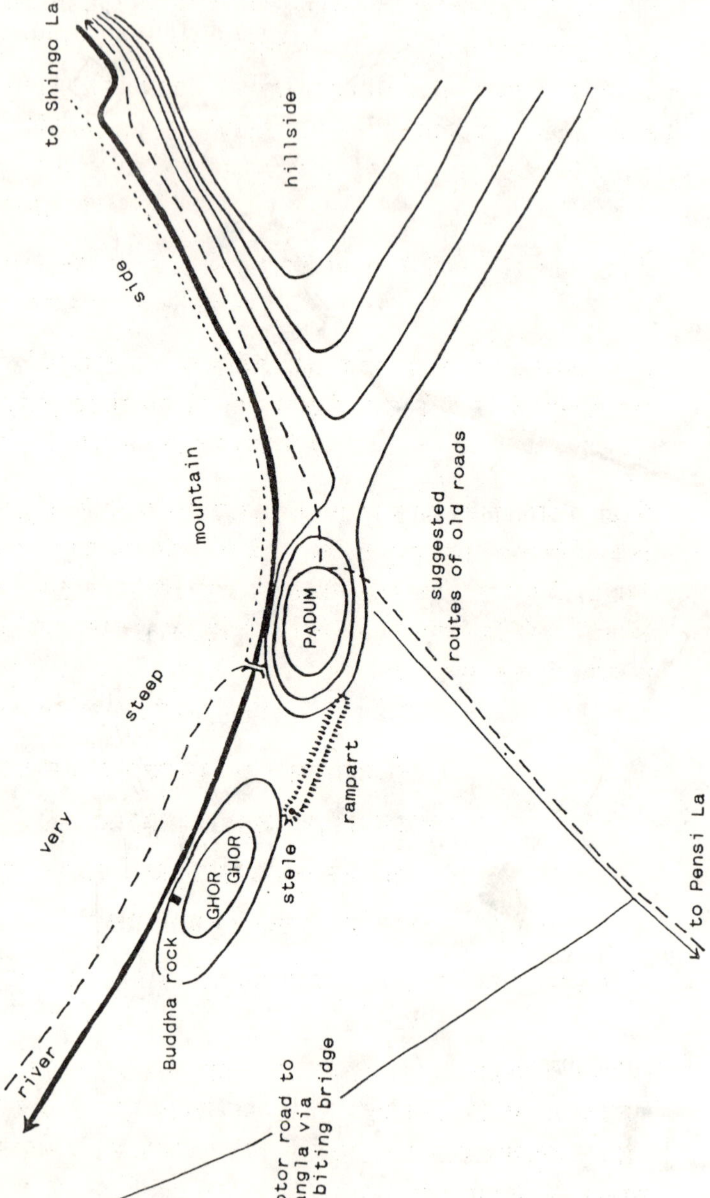

Fig. 7 Suggested reconstruction of the defences of Padum,

N.Howard Fig. 7:, Padum.

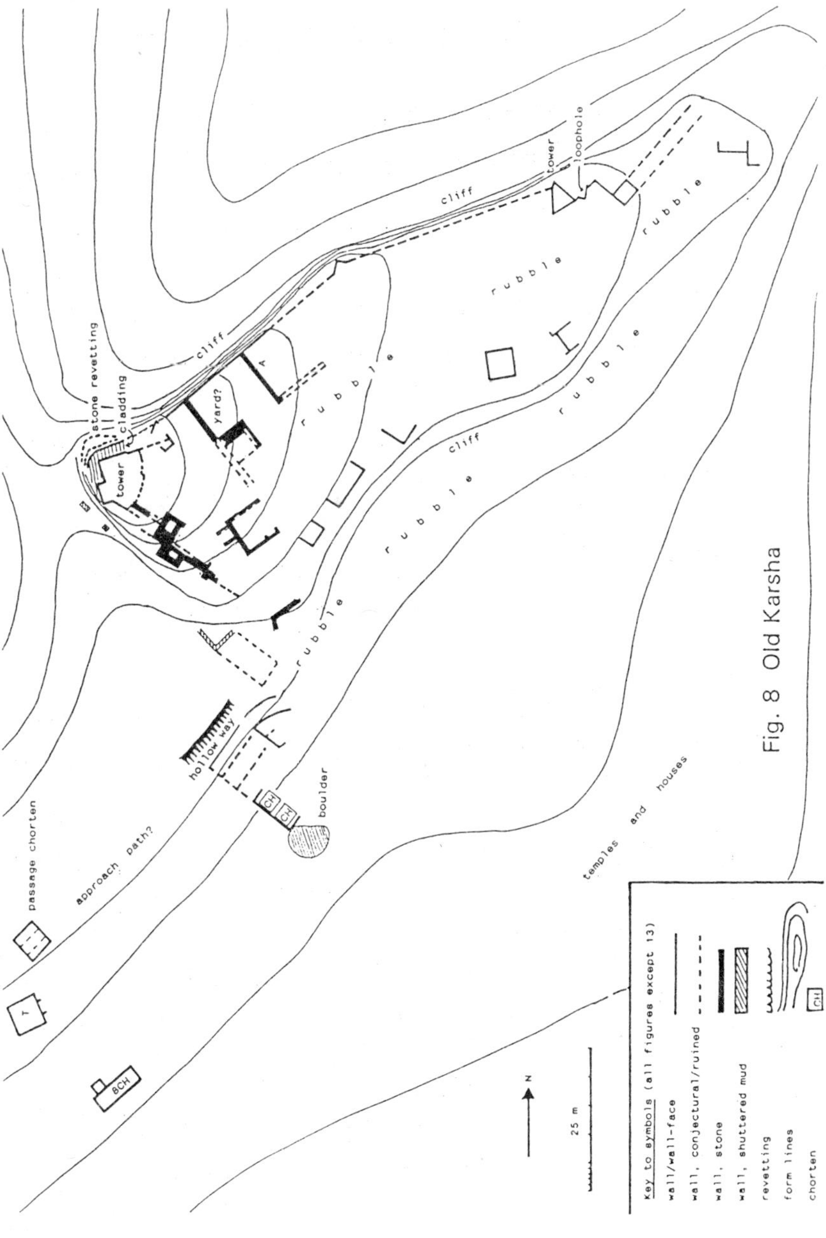

N.Howard Fig. 8: Karsha.

L'HOMME DANS LE MONDE SURNATUREL LADAKHI

Patrick Kaplanian[1]

English Abstract

The traditional supernatural world of the Ladakhi people comprises three main groups of beings (*lha, tsan, lhu*) inhabiting three different levels. The gods (*lha*) live in the sky (*stanlha*); beneath the Buddhist pantheon are the minor deities considered here, comprising six groups each with its distinct social role, five of them being honoured by special altars (*lhato*). The red demons, like many other ogres, fairies etc., live in the human world, and are ceaselessly on the prowl. Seen from the front they are beautiful but it is terrible and often fatal to see them from behind as they have no backs and all their organs are exposed. The deities of water, earth and fertility (*lhu*) live in the waters and the underworld (*yoklhu*); in general they have the forms of fish or reptiles but may assume a human likeness. They can bring good or bad luck and to avoid the latter one must carefully avoid harming *lhu* or defiling the places where they live. Both *lha* and *lhu* are thought of as inhabitants of structurally and socially organised worlds, resembling and interwoven with the human world, while the solitary *tsan* are a kind of failed men or even "anti-men".

....

La publication de trois articles spécialisés sur certains aspects du monde surnaturel Ladakhi[2] m'amène à reconsidérer une vue d'ensemble sur le sujet qui aurait due être présentée avant d'attaquer ces sujets très pointus.

Le chapitre consacré au monde surnaturel dans mon livre *Les Ladakhi du Cachemire* (Paris 1981) est un effet en grande partie dépassé par de nombreuses recherches récentes sur le sujet en

---

1. 4, rue neuve Popincourt, 75011 Paris, France.

2. "Entre lha et lhu". Actes du premier colloque d'anthropologie médicale. Paris 1987.

"La maladie en tant que *(s)notpa*". L.Icke-Schwalbe & G.Meier (eds) *Wissenschaftsgesichte und gegenwärtige Forschungen in Nordwest-indien.* Dresden Museum of Ethnology, 1990.

"Les vérités de l'interprétation : jalousie: possession et guérison au Ladakh". A paraître.

particulier la thèse de S.Day[3].

Cet article se limitera à l'armature du système qu'est le monde surnaturel ladakhi c'est-à-dire la triade *lhu-tsan-lha* et au statut de l'homme - ou à son identité comme on voudra - rapport à cette triade.

Le monde se divise en trois niveaux. Le premier est celui d'en-haut, le ciel où vivent les dieux (*lha*) : c'est le *stanlha*. Le second est celui d'ici-bas, le monde des humains et des démons rouges (*tsan*). Dans le troisième, souterrain et aquatique, vivent les *lhu* (*klu*) ou les *naga*, divinités de l'eau, du sous-sol et de la fertilité : c'est le *yoklhu*, parfois appelé *yokdjoklhu*.

Les trois mondes sont souvent associés. C'est par exemple une coutume pieuse de tremper l'annulaire dans le *chhang* avant de le boire et de faire gicler une goutte vers le haut - pour les *lha* -, horizontalement - pour les *tsan* (*btsan*) - et vers le sol - pour les *lhu* -, en frottant le pouce sur l'annulaire. Ce rite, ordinairement facultatif, est d'un emploi quasi-obligé pendant les mariages avant de commencer la grande beuverie. Une chanson l'accompagne, saluant les trois ordres de divinités.

Les *Lha*

Le mot *lha* est un terme très général qui se traduit par dieu. Il désigne tout d'abord les grandes figures du panthéon bouddhiste ; et aussi les divinités mineures. Pour les grandes divinités les Ladakhi préfèrent le mot *chhoskyong* ce qui en pur tibétain classique serait une erreur, *chhos-skyong* désignant une catégorie bien précise de divinités.

Pour les Ladakhi les *lha* mineurs, ceux qui nous intéressent ici, habitent un monde féérique. Dans certains contes, le ciel est peuplé de villages, de palais habités par des rois et des princesses. Ce sont des êtres plus ou moins purs qui ont des ailes pour voler et une coiffure spéciale à cinq pans.

Sauf dans ce cadre des légendes, les *lha* ont des rôles bien précis. En les classant selon leurs fonctions, il est possible de distinguer six sortes de *lha* protecteurs, divinités tutélaires des monastères, des palais, des villages, des quartiers, des *phaspun* et des individus.

Le *gonlha* protège un monastère et chaque *gonpa* a le sien propre. A l'extérieur des monastères, le plus souvent sur une colline le dominant, on trouve une structure cubique peinte en rouge : c'est le *lhatho* ou autel extérieur qui abrite le *lha*. Son visage est peint sur l'une des faces, parfois sur les quatre ; masque féroce avec un

3. S. Day. *Embodying Spirits*. Thèse non publiée. London School of Economics. Londres 1989.

troisième oeil et des canines apparentes pour lui donner un aspect terrifiant ; car les *gonlha* sont toujours des êtres effrayants, dompteurs de démons.

Les palais sont protégés par les *tselha*, qui sont également les divinités tutélaires des familles de sang royal. Le plus souvent, le *tselha* n'est représenté que dans le temple domestique du palais, mais on peut trouver des *lhatho* sur ses terrasses.

Le village (*yul*) a pour protecteur un *yullha*. Toute agglomération possède un *lhatho* qui la domine, dressé sur une éminence. Certains villages en ont même plusieurs, Stok par exemple, où l'on en trouve quatre ; dans ce cas, certains *lhato* protègent l'ensemble du village et d'autres seulement des quartiers.

Le *phazlha* ou *phalha (pha-lha)* est la divinité tutélaire du "clan" (*phaspun*) qui regroupe quelques maisons. Chaque "clan" a son *lha* et les autels sont placés sur les terrasses des maisons. Il est très rare qu'ils soient enfermés dans des pièces spéciales. Toutes les maisons du "clan" n'ont pas de *lhatho* et celles qui en ont un ne sont pas nécessairement les plus riches.

Les *lhatho*, à l'exception de ceux des monastères, sont blancs. On peut relever quelques cas de *yullhatho* rouges et, dans ce cas, on considère qu'il s'agit de divinités terribles, de protecteurs puissants. Le cube de pierre est surmonté d'un paquet de branches fagotées ensemble par des écharpes cérémonielles blanches (*khataks*). Aux branches sont souvent mélangées des lances et des flèches, la pointe tournée vers le bas. Les fagots se composent généralement de branches de *shukpa*, le cèdre-encens (*Juniperus wallichiana*), arbre à feuilles persistantes qui sert d'encens local. On les change au jour de l'an ladakhi (vers décembre).

A l'intérieur du *lhatho*, se trouve un pot contenant de l'orge ; soigneusement scellé, il est changé au Nouvel An. Selon l'état de l'orge, on peut faire des prédictions sur la prochaine récolte. L'orge a gonflé ou diminué : la récolte sera bonne ou mauvaise ; on y trouve des cheveux : il y aura beaucoup de mauvaises herbes, etc. Posés verticalement sur le tissu qui scelle le pot, sont placés une grosse flèche sans pointe et dont l'empennage est replié, ou un couteau sacrificiel à triple lame (*phurba*), en bois, qui est la divinité même, son âme ou son esprit, sa vie, concept que les Ladakhi rendent par le mot *srok*. On parle alors de *srokshing* (*shing* = bois).

Pour les *yullhatho*, on utilise le plus souvent des rameaux de peuplier ou de saule changés en été, à des dates qui varient suivant les villages. Cette opposition entre l'utilisation d'arbres à feuilles caduques et d'essences à feuilles persistantes renforce une opposition été/hiver qui reste encore à expliciter.

Les cinq premières catégories de *lha* ont donc un *lhatho*, reste le *skyelha (de skyeches*, naître) *lha* individuel, sorte d'ange gardien qui ne fait l'objet d'aucun culte et qui n'a pas de *lhato*.

L'individu, le "clan", le quartier et le village, on voit que le *lha* est la divinité tutélaire des principales institutions sociales, y compris l'individu, la plus simple et la plus triviale. A cette liste s'ajoutent deux institutions parallèles et essentielles : le palais et le monastère. On constatera néanmoins une curieuse absence dans cette liste : la maison, la famille l'un et l'autre revenant à peu près au même puisque l'on sait[4] que la société bouddhiste Ladakhi est une société "à maison" au sens ou Lévi-Strauss a défini ce concept. Le mot *khyimlha* pourrait se traduire par "*lha* de la maison" mais il désigne en fait la *pha(z) lha*. Si les *lha* revoient aux institutions et à l'ordre social nous allons voir que les *lhu* revoient au corps.

Les *Lhu*

Les *lhu* sont des divinités tantôt anthropomorphes tantôt zoomorphes. Dans les contes (*runs* ; *sgrung*) ils apparaissent le plus souvent sous une forme humaine. Ils constituent un monde parallèle en dessous avec des palais, des villages, une hiérarchie sociale etc. Dans la vie quotidienne ils sont surtout décrits comme zoomorphes. Ce sont tous les animaux qui vivent dans l'eau (poissons) ou en contact étroit avec le sol (lézards, serpents). Ils sont sensibles à la violence, au fer, au sang et à la polution (saleté, urine, excréments). Un certain nombre de précautions doivent être prises pour ne pas souiller les lieux qu'ils fréquentent (*lhusa*) ou les blesser (d'un coup de pioche par exemple). Par contre ils apprécient beaucoup le lait, les fruits et les fumigations d'encens, de santal ou de *shukpa* (cèdre-encens *Juniperus wallichiana*). Ils sont dispensateurs de richesse et de fertilité. Ils frappent leurs victimes de pauvreté ou de misère. Ils sont aussi à l'origine de la majorité des maladies des membres inférieurs et des maladies de peau.

Les *lhu* réagissent de manière quasi-automatique aux blessures et aux souillures qui leur sont infligées. Ils renvoient en quelque sorte la blessure ou la souillure qui les a frappés. Leur horreur du fer, du sang, des excréments, de la saleté n'est que l'expression de ce renvoi. En d'autres termes ce qui importe pour les *lhu* c'est l'intégrité de leur corps. Tout fonctionne comme si - et cela est dit explicitement par les Ladakhi - le corps des *lhu* était le doublet du corps humain. A des lésions réelles (blessures) ou symboliques (souillures) du corps d'un *lhu* vont correspondre d'autres lésions du corps de l'homme auteur du méfait.

---

4. Voir à ce sujet, en particulier, les travaux de M.Phylactou.

Le seul moyen d'éviter d'être frappé par un *lhu* est un entretien scrupuleux des lieux fréquentés par ces divinités du monde souterrain. On évite soigneusement de souiller les cours et les points d'eau (tout particulièrement les sources) et tout lieu consacré à un *lhu* (*lhusa*). On entretient avec minutie les *lhubang* petites habitations de pierre qui leur sont consarées.

L'intégrité du corps des *lhu* renvoie donc à l'intégrité du corps humain. Il ne s'agit pas de propreté ou d'hygiène au sens où on pourrait l'entendre en Occident mais de pureté versus souillure. Les blessures réelles et les souillures symboliques ne forment qu'une seule et même catégorie pour les Ladakhi. Il s'agit en fait de définir les limites du corps. Tout ce dont les *lhu* ont horreur - sang, excréments - vient de l'intérieur du corps. D'ailleurs les *lhu* rejettent aussi la viande. Et il y a vraisemblablement une articulation entre le fait que ce qui vient de l'intérieur du corps souille et le fait que c'est au niveau des limites de ce corps (de la peau) que les *lhu* frappent.

Dans les cas des *lhu* (pas plus que dans celui des *lha* d'ailleurs) il n'y a pas à proprement parler de "responsabilité" de la victime. Que quelqu'un ait blessé un *lhu* sans le vouloir par inadvertance ne changera rien à la réplique de ce dernier. Ainsi Dolma une petite fille de quatre ans est paralysée des jambes (peut-être un cas de poliomyélite). Elle se traîne par terre en s'aidant de ses bras. Son père est convaincu qu'elle a été victime des *lhu* parce qu'elle avait uriné dans un ruisseau étant toute petite fille. On voit bien qu'il s'agit de causalité d'étiologie mais en aucun cas de "culpabilité" de "morale".

L'"innocence" n'a pas empêché les *lhu* pourtant êtres subjectifs doués d'intentionnalité et de désir de frapper l'enfant. L'attitude de l'instance supérieure a quelque chose d'aussi aveugle et systématique que la causalité scientifique occidentale. Mais le processus est présenté comme intentionnel même s'il est systématique.

Entre *Lha* et *Lhu*

Cette opposition entre le haut et le bas qui recoupe une opposition entre les institutions sociales et le corps est doublée d'une opposition masculin/féminin.

Les Ladakhi disent que les *lha* sont les prototypes des hommes et les *lhu* ceux des femmes. Les hommes étaient jadis habillés de blanc comme les *lha* (ce costume blanc n'a pas tout à fait disparu d'ailleurs). Quant aux femmes elles portent le *perak* qui imite le serpent-naga, des bracelets de conques sciées — animal marin aquatique — aux bras.

Il ne s'agit bien sûr pas que de ressemblance les hommes aux *lha* et les femmes aux *lhu* par le costume. Les *lha* sont liés aux intitutions et les hommes au politique (au sens le plus large de ce mot). Les femmes quant à elles sont bien entendues liées comme les *lhu* à la fécondité. Le politique l'organisation sociale sont affaire masculine. La fécondité dont les *lhu* sont dispensateurs est affaire féminine.

L'être humain a un corps. Il est aussi marqué par une organisation sociale. Il est donc à mi-chemin entre le monde d'en haut celui des *lha* celui qui renvoie à l'organisation sociale par toute une série de divinités qui coiffent les intitutions depuis l'individu jusqu'au village et le monde d'en bas qui revoie au corps[5].

L'être humain est par ailleurs homme et femme qui ont respectivement pour paradigme les *lha* d'en haut et les *lhu* d'en bas. L'être humain est à mi-chemin : il appartient au monde du milieu.

Les *Tsan*

Mais si le monde d'en haut et le monde d'en bas sont relativement simples à décrire parce qu'homogènes, peuplés l'un comme l'autre de divinités clairement définies, le monde du milieu est d'une complexité effarante. On y trouve outre les hommes et les *tsan* dont nous allons parler, toutes sortes de lutins, fées, ogres, fantômes, démons etc.

Et d'abord pourquoi le monde du milieu s'appelle-t-il *bartsan* de *bar* (milieu) et *tsan/(btsan* un démon rouge bien précis) ? Pourquoi pas le *barmi* (*mi* personne, gens, humains). Il convient tout d'abord de définir les *tsan*.

Les *tsan* sont des êtres ambigus. Vus de face ils sont très beaux et même masculins paraissent efféminés. Ils se déplacent souvent à cheval et portent aux pieds des petites clochettes comme celles des danseuses indiennes (*tipshil*). Certains prétendent qu'ils sont de couleur rouge et qu'ils portent des cornes, les mêmes cornes que nous retrouverons sur les *tsandos* (voir plus bas).

Mais vus de dos ce sont des êtres horribles car ils sont en fait dépourvus de dos ; leur coeur, leurs poumons et tous leurs viscères apparaissent bien visibles. Comme ils se déplacent le soir ou la nuit il faut éviter de se retourner après avoir croisé un inconnu aux heures tardives : il pourrait être *tsan* et le malheur, la maladie voire la mort s'abattrait sur celui qui verrait le dos d'un tel démon. Le *tsan* est considéré comme le principal responsable des morts prématurées.

Toutefois seules les personnes de basse spiritualité (de bas *sparkha*) peuvent voir un *tsan* ou en être victime. Ceux qui ont progressé spirituellement ne les voient pas et n'en souffriraient pas

---

5. Pour employer un langage bien connu on pourrait dire que les hommes sont à mi-chemin entre la nature (le corps) et culture (les institutions).

s'ils en voyaient.

Les *tsan* sont donc ambigus dans leur aspect physique qui oppose la face au dos et par leur caractère. De ce point de vue ils ressemblent aux hommes car ils sont tantôt bienveillants tantôt malfaisants selon la façon dont on se comporte avec eux.

L'absence de dos est la marque parfaite du *tsan* : elle revient comme un leitmotiv dans la bouche de tous les Ladakhi. Ceci est propre au Ladakh car Nebesky-Wojkowitz[6] dans son chapitre sur les *tsan* ne la mentionne pas. Il parle d'être rouges qui boivent du sang et habitent des châteaux de cuivre. Au Ladakh les *tsan* ne vivent pas dans un monde parallèle au nôtre : ils errent et rôdent autour du monde des humains comme ceux décrits par C. Jest au Dolpo[7].

Les *tsan* sont des êtres qui errent parmi les humains. Sans point fixe sans attache particulière ils rôdent sans arrêt et parcourent des chemins. Ces "chemins de *tsan*" (*tsanlam*) s'opposent radicalement aux maisons des humains. Aux *tsan* l'errance, le chemin ; aux hommes le point fixe, l'intérieur, le dedans (*nang*). Le fait d'habiter des maisons points fixes creux et clos est le critère de civilisation le plus important. Il existe au Ladakh une caste de chanteurs mendiants appelés *beda*. Ces *beda* sont tout en bas de la hiérarchie sociale parce qu'ils n'ont soit-disant pas de domicile fixe, de maison, de lieu d'attache et de fonction sociale particulière[8].

On trouve chez les uns et les autres le thème de l'errance, de l'absence de maison qui font des uns un monde parallèle à celui des humains une image inversée située au même niveau (le *bartsan*) et des autres une catégorie sociale inférieure à la limite de l'humain. De plus les *tsan* ne sont pas organisés en société (alors que les *lhu*, les humains et les *lha* le sont). Bien au contraire ils se fuient les uns les autres. Pour éviter les *tsan* on pose des pierres triangulaires rouge (*tsandos* ; *btsan-mdos*) ou bien on barbouille une partie des murs de rouge. Le rouge étant la couleur des *tsan* un *tsan* voyant ce rouge ne rentre pas dans la maison pensant qu'elle est occupée par un autre *tsan*.

Le monde des *lhu* et le monde des *lha* constituent deux mondes parallèles au monde humain, tandis que les *tsan* constituent une anti-société, un monde inverse - Les humains dans leur ensemble sont analogues aux *lhu* et aux *lha*, les premiers reflètant le corps, les seconds l'organisation sociale, les premiers étant les prototypes des femmes, les seconds les prototypes des hommes.

---

6. Nebesky-Wojkowitz. *Oracles and Demons of Tibet.* Graz 1962.
7. C.Jest. *Dolpo. Communautés de langue Tibétaine du Nepal.* Paris 1972.
8. Disent les Ladakhi. En fait cela n'est pas toujours vrai.

Mais les hommes sont aussi autochtones. L'image qui assimile la femme à la terre, si répandue de par le monde, existe aussi au Ladakh - Elle se manifeste entre autres par l'interdiction stricte faite aux femmes de labourer, voire simplement de toucher une charrue. Or le *tsan* rouge est en terre. C'est avec de la terre brûlée (donc cuite) que l'on colore les *tsandos*.

Les *tsan* sont en fait des "anti-hommes", des hommes ratés, inachevés d'abord (l'absence de dos) et incapables de s'organiser en société à l'image des institutions que fondent les *lha*. Leur corps ne présentent pas l'intégrité que garantissent les *lhu*.

Ainsi l'homme est tissé dans un système d'homologies entre *lha* et *lhu* et défini par rapport à une image inverse (sur le plan social) et déformée (sur le plan du corps) que sont les *tsan*.

ECOLOGY AND CONSERVATION IN LADAKH

David Mallon[1] *and Roger Prodon*[2]

Introduction

Ladakh has often been described as a high-altitude desert, and the combined effects of altitude and aridity have formed a relatively unproductive environment, shown by a restricted variety of plant and animal species, and low densities of those species which do occur.

We were unable to visit the high plains of Rupshu and the Nubra valley, and so this paper refers mainly to that part of Ladakh open to foreigners. The whole of this area is mountainous, with elevations from c.2800m to over 6000m. These mountains contain a series of arid-montane habitats, with limited zonation compared to wetter slopes on the southern side of the Himalaya. Ladakh shows close ecological affinities with Tibet and Central Asia, and from a biogeographical point of view, it is a part of the Palaearctic Region.

Flora

The flora of Ladakh is conventionally divided into three types: arid, alpine, and oasitic. Arid vegetation types (sometimes further divided into desert and semidesert types) are the most common, and cover large areas of Ladakh; typical examples are those dominated by *Artemisia* (Ladakhi: *burtse)* and *Caragana* (Lad: *drama*).

Oasitic vegetation occurs around villages and irrigated areas, while alpine vegetation is found on some hill slopes where meltwater from glaciers or snow patches allows a richer plant growth to develop. It is here that many of the summer pastures are situated.

There is an increase in aridity northwards and eastwards away from the main Himalayan range, and this is matched by a similar reduction in the amount of vegetation (Hartmann, 1983). A more detailed account of the flora of Ladakh can be found in Kachroo *et al.* (1977), while much information useful for identification is contained in Polunin & Stainton (1984) and Stainton (1988).

Trees are few, but not absent altogether. The only wild trees growing widely throughout the area are species of Willow *Salix*, (Ladakhi: *lchan-ma)* and Juniper *Juniperus* (Lad: *shugpa*).

Poplars *Populus* (Lad: *yerpa*) and Birch *Betula utilis* (Lad:

---

1. 3 Acre Street, Glossop, Derbyshire SK13 8JS, U.K.

2. Laboratoire Arago, 66650 - Banyuls sur Mer, FRANCE

stakpa) occur in a few places. The main cultivated species are Willows, Poplars and Apricot with Mulberry, Walnut and Apple at lower altitudes. The J & K Forest Department has established extensive plantations of Willow and Poplar in many places.

In the wild, trees occur in two situations: along valley bottoms and old Junipers on hill slopes. Old specimens of Juniper protected for religious reasons are found in several places, such as at Likir and Phugtal Gompas, and there are groves of over a hundred trees at the villages of Hemis Shugpa Chen and Nierak. Regeneration of these is prevented by livestock grazing. In addition, isolated Junipers and scattered groups of up to several hundred trees grow on cliffs and steep slopes in a few places. In one particularly remote part of the Zanskar gorge, there are large numbers of Junipers growing in thin stands. These appear to be the remnants of steppe Juniper forest, a vegetation type found widely in dry, mountainous areas in the Transhimalaya and Central Asia. Many of these trees in Ladakh are dead or dying, and there is little regeneration. It seems therefore, that these steppe forest remnants may be dying out from natural causes, although there is abundant regeneration of juniper in the upper Nubra valley (H.A.Osmaston, pers. comm.). Juniper wood is of great value as building timber and the fact that most of the remaining trees are found in the remotest areas and on inaccessible cliffs suggests that human agency has also contributed to the removal of of this type of vegetation from many areas. Similarly, groups or groves of birch trees can be seen on a few remote hill slopes, near Wanla, Photoksur and Pidmu in Zangskar.

Thin strips of trees grow along river valleys, made up mainly of Willows with bushes of Tamarisk *Myricaria* species (Lad: *umbuk)*, Buckthorn *Hippophae rhamnoides* (Lad: *tsermang)*, and Rose *Rosa* species (Lad: *se-a)* with occasional Poplars and Junipers, and more rarely, Birch. There are small patches of such woodland in several valleys, but the only extensive examples occur in the remote and almost uninhabited Chang Chu and Oma Chu valleys, where tree growth in a few places is thick enough to impede movement. Unlike the Juniper, this woodland appears to be regenerating satisfactorily. This type of vegetation probably once grew in all or most river valleys in Ladakh, and its absence now is likely to be the result of removal by human agency.

Fauna

There is no detailed work covering all the mammals of Ladakh, but some information can be found in Ganhar (1979), Gergan (1962), and Osborne *et al.* (1983).

A few mammal and bird species typical of the Tibetan Plateau are resident in Rupshu, but not elsewhere in Ladakh. Three of these mammals, Wild Yak (Lad: *dong) Bos grunniens*, Tibetan Antelope (Lad: *tsos) Pantholops hodgsoni* and Tibetan Gazelle (Lad: *goa) Procapra picticaudata* are now extremely rare. Two other species of the eastern plateau, Tibetan Wild Ass (Lad: *kyang) Equus kiang* and Tibetan Argali (Lad: *nyan) Ovis ammon hodgsoni* are found in greater numbers, and important populations survive in Ladakh.

The rest of the mammal fauna is typically Transhimalayan. The Ibex (Lad: *skyin) Capra ibex* and Bharal (Lad: *napo) Pseudois nayaur* are widespread; the Ladakh Urial (Lad: *shapu*) *Ovis vignei* is confined to the Indus valley. Wolf (Lad: *shangku) Canis lupus* and Snow Leopard (Lad: *shan*) *Panthera uncia* are also widespread, but rare. Bears (Lad: *drinmo) Ursus arctos* have been reported from Zanskar, and other species occurring include Fox, Marmot, Hare, Weasel and Pika.

While animal numbers in Ladakh are low in absolute terms, this is a reflection of the harsh, unproductive environment, and in relative terms, populations are extensive and unfragmented, in many cases comparing favourably with other parts of the Himalayan region. There has inevitably been some decrease in numbers of wildlife around major population centres and along the line of the roads from Srinagar—Leh and Kargil—Padum. Otherwise, however, with one exception, we did not find any evidence of a significant decline in animal numbers in recent years, and Ladakh contains important Ibex, Bharal and Snow Leopard populations. This is in the main due to demographic patterns and social attitudes which have had important consequences for the wildlife. Firstly, the sparsely distributed human population and the location of most settlements in the major river valleys has left large areas available for wildlife. Some particularly inaccessible valleys are so little disturbed that they can be regarded as a kind of natural sanctuary. Secondly, Buddhist prohibitions on killing have meant that hunters have traditionally been few, and hunting is futher discouraged by strict laws, enforced by the Forest Department. While some illegal hunting undoubtedly goes on, it is only on a small scale, and Ladakh has been spared the systematic onslaught on wildlife that has severely reduced large animal populations in many parts of the Himalayan region.

The one exception to the above is the Ladakh Urial, or *shapu*, which has suffered from overshooting and now survives in pockets of its former range (Mallon, 1983). The habitat of this species is in the low hills along the Indus valley which are easily reached from the main road. The blame for this was put on the Indian army (Ranjitsinh

1981), though now the Army in Ladakh is under orders not to shoot wildlife, and the *shapu* population appears to be recovering.

The State Directorate of Wildlife Protection has designated a series of national parks and sanctuaries for Ladakh which will preserve representative habitats and important wildlife areas. The DWP recognises that these will have to managed in sympathy with the needs of the local population.

Around 270 bird species have occurred in Ladakh, of which only about 35% are known to breed, the rest being migrants or rare visitors. A few pairs of the endangered Black-necked Crane breed in marshy areas near the border with Tibet. Some former breeding species have declined sharply in numbers and the possibility that this is connected with removal of scrub was discussed by Delany *et al.* (1982). Further information on the birds of Ladakh can be found in Holmes (1986), Mallon (1987) and Prodon (1984).

Human impact on the environment

In all parts of Ladakh, trees, shrubs and plants are used for fuel, building, grazing, fodder and incense. The location of the densest remaining trees in the most sparsely populated areas, the presence of tree stumps in many valleys, and documentary and oral evidence all indicate that the cumulative effects have been the removal of tree and shrub cover in many valleys. For example, Hemischu and Uleh Tokpo valleys show signs of cut out trees and bushes; in Sani, Zanskar, villagers speak of having to go farther and farther into the valley each year to fetch fuel wood, and a few straggling trees and bushes in the valley show where the recent limit of the trees was situated. Workman (1908) said that the marshy areas near Rangdum were covered in Willow scrub two to six feet high, but this has now disappeared.

Overall, wood for fuel and building is in short supply in Ladakh, but there are exceptions, such as the Markha valley, where good supplies of wood are carefully managed, and some can be sold in Leh in winter. In Zanskar, and other areas where trees are few, villagers have to travel far and wide in search of wood, or use more dung and shrubs for fuel, which may be less efficient and more unhealthy. In the Lingshed area, villagers travel for 2-3 days to obtain building timber which must then be hauled all the way back to the village. In some places, people also spoke of having to travel further and further in order to obtain an adequate supply of woody plants such as *burtse* (*Artemisia*), and *lonze* (*Acantholimon*). This clearly has a negative effect on the workload of villagers, who must travel and carry over greater distances.

In recent years, the import into Ladakh of coal, kerosene and wood has provided alternative sources of fuel in places along the main roads, and tree planting by the Forest Department has gone some way to offset removal of natural tree cover.

Hill slopes are also widely used for grazing by domestic animals. A few signs of overgrazing were noted, but the areas concerned were small and there was no sign of large-scale degradation of pastures. However, a full assessment would require a detailed agro-botanical study of the grazing lands, comparing the availability of palatable grasses etc. in different areas. Several signs of good practice were seen, suggesting that grazing pressure was not excessive, e.g. a valley may be left fallow for a period each year, and in the east, where livestock rearing is more important, herds are moved around different areas in rotation, allowing them to recover. One negative trend has been the arrival in the upper Suru valley in recent years of Bakkarwal seasonal grazers from the southern side of the Himalaya, bringing with them several thousand head of livestock, which greatly increases competition for grazing and which has led to some tension with the local population.

Many changes have taken place in Ladakh since 1962, following the influx of military personnel and administrators from outside the area, the growth of a cash economy, the influence of modern mass communications and the opening of the area to foreign tourists. Among these changes has been a sharp increase in the population, which rose by 17% between the 1961 and 1971 censuses. At such a time of rapid social and economic change it is not easy to draw firm conclusions, but it seems clear that much of the population increase has been absorbed by job opportunities with the administration, armed forces and tourism in the main centres, and this has so far prevented a correspondingly sharp increase in pressure on the land. Village expansion has been limited by the availability of water for irrigation, and livestock numbers do not appear to have increased significantly.

Whatever their effect on the traditional way of life of Ladakh, tourists have made little direct impact on the environment, except for the leaving of litter at popular camping places.

Conclusions

Surviving wildlife populations in Ladakh appear to be good, and given a continued ban on hunting, there is no reason why they should not remain so. There is as yet no evidence of severe environmental damage, but in places there are problems with the supply of fuel wood and these need to be addressed by planting schemes or the provision of alternative energy sources.

It seems obvious that the population will continue to expand and, while migration to the towns is continuing, pressure on the land will increase, particularly where new irrigation schemes allow development of new fields and the expansion of villages to take place. Villagers will also no doubt seek the extension of road building programmes to their own areas, improving access, and bringing both benefits and disadvantages.

Although the land in Ladakh is not susceptible to the serious degradation caused by the cycle of forest removal and soil erosion which is prevalent on the monsoon slopes, the environment is still fragile, and conditions are near the limits of both aridity and altitude for practical cultivation and habitation. Obviously, it is in the direct interests of those people who depend on the land for some of their needs that no overuse should threaten its future productivity. This will require extended tree planting, monitoring of pastures and grazing lands, and the improvement in quality of livestock herds. While the people of Ladakh should not be denied an increase in their prosperity, there is a need for development to proceed not only with the best aspects of the traditional way of life intact, but also without the damage to the environment which has seriously affected the standard and quality of life in many other places.

Bibliography

DELANY, S.N., C.A.DENBY & J.A.NORTON (1982) "Ornithology." *University of Southampton Himalayan Expedition 1980 Report:* 5-153.

GANHAR, J.N. (1979) *The Wildlife of Ladakh.* Srinagar, Haramukh Publications.

GERGAN, S.S. (1962) *Big Game of Jammu and Kashmir.* Srinagar, Forest Dept.

HARTMANN, H. (1983) "Pflanzengesellschaften entlang der Kaschmirrroute in Ladakh." *Jahrb. Vereins zum Schutz der Bergwelt (München)* 48: 131-173.

HOLMES, P.R. (1986) "The avifauna of the Suru river valley, Ladakh." *Forktail* 2: 21-41.

KACHROO, P., B.L.SAPRU & U.DHAR (1977) *Flora of Ladakh.* Dehra Dun, Bishen Singh Mahendra Pal Singh.

MALLON, D.P. (1983) "The status of the Ladakh urial *Ovis orientalis vignei* in Ladakh, India." *Biol. Conservation*. 27: 373-381.

MALLON, D.P. (1987) "The winter birds of Ladakh." *Forktail* 3: 27-41.

OSBORNE, B.C., D.P MALLON & S.J.R.FRASER, (1983) "Ladakh, threatened stronghold of Himalayan wildlife." *Oryx* 17: 182-189.

POLUNIN, O. & A. STAINTON (1984) *Flowers of the Himalaya.* Delhi, Oxford University Press.

PRODON, R. (1984) "Sur la composition et la biogéographie de l'avifaune du Ladakh (Inde)." *Acta Biol. Mont.* 1984(4): 573-581.

RANJITSINGH, M.K. (1981) "Himalayan Fauna." *The Himalaya: aspects of change.* ed. by J.S.Lall, Delhi, Oxford University Press: 64-76.

STAINTON, A. (1988) *Flowers of the Himalaya: a supplement.* Delhi, Oxford U.P.

SOZIALSTRUKTUREN IN HUNZA, PAKISTAN

*Gudrun Meier**

English Summary

Social structures in Hunza, Pakistan

The history of Hunza can be divided into four phases. In the first phase society was organised in clans. The three original villages in Hunza were Altit, Baltit and Ganish, and the original clans were Thapkianc, Baratalin and Buroon — to which the Qurikuc were added later. All three villages shared a common irrigation system, and this demanded a high degree of social organisation.

The second phase began in around 1200 AD when two nephews of the Shina-speaking rulers of Gilgit established themselves in Hunza and Nagar. The rulers (known as *tham*) never had absolute authority; the *tham* shared the ritual "first ploughing" in spring with the Wazir, a member of the Thapkianc clan.

The third phase ran from 1761 to 1891. In the second half of the 18th century China conquered East Turkestan (Xinjiang). The *Taotai*, the most senior Chinese official in the region, accepted Tham Silum Khan III of Hunza as a tributary. Every year Hunza sent 15 bags of gold dust to the Taotai for onward transmission to the Chinese court. New trading opportunities transformed the economic basis of Hunza. A surplus of manpower meant that more men were available for military purposes. The people of Hunza extended the radius of their armed raids — including raids on the road from Leh to Yarkand. Increased prosperity resulted in the creation of a new social stratum.

Friedrich Engels described one of the transitional stages between a "gentry"-based society (*Gentilgesellschaft*) and a class-based society as "military democracy". This concept is controversial but, for lack of a better term, it seems to fit Hunza during this period. Within Hunza there was a degree of democracy in village councils and among the elders in the court (see tables at end), but this was combined with extensive external military activity.

In 1891 Hunza came under British colonial rule, and the older social structures began to lose their significance. It was formally absorbed into Pakistan in 1954 and the last 'king' of Hunza lost his position in 1972.

Summary by John Bray

---

* Staatliches Museum für Völkerkunde, Japanisches Palais, Palaisplatz, 01097 Dresden, GERMANY.

Einleitung

Das Hunza-Tal im Nordwest-Karakorum hat dank seiner geographischen Lage am Rande großer Imperien und südlich der Seidenstraße frühzeitig Interesse bei Chinesen, Briten und Abgesandten des zaristischen Rußland gefunden, die aus strategischen Erwägungen Verbindungen zu den Hunzukuc aufnahmen. Forschungen in diesem Gebiet galten in erster Linie den Hochgebirgspässen, die den Übergang in die Interessensphäre der jeweils anderen Seite gestatteten. Die Beobachtungen zur Bevölkerung des Gebietes und zu den potten und Gebräuchen wurden meist aus persönlichem Interesse der Kundschafter gemacht. Man hat diese Berichte später als "Offiziers-Ethnologie" bezeichnet. Sie enthalten aber trotz allem wichtiges Material, an dem kein Forscher vorbeigehen kann. Beobachtungen zu den gesellschaftlichen Verhältnissen finden sich da aber noch wenig. Spätere Forschungen, insbesondere die Arbeiten von Lorimer aus den zwanziger und dreißiger Jahren dieses Jahrhunderts, bauen auf Informationen, die ihnen die geschichtsbewußten Vertreter des Königshauses und der traditionellen Führungskräfte gaben. Diese Sicht der Historie ist zwangslaufig einseitig auf die Herausstellung eigener Verdienste und auf die Idealisierung der traditionellen Verhältnisse angelegt. Erst der Vergleich mit den gesellschaftlichen Verhältnissen in den benachbarten Tälern und das Bekanntwerden der engen Verknüpfungen der Geschichte Hunzas mit dem chinesischen Reich durch die Publikationen von Snoy, Müller-Stellrecht, Jettmar u.a. lassen jetzt den Versuch sinnvoll erscheinen, die Entwicklung der gesellschaftlichen Verhältnisse in Hunza erneut zu untersuchen.

In der Geschichte Hunzas sind bisher vier wesentliche Abschnitte der Entwicklung festzustellen:

1. die Zeit von der Einwanderung in das Hunzatal bis zur Errichtung einer Shina-Sprecher-Herrschaft um 1200.
2. die Herrschaftszeit der Shina-Sprecher bis zur Unterstellung unter die chinesische Oberherrschaft 1761.
3. die Entwicklung Hunzas als Tributär Chinas und Beauftragtem zur Sicherung der Seidenstraße und der chinesischen Südgrenze am Kleinen Pamir bis 1871.
4. der "State of Hunza" von 1891 bis 1954.

Die Entwicklung Hunzas bis 1200 AD

In der Geschichte Hunzas, deren Anfänge in Legenden und fiktiven Genealogien nur schwer faßbar ist, ist das erste sichere Datum das Jahr 763. In diesem Jahr zog ein chinesisches Heer weit nach Süden und berührte dabei auch das Hunzatal. Ein vorübergehender Tributkontakt soll zustandegekommen sein, der aber wohl kaum

Spuren hinterließ - mit Ausnahme der Notiz in den chinesischen Annalen.

Es gab in dieser Zeit auf der Hunza-Seite des Tales - die andere Flußseite war von den Nagerkuc besiedelt - die drei "Urdörfer" Altit, Baltit und Ganish mit den drei "Ursippen" der Thapkianc, Baratalin und Buroon, zu denen später die Qurokuc kamen, die sich aus verschiedenen Splittergruppen ohne gemeinsamen Ahnen zusammensetzten. Der rituelle Mittelpunkt dieses Talhaushaltes war Baltit.

Alle drei Dörfer lagen an einem gemeinsamen Bewässerungssystem, dem Harchi Har, dem Gletscherbach des Ultar-Gletschers, von dem aus Stichkanäle zu den Feldern führten. Bewässerungsanlagen waren die erste Voraussetzung für das Leben in diesem wüstenhaften Hochgebirgstal. Der Hunzafluß, dessen Flußbett etwa 70 m unterhalb der nutzbaren Talterrassen liegt, war dafür nicht nutzbar. So mußten die Gletscherschmelzwässer am Gletschertor gefaßt und in Kanälen zu den Feldern geleitet werden. Solche Arbeiten setzen ein gut organisiertes Gemeinwesen voraus. Die Sozialstruktur der Urdörfer basierte auf den Sippen/Clans. Die Wirtschaftseinheit war die patriarchale Großfamilie. Vergleicht man die Verhältnisse im benachbarten Bagrottal und die Reste der alten Bebauung der Urdörfer, kann man schlußfolgern, daß die Sippen/Clans innerhalb der Dörfer in Clanquartieren wohnten, die festungsartigen Charakter hatten und über Wehrtürme verfügten.

Der Rat der Familienoberhäupter befand über die Angelegenheiten der Sippe. Der Rat der Sippenältesten nahm sich aller Probleme des Talhaushaltes an; war oberste Instanz in Rechtsfragen; wählte den "ersten Pflüger" und bestimmte aus seinen Reihen den "Kadako" — "einen, der das letzte Wort hat"- also eine Institution, die dem Häuptling nahekommt. Es ist nicht bekannt, ob das eine Wahl auf Lebenszeit war oder ob diese Funktion nur für eine gewisse Zeit galt oder ein solcher "Führer" nur bei größeren Gemeinschaftsaufgaben - Kanalbau, Beutezüge usw. - gewählt wurde.

Das Amt des "ersten Pflügers", das nach den Berichten jährlich neu von einer Sippe übernommen wurde und dessen Inhaber die Fruchtbarkeit für das Land verbürgen mußte, wurde später eine ständige Aufgabe der Thapkianc-Sippe. Ihre Vertreter sollen jeweils den größten Erfolg in ihrer Amtszeit gehabt haben.

Die Sippen/Clans waren exogam und tauschten nach bestimmten Regeln ihre Töchter aus. Die patriarchale Erbfolge schloß Töchter vom Besitz an Sippenland aus. Die Eltern, die Söhne und ihre Familien und unverheiratete Familienmitglieder bewirtschafteten gemeinsam den Boden. Sippeneigentum waren die Almen, sie wurden in einem Rotationssystem benutzt. Da die Herden klein waren, schlossen sich die Familien zu gemeinsamer Almnutzung zusammen.

1200 bis 1781

Das Zusammenleben der Sippen/Clans im Talhaushalt war sicher nicht so problemlos, wie es nach dieser Darstellung erscheinen könnte. Eine erste Vormachtstellung der Thapkianc-Sippe ergab sich nach der endgültigen Übernahme des Amtes als "erster Pflüger". Ebenso kann an eine zeitweilige Herrschaft durch einen erfolgreichen Anführer von Raubzügen in Nachbartäler, der dieses Amt nicht an den Sippenältesten zurückgeben wollte, gedacht werden.

Das Streben der Thapkianc-Sippe nach Herrschaft und die dadurch ausgelösten Auseinandersetzungen mit den anderen Sippen scheint der Shin-Dynastie in Gilgit, dem Machtzentrum der Region, ein willkommener Anlaß gewesen zu sein, einzugreifen. Schon zuvor hatten sie mehrfach den Versuch zur Beherrschung der nördlich gelegenen Gebirgstäler unternommen. Jetzt, etwa um 1200, wurden zwei Neffen des Herrschers als Vertreter Gilgits im Hunzatal eingesetzt. Maglot verwaltete Nagar, Girkis Hunza. Beide lösten sich jedoch sehr schnell von Gilgit und versuchten mit einer Gefolgschaft aus unzufriedenen Sippengenossen eigene Dynastien in Hunza und Nagar zu errichten. Trotz starken Widerstandes in Hunza, insbesondere durch die Thapkianc-Sippe, die dabei fast ausgerottet worden sein soll, gelang es Girkis, die Herrschaft an sich zu bringen. Gesichert war diese Herrschaft nie absolut, ohne die Respektierung der bestehenden Sippenordnung hätte die Ayaso-Dynastie keinen Bestand gehabt. Neben der anderen Sprache, dem Shina, einer Dardsprache, die sie in dieses Kernland der Burushaski-Sprache, einer auch heute noch nicht zugeordneten Sprache, mitbrachten, waren es vor allem die geistigen Vorstellungen der Darden mit Feenglauben, Wildziegenverehrung, Rindermeidung, Verdienstfestwesen und Rangsystem, mit dem sich die Hunzukuc auseinandersetzen mußten. Girkis und seine Nachfolger als "Könige" zu bezeichnen, wie es in der Literatur allgemein getan wird, entspricht kaum ihrem wahren Status zu dieser Zeit und ist wohl mehr eine Umschreibung im Hinblick auf den europäischen Leser.

Nur wenn der tham - so die Burushaski-Bezeichnung - gemeinsam mit dem Wazir, einem Mitglied der Thapkianc-Sippe, das Ritual des ersten Pflügens vollzieht, ist für ausreichende Fruchtbarkeit des Bodens gesorgt.

Die innere Struktur der drei Dörfer ändert sich in dieser Zeit fast nicht. Die schwache ökonomische Basis des Landes läßt weder die Installation aufwendiger Verdienstfeste, noch die Errichtung einer umfangreichen Hofhaltung zu.

Die Gefolgschaft des tham ist eine kleine Gruppe junger Männer, die zeitweilig als Hirten und Jäger in Baltit dienen und ihn gelegentlich zu Beutezügen in die Nachbartäler oder an die Seidenstraße begleiten.

Die Verbindung zu den führenden Familien der Sippen wird durch die Vergabe von Milchelternschaften für die Prinzen und Prinzessinnen hergestellt. Diese Verwandtschaftsform ist bindender als die Blutsverwandtschaft und sichert dem Milchkind eine lebenslänglich treue Gefolgschaft.

Steuern sind als "Gabe der ersten Früchte" und als Verpflichtung zur gemeinsamen Bestellung des "Königslandes durch die Bewohner des Dorfes, in dem sich das Feld befindet, keine drückende Last. Man darf annehmen, daß es sich bei diesem Königsland um das ehemalige Sippenfeld handelt, dessen Erträge früher bei den gemeinsamen Sippenfesten verwendet wurden. Nun stehen diese Erträge als Mittel zur Linderung der alljährlich wiederkehrenden Hungersnöte im Frühjahr, als Saatguthilfe und zur Verpflegung von Gästen zur Verfügung des tham.

Um 1700 erfolgte - aus Baltistan kommend - die Einwanderung einer Gruppe von Berico oder Dom, Schmieden und Musikanten, die kastenartig organisiert waren. Sie wurden nicht in das bestehende Sozialgefüge integriert und waren als "Fremde" am unteren Ende der sozialen Stufenleiter angesiedelt. Sie bauten in Niederhunza ein eigenes Dorf und kamen als Spezialisten zur Arbeit in die Hunza-Dörfer. Für ihre Tätigkeit wurden sie mit Naturalien entlohnt. Es wurden keine Heiratsbeziehungen zu den Berico aufgebaut.

Sklaven gab es in Hunza nicht, gelegentlich gemachte Kriegsgefangene verkaufte man allerdings an Sklavenhändler, die diese Menschen dann nach dem Wakhan oder Ostturkestan verhandelten. In Hunza hätten die Gefangenen die Wirtschaft belastet.

1761 bis 1891 AD

In der zweiten Hälfte des 18. Jahrhunderts, 1759, eroberte China Ostturkestan, ohne allerdings mit ausreichend Truppenpräsens den Landgewinn absichern zu können. Hunza, das in Auseinandersetzungen mit den Kirkisen auf dem Tagdumbash um die Nutzung von Weidegebieten verwickelt war und zudem durch gelegentliche Überfälle auf die Karawanenzüge der Seidenstraße die Aufmerksamkeit der Chinesen geweckt hatte, machte dem Taotai in Kashgar, dem höchsten chinesischen Beamten an der Südgrenze, ein Unterwerfungsangebot. Der tham tat dies, obwohl keine chinesischen Truppen bis Hunza vorgedrungen waren. Er erhoffte sich mit diesem diplomatischen Schachzug wohl nicht nur Unterstützung bei seinen Forderungen gegenüber den Kirgisen, sondern auch Handlungsfreiheit bei anderen Unternehmungen. Tham Silum Khan III. wurde vom chinesischen Kaiser als Tributär angenommen und hatte jährlich 15 Säckchen Goldstaub an den Taotai für den chinesischen Hof zu übergeben. Zusätzlich wurde er mit dem Schutz der chinesischen Südgrenze am Kleinen Pamir, dem Schutz der Handelswege und der Niederhaltung der Kirgisen-Nomaden auf dem Tagdumbash beauftragt. Dafür wurden Hunza die Weiderechte auf dem Tagdumbash bestätigt und ein Tributrecht gegenüber den Kirgisen-Nomaden eingeräumt. Dazu kam das Recht auf die Beute bei den Einsätzen an der Grenze und Vorzugsbedingungen auf den chinesischen Märkten.

Als Geschenke des chinesischen Kaisers erhielt die Tributgesandtschaft in Kashgar Pferde, Gewehre, Kleidung, Seidenrollen, Porzellan, Tee u.a., dazu kamen Geschenke der chinesischen Beamten.

Damit ergibt sich nach 1761, dem Datum der Aufnahme der Tributbeziehungen, eine völlig neue Situation für Hunza.

Durch die Verbesserung der Lebensbedingungen für die Bevölkerung, insbesondere eine stabilere Lebensmittelversorgung über den Großteil des Jahres durch die neuen Handelsmöglichkeiten, die aus der eigenen ökonomischen Basis nicht zu erreichen gewesen wäre, nahmen die Alters- und die Säuglingssterblichkeit ab und die Geburtenhäufigkeit zu. Innerhalb von ungefähr 40 Jahren kommt es so zu einem bedeutenden Bevölkerungszuwachs. Die Urdörfer werden zu eng. Unter Silum Khan III. wird ein neuer Bewässerungskanal, der Dala oder Samarkand, gebaut, an dem neue Dörfer errichtet werden können. Mehr Männer stehen für Kriegs- und Beutezüge zur Verfügung. Die Hunzukuc weiten ihre Raubzüge meist getarnt als Grenzschutzutzunternehmen, nach Osten bis zu den Pakhpo und an den südlichen Zweig der Handelsstraße, die von Leh kommend nach Yarkand führt, aus. Kriegsgegangene werden mit gutem Gewinn auf den Sklavenmärkten in Badakhshan und Turkestan verkauft. Die Beute wird zwischen dem tham und der Mannschaft im Verhältnis 1/3 zu 2/3 verteilt. Anhäufung von Reichtum wird möglich, eine Schichtung der Gesellschaft quer durch die alte Sippenstruktur setzt ein, Verdienstfeste werden möglich.

Diese entscheidende Änderung in der Sozialstruktur der Hunzukuc, die eindeutig von äußeren Einflüssen ausgelöst wurde, und die die Voraussetzungen für eine weitere Schichtung der Gesellschaft schufen, sind von dem ehemaligen Political Agent und späteren Sprachforscher Lorimer erforscht und von Irmtraut Müller-Stellrecht aufgearbeitet und publiziert worden. Hieraufbasieren diese Ausführungen.

Friedrich Engels hat in seinem Werk "Der Ursprung der Familie, des Privateigentums und des Staates", das sich stark an L.H. Morgan's "Ancient Society" orientierte, diese Form des Übergangs von der Gentilgesellschaft zur Klassengesellschaft als "Militärische Demokratie" bezeichnet. Über den Begriff ist viel gestritten worden und viele Historiker lehnen ihn ab. Betrachtet man jedoch, was Engels als Begriffsinhalt ansieht - nämlich eine funktionsfähige Gentilverfassung nach innen und militärische Aktionen nach außen - dann scheint Hunza in der Zeit nach 1761 ein gutes Beispiel dafür zu sein, wie eine solche Übergangsperiode ausgesehen haben kann. Die Beobachtung, daß besonders in den Randgebieten und unter besonderen historischen Konstellationen diese Entwicklung vor sich ging, zeigt, daß es sich dabei um eine der möglichen Übergangsformen handelt.

1891 bis 1954

Die Sinnentleerung vieler gentiler Institutionen und die "Aufweichung" gentiler Strukturen durch die Machtstellung des tham/Khan unter der Protektion der britischen Kolonialmacht nach 1891 einerseits und die Durchsetzung islamischer Lebens- und Rechtsnormen andererseits haben zu Formen des gesellschaftlichen Lebens geführt, die von den Forschern mit "halbfeudal mit archaischen Resten" umschrieben werden. Welche Folgen für die innere Struktur der Hunzadörfer dieses Tourismus-Werbe-Etikett hat, ist gegenwärtig zu beobachten.

Bereits 1954 wurde Hunza Teil des Staates Pakistan. Der letzte König von Hunza verlor seine Funktion 1972.

TABLE 1. SOCIAL STRUCTURES IN HUNZA VILLAGES

Till 1200 AD

3 villages Áltit, Báltit, Gánish	with	4 "tribes" = clans Thápkianc Barátalin Buroon Qúrokuc
council of the headmen of the clans kadáko "the man who had the last word"		council of the headmen of the families

From 1200 to 1761 AD

Áyaso - Dynastie
(from tham Girkis, who came from
Gilgit, to tham Silum Khan III.)

3 villages council of the headmen of the clans	with	4 "tribes" = clans council of the headmen of the families

officials:
wázir = "Prime minister"
lambadar = "chief" of a village
speaker = told the people what to do

From 1761 to 1891 AD

the tham,
his first wife her children
his other wives and their children

the Greats the Baldákuin the Ṣádarisó	4 "tribes" = clans patri-lineages council of the headmen of the families
the yatkuin - Bǎaře sis rank system = dynamic	gentil system = static

TABLE 2. OFFICIALDOM IN HUNZA

Officials of the "state of Hunza":

tham = Khan = chief
wázir = "Prime minister"
thránphá (2 in each village)
cárbù (the speaker of the tránphá)
kadáko = the first under the headmen of the clans

Officials of the tham's household:

farrāsh = the man who has the keys
yarpá = steward on each of the tham's properties
ġulćin = head cook
bread gulcin = head baker
royal herdsman
gumáali = men who fetch water for the tham
yasòol = men who give food in the public assembly
diwan begi = a man used to keep guard over the plundered property and personally bring it to the tham.

Wichtige Literatur

ENGELS, FRIEDRICH 1956 "Der Ursprung der Familie, des Privat eigentums und des Staates", in: *Marx-Engels-Werke* (MEW), Bd. 21

BIDDULPH, J. 1880 *Tribes of the Hindoo Koosh.* Reprint Graz 1971.

JETTMAR, KARL 1975 "Die Religionen des Hindukusch" in: *Die Religionen der Menschheit*, Bd. 4,1.

MÜLLER-STELLRECHT, IRMTRAUD 1975 "Feste in Dardistan: Darstellung und kulturgeschichtliche Analyse" aus: *Arbeiten aus dem Seminar für Völkerkunde* der J.W.v. Goethe-Universität Frankfurt a.M. Bd.5

MÜLLER-STELLRECHT, IRMTRAUD 1978 "Hunza und China (1761-1891)" in: *Beiträge zur Südasien-Forschung*, Südasien-Institut, Universität Heidelberg, Bd. 44.

MÜLLER-STELLRECHT, IRMTRAUD 1979 "Materialien zur Ethnographie Dardistans (Pakistan)" aus den *nachgelassenen Aufzeichnungen von D.L.R.Lorimer*. Graz, Adeva.

SNOY, PETER 1983 (Herausg.), *Ethnologie und Geschichte - Festschrift für Karl Jettmar*.

SNOY, PETER 1975 *Bagrot - Eine dardische Talschaft im Karakorum.* Graz, Adeva.

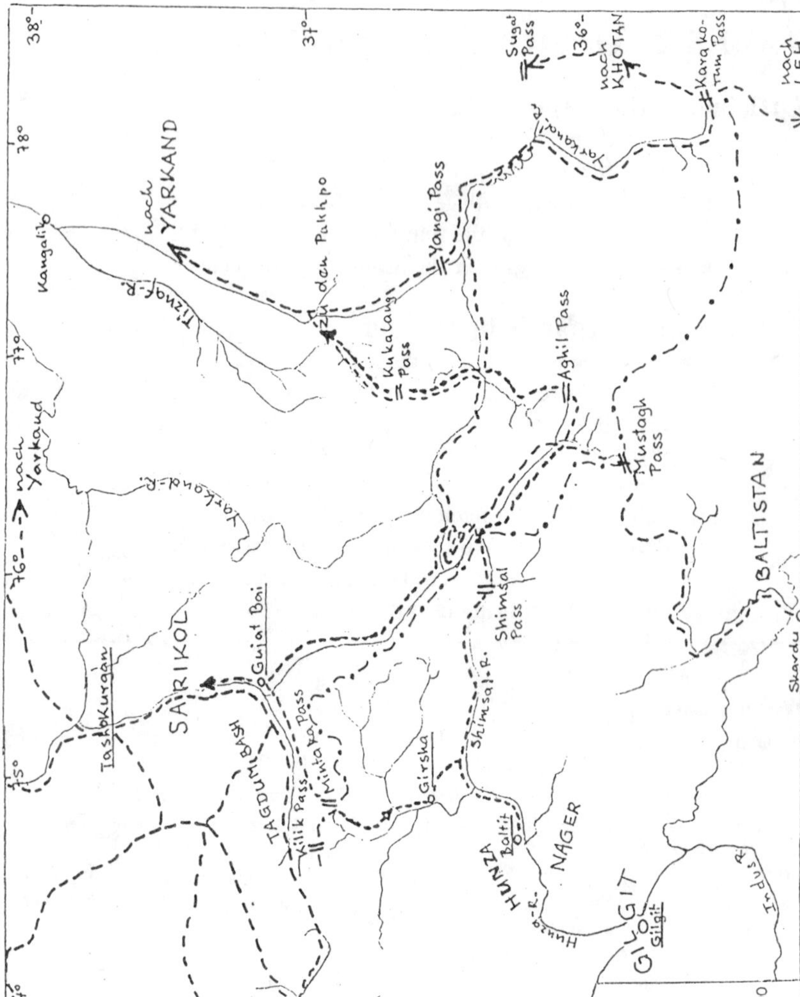

G.Meier Fig. 1: Routes to the North and East from Hunza.

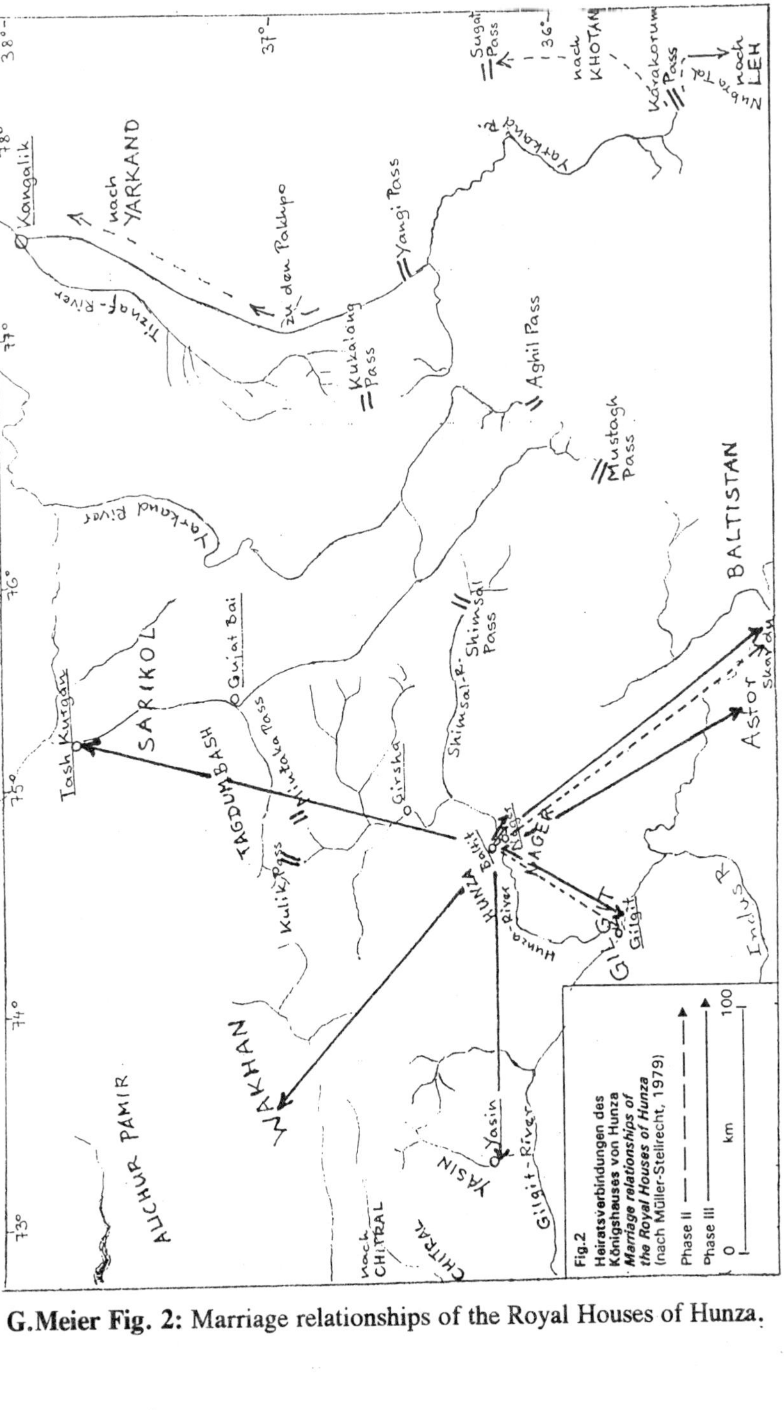

G.Meier Fig. 2: Marriage relationships of the Royal Houses of Hunza.

FARMING, NUTRITION & HEALTH IN LADAKH, TIBET & LOWLAND CHINA
A review

Henry Osmaston[1]

Summary

The people of the high montane areas (3500-5000m) of Tibet and Ladakh are small by American and European standards, as are the people of lowland China; the children show a serious check in growth at weaning and in the montane areas a high incidence of disease and mortality. Malnutrition has been suggested as an important factor in all these, though the possible contribution of ethnicity is unknown. Detailed statistical evidence is presented from a variety of sources. All three areas have a productive agriculture, adversely affected by political action, but reliable knowledge is scanty about the diet in the montane areas, especially of children. Recommendations are made for future investigation and action in Ladakh.

Introduction

Farming is a means of using natural resources sustainably to sustain human existence, principally by the production of food and thus the maintenance of health. To consider farming, nutrition or health in isolation can lead to erroneous conclusions and hence mistaken policies. In a region such as Ladakh, peopled by mainly subsistence farmers, nutrition and health are largely dependent on adequate food production from their own crops and livestock. However it is remarkable that in such a relatively peaceful and well administered region, there is still so little reliable knowledge about the basic facts of agricultural production and food consumption. Official perceptions of agriculture in Ladakh have been that it is primitive and unproductive, needs Western technology to improve it, and needs supplementing by imported food to meet local food requirements. Official fiscal and technical policies have been based on these beliefs, but new evidence shows that they are wrong. However much more reliable and detailed information about domestic food consumption and other uses of agricultural produce is still required.

The improvement of people's health is a popular and common aim both of governments and of many non-governmental organisations. Some major and conspicuous health problems are susceptible to direct attack and sometimes spectacular cure or prevention by surgery,

---

1. Dr.H.A.Osmaston, Finsthwaite Cottage, Finsthwaite, Ulverston, Cumbria LA12 8BN, UK.

inoculation or micro-nutrient supplementation. Rapid epidemiological or demographic surveys may demonstrate the existence of other problems of community health such as liability to cardio-vascular disease, bronchial conditions, specific cancers, subnormal growth and high infant mortality, but to identify the causal agents or conditions is often much more difficult, especially because complex environmental, social, economic and traditional factors are often involved. It may even be difficult to decide whether a particular condition, e.g. small stature or thinness, is or is not a disadvantage in a particular environment, whether it is primarily due to genetic or environmental causes (the old nature v. nurture argument), and if the latter what those causes are and whether remedial measures are appropriate.

In Ladakh these uncertainties have led to controversy over the question of childhood malnutrition. It is evident to any visitor to Ladakh that adult Ladakhis are typically short and slight compared with Europeans. One view is that Ladakhis are small because of childhood malnutrition, but the use of the technical medical word for this — '*stunting*', which in everyday English has a derogatory implication, — has aroused particular antagonism. The opposing view is that Ladakhis are genetically small thanks to natural selection of a body form which is best adapted to the montane environment; or alternatively that smaller size may indeed be nutritionally or environmentally determined but is nevertheless an advantageous and acceptable adaptation or accommodation to the environment. The first view has provided justification on limited evidence for an aid programme providing supplementary food for children, besides the large scale issue of subsidised government rations, which have come under some criticism. This divergence of views is not exclusive to Ladakh but has arisen about other montane communities, for example in the Andes. This paper reviews additional evidence about the question in the Himalaya, and suggests alternative policies.

Food Production

One popular image of the past, up to Ladakh's abrupt precipitation into the modern world by the Indo-Pakistan and Indo-Chinese military confrontations of 1948 and 1962, which converted it from a political backwater to a vitally strategic frontier zone, is one of food adequacy and indeed surplus. The traditional phrase quoted about former times by many elderly Ladakhis is *"za.bos thung.bos"* — "food enough; drink enough", that is apart from brief shortages due to natural disasters, such as the heavy snows in Zangskar in the spring of 1955 when many livestock died. A counterblast to this rosy-tinted view of the past is given by Sonam Wangyal (in press), who, while not denying the agricultural productivity, describes it as overborne by the oppressive exactions of Dogra and Kashmiri officials, landlords and money lenders between 1839 and 1949 (when land was redistributed and agricultural taxation effectively ended). Leh's importance as an *entrepôt* of trans-Himalayan trade resulted in a considerable demand for food and forage to supply the caravans, estimated at over 300 tonnes of grain annually, about 5% of the district's production, at the beginning of this century (Warikoo, this volume), nearly half of this being acquired compulsorily by the government as land taxes. In addition to this every settled household annually traded grain for wool and salt brought by the Ladakhi nomads from Rupshu and Changthang by sheep and yak caravans (Rizvi, 1983, 1985). On a wider scale substantial quantities were traded with Tibet, Rudok being heavily dependent on this import, any interruption of it causing international repercussions (Bray, this vol.). Though individual farmers (every Ladakhi farmed either directly or through tenants) primarily produced their own subsistence needs, many of them and the region as a whole produced a surplus, and current yields show how productive the traditional agriculture was and is.

Ladakhi farmers themselves have always traditionally thought of yields in terms of yield ratios (the amount harvested per unit sown). They commonly estimate their yield ratios as being in the range of 5:1 to 10:1; even lower ratios (2.3:1 to 6.7:1) were indicated by observations carried out on farms by Ladakh Ecological Development Group (LEDeG) staff in 1990. These are extrordinarily low in comparison with a typical western ratio of 50, and in view of the fact that one good ear of Ladakhi 6-row barley, grown from a single grain sown, may produce 50 grains. However yield ratios are not reliable guides to yields per hectare since yield is nearly constant over a considerable range of sowing rates, because open sown crops grow more tillers (branches) and ears per plant than close ones. Other data from the Markha and Zangskar valleys indicate much lower sowing rates (Southampton, 1979; Osmaston 1994).

Official government statistics of grain yields in Ladakh are 0.7 t/ha for barley and wheat (Census of India 1961; Leh District Planning Commission 1984), though Agricultural Dept. staff will admit that these are too low and higher figures of 1.2 to 1.5 t/ha are given in a recent agricultural handbook (SKUAST, 1987). Farmers, if pressed, will often admit to yields of about 2-3 t/ha in the more fertile villages. This is confirmed by estimates of yields from small sample plots (c.1m^2) in crops in Zangskar (Chalmers & Ramm 1984; Osmaston 1985, 1989, 1994) and by Goering in the Indus valley (Norberg Hodge et al. 1989) which indicate that yields in average crops in good agricultural areas are about 3-3.5 t/ha. These exceed the 2-3 t/ha yields in the Punjab, India's main producer, and are similar to yields in developed countries from intensive agriculture before the 1950's. They much exceed the 1-2 t/ha yields typical of the prairies of the USA or the steppes of Russia. These samples were complemented by measurements of all the stacked harvested crops in 1981 at sTongde village, Zangskar, which gave estimated yields of about 3 t/ha for barley and wheat (Osmaston 1994).

It is difficult to reconcile this good evidence of satisfactory yields with other other reports of low yield ratios. It suggests that Ladakhi farmers are sowing many times more densely than normal (and perhaps than necessary). However plant populations are fairly uniform and normal, and do not indicate dense sowing; there are no obvious pests or other causes of heavy losses in the seedbed. If such heavy sowing is indeed practised, remedying the actual or perceived need for this could make an immense contribution to the efficiency of Ladakhi agriculture.

The productivity of traditional agriculture is evidently good by world standards, thanks to a very effective and efficient system of nutrient conservation and recycling using livestock dung, human excreta and domestic waste; fields are normally cropped continually from year to year without deterioration or need for fallows. The hardy livestock are an essential component of this closely integrated system, breaking down straw into manure (natural decay is slow in this climate), and providing draught power and dung fuel (Osmaston 1985; 1989; 1994). Government policy however, influenced by the low official perception of yields, is to introduce delicate Jersey cattle and to promote the use of synthetic fertilisers imported by road over the Himalaya at high cost from lowland India (e.g. SKUAST 1987), which are distributed at greatly subsidised prices to farmers. So far adoption of fertiliser use has been at a low level, except in the peri-urban area of Leh where alternative employment for a farmer's family is attractive and labour for tending cattle and spreading manure is expensive. The opposition of the Ladakh Ecological Development Group has recently moderated official enthusiasm and restrained adoption.

Total agricultural production is however constrained by the predominantly steep and rocky landscape and by limited water supplies for irrigation. Only ¼% of the area of Ladakh is currently cultivated and even if further water supplies could be harnessed, only 1% is potentially cultivable (Osmaston 1990).

In Tibet, where most farmers and nomads were previously the closely constrained tenants or serfs of big landowners or monasteries, farming has undergone three revolutions since the take-over by the

Chinese in 1959. First the expropriation of the landlords and redistribution of their land; for many poor farmers this was an improvement. Then starting in 1966 came the Cultural Revolution and forced collectivisation into communes, when there were crop failures and famines due to bureaucratic mismanagement and attempts to replace barley crops by wheat. Since 1980 the land and livestock have been redistributed to farmers under the Individual Responsibility policy and information gathered personally during consultancies in Tibet in 1990 and 1991 showed that this has resulted in quite prosperous conditions for farmers and herdsmen (Clarke & Osmaston, in prep.; also see Goldstein & Beall 1990). Livestock production has risen and grain yields in the three main valleys (Yarlung Tsangpo, Lhasa and Gyantse) are good (about 3t/ha according to a local farmer, i.e. very similar to Ladakh; up to 4.5t/ha according to Lhasa Municipality officials). Official policy is however constrained by the objective of meeting the needs of the growing immigrant Han Chinese civil and military population. Huge irrigation development projects are planned with international aid in the major valleys, with emphasis on the production of wheat, instead of the traditional barley, while the use of subsidised imported fertilisers is promoted to replace the traditional organic manures which have successfully maintained fertility for millennia in this light loessic soil (see 'Peatfield' 1995). Meanwhile the increased cattle population is causing overgrazing and the start of potentially disastrous erosion in the hills.

Food Consumption

Direct and reliable quantitative information about the diet of Ladakhis is scarce. A short term study was done in 1980 in the village of sTongde, Zangskar, where 119 person-meals in sample households were weighed and analysed, and further questionnaire data collected for the rest of the year (Attenborough 1994). This indicated that the diet as a whole (corrected for age but not sex, and excluding alcohol) was adequate with respect to protein, fat and some water-soluble vitamins; possibly inadequate with regard to vitamin A; probably inadequate with regard to iron, calcium and vitamin B_{12}; and might contain an excess of sodium. The energy content for adults was 1545 Kcal/day (1100 from home-grown grain), but it should be noted that the study was immediately pre-harvest when farmers may be too busy to eat fully, even if food is not short; some farmers in Ladakh carry large stocks of grain from year to year. This is however only 58% of the 2650 Kcal/day which is now recommended (FAO/WHO/UNO 1985) for an adult male subsistence farmer doing moderate work (corrected for a mean weight of 53kg. — see Table

1)); and 74% of the 2100 Kcal/day recommended for a rural woman in a developing country (corrected for mean weight of 47kg). Goldstein & Beall (see below) have recorded very large seasonal variations in energy intake in nomads in Tibet, but the large excess in winter is largely due to eating the meat from the major slaughter time in autumn, not available to Ladakhi arable farmers. There is still great controversy about this subject and the extent to which there may be 'adaptation' or 'accommodation' to a low calorie diet (see Dasgupta & Ray, 1986, for a detailed review).

There is however much variation in the prosperity of both households and villages, though the highest and remotest villages are not necessarily the poorest (Osmaston & Crook 1994). Some households always have to borrow seed from others or the local monastery, to be repaid at harvest with substantial interest; some even have to borrow food grain in the last weeks before harvest.

In contrast to these figures, the grain production of sTongde village (a particularly prosperous one) was estimated as described above, in 1981 before the impact of road transport and easy imports, as being sufficient to supply 4000 Kcal/day for working adults, four times actual consumption estimated from the food survey. Although some of the grain is traded with nomads for wool and salt, and some is given as tithes to the monastery (although the consumption of monks from sTongde village has been included with their families), the remaining discrepancy is huge. It is striking that the Muslim Agricultural Officer at Padum said that "75% of the grain harvest was wasted by brewing beer" (Parr 1990); however besides the importance of moderate human consumption in providing vitamin B not readily available from other sources, a Veterinary Officer might well consider that the spent grain was a vital food supplement for livestock. Certainly large quantities of barley are used for brewing beer for daily domestic consumption and for communal parties and festivals. S.Homewood (pers. comm.) has been told by several Ladakhis that farmers commonly use over half the barley crop for brewing; Crowden (this vol. and in press) reports that a rather atypical household in Padum uses 20-40%. Even in efficient commercial brewing a third of the malt is lost as CO_2 during the process of fermentation, a third of it remains in the spent grains (sometimes used for human food but usually for animals) and only a third goes into the beer as alcohol and soluble carbohydrates, though these contain 40% of the original energy. Home-brewed Ladakhi beer is unlikely to contain more than 30% of the energy in the unmalted barley. Thus if 50% of the grain crop is used for home-brewing, it could raise the human food energy derived from grain from 50% to 65% of the crop energy content, or say from 1000 to 1300 Kcal/day. This would correspond to drinking nearly a litre of *chang* daily (or half a litre plus occasional parties), a likely amount for men but women drink much less (Crowden pers.comm.). Much *chang* is drunk between meals, so it may be missed by a meal survey. In the Leh area much beer is brewed for sale as this is a more profitable use for barley than sale or exchange as food; some *chang* is also distilled into *arak*.

Since 1948 the previous food consumption patterns in Ladakh have been changed by the huge military forces, by the influx of civil servants and more recently by the flood of tourists, Kashmiri businessmen and labourers; in 1971-81 the Census of India recorded a 24% increase in females but 40% in males, excluding the army, to a total of 68,000. Few of them like the traditional staple food, barley. Besides these there is the movement of rural farmers, especially younger sons, into Leh, who also soon develop a preference for wheat and rice. Of these groups the army is largely self-sufficient with food imported from lowland India, as is much tourist food. The demands of the other groups have been met by the government importing large quantities of cheap grain from the Punjab and other food, and heavily subsidising the transport costs which would otherwise be prohibitive. These are then available to the public in rationed quantities at low prices, which undercut the prices of locally grown staples. 6000 tonnes of rice were imported into Ladakh in the 1985/86 year, besides large quantities of wheat flour (see also Crowden in this vol. and in press). Because of transport costs and traditional preferences, most is consumed in Leh and other main-roadside villages, but now it is distributed even to the remotest villages in Zangskar by trains of pack-mules hired from Kulu and the degree of dependency which has developed is a serious problem. In the severe winter of 1986-87 there were riots in Leh over the food shortage due to the prolonged blockage of the passes. Butter was flown in (tinned 'Amul' butter is normally only half the price of local butter, though less liked by Ladakhis) and Leh residents had to resort to buying other food from country villages. Farmers complain that the availability of these cheap imports is depressing local agricultural production, both for home consumption and for any surplus that might otherwise be traded, although the rising demand for fresh vegetables in Leh is some compensation for farmers in that area. Subsidising both imported food and imported fertilisers, undermines traditional agriculture on both the economic and technical fronts; if the government subsidised the price of **local** food for issue as rations (if these are really considered necessary), this would encourage local traditional farming and reducing dependence on imports from lowland India. Rice could be a fully priced food.

Such measures would be unpopular with urbanised Ladakhis and with non-Ladakhis including some government staff. However, if as seems likely the internal security and external military situations improve, the central government may feel it less necessary to spend these subsidies which currently foster Ladakh's dependency. In the long term it is very doubtful whether the Punjab's present abundant harvests will keep pace with India's soaring population and permit the continuation of the nation-wide policy of food-subsidy. In neighbouring Muslim Hunza, Pakistan, a greater population increase, partly due to immigration, has resulted in none of these valley communities now being self-sufficient in food (Kreutzmann 1994).

In Tibet before 1959 food supplies, primarily barley, seem to have been adequate. During communisation the official target allowance (often not attained) was 170 kg of grain a year for each person, which would have yielded about 1500 Kcal/day after allowing for milling and waste, but a recent farmers' discussion group estimated that 50% more than this is desirable in the 6 months of spring and autumn when work is heaviest (Kolsteren *et al.* 1990). Now rural supplies of traditional foods seem adequate, but the needs of the urban and military populations are only partly met by compulsory levies on production, and huge additional imports of grain, mainly wheat, from lowland China are necessary. As in Ladakh, substantial quantities of barley are used for home-brewing.

The Tibetans' diet, despite their Buddhism, includes a substantial element of meat. Sir Charles Bell (1928, p.217) wrote "The staple diet of the ordinary Tibetan is yak's meat, mutton, barley flour, cheese and — most of all — tea," though as regards meat this glosses over its very seasonal consumption and differences between arable farmers and nomads. The official current estimate of consumption of yak meat in the Lhasa region of Tibet is 50kg per person a year (Lhasa Mun. pers. comm.); this was supported by our own household survey in which the stated beef consumption (excluding sheep- and goat-meat which are also considerable) in a prosperous arable household was equivalent to 35kg/adult/year but in two pastoral households was 55 and 100kg/adult/year (the latter was 5 yak for 8 adults!). In Lhasa itself and other towns, roadside butchers' stalls are a common sight. These figures are corroborated by observations of pastoral nomads on the plateau (Goldstein & Beall 1990, Beall & Glodstein 1993, Beall *et al.* 1995) who found that in summer, when most work is done, food included very little meat, and was sometimes not enough even to meet estimated or measured BMR needs (summer BMR, 18-59 years, males 1423, females 1237 Kcal/day), whereas in winter men have a daily intake of c.1750 Kcal from meat alone with a total of over 4000 Kcal, part of which is used for the accumulation of body-fat, for expenditure next summer. However the small summer diet does not result from shortage of food or cause hunger.

This contrasts with Ladakh where Buddhist principles are more closely adhered to, though at least partly from force of circumstances. The lower rainfall there results in scantier grazing, and hence lower rates of reproduction and growth of livestock; in many villages farmers often have no surplus for sale and even have difficulty in maintaining their herd numbers (Osmaston 1985; Osmaston, Frazer & Wilkinson 1994). Consequently even a prosperous farmer may only slaughter one of his cattle in alternate years, to be shared with a neighbour, and an occasional goat or sheep for special occasions. The influence of the Hindu regard for the sanctity of cattle also constrains official attitudes to possible schemes for beef production. The food survey at sTongde (Attenborough & Leeds 1994) indicated a consumption of only about 2kg of mutton per person a year while beef did not figure at all.

Lowland China has been through similar farming and dietary changes, with calamitous famines during the Great Leap Forward and the Cultural Revolution. The Individual Responsibility policy has encouraged farmers to boost production, and for a time China's staple food problem seemed to be solved, but there are reports now that some farmers are finding diversification into other crops and activities more profitable so that production is falling. In both town and country in the Han lowlands the diet still centres on rice with some white wheat flour, but plenty of vegetables supply variety and roughage.

These nutritional vicissitudes may be reflected in the heights attained by different adult age groups but as far as the current generation of children is concerned their food supply should have been fairly good. Urban Tibetans and Han immigrants have access to a large variety of locally grown and imported vegetables as do people in Leh, though in neither Tibet nor Ladakh has this yet had much effect on those in the more remote villages.

Body Size and Health

Several investigators have gathered demographic, mortality, ill-health or anthropometric statistics in Ladakh and Tibet which are markedly 'inferior' to certain reference standards. From experience elsewhere, particularly the 'improvements' seen in emigrant populations living in more prosperous conditions than before (e.g. Japanese in U.S.A.), it is often inferred that 'malnutrition' is a causative factor, a deficiency of energy, protein or other nutrients.

Adults

Table 1 gives the results of several such studies: a 1993 survey of pastoral nomads at Phala (5000m) in Tibet (Beall *et al.* 1995); a 1981 study in Kumik, a remote village in Zangskar (Ball & Elford 1994); part of a very rigorous world-wide study of blood pressure, using a probably rural but less remote Indus Valley sample (INTERSALT, Anon 1988); and three surveys from the Indus Valley (Ball 1989, reporting data collected by Norboo & Baw; Wiley 1994a,b). Comparative data from lowland China, Britain and the USA are also given.

The table confirms that adult rural Ladakhis and Tibetans are short and very light compared with British and American whites, and are slightly shorter and lighter than Chinese. The precise significance of BMI is debatable[3], but Ladakhis had the lowest value of 52 ethnic groups in the INTERSALT survey, the mean being about 25 and the highest Hawaiians with 31. The only other groups with BMI's less than 22 are some Kenyans, some Amerindians, some New Guineans and some lowland Chinese. There are discrepancies between the two China surveys; the data given in Anon (1979) fall at the upper limit of the INTERSALT figures for height, and at the lower limit for weight (therefore yielding low BMI's). Given the date and source of the former survey it is possible that the figures were adjusted to conform with an arbitrary ideal Chinese form. Despite evidence that food is abundant, the Tibetan sample has an even lower mean adult BMI of 18.5, the 36% of individuals below this being in the range which has been suggested to indicate CED/PED (chronic/protein energy deficiency). Similarly in the healthy Ladakh Kumik sample 12% of males and 20% of females were below 18.5 For such short people this statistic is misleading. Only 10% of the Tibetans and 5% of the Ladakhis had BMIs less than 17, a more appropriate cut-off[3].

The Phala and five Ladakh surveys form a suggestive series with each of the statistics rising progressively from the remotest and highest community, to the urban men of Leh, though the sample of the latter was small and not well defined, so it is possible that other factors played a part. The Leh population is drawn from a variety of local and neighbouring sources.

In view of the indication that diet in Zangskar may be deficient in iron, studies of anaemia in the Lhasa and Leh areas, both at about 3,500m, are of interest. Humans from low altitudes, where mean haemoglobin levels range from 12% in children to 14% in adults, usually adapt to these high altitudes by developing a haemoglobin (Hb) level about 2% higher (Hb% = g/dl); the Quechuan Indians who now live permanently at high altitudes in the Andes show a greatly raised level; 18.8% at 3,700m and more at higher altitudes. However

Himalayan Sherpas and Tibetans show a smaller increase: nomads at Phala, Tibet, (c.5,000m) have a mean Hb of 18.2%, but also have a higher than expected oxygen saturation so that the blood oxygen content is about 5% higher than in typical adults at sea-level (Beall & Goldstein 1990). It is surmised that they have evolved this additional adaptation over a long period and there is evidence that this is carried by a major gene (Beall *et al.*1994).

Studies of 2772 children and 625 non-pregnant women in Lhasa municipality showed Hb levels similar to or only slightly above those of people living at sea level, approximately 12% and 14% respectively. Application of the recommended WHO altitude-adjusted cut-off levels (CDC Atlanta,1989, recommended cut-off for children and child-bearing women: 11% + (0.55% x 3.7) = 13% @ 3,700m.alt.) to diagnose anaemia would imply that half or more of the population are anaemic (Kolsteren *et. al.* 1990, 1992, in press). Instead the authors infer that the Lhasa population do not exhibit altitudinally raised Hb levels and that only about 10% suffer from anaemia. In Ladakh, in a village near Leh, the mean Hb level for 42 women was 12.8% and for 28 men was 14.9% (Tsering Dolma *et al.* 1990). Two further surveys of 355 and 467 individuals near Leh (Tsering Norboo, personal comm.) gave Hb means of 13.4% and about 12% for both sexes together. In the former survey men were about 1% higher and women about 1% lower than the mean. The reason for the discrepancy between the surveys is obscure; different types of haemoglobinometer were used. These limited data indicate that Ladakhis too may not exhibit altitudinally raised Hb levels. Confirmation of this is important before valid conclusions can be drawn from studies of possible dietary iron deficiency and anaemia. This question is also discussed by Dirren *et al.* (1994).

Children

Data in Table 2 for 115 children aged 2-7 years in Ladakhi villages in the Indus valley (Padfield, this vol.) show that they too are short for their age, in that two-thirds are less than 90% of the height of the Harvard reference standard based on healthy children in the U.S.A. (close to but not identical with the widely used USA National Center for Health Statistics (NCHS) standards)[2], and a quarter are less than 85% of that. By the standards of the U.S.A. and north European countries these categories would be classified as 'stunted' and 'severely stunted' respectively. Direct comparisons between these figures and Table 1 are difficult but they suggest that 'stunting' may decrease in percentage terms between childhood (median height and probably mean height between 85% and 90%, probably about 88% of

NCHS) and adulthood (mean height about 93% of NCHS). It may therefore be more appropriate to describe the differences in absolute terms; a loss of so many centimetres in childhood which persists throughout life. However there are some indications from other mountain communities that such youths may continue growth for a couple of years longer than lowland youths, thus making up some of their loss. 1Weights of Indus Valley children were low at all ages, particularly in the age groups 0-1 and 1-2 years, when one third and two thirds respectively of the children were less than 80% of the reference standard, i.e. apparently suffering from increasing malnutrition. Ratios of weight to height were low but not remarkably so because both variables were low. Other studies of skinfold thickness have confirmed the light build of Ladakhi children. Though the statistics for Ladakhi children are significantly worse than those of Lhasa valley Tibetans, very similar peoples in nearly identical environments, they could be closer to Tibetan nomads at Phala (5000m) where insufficient child data are available, but adults are even lighter than Ladakhis.

Though weights of a small sample (7) of infants 0-5m in this survey averaged over 100% of NCHS, a much larger sample (168, but 14% non-Ladakhi) of healthy infants born in Leh hospital and recorded by Wiley (1994a,b) averaged 2.75kg birthweight, only 84% of NCHS and much below both Lhasa Tibetans and Andean birthweights. However mean length was 48.4cm, 97% of NCHS, so that infants were thin (PI 24). Infant mortality was about 182/1000; about 82% of this was neonatal; 66% of deaths were in those whose birthweights were less than the mean; and 69% of hospital deaths were due to respiratory disorders. Females, though smaller than males on average, survived equally well. Small birthweights were significantly related to small maternal size and hard work during pregnancy; eating more than usual during pregnancy produced larger babies but a relative increase in high energy or protein foods did not, though Norberg-Hodge & Russell (1994) were told in sTongde that pregnant mothers were given especially rich and nutritious food such as butter and meat.

In their summary of health in Kumik Ball & Elford (1994) say "Those who survived early childhood could look forward to an adult life almost completely free of malnutrition or obesity, severe respiratory disease or hypertension". However the proviso of surviving childhood was very necessary as infantile (0-1yr) deaths were 180/1000 and childhood (1-5yr) deaths about the same, figures that exceed both neighbouring Nepal and lowland India. The primary causes were measles and respiratory diseases (although malnutrition could have affected susceptibility to both). A similar study in the neighbouring but more prosperous sTongde village (Attenborough 1994) found infantile death rates of 88/1000 and childhood deaths of about 115/1000. In the Indus valley, infantile deaths in the higher and more remote villages averaged 200/1000, whereas in Alchi and lower Wanla (more accessible and probably with more varied and productive agriculture) it was only 100/1000. Child deaths were about 70/1000 for both areas (Padfield, this vol.). Other infants, though surviving, suffered from debilitating diseases and consequent growth checks.

Two much larger surveys of children in the Lhasa Prefecture or Municipality of Tibet, which includes a huge rural area besides the city (over 30,000 sq.km) provide interesting comparisons with a neighbouring population of similar though not identical ethnic origins, in similar natural environmental conditions and with a generally similar traditional diet but with major recent social and economic changes (Kolsteren *et al.* 1990). Because of the large samples these data are statistically more reliable than the Ladakh data, with smaller errors and smoother curves, while in view of their dates, authorship and unflattering conclusions one can have confidence that they have not been adjusted for political reasons. The similarities between the Tibet and Ladakh data therefore lend support to the latter, and confirm that they are examples of a real and widespread pattern of growth in similar peoples, environments and cultures.

The first survey of Tibetan children aged 0-7 years was carried out in 1986 by Tibetan Government Authorities (Table 3). Samples comprised 4,600 urban Tibetans, 4,400 rural Tibetans, and 900 immigrant urban Han (lowland Chinese). The following comparisons were made with the NCHS data[2] recommended by W.H.O. (Waterlow *et al.* 1977) based on large numbers of American children, presumed to be well nourished, see Table 3 and Figs. 1,2,3. The uncertain appropriateness of these comparisons was noted; in particular the typically larger size of American boys than girls is not repeated in Tibetans; indeed the reverse, girls being distinctly heavier and slightly taller. Both urban and rural Tibetan children have weights-for-age **exceeding** NCHS values for their first 3-4 months, suggesting that Tibetan mothers are not malnourished (see also Moore 1990, Zamudio et al.1993 for similar reports). However weight-for-age in Tibet then drops steeply to 80-90% at 15 months, then slightly rising before a final fall to 76-85% at 7 years. Height-for-age also equals NCHS values at birth, falling slowly to 95% (urban) and 90% (rural) of NCHS values at 7 years. Weight-for-height was well above NCHS for the first 5 months, falling steeply to 91% at about 1 year and thereafter rising slightly to c.94%. Though Tibetan children are shorter and lighter than Han children in lowland China, and Han children in Lhasa have mostly spent their first two years in the lowlands, by the age of 3 years the Lhasa Han have dropped substantially behind Tibetan children in weight, often suffering from intestinal complaints and other problems arising from the unaccustomed environment.

The second survey was carried out by SCF staff and the Lhasa Health Bureau in 1990. All children under 7 years in 637 rural households in the World Food Project 3357 area (Lhasa valley) were weighed and measured, giving a sample of 479 children. Results are presented in Table 2 as comparisons between mean Weight-for-age and mean Height-for-age with NHCS standards at various ages. Both urban and rural Tibetan infants appear well nourished at first but drop to low weights-for-age after weaning, especially the rural ones, but their heights-for-age are only slightly below standard and are closely similar to those for lowland Chinese children. Their weights-for-height show a similar but less acute pattern to weight-for-age. It is generally considered that low weight-for-height ('wasting'), a measure of how thin children are (like BMI), reflects acute or short-term problems of nutrition, while low height-for-age reflects chronic or long-term inadequate nutrition, and low weight-for-age represents a combination of both. These figures do not indicate that Tibetan children are suffering more from malnutrition than lowland Chinese (if this is indeed the main factor in height and weight differences) and they appear to be considerably better off than Ladakhis.

A more recent study in 1993 (Harris 1994) of 341 urban and rural Tibetan children showed generally similar results, except that Height-for-age after 1 year was very significantly below NCHS standards, constituting serious stunting: 61% lay more than 2 SD below WHO standards. This was paralleled by the results of a smaller study in a single village by the Woodlands Mountain Institute. Over 40% of children showed other signs of malnutrition such as rickets and depigmentation of hair. However, because both height and weight for age were equally low, weight for height was normal. The consequence of this is the commonly observed phenomenon that Tibetan and Ladakhi children do not generally appear thin and wasted; it is only after enquiry that one realises how small they are for their age; possibly this indicates micro-nutrient rather than energy deficiency. The infantile mortality rate is reported to be 91/1000 with a further 35/1000 up to age 5 years, very many fewer than in Ladakh, though still three times the levels in lowland China. This study is being continued in close cooperation with the Tibetan medical authorities, together with remedial trials.

The data for China, though from relative lowlands, are especially relevant to Ladakh and Tibet because they too are for a largely rural population, with low adult heights and very low BMI's by world standards. As distinct from comparative data for segments of population after immigration to a totally new country and environment compared with those remaining, these refer to children in various residential sectors of the same population at different times, only slightly affected by migration and with rather similar overall economic vicissitudes. The principal points of interest are first the increase of 1.5 - 2.0 % in height of all sectors over the period 1975-1985, corresponding to age classes of children reared during the disasters of the Cultural Revolution and after its end; and second the consistent and progressive reductions in height in all age classes between the city, urban, suburban and rural children (noting that, in contrast to some developed countries, suburban people may be less prosperous than urban ones, though not so disadvantaged as in the peri-urban shanty towns of many 3W countries). It is reasonable to infer that the greater height growth may be the result of improvements in national nutrition and child care over time and of a better and more varied diet, with better access to health-care facilities, associated with urbanisation, although all sectors still show a check at 1-3 years.

Norboo and Baw's data (Ball 1989) for urban and rural Ladakh show a similar difference in height, associated with distinct differences in diet and life-style for men living in Leh (pop. c.20,000), although the main changes in Leh postdate the infancy of most of the sample men. Besides being taller, they were heavier and stouter, imported rice replaced wholemeal barley flour in their diet, 80% led sedentary lives compared with the 100% of rural men who were active, and they had significantly higher serum cholesterol levels, 5.15 against 3.75 m.mol. More time and data will be required to judge whether the gain in stature, probably accompanied by a decrease in infant mortality, is balanced by an increased adult death rate from coronary heart disease and other complaints associated with low fibre diets and sedentary habits. In principle, some nutritional improvements should be possible without adding to these risks. Hypertension already presents problems in the rural population[4].

On the evidence available it is difficult to discriminate in any of these countries between the effects of any improvements in nutrition and in child health care in the past. For the immediate future, any proposals for action to increase the height, weight, health and survival of rural Ladakhi infants must target both these probable factors.

Hitherto the only serious attempt in Ladakh at effecting this has met with limited success. The Leh Nutrition Project (LNP) (Padfield this vol.) was started by Save the Children Fund (SCF) in response to serious flood damage to crops and fields in 1979, as an emergency relief programme supplying food, clothes etc. at the request of Ladakhi villagers. The Indian Council for Child Welfare then asked SCF to implement their School Feeding Programme (SFP) already functioning widely in lowland India. Apart from its expected direct benefits to children, this provided a valuable *entrée* to village communities, first for monitoring child health and effecting such measures as inoculation and encouraging vegetable growing and eating; second for more general attempts at rural development. The feeding programme comprised village kitchens where a nutritrious stew, *tukpa*, based mainly on imported rice but supplemented with local vegetables and grain, was fed to all school-children, besides any younger ones who came or were brought.

The monthly monitoring of health, height, weight and mid-upper-arm circumference, together with specific surveys (Padfield, this vol.) confirmed serious infant ill-health, under-size and mortality, and, on limited evidence, probably some child malnutrition. Child weights and arm circumferences were greatest in autumn after the harvest and least in spring and summer when food supplies were low and mothers had most other work to do. Height growth was greatest in spring. Like many feeding projects the SFP was subject to some criticism, partly questioning its necessity, partly deprecating its use of imported food and erosion of traditional self-sufficiency and independence. By the late 1980's it was claimed that the improved health care had resulted in reductions in infant mortality, but it appeared, again on limited analysis of the evidence, that the actual feeding programme was having little direct effect on child growth and health and it has been progressively reduced. The failure of the feeding programme may have been due to three factors, which carry important lessons for future schemes:

a) Infancy, not school-age, seems to be the critical age for growth and health problems, but there was great difficulty and little success in reaching infants.

b) There are traditional cultural prejudices against certain foods as being 'too rich' and therefore indigestible or unsuitable for small children, partly due to the traditional lore of the *amchi* (village doctors practising Buddhist medicine). In sTongde village Norberg-Hodge & Russell (1994) found that women breast-fed infants for an average of 3.4 years, but started supplementary feeding at 2-3 months, usually with water or goats milk and a little sugar. Yoghurt, buttermilk and vegetables are however considered indigestible and are never given (but see Law & Tsewang Smanla, 1987, p.62, for recommendation of a wide variety of nutritious foods).

c) Perhaps busy families treated the childrens' school meals as a substitute for home meals rather than a supplement to them.

Discussion

Until recently Ladakh could be regarded as having a population of short but healthy, well proportioned, active, well-adapted and apparently adequately fed adults, with numbers stabilised by Buddhist monasticism and polyandry, low fertility and high infantile mortality (Crook & Osmaston 1994). Now, external economic and medical resources prompt instinctive practical responses to the small weights of Ladakhi infants, the severe growth checks at weaning, the serious disease and mortality experienced by infants and children in Ladakh (in all these Ladakh is significantly worse than central Tibet and lowland China) and the view (particularly among non-Ladakhis) that all adults *should* be as big as Westerners and that if maternal and childhood problems were remedied they *would* be. However we are still uncertain about the basic causes of these problems and of their remedies. In view of evidence of genetically controlled adaptation to hypoxia, and perhaps of infant size in the Andes, it would be rash to exclude the possibility of genetic control of small adult size. Similarly the apparent contradiction in rural Ladakh between abundant agricultural production but low food consumption is still an open question.

Besides these, there are more problematic questions. For example, how far is any energy deficiency a cultural choice, if many Ladakhis really choose to devote half or more of their nutritional energy resources to brewing beer? Could stunting and ill-health be partly the otherwise avoidable consequences of this choice? Does the demand for imported government rations also arise from this diversion of homegrown food, perhaps to the extent of releasing even more for brewing? These questions also serve to illustrate the different approaches of the paediatrician and nutritionist on the one hand, and the anthropologist and socio-biologist on the other. To the former the immediate health of the current generation is the primary consideration, and the only one for which sufficiently reliable information can be obtained for identifying and planning effective action. For the latter the 'fitness' of the current generation is maximised by those adaptations or accommodations to the environment which best ensure the transmission of the genotype through future generations; this may involve subordinating the perfect health or even survival of individuals to the welfare of their progeny and the community. In this context the beer drunk at formal occasions and in traditional hospitality is a social cement, important to the continuing strength and structure of the community (c.f. Ripley, this vol. and Ardussi, 1977), and perhaps more important than the debatable disadvantages of stunting.

There is evidence from elsewhere that small size is a strong indicator of greater liability to childhood ill-health and mental deficiency (e.g. Tomkins 1988) and death (e.g. Vella et al. 1994), presumably arising from the same or related causes, but the question of whether small stature is *per se* a disadvantage is not clear, if it is accompanied by a 'normal' or near normal weight-for-height, i.e. an appropriate 'well proportioned' physique. Tuffrey (1994, see also Strickland & Tuffrey, in prep.) lists five studies in which small stature was associated with particular advantages, ranging from lower energy costs to a lower risk of cancer from hormone related cancers, and ten studies showing the reverse, ranging from poorer brain growth to lower chances of employment; some in each group were directly opposed. FAO/WHO/UNO (1985, p.28) quotes studies showing that once the hazards of early childhood are past, stunted children have a better physical performance than larger better nourished ones.

The energetic efficiency of small size and light build have been demonstrated in other mountain dwelling peoples. Rebecca Stephens in her account of her ascent of Everest (the first by a British woman) writes "These Sherpas were twice as strong and twice as fast on the hill as any man I had met and always smiling. They were so dextrous. They were small — Tchering Zhambu was tiny, about 5ft. 2in. [1.57m] — but the efficiency of their movements fascinated me." (Stephens 1994). From a more scientific approach, Brooke Thomas (1973) justified the use of children for herding in the Andes. Nutritional studies on animals ranging from rats to dairy heifers have shown health advantages in adult life consequent on lower nutritional levels in youth, and obesity in human youth has been shown to be particularly deleterious to health (Anon 1983). Thus it seems that sub-maximal growth, at least in moderation, may not be a <u>wholly</u> negative phenomenon in the Himalayan environment, with high activity requirements and limited food resources; and growth to the potential maximum may not lead to optimal 'fitness', used in the sociobiological sense of success in survival and reproduction.

Recent economic and social changes have reduced monasticism and polyandry and improved health care: the population of Leh District increased at only 0.66%/yr 1901-61, but at over 2%/yr in 1961-81, only partly due to immigration. The persisting high infant and child mortality is a clear target for humanitarian action, but unless this is accompanied by effective family planning it will be a questionable advantage to the

Ladakhi people in their land of very restricted natural resources and carrying capacity (for a discussion of this ethical and practical problem on a global scale see King 1990). Population control in Ladakh is unfortunately vexed by political rivalries and marital differences between the two main religious groups, Buddhists and Muslims.

However, irrespective of what view is taken of these questions, our ignorance of the factors involved is such that only limited effective action can be taken without more reliable information. In both Ladakh and Tibet the two priorities are for a review of official policies which are adversely affecting farming, and for well designed and executed studies of food production, food consumption, nutrition and health.

SUMMARY OF CONCLUSIONS & RECOMMENDATIONS FOR LADAKH

Farming

1. The traditional agricultural system is very effective, conservative and productive, but suffers from competition from imported subsidised food and an unjustifiably poor official and hence public image. It needs support by

(a) officially recognising its productivity and raising its public image.

(b) encouraging the traditional recycling of nutrients rather than subsidising synthetic fertilisers.

(c) encouraging livestock as much for manure production as for milk; thus longevity and hardiness may be more important than high milk production.

(d) improving the market for local produce, if necessary by subsidies. The cost of this could be offset by reductions in subsidies on imported food.

2. Sowing rates seem unnecessarily high and probably wasteful. These need investigation.

3. Further integrated and detailed studies of the farming system, including animal husbandry, are required, together with its total inputs and outputs of all kinds of produce, fuel and draught power.

Food

3. There is still too little quantitative information on what Ladakhis, especially children, eat and drink to draw reliable conclusions. Adults appear to be adequately fed and there is no convincing evidence of rural food shortages except after natural disasters and (as everywhere) in the poorest families. Much less meat is eaten than in Tibet.

4. Year-long surveys are required of the food consumption of sample families in different communities, including all food bought, sold, exchanged and produced. The nutritional value and adequacy of these diets needs assessment, especially infant and child diets.

5. The necessity for the issue of imported subsidised food rations to farners, and their possible replacement for townspeople by locally grown food (perhaps subsidised) need critical consideration.

6. The quantity of grain used for home-brewing is large but unknown, as is its contribution to nutrition. This needs assessment.

Health

7. Three similar and primarily rural peoples, lowland Chinese, Tibetans and Ladakhis are very short and light by Western international reference data.

8. In all three peoples most of the relative loss in height and weight is concentrated in early childhood between the ages of 9 months and 3 years, the period of weaning. In Ladakh there is also a low birth weight and high infant and child mortality, particularly in remote rural villages. Rural adults in Ladakh appear to be healthy.

9. In all three peoples there is evidence that this shortness and lightness decreases with increasing urbanisation. The latter is associated with changes in diet and better health care which are likely to be factors in the height and weight changes. In China improved height growth is also associated with economic and political changes in both urban and rural populations. However there may be adverse effects of the dietary and life-style changes usually associated with urbanisation.

10. Current rural health-care measures should be continued, also seeking ways of influencing traditional ideas on infant care, especially the advice given by *amchi* to mothers. Further studies of infantile and child mortality, health and growth are required.

11. Haemoglobin levels in healthy Tibetans and Ladakhis at high altitudes seem for genetic reasons to be about 2% below those expected. Surveys of anaemia should confirm and take account of this.

General

12. Farming, food and health are of such fundamental importance to the wellbeing of all Ladakhis and are so interconnected that a major integrated study and consequent long term development programme are needed for their improvement, and this should be a top priority for Government and NGO's.

References (*CO* = Crook & Osmaston *q.v.*)

ANON (INTERSALT COOPERATIVE RESEARCH GROUP) 1988 "Intersalt. an international study of electrolyte excretion and blood pressure. Results for 24 hour urinary sodium and potassium excretion". *British Medical J.* 297, 319-328. (also supp. infm. from Dr.Paul Elliott)

ANON 1979 *A general description of the physical shapes, functions and qualities of Chinese children and youth.* Research Group for the study of the physique of Chinese children and youth of the National Research Institute of Sports Science. Beijing. [quoted in Jamison *et al. q.v.*]

ANON 1983 "Obesity". *Journal Royal College of Physicians of London*, 17, 3-58.

ANON 1989 *Children and women of China.* UNICEF, Beijing.

ARDUSSI, J. 1977 "Brewing and drinking the beer of enlightenment in Tibetan Buddhism". *J. Amer. Oriental Soc.* 97, 115-124.

ATTENBOROUGH, R. 1994 "The population of sTongde, Zangskar". Ch.9 in *CO*.

——— R. & M., & A.R.LEEDS 1994 "Nutrition in sTongde". Ch.12 in *CO*.

BALL, K. 1989 "Can Ladakh avoid western health hazards?" *The Future of Agriculture in Ladakh*, 31-36. Internat. Wksp 1989, Ladakh Ecological Development Group and the Ladakh Project. (21 Victoria Sq., Bristol, UK.)

BALL, K. & J.ELFORD "Health in Zangskar". 1994. Ch.13 in *CO*.

BEALL, C.M. 1990 "Variation in hemoglobin concentration among samples of high altitude natives in the Andes and Himalayas". *Am.J.Hum.Biol.* 2, 639-651.

——— & M.C.GOLDSTEIN 1990 "Hemoglobin concentration, percent oxygen saturation and arterial oxygen content of Tibetan nomads at 4,850-5,450m". Ch.11 in *Hypoxia: the adaptations*, Decker, Toronto.

——— & M.C.GOLDSTEIN 1993 "Dietary seasonality among Tibetan nomads". *Nat. Geogr. Res. & Explor.* 9(4), 475-480.

——— *et al.* 1987 1987 Haemoglobin concentration of pastoral nomads permanently resident at 4850-5450 meters in Tibet. *Amer. J. Phys. Anthr.* 73, 433-438.

——— *et al.* 1994 "Major gene for percent of oxygen saturation of arterial hemoglobin in Tibetan Highlanders". *Am. J. Phys. Anthrop.*, 95, 271-276.

——— *et al.* 1995 "Basal metabolic rate and dietary seasonality among Tibetan nomads". *Amer. J. Hum. Biol.* 7.

BELL, Sir CHARLES 1928 *The people of Tibet.* Oxford University Press.

BRAY, J. (this vol) "Kashmir, Ladakh and Western Tibet: episodes in frontier diplomacy during British rule in India".

BROOKE-THOMAS, R. 1973 *Human adaptation to a high Andean energy flow system.* Occas. papers in Anthrop. 7. Pennsylvania State University, USA.

CDC 1989 "Criteria for anaemia in children and child-bearing aged women". *Mortality and Morbidity Weekly Report* 38, 22, 400-404.

CHALMERS, H. & C.RAMM, 1984 *Zangskar 1983: report of an agricultural study made during a visit to Zangskar, Kashmir, June-July 1983.* Held in Edinburgh Univ. Library. Mimeo, 24pp.

CLARKE, G.H. & H.A.OSMASTON (in prep.) (eds.) *Development, society and the environment in Tibet.* Proc. 7th Seminar, Int.Ass Tib.Studies.

CROOK, J.H. & H.A.OSMASTON (eds.) 1994 *Himalayan Buddhist Villages: Environment, Resources, Society and Religious Life in Zangskar, Ladakh.* Univ. Bristol, Bristol, & Motilal Banarsidass, Delhi. 976p.

CROWDEN, J. 1989 "The viability of traditional agriculture with special emphasis on Ladakh and in particular the productivity of the Zangskar Valley". In *The future of agriculture in Ladakh*, International Workshop, Leh 1989, 11-18. The Ladakh Ecological Development Group & the Ladakh Project.

——— (this vol.) "Development and change in Zangskar, 1977-1989".

——— (in press) "The road to Padum". *Recent Research in Ladakh 6.*

DASGUPTA, P. and D.RAY 1986 *Adapting to undernutrition: the clinical evidence and its implications.* World Instit. for Dev. Econ. Res., 78 pp. Helsinki.

DIRREN, H., M.H.G.M.LONGMAN, D.V.BARCLAY & W.B.FREIRE 1994 "Altitude correction for hemoglobin". *Eur. J. Clin. Nutr.*48, 625-632.

FAO/WHO/UNO 1985 *Energy and protein requirements.* Tech. Rep. 724, WHO.

FERRO-LUZZI, A. *et al.* 1992 "A simplified approach of assessing adult chronic energy deficiency". *Eur. J. Clin. Nutr.* 46, 173-186.

GARROW, J.S. & J.WEBSTER 1985 "Quetelet's Index (W/H^2) as a measure of obesity". *Int.J.Obesity*, 147-153.

GOLDSTEIN, M.C., & C.M.BEALL 1990 *Nomads of Western Tibet.* Serindia, London.

HARRIS, N. 1994 *Prospectus: Tibet child nutrition & collaborative health project.* Western Consortium for Public Health, University of California, USA. 5p.

JAMISON,D.T. *et al.* c.1980 *China: the health sector.* World Bank, Washington, DC.

KING, M. 1990 "Health is a sustainable state" *Lancet* 336, 664-667. (also the accompanying editorial "Nothing is unthinkable").

KREUTZMANN, H. 1994 "Habitat conditions and settlement processes in the Hindukush—Karakoram." *Petermanns Geogr. Mitt.* 138, 337-356.

KOLSTEREN, P., S.ATKINSON & K.MASKALL 1990 *Nutrition, health, water & sanitation assessment in the Lhasa Valley.* Save the Children Fund/Lhasa Health Bureau. Mimeo 104pp.+ apps.

——— 1992 "Une enquête nutritionelle au Tibet". *5èmes Journées scientifiques internationales du GERM. 22-28 nov. 1992.*

KOLSTEREN, P. & P.VAN DER STUYFT (in press) "Le diagnostic de l'anémie en haut altitude: problèmes rencontrés au Tibet".

LAW,A. & TSEWANG SMANLA 1987 *A Tibetan guide to health. Diet and nutrition in Ladakh according to the amchi system of medicine.* Save the Children Fund, London. mimeo 76p.

MOORE, L.G. 1990 "Maternal O_2 transport and fetal growth in Colorado, Peru and Tibet high altitude residents". *Am.J.Hum.Biol.* 2, 627-637.

NCHS 1977 *NCHS Growth curves for children, birth - 18 years, United States.* National Center for Health Statistics, Public Health Service, U.S. Dept. of Health and Human Services.

NORBERG HODGE, H., J.PAGE, & P.GOERING 1989 *Agriculture: Global trends and Ladakh's future.* 42p mimeo. The Ladakh Project, 21 Victoria Sq., Bristol.

——— with H.RUSSELL 1994 "Birth and child-rearing in Zangskar". Ch.16 in ***CO***.

NORBOO, TSERING & TSERING MORUP (in press) "Culture, health and illness in Ladakh". *Recent Research in Ladakh 6.*

OSMASTON, H.A. 1985 "The productivity of the agricultural and pastoral system in Zangskar". *Acta Biologica Montana* 5, 75-89. Univ. of Pau, France.

——— 1989 "Agriculture in Ladakh: building a coherent policy". In *The future of agriculture in Ladakh,* International Workshop, Leh 1989, 4-10. The Ladakh Project & Ladakh Ecological Development Group.

——— 1990 "Environmental Determinism and Economic Possibilism in Ladakh". In L.Icke-Schwalbe & G.Meier (eds.) *Wissenschaftsgesichte und gegenwärtige Forschungen in Nordwest-Indien (Proc. Third Coll. on Ladakh).* Dresden Museum of Ethnology, p.141-150.

——— 1994 "The agricultural system". Ch.5 in ***CO***.

OSMASTON, H.A. & J.H.CROOK 1994 "Sha-de: meagre subsistence or Garden of Eden?" Ch.7 in ***CO***.

OSMASTON, H.A., R.FISHER, J.FRAZER & T.WILKINSON 1994 "Animal Husbandry in Zangskar". Ch.6 in *CO*.

PADFIELD, N. (this vol.) "Child health and nutrition in Ladakhi villages".

PARR, J. 1990 *A study of the high altitude farming system in Zanskar, India.* Dissertation, Dept. of Geography (ref. 2867), Univ. Birmingham, U.K. 77p.

PEATFIELD, P. (*nom de plume*) 1995 "Save our tsampa". *Tib. Rev.*, May 1995, 13-19.

RIPLEY, A. (this vol.) "Food as ritual".

RIZVI, J. 1983 *Ladakh. Crossroads of High Asia.* Oxford University Press, Delhi

_______ 1985 "Peasant traders of Ladakh". *India International Centre Quarterly* 12, 1, 13-27.

SKUAST (c.1987) *Package of practices for crops of Leh & Kargil.* Sher-e-Kashmir Univ. of Agric. Sc. & Tech., Shalimar, Srinagar. Vishinath Press 23p.

SONAM WANGYAL (in press) "Political evolution in post-independence Ladakh" *Proc. 7th Int. Coll. on Ladakh,* Bonn, 1995.

SOUTHAMPTON UNIVERSITY 1979 *Himalayan Expedition, 1977.* (ed. S. Fraser) University of Southampton, 141 pp.

STEPHENS, R. 1994 "A British woman on Everest". *Alpine J.* 99 (343), 125-129.

STRICKLAND, S.S. & V.R.TUFFREY (in prep.) *Form and function: a study of nutrition, adaptation and social inequality in three Gurung villages of the Nepal Himalayas.* Smith Gordon, London.

TOMKINS, A.M. 1988 "The risk of morbidity in a stunted child". p.185-199 in *Linear growth retardation in less developed countries.* Ed. J.C.Waterlow. Raven Press, New York.

TSERING DOLMA *et al.* 1990 "Seasonal koilonychia in Ladakh". *Contact Dermatitis* 22, 78-80.

TUFFREY, V.R. 1994 "*Seasonality, anthropometric status and household welfare in rural Nepal*". D.Phil. thesis, Faculty of Medicine, University of London.

VELLA, V., *et al.*1994 "Anthropometry as a predictor for mortality among Uganda children, allowing for socio-economic variables". *European J. Clinical Nutrition*, 48, 189-197.

WARIKOO, K. (this vol.) "Gateway to Central Asia: the Trans-Himalayan Trade of Ladakh".

WATERLOW, J.C. *et al.*"The presentation and use of of height and weight data for comparing the nutritional status of groups of children under the age of 10 years". *Bull.WHO 55*, 489-498.

WILEY, A.S. 1994a "Neonatal size and infant mortality at high altitude in the western Himalaya". *Am.J. Phys.Anthrop,* 94, 289-305.

WILEY, A.S. 1994b "Neonatal and maternal anthropometric characteristics in a high altitude population of the western Himalaya." *Amer.J.Hum.Biol.* 6, 499-510.

ZAMUDIO, S. *et al.* 1993 "Protection from intrauterine growth retardation in Tibetans at high altitude". *Amer. J. Phys. Anthrop.* 91, 215-224.

Table 1 BODY MEASUREMENTS OF LADAKHI AND OTHER ADULTS
Group Mean or Range (Standard Error)

	Sample Number	Height (cm)	Weight (kg)	BMI[4]	PI[5]
Tibet (Phala, Tibetan nomads, c.5000m) (Beall *et al.* 1995)					
Males aged 18-59	19	c.161	50	19.2	12.0
Females aged 18-59	19	c.149	40	18.0	12.1
Ladakh (Kumik, Zangskar, rural Ladakhis 3750m) (Ball & Elford 1994)					
Males over 15 years	45	162(1)	53(1)	20.2(0.2)	12.5
Females over 15 years	39	148(1)	47(1)	21.5(0.2)	14.5
Ladakh (Indus Valley, rural ? Ladakhis c.3000m) (INTERSALT, Anon 1988 & supp.)					
Males aged 20-59	100	164(1)	55(1)	20.4(0.2)	12.5
Females aged 20-59	100	153(1)	46(1)	19.6(0.2)	12.8
Ladakh (Wanla, Indus Valley, rural Ladakhis [1,3], 3300m) (Ball 1989)					
Males aged 23-50	36	166	57	21	12.9
Ladakh (Indus Valley, Leh Hospital maternity patients, mostly Ladakhis, mostly rural) (Wiley 1994a,b)					
Females aged 25 * possibly more than usual as <24hrs after birth	145	153	49*	21*	13.7*
Ladakh (Leh, Indus Valley, urban Ladakhis[2,3], 3300m) (Ball 1989)					
Males aged 23-50	23	170	69	24	14.0
China (INTERSALT, Anon 1988 & supp.)					
Males aged 20-59	3x100	166-170	59-68	21.3-23.6	13.4
Females aged 20-59	3x100	155-159	52-61	21.4-24.1	14.5
China (urban) (Jamison *et al.* c.1980 quoting Anon 1979)					
Males aged 18-25		170	59	20.4	12.0
Females aged 18-25		159	51	20.2	12.7
United Kingdom (white?) (INTERSALT, Anon 1988 & supp.)					
Males aged 20-59	3x100	172-174	73-79	25-26	14.7
Females aged 20-59	3x100	[illegible]	[illegible]	[illegible]	[illegible]

Table 1 (cont.) BODY MEASUREMENTS OF LADAKHI AND OTHER ADULTS

		Height (cm)	Weight (kg)	BMI[4]	PI[5]
U.S.A.(white) (INTERSALT, Anon 1988 & supp.)					
Males aged 20-59	3x100	173-177	81-84	25-26	15.4
Females aged 20-59	3x100	158-164	66-71	24-28	16.4
NCHS data (NCHS 1977)					
Males, 18yr.		177	68↑	21.7↑	12.3
Females, 18 yr.		163↑	57	21.5↓	13.2
COMPARISONS[5,7]					
Ladakhi rural/NCHS %					
Male		92%	81%	94%	102%
Female		92%	82%	95%	110%
Ladakhi rural/UK (INTERSALT) %					
Male		95%	72%	80%	85%
Female		94%	72%	82%	86%
Ladakhi rural/USA (INTERSALT) %					
Male		94%	67%	80%	81%
Female		93%	68%	79%	83%

NOTES

1. 32 were active farmers.
2. 17 were sedentary professional and commercial.
3. Leh men consumed more rice, meat and fat than Wanla men and had higher serum cholesterol.
4. Body Mass Index (BMI) is Weight(kg) ÷ $Height(m)^2$, often used as an index of obesity or thinness.
5. Ponderal Index (PI) is Weight(kg) ÷ $Height(m)^3$, a less commonly used but better index of obesity or thinness. For females, who are shorter and lighter than males, but whose physique is normally fatter, the table shows their BMIs are sometimes less, sometimes more, than males. Their PIs however are consistently and probably correctly more than males. See main notes.
6. Differences of less than 3% in the comparisons are probably not significant.
7. Comparison of active Ladakhis with healthy USA NCHS youths may be more appropriate than with possibly obese middle-aged USA and UK Intersalt adults. It is particularly noteworthy that rural Ladakhi's PIs are greater than NCHS ones, indicating that **for their height** they are not over-thin.

↑↓ = figure still rising/falling at age 18yrs.

Table 2. CHILDREN IN LADAKH & LHASA PREFECTURE
Percentages below Harvard and WHO NCHS reference data
(Ladakh — col.1 Wiley 1994a,b; cols.2-5 Padfield this vol.: Tibet — Kolsteren *et al.* 1990)

	WFA birth	WFA 0-4m	WFA 0-2 yr	HFA 2-7 yr	WFH 2-7 yr
(a) Standard Cutoff	**80%**	**80%**	**80%**	**90%**	**80%**
Ladakhis — Indus Valley ()					
(b) Percent below cutoff	c.40%	-	55%	60%	2%
(c) Mean as % of ref. mean	84%(n=168)	>100%(n=7)	78%	88%	96%
Tibetans - Lhasa Valley (0-7 yr)					
(b) Percent below cutoff			35%	35%	4%
(c) Mean as % of ref. mean	see Table 3	see Table 3	86%	92%	99%

Notes
(a) Commonly used but arbitrary cutoff values of mean weight for age (WFA), height for age (HFA) and weight for height (WFH) as percentages of the reference values. In standard populations the cutoffs are about 2 Standard Deviations below the mean.
(b) Percentages of individuals in the sample who fall below these cutoffs and are considered stunted.
(c) Sample means for WFA, HFA and WFH as percentages of the reference values.
(d) Kolsteren noted that the standard errors of the percentages below cutoff points for Lhasa children were very large, making them difficult to interpret reliably. However the much larger percentages below cutoff found in Ladakhis will be more precise, as will the means of both races.

NCHS data		**Birth**	**3m**	**6m**	**15m**	**5yr**	**7yr**
Weights (kg)	F	3.3	5.3	7.2	10.2	17.5	22
	M	3.3	6.0	7.8	10.9	18	23
Height (cm)	F	50	59	66	78	108	121
(or length)	M	51	61	68	79	110	123
BMI*	F	13.2	15.2	16.5	16.8	15	15
	M	12.7	16.1	16.9	17.5	14.9	15.2
PI*	F	26.4	25.8	25.0	21.5	13.9	12.4
	M	24.9	26.4	24.8	22.1	13.5	12.4

***Estimated from NCHS data above.** Note that BMI of healthy chubby babies is misleadingly low, 13 at birth and

Table 3. CHILDREN IN LHASA PREFECTURE, TIBET, AND LOWLAND CHINA
Mean measurements compared with NCHS
(Tibet: Kolsteren *et al.* 1990. Lowland China: Anon 1979)

Age	Birth	3 months	6 m	15m	5 yr	7yr
WEIGHT for AGE						
Urban Tibetans	100% F	105% F	99% F	89% F		85% F
	100% M	97% M	97% M	85% M		82% M
Rural Tibetans	105% F	106% F	95% F	80% F		80% F
	100% M	100% M	90% M	82% M		76% M
HEIGHT for AGE (F & M similar, so meaned)						
Urban Tibetans	99%	100%	99%	97%		95%
Rural Tibetans	100%	100%	97%	94%		90%
Lowland Chinese[1]						
City	100%			98%	97%	
Urban	100%			97%	96%	
Suburban	100%			95%	94%	
Rural	100%			94%	92%	
WEIGHT for HEIGHT (F & M similar, so meaned)						
Urban Tibetans	97%	103%	97%	92%		93%
Rural Tibetans	99%	105%	97%	91%		94%

1. Males were consistently 1cm taller than females.

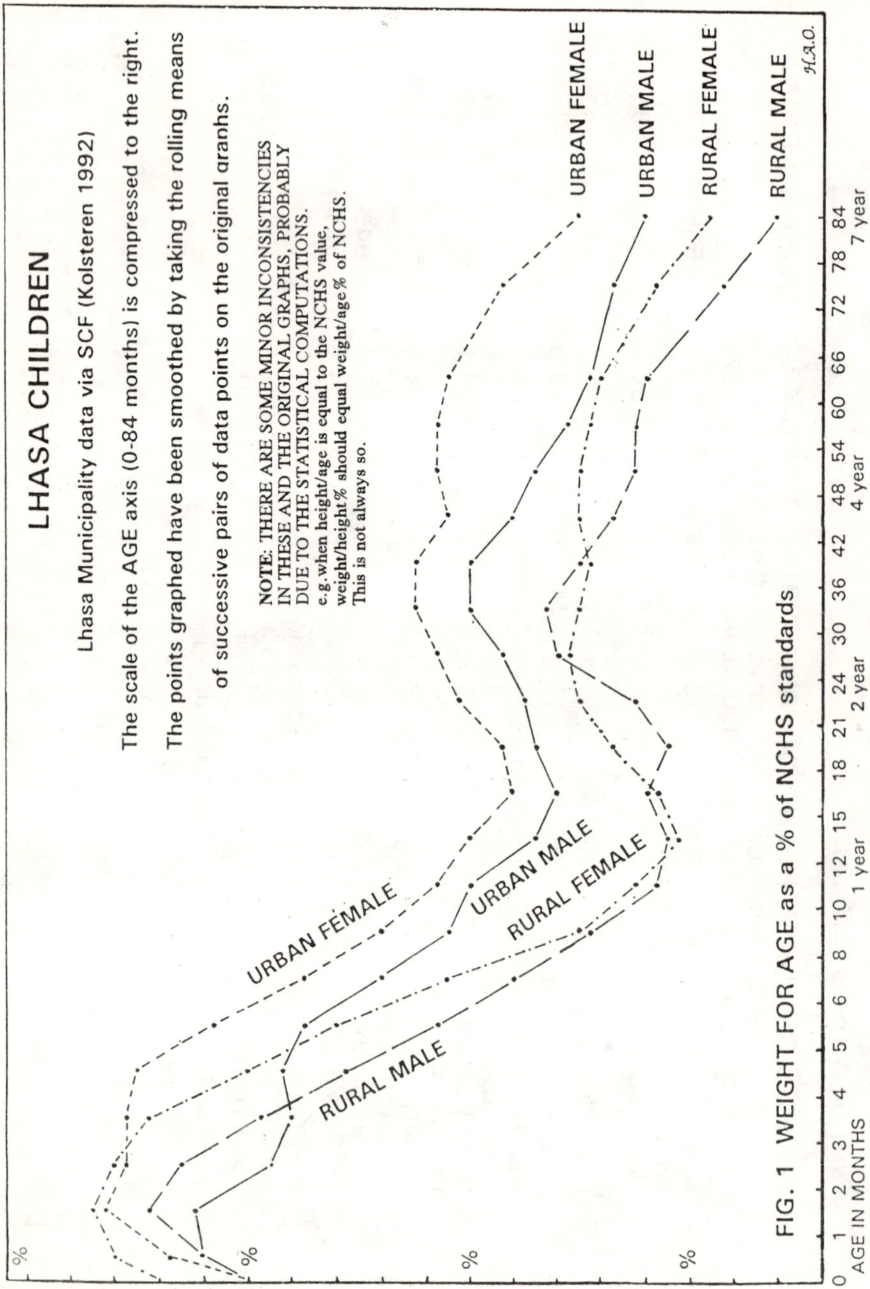

H.A.Osmaston Fig. 1: Lhasa children, Weight for Age.

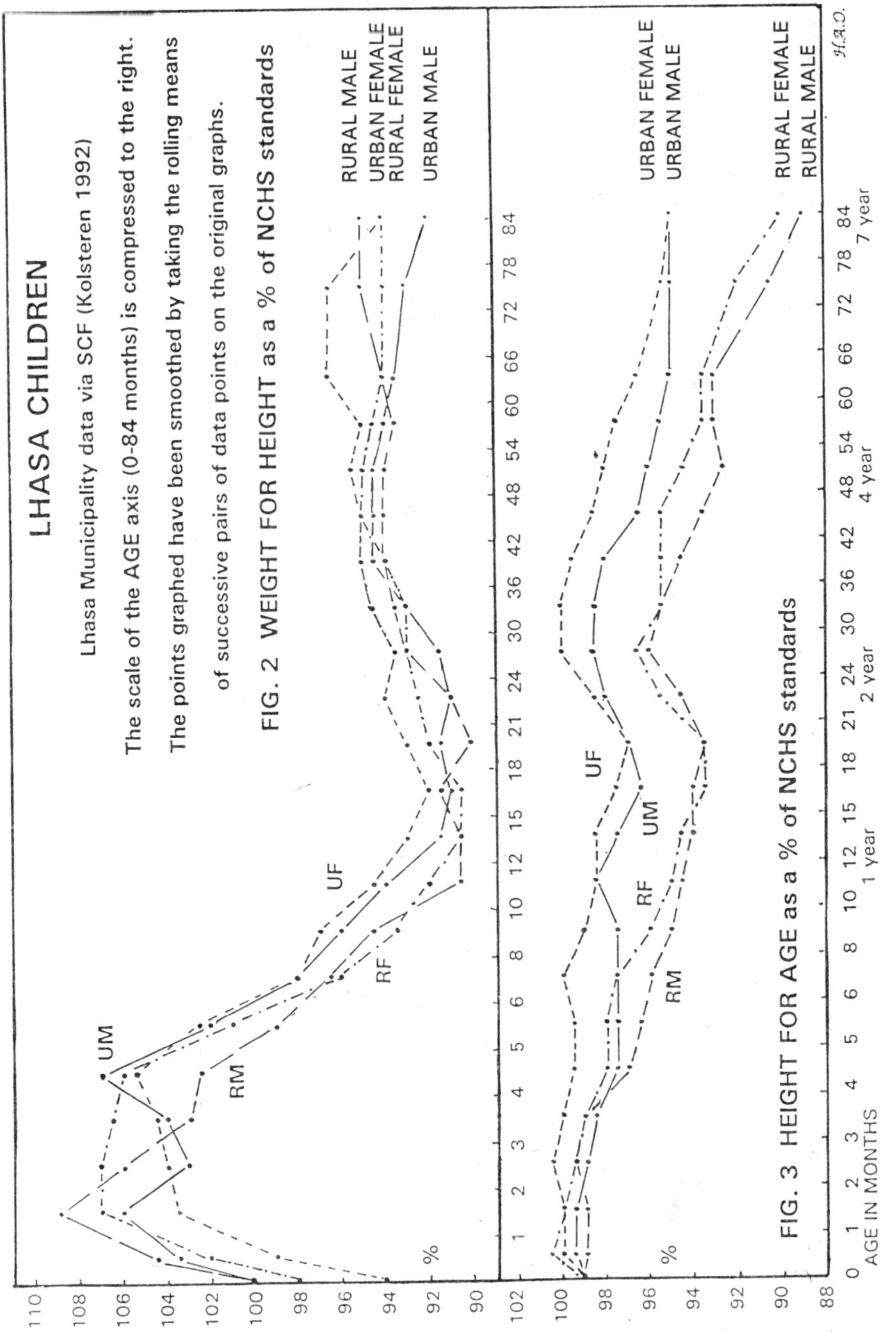

H.A.Osmaston Figs. 3 & 4: Weight for height & Height for Age.

NOTES

1. Acknowledgements

I thank Dr.Keith Ball, Prof.Cynthia Beall, Dr.Graham Clarke, Mr.James Crowden, Prof.Melvyn Goldstein, Mr.Stephen Homewood, Dr.P.Kolsteren, Dr.Tony Leeds, Dr.Nigel Padfield, Mr.Tsering Dalha, Dr.Tsering Norboo, Dr.Veronica Tuffrey and many others for help with and critical comments on this paper; also for the loan of Dr.Tuffrey's thesis and for the use of Dr.Padfield's unpublished data; Dr.Paul Elliott for supplementary INTERSALT results; the SCF for a copy of the report by Dr.Kolsteren *et al.* on Lhasa; Mr.Robbie Barnett for copies of reports on China; the University of Bristol and the Harry Guggenheim Foundation for support in Ladakh; and the International Development Centre, University of Oxford, for support in Tibet.

2. NCHS Growth Curves (see ref. below)

This publication is not readily obtainable in U.K. but the British Library has a microfiche 4147-11-169. The curves have also been republished by WHO, and closely resemble those of Castlemead Pubs., often used in the U.K. The report is based on two different sets of data: one from birth to three years based on 867 middle-class white children living near Yellow Springs, Ohio, USA; the other from 2-18 years based on very much larger samples drawn from all over the USA.

The curves of Weight/Height only include children considered to be pre-pubescent, i.e. less than about 10 yrs. These curves are nearly independent of age, so it is suggested that they may be of special use in studying the nutritional status of children whose date of birth may be unknown or unreliable.

The increases of height recorded in the past in successive generations of American children have now nearly ceased, suggesting that they are attaining their maximum genetic potential. Body sizes significantly smaller than these NCHS reference values are sometimes described as having "Low anthropometric status".

3. BMI (Body Mass Index) and PI (Ponderal Index)

BMI = Weight (kg) ÷ Height (m)^2 PI = Weight (kg) ÷ Height (m)^3

PI (also known as Body Form) has a theoretical advantage over BMI in being a surrogate volume (mass) ÷ length^3, so non-dimensional, a desirable characteristic for a scientific index. For all groups of bodies of **exactly** the same shape, whether spheres, rods or humans, PI is constant for each, dependent only on shape and independent of size. BMI however must increase with size; it is thus a statistical abstraction, not a true index of shape. However in most human groups tall humans tend to be leaner than similarly nourished short ones (i.e. PI falls with increasing height) thus cancelling out the expected increase in BMI, which consequently appears to be nearly independent of height. This seems convenient for those studying nutritional status, but it conceals a real difference between short and tall individuals or groups, which is often overlooked and can lead to problems if individuals of different heights are compared or grouped by BMI. Besides being used as a criterion of obesity (e.g. Garrow & Webster, 1985), BMI is often used as an indicator of Protein-Energy-Deficiency when BMI is below 18.5 (e.g Ferro-Luzzi *et al.* 1992), though because Ladakhis and Tibetans are small (adults 8% shorter than NHCS, see Table 1) it is arguable that for the same body shape their cutoff should be 18.5 x .92 = 17.0 See p.136; Table 1, notes 5 & 6; Table 2, note to NCHS.

4. Hypertension

The INTERSALT survey reported a mean blood pressure of only 112/71 for the rural Ladakhi sample, with 10% exceeding 140/90 mm/Hg . However Norboo (in press) reports that 16% of his mostly rural patients are hypertensive, a higher proportion than in other similarly under-developed regions. The customary drinking of salt-butter-tea may contribute to hypertension here. Urinary sodium was the fourth highest in the INTERSALT survey at 194mmol/24h.

CHILD HEALTH AND NUTRITION in some Ladakhi Villages

*Nigel Padfield**

Background

In 1978, following a catastrophic flood of the river Indus, Save the Children Fund (UK) was asked by the Ladakh authorities to assist the emergency relief effort by the provision of food, clothing etc. When the emergency was over, SCF was asked to undertake a longer term supplementary feeding programme for children in conjunction with the Indian Council for Child Welfare. They agreed to do so on condition that they also be allowed to promote "applied nutrition", i.e. community development activities designed to enhance villagers' self-sufficiency.

These were the origins of the Leh Nutrition Project (LNP), which started in 1979. In addition to a supplementary feeding programme other LNP activities in the early stages included the promotion of vegetable growing, irrigation channel repairs, non-formal pre-school education and a community yak programme. By 1981 about 30 villages south of the Indus were involved and villagers were asking for a health component to be added to the programme.

In response to this request an LNP team assisted by the author carried out two surveys in the autumn of 1981 and the summer of 1982 to investigate the health and nutrition status of children in villages in which LNP was working or proposing to work and to determine what, if any, health activities would be appropriate. This paper reports on some of the findings of these surveys.

Methods

The first survey in October-November 1981 was carried out in the following 8 villages:-

Stakna	Rumbak	Martselang	Mangu
Alchi	Markha	Skiukaya	Hankar

In June 1982 a second somewhat shorter survey was carried out in 8 villages in Wanla. 6 were in the lower Wanla valley up to and including Phangila. The other villages were Urtse and Hanupattar in

---

* Dr. N.Padfield (S.C.F. Consultant 1981-82), Grove End Cottage, Scotsgrove, Thame, Oxon, U.K.

"upper" Wanla.

All the children that could be found in each village aged 0-95 months were weighed, measured and physically examined. In addition a questionnaire was administered to their mothers to determine *inter alia* the number and age of all their living children; the number of their children who had died together with their age of death and cause of death and illnesses that had occurred to their children in the previous month.

The choice of nutrition status indicators was determined by practical considerations. As none of the villages had ever previously experienced a nutrition survey and many had never seen a trained health worker before, it was decided that the survey must be as non-intrusive as possible. No attempt was, therefore, made to measure the height of children less than 2 years old as this would have meant subjecting them to a possibly traumatic supine length measurement.

For these reasons the following nutrition status indicators were used in the 1981 survey

Children aged 0-23 months - weight for age (W/A)

Children aged 24-95 months - weight for height (W/H) and height for age (H/A)

In the more rapid 1982 survey the same indicators were used except that heights, and therefore H/As, were not measured.

Children were weighed in light underclothing to the nearest 0.1kg on a Salter hanging scale. Height was measured to the nearest cm using a locally made height stick with a sliding headboard. Weight for height was determined in both surveys using a Nabarro colour-coded wall chart. In the 1981 survey, where heights were measured, W/H was also calculated directly from the weights and heights obtained. All W/A, W/H and H/A calculations were made using Harvard standards, i.e. a reference population of healthy American children. These are almost identical to, but have now largely been superseded by the NCHS standards (National Center for Health Statistics, USA).

Findings

For the sake of simplicity the main findings of the two surveys have been combined wherever possible:-

1. Weight for age.

W/A is said to be "normal" if it is 80% or more than the reference value, i.e. if the child's weight is 80% or more of the median weight attained by a reference population child of the same age. Grade 1 malnutrition (MN) denotes 70-79% of the reference value; grade 2 MN denotes 60-69% of the reference value and grade 3 MN is less than 60%.

TABLE 1

2 surveys combined. 98 children aged 0-23 months.

Nutrition status	**0-11m**	**12-23m**	**Total**
Normal	28 (65%)	16 (29%)	44 (45%)
Grade 1 malnutrition	11 (26%)	22 (40%)	33 (34%)
Grade 2 malnutrition	4 (9%)	12 (22%)	16 (16%)
Grade 3 malnutrition	—	5 (9%)	5 (5%)
TOTAL	**43**	**55**	**98**

It is clear from table 1 that nutrition status is considerably worse in the second year of life than in the first. Among children aged 12-23 months less than 30% had a normal W/A. The mean W/As of children of different ages in the 1981 survey (table 2) illustrate the age-specific differences more clearly.

TABLE 2

Age (months)	**No of children**	**Mean W/A(%)**
2-5m	7	102.7%
6-11m	18	82.2%
12-17m	16	80.5%
18-23m	24	70.5%
TOTAL	**65**	**79.4%**

Among the small sample of children less than 4 months old mean W/A is actually GREATER than that of the reference population. However, there is then a progressive deterioration in nutrition status in comparison with the reference population.

A similar picture was seen in the 1982 survey. The mean W/A of 18 children aged 0-11 months was 80.4% whereas the mean W/A of 15 children aged 12-23 months was 71.7%.

2. Weight for height. 2 surveys combined. 248 children aged 24-95 months.

243 children (98.0%) had a normal nutrition status by W/H criteria, i.e. their W/H was 80% or more of the reference value. The remaining 5 children (2%) had a W/H of less than 80% and were said to be "wasted". This figure includes 2 children who were clinically "wasted", but whom it was not possible to measure as they were both

suffering from multiple painful boils.

Mean W/H by **age group** was calculated for the 164 children in the 1981 survey. This was considerably lower among children aged 24-35 months than among older children (table 3).

TABLE 3

Age (months)	No. of children	Mean W/H(%)
24-35m	23	92.7%
36-47m	30	97.1%
48-59m	29	97.1%
60-71m	29	96.6%
72-83m	22	96.7%
84-95m	31	97.3%
TOTAL	**164**	**96.4%**

3. Height for age. 1981 survey only. 108 children aged 24-95 months.

There were some difficulties determining exact age, particularly among older children. Children were excluded, if there were doubts about their age. The results obtained from the remainder are presented in table 4.

TABLE 4

Age (months)	No.	> 90% H/A	85-89% H/A	<85% H/A
24-35m	20	12 (60.0%)	4 (20.0%)	4 (20.0%)
36-47m	24	8 (33.3%)	10 (41.7%)	6(25.0%)
48-71m	37	14 (37.8%)	15 (40.5%)	8 (21.6%)
72-95m	27	9 (33.3%)	9 (33.3%)	9 (33.3%)
TOTAL	**108**	**43 (39.8%)**	**38 (35.2%)**	**24 (25.0%)**

For height for age the generally accepted cut-off point is 90% of the reference value. Those with H/A less than 90% are said to be "stunted". 60.2% of the sample fell into this category. Those with H/A less than 85% are said to be "severely stunted". 25.0% fell into this category.

4. Infant and child mortality. A very crude estimate of infant and child mortality rates was obtained by relating the number of reported infant (< 1 year) and child deaths to the number of children ever born (NEB), as shown in table 5.

TABLE 5

	1981 survey	1982 survey
No. of children ever born (NEB)	504	259
Infant deaths (< 1 year)	89 (17.7%)	28 (10.8%)
Child deaths (> 1 year)	33 (6.5%)	19 (7.3%)
Total deaths	**122 (24.2%)**	**47 (18.1%)**

Since almost all child deaths occur before the age of 5 years, it is generally accepted in surveys of this sort that the number of reported deaths in children aged more than 1 year is a reasonable approximation of the number of 1-4 years deaths. The figures, therefore, suggest that in the 1981 survey villages almost a quarter of children had died before their fifth birthday. This compares with 18.1% for the Wanla villages.

Most deaths occurred in the first year of life. The crude estimate of infant mortality rate (IMR) obtained from these figures was 174 per 100 in the 1981 survey and 108 per 1000 for the Wanla villages. The differences in estimated IMRs in different areas is further illustrated in table 6.

TABLE 6

	NEB	Infant deaths/NEB
Skiumarkha valley + Rumbak	171	21.1%
Mangu + Martselang	170	19.4%
"Upper Wanla"	70	18.6%
Alchi	163	12.3%
Lower Wanla villages	189	7.9%

The estimated IMR figures are high in all areas except Alchi and the Lower Wanla villages. These are the ones at lowest altitude. They are also comparatively wealthy with greater scope for food production.

Chest infections were the most commonly reported cause of death followed closely by measles. However, in many cases the cause of death was unknown.

5. Health problems. The health problems most commonly observed or reported in the previous month were:-

Respiratory tract infections	Worms
Diarrhoea diseases	Eye infections

Anaemia Ear infections

Respiratory tract infections were the most commonly reported health problem (30% in the 1981 survey) as well as the main reported cause of death. Diarrhoea was reported far more frequently in the Indus valley villages than in the more remote areas. Anaemia, almost certainly nutritional in origin, was found in 10% of the children. Worms were particularly common in the more low-lying areas such as Wanla. Eye infections are important because, if untreated, they may lead to blindness. One child was seen to whom this had happened. Ear infections, if untreated, may lead to deafness.

Discussion of Findings

The surveys were not carried out for research purposes, but to provide LNP with some practical information to assist in programme planning. The result is that the methodology used was not ideal for making comparisons with surveys done in other places and the numbers of children seen were small. The findings must, therefore, be treated with caution. Nevertheless some tentative conclusions may be drawn:-

Nutrition status. The nutrition status indicators used provide different types of information. A W/H of less than 80% of the reference value ("wasting") denotes acute malnutrition, i.e. malnutrition that has resulted from a severe nutritional deficit in the previous 2-3 months. The prevalence of "wasting" may, therefore, vary seasonally. At the time of the surveys only 2% of the children were "wasted", which suggests a low level of acute malnutrition at that time of year in children over 2 years old.

A H/A of less than 90% of the reference value ("stunting") denotes chronic malnutrition, i.e. less than adequate food intake over a long period of time. This in turn is often associated with factors like poor weaning practices and frequent episodes of illness. The "stunting" level found in the survey (60.2%) was as high as is found anywhere in the world. However, it should be noted that the sample size was small and there were difficulties obtaining accurate ages particularly among older children.

W/A is a composite indicator which may denote either acute or chronic malnutrition. The findings suggest that there are few nutritional problems in the first 6 months of life when breast milk supplies all nutritional needs. Nutritional status then deteriorates, particularly during the second year of life. This is at the height of the weaning period when children are also vulnerable to frequent episodes of illness.

The data from table 3 suggest that nutrition problems continue for children aged 24-35 months, but that those who survive to their third birthday appear to be reasonably well nourished thereafter. The high stunting levels in older children are perhaps best seen as a legacy of the period of nutritional vulnerability between 6-35 months.

Mortality. It is difficult to draw firm conclusions from a retrospective survey involving such a small sample. However, the data suggest high levels of infant mortality (more than 180 per 1000) in the higher and more remote villages. The IMR for India as a whole at the time of the survey was 129 per 1000.

The most commonly reported causes of death — chest infectionsand measles — are amenable either to simple treatment or to prevention by immunisation. One family reported having lost four children during a measles epidemic.

Health problems. The health problems encountered are similar to those found in other parts of India, although chest infections appear to be particularly prevalent and diarrhoea in the more remote villages may be less of a problem than elsewhere, perhaps due to their having a plentiful and uncontaminated water supply.

Although the problems are all either preventable or easily treated, most of the villages in which LNP was working were without any access to health care apart from that provided by traditional practitioners such as Amchis. Amchis are skilled, respected and treat many ailments effectively. However, their medical system lacks the antibiotics needed to cure conditions such as chest infections and lacks also the immunisation capacity to prevent diseases such as measles.

The LNP team concluded as a result of the surveys that the villagers' request for a health programme was justified. This would be best achieved by supporting the Amchi system and, where necessary, providing Amchis with additional allopathic skills. In addition support should be given to the District measles immunisation programme and to the Rehbarisehat scheme for providing primary school teachers in remote villages with a basic first aid training.

FOOD AS RITUAL

Abby Ripley[1]

For anyone who has been a guest in a Ladakhi household, there is no denying that food and drink are the basis of hospitality. How many of us have thought we just couldn't drink another cup of tea or eat another spoonful of rice? Yet in a broader perspective this generous outlay is also characteristic of many other societies and cultures, e.g. Indian Kashmiri or Punjabi, Nepalese Tibetan or Sherpa, Chinese. All of these peoples, like the Ladakhis, take particular pride and pleasure in sharing and consuming food, in feasts and feasting. This is not an uncommon social phenomenon or one which has been overlooked by other scholars.[2]

In so far as Ladakh is concerned, the use of food socially is

---

1. Ms. A. Ripley, Dept. of Anthropology, Rutgers University, New Brunswick, N.J. U.S.A.

or Box 431 New Milford, CT 06776, U.S.A.

2. To cite a select few, see R. S. Khare, *The Hindu Hearth and Home.* New Delhi: Vikas, 1976; R. S. Khare and M. S. A. Rao (eds.), *Food, Society. and Culture.* Durham, N.C. : Carolina Academic Press, 1986 (this reference contains a comprehensive bibliography of food and nutrition in South Asia); Rinjing Dorjc, *Food in Tibetan Life.* London: Prospect Books, 1985; K. C. Chang (ed.), *Food in Chinese Culture: Anthropological and Historical Perspective.* New Haven: Yale University Press, 1977; Brenda Beck, "Colour and heat in South Indian ritual," *Man*, 4 (1969): 553-572; John Ardussi , "Brewing and drinking the beer of enlightenment in Tibetan Buddhism, " *Journal of the American Oriental Society,* 97 (1977) :115-124; Linda Stone, "Food symbolism in hindu Nepal," *Contributions to Nepalese Studies*, 6 (1978) :47-65 ; John Robson (ed.), *Food, Ecology and Culture: Readings in the Anthropology of Dietary Practices.* New York : Gordon and Breach, 1980; T. Fitzgerald (ed.), *Nutrition and Anthropology in Action.* Amsterdam: Van Gorcum, 1977; Marvin Harris, *Good to Eat.* New York: Simon and Schuster, 1985; L Sherry Ortner, *Sherpas Through Their Rituals* . London : Cambridge University Press, 1978 ; Jack Goody, *Cooking, Cuisine and Class.* New York: Cambridge University Press, 1982; Lawrence Babb, "The food of the gods in Chhattisgarh: some structural features of Hindu ritual, " *Southwestern Journal of Anthropology*, 26 (1970) :287-304; Gabriella Eichinger Ferro-Luzzi, "Ritual as language: the case of South Indian food offerings," *Current Anthropology,* 18 (1977) :507-514; T. Selwyn, "The order of men and the order of things: an examination of food transactions in an Indian village, " *International Journal of the Sociology of Law,* 8 (1980) :297-317; Frederick Simoons, *Eat Not This Flesh.* Madison: University of Wisconsin Press, 1961; Audrey Cantlie, "The moral significance of food among Assamese Hindus, " in *Culture and Morality* ed. Adrian Mayer. New Delhi: Oxford University Press, 1981; McKim Marriott, "Caste ranking and food transactions: a matrix analysis, " in *Structure and Change in Indian Society,* eds. M. Singer and B. S. Cohn. Chicago: Aldine, 1968; Edward Harper, "Ritual pollution as an integrator of caste and religion, " in *Religion in South Asia,* ed. Edward Harper. Seattle: University of Washington Press, 1964.

noteworthy only if seen in a larger context and not just as a necessity, an enjoyment, or even as a manifestation of culturally conditioned generosity or the Buddhist ethic. It could be argued that in a land where extreme climatic conditions make scarcity a basic contingency of life, there is an overwhelming awareness of food - why else the inviolability of the Ladakh *zot* or pantry?[3] This concern with food, however, goes beyond the perennial food deficits in many households to the extraordinary activities and attitudes associated with food itself. It is these activities that interest me, and particularly what they convey as meaning - the form of perception which constitutes and organises the mental, physical, and cultural life of humans; in this instance, the way of "seeing" the world, the interactions within it.

The elemental unit of meaning is a point of reference which is known either for its empirical self or inferred by analogy. The former yields a simple, straightforward image with a restricted meaning because it pertains to the microcosmic world of man. The latter opens up a world of multiple meanings which expand into even larger (macrocosmic) frames of reference. Together they form a symbolic continuum in which the points of reference become increasingly relational and metaphorical as they either equate or substitute one for the other (Wagner, 1986).

Food is a point of reference in Ladakhi culture, and a very significant one. As a generic reference food is sustenance; food is hospitality; food is an item of exchange. In these various capacities food generates meaning - for example, it is perceived as providing health, happiness and wealth. In turn these meanings become the referents for food or, alternatively, food becomes the symbol for either one or all of them. However, culture encompasses discrete categories so that particular foods become appropriate for particular occasions, increasing the points of reference and expanding the significance of the symbol. Hence, *mar-zan* is specific nourishment for the celebrants of a birth; *don* is a specially prepared meal for guests; and *geg-stor* is food exchanged for a favour. In order to accommodate numerous differentiated references such as these within the cultural frame, food as the common denominator must become a symbol which is, at one and the same time, more intensive and more extensive. Accordingly its image becomes fixed and iconographic like that of *khar-chor* and

---

3. As part of the *Lo-sar* celebrations, a stone or piece of ice referred to as a "golden rock" (*ser-pa long*) is brought from outdoors into the *zot* and represents the coming of riches into the household larder — an auspicious beginning of a new year. Actually a historical precedent for guarding the *zot* or keeping it off-limits (sometimes locked) might be the intrusive demands made by hostile armies needing food.

tshogs, and the primary meanings of food - health, wealth and happiness - are conflated to form a new, expanded signification - that of "offering" which includes the former meanings in addition to the ones of auspice and conciliation. Within the macrocosmic cultural milieu of Mahayana Buddhism, where processes are thought to be cyclical and recursive, the act of offering connotes repayment and/or redistribution which, in turn, implies a reciprocal relationship. Therefore, any symbolic offering which (1) represents many meanings and actions; (2) unites disparate but analogous qualities or associations; (3) counterbalances conceptual meanings (e.g. moral or social ideologies) with perceptual ones (e.g. those related to the sensory experience, especially emotions) becomes a dominant symbol (Turner, 1967).

For Ladakhis such a symbol is the *dun-ges*. Esoterically its three-dimensional shape is that of a *chorten* ; its two-dimensional one a mandala - both representative of the universe or cosmos. As a vertical structure it symbolizes the Buddha's three-fold body: Body, Speech, and Mind; as a horizontal plan, it symbolically locates the Buddha or one of his manifestations, a *bodhisattva* at the center where he mediates between the Absolute (i.e the threshold of *nirvana*), and the phenomenal world.[4] Commonly the *dun-ges* is regarded as an auspicious symbol which bestows good luck or a blessing when portions of it are distributed among villagers. For that purpose it is made from dough (out of ingredients donated by laymen) into a kind of cake, completely edible. Through the formation and dedication of this "mega"-symbol by a *lama* who, through his power and authority, charges it with positive *karma* or merit, the *dun-ges* becomes a ritual object, along with other symbols, for ceremonial occasions. At the conclusion of these ceremonies the *dun-ges* is cut into pieces and eaten by participants or taken home. Once again, esoterically, it is a symbol of the vow and beneficence of the *dhyani-bodhisattva* who transfers the accumulated merit to human beings.

---

4. Anna Grimshaw in her PhD dissertation (1983) points out that one of the distinguishing features of Mahayana Buddhism and Tantrism is their emphasis on the body, particularly as a "focus for ritual attention" (p. 130). In that regard it is not surprising that food has an important function in the rituals of both. Furthermore, of the three Buddha bodies, the intermediate one (*sambhogakaya)*, whether translated into English as the "Body of Reciprocal Enjoyment" (Grimshaw, 1983) or the "Complete Enjoyment Body" (Cozort, 1986), experiences a state of satisfaction through its Form Body which is the result of the collections of merit (see p. 25, Cozort). Since the merit is returned to his human benefactors through the medium of food, I wonder if the "enjoyment" may be as much a capacity to "accept" or "ingest" food (as a human body would) as an ability to return the food transformed as merit or blessing (see continuation of text).

Because it accomplishes much, so to speak, the dominant symbol becomes the basic unit of ritual action, and like ritual symbols in general, it is "...essentially involved in social process... associated with human interests, purposes, ends, and means...." (Turner, 1967:20). There are many dominant symbols in Ladakhi culture just as there are numerous lesser ones. What I propose to do for the remainder of this paper is to describe a variety of food items or foodstuffs which serve as symbolic points of reference or highlights in the cultural matrix of Ladakhi meaning and experience, and to discuss how they form the basis of ritualized social behavior. Let me say that the complex of symbols and ritual allows that certain symbols are used although the meaning of what they symbolize has been long forgotten. It is through the empowerment of the ritual that some symbols are validated and sometimes even interpreted, but for the ordinary villager it is tradition that counts - with or without a detailed explanation.

Nowhere is the display and distribution of food more obvious than at feasts or *don-thang*, and nowhere is it more formalized, i.e. ritualized, than on those occasions. For that reason feasts will be discussed last. However, in addition to feasts which are fundamentally gifts of food on a large scale, there are other, smaller gifts of food such as *mar-zan* given for the event of birth. *Mar-zan* or food *(zan)* with butter *(mar)* is a classification encompassing *amay mar-zan* and *drasil,* but which has also come to designate small quantities of butter, sugar, flour, or rice brought to a household where a birth has taken place. Traditionally *amay mar-zan,* made from *tsampa* cooked in water with salt and ghee added, was given to a woman by her mother on the day after delivery. Practically it is to abet the new mother's recovery, but also as a symbol of vitality and good fortune, it is sometimes smeared on the brows of those present much like *ru-ma* or *yar* are dabbed on the foreheads of participants in *Saka,* the Spring plowing ritual. In the latter instance the *ru-ma* is made from *tsampa*, butter and *chang*, and is unceremoniously applied along with a handful of flour in a spirit of boisterous conviviality, characteristic of *Saka* activities. *Yar*, on the other hand, is a piece of butter solemnly rubbed into the forehead and over the face and hands. When used as an auspicious signifier butter is referred to as *yar,* and most commonly employed to garnish offerings such as *chot-pa* and *chang*. Incidently the *dzo* which perform for *Saka* are similarly consecrated, i.e. their horns oiled, their foreheads dabbed with *ru-ma*.

Returning, however, to the gifts of *mar-zan*, on the seventh day after birth the closest relatives bring *drasil*, a favorite dish prepared from boiled white rice, butter, and sugar to which stewed apricots and/or peanuts are added. On the fifteenth day other relatives, friends, and fellow villagers offer the basic raw materials of *mar-zan* mentioned above, i.e. flour, butter, sugar, and rice. In another context *amay mar-zan* and *drasil* can be considered restorative or curative foods as can *stay-zan* which is a paste of cooked barley flour and ghee placed upon the navel of the newborn to hasten healing by protecting it from moisture and dirt.

Other examples of food gifts are *pin-don* and *pak-don* or *pak-zan*. The former is typically a presentation of seven *cambir* (baked wheat bread) draped with *khar-tuk* (ceremonial scarf) to the mother or father of an infant. In some villages where the New Year *don* provides a socially convenient moment, the host household will offer *pin-don* to the parent(s) of any child born within the year. If a child's grandparent is also present, sometimes a lesser gift, e.g. *kul-cha* (sweet biscuit), will be given to him/her. Likewise, *pak-zan* is given to a woman who has married during the year, and is usually presented in the house of the bride's relative. *Pak-zan* is any prepared meal, e.g. *cambir* along with rice and dal, which can be conveniently taken away by the visiting *pak-ma* (bride). Before going any further let me note that the word *zan* broadly means "food" but usually cooked food made up of more than one ingredient such as *pak-zan*. In comparison *pak-don* or *pin-don* are derived from *don-thong*, but as single gifts of food represent celebratory feasts on a miniature scale or in symbolic proportions.

Cooked or prepared food as opposed to foodstuff is the primary medium by which pollution is transmitted hence the socially imposed *zem-ches* which disallows non-*pha-spun* members from eating or drinking in a house defiled by the blood of childbirth (*bang-thip)* or a corpse (*ro-thip)*. Secondary conveyors of pollution or *thip* are humans who, if contaminated, also contaminate their domestic gods, *kim-lha* or *phas-lha*. Depending upon the sensitivity of their family and/or *pha-spun* gods, householders may not take food in a defiled house for seven to thirty days. To alleviate the stricture of *zem-ches*, at least one village has devised a system whereby half of the village households will desist from any food or drink on the occasion of a birth celebration while the other half will do the same for death. This arrangement enables villagers to "safely" carry out their social obligation of being supportive by attending the various functions associated with life crisis events, at which food and drink are customarily offered by the celebrant household. In that case a number of special arrangements are made, facilitated by traditional social institutions such as the *pha-spun* whose responsibility it is to prepare meals, among other things, for the household in crisis. As patrons of the same *phas-lha* they are exempt from godly retribution, but at the same time can assist in meal preparation under certain circumstances - those circumstances being the temporary establishment of a kitchen outside the defiled house where "pure" food and tea can be prepared for guests. Paradoxically, in spite of *zem-ches* sanctions, of which the avoidance of contaminated food is just one aspect (the other involves avoiding fields and streams), much planning and labor goes into food preparation. For example, at the event of death, closest relatives of the deceased consult with one another to decide in what order they will sponsor meals on various days of the *cho-ga* (cremation ritual), what kinds of food should be offered, and how the foodstuffs will be made available to the *pha-spun* and others who will make the preparations.

Marriage, the actual ceremony rather than the public celebration, provides us with one of the most potent functions of food in the secular domain. It is used to seal or confirm the marriage bond. Before the *go-ras* or nuptial head-dresses are untied the leader of the bridal party sings a song pertaining to the enactment of *sangma tok* or the symbolic taking of food. For that one plate of food, one spoon, and one cup of tea and/or *chang* are placed before the seated couple, and they are urged to feed one another. Whether the groom complies first or the bride, the small amounts ingested from their communal meal signal to all present their acceptance of the marriage alliance. At that point the *go-ras* are removed, and in the ceremony which I witnessed the groom's or *mag-pa*'s mother-in-law stepped forward to present them with *babs- zan*, a plate of an odd-number of small round cakes or patties made from *paba* (the flour of partially roasted barley cooked slowly in water) and adorned with *yar*. Afterwards these were distributed among the guests. Apparently in an earlier era and in remote villages today, the bride and groom are given the "soft" *paba* or the *paba* made with butter for *sangma tok*.. At any rate it is interesting to note that *paba,* the most common, cooked food in Ladakh, is alternatively referred to as *zan*.

Celebration of the Ladakhi new year is a grand feast for villagers and for their gods and spirits, epitomized by the greeting, *Lo-sar-la jal sKyit* or "Happy Feast of *Lo-sar*." In spirit and events it is a time for excess and indulgence; for extroversion and generosity toward all sentient beings, expressible through a number of activities, the focus of which is food.

One of these is the making of *skyen*, or ibex, from dough and arranging them on a shelf in the kitchen along with a typical offering to the divinities, like *gee-nas*. An odd number of *skyen* are fashioned by the mistress of the house or a fertile female as dictated by an ancient belief that the symbolic image of the ibex fosters fertility. In that connection it is interesting to note that on the third day of *Lo-sar* the *skyen* are turned on their sides, signaling, as it were, the birth of a new year. Normally children - the very object of this magical projection - are given the tiny ibex as food to play with. When a female in the house is pregnant the *skyen* remain untouched until after the birth. As a symbol of fecundity the *skyen* is not unlike the *orza*, the earthen jug used to hold ceremonial *chang*. Since it is normally regarded as an auspicious symbol, I conjecture that because of its womb-like shape it also symbolizes birth, especially when it is turned on its side to indicate empty content or the delivery of its content. This, in fact, was an action taken at a funeral that I attended. It occurred following the cremation of the deceased, when the males, including relatives, returned to the deceased's house and sat around an open space in a nearby field in which a *chang* jug smaller than the *orza* had been placed. The act was particularly significant in view of its context, death, if it can be interpreted as a portent of new life or rebirth. Antithetical to that is the small clay pot *(galu)* containing a residue of fermented barley kernels used in making *chang* which is broken and cast to evil spirits before the bride enters the house. Since these covetous, potentially harmful spirits must be diverted, what better way to satisfy them than to abort the symbolic womb. As in other ransoming rituals, the over eager spirits are easily fooled.

For the *pak-ston* or public marriage celebration yet another pot of *chang* has an additional function. Traditionally the groom's uncle provides an *orza* into which gifts of *chang* are poured, and at some point in the festivities, it is expected that male guests will dance around it. On this occasion custom demands the largest *chang* pot available, and it sits upright, the better to receive the *khar-chor*, the "white offering," in this case, *chang*. Obviously here *chang* may be seen to represent semen since the hoped-for result of the marriage is children. Before returning to the activities of *Lo-sar*, let me point out that, in general, *khar-chor* is an offering that precedes every favorable event, and it appears in different guises. In addition to *chang*, which is brought to a *pak-ston*, flour, butter, and sugar are also given (much like the items of *mar-zan*, making it also a kind of *khar-chor)*. On the other hand, *khar-chor* as an auspicious presentation is not appropriate for funerals. The very simplest *khar-chor* is a gestural offering only and may consist of a bowl of water. In earlier times, when milk was more abundant, a bowl of buttermilk or curd and a pitcher of *chang* were the representative *khar-chor* (male, female symbols); nowadays mostly, a container of flour has replaced the milk. The male-female symbolism can also be seen in the simultaneous offering of burning incense *(poks)* - smoke is also white - by a boy or man *(poks-pa)*, while a girl or woman *(khar-chor-ma)* offers the *khar-chor*.

Lo-sar encompasses a series of enactments with obvious roots in the Ladakhi or regional folk tradition of the distant past. The presentation of *thap-zan* is one of these customs. Here common food *(zan)* of the common household hearth *(thap)* is presented to kin who are no longer members of the ancestral or focal residence, i.e. they have married out. As custom dictates these individuals are invited to return singly or in groups in order to receive food. Among the ordinary villagers relatives are usually given *paba* made rich with a hollow of ghee at its center along with an odd-number of *cambir*, but some Ladakhis say that at one time hierarchial cuts of meat were also distributed, e.g. shoulder meat to a married daughter; ribs to an uncle or aunt. These cuts were further sub-divided for lesser relatives such as nephews. (In hunting societies it is customary that the hunter distributes his kill according to some kind of social ranking, keeping the most prized piece for himself.) Among the *sku-tak*, instead of *paba*, a plate of *ku-ra* arranged as a *chorten* used to be presented. It should be noted that *ku-ra* is in the shape of an endless knot, the Tibetan Buddhist symbol for longevity. Nowadays, rice with a meat or vegetable sauce is a permissible gift of *thap-zan*.

Of course the *thap* itself, the abode of the *thap-lha*, is an object of veneration (through *chak)* during *Lo-sar*. It receives an offering of butter and *chang* and is greeted respectfully: *thap lha-gamo o-ma ju; thap-lha gyapo o-ma ju*. Afterwards other members of the household are similarly greeted and toasted with *yar*, embellished cups of chang. This simple enactment illustrates two things: first, the offering formula - gods before humans; secondly, the mirror reflections of secular and sacred rituals. Of the former let me say that ritual is a performative act utilizing the spoken word along with actions which are highly structured, i.e. made up of predictable patterns or sequences; it is also a hypercodified act, i.e. made up either of symbols - meaningful objects and locations - or conventions that are exaggerated, condensed, and/or redundant in form or content (Tambiah, 1985). In other words ritual is an attempt to communicate an important ideology with as little ambiguity and margin of error as possible so as not to disrupt or discontinue its power to transform or transmit: in this example to transform food into a substance easily conveyed to the spirit or god for the purpose of conciliation.

In looking at the analogous components in rituals performed by the laity and those performed by ritual specialists such as the *lamas,* I am not concerned with traditional arguments about the dialectic between sacred and secular domains; rather, I see the common elements as stemming from a cultural consensus that certain procedures are important for the maintenance of society and that a division of labor or responsibility for that maintenance is only expedient. Therefore, laymen attend to one set of rituals, and the *lamas* to another, utilizing similar repertories which are distinguishable by the skill and knowledge of the ritualists. (In most cases the clergy-performed rituals are more sophisticated.)

The cultural consensus owes its existence to the fact that, in the words of Tambiah (1985:129), "...all societies have cosmologies which in their several different classificatory ways relate man to man, man with nature and animals, and man with the gods and demons and other nonhuman agencies." These cosmological conceptions are composites of beliefs, myths, orienting principles, and other sacrosanct phenomena which actuate and legitimate the pragmatic world. The paradigm of this cultural achievement is the ritual. In reference to the ethnographic data which I have just given some samples of, it is clear that the cosmological or ideological construct behind the ritualization of food in Ladakh pertains to offering. This undoubtedly has its origins in the Vedic past when cosmological divinities were worshipped through the medium of offerings, as later were the deities of Indian Buddhism and Tantra, and finally Bon and the Buddhism of China, Tibet, Japan; the quintessential offering being that of the *homa* or fire ritual. The *chin-sek*, as it is called in Tibetan, takes a variety of forms, but most notably, as far as the ordinary villager is concerned, in the cremation rites for the dead. Various consecrated materials, mainly foodstuffs (*chang*, curd, *paba*, ghee, *tsampa*, etc.) are offered to the *may-lha* or fire god through the open mouth of the chimney, sometimes with spoons. To carry the anthropomorphic image further, the heat of the fire can be likened to the digestive juices of the belly. A less elaborate form of the *chin-sek* is the offering of *geg-stor*, the sacrifice to mischievious spirits who might interfere with any ritual or ceremony, for example, before the bride enters a house for marriage. The *geg-stor*, in fact, as a kind of *storma* is basically food used to lure or entice much like *surr* and *shi-mi* (i.e. the food for the dead). At any rate the act of offering (*pul-ches* or *sol-ches)* implements rules of procedure as well as distribution. In formal rituals such as *dol-choke*, Tara is invited and seated (*chan-den*), washed (*too-sol)*, given food (*chot-pa pul-ches)*, requested to grant a favor (*sol-dip)*, and sent back (*sheck-sol)*, in that order. For Tantric rituals which are more forceful the procedural order is a little different. Using *skang-sol* as an example, the Dharmapalas or *chos- skyong/schung-ma* are invited, asked for forgiveness of sins (*shaks-pa)*, offered food (*skang-wa* or *sol-chot)* and drink (*ser-kem)*, and then reminded of their duty to protect the Dharma and humans--in general to be helpful (*skool)*, and finally praised (*stot-pa)* and sent back (*sheck-sol)*. The offerings are prepared and purified before the start of the ritual. In the case of *skang-sol*, many *chot-pa* - the food of the religious protectors - are prepared for the feast at the ritually appropriate moment of *skang-wa*. Likewise for the offering of *tsogs* (*tsogs pul-ches)* various food items are readied, among them being: *tsogs yos* (snacks); *tsogs keer* (bread); *tsogs chang*; *tsogs sha* (raw meat); *tsogs jo* (curd); and *tsogs* (a cake-like offering, symbolic of the human breast). The *chot-pa* and *tsogs* along with the *dun-ges,* in fact, represent life-giving qualities - protection, sustenance, and happiness through the assistance of gods, mothers, and the attainment of perfection. Although *chot-pa* (*storma*) are the featured, fancy food, so to speak, of specific rituals and therefore assume various shapes, colors, and ornamentation, the fundamental altar offering of *nair-chot* includes simple foods as well as other items for the satisfaction of the deities. The abbreviated or basc offering is a flower (*mentoke)* and incense (*duk-spos)* for smelling; butterlamp (*chot-may)* for seeing; water or *chang* (*ti-jap)* for thirst; and food (*jal-zas)* for hunger - five in number which symbolically corresponds to the five *skandhas* or aggregates of self posited by Buddhist philosophy. However, with the addition of water (*jap-sil)* for washing (thereby touching) and music (*rol-mo)* for listening, the full offering corresponds to the organs of sense and the body in which they are located (philosophically, *rupa,* the first *skandha)*. (This same numerical ccnfiguration occurs with *dun-sar snah*, an offering of five sets of seven bowls arranged on the household altar.) At any rate for the ritual offering itself, there is a hierarchy of distribution, i.e. from the highest spiritual being to the lowest (e.g. *kondo* to *yi-dak)* as well as from the most delicious, grandly presented to the least (e.g. *tsogs* to *tsogs-lak)*. Finally after the gods and spirits have feasted, humans feast on the blessed leftovers (*chin-lab)*.

Many of these same ritual patterns and sequences are employed by villagers. In the enactment of *lha sol-ches* the vicinal gods (lhas), both household and village categories, are propitiated with food offerings. For the household ceremony several choice -foods are prepared and purified with the smoke of juniper (*shuk-pa)* then offered to the domestic gods. Afterwards household members partake of the banquet. Similarly, for the village *lha sol ches* and *lha spo-ches* (i.e. changing of the *lha*) small amounts of meat, bread, and *chang* as well as a pseudo *chot-pa* referred to as *lha-bon* are presented to the *yul-lha* or *phas-lha*, after which the participants share in the leftovers, if only symbolically since the offerings were so small in the first place.

At *shi-mi* when families play host to their dead, a full-scale meal of tea and *chang*, bread and *paba*, and perhaps meat and rice ("*thap-zan* for our dead relatives" as one Ladakhi described it) is carried to the cemetery. *Surr* is offered to the "smelleaters", the cooked foods are purified with the mantra *Om ma hum* then offered first to the Buddhas, Bodhisattvas, Dharmapalas, etc. and then to the spirits of the deceased. Afterwards the living eat.

At the level of purely secular transactions or affairs the ritualization of food persists. When villagers are assembled for a *don-thang*, not only are they seated according to social rank, but food and drink are served in a descending hierarchy from *sku-tak* to *rig-ngan* - diagramatically from the center to the periphery or from the throne to the earth floor as when the deities of the *homa* mandala are saluted. Moreover, the formality of the *don-thang* implicitly mirrors the ritual order of feasts provided for the deities - that is, invited guests are seated as described above and sometimes given the opportunity to wash before they are offered food which renews or establishes a relationship between host and guest, and then the (happy) guests return to their own households, often with leftovers - a kind of gift referred to as *skes* - to distribute among those at home (like a secular *chin-lab).* As a final correspondence, the Ladakhi *don-thang*, or ceremonial meal, requires the use of seven different food items, such as *ko-lak, mok mok, chapatis* with vegetables and meat, *pay-mar, phating, cambir,* and rice or *chapatis* with meat and vegetables — the same number as in altar offerings.

Let me conclude by commenting that in view of how much food and foodstuffs are given away on ceremonial occasions - and I've given you only a partial accounting - it's no wonder that Ladakhi households experience food shortages, except that food is really an exchange commodity, and therein lies the key to village economy - another paper topic for another time.

Bibliography

COZORT, Daniel. 1986. *Highest Yoga Tantra.* Ithaca, N.Y.: Snow Lion Publications.

GRIMSHAW, Anna. 1983. *Rizong: A Monastic Community in Ladakh.* Unpublished Ph.D. dissertation, University of Cambridge.

TAMBIAH, Stanley. 1985. *Culture, Thought and Social Action.* Cambridge: Harvard University Press.

TURNER, Victor. 1967. *The Forest of Symbols.* Ithaca, N. Y.: Cornell University Press.

WAGNER, Roy. 1986. *Symbols That Stand For Themselves.* Chicago: University of Chicago Press.

LADAKH IN 1936

*Robert Roaf**

In 1936 Ladakh had changed little from what Moorcroft had found in 1820. The main economic activity was self-subsistent agriculture, but there were also local craftsmen - metal and wood workers; wool spinning and weaving were universal. Almost everything was locally made. There were no roads, wheeled vehicles or cars, no machinery, no electricity, no piped water, no radios, no telephones nor any of the other irritations of modern life. Apart from agriculture the other economic activity was the caravan and entrepot trade, which was centred on Leh where the Karakoram,Tibet and Kashmir trails converged.

As memory can be fallacious I will stick to what I recorded in my diary; the account will therefore be chronological rather than logical.

To reach Ladakh one had first to cross the Zoji La. In places the path was frightening - a narrow strip cut in the side of a cliff, hundreds of feet below the valley was like a chess board of white skeletons and black vultures. Mules walk on the extreme outer edge of a path which avoids the inner saddle bag being rubbed against the cliff side; to ride a mule under such circumstances is terrifying. At the top the pass opens out but it was still bitterly cold. Once the Himalayas have been crossed the scenery changes and after the delightful alp of wild flowers at Matapan the scenery becomes bleak. Dras had a bad reputation for fleecing travellers - particularly their co-religionists from Central Asia who were going on the pilgrimage to Mecca. We did not like the Baltis who were unreliable porters addicted to petty thieving (Moorcroft found the same in 1820). We did however discover that their language was very similar to Tibetan with all the silent consonants being pronounced so that we were able to communicate.

Kargil was then as now the administrative centre, the ground was fertile and the crops were abundant. We had to show our passes as there was a sensible policy of severely limiting the number of Europeans visiting Ladakh. Here there was also some north south trade from Gilgit through Kargil to Zangskar and over the Bara Lacha and Rohtang passes to Kulu - Moorcroft's route in 1820. After Kargil

---

* Professor R.Roaf, 219 Speke Road, Liverpool L25 0LA, U.K.

one is in Ladakh proper and we were much cheered by the sight of Mulbek Monastery and the rock carvings of Chamba. The approach to each village was indicated by a mani wall and chortens or chorten gate-ways. We were told that they kept out the evil influences from the West. There were also Mani carvings on rocks. We usually stopped a couple of nights at any village which was close to a main monastery so that we had ample time to visit the local monastery. In the evenings there were always crowds of patients. Likhir was then, as now, well kept and full of tankas, frescoes, wall and ceiling hangings and carpets. At P'yang we found a talented monk painter - Konchog Gyaltsen. Later we stayed in P'yang monastery and took lessons in Tibetan painting from Gyaltsen.

At Spitok we met the bursar - Dawa - a man of outstanding ability and spirituality, who also had a trenchant sense of humour. He was also a Tibetan doctor and later practiced in Lhasa; after the Chinese invasion he was imprisoned and tortured but, as an Indian citizen, was finally released but did not survive very long.

Leh was a magnificent sight. It was much smaller in area than nowadays and the relatively few houses were surounded by orchards, fields and trees. We camped in a delightful orchard owned by Ghulam. The only drawback was unexpected irrigation.

On our journey we had met many Tibetans and Yarkandis and in Leh we saw many different races each with their characteristic dress and culture. The Yarkandis were large fine looking men with larger horses. Although they had typical Mongolian features, many had fair complexions and hair and green or blue eyes. In their caravans there was always at least one Samovar strapped on the back of a pony or mule.

Haji Mohammed Siddiq was a highly respected head of a trading business with links with Lhasa, Central Asia and Kashmir. It is interesting that a Muslim business should be chosen to carry the Lopchak to Lhasa. At one time the family owned more than fifty mules. His grandson Abdul Wahid has written a fascinating account of the caravan journey to Lhasa with the Lopchak.

Another prominent merchant was Nono Toniat, who had been to Lhasa five times and whose Tibetan partner, a former monk from Shigatse, was busy loading forty mules for a journey to Lhasa and back which would occupy a year altogether. The vast number of animals - yaks, dzos, mules, ponies, goats and sheep - were an outstanding feature, producing sufficient dung, both for cooking and for fertilizing the fields.

We were very impressed by the scholarly Joseph Gergen, who had nearly completed the translation of the Bible into Ladakhi.

It was a great privilege to have had the experience of a pre-industrial, pre-monetarist society which had not only internal harmony but also a respect for the environment, knowing that it must not be destroyed if the community was to survive.

Although I saw a considerable number of patients they were mainly from the larger villages and Leh and conditions may have been different in outlying villages.

Naturally one saw a large number of superficial infections of the skin and eyes. I also saw some of the disorders of old age - such as cataract and heart failure. I did not see any evidence of malnutrition; the children appeared to be lively and well nourished, the women worked in the fields just as much as the men. I did not see any evidence of old rickets, such as one sees in countries where malnutrition is common and I did not see any evidence of tuberculosis or of the sequelae of poliomyelitis. There may have been such patients lying at home in remote houses but if they were common I would have expected to see some. This very incomplete account suggests that present day health problems may be different.

THE SIGNIFICANCE OF KHUKSHO in the Cultural History of Ladakh

Nawang Tsering Shakspo[1]

The village of Khuksho is inhahited by descendants of Aryan Dards known locally as Drokpa (*'Brog pa)* and lies on the left bank of the "Lion River" Indus ahout 120 km. from Leh, the capital of Ladakh, and 25 km frcm Skurbuchan village. Recently this small village has attracted the attention of many scholars and researchers interested in the centuries-old history of Buddhist/Muslim co-existence and their cultural legacy in Ladakh .

In September 1988, I and Sonam Phuntsog, my scholar friend from Achinathang, paid a week-long visit to Khuksho. From Ledo village the route to Khuksho followed the left bank of the river Indus. It was a difficult trek: in several places the strong current of the river had narrowed down the footpath and before we could reach Khuksho we had to cross two stiff passes, which took us about four hours . However, my informant kept me interested by telling many interesting stories about his earlier visits to the village and this seemed to cut down the arduous journey. I learnt that, apart from Ledo, which lies to the east, Khuksho's other immediate neighhours are Pachari and Dargo. While the small village of Dargo is inhabited only by Muslims, Pachari is a Buddhist village with one Muslim family. Khuksho itself has about fifty families half of whom are Buddhists and half Muslims. For administrative purposes the three villages of Khuksho, Pachari and Dargo come under the command of a single village head.

Khuksho has a beautiful landscape. The stream from Thebchung peak just above flows through the centre of the village. On the other side of the valley we can see the Brogyul peaks with juniper plants growing in abundance. Other common trees and pants in the area include birch, apple, apricot, willow and wild roses.

On the outskirts of Khuksho we saw a ruined castle built by Tha-tha Khan, the first settler of the village, in the ninth century. After this we saw some chortens (*rig gsum mgon po*), a Matam Sarai and finally a new gonpa and prayer wheel in the middle of the village. Among the old monuments of the village are a gonpa, built by one Lama Samphel around 1841, and a mosque.

---

1. Ayu-Chang-Chung, Sabu, Leh 194101, Ladakh, INDIA

A mixed Buddhist/Muslim religious tradition

During our visit we saw that the people of the village observe a mixed religious tradition derived from both Buddhism and Islam. The Muslims of the area belong to the Shia faith while the Buddhists belong to the Drigungpa sect of the Kargyud tradition in the Mahayana school. Lamayuru monastery provides a monk to conduct prayers and perform rituals. Many folk traditions, particularly those connected with various stages of the agricultural cycle, are popular with the villagers, as are stories connected with the Buddha and the bodhisattvas such as the story of Gyalbu Norzang (*Rgyal-bu nor-bzang*) and the Kesar Saga.

It is a well-known fact that Buddhism once prevailed in the entire Purig region, of which Khuksho is a part. Missionaries from Kashmir and Baltistan introduced Islam around the middle of the 16th century. The descendants of the missionaries, locally called Aghas, still have considerable influence on the life of the Muslim population of the area. The Chigtan Cho (the chief of Chigtan) was a Muslim and once had great political influence on the villages on the left bank of the Indus who came under his authority as far as Tagmachig. It was perhaps this strong influence which facilitated the spreading of Islam. As A.H.Francke comments, "The people of Tagmachig, who were subject to these chiefs, did not like the change of religion, and, as their now lost inscription is said to have told, they went to the Ladakhi king, Jamyang's successor, and asked him to allow them to become his subjects. They were accepted, and remained Buddhists".[2]

Buddhist influence has been revived in contemporary Khuksho with the return of Lama Smonlam Stanzin to his native land after 19 years of religious study in Nepal under Lama Padma Lungtsob Gyatso, a Tibetan lama from Kham. I was astonished to learn that Lama Smonlam Stanzin's father was the village's first Haji (the title obtained by Muslims after making the pilgrimage to Mecca): Haji Ghulam Ali was a convert from Buddhism and his original name was Stanzin Phuntsog. His brothers were called Qasim and Tundup, one a Muslim and the other a Buddhist name. It is interesting to note that although Haji Ghulam Ali and Qasim were Muslims they shared a polyandrous marriage with Tondup, their Buddhist brother.

I was told that the lama had entered the priesthood at the age of 13. Two years later he left the village on a pilgrimage to the Buddhist holy places and on to Nepal to pursue his religious studies. I was naturally very keen to meet him, but was disappointed to learn

---

2. A.H.Francke, *A History of Western Tibet.* London: A.H.Partridge, 1907, p. 95.

that he had gone to a Shia family near Kargil to perform *bsangs* (purification) and *lu stor* (Naga/spirit) rituals. Even now a large number of Shia Muslims in the Purig region continue to show great respect and devotion to Buddhist rituals connected with health and wealth. Their faith in oracle-healers, popularly known as *lha-ba* and *lha-mo*, is particularly noteworthy.

It was also interesting to learn that the Akhon, the Muslim religious leader, practises traditional Ladakhi *am chi* medicine as well as performing Shia rituals. The Akhon and the Buddhist monk of the village command equal respect and confidence from the villagers.

Both communities pay profound respect to spirits known as *lha*. My informant told me that the village Muslims as well as the Buddhists make sacrifices and food-offerings to the village *lha* on the fifteenth day of the first month, the seventh day of the fifth month and the fifteenth day of the sixth month of the traditional Ladakhi/Tibetan calendar. However, only a Muslim could make the animal sacrifices and he would only use "halal" meat.

According to village custom the eldest son of the family receives a Muslim name. Others would have "mixed" names such as Ali Tsering, Musa Namgyal, Sonam Bibi, Fatima Tsering and so on. Traditionally the Lhardak *(lha bdag* - the man responsible for prayers to the village *lha*) would be a Muslim and would make sacrifices according to Islamic custom as well as offering Buddhist prayers. However, the current Lhardak, who was formerly known as Issa Mohammed, embraced Buddhism at the age of 27 and is now called Tsering Motup. So Lhardak Tsering Motup invites a Muslim butcher for the *lha* offering.

Some peole think that the village *lha*, Stagpa Lhachen *(Stag-pa lha-chen*) belongs to the Dog-lha *('Brog-lha*) family of *lha*. The people of Khuksho therefore follow Dard *('Brog-pa*) traditions such as abstaining from eating beef and chicken or drinking cows' milk for seven days after confinement. According to my informant, Stagpa Lhachen has two brothers: Zangpa Lhachen *(Bzang-pa lha-chen*) and Zangnam *(Bzang-nam*) who reside in the villages of Hanu and Skurbachen respectively.

The *lha-mo*

In Khuksho we found a *lha-mo* who, besides making predictions, possessed healing pwer and could cure sick men and animals. In response to repeated requests from Sonam Phuntsog, my informant, the *lha-mo* came into trance and answered some of our questions. She is a middle-aged housewife who acquired the spirit power about ten years ago. When she was in trance she announced that she wasa possessed by a *lha* called *Kyi-gu lha-kyong-he*. The other *lha* who possess her include the lha of Haqnis (which is now predominantly Shia Muslim), Haqnis Chomo and Kangri Lhachen.

Unlike the oracles of the Leh area, the Khuksho *lha-mo* does not need special clothes, ornaments and instruments such as the crown, *damaru* (drum) and bell. Instead she covers herself with a veil during the trance. Her style of performance was simple, requiring only a plateful of grain, barley flour, black tea, chang (a light alcoholic beverage made of barley) and water in offering bowls. She also lights a butter lamp and juniper twigs for fragrance and purification.

The villagers told us that the *lha-mo* had been very useful in healing both people and animals, Her role and presnce during confinement is particularly appreciated. Like many of the oracles of Upper Ladakh, she is an illiterate housewife. When she was in trance, she advised us to recite *Om vajra sattva hung*, the famous mantra of Dorje Sempa and announced that the *lha* 's diet was Juniper. To cure a person or an animal she uses an arrow *(mda' dar*) as the healing instrument.

In the course of our discussion with her, the *lha-mo* revealed that spices such as garlic and onion are prohibited for her when she is calling up the spirit because this would delay the invocation. She said that she first felt the spirit in her when she was quite young but was not fully aware of it. Eventually, when other people felt its presence, she was taken to Leh by her relatives and the village headman. She was blessed by Bakula Rinpoche and Togdan *(rTog-ldan*) Rinpoche. Both Lamas gave her certain instructions and advised her to keep herself clean. On auspicious days such as the 8th, 10th, 15th, 25th and 30th of the month she would invoke more than one *lha*. Initially she hesitated to perform, but now she is more relaxed, and even earns some money from people who have benefitted through her trances.

Mohammed Hussain's reminiscences

Other fascinating aspects of the social life of Khuksho were revealed by Mohammed Hussain, who was now aged 70 and had been village headman when he was younger. In our talk he revealed that he had been born into a Buddhist family and had been given the name Sonam Tsering. However, when he was still young he had fallen seriously ill, and he believes that someone advised his father to change the name of his son in order to save his life. He recalled that during his youth he would sing and play various musical instruments, such as the Surna (a sort of flageolet), and attend both Buddhist and Muslim marriages. At some Buddhist marriages he had the privilege of acting as *nyo pa*, the wedding assistant, and had consumed chang. Such were the close links between the two communities.

Besides Urdu, Mohammed Hussain knew Tibetan/Ladakhi script which he had learnt from Cho Jaffar Khan, the chief of Chigtan. He linked the script to his own culture but agreed that only a handful of Muslims in the region could read it. He had himself taught it to his son Mehdi, who is the present village headman, and to one of his nephews who is working for the Jammu and Kashmir government in Kargil. Mehdi is also a keen Surna player and had played for the village festivals for a long time. Some years ago the government tourism department organised a festival at Kargil and Mehdi had played a key role as a member of the Khuksho cultural troupe.

Mohammed Hussain knew several folk-songs and stories as well as the Kesar Saga. He said that the people of the village had been very liberal in their religious beliefs. Inter-marriages between Buddhists and Muslims were therefore common, and he feels that this brought people closer to each other rather than causing conflict. Polyandry also was prevalent with brothers practising different religions living together. He said that whereas Muslims preferred wives from Chigtan, Samra and Haqnis, Buddhists liked girls from Ledo, Pachari, Achinathang, Skurbachan and Tagmachig.

He said that from time immemorial both Buddhists and Muslims had lived together in Khuksho and the village was known for this to all the Ladakhis in the Indus valley as well as the people in the Kargil region. Until recently one could see members of both communities living together under a single roof. I asked him about the common belief that in the old days families with members in both communities would reside in a single household and cook their food in the same pot: when preparing meat they would only put an identification mark on the halal meat for the Muslims of the family. Mohammed Hussain denied knowledge of such a tradition. However, he said that in the past when people from other parts of Ladakh asked Skardu fruit dealers about the quality of their apricot kernels, the traders would reply that the kernels were as good as the people of Khuksho, who were known for their sweet nature.

Ihad another discussion on marriage connections with a 65 year-old blind Muslim woman called Khati. She said that of her two children the son, Tashi Phuntsog, was a Buddhist whereas her daughter, Rokhe, was a Muslim. She told me that the young appeared more inclined to Buddhism. One reason for this was that the villagers had easier access to the Leh area, which is a predominantly Buddhist region, than to their district headquarters in the Muslim town of Kargil. I gathered that a large number of Khuksho young people were employed as labourers with army units at Spituk near Leh where they had apparently succeeded in establishing a "Khuksho Dong" (Khuksho Colony).

Mohammed Hussain told me that traditionally the people of Khuksho had close ties with other neighbouring regions which were renowned for various trade goods: the villagers would go to Shigar in Baltistan for apricots; to Zanskar for butter; to Purig for wheat; to Nubra for soda; and to Changthang for salt. In this way they had established close religious and cultural ties with all the neighbouring regions of Ladakh.

Festivals

While I was talking to Muhammed Hussain in his guest room, he pointed out some old trees on the left bank of the village stream close to his house. They were birch trees, which are rarely seen in Ladakh, but are abundant in this village. He believes that the god Stagpa Lhachen resides under one of these trees, and the birch grove is the focal point of all the traditional social and cultural celebrations of the village.

The villagers organise their spring festival in the fifth month when the entire valley is blooming with wild roses. Well before the festival begins, the girls of the village collect flowers and make garlands to offer to the village god at the *sngo lha* summer festival which is celebrated on the seventh day of the sixth month. Several days before the beginning of the festival, eighteen specially selected young men who were born in the Tiger year go to the mountains, where they spend the night, to collect various types of wild flowers. If a youth is joining the group for the first time he has to organise a feast for his friends and relatives on returning to the village. Similarly, eighteen young maidens born in the Sheep year also collect flowers to offer garlands to the village god to fulfil their aspirations and to pray for the village's peace and prosperity.

All the villagers assemble at the festival site dressed in their best clothes to offer respect to the god. The Lhardak then offers libations and recites a text called *lha gsol* which lauds the names of various village and local gods: Haqnis Chomo; Fokar Chomo; Dragnag Chomo of Khaltsi; Yagra Chomo of Domkhar; Lhamo of Dargo; Zangnam of Skurbachen; Zangldan of Hanu; and Stagpa Lhachen of Khuksho. After the *lha gsol* ceremony they perform special folk dances and, holding flowers in their hands, sing songs in honour of the village gods. They also drink a lot of chang.

It is interesting to note that married women are not permitted to offer flowers, or even to come close to the particular birch tree under which the village *lha* is believed to be residing. Similarly a girl whose engagement is fixed would offer her last prayer for happiness on going to her new house and for prosperity for the village. She would pray for the protection of the village *lha* and seek help to overcome difficulties. The young girl would sing melancholy songs before the village people. Birch and juniper trees were considered holy according to village tradition, and no one was allowed to cut these trees or burn them.

The other important festivals of the village are the harvest festival, which is organised in the eighth month; Losar, the New Year, which is celebrated on the first day of the eleventh month; and Nauroj, a Muslim festival which falls on 21 March.

On the third day of the twelfth month the villagers organise *Ma ma ne pa*. This was originally a Dard *('Brog pa)* festival and is celebrated with great enthusiasm in all the villages on the left bank of the Indus from Khaltsi up to Baltistan. In conjunction with this festival the villagers organise feasts for close relatives and make food offerings to the deceased.

Looking back, Mohammed Hussain said that Muslims and Buddhists used to organise *Sngo lha* and other festivals jointly, and the whole village would take part in all the festivities. But now, with a grim expression on his face, he said that the good old days were over and he believed that external influences were gradually eroding the old traditions. Muslims now attend the festivals only as spectators and were gradually disassociating themselves from village customs. He himself, being a keen lover of folk-lore and folk-songs, felt strongly that the traditions which bound the village together must be kept alive for posterity.

A BRIEF HISTORY OF MUSLIMS IN LADAKH

*Abdul Ghani Sheikh**

The date of the advent of Islam in Ladakh cannot be given precisely but it can safely be said that the first Muslims set foot in the area more than 600 years ago. Mir Syed Ali Hamdani was the first to make Muslim converts in Ladakh after his second visit to Kashmir when he passed through in 1394 A.D. on his way to Kashgar, Chinese Turkestan. He is often described as the founder of the Islamic faith in Kashmir and, according to local tradition, built several mosques in Ladakh including one at Padum (Zanskar) and one in Shey. Shey was the capital of Ladakh at this time.

Syed Ali Hamdani was followed by his principal disciple, Syed Mohammed Noor Baksh, who visited Purig and Baltistan and he rapidly converted the Baltis to Islam (Gergan 1976). His followers are known as Noorbakshi and are found only in Baltistan and Ladakh. The reference to Baltistan is significant because the Baltis and Ladakhis are closely related ethnologically and their culture, language and mode of living are by and large identical.

In his youth Sultan Zain-ul-Abidin (1423-1475) of Kashmir is reported to have ordered the expulsion of the mystic Sheikh Zain Shahwalli for showing disrespect to him. The Sheikh went to Ladakh and converted many people to Islam. In 1505 Shamsud Din Iraqi, a noted Shia scholar, visited Baltistan and Purig. He was responsible for spreading the Shia cult in Kashmir and converted the overwhelming majority of Muslims in Baltistan to his school of thought.

The propagation of Islam in the Leh area appears to have suffered a setback in the sixteenth century for we find no references to mosques, Muslims or their culture in the *Tarikh-i-Rashidi* by Mirza Haider Dughlat who invaded and briefly conquered Ladakh in 1532, 1545 and 1548. However, the situation was quite different in Baltistan and Purig where Shia Islam and the Nurbakshi sect continued to flourish.

The chiefs of Baltistan and Purig occasionally invited Muslim scholars and preachers and this practice continued until Zorawar

---

* Yasmin Guest House, Leh 194101, Ladakh, INDIA.

Singh's invasion of Ladakh in 1834. They were granted land to settle down in the local villages and often married daughters of the chiefs. After their conversion to Islam, the chiefs of the Purig area styled themselves "Sultan" and claimed to be independent from the King of Ladakh.

In the beginning of the 17th century Islam began to take root in the Leh area after King Jamyang Namgyal's defeat in in a war with Baltistan. Jamyang Namgyal was taken prisoner and Ali Sher Khan, the Muslim ruler of Skardu, offered his daughter Gyal Khatun to him in marriage. Ali Sher Khan sent a bevy of Muslim maids, a host of male servants and a band of Balti musicians back to Ladakh with the marriage party. Gyal Khatun retained her religion until her death and private mosques were built for her and her servants in Leh and Shey. Later Muslim queens of Ladakh used to offer prayer in these mosques. The Muslim musicians settled in Leh and their status was elevated to "Kharmon" or "royal musicians".

Several hundred Balti Muslims are thought to have migrated from Baltistan and Purig to Shey and Chhushot during the reign of Jamyang Namgyal. Their descendants' number has now swelled to some 6,000. According to oral tradition, the King also granted land to Kashmiri Muslim traders to settle permanently in Leh. These traders were called "Kharchongpa" or "palace/royal" traders. They received special trade privileges in return for some service to the royal family. In addition to Leh, they had houses in Rudok, a trade centre in Western Tibet. The names of the families who are descended from these traders are: Rili, Shanku, Khalsawar, Sotey, Banaras, Hangol and - possibly - Bungur. Now these families have divided and sub-divided into many branches and are settled in Thikse, Chhushot, Phyang and Sabu villages as well as Leh itself.

The Muslims were invited to Ladakh for different purposes. The ancestor of the Khwaja family of Leh was invited from Srinagar to write the King's Persian correspondence with the Moghul governors of Kashmir. A man called Ismail Zergar was brought to Leh from Kashmir in the seventeenth century to strike coins. Another man called Malik was brought to work as a butcher. These people were granted land to build houses and provided with basic amenities. The social status of these Muslims was by and large equivalent to that of the high caste Buddhists.

There are about 45 Muslim families in Padum, Zanskar. According to Hashmatullah Khan, the author of *Tarikh Jammun, Kashmir, Laddakh aur Baltistan*, a trader called Razaq Joo was the first Muslim to settle in Padum. The story of his arrival in Zanskar is very interesting. After King Senge Namgyal had captured Zanskar he deputed his son Dechok Namgyal to be the local governor. But Prince Dechok could not adjust to what he held to be the colourless and boring environment of Zanskar and he begged his father to let him come back to Leh. In those days Razaq Joo used to come to trade in Leh and, since he was a very witty and good-humoured person, Sengge Namgyal persuaded him to settle in Padum to keep Prince Dechok company and provided him with financial incentives to do so. Razaq Joo settled in Padum permanently, married there and was very successful in his mission.

The Tibeto-Mongolian invasion in 1681 strengthened the position of the Muslims in Ladakh. The invading army advanced to Leh and Basgo. Failing to repulse the enemy, Shakya Gyatso, the Prime Minister of Ladakh, went down to Kashmir to seek assistance from the Moghul Emperor Aurangzeb. In 1684, a large army under the command of Nawab Fidai Khan was sent to Ladakh and the combined Tibeto-Mongolian forces were routed and fled to Tibet.

In return for his assistance, the Moghul Emperor placed severe conditions on Delegs Namgyal, the King of Ladakh. The King had to issue currency in the name of the Emperor and he himself had to become a Muslim with the new name of Aqbat Mahmud Khan. He also had to introduce "Khutba" or the mention of the Emperor in the Friday sermon in the mosque. Prince Jigsdol was taken to Kashmir as a hostage to make sure that the King stuck to his committments.

In 1715 two Europeans, Father Ippolito Desideri and Father Freyre visited Leh. Desideri writes, "A number of merchants from Kashmir engaged in the wool trade live in this kingdom and they are allowed to have mosques and openly to hold their religion".

After the final conquest of Ladakh by the Dogra army in 1842, some Muslim soldiers remained in Leh and settled down there permanently. Many Muslims of Kashmiri or Turki origin (from Xinjiang) married Ladakhi Buddhist women. Their offspring are known as "Arghon".

Frederic Drew who was Governor of Ladakh in the 1860s observes in his book, *The Jammu and Kashmir Territories, a Geographical Account,* that after marriage Ladakhi Buddhist women and Arghon Muslims would adapt to each other's way of life. The man kept his religion but in other respects adopted the food, language and social customs of his wife. Many Arghon Muslims and Buddhists are blood relations.

In the late nineteenth and early twentieth centuries, the Arghons produced several distinguished adventurers and enterprising travellers who accompanied European expeditions to Central Asia and Tibet as caravan leaders, interpreters, guides and porters. Galwan

Rasul, Mohammed Issa and Qalam Rasul were the most famous of these.

There were occasional conflicts between the rulers of Ladakh and those of Skardu and Purig but these did not leave any lasting legacy of bitterness among the warring groups and there were long periods of co-existence and friendship. Occasional intermarriages between Muslim chiefs of Purig and Baltistan and the Buddhist royal family of Ladakh helped reduce tensions. The common people followed the example of religious tolerance set by their rulers.

The Muslims have inherited many things from Buddhist Ladakh but they have themselves made significant contributions to local culture. For example, many Kashmiri dishes, such as *gosht kebab, yakhni* and *samosas* are popular in Ladakh. Several Kashmiri words - such as *thul* (egg), *handang* (dumb), and *chanda* (pocket) - have entered Ladakhi vocabulary. Persian words in common use include *surna* (a type of musical instrument) and *daman* (drum). Turki words include *charog* (shoe) and *chaqman* (cloth) Ladakhi folk music shows Muslim influence and the mosques and imambaras of Ladakh are important examples of local architecture. For all their religious differences, Ladakh's Buddhist and Muslim communities are heirs to a common cultural heritage.

Bibliography

DESIDERI, IPPOLITO. *The Travels of Ippolito of Pistoia S.J. 1712-1727.* Edited by Filippo de Filippi, with an introduction by C. Wessels S.J. London: Routledge, 1937.

DREW, FREDERICK. *The Jummoo and Kashmir Territories, a Geographical Account.* London: Edward Stanford, 1875.

DUGHLAT, MIRZA HAIDER. *Tarikh-i-Rashidi. A History of the Moghuls of Central Asia.* Translated by E. Denison Ross. Edited with a commentary by Ney Elias. London: Low Marston, 1895.

GERGAN, YOSEB. *La dvags rgyal rabs chi med gter.* Edited by S.S.Gergan. Srinagar, 1976.

KHAN, HASHMUTALLAH. *Tarikh Jammun, Kashmir, Laddakh aur Baltistan.* Lucknow, 1939.

ECOLOGICAL SET-UP AND AGRARIAN STRUCTURE
of High Altitude Villages of Ladakh[1]

Harjit Singh[2]

Land provides the stage on which man-nature interaction takes place. Man uses it for all his activities, thus for his survival. He, unlike animals, does not adapt himself to nature but interacts with it, modifies it and gets transformed in the process. This relationship is not static but has its own dynamics which get reflected in the land use particularly for economic activities. Human response varies in space and is region-specific depending on the prevailing environmental conditions on one hand and the level and nature of available technology on the other. In initial stages of development, man is generally at the receiving end in the process of man-nature interaction where he simply adapts himself to environmental requirements without altering much the latter. If it is a mountainous region with cold arid climate, he responds either by becoming a pastoral nomad depending mainly on limited available pastures or by carrying out subsistence farming wherever the environment permits. Ladakh[3] is typical of such areas where nature is hostile and man is by and large at early stages of development having low level of technology. Hence, man adapted himself by becoming a pastoral nomad in its eastern part, where farming is not possible due to very high altitude and cold climate, and by tilling land in relatively lower warmer valleys.

Though the entire region seems to be backward, recent developments and certain socio-cultural factors have brought about significant changes in the traditional land use. The present study is an attempt to understand the process of interaction as reflected by land use particularly in terms of agriculture and to comprehend the relationship that man evolved with nature by developing a certain type of agricultural system. In the light of the above, it is important to

---

1. Some of this material has been published in *Dynamics of Mountain Geosystems*, ed. R.B.Singh.

2. Assoc. Prof., Centre for the Study of Regional Development, Jawaharlal Nehru University, New Delhi - 110067, INDIA.

3. Here Ladakh refers to the region consisting of Leh (which includes Shyok and Nubra) and Kargil (which includes Zangskar) districts, i.e. all except those areas occupied by Pakistan.

analyse the following:

i) the nature and the level of natural constraints on land use in general and on agriculture in particular;

ii) the historical harmony that man evolved with nature in his economic response to harsh environment;

iii) the agricultural structure mainly in terms of land use, distribution of of land holdings, cropping pattern and agricultural inputs and finally;

iv) the traditional agricultural system and the recent changes therein.

The study mainly deals with three villages of Ladakh and is based on data collected through field work conducted during June-July 1988. The villages are:

i) Stok - situated near Leh Town on an alluvial fan. It was formerly the summer capital of Ladakh. This is also one of the villages which have undergone lot of changes in recent times because of its proximity to the most important urban centre of the region and also by its being a tourist attraction.

ii) Rangdum - a backward monastery village situated on the valley floor in the relatively more isolated upper Suru Valley. The land is flat but due to its altitude of over 4,000 metres resulting in very cold climate which is also the result of physiographic configuration, it has very poor agricultural base.

iii) Parkachik - a muslim village situated on a river terrace and an alluvial fan in the higher parts Suru Valley. It is comparable with Stok in terms of physical environment and in fact is slightly better off as it receives more precipitation but due to relatively more isolation it remains backward.

As mentioned above, Ladakh has a hostile environment due to high altitude and extremely rugged terrain on the one hand and cold arid climate on the other. In general, the entire region is an elevated territory presenting a system of alternating valleys and mountain ranges except in the eastern part which is a plateau. The mountain ranges form the most important physiographic feature of Ladakh in terms of the areal coverage. Though presenting positive physical relief, these ranges are almost totally negative from the point of view of agricultural activity. The ranges, running nearly parallel to each other, traverse Ladakh with south-east to north-west trend. The following are the important ranges of Ladakh;

i) the Zanskar Range

ii) the Ladakh Range

iii) northern face of the Great Himalayan Range, and

v) the Saltoro range and the southern slopes of the

Karakoram Range.

All these ranges provide barren rocky surfaces largely devoid of soil and vegetation cover as well as human settlements. The eastern part of Ladakh namely Changthang may also be regarded largely negative from an agricultutral point of view. The terrain and climatic constraints do not favour settled agriculture, the economy, therefore, is largely nomadic. The nomads called Changpas in this region, keep wandering in search of grazing lands which are found in the valleys of small rivulets or near the lakes. The plateau is less rugged compared to the mountains yet it is of little use for agriculture mainly because of very high altitude (generally above 4500 metres), high aridity and extensive rocky surfaces.

Because of the factors mentioned above, nearly 68 per cent of the total land lies above 5000 meters above sea level and is virtually unfit for vegetative and human life. Land lying between 4500 metres to 5000 metres, constituting approximately 5 per cent of the total area, permits some pastoralism. Settled agriculture is confined to areas below 4500 metres in height.[4]

The second major constraint on agriculture in Ladakh is imposed by the cold and arid high altitude climate. Climate exerts significant influence on the land use, especially on agriculture. Major climatic elements influencing growth of plants in the region are temperature and precipitation. Temperature is most significant in Ladakh because of the occurrence of lower than the required values over a substantial part of a year and of high fluctuation in it. Temperature generally does not exceed 29.7C. July and August are the hottest months having mean temperatures of 19.4C and 19.0C respectively. January and February are the coldest months with mean temperature of -10.9C and -8.5C (mean of records at Leh, Dras and Kargil). Most of the plants require minimum of 6C temperature for the germination of seeds and the plants to grow.[5] Lowest temperature values touch and go below the lethal limit for the growth of active plant cells in most of Ladakh for a significant part of a year. Moreover, a high diurnal range of temperature makes mean temperature values quite deceptive.[6] It is, therefore, not surprising that the growing season in Ladakh is restricted to less than 6 months in

---

4. For details see Harjit Singh (1981) "Environmental Constraints in a Cold Desert - A Case Study of Ladakh", *Perspectives in Agricultural Geography* ed. by Noor Mohammad, New Delhi.
5. K.H.W. Klages (1948) *Ecological Crop Geography*, New York.
6. Harjit Singh (1981), *op. cit.*

a year.[7]

Precipitation is another important element of climate, and its low amount acts as a strong constraint on the economy of Ladakh. The region falls in the rain shadow zone and a large part of Ladakh, especially its central and eastern part, receives less than 10 cms. of annual precipitation. Villages situated in the southwestern part are slightly better off as Kargil gets 23.9 cms. of annual precipitation. Unfortunately, a large amount of precipitation occurs in the form of snow during winter months which is agriculturally off season. Precipitation, therefore, plays a marginal direct role in the agricultural economy of Ladakh.

As a result of the environmental constraints discussed above, most of the land in Ladakh is uninhabitable. Only 577 sq. kms. land, accounting for 0.6 per cent of the total geographical area, is inhabited. Even within the assessed area[8] of 577 sq. kms., only 28 per cent of the land is under cultivation. It is mainly because permanent settlements in general and agricultural activity in particular have certain prerequisites in Ladakh. These include;

i) relatively lower altitude where temperature is high enough, even for a short period, to permit the crops to mature;

ii) relatively gentler slope where land could either be levelled or agricultural terraces be cut;

iii) proximity to water as irrigation is a precondition for cultivation because of the arid climate;

iv) adequate soil cover to sustain plant cover as large tracts lie in the form of bare rocky surfaces.

The above mentioned conditions are met in the river valleys especially on the valley floor, river terraces and alluvial fans. Consequently all permanent settlements and agricultural land are found on the above mentioned geomorphic features. As stated earlier, all the three villages selected for detailed analysis are also associated with these features. Stok and Parkachik are situated at an altitude of around 3,800 metres and Rangdum at about 4,000 metres above sea level. Stok has very arid climate while Parkachik and Rangdum are a little better off in terms of precipitation as these are situated close to the Great Himalayan Range which is the main climatic barrier. Rangdum,

---

7. *Ibid.*

8. Assessed Area refers to land lying within village boundaries; the total figure has been arrived at by adding the area of all villages of the region. [This is a Revenue Dept. term used by the Census of India but of unclear definition; the village boundaries appear arbitrary. All the very extensive land excluded is curently rough grazing or waste land. Some would be cultivable if it were irrigated. Ed.]

though situated in a wide flat valley, experiences a very cold climate due to its higher elevation and physiographic configuration. It is enclosed by high permanently snow covered ranges from where the cold air descends making the valley its reservoir.

Even in this region of hostile environment man settled down and developed harmonious relations with the former by orienting his socio-economic set-up to fit into limits laid down by nature. He levelled and terraced the land and constructed an intricate network of Kuls[9] for irrigation. Since this work was not possible at an individual level, he went in for collective effort under the supervision and guidance of "the Community Centre" which came up in the form of the *gompa*.[10] He selected favourable sites and started carrying out subsistence farming to eke out his livlihood. Land use in the villages was simple where relatively flat areas with adequate soil cover were put to cultivation. Land with bare rock outcrops was used for building houses or was left unused. Since cultivable land was limited and scattered, the settlements took the form of hamlets. Water for irrigation was diverted from the higher reaches of streams/nallas and brought to agricultural fields through Kuls using gravitational force.

As expected agricultural land is used mainly for growing food crops namely *grim* (naked barley), wheat and peas. Less fertile land is used for raising fodder crop of *oal* (Alfalfa) for feeding livestock during winter months when pastures are not available. Trees were planted along the course of streams and nallas to get wood. Agricultural land was limited and land holdings small, therefore, fragmentation of land was not viable. Man, therefore, went in for a polyandrous marriage system with property passing only to the eldest son in the family.[11]

This system checked the fragmentation of land on the one hand and the size of population on the other. This way villages developed into, by and large, self sustained units with limited interaction with the outside world. Ladakh thus remained in relative isolation for centuries and changes started coming about only during the last three decades. These were mainly due to:

---

9. Kuls are narrow channels constructed for taking water to agricultural fields.

10. *Gompa* refers to a Buddhist Monastery. Though it is a religious institution it plays a very important role in all temporal aspects of life of Ladakhi Buddhists. For details see H. Singh (1977) "Territorial Organisation of Gompas in Ladakh" *Himalaya Ecologie et Ethnologie*, Paris.

11. Buddhists in Ladakh traditionally had a polyandrous marriage system. In this system only the eldest son in a family used to get married. His younger brothers - generally not more than two - used to become co-husbands of the eldest brother's wife. In case the number of brothers was more than three, the youngest used to leave the house to join the *gompa* by becoming a Lama.

i) the Indo-China border dispute of 1962 because of which the strategic significance of Ladakh was realised. Consequently a lot of army moved in bringing with it outside influence in a big way. A more important fact was massive road construction activity which started in the region in the post-1962 period. The Srinagar-Leh Highway was completed and regular traffic on it started in 1966. This also brought significant changes.

ii) Opening up of the region to tourists in 1974. Prior to this, Ladakh was a restricted area even for non-Ladakhi Indians. A large part of the region was opened to tourists in 1974. Since it is rich in natural beauty and has an unspoiled Lamaistic Buddhist Culture akin to Tibet, it started attracting a large number of tourists. Presently, about 15,000 foreign tourists visit Ladakh every year. This brought about significant changes in the region. A number of hotels, restaurants and guest houses were established. A well developed market came up to meet the demand of tourists.

These changes also influenced the village economy and the land use. They made the local population aware of new developments and of inputs in agriculture and generated demand for certain agricultural products, particularly vegetables and fruits. Therefore, they also affected the cropping pattern to some extent. These changes were, however, felt more in accessible villages or in those situated near urban centres or places of tourist interest. Let us look at the agricultural structure of the three villages and see the changes if any therein.

Land use and agricultural structure of the three villages

Intensity of land use is low and it varies within the region. It mainly depends upon the level and nature of natural contstraints on the one hand and that of available technology on the other.

TABLE 1. LAND USE 1988 (hectares)

Village	Area	Cropped area	Cultivable waste	Not cultivable	Tree crops
Stok	584	332	61	173	18
Rangdum	290	94	910	105	-
Parkachik	197	74	49	75	-

Source: Patwari Records

Less than 40 per cent of total land was found to be under the plough in Rangdum and Parkachik. It was only in Stok that the area under cultivation accounted for 57 per cent of total land. No land in any of the villages was recorded to be occupied by forest.

Stok is a fairly large village with a population of 1056 persons situated on the northern slopes of Zanskar range in the Indus Valley at a distance of about 20 kms. from Leh. It occupies a site on the higher parts of a big alluvial fan. There are four main clusters of houses and some isolated houses in the village. Most of the houses occupy rocky land and break-of-slope points. The village also has the palace of the former ruler of Ladakh occupying a high place on its western end. The Stok *gompa* occupies the higher part of the alluvial fan to the south of the main village. Land lying in between the house clusters is being used for cultivation. A number of trees, mainly willow, poplar and fruit trees like apricot, have been planted recently either in the courtyards of houses or on less fertile land. Tree crops covered nearly 3.1 per cent of total area of the village. Some land has also been reclaimed recently for agricultural purposes in the peripheral part of the village. The lower part of the alluvial fan is still lying unutilized due to scarcity of water for irrigation.

Parkachik village is comparable with Stok in terms of environmental conditions but it was cultivating only 37.3 per cent of its total land. The village is a fragmented one with four hamlets and a few isolated houses acccommodating in all 642 persons in 125 households. Agricultural land is found on the river terrace of the Suru and on an alluvial fan. Though it is situated on Kargil-Padam route no significant change is noticed. A large area accounting for nearly 45.9 per cent of total land is lying as culturable waste.

Rangdum is a very backward village with 32.5 per cent of the total land under plough. It is situated in a wide valley where a number of streams join Suru and is made of two hamlets namely Juldo and Tshi Tungda situated at a distance of about 9 kms from each other. In between the two hamlets is situated Rangdum *gompa* on a hillock. The land is full of boulders and pebbles and is not very fertile. Moreover, due to the very cold climate crops, at times, do not mature and have to be used as fodder. All land is owned by the *gompa* and the villagers work on it as tenants. The village presents a very desolate picture with very little greenery and no tree vegetation at all.

Distribution of land holdings

Distribution of land is unequal and most peasants cultivate small land holdings.

TABLE 2: Size of Land Holdings and Distribution of Agricultural Land (%)

(The first column under each village gives % of total number of land holdings (households) in each size group; the second column gives % of total area of land in each size group.)

Size (Acres)	Stok		Parkachik		Rangdum (Leased)	
<1	24	4	31	10	68	35.8
1 - 2.5	36	21	38	26	27	32.7
2.5 - 5	28	37	18	26	-	-
5 - 10	9	22	13	38	5	31.4
>10	2	16	-	-	-	-

1 acre = 0.405 hectares.
Source: Field survey (i.e. farmers' responses) and Patwari Records.

Table 2 shows that over 95.5 per cent of peasants in Rangdum were cultivating land measuring less than 2.5 acres. In fact 68.2 per cent had very small land holdings i.e. less than one acre. Nearly 69 per cent of the total agricultural households in Parkachik and 60.1 per cent in Stok had land holdings of less than 2.5 acres in size. It may be noted from the table that small farmers owning less than one acre of land and accounting for 24.1 per cent in Stok and 31.1 per cent in Parkachik, were owning only 4.6 per cent and 9.6 per cent of the total agricultural land in these villages respectively. It is also interesting that large farmers cultivating over 10 acres of land were absent both in Parkachik and Rangdum villages while they accounted for 1.5 per cent of total land owners in Stok owning 16.1 per cent of total agriculture land. It also shows that land inequalities are more pronounced in Stok village which was formerly the headquarters of a feudal state. The average size of land holdings was found to be largest in Stok with 3.6 acres followed by Parkachik and Rangdum with average size of 2.2 acres and 0.9 acres respectively.

In order to look at the disparities in the distribution of land holdings, the Coefficient of Variation (C.V.) was calculated.[12] C.V. was found to be 163 per cent for Stok, 137 per cent for Rangdum and 91 per cent for Parkachik. One can infer from this that distribution of land holdings is very inconsistent in Stok compared to the other two

12. Coefficient of variation was calculated by using the following formula:
C.V. = (S.D. ÷ Mean) x 100

villages. In order to find out inequalities in distribution, Lorenz Curves were drawn and Gini coefficient (a measure of inequality) calculated[13]. The value of the Gini Coefficient was found to be 0.505 for Stok, 0.466 for Rangdum and 0.443 for Parkachik. It shows that highest disparities in the distribution of land holdings are in Stok. The reason for this is that the former ruler still owns large holdings in Stok. Moreover Stok *gompa* also owns a large tract of land there. Apart from this, it seems that some land has got concentrated in a few hands either by buying it from poor peasants or by reclaiming new lands with the help of irrigation.

Disparities were found to be least in Parkachik village. It is a poor village inhabited by a muslim population and most of the farmers are cultivating small land holdings.

Rangdum village presents an entirely different case. In fact, as stated earlier, the entire land is owned by the *gompa,* therefore, strictly speaking, it is not comparable with other two villages. Farmers are only cultivating land leased in from the *gompa*. Since it is almost like a permanent lease running through generations on hereditary basis, it has been included in the present study. Here again disparities, in fact, are low and it was found that out of 22 sample households, accounting for a little over 70 per cent of the total households, 21 households were operating land holdings measuring less than 1.25 acres. There was only one household which was cultivating 6.25 acres of land and it was mainly the effect of the latter which explains somewhat the disparities in the distribution of land holdings.

It can be concluded from the above that inequalities are marked in the more developed village of Stok. The majority of peasants continue to cultivate small land holdings in all villages of Ladakh. The lower disparities, in fact, are because of the overwhelming number of poor peasants both in Parkachik and Rangdum.

Cropping pattern

Ladakh being made up of self subsistence villages has been traditionally growing food crops only. Important food crops grown in the region included *grim* (naked barley), wheat and peas. It may be

---

13. Gini Coefficient was calculated in the following way:

$$Gr = [!X_i\, Y(i+1) - X(i+1)\, Y_i] \div [100 \times 100]$$

Where X_i = cumulative % of number of households (landholdings) up to '*i*'th class of households; and Y_i = cumulative % of area of landholdings up to '*i*'th class of landholdings.

pointed out that peas are grown not as a vegetable but are used for making *tsampa (sattu)* just like *grim* and wheat. The pea crop is also quite often used as fodder as frequently it does not mature due to the very cold climate. *Grim*, wheat and peas are roasted then ground to make *tsampa* which forms the main food. *Grim* is also used for fermenting to make *chang* which is very popular drink with the Buddhists of the region. Other crops include *oal* (alfalfa) for fodder and also some *trumba* (buckwheat) and *garas/bakla* (beans). Let us look at the cropping pattern of the three villages.

TABLE 3: Percentage Area Under Each Crop (1988)

Village	*Grim*	Wheat	Peas	*Trumba*	*Garas/ Bakla*	Fodder	Veg.	Other
Stok	53	28	0.5	1	0.5	11	5	1
Parkachik	65	16	12	2	-	3	2	-
Rangdum	65	2	23	-	4	5	-	1.4

Source of data: field survey (i.e. farmers' responses) and Patwari records.

As expected, crops here were grown mainly for self consumption. It is only recently that some vegetable crops have been introduced to meet the demand of the army and the tourists. Some locals have also started consuming vegetables. It may be mentioned that the region is highly suitable for vegetable cultivation. But it has begun mainly in more accessible villages situated near urban centres. Market facilities in places like Leh and Kargil have also played important role in vegetable growing. Till the early 1960s, the farmers had no place to sell vegetables nor could they buy food as there was no market.

As stated earlier, agriculture is a seasonal activity which extends for less than five months in a year in all the three villages. The above table shows that diversification in the cropping pattern is low both in Parkachik and Rangdum villages. Food crops, mainly *grim* and wheat, have overwhelming predominance. The third most important crop in the two villages is peas. Wheat, considered to be a superior crop by the locals, is becoming an important crop in Stok. The most significant factor showing recent changes is the area under vegetable cultivation. It was nearly unknown before the 1960s. Today, nearly 4.7 per cent of total cultivated land is occupied by vegetables in Stok. The main vegetables grown in this village include cabbage, turnips and cauliflower. Fodder is important and is grown for use during the winter months because at that time natural pastures are not available. The level of diversification was found to be highest in Stok. It was mainly because of its proximity to Leh - the main market centre, administrative headquarters and main place of attraction to tourists. Parkachik and Rangdum were found to be still largely carrying out subsistence farming.

Apart from irrigation which is a prerequisite for agriculture in the cold desert of Ladakh, the use of modern inputs, such as chemical fertilizers, improved seeds and implements was found to be low especially in Parkachik and Rangdum. Nearly 74 per cent of farmers are using chemical fertilizers in Stok. The figure for Parkachik was a little less than 60 per cent. Use of fertilizer was completely unknown in Rangdum village. It was also noticed that farmers mainly in Stok village were sowing improved varieties of seeds especially for growing wheat and vegetables. Government stores are the main supplier of these modern inputs. Use of improved varieties of seeds was very low in Parkachik and nearly non-existent in Rangdum. Low use of modern inputs is mainly because of the strong control of the *gompa* in Rangdum and also poverty and lack of awareness there as well as in Parkachik. Peasants in Rangdum seem to be totally indifferent towards improvement of land as well as of agriculture. It probably is because they do not feel attached to land as they do not own it. It is interesting to note that both Stok and Rangdum have strong *gompa* control but the former is changing rapidly and is accepting many modern agricultural inputs mainly due to its location near Leh which is developing very fast.

On the basis of the above, a model of a traditional self-sustained agricultural system has been developed showing different linkages. An attempt has also been made to show recent changes which are coming about and are altering this system. It highlights that in the man-nature interaction process, the harsh environment leads to the development of two main economic activities i.e. self-subsistence agriculture and livestock rearing. Man responds to the low carrying capacity of land by having small size of human population. Limited agricultural land is owned either by individual farmers or by the *gompa*. Basic inputs are:

i) Animal power of Yak or Dzo for ploughing and for threshing.

ii) Human labour contributed by owner cultivators themselves in most cases. Another important factor is the *phaspun* which is a group of families joining together in a village to complete more labour intensive work such as harvesting etc. in turns. The *phaspun* highlights collective effort and consists of families extending up to first or second cousins. Land owned by *gompas* is always cultivated by tenants/agricultural labour.[14] Land is generally leased out to peasants who are responsible for most of agricultural work and in return those tenants pay part of the produce, which at times can be as high as 50 per cent of total produce to the *gompa*. As expected this practice was observed both in Rangdum and Stok. The work is carried out under the general supervision and guidance of the *chak-zod* - a senior lama who is assigned this task by the *gompa*[15]. It is interesting to note that some cases of employing agricultural labour on wages by large land owners, were observed in Stok village. This again seems to be a recent practice. However, no wage labour in agriculture was noticed in Parkachik and Rangdum villages.

iii) Manure: It forms an important input in agriculture throughout Ladakh. Manure consists of animal dung/droppings and night soil. It is again an environmental compulsion that like many other rural areas of India, the people of Ladakh cannot use agriculture fields to attend to natural call during winter months when it is too cold. Therefore, every house must have a toilet. The toilet is generally built on the first floor with a hole in the wooden floor. Excreta gets collected in the lower ground floor. This is mixed with soil and used as manure. Since the climate is very cold and arid, it therefore, does not emanate too much stink. As stated earlier, villages have started using chemical fertilizers. Though the quantity used was small, usage was quite extensive in Stok and is picking up in Parkachik.

iv) Locally grown seed, which is taken from the previous year's production, is extensively used. Improved varieties of seeds were sown in many cases only in developed pockets as shown by the case of Stok.

v) Simple agricultural implements.

As a result of low inputs, agricultural production is limited. The model shows that most of the produce is used as food. Only limited trade takes place.

The other important component of economy is livestock rearing. Most of the livestock, except those required for agricultural operations, are taken to natural pastures situated in higher areas during the summer months. One family from each village takes the cattle to

---

14. No lama is supposed to do any manual work. It is believed to be written in the code of conduct of Lamas that if he undertakes any manual work, it would lead to death of numerous life bearing objects. For details see, Harjit Singh (1977), *op. cit*.

15. A *chak-zod* is a manager-Lama looking after financial matters of the monastery. See *ibid*.

summer pastures and lives there in a hut, called Doksa, built for this purpose. This duty rotates among all families of the village on yearly basis. Milk products such as butter and cheese etc. are made in the Doksa. The model clearly shows different uses of livestock. Cattle are stall-fed during winter months using fodder grown on agricultural fields.

The model shows significant changes coming about in the traditional agricultural system. The role of the *phaspun* is declining and it is getting replaced with hired labour. Positive changes include expansion of agricultural land with the help of irrigation, introduction of fertilizers and improved varieties of seed and of new crops especially vegetables leading to increase in production and trade. These changes, however, are occurring mainly in villages having locational advantages and where general development is taking place. It is interesting to note that in spite of having similar environmental constraints some villages are changing rapidly due to certain human interventions. The above point is amply proved by the case of Stok village.

It can be concluded from the study that intensity of land use continues to be low. By and large, villages are carrying out subsistence farming. Recent changes are occuring only in villages situated near urban centres, main transport roads or in and around places of tourist interest. This highlights the significance of human efforts in areas of hostile environment.

The author acknowledges his gratitude to M.A. (Geography) students of 1987-89 batch of the Centre for the Study of Regional Development, Jawaharlal Nehru University, for helping in data collection.

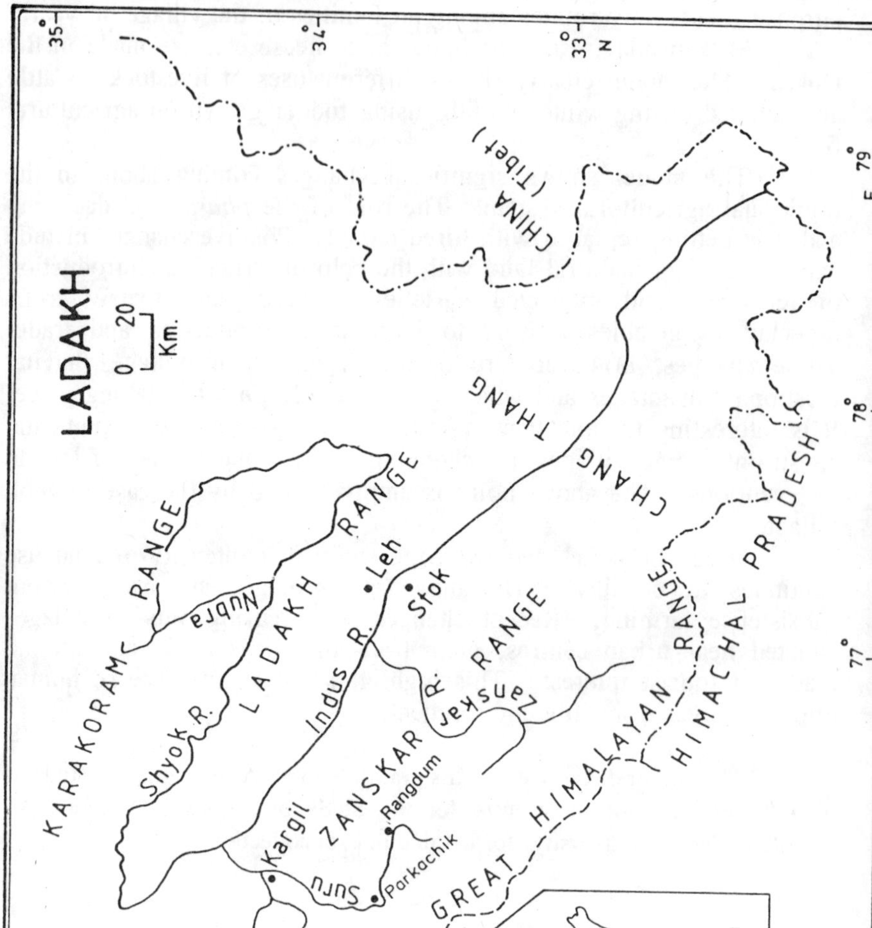

Harjit Singh, Fig.1. Map of Ladakh

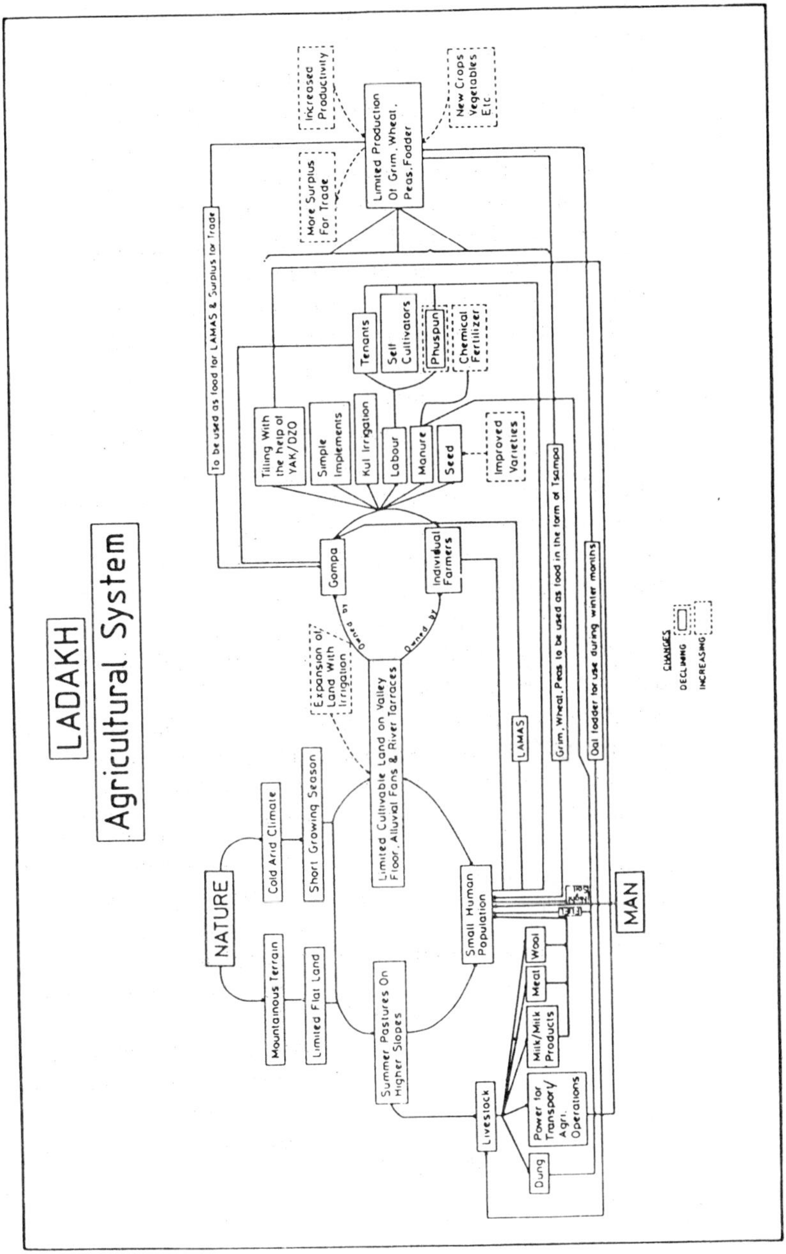

Harjit Singh Fig. 2. Ladakh - the agricultural system.

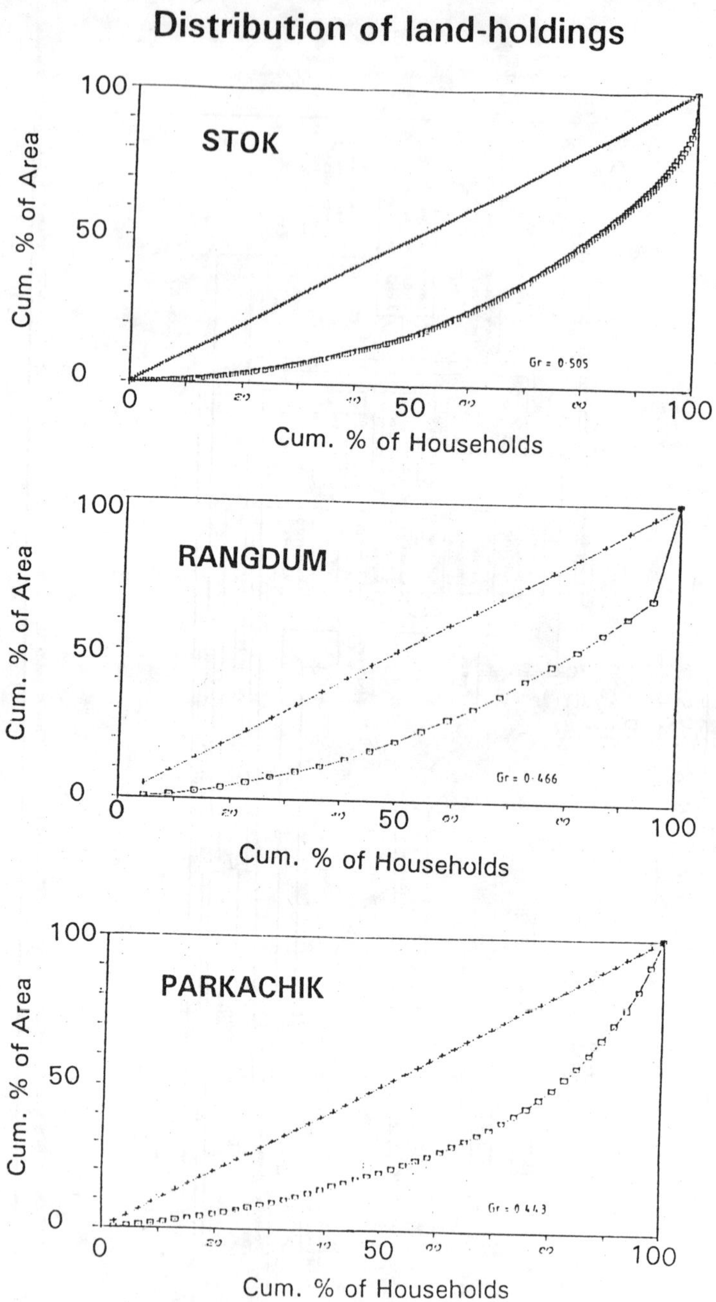

Harjit Singh Fig. 3. Distribution of landholdings.

THE FATE OF TRADITIONAL EDUCATION IN LADAKH

*Nawang Tsering**

In Ladakh, traditional education implies the fivefold sciences of Buddhist knowledge: medicine, fine arts, logic, language and religion. In ancient times many Tibetan students visited India with the aim of receiving first-hand knowledge of these sciences, and one can still read accounts of their hazardous journeys. Many perished on the way before they could even reach the land of the Buddha.

Tibetans' quest for knowledge continued between the 7th-12th centuries. According to historians, the disintegration of Buddhism was almost complete in Central India by the 11th century, and several erudite Indian scholars began migrating to the Himalayas and Tibet. Tibetans were very fortunate, as they had already received the complete works of Indian Buddhist sciences before Buddhism was expelled from its own soil by the 12th century. In Tibet, pious kings had Buddhist texts translated into the Tibetan language. Without deviating from original Buddhist thinking, Tibetan scholars devised a comprehensive system of teaching Buddhist knowledge more effectively. Besides translating Buddhist texts, they produced hundreds of commentaries and sub-commentaries on important texts concerning all forms of knowledge. Manuals of Buddhist logic were also prepared.

The verses of Maitriyanath explain the importance of Buddhist learning: "The bodhisattvas who do not master the five-fold sciences of Buddhist knowledge cannot expect to attain Enlightenment". The highest goal for a Mahayanist was the attainment of enlightenment, that is, a state of Buddhahood, and five-fold Buddhist knowledge was the means to accomplish this end. Ladakh's contemporary educational and religious tradition almost duplicates Tibetan cultural and religious practices. Yet various surviving Buddhist sites at Dras, Mulbek and Alchi, and the arts of image-making, murals and rock-carving, indicate that Ladakh once had direct links with Kashmir and Gandhara. Rinchen Zangpo, whose field of dharmadatu activities was the ancient kingdom of mNga'-ris, was said to have brought over a number of artists from Kashmir.

---

* Dr.Nawang Tsering, Central Institute of Buddhist Studies, Choglamsar, Leh 194101, Ladakh, INDIA.

This suggests that until the onset of Tibetan influence in the 10th and 11th centuries, Ladakh drew its cultural and religious strength from these neighbouring states. From the 13th century onwards, there are accounts of students moving from Ladakh to Central Tibet for higher studies, as well as ordination. The teacher-student relationship between Tibet and Ladakh continued up until the middle of this century. While several Ladakhi monks made Tibet their permanent home, many would return after staying in Tibetan monasteries for several years. A few achieved distinction in different branches of Buddhist knowledge, and are said to have become abbots of philosophical institutions in Tibet. Even now, those Ladakhi monks who were fortunate enough to study in Tibet, remember those times with nostalgia. A few Ladakhi monks were able to obtain the degrees of lha-rams-pa or bka'-chen in Tibetan monasteries. The five-fold philosophical subjects: the Pramanasastra, Madhyamikasastra, Prajnaparamita-sastra, Abhidharma and Vinaya, were difficult to master. Sras Rinpoche of Ridzong monastery, and bka'-chen bZod-pa of Tikse, are of the few who have achieved thorough knowldege of these philosophical subjects in Tibet. The works of bka'-chen bZod-pa on Pramanasastra, tantra, grammar and history, have been published in India. In most of the gonpas it is still possible to find one or two trained dge-bshes or mkhan-po who are more than willing to teach, and a significant number of monks benefit from their scholarship. Monks, it seems, are the least apprehensive about the future of the teaching tradition in the monasteries. Sras Rinpoche lives away from his monastery, whilst bka'-chen bZodpa spends much of his time at his ancestral home, and busies himself reading and writing. In recent times, a dge-bshes at Temisgam was said to have complained, "I have knowledge, but what is the use of it - no one seems to need it any more". This speaks for the present state of traditional education in the monasteries of Himalayan states. In some respects the ritually-oriented and established system hinders the improvement of academic life in these monasteries.

The sprul-sku who have enjoyed an extraordinary place in Ladakhi society, limit their role to bestowing routine dbang. Each gonpa has no less than fifty monks on its roll, but at any one time hardly five monks are to be found residing there. Individual monks cannot afford the necessary time for the study of the subtle points of Buddhist philosophy. A monk's days are spent shuttling between village and gonpa, an activity indispensible for subsistence. A villager would not support a monk who does not come out to perform rites for the welfare of his family.

In such circumstances, a section of the Buddhist population is exploring alternatives to the existing system. Some important suggestions have come up during a series of seminars in the monasteries, in which monks and sprul-sku have been present. The alternatives discussed in the seminars are: (i) limiting house to house visits by monks for the performance of rites, (ii) instructing laypeople to come themselves to the monasteries and donate, instead of providing food and money on invitation, (iii) organising short-term teaching on Buddhist history, literature, philosophy and languages, (iv) providing facilities in the monasteries for teaching the Amchi system of medicine, thanka painting, and sculpture, and (v) opening primary schools in all the monasteries. The last point is being currently implemented. 24 primary schools, financed by the Department of Culture of the Government of India, have opened in different monasteries. The Central Institute of Buddhist Studies at Leh has taken the responsibility of preparing the syllabuses for these schools.

The School of Buddhist Philosophy, now known as the Central Institute of Buddhist Studies, was established in 1959 at Leh. The unfortunate events that took place in Tibet in that year, shattered the myth that Tibet would remain a permanent spiritual home to Himalayan people. Tibet, the home of hundreds of lamas from these highland regions, had never treated them as outsiders. The doors of the monasteries in Tibet were suddenly closed, and the foreign lamas were forced to quit the country, a reminder of the Buddha's word that parting with one's near and dear is sorrow.

For the first time, people from Himalayan states came to realise that Tibet was politically separate, and they were saddened by the reality of the existence of two different countries. As they were cut off from the source of their culture and religion, the spiritual leaders of the gonpas of Ladakh called a council of the Sangha to consider the changed situation and to find ways and means of keeping alight the torch of Mahayana on the roof of the world.

This council, under the spiritual leadership of the Venerable Kushok Bakula, took a concensus decision to establish an institution in Leh for traditional monastic education with ten students drawn from ten gonpa. ***Mtshan-nyid slob-grwa-khang*** (The School of Buddhist Philosophy), was born in a few rooms in a mud house at Leh in October, 1959. Fortunately, two Tibetan masters of philosophy, dge-bshes Ye-shes thub, and dge-bshes Ye-bshes thub-mkhas, accepted the invitation to take charge of the school.

The aim and objective of establishing this was to teach Buddhist philosophy by preserving the Tibetan scholastic tradition, and thereby to reintroduce Indian Buddhist philosophy on to its own soil.

Some of the founders of this institute were probably aware that important Buddhist-Sanskrit texts discovered in India, Tibet and Central Asia, had become virtually foreign to scholars other than those familiar with Tibetan.

In order to transmit such knowledge to future generations, it is essential to maintain continuity in the learning processes themselves. These include debating, disputation, and learning basic texts by heart. By adopting age old methodological learning processes, it is possible to achieve clarity of mind for understanding Buddhist philosophical texts.

However, with the increase in numbers of students and staff (due to a large number of new arrivals from Tibet), the already overburdened monastic community was in no position to provide food, clothing and other necessities for the school. In these circumstances, the Department of Culture and the Ministry of Education of the Government of India helped by taking over the Institute in 1963. And with the aim of further expansion and degree recognition, the Institute was affiliated to the Sanskrit University in Varanasi. New subjects were introduced and admission was opened to all students, including girls.

In this changed context, monasteries refrained from sending young students from the gonpa, preferring to send them to various Tibetan settlements in India instead, where more traditional schools were being established. To see to it that young lamas from the gonpas study at the Leh Institute, the School authority opened a new wing reintroducing the old courses of study along traditional lines. Since then, fifty young lamas have been receiving traditional education at the Institute.

Thirty years is a relatively long period in the life of an institute, and various questions arise. What major steps have the authorities of the Institute taken towards achieving the original goals, and what are its successes and failures?

During these years, classes have been upgraded to Acharya degrees. This degree is only given in Buddhist Philosophy, and it entails 12 years study, beginning in 6th class. There are also a few research fellows who have been carrying out research work in different subjects of Buddhism. The proceedings of the annual All India Seminar on Buddhist subjects and Ladakhi culture, are published under the title of Ladakh Prabha, Dawn of Ladakh. The Institute has also published Hindi translations of Buddhist texts. It has produced dozens of trained graduates in Tibetan language and literature. When the State Government introduced Ladakhi language in schools, the graduates from the Institute came forward to teach the language. Had the Institute not existed, Ladakh could not have trained teachers to teach Ladakhi in schools. The Ladakhi language has been gaining popularity, especially in rural areas. The situation has changed much since a Tibetan gentleman remarked about the knowledge of this language among Ladakhis, "I have found no one in Ladakh who does not read and write, but there is no one who writes this language correctly". As for fine arts, the Institute has appointed a painter and a sculptor. A teacher in the Amchi system of medicine has also been appointed.

In the years to come, the Institute will be able to produce scholars in Buddhist philosophy, history, language, fine arts and medicine. Other centres which have been active in promoting traditional learning are: The Cultural Academy of Leh, the SECMOL Group, the Ladakh Ecological development Group, and the Amchi Society of Leh. All India Radio, Leh, has also played a major role in promoting knowledge of traditional culture. Almost every village has a welfare society which looks after the preservation of the old mchod-rten. Ladakhis are very enthusiastic about their cultural heritage. Throughout Ladakhi history, there have never been such combined efforts and interest in the preservation of Ladakhi culture and religion. Now, ancient learning is no longer the exclusive domain of clergymen.

EARLY HISTORY OF LADAKH: MYTHIC LORE & FABULATION

A preliminary note on the conjectural history of the 1st millennium A.D.

Rohit Vohra[1]

The present paper attempts to present legends based on folk lore of the local population of Ladakh. These cannot, at the present state of our knowledge, be fully integrated with scientific history. However scientific history does not provide us with any insight on the pre-11th century period aside from fragmentary pieces of information. We are informed about descendants of Gesar ruling Ladakh during this period. There are the legends of Wanla Cho and rGya-pa Cho ruling in Ladakh prior to the coming of Nyi-ma mgon and it is said that it is they who invited the latter to settle in Ladakh.

At some time prior to this Tha Tha Khan, a scion of the Gilgit royal family migrated to Purig. In Purig there is widespread knowledge of the settlement of the area by his descendants. In Nubra and Purig there are the folk legends about Cho Bongskang and Su-Malik who can be connected with the rulers of Gilgit. I am aware that there are several other legends and stories[2] of petty chiefs which could be adjusted within the framework of the above period. However the present paper must restrict itself to the above as otherwise the entire subject matter would become too unwieldy.

---

1. Dr.Rohit Vohra, P.O. Box 66, Ettelbruck, Luxembourg.

2. Some of the early local rulers mentioned by the Buddhist 'Brog-pa Dard informants are Shar Lha-chen (=Ladakh rGya-po), Purig Sultan (=Chigtan Cho) and Brag-mag-pon (also Ra Mag-pon, i.e., Skardu Cho) at Rong-chu-rgyat.

There are names of other rulers mentioned in the various works of A.H. Francke: rGya-shin, Shirima, Suryamati from the area around Khalatse for which inscriptions were found. Then there is the ruler Bandel from near Saspol who is reputed to have constructed the ancient fort at Alchi called Alchi mKhar-gog. There were chiefs at Kartse called Tri-rgyal who changed their name to Tri Sultan after the coming of Islam. We also have the mention of the Hasora chiefs as well as the Minaro chiefs at mDa-Garkun.

Part I: Gesar

Introduction

In the Chronicles of Ladakh (La-dvags rgyal-rabs:35.9-10; Francke 1914 & 1926) we have the mention of the descendants of Gesar ruling Ladakh prior to the coming of sKyid-lde Nyi-ma-mgon[3]. Gesar (Kesar) as an epic hero and a living spirit is well known in Ladakh. Various versions of the legend are available from the Changthang Nomads, Nubra, Central Ladakh and other versions from Purig, Baltistan and Hunza (Müller-Stellrecht 1979 & 1980). In an earlier paper I had identified the numerous sites along the banks of the river Indus associated with the memory of Gesar in Purig (Vohra 1983:66-68). Similar associations with Gesar are known from other parts of Ladakh and Baltistan not to mention Tibet (Kvaerne 1970:221-229). George Roerich made a most comprehensive survey on Gesar and of published literature (Roerich 1942:277-315).

Academic discussions on the origin of the title, Phrom ('Phrom/Khrom) and the name Gesar have principally centered around the question of its origin or its derivation from the Roman Ceaser and its subsequent arrival in east Tibet to provide the genesis of the epic. Other arguments have concentrated efforts on identifying the Turki Gesar's origin and the epic form through the system of the four cardinal points[4], an idea first formulated by R.A. Stein. Subsequent papers by R.A. Stein, Ariane Macdonald, Géza Uray and Róna-Tas among others have contributed on the subject[5].

Gesar in Texts

Scientific evidence to support the existence of Gesar as a historical personality is at the present state of our knowledge not sufficient. It is however deemed necessary to use the legendary material available to throw some light on the pre-10th century historical background of the region. There are several works of the ancient past which make historical references to Gesar. In the documents concerning Chinese Turkestan, Phrom Gesar finds presence in the text *Prophecy of the Li country*(i.e., Khotan *Li-yul-lun-bstan-*

---

3. In connection with Gesar Saga in Ladakh there are also several tales of the legendary hero Api Cho who seems to have been a daring rival of Gesar.

4. The four Great Kings of the four different heavens, a theory that spread to different parts of Asia. For the overview of its spread in Tibet see Stein (1959:252-260;303-305).

5. Here I will refrain from the discussion conducted by the above mentioned authors and restrict myself to Ladakh. A.H. Francke's efforts to contribute to the discussion and the possibility that Gesar epic has its origin in Ladakh are to be mentioned.

pa). This text along with certain others were compiled during the 9th or the 10th century (Thomas Pt.I:73-74; Emmerick 1967; Hill 1988).

In Sarat Chandra Das's *Tibetan Dictionary* we are informed that Phrom is the name of the country situated to the north-east of Yarkand and to the north of Tibet. This country during the 6th century (according to others 7th century) is said to have been ruled by King Gesar (Das 1902:845). F.W. Thomas seems to agree with the above statement and proposes the hypothesis of identifying the region with Guchen and/or Turfan (Thomas Pt.II: 286-291) which is known from Chinese and other sources to have been dominated by the Dru-gu, i.e., Turks. However Uray following the suggestion of Sato and Harmatta is inclined to identify the lands either with the Turk area Küsen or the former Kushana countries of Gandhara and Udayana (Uray 1979:281). It is to the Turk ethnic stock that Gesar is supposed to have belonged. In the *Prophecy of the Li country* and the *Annals of the Li country*, which are original Tibetan works compiled in Khotan during the time of the Tibetan influence in that region, we are informed that the king of Khotan Vijaya Sangrama, builder of the Hgu-gzan monastery, had as his consort Hu-rod-ga (or Hu-rong-ga), the daughter of Phrom Gesar (Thomas Pt.I: 131; Emmerick 1967:69).

During this period there was a special amity between Khotan and Phrom Gesar. There is evidence of the copying of a Saka Khotani text by the order of a member of the Gesar lineage which may have been a result of that intimacy (Thomas Pt.III:79). Vijaya Samgrama's younger brother's consort was a drugu-mo which further strengthens the question of close ties between Khotan, Phrom Gesar and the Turks in general. In *Padma-thang-yig* we have information of the Tibetan army subduing Gesar, which finds mention in the text *Rgyal-po'i-bka'i-than-yig* (Pronouncements concerning Kings). Gesar, as is evident from these documents, could be a dynastic name not of Tibetan origin and should be traceable in Dru-gu connections. Phrom could have been the name of Gesar country (Thomas Pt.III:80-83).

Coins and Tamgas connected with Gesar

Certain emissions of coins bearing the title Fromo Kesaro have been identified with the successor of Sahi Tegin (Humbach 1966:20-23;64-65; Harmatta 1969:409-412;431-432) who was the ruler of the Second Turki Sahi dynasty at Kapisa-Udyana ruling between 738 and 745 A.D. He is identical with Fu-lin-ki-p'o and received the investiture from the Chinese court in 738 as King Wu-san T'e-k'in Sha just as his father Sahi Tegin (700-738) and subsequently his son in 745 as "King of Ki-pin (Kapisa) and of the kingdom of Wu-ch'ang (Udyana)" (Chavannes 1903:132, 213-214; 1904:59). It is during this ruler's time that many temples were constructed in the region as is reported by Ou-k'ong (Chavannes 1903:198) and this confirms the Buddhist confession of the rulers (Chavannes 1895:356; Fuchs 1938:444-449). As has been suggested this Fromo Kesaro must have been the father-in-law of the King of Khotan, Vijaya Sangrama, ruling about the mid-8th century (Uray 1979:296-297).

There are altogether five coins (Emissions 247-251: Phromo Kesoro) bearing the title Fromo Kesaro (Göbl 1967 Bd.I:170-173). Although Humbach would like to associate certain other emissions (288 and 289 in Göbl 1967) with the title Fromo Kesaro (Humbach 1983:303-309). These emmissions now identified with the sucessor of Sahi Tegin, Fromo Kesaro, further raise the question regarding Tamga 61d. This tamga we find on the reverse of a coin of Sahi Tegin (Emission 245) and it has also been found engraved twice at Tangtse in Ladakh. One engraving is close to a Sogdian inscription (Vohra 1992a: Plate 19; 1993: Plate 8) and a second amidst Tamgas and other symbols (Vohra 1995: Plate 1). Furthermore it is to be noted that there are four other variations of this same tamga (Göbl Bd.IV: Tafel 17, Tamga 61-61c) and all of them only appear on emissions of coins of Sahi Tegin and his vassal (Göbl 1967 Bd.I: 25).

Lineal descent from Gesar and kinship in the region.

In the beginning of the records of the various rulers of the area, Ladakh (rGya, Zanskar etc.), Baltistan (Shigar) and Gilgit, there are direct references to descent or kinship to Gesar or dealings with Gesar. The earliest rulers of rGya and Zanskar trace their descent and kinship with Gesar while the Shigarnama, of Baltistan, informs us of Amacha Testay Cho during whose time Gesar of Ladakh is supposed to have married and lived in Shigar and later returned to Ladakh. Api Cho, ruler of Shigar, went to bring the daughter of Amacha Testey Cho and later looted and set fire to his palace (Schuler 1978:107). In 1979 and 1980 while documenting the local folklore on Gesar in Purig I was often informed about his contemporary in Baltistan called Api Cho with whom Gesar often went to war.

We know that the rulers of Khotan, Skardu, Gandhara (Sachau 1910,Vol.II:10), Suvarnagotra (Thomas 1935,1951) and Kashmir (Stein, M.A. 1973:13-20) had intimate relations with each other. In the Tibetan texts concerning Khotan and the *Rajatarangini* there is evidance of marital ties between the rulers of these kingdoms (Vohra 1983:61-65; 1988:538-543). The information on Gesar originating from a couple of centuries prior to the coming of Nyi-ma-mgon to Ladakh is further strengthened by the fact that contemporary to the above events the ruler at Skardu was Isvara-varman who, together with his eldest son and the King of Khotan, died resisting the Tibetan occupation of Khotan. This event is followed by a strife between the new rulers of Khotan and Skardu, i.e., Vijaya-kirti and Vijaya-varman, leading to the victory of the former (Thomas Pt.II:142-143)[6].

These close ties between the rulers of Khotan and Skardu are to be attested in the fact that the dynastic history of Shigar (Khan 1939:602 ff; Schuler 1978:103-109), a neighbour of Skardu, mentions the earliest rulers bearing the title Amacha (< Skt.:Amatya). The usage of this title continued until 1841. The title Amacha was used by the rulers of Khotan and was endorsed by Chinese imperial decrees (Thomas 1951:191, 261-262,313; Uray 1979:f.n.80). The close ties between the rulers of Khapalu, Skardu and Shigar with the regions across the Karakoram mountains, i.e., Yarkand, Khotan and Kashgarh, were maintained over the route crossing the Mustag pass. I had, in a paper delivered at Herrnhut in 1987, provided geographical arguments regarding the route across the Mustag pass connecting these communities which was in use until the 19th century (Vohra 1987:268-276; 1990:125-128; Thomas 1951 Pt.II:143).

The coexistence of Chinese and Indian elements in Khotan, as attested by coins bearing Chinese legends on the obverse and Indian Prakrit written in Kharoshti script on the reverse[7], must have had as one of the sources of its dissemination through the Darada kingdom of Gilgit-Skardu-Kishanganga from the mid-first millennium A.D. The recent documentation of inscriptions from Gilgit-Skardu-Chilas areas by Jettmar and the translations by Fussmann and Oskar von Hinüber reveal a flourishing Indian cultural tradition among the royal dynasties of the area[8]. At the present state of our knowledge one cannot with any certainty say if there existed contacts between the Patola Sahi rulers of Gilgit-Baltistan and the Kabul Sahi of Kapisa-Gandhara though both these maintained relations with Kashmir.

---

6. On the question of the Tibetan expansion over Skardu-Gilgit and to the final occupation of the Four Garrisons (Chavannes 1903: 150-151) which are attested to from the T'ang Annals (T'ang-shu) and for other related information in connection with the contemporary rulers of Baltistan-Gilgit region see Vohra (1988).

7. These coins are to be dated to the first centuries A.D.(Stein M.A. 1907:204-205;Thomas 1944:82-98). To approximately the same period belongs the Kharoshti inscription at Alam Bridge, at the junction of Gilgit and the Indus rivers, which mentions Daradaraya <Darada Raja> (Fussmann 1978:18-19).

8. For the treatment of the material and the literature on the above see Vohra (1988) and a detailed bibliography in Jettmar 1989 and 1993.

PART II: rGya-pa Cho

A. rGya-pa Cho - Wanla Cho - sKyid-lde Nyi-ma-mgon

In ancient times, prior to the coming of sKyid-lde Nyi-ma-mgon, rGya-pa Cho ruled from rGya. One of his contemporaries was the Wanla Cho or Cho Brag-dar Skyaps. At this time there were other minor chiefs ruling in Purig. rGya was an important capital of the region and revenue in the form of grain was brought there. rGya-pa Cho's granary was located at a place called Kagyali.

rGya-pa Cho had kinship ties to Gesar rGyal-po. A contemporary of theirs was Api Cho in Baltistan who is said to have fought several times with Gesar. There are many epic stories related about their encounters. In Zanskar ruled a descendant of rGya-pa Cho and Gesar and this Zanskar Cho separated his lands from those of rGya-pa Cho, hence claiming independance.

Brag-dar Cho gave land to Lotsava Rin-chen bzan-po in Wanla. In the monastery on the hill at Wanla there is an inscription regarding Wanla Cho. Brag-dar Cho had four brothers.

One winter Yarkandi forces invaded Ladakh but due to heavy snowfall the Yarkandis were at a disadvantage and rGya-pa Cho was able to defeat them. Sometime later rGya-pa Cho received information on another impending invasion by the Yarkandi forces.

In the Cho-rabs section of Gergan's work we are informed that at this time the ruler of Purang[9] was a descendant from the royal house of Lhasa. The ruler, Nyi-ma-mgon, was invited to assist in defeating the Yarkandis. Later rGya-pa Cho gave Nyi-ma-mgon the Shey-Thikse area which was barren land (Gergan 1976:177). Here Shey mKhar was built and the Shey-Chushot canal was dug for water supply.

When Nyi-ma-mgon came to Ladakh he had an inscription engraved at the sMan-la statue (at the sharp turn after leaving Chuglamsar) which says "Nyathi-chan's descendant sKyid-lde Nyi-ma-mgon is for the benefit and welfare of the people of Nari skor-sum" (Gergan 1976:177).

rGya-pa Cho was a severe ruler and his subjects, being dissatisfied with him, preferred to follow Nyi-ma-mgon. Due to his benign rule sKyid-lde Nyi-ma-mgon was able to bring the whole of upper Ladakh (Stod) under his control and later his three sons divided the kingdom amongst themselves.

---

9. Here I would only mention the fact briefly regarding the instrumental role of the 'Bro clan of Zan-zun (Guge-Purang) who were one of the chief players among the aristocratic clans determining the ruler of Tibet. It was their influence which caused Nyi-ma-mgon's line of royal descendants to take refuge in Purang. We know that the 'Bro clan was chiefly responsible for the revival of Buddhism in Ladakh at least at the beginning of 2nd millennium A.D.

When I visited rGya in 1980 and again in 1983 I collected the above and some other data on rGya-pa Cho. It is said that he fought several battles with the rulers of Purig, i.e., Suru, Kartse, Chigtan as well as the Baltis. rGya-pa Cho did not have any children and his younger brother who ruled at Tiri received the lands. His lineage still exists today and his descendants are known in the area.

I was informed that the place derived its name from the number 100 (=rGya) as there existed one hundred houses. rGya-pa Cho also had land in Photogsa and Lingshed. The Zims-khang of rGya-pa Cho is in the village. The Rum-khang of rGya-pa Cho is located near the great Mani wall in the village. Kang-ju is the Pha-Lha of rGya-pa Cho and the Lha-tho was kept in the mKhar where there was a mark. Now the mKhar, which is very high upon a hill, has been converted into a monastery and the Lha-tho has been removed to the roof top. During the Lo-gsar celebrations the villagers traditionally conduct a horse race in the village grounds and play polo in memory of rGya-pa Cho. One of rGya-pa Cho's pastimes was hunting rabbits and this has now become a tradition. Hence during the month of April the villagers hunt rabbits and this practice is called "Rigar". This activity has its practical side as well as it keeps down the number of rabbits which are thus prevented from destroying their crops.

Part III: Tha Tha Khan

In the Minor Chronicles of Ladakh we find the numerous chiefdoms of Purig referring to their apical dynastic ancestors as coming from the west, i.e., Baltistan, Gflet (or Gelat = Gilgit) which region had as its ancient name Sarjan.

There is further the mention of a certain Ka-cho Tha Tha Khan belonging to the ruling house of Gilgit who migrated to Purig. According to Hashmatullah Khan's calculation this migration took place approximately 250 years prior to the coming of Nyi-ma-mgon to Ladakh. The dating method of Hashmatullah Khan is highly questionable and all that we may more confidently state is that Tha Tha Khan's migration took place some time prior to Nyi-ma-mgon.

Genealogy of the rulers of Gilgit

The genealogical data in the following table were collected by Hashmatullah Khan from 1894 onwards (Khan 1939:758 ff.), and are given here with some modifications.

Circumstances leading to the migration of Tha Tha Khan from Gilgit

The legend of Ka-cho Tha Tha Khan is well known throughout

Genealogy of the rulers of Gilgit

(after Khan 1939:758 ff.).

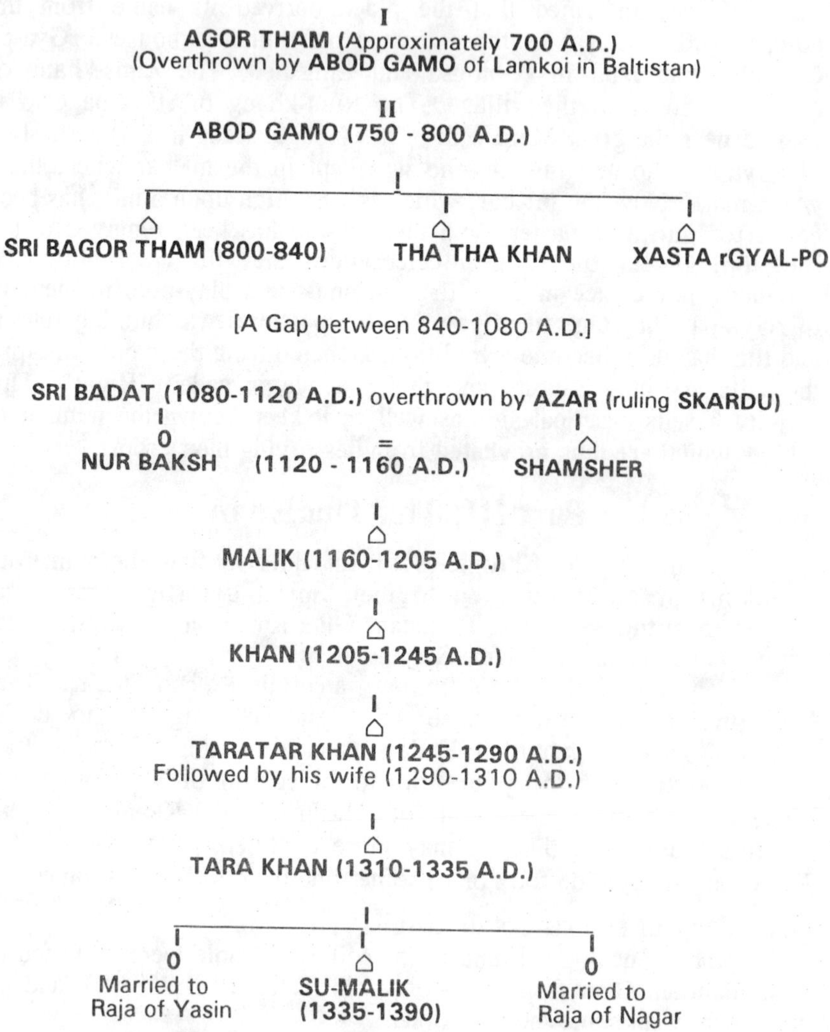

Key: △ = male 0 = female

Purig.[10] Hashmatullah Khan has provided a detailed version about the reasons for Tha Tha Khan leaving Gilgit, his arrival in Sod and the establishment of castles (Ladakhi: *mKhar*) and settlements in Purig.

I - Hashmatullah Khan relates in one version that Thakan was the prince of Gilgit who was deprived of rule by Sri Bagor Tham and was forced to leave the country.

II - Another version is that Abod Gamo went with his son Sri Bagor Tham to Gilgit where he killed the ruler Agor Tham and married his widow. From this marriage Tha Tha Khan was born. Upon the death of Abod Gamo Sri Bagor Tham succeeded him and the enemies of Tha Tha Khan, due to his connections with the former regime, wanted to get rid of him and so he fled Gilgit (Khan 1939:710).

III - Earlier to these two versions we find related that one of the Rajas of Gilgit was very cruel and was told by an astrologer that his rule would be harmed by a specific person called Ka-cho-pa. The characteristics of this enemy, forseen by the astrologer, were found in Tha Tha Khan. The ruler intended to kill him but Tha Tha Khan learned of the plot in time and fled Gilgit (Khan 1939: 709).

Hashmatullah Khan is of the opinion that the very first version is probably the one which is most convincing, "as the two names Tha Tha Khan and Thakan are two variations of the same" (Khan 1939:710).

Prof.Emerson who did research work in Baltistan during the 1970s and 1980s is informative in this connection and we find that there is no dichotomy between the various versions. In fact these are not different versions but all fit in well with one another and relate about one single event. I derive the following interpretation from the above:

Sri Bagor Tham succeeded his father Abod Gamo. His brother or rather his step-brother Tha Tha Khan represented a threatening aspect to his rule and the throne. Perhaps as recounted in Version - III, that the astrologer saw Sri Bagor Tham's rule threatened by a certain Ka-cho whose characteristics were recognised in Tha Tha Khan can be explained in the title Ka-cho.

Prof Emerson remarks that Ka-cho (Ka = brother; Cho = chief, i.e., brothers of the chief) were the male descendants or the brothers of the chief. Thus in any given generation, the Ka-cho class would include the ruler's real brothers (if any), his paternal uncles and male cousins of the 1st, 2nd....nth order. Thus the title of Ka-cho is

---

10. e.g. The former Assistant Commissioner Kacho Sikander Khan of Sanjak.

used by any one who has acknowledged patrilineal kin-ties to the chief (=cho), no matter how great the kin-distance. These Ka-chos represented a class and formed the standing army (Emerson 1984:106-107).

Thus Ka-cho Tha Tha Khan was possibly the step-brother of Sri Bagor Tham, born from the widow of Agor Tham, the previous ruler, and their father in common Abod Gamo. When Sri Bagor Tham ascended the throne, Ka-cho Tha Tha Khan represented a threat to his authority. This must have been particularly important as far as his legitimate rights were concerned. Though Sri Bagor Tham must have been older and thus was able to gain some support, however in the eyes of the local population Tha Tha Khan must have been the more appropriate heir to the throne, as in him they would have seen the descendant of the old ruling house. Thus the extermination of his kinsman Tha Tha Khan must have seemed evident to him in order to secure his hold upon the throne. However Tha Tha Khan got wind of the impending danger and escaped to the east, finally arriving in Purig.

Migration of Tha Tha Khan to Purig

Here below is reproduced the most detailed version recorded by Hashmatullah Khan to which I was able to add some details collected during my field work between 1979-1986 (Vohra 1985).

It is said that Tha Tha Khan was 12 years old when he came to Purig in the company of his foster brother and foster father. According to the version recorded by me from Kuksho it is said that Tha Tha Khan came with Balti-mi, Stag Lha-chen[11] and Mon-po to the area. When they reached the area opposite village Dargo in the Kuksho region (this area was unpopulated at that time) on the banks of the river Indus, they liked it because of the evenness of the land, the bushes and the flowing water. However as the river Indus lay in between it seemed difficult to reach Dargo. It was the beginning of Spring and in this season glacial waters flow down into the Indus with often chunks of ice floating on the surface. Sitting on the bank they were just contemplating how to cross the Indus when a giant chunk of ice floated past them. They interpreted this as a sign of heavenly help and using that ice block as a boat succeeded in crossing to the other side. However they found it impossible to remain in that unpopulated

11. According to the version from Kuksho, recorded in 17.08.83, Stag Lha-chen is 'brog-lha of Gilgit. Tha Tha Khan was a Lha-phru, i.e., he was not born of any human parents. He was exiled by the Cho of Gilgit. Along with Tha Tha Khan came 9 other households: Gasho-pa, Baltistan-pa, Miyara-pa (bearded one), Skya-pa, Shokbar-pa, Stamo-pa, Tschangya-pa, Rablon-pa and Sumbran-pa. At that time no differences existed among the human beings and all knew what each thought and did. The differences were later created by excessive taking from the poor.

place due to the lack of provisions and continued further in search of the inhabited part of the region. Tha Tha Khan had a walnut in his pocket which he took out and buried in the ground by the side of a fresh water spring. They went on and reached the place where at present village Kuksho exists. They liked the place as well. Tha Tha Khan had a green stick of the Bhoj tree in his hand which he planted at that place and went further with his companions. Next they reached Yarobaltic where two families had already settled. The head of those two families was their fellow countryman who gave them a job and promised them his help. Tha Tha Khan and his foster brother worked as shepherds while the foster father did the household work for the man. The place where those two families' houses were situated is known now as Shagmela and the area around those houses is now called Loto Thang Bo.

Tha Tha Khan always took the goats to a hill for grazing. Once he fell asleep while herding the goats and saw in his dream that he was lying all alone on dusty ground which was littered with stones. When he went back to his employer and told him about his dream the man interpreted it as meaning that one day he would be raja of that country. Henceforth his employer took more interest in Tha Tha Khan's education.

In the meanwhile some other friends of Tha Tha Khan, who had been banished from Gilgit, reached the area and thus joined him. The company of his friends gave him courage and taking some provisions from his master he left for Dargo. En route he climbed the mountain Nin Dum and from its top he could see the whole area below. On one side he could see up to Goniyal in the valley of Dras, then Kondoce in the valley of the river Suru and Khalatse in the Indus valley. Interpreting this as a sign of good luck he proceeded further. When he reached Kuksho he found that the stick he had planted had turned into a tree and similarly in Dargo a walnut tree had grown by the side of the spring. In Kuksho he built two houses. One towards the north of the stream which he named Tho Tho mKhar where he settled himself. The other house he built south of the stream which he called Pato mKhar and here his companions settled. Later when Pato mKhar was further populated the name was changed to Kokas Kasog meaning the settlement of the castle. This name later changed to Kuksho. The tree which Tha Tha Khan had planted grew very big and its shadow encompased a huge area. It is said that when in the family of Gasho-pa (Ka-cho-pa) a child is born then a new branch sprouts and when someone dies then a branch dries up. The Walnut tree at Dargo existed until the invasion of Zorowar Singh when during his conquest of the area it was destroyed and in its memory the people built a tower.

PART IV: Cho Bongskang

In the history of Gilgit there is a gap of several generations after Sri Bagor Tham, of the 9th century, to his next known sucessor Sri Badat (11th - 12th century). It is interesting to note that the little information we have on the previous ruler is about the change in the rule which occured. Similarly in the case of Sri Badat his rule and its termination by Azur Jamshed is characteristic for the survival of the historical event (Khan 1939:766 ff).

Sri Badat and Cho Bongskang

It is related that Sri Badat was a devout Buddhist which is in contradiction to the mythic lore as we find related below where he is seen as relishing human flesh. It is said that as an expression of his devotion he had had erected two massive Buddha reliefs on either side of the Kargo stream (Khan 1939:767). The image on the western side still exists and is located near the village Naupur. This image is similar in artistic style and skill of execution to the Mulbec Maitreya. Sri Badat's splendid palace was located near the mountain south of Gilgit and its ruins were seen by Hashmatullah Khan. It is said that at a point in time Sri Badat became an extremely oppressive and cruel ruler and terrorised the local population, confiscating their property by force. This led the Tarakani family of Skardu to overthrow him. Shamsher of this family then married the daughter of Sri Badat, named Nur Baksh, thus legitmizing his rule.

The mythic lore concerning Sri Badat is available from the works of several authors based on information collected in Baltistan, Gilgit and Hunza during the past century. Differing versions were noted by Leitner, Guhlam Muhammad, Biddulph, Schomberg, Haughton and Marsh. However it is the version provided by Leitner (Leitner 1978:9-16) which is the most comprehensive and detailed.[12] The thematic detail is identical to the mythic lore of Cho Bongskang recorded by me in Nubra. Here I will limit myself to recounting the Nubra version of Cho Bongskang (Vohra 1985a).

Cho Bonskang[13]

At Teb-lé there once lived the wicked ruler Cho Bongskang, who had come from a distant land. He was invincible as his body was

12. For a detailed study of the topic see Müller-Stellrecht (1973).

13. This is an amended version of the lore included in a paper "Mythic lore and Historical Documents from the Nubra Valley in Ladakh" presented at the Bicentenary Csoma de Körös Symposium, Visegrád - Budapest, 13 - 19 September 1984.

made of steel and he terrorised the local population. Contemporary to this ruler in the Tshrka area where he had his fort, there was also the fortress of the more benign ruler at Charasa in the Farka area.

As the sun's rays fell very late on his fort at Teb-lé, due to the obstruction by a hill, he demanded forced labour from the local population and made them level down the hill. The people were tired of this ruler and his egocentric demands. Once he wanted to have shoes made and the villagers engaged themselves in making shoes for him but none of the shoes would fit him. Ultimately an old woman made a pair of round shoes which fitted his feet and which resembled the hooves of a donkey. This is also indicated in his name, i.e., Cho Bong Skang (= Chief Donkey Feet).

As regular tribute each household from the village had to provide him with a kid goat for his royal meals. One day the cook prepared the usual dish of goat meat which tasted unusually good to him. He immediately summoned the cook and demanded as to what meat it was that had such a good flavour. The cook replied that it was meat from the kid provided as tribute by the poor woman of the village whose child had recently died. However as to why the flesh tasted so good to Cho Bongskang the cook could provide no answer. So Cho Bonskang demanded that the woman be brought into his presence immediately. The poor woman was alarmed at being summoned and full of fear appeared before the chief at the fortress. However as Cho Bongskang spoke gently and asked to know the reason for the special flavour of the meat she was at once relieved. She replied that since her only goat had died while giving birth to the kid, she had fed the kid with her own milk. Upon learning that the flesh of the kid tasted so delicious after being fed on human milk he wondered how good the flesh of young babies would taste.

Following this incident he began to demand young babies as tribute from the villagers instead of a kid. Thus each household had to deliver a child, in rotation, to Cho Bongskang for his meals. The people became weary of this cannibal they had for a chief and wanted to get rid of him but as he was made of iron they were at a loss as to how they would accomplish their task.

An old woman who knew the secret about Cho Bongskang's vulnerability then took the task of appealing to the ruler at Charasa on behalf of the villagers. She conspired with the Charasa chief and informed him about Cho Bongskang's heart (used in the sense of the soul) being made of lac (Ladakhi: *la-cha*), the only weak point in an otherwise invincible body. It was due to this fact that Bongskang had a great fear of fire which could melt his heart and thus cause his death.

The ruler of Charasa then plotted to have ditch dug just inside the gateway of the fort and this he planned to do on the next occasion when Bongskang went to collect his tribute of a child. Hence on the next moonless night as Bongskang left his fort to collect the tribute from the village one body of the villagers went to the fort to dig a large ditch and cover it with branches and leaves.

A second party of villagers were assembled in the village premises with bundles of juniper (Ladakhi: *shuk-pa*) branches. As the assembled villagers saw Cho Bongskang approach the village they lit the juniper branches and chased him. In his fear of fire Bongskang ran to take shelter in his fort followed by the villagers with the juniper torches. Upon entering the threshhold of the fortress he fell into the ditch prepared for him by the villagers. As the villagers approached they began throwing their well lit torches into the ditch where Bongskang struggled amidst the flames. As Bongskang died in agony the villagers threw stones upon him thus burying him in his fortress.

In memory of the success in getting rid of the evil cannibal Cho Bongskang the festival Dong-me is celebrated every year. This takes place on the first day of the New Year festival celebrations. The villagers prepare from dough of sattu flour representations of the Sun and the Moon and place them in their houses so that no evil influences can enter their homes. In the evening they walk in a procession with juniper torches to commemorate the driving away of the evil ruler Cho Bongskang and at the end throw their torches into a bonfire symbolising his death.

I was informed that there are more detailed versions of this myth which are recited in the village Charasa during the winter months. These need to be recorded in detail in order to get a proper insight into the thematic of the myth. This is essential in order to compare it with the almost identical versions of the myth which are available from Gilgit where the evil ruler is named Sri Badat. Oral traditions about this Buddhist ruler of Gilgit[14] were recorded by several authors following the mid-19th century as has been mentioned at the beginning of the present enumeration. The basic theme is that Sri Badat was a cannibal and an oppressive ruler who was put to death with the aid of a neighbouring chief and the old woman. The old woman knew the secret of his heart being made of lac which would melt if he came in contact with fire and thus similarly as above the village population drove him to his death with lighted torches. Other characteristics of Cho Bongskang are identical with those of Sri Badat

14. Jettmar (1975:242) provides a detailed analysis of the myth in the context of the festivals related to Sri Badat in Gilgit and the neighbouring areas. Also see Müller-Stellrecht (1973).

as both had feet like those of a donkey (Ghulam Muhammad 1980:39; Jettmar 1975:242), they were oppressive and ate human flesh, their heart was made of a substance which melts and therefore they had great fear of fire (Leitner 1978:9-16; Ghulam Muhammad 1980:41; Biddulph 1880:109; Jettmar 1975:240-244; Müller-Stellrecht 1973:5-13).

The incidents which take place in both versions of the myths have an indisputable identity. Both oppressive chiefs are regularly supplied with lamb or kid flesh by the villagers as tribute. Once in the royal kitchen is cooked a kid which has been fed with human milk by a woman who has lost her child. Eating this flesh converts him into a cannibal chief who henceforth demands flesh of children of tender years as tribute from the villagers. Thus both rulers are accidentally brought to enjoy the taste of human flesh (Leitner 1978:9; Ghulam Muhammad 1980:41). The oppressive ruler cannot be tolerated any longer and a woman, who comes to know the secret of the vulnerability of the chief's heart (as he is made of steel, Leitner 1978:16; Jettmar 1975:240-241) connives with a neighbouring chief and the local populace to dig a pit into which he is chased with a juniper torch procession and falling into the pit dies in the fire of the torches thrown upon him.

In memory of this event, at the beginning of the New Year festive celebrations, a juniper (Ladakhi: *shuk-pa*; Shina: *chilli*) torch procession takes place in Gilgit along the banks of the river whereby the memory of the driving away of the evil chief is revived (Leitnar 1978:16; Ghulam Muhammad 1980:47; Biddulph 1880:100-101; Jettmar 1975:242,265; Müller-Stellrecht 1973:5-13). The element of the chasing of the evil king is very similarly celebrated by the Binan speaking Lahulis, during the new year celebrations, when they sing a song cursing an evil ruler (Asboe 1933:191; Vohra 1989a). Apart from the connection of the fire procession to drive away a former wicked ruler, in the different areas of the Himalayas, fire plays an important role during the New Year celebrations, in driving away or the destruction of the evil of the previous year. This fact can also be noted for the Kalash Kafirs (Jettmar 1975:379-386), to the west of the Dards (Jettmar 1975:261-266) as well as for the Ladakhis and the Tibetans (Stein 1972: 220,217).

PART V: Su-Malik

Su-Malik is the ruler of Gilgit about whom we hear next. According to the approximate dating provided by Hashmatullah Khan we can attribute to him a reign from 1335-1390 A.D. The rule of Su-Malik during the 14th century is confirmed through the history of Mirza Gurfan according to whom he is said to have been the last local ruler of Chitral in Mulkho and Turikho (Jettmar 1975:455). At this time Shah Nadir, following in the footsteps of the earlier invader, Taj Mughal, invaded the area and established the Shah Rais (Ra'is) dynasty. However according to Hasmatullah Khan it was Taj Mughal's second attack on this area. Taj Mughal of Badakhshan was defeated in battle by Su-Malik and the former retreated. However Su-Malik pursued him upto Kotal-Darkot where he lost consciousness and fell from his horse and was captured and taken prisoner to Badakhshan. It is related that he served in the royal kitchen as supplier of wood for two years.

Later, as he was an expert in handling and the care of horses, he was appointed as chief of royal stables, a post which he held for two years. Then one day he took the horse, Togar, and escaped to Gilgit. Riders were sent in his pursuit to capture him and finally on the 8th day one rider, through some trick, was able to approach him but Su-Malik cleverly bribed him and thus saved his life. He then went to Yasin where his sister was married to the ruler and spent a few days. Then he took his brother-in-law to Gilgit where his wife had been ruling in his absence and thus regained the throne (Khan 1939:771-773).

The songs to Su-Malik are sung during festive occasions in the Chorbat area when prayers are offered to this ruler. The following song of Su-Malik was recorded from the inhabitants of Turtuk and Tyakshi in Nubra (Vohra 1992).

Su-Malik where have you come from ?
Su-Malik where will you go ?
Su-Malik, water, earth and three trees (Chang-ma, Shuk-pa and Chu-li).
Three mountains of earth.
Three stone mountains.
Su-Malik where have you come from ?

Su-Malik came from the mountain
Like the smell of incense in the smoke of the red mountain came Su-Malik.

Su-Malik came with a bull.
What will you do with the meat which is like medicine ?
Divide it among the people.
Red earth on top of the mountain.
Who is coming ?
A horse is coming with a trader.

References to the ruler Su-Malik (also called Su-rGyal) are to be found in the Bononah hymns sung by the Buddhist Dards of Ladakh in the villages of mDa and Garkun (Vohra 1989:97, 37-138).

Concluding Remarks

Recent discoveries in the northern areas of Pakistan of inscription mentioning the Patola Shahi rulers from the 6th century onwards, with an interval of two centuries, until the 12th century have established a reasonably concrete chronology (v.Hinüber 1986; Jettmar 1993). I had attempted to catalogue the rulers in relative chronology in 1985 in a paper delivered at the 4th Seminar of the International Association for Tibetan Studies (Vohra 1988:537-539,f.n.24). This however raises the question of the reliability of the folklore and the conjectural dating for the rulers mentioned therein. An attempt in this direction for the early period has been attempted by Prof. Dani based upon Shah Rais Khan's *History of Gilgit* (Dani 1987:116). At the present state of our knowledge there seem to be no convincing ground for equating the rulers of the inscriptions with those of the folk legends.

Bibliography

ASBOE, W. 1933 Social Functions in Lahul, Kangra district, Punjab. *The Journal of the Royal Anthropological Institute of Great Britian and Ireland* Vol.LXIII.

BIDDULPH, J. 1880 *Tribes of the Hindoo Koosh.* Calcutta.

CHAVANNES, E. 1895 L'Itinéraire d'Ou-K'ong, together with S. Lévi, *Journal Asiatique*. IV. Paris.

——— 1903 *Documents sur les Tou-kiue (Turcs) Occidentaux, recueillis et commentés, Librairie d'Amérique et d'Orient*. Paris.

——— 1904 Notes Additionelles sur les Tou-kieu (Turcs) Occidentaux. *T'oung Pao* Serie II, Vol.II.

DANI, A.H. 1987 Mediaeval Kingship in Gilgit. *Journal of Asiatic Society of Bangladesh* (Hum.) Vol.XXXII, No.2.

DAS, Sarat Chandra. 1902 *Tibetan-English Dictionary*. Calcutta.

EMERSON, Richard M. 1984 Charismatic Kingship:A study of State-Formation and Authority in Baltistan, *Journal of Central Asia* Vol. VII, No.2, Dec.

EMMERICK, R.E. 1967 Tibetan Texts concerning Khotan. *London Oriental Series* Vol.19, Oxford University Press, London, New York, Toronto.

FRANCKE, A.H. 1914 & 1926 *Antiquities of Indian Tibet*. Vol.I & II, Calcutta.

FUCHS, Walter. 1938 *Huei-ch'ao's Pilgerreise durch Nordwest-Indien und Zentral-Asien um 726.* Sitzungsberichte der Preußischen Academie der Wissenschaften Phil-Hist Klasse, Berlin.

FUSSMAN, G. 1978 Inscriptions de Gilgit, *Bulletin de l'Ecole Francaise d'Extreme Orient*, Tome LXV, Fasc.-p.1-64.

GERGAN, Joseph. 1976 *Bla-dvags rgyal-rabs 'c'i-med gter*. New Delhi.

GHULAM MUHAMMAD. 1905-1907/reprint 1980 Festivals and Folklore of Gilgit. *Memoirs of the Asiatic Society of Bengal* I, No.7, Reprint by National Institut of Folk Heritage, Islamabad.

GÖBL, Robert. 1967 *Dokumente zur Geschichte der Iranischen Hunnen in Baktrien und Indien*. Bd I-IV, Otto Harrassowitz, Wiesbaden.

HILL, J.E. 1988 Notes on the dating of Khotanese history. *Indo-Iranian Journal* 31/3, 179-190.

HARMATTA, J. 1969 Late Bactrian Inscriptions. *Acta Antiqua Academiae Scientiarum Hungaricae* 17.

HAUGHTON, H.L. 1913 *Sport and Folklore in the Himalaya*. London.

HUMBACH, H. 1966 *Baktrische Sprachdenkmäler*, 1, Wiesbaden.

——— 1983 Phrom Gesar and the Bactrian Rome. *Ethnologie und Geschichte Festschrift für Karl Jettmar*, Herausgegeben von Peter SNOY, Franz Steiner Verlag, Wiesbaden.

JETTMAR, K. 1975 Die Religionen des Hindukusch. *Die Religionen der Menschheit* Bd.4,1, Verlag W. Kohlhammer, Stuttgart.

——— 1989 *Antiquities of Northern Pakistan*. Reports and Studies, Vol 1, Text & Plates, Phillip von Zabern, Mainz.

——— 1993 *Antiquities of Northern Pakistan*. Reports and Studies, Vol 2, Phillip von Zabern, Mainz.

KHAN, Hashmatullah. 1939 *Tarikh-i Jammun wa Kashmir, or the History of Jammu and Kashmir, and of the other conquered territories including the area of Tibet* (in Urdu). Lucknow.

KVAERNE, Per. 1970 Un nouveau document relatif a l'Épopée Tibétaine de Gesar. *Bulletin de l'Ecole Francaise d'Extreme-Orient* Tome LVII, p.221-229, Paris.

LEITNER, G.W. reprint/1978 *Dardistan in 1866, 1886 and 1893*. reprint by Manjusri Publishing House, New Delhi.

MARSH, H.C. 1876 *Description of a trip to the Gilgit Valley, a dependancy of the Maharaja of Kashmir*. JASB,45.

MÜLLER-STELLRECHT, I. 1973 *Feste in Dardistan. Darstellung und kulturgeshichtliche Analyse*. Frankfurt am Main,5, Wiesbaden.

——— 1979 *Materialien zur Ethnographie von Dardistan (Pakistan), Aus den nachgelassenen Aufzeichnungen von D.L.R. Lorimer*, Teil I. Hunza, Graz.

———1980 *Materialien zur Ethnographie von Dardistan (Pakistan), Aus den nachgelassenen Aufzeichnungen von D.L.R. Lorimer*, Teil II. Gilgit, Teil.III Chitral und Yasin. Graz.

ROERICH, George N. 1942 The Epic of King Kesar of Ling. *Journal of the Royal Asiatic Society of Bengal* Vol.VIII, Article No.7,p.277-314.

RóNA-TAS, A. 1984 *On the birth of the Ge-sar epic*, Unpublished manuscript of a paper read at Visegrád-Budapest.

SACHAU, E.C. 1910/reprint 1983 *Alberuni's India*, Vol. I & II, Reprint Munshiram Manoharlal, Delhi.

SCHOMBERG, R.C.F. 1935 *Between the Oxus and the Indus*. London.

——— 1936 *Unknown Karakoram*. London.

——— 1938 *Kafirs and glaciers, travels in Chitral*. London.

SCHULER, Sidney. 1978 The "Story of the creation of Shigar" of Wazir Ahmad. *Central Asiatic Journal*, Vol.XXII, 1978.

STEIN, M.A. 1907 *Ancient Khotan*, Vol. I, Oxford.

——— 1973 A Contribution to the History of the Sahis of Kabul. *East & West*,

Vol.XXIII, No. 1-2. Roma.

STEIN, R.A. 1959 *Recherches sur l'épopée et le barde au Tibet*. Thèse pour le Doctorat ès Lettres présentée à la Faculté des Lettres de l'Université de Paris. Paris.

——— 1972 *Tibetan Civilization*, London.

THOMAS, F.W. 1935/1951/1955 *Tibetan Literary Texts and Documents concerning Chinese Turkestan*. Part I, Vol. XII/1935; Part II,Vol.XXXVII/1951; Part III, Vol.XL/1955, The Royal Asiatic Society, London.

——— 1944 Sino-Kharoshti coins. *Numismatic Chronicle*, IV,p.83-98.

URAY, Géza. 1979 The Old Tibetan Sources of the History of Central Asia up to 751 A.D. *Prolegomena to the Sources on the History of Pre-Islamic Central Asia*, ed. J.Harmatta, 41-60, Akadémiai Kiadó, Budapest.

——— 1985 Vom Römischen Kaiser bis zum König Ge-sar von Glin. *Fragen der Mongolischen Heldendichtung*, Teil III, Herausgegeben von Walter Heissig, Otto Harrassowitz, Wiesbaden.

VOHRA, R. 1983 History of the Dards and the concept of Minaro traditions among the Buddhist Dards in Ladakh. *Recent Research on Ladakh*, ed. by D.Kantowsky and R.Sander in Shriftenreihe Internationales Asienforum, Bd.I, Weltforum Verlag, Köln.

——— 1985 *Historical Documents from the Nubra Valley*. Part.I: Facsimile Edition of Stone inscriptions and the Manuscript of the History of bDe-skyid Monastery; Archiv für Zentralasiatische Geschichtsforschung, VGH Wissenschaftsverlag, St. Augustin, Germany.

——— 1985a Ethno-historical notes on Nubra in Ladakh. *Acta Biologica*, Vol.5, 2nd Ladakh Workshop, Pau, France.

——— 1987 An Old Route Across Karakoram Mountains, from Khapalu in Baltistan to Yarkand. *United Services of India Journal* (USI), 268-276.

——— 1988 Ethno-Historicity of the Dards in Ladakh-Baltistan: Observations and Analysis. *Tibetan Studies*, Band II, Proceedings of the 4th Seminar of the International Association for Tibetan Studies, ed. by H.Uebach & Jampa L. Panglung, Munich 1988.

——— 1989 *The Religion of the Dards in Ladakh, Investigations into their pre-Buddhist 'Brog-pa Traditions*. Skydie Brown International, Ettelbruck, Luxembourg.

——— 1989a *An Ethnography, The Buddhist Dards of Ladakh, Mythic lore - Household - Alliance System - Kinship*. Skydie Brown International, P.O.Box.66, Ettelbruck, Luxembourg.

——— 1990 An Old Route across the Karakoram Mountains from Khapalu in Baltistan to Yarkand. *Wissenschaftsgeschichte und gegenwärtige Forschungen in Nordwest-Indien*. Herausgegeben Lydia Icke-Schwalbe und Gudrun Meier, Staatliches Museum für Völkerkunde, Dresden, 125-128.

——— 1992 *Ethnic Festivals in Ladakh: The Buddhist 'Brog-pa. 166 page Unpublished Manuscript* (Draft Sept.1992) presented to the Indian Council of Social Science Research for a Senior Fellowship awarded for the years 1990-1992.

——— 1992a (Forthcoming) *Sogdian Inscriptions from Tangtse in Ladakh*. Paper delivered at the Sixth Conference of the International Association of Tibetan Studies, Fagernes, Norway, August 21-28th, 1992.

——— 1993 Antiquities on the Southern Arteries of the Silk Route: Ethnic movements and New Discoveries. *Anthropology of Tibet and Himalaya*, ed. Charles Ramble and Martin Brauen. Ethnological Museum of the University of Zurich, Zurich.

——— 1995 (this volume) Arabic Inscriptions of the Late First Millenium A.D. from Tangtse in Ladakh.

GATEWAY TO CENTRAL ASIA
the Transhimalayan Trade of Ladakh, 1846 - 1947

K. Warikoo[1]

Its contiguity with Central Asia and Tibet and its proximity to the Silk route turned Ladakh into a major gateway in the Indo-Central Asian exchange of men and materials through the ages. Enjoying a central position in the network of caravan trails, Leh - the capital of Ladakh - was an important transit emporium where Indian traders met their counterparts from Tibet, Central Asia and Afghanistan. Undaunted by numerous physical obstacles these traders peddled across the lofty Himalayan and Karakoram mountains and the barren deserts displaying a unique adventurous spirit. Usually the traders would exchange or sell their goods at Leh, thus making it the terminal point of the multilateral trade carried between India, Tibet and Central Asia. This paper seeks to analyse the extent and pattern of foreign trade carried through Ladakh with adjoining territories of Chinese Turkestan and Tibet, and also to assess the impact of this transhimalayan trade on the society and culture of Ladakh.

Trade routes

Numerous caravan routes that converged near Leh acted as the channels of communication between India and Central Asia. From the Indian side the bulk of the trade passed through the Srinagar-Leh route, though traders from Skardu, Kishtwar, Kulu, Lahoul, Spiti, Nurpur and Bushahr used to carry on their business with Ladakh directly through the Khapalu-Chorbat-Nubra, Kishtwar-Zanskar and Kulu-Rohtang pass-Lahoul-Keylong-Bara Lacha pass-Rupshu-Longa Lacha pass-Thung Lung La and Leh routes respectively. To the east of Ladakh a caravan trail passed through Gartok towards Lhasa, the capital of Tibet. In the north Ladakh stood connected with the Silk route at Yarkand by a caravan route running across the Karakoram pass. From Leh there existed three paths leading to Yarkand - the nearest big trading centre of Central Asia. Those traders and passers-by who opted to travel to Yarkand in winter would cross the Digar La

---

1. Assoc. Prof., Central Asian Studies Division, School of International Studies, Jawaharlal Nehru University, New Delhi 110067, INDIA.

and follow the narrow and winding valleys of the Shyok river. The Shyok, which was frozen during winter, had to be crossed and recrossed several times. After negotiating the Karakoram pass traders would start their descent towards Yarkand passing through Kugiar and Karghalik. But it was usual for the Central Asian and Indian traders to bring their caravans to Ladakh in summer and start their return journey homewards in the autumn. The summer route from Leh to Yarkand passed through Khardung La, Nubra valley, Saser La, Karakoram pass and the Suget pass. Yet another route ran across the Changla pass, the Chang Chenmo valley and Lingzithang plains to join the Leh-Yarkand summer route at Shahidulla. The Chang Chenmo valley route to Eastern Turkestan was improved considerably after the conclusion of a treaty between the Kashmir Durbar and the British Indian government in 1870. Under the treaty this route was also declared a free highway. Efforts were made to establish this track as the main trade route hetween Leh and Yarkand, as it was easier than those by the Shyok or Saser pass. But, being relatively longer in distance, and fuel, grass and water not being so abundantly available on this route, it did not become so popular with the traders, excepting those who used camels to transport their goods.

Notwithstanding its physical difficulties, the Srinagar-Leh-Yarkand route was the most important and long established thoroughfare between India and Central Asia. Even though the British authorities took numerous steps to improve the Kulu-Leh route with a view to encourage direct trading between British India and Central Asia, traders continued to use the Srinagar-Leh route as it was "the easiest and best supplied as to grass, provisions etc. and thoroughly open for two or three months longer than the Kulu route".[2] It. was through this route that the Kashmir shawl industry received its supplies of pashm wool that was imported into Ladakh from Tibet and Yarkand. Soon after his conquest of Ladakh, the Dogra general, Wazir Zorawar Singh, improved this route to make it an easy passage for mounted travellers[3]. This road was kept in excellent repair throughout the period of Dogra rule in Kashmir. As a sequel to the treaty concluded between Maharaja Ranbir Singh and T.Forsyth in April 1873, the Kashmir government allocated a yearly sum of 2,500 rupees for maintenance of roads and sarais along the Indo-Central Asian trade route which came to be known as the Treaty Road. In the

---

2. T.G.Montgomerie, Supt. G.T. Survey of India, Dehradun to the Lt.Governor, Punjab dated April 6, 1871. See *Foreign and Political A*. June 1871, 560-597 (National Archives of India).

3. Alexander Cunningham, *Ladak*, London 1854, p. 149.

late nineteenth century an extra annual grant of 5,000 rupees was made available by the Kashmir Durbar for this purpose[4]. There were two big caravan-sarais each at Leh and Srinagar for accommodating the traders and Central Asian pilgrims. Besides, godowns, stables, dak bungalows and inns were established at various stages of the route where traders received shelter and supplies of grain and forage for the ponies at subsidised rates. Similarly the villagers living in and around a particular stage of the trade route in Ladakh were responsible for supplying pony and coolie transport to traders and travellers at reasonable rates. It became known as "Res" system under which 15 to 20 ponies would always be available at each stage for use of the traders, public servants and travellers enjoying official patronage[5]. Such was the safety of this route that in the event of unfavourable weather or death of ponies, traders would march on to the next safer stage leaving behind their goods which were fetched after the climate became favourable or substitute transport became available. As a result the Srinagar-Leh route became the most important thoroughfare between India and Central Asia during Dogra rule in Kashmir.

Extent and pattern of trade

Ladakh's place in the Indo-Central Asian trade was only that of a transit emporium, as it did not produce or consume much to make any indigenous trade of importance. Traders from Tibet, Central Asia and India gathered at Leh to exchange their merchandise. This commercial intercourse also provided strong support to the local trade passing between Leh and Skardu (Baltistan) which formed a Tehsil of the Ladakh Wazarat of the State of Jammu and Kashmir during Dogra rule[6].

Local trade with Baltistan

The domestic trade between Leh and Skardu was similar in nature to what was carried between Leh and adjoining areas like Nubra, Zanskar, Purig and Chang Thang. It passed through two channels: (i) Leh-Indus Valley-Skardu; and (ii) Leh-Nubra-Chorbat-Khapalu. A substantial number of Baltis would visit Leh throughout the year. Balti peasants and petty traders brought for sale to Ladakh the produce of their farms and households such as apricots, apricot oil,

---

4. R.L.Kennion to A.C.Talbot, Resident in Kashmir dated August 16, 1900 See *Foreign Extl.* B, February 1901, 339-340 (National Archives of India).
5. E.Joldan, *Harvest Festival of Buddhist Dards of Ladakh and other essays*. Srinagar 1985, pp. 64-5.
6. *Census of India, 1941* Vol XXII, Jammu & Kashmir 1943 p. 481.

butter, grapes, almonds, barley, tea cups, stone vessels for cooking, woollen cloth and coarse shawls. They took back in exchange Indian cotton cloths and other piece goods, tea, gold and silver thread, Yarkandi leatherware, sheeps' wool and also some quantity of Yarkandi wool which was used in the manufacture of Balti shawls. From Leh these apricots and coarse shawls were transmitted to Lhasa and Yarkand through the medium of regular trade channels. Some adventurous Baltis went as far as Yarkand in search of employment and stayed there for a few years to work as manual labour. On their return home these Baltis used to invest their savings in purchasing merchandise which they carried to and sold in Baltistan. Unemployed Baltis would earn their livelihood by working as porters and pony drivers for traders. The trans-Himalayan trade that passed through Ladakh further integrated its economy with that of Baltistan which was already under its administrative jurisdiction.

Trade with Tibet

Ladakh's trade with Tibet was regulated by the Treaty of Tingmosgang concluded in 1684, under which Ladakh got the monopoly over shawl-wool produced in Tibet, and the Tibetans acquired the exclusive right to the brick-tea trade with Ladakh[7]. The treaty also provided for the despatch of periodical missions by Ladakh to Lhasa carrying presents for the Dalai Lama[8]. Since the bearers of this religious mission were allowed to carry merchandise, it soon acquired a commercial character. The shawl-wool that was imported into Ladakh was exclusively exported to Kashmir through the agency of Kashmiri merchants. Brick-tea imported from Tibet was almost entirely consumed within Ladakh and also forwarded to Kashmir. Such trade ties between Ladakh and Tibet were reinforced by the Treaty of 1842 concluded between the Dogra and Tibetan officials. Under this treaty semi-official trade missions were exchanged at intervals between Leh and Lhasa[9]. The triennial mission which left Leh for Lhasa carrying presents and merchandise was known as the *lopchak* mission. The annual Tibetan caravan coming to Leh with brick-tea and other goods was called *chaba.* Whereas the Ladakhi traders were entitled to free transport, and accommodation during their travel and stay in Tibet, traders from Tibet enjoyed similar facilities

---

7. A.H.Francke, *Antiquities of Indian Tibet*, 1926 vol. 2, pp. 116-7.
   M.W.Fisher, Leo E.Rose and R.A.Huttenback, *Himalayan battleground: Sino-Indian rivalry in Ladakh*. London 1963, p. 39.
8. *Ibid.*, p. 40.
9. *Ibid.,* p. 55-6.

during their sojourn in Ladakh. After the final annexation of Ladakh by the Dogras in 1842, the *lopchak* mission lost its religious character. It was now being managed by professional traders, mainly Kashmiri Muslims settled in Leh, who earned large profits in the transactions. Sven Hedin who called on the well-known Muslim merchant, Haji Nazer Shah, at Leh during a stopover in his journey to Tibet in 1906 was astonished to see in his commercial house "chests full of silver and gold dust, turquoise and coral, materials and goods" to be sold in Tibet[10]. He soon found that the source of this wealth was their monopoly over the *lopchak* mission which fetched them an annual profit of about 25,000 rupees[11]. This Muslim family of about one hundred members, which was headed by Nazer Shah, was entrusted "the duty of carrying out the *lopchak* mission" by the Mahaharaja of Kashmir and at the time of Sven Hedin's visit they had been retaining this confidential post "for some fifty years"[12]. The close involvement of Kashmiri Muslim settlers in the trade with Tibet can be gauged from the fact that even as late as in 1959 about 129 such families having about 600 members were residing in Lhasa-Shigatse area of Tibet[13].

The Ladakhi imports from Tibet comprised fine pashm wool, brick-tea, salt, China silks, tea cups, carpets, paper and musk[14]. Strachey who visited Ladakh in 1847 estimated the value of such imports as one and a quarter lakh rupees[15]. Ladakh's exports to Tibet comprised silver bullion (*yambus*), gold, China silk and coarse cotton goods received from Eastern Turkestan, glass-ware, coral, cotton cloths, chintzes, brocades, goatskins and furs imported from British India, saffron and rice from Kashmir and apricots and barley of Ladakh and Baltistan[16]. Apricots, Chinese silver, Turkestan-made cotton goods and silk cloth and Kashmir saffron constituted the bulk of Ladakhi exports to Tibet. Much of this trade was generated by the heavy demand for pashm wool in Kashmir which had developed into

---

10. Sven Hedin, *Trans Himalaya*. London 1909, vol. I, p. 57.
11. *Ibid.*, p. 59.
12. *Ibid.*, p. 58.
13. For further details see *Note given by the Ministry of External Affairs, New Delhi, to the Embassy of China in India, September 24 1959*. (India, Ministry of External Affairs, *Notes, memoranda & letters exchanged between the Governments of India & China, Sept. to Nov. 1959. White paper II*. New Delhi 1959, pp. 88-96.)
14. H.Strachey, *Account of Ladakh trade. Foreign S.C.* 12 Sept. 1852, 153-6 (National Archives of India).
15. *Ibid.*
16. *Ibid.*

the main centre of shawl production. The assured supplies of pashm wool from Tibet not only sustained Kashmir's shawl industry, but also provided new avenues of employment to skilled and unskilled workers in Ladakh and Kashmir. Tibet was dependent on Ladakh and Kashmir for supplies of essential goods like food grains, saffron, coarse cotton cloth, leather and apricots. That the cotton and silk fabrics produced in Kashgar and Khotan were also transmitted to Tibet through Ladakh, shows that there existed no direct communication between Western Tibet and Eastern Turkestan during this period. The annual turnover of Ladakh's trade with Tibet during Dogra rule amounted to several lakh rupees. This trade suffered heavily after the Chinese troops occupied Tibet in 1950. It continued to operate however, though under strains, until it came to a standstill in 1959 following disturbances in Tibet.

Indian — Central Asian trade in Ladakh

The bulk of Indian trade with Central Asian towns of Yarkand, Kashgar and Khotan was carried through Ladakh. Central Asian exports to Ladakh comprised gold and silver, cannabis hemp drug (*charas*), shawl wool, carpets and felts, tea, Chinese tea-cups, leather-ware, coarse cotton cloths, raw silk and ponies Out of these items bullion, *charas* and shawl-wool constituted the major imports. The Yarkandi and Andijani traders used to bring these goods to Ladakh where they exchanged the same with their Indian counterparts. Occasionally the Central Asian traders would move forward to Kashmir and Punjab in the hope of realising better profits. Similarly Indian traders would also proceed beyond Ladakh towards Yarkand to make direct purchases at relatively lower prices. Indian traders brought to Leh Indian and British-made cotton cloths, brocades, Kashmir shawls, indigo, spices, dyed goatskins, opium, preserved fruits, coral, indigenous medicines, sugar and books. Whereas most of the Indian imports were exported to Yarkand, part of them also went to Lhasa.

In the late 1840s merchandise valued at about seven and a half lakh rupees exchanged hands in Ladakh each year[17]. Out of this figure, the imports from Yarkand and India via Kishtwar, Nurpur, Kulu and Bushahr represented the amount of 1.75 and 4.50 lakhs respectively[18]. Another contemporary estimate of trade passing through Ladakh has been provided by Cunningham who visited Leh twice during the years 1846-47. According to him annual Indian

17. *Ibid.*
18. *Ibid.*

imports into Ladakh averaged 220,000 rupees, whereas the Central Asian exports to India via Ladakh were valued at 238,000 rupees[19]. This meant an annual trade turnover of a little more than four and a half lakh rupees. Though Cunningham's estimate is much less than that of Strachey, we get a rough assessment of the volume of annual trade passing through Ladakh in the 1840s which can be safely put between six to seven lakh rupees. (1 lakh = 100,000.)

The extent and pattern of overland Indo-Central Asian trade carried through Ladakh fluctuated from time to time due to the changing political situation in Central Asia. In the early nineteenth century, when the relations betueen Omar Khan, the ruler of Kokand and the Chinese authorities in Eastern Turkestan had become strained, all the Andijani traders left Yarkand for their country and abandoned their business trips to Ladakh[20]. This resulted in a considerable decrease in Yarkandi exports to Ladakh[21]. Such disruptions in trade occurred even afterwards when Eastern Turkestan was rife with turmoil caused due to Khoja uprisings against the Chinese rulers.

Till the late 1860s Yarkandi exports to Ladakh were mainly in the form of Bukharan and Kokandi gold coins, Khotanese gold dust and jade, Chinese silver ingots, tea, hemp drug, China silk, Russian leather etc. Chinese silver *yambus* were abundantly available in Ladakh at the rate of about 170 rupees each. These were largely exported to Kashmir where they were melted and manufactured into silverware. According to Hugel, an Austrian traveller who visited Kashmir in 1830s, these silver ingots bearing Chinese stamp markings were made into coins in Kashmir[22]. It was during this period that large quantities of opium produced in Kishtwar and Bushahr were exported to Eastern Turkestan where it was consumed by the Chinese traders and civil and military officials. Despite the Chinese prohibition imposed in 1839 on the import of opium this drug was exported to Eastern Turkestan by Indian traders to the extent of 210 maunds (8 tonnes) per year with the connivance of Chinese customs officials[23]. During Yakub Beg's rule in Kashgaria (1867-77) little or

---

19. A.Cunningham, *Ladak*, p. 251.
20. W.Moorcroft, *Travels*. London 1841, vol. I. p. 253.
21. Moorcroft, who was in Leh at about the same time, was witness to the delayed arrival of a small caravan of 25 horses laden with shawl-wool, felts, tea and silk at Leh in the autumn of 1820 from the direction of Yarkand. See his *Travels*, vol. I, p. 252.
22. C.B.Hugel, *Kashmir under Maharaja Ranjit Singh: its artistic products, taxation system, imports, exports and trade*. Translated from the German and annoted by D.C.Sharma. New Delhi 1984, p. 61.
23. R.H.Davies, *Report on the trade and resources of the countries on the north-*

no opium was exported to that place. But soon after, the value of Indian opium exported to Chinese Turkestan during the years 1878 to 1880 reached the figure of 86,000 rupees because the Chinese consumers had reappeared in Kashgaria[24].

The volume of trade between India and Kashgaria registered a steady increase after the Chinese were driven out of that country by Yakub Beg in 1867. This was owing to the stoppage of all Chinese imports into Eastern Turkestan and also due to the development of harmonious relations between Yakub Beg and the British Indian authorities. The abolition of all transit duties on merchandise passing to and from Central Asia through Kashmir and Ladakh by Maharaja Ranbir Singh also encouraged this trade. During the rule of Yakub Beg in Kashgaria export of Indian tea to that quarter increased considerably. Even the Chinese tea imported into Ladakh via Lhasa and Punjab was exported to Eastern Turkestan to meet the shortages caused there by the cessation of its trade with China. The British-manufactured cotton and silk cloths now began to substitute the Indian cotton prints and silks. However, *charas*, pashm wool and ponies continued to be imported into Ladakh from Eastern Turkestan as heretofore. Indian exports to Eastern Turkestan shot up to an unprecedented figure of more than 8 lakh rupees during the year 1874.[25] This included arms and ammunition worth 120,000 rupees imported by Yakub Beg for his army[26]. Such an unusual increase in Indian exports was largely due to the fact that a British merchant named Russell took a large quantity of English cotton goods and silks to Eastern Turkestan for sale via Ladakh[27]. However, Ladakh's import and export trade with Eastern Turkestan decreased by more than four and a half lakh rupees in 1877 when unsettled political conditions prevailed there on account of a war between Yakub Beg and the Chinese forces[28].

The death of Yakub Beg in 1877 and the subsequent re-occupation of Eastern Turkestan by the Chinese did not result in any adverse impact on the Indo-Central Asian trade. Several factors were responsible for the continuance of this trade even after Sinkiang had become a Chinese possession in 1878. Firstly, the Chinese authorities

---

western boundary of British India. Lahore 1862, p. 65.

24. N.Elias, British Joint Commissioner, Ladakh to the Officer on Special Duty in Kashmir, 12 July 1881. *Foreign Genl. B*. September 1881, 144-5 (National Archives of India).
25. *Foreign Pol. A*. September 1875, 21-24 (National Archives of India).
26. *Ibid*.
27. *Ibid*.
28. *Foreign Pol. A*. September 1878, 45-69 (National Archives of India).

did not interfere in the long established trade between India and the southern oasis-towns of Sinkiang. Their restrictions on the import of Indian tea and opium also proved ineffective in the face of smuggling of these commodities in connivance with the Chinese customs officials.

Secondly, Sinkiang did not possess an industrial base to cater to its demand for manufactured and other piece goods that were imported mainly from Russia through the Kokand-Kashgar route and partly from India through the Srinagar-Leh-Yarkand route.

Thirdly, Indian trade with Bukhara, Kokand and other parts of Russian Central Asia which was hitherto carried through the Peshawar-Kab-Bukhara route was partly diverted to the Srinagar-Leh-Yarkand route after the Russians imposed strict restrictions on the import of British Indian goods into Russian Central Asia.

Fourthly, the arrival at Leh of Central Asian pilgrims on their Haj Pilgrimage to Mecca via India also contributed to the increased Central Asian imports into Ladakh as they brought along with them a large quantity of bullion, silks and ponies for sale in Leh or Srinagar.

Fifthly, the complete security of the Srinagar-Leh-Yarkand route which was devoid of robbers and the facilities available at various stages of this route so far as the supply of ponies, porters, food and fodder was concerned, also helped in the development of Ladakh as an important trading centre.

After the conclusion of the Russo-Chinese treaty at St.Petersburgh in 1881 the bilateral overland trade between Sinkiang and Russia scaled new heights. This in turn affected Indian trade with Sinkiang in more than one way, as it had now to face stiff competition from Russia in that quarter. Now the import of Khotanese gold dust and Chinese silver ingots into Ladakh was substituted by that of Russian gold and paper roubles. The Yarkandi felts and Khotanese carpets became dearer in Ladakh and Kashmir as their prices appreciated due to increased demand in the Russian markets. And a lesser quantity of Turfani fine wool was imported into Ladakh, as the same was being supplied to Russian Turkestan in large quantities. Import of coarse wool and pashm from Chinese Turkestan dropped considerably in value from 1930 onwards. But the prosperity of the Russo-Sinkiang trade also meant a corresponding increase in Indian trade with Sinkiang. Since Sinkiang's exports to Russia far exceeded the imports from that end, the balance was met by rouble payments which ensured a regular and abundant supply of Russian currency in the markets of Kashgaria. This in turn led to increased imports from India which were now paid back largely in Russian gold and paper roubles and raw silk. However, *charas* continued to be imported into Ladakh despite its heavy taxation in India. An average of 3,000 to

3,500 maunds of *charas* (115-135 tonnes) was annually imported into Ladakh from Chinese Turkestan during the years 1882 to 1932. Most of this *charas* was consumed in the Punjab and Oudh whence it was carried by Indian traders via the Leh-Kulu route.

The years 1890 to 1908 saw an unusual increase in coral exports to Chinese Turkestan from India. During this period coral worth about twenty-four lakh rupees was exported. There existed a strong tradition among the Central Asians to use coral ornaments. About half of the coral exported to Chinese Turkestan was re-exported from there to Russian Turkestan. But this trade, which was entirely in the hands of Indian merchants, reached lts lowest point in 1918 when coral worth about 180 rupees only was exported from Ladakh[29]. At the close of the nineteenth century Russian currency began to occupy an important place in the Indian imports from Chinese Turkestan. Rouble import was resorted to by the Indian traders as a forced medium for sending back their sale proceeds to India. Russian gold and paper roubles worth about 80 lakh rupees were imported into India via Ladakh during the years 1897 to 1919.

With the establishment of Soviet power in Central Asia, the bilateral trade between Sinkiang and Russian Turkestan received a setback. It was now diverted to Ladakh. This resulted in an unusual increase in the Indian exports to Sinkiang through Ladakh. During the years 1917 to 1931 goods worth about 285 lakhs of rupees were exported from India to Chinese Turkestan through Ladakh of which European cotton goods and silks, dyed skins, indigo, spices and tea constituted the main items. In the same period merchandise valued at about 330 lakh rupees was imported from Chinese Turkestan into Ladakh of which *charas,* Russian gold and paper roubles, gold dust, raw silk, carpets and felts were the main items. The balance of trade thus stood in Sinkiang's favour. The Indo-Central Asian trade through Ladakh, which had scaled an unprecedented height of more than 68 lakh rupees during the year 1920-21[30], began to decline in value soon after the opening of Russian overland trade with Sinkiang. From the late 1930s onwards internal disorders in Sinkiang began to act as a stumbling block to this trade which finally ceased to flow from 1949 following the Communist takeover of Sinkiang and the subsequent closure of Sinkiang to outside traffic. This deprived Ladakh of its importance as an emporium of the Indo-Central Asian trade that passed through a network of caravan trails crisscrossing Ladakh.

---

29. *Foreign Frontr. B.* February 1920, 125-7 (National Archives of India).
30. *Foreign Pol. Frontr.* B. November 1921, 16-18 (National Archives of India).

The impact of trade on Ladakh's society and culture

The passage of a lucrative trade between India and Central Asia through Ladakh left a distinct impression upon its socio-economic life. Leh, the capital of Ladakh, acquired a cosmopolitan character during the trading season when merchants of different nationalities coming from Bukhara, Andijan, Kashgar, Yarkand, Kabul, Badakhshan, Tibet, Amritsar, Hoshiarpur, Kulu, Nurpur, Bushahr and Kashmir arrived at Ladakh to sell their goods. The sparsely populated town of Leh suddenly hummed with activity which lasted throughout the summer months. This trade brought economic prosperity to all those who were in one way or the other involved in it. However, Ladakhis benefitted from this trade only partially because very few of them carried on their own businesses. Most of the Ladakhis being poor and illiterate contented themselves to act as pony-drivers and porters, or as suppliers of pack animals and forage to traders. Those Ladakhis, Arghuns and Kashmiri settlers in Leh who traded with Central Asia and Tibet turned into a richer and affluent class as compared to the majority of Ladakh's population which was poor. Buddhist traders of Ladakh were generally engaged in domestic trade. As against this, the Muslim traders of Leh were involved in trade on all routes and they maintained family and trade links in Skardu, Kashmir, Lahaul, Nurpur, Yarkand and Tibet. They wielded considerable influence in Ladakh which was quite disproportionate to their smaller numbers.

Due to circumstances of trade a number of Central Asian, Hoshiarpuri and Kashmiri merchants were obliged to take up their abode in Leh. Most of these traders indulged in marriages of convenience with the local Ladakhi girls and became an inseparable part of the Ladakhi society. Among them were such Kashmiri Muslims as traded with Tibet and exported pashmina wool and tea to Kashmir. Similarly some Central Asian merchants would stay back in Ladakh in times of political uncertainty in their homeland or owing to the closure of passes and take temporary Ladakhi wives. As a result a new hybrid class of Arghuns came into being. They were the offspring of Kashmiri or Central Asian traders who had taken Ladakhi wives, temporary or permanent. By and large the Arghuns continued with the tradition of trading with Central Asia or Tibet. Some of them also acted as the carriers of merchandise that belonged to traders.

The passage of trade through Ladakh influenced the dress, food and drinking habits of its people. Machine-made cloth brought by Indian traders, velvets, otter-skin hats, Khotanese or Chinese silk fabrics and Yarkandi cotton cloths were increasingly used by the local people, particularly the elite classes as their dress material. Chinese brick-tea imported from Lhasa and Yarkand was largely consumed within Ladakh. Part of this tea was also sent to Kashmir. Similarly, Yarkandi *pilau* (rice cooked with meat and spices) became an important addition to the Ladakhi cuisine. The use of steamed dumplings of meat locally called *mok mok* also became common in Ladakh. The affluent sections of Ladakhi society used to wear long leather boots that were imported from Yarkand. Some items of Yarkandi dress such as *pichak tungyu* (conch-handled knife) and *kosa masi* (long calf-leather footwear with a separate pair of leather slippers) became a fancy item of Ladakhi dress. The use of Chinese tea cups, jade articles from Khotan and Lhasa, Yarkandi steamers and teapots was also introduced in Ladakh. Central Asian visitors and Arghuns who frequented the route between Sinkiang and Ladakh introduced in Leh certain dance forms, such as tall-man, dragon, lion and *kishti* (boat) which were prevalent in Sinkiang.[31]

The farmers in Leh and surrounding villages like Stok, Shey, Spitok, Chushot, Choklamsar and other villages situated along the trade routes took to extensive cultivation of lucerne. The large-scale introduction of a perennial variety of this called Yarkandi *ol* is obviously the direct result of Ladakh's commercial intercourse with Yarkand.[32] The agriculturalists profited by leasing out their grass fields to traders and pony drivers to feed their ponies on. But this trade put a drain on the food resources of Ladakh. During the Dogra rule an average quantity of three to four thousand maunds of barley grain was collected as land revenue from Ladakhi peasants.[33] It amounted to less than half of the actual requirements of the traders.[34] The deficit was met partly by forced procurement of barley from Ladakhi cultivators at much lower prices than the actual market rates.[35] The result was that Ladakhi agriculturalists faced immense hardships as they were also required to deliver the grain at the godowns. State granaries were located at Leh, Saspol and Lamayuru, where barley was supplied to traders at fair prices.

Ladakhis indulged in large-scale weaving of coarse woollen cloth and blankets. They also manufactured sacking which was in constant demand from the traders who required the same for packing

---

31. E.Joldan, *op. cit*. p. 54.
32. Janet Rizvi, *Ladakh: Crossroads of High Asia*, Delhi 1983, p. 103.
33. E.G.Colvin, Resident in Kashmir to the Secretary to the Government of India, Foreign Department dated 17 May 1904. *Foreign Frontr. A*. June 1904, 110-111 (National Archives of India). 3-4,000 maunds = 110-150 tonnes.
34. *Ibid*.
35. *Ibid*

their goods. According to Cunningham, the quantity of blanketing and sacking annually consumed in Ladakh in connection with the carrying trade amounted to about 1,20,000 yards of one foot width in the manufacture of which about six and a half lakh pounds (300 tonnes) of wool were consumed.[36] But for this home made wool, Ladakhis were almost wholly dependent upon imports for their day-to-day requirements such as manufactured cotton cloth and silk, tea, spices, utensils, leather goods, felts, carpets, etc. Since these commodities were abundantly available at cheaper prices in the Leh market, no incentive was thereby left to promote local industry.

36. A.Cunningham, *Ladak*, p.23

Clarke Pl.1: Steel stove decorated with brass, early 1980's, kitchen of Standzin Bangmo, Leh.

Clarke Pl.2: *mChod-rten* made in 1981 for the Langto family in Changspa by *Phun-tshogs dPal-bzang*. 1 meter high, copper gilt.

Clarke Pl.3: *Phun-tshogs dPal-bzang* in his winter workshop at Chiling, in 1987

Clarke Pl.4: Teapot (*'Brug-lung-ma*) by *mGon-po bKra-shis* c. 1910. Copper from the Zangskar river and silver, 34 cm. high. Property of *Rig-'dzin rNam-rgyal bKa'-blon, Leh.*

Clarke Pl.5: Detail from no. 4, silver plaque with kinnara figure.

Clarke Pl.6: Cup cover, embossed silver by *mGon-po bKra-shis*, 10.5 cm. diameter. Property of *Rig-'dzin rNam-rgyal bKa'-blon*, Leh.

K.Howard Pl.1: Basgo: *Rag-po.*

K.Howard Pl.2: Stok: Lotsava *mChod-rten* (chorten) with cruciform type at right.

K.Howard Pl.3: Nyarma: Lotsava *mChod-rten*.

K.Howard Pl.4: Basgo: Ancient *mChod-rten*, similar to that at Man-gyu.

K.Howard Pl.5a: *lha-bab mChod-rten-* plinth type.

K.Howard Pl.5b: Shey: *lha-bab mChod-rten-* plinth type (lhaba chorten)-without plinth; stupa mandala in foreground.

K.Howard Pl.6: Chanspa: *bkra-shis-sgo-man* (tashi goma).

K.Howard Pl.7: Shey: stepped *mChod-rten.*

K.Howard Pl.8: Tisseru.

K.Howard Pl.9: Karsha: passage *mChod-rten*.

K.Howard Pl.10: Shey: hollow *mChod-rten* near gonpa.

K.Howard Pl.11: Sabu: lotus decoration.

K.Howard Pl.12: Taru: *mChod-rten* types: circular plinth (2nd left); *lha-bab* with lotus pattern (4th from right)

N.Howard Pl.1: Bardan Monastery, the gate-house is on the right; the revetting/wall and the outer gate below it; the flank wall runs down the edge of the hill, bottom right.

N.Howard Pl.2: Tarungtse, view from the north, ruins along the ridge of moraine; the tower (?) and the enclosure wall are to the right; the buildings, at A-A1 on Fig.1, to the left.

N.Howard Pl.3: Tarungtse, unbroken outer wall of buildings around A1 (north side looking west); note the stones are not dressed and little, if any, mud mortar has been used.

N.Howard Pl.4: Tower, opposite **Tungri,** view of tower from the north; the ruins of the lesser buildings run down the ridge to the left.

N.Howard Pl.5: Castle (?) opposite **Tungri,** view from south-east. From left: the ditched (?) saddle, massive wall with facetted trace and the gentler slope with remains of dwellings.

N.Howard Pl.6: Castle (?) opposite **Tungri,** loophole from inside, note: the stones appear to have been somewhat dressed and much of the mud mortar has weathered out.

N.Howard Pl.7: Umatanche tower, view from north, note loopholes and remaining mud mortar on left, windows on right.

N.Howard Pl.8: Umatanche tower, back view

N.Howard Pl.9: Tsha-zar, view from north.

N.Howard Pl.10: Zangla, view from west; chortens and approach path centre and left; the white building on the rock is the palace; the outer walls of the buildings of the town (the defensible settlement) are before it to right.

N.Howard Pl.11: Zangla palace, shuttered mud extensions on right; the blocked window with balcony and column capital is to left of flag pole; timber lacing can be seen in the near corner on left.

N.Howard Pl.12: Karsha monastery, upper tower, and triangular loopholes.

N.Howard Pl.13: Karsha monastery, lower tower, mud wall on left; the other wall of the V plan runs down the edge of the rock towards bottom right.

N.Howard Pl.14: Karsha monastery, banded texture masonry below towers.

N.Howard Pl.15: Karsha old castle, north-western apex tower, from north-east (ie. inside); window on left; the mud and brick cladding is the lighter material on the right.

N.Howard Pl.16: Phima Ralagung tower, the outbuildings were beyond the tower, where the rock is hidden.

N.Howard Pl.17: Padum hill-top temple, banded texture masonry.

The Fifth International Colloquium on Ladakh

SOAS, London 1992

5TH COLLOQUIUM

CONTENTS

The Fifth International Colloquium on Ladakh

Introduction

Prompted by Peter Marczell of Geneva, a colloquium was organised at SOAS on 1-2 June 1992, to mark the 150th anniversary of the death of Alexander Csoma de Kôrös the Hungarian scholar and linguist who, from studies mainly carried out in Zangskar, Ladakh, laid the foundations of the formal study of Tibetan.

Csoma de Kôrös, who already had command of thirteen languages, left Hungary in 1819 to seek for the origins of his people in central Asia. He reached Leh in 1822 but, foiled in his hopes to proceed to Yarkand, was returning to Srinagar when he met William Moorcroft at Dras. Encouraged and helped by Moorcroft he decided to decided embark on a study of Tibetan. He arrived in Leh for the second time on 1 June 1823 and was advised to study at Zangla in Zangskar under Lama Sangs-rgyas-phun-tshogs, a scholar, amchi and onpo who had himself studied classical Tibetan in Tibet. He was given a small room in the palace and studied there and at Dzonkhul monastery till the autumn of 1824.

After wintering in the more genial climate of Kulu he returned to Zangskar and spent a year studying at the spectacular monastery of Phugtal, eventually completing his studies after a further three years at Kanum in Lahul. During this time he received support from the British Government of India which also undertook the publication of his two main works, the Grammar and the Dictionary.

Although these concerned classical Tibetan rather than Ladakhi, their preparation depended on the ease of access to Ladakh and his welcome there, compared with Tibet itself, so that it is entirely appropriate that his memory should be linked closely with the former. The Dictionary has recently been republished in Delhi.

The following papers were presented to an audience numbering over sixty.

The colloquium was organised in four half-day sessions, respectively devoted to the subjects of Alexander Csoma de Kôrös; Ladakhi history; anthropology; and the arts. In the first session, as well as the papers by Peter Marczell and Elizabeth Tóth reproduced below, Dr.G.Bethlenfalvy of Budapest spoke on the topic of the early period of Tibetan Studies in which Csoma played such an important part, while Prof.G.Benedek from the University of Georgia, USA, drew attention to the present situation in Csoma's homeland of Transylvania, now part of Romania. The paper by Bernard Le Calloc'h was read in his absence.

The historical session comprised the papers by Philip Denwood, Neil Howard, John Bray and Gudrun Meier; the anthropological session those by Nicky Grist, Pascale Dollfus, James Crowden and Kim Gutschow, all reproduced below.

The session on the arts, as well as the papers by Rohit Vohra and Mark Trewin, included papers by Roger Goepper on inscriptions at the Great Stupa at Alchi (now published elsewhere*), and by James Crowden on early art from Zangskar.

The "Projekt Save Alchi" run by Roger Goepper and Jaroslav Poncar of Cologne contributed an exhibition of the latter's colour photographs and a video of restoration work at Alchi. Other videos shown were "The Bononah Festival of the Buddhist Dards in Ladakh" by Rohit Vohra, and "Near to The Top of the World" a film about the life of Alexander Csoma de Kôrös by Ferencz Nemenyi.

The Colloquium was made possible through the generosity of the School of Oriental and African Studies, the British Academy, the Hungarian Ministry of Culture and Public Education, the Embassy of the Republic of Hungary in London, and Hibtrade International Ltd. of London. The organising Committee were Hilary Armstrong, John Bray, Philip Denwood, Clare Harris, Mary Hood, Maria Phylactou, and Mark Trewin. I would particularly like to thank Clare Harris and Maria Phylactou for much hard work in preparing the Colloquium and this publication, and Peter Marczell for his initiative and enthusiasm.

Philip Denwood
Lecturer in Tibetan

School of Oriental & African Studies
Thornhaugh Street, Russell Square,
London WC1H 0XG U.K.

* "The 'Great Stupa' at Alchi". *Artibus Asiae LIII*, 1/2, 1993.

KASHMIR, LADAKH AND WESTERN TIBET
Episodes in Frontier Diplomacy during British Rule in India

John Bray[1]

The Ladakhi-Tibetan frontier was free from military conflict from 1842, when the Tibetan government signed a peace treaty with Jammu, until the outbreak of war between India and China 120 years later. *Pax Britannica* meant that the inhabitants of the border regions were able to concentrate on trade and their shared religious links rather than war. However, from the British point of view, relations between Ladakh and Tibet were frequently confused, and at times controversial. In an earlier article I discussed the Government of India's concern in the 1880s and the 1890s that the triennial *lo phyag* mission from Leh to Lhasa might imply Ladakh's subordination to Lhasa.[2] This article, which is based on the India Office Records in London, continues the story with an analysis of Ladakh frontier diplomacy between the 1890s and the 1940s.[3] Professor Alistair Lamb has previously drawn on the India Office records in his two magisterial studies of India's relations with Tibet.[4] In this paper I hope to

---

1. 8 Glendall Street, Brixton, London SW9 8AJ, U.K.

2. John Bray, "The Lapchak Mission from Ladakh to Lhasa in British Indian Foreign Policy." *The Tibet Journal*, 15 (1990) No. 4, pp. 75-96.

3. The India Office records referring to Ladakhi/Tibetan border issues come into two main categories: "Political and Secret" files concerned with India's external affairs; and files from the British Residency in Kashmir, a selection of which were sent to London after independence in 1947. Both sets of files have certain limitations. First, and most obviously, they represent the British rather than the Kashmiri, Ladakhi or Tibetan points of view. Secondly, the records are far from comprehensive. Officials from the Government of India's External Affairs Department selected only the most important information to send back to London and, from their perspective, Ladakhi border issues rarely came into this category. Moreover, one of the Residency files listed in the India Office index has been lost or mislaid (R/2 1068/113. File No. 140 of 1936-1940. Matters in dispute between Ladakh and Tibet). This paper therefore cannot claim to offer a complete history of Ladakhi frontier affairs, but it is hoped that it will point the way to more detailed research based on archives in India.

4. Alistair Lamb, *British India and Tibet , 1766-1910* (Revised edition. London and New York: Routledge & Kegan Paul, 1986); *Tibet China & India. A History of Imperial Diplomacy* (Hertingfordbury: Roxford Books, 1989) - see especially pp. 350-362. See also his *Sino-Indian Border in Ladakh* (Canberra: Australian

complement Lamb's work by examining Ladakhi local issues in greater detail.

Traditional political and commercial links between Ladakh and Western Tibet

The basis of Ladakh's relationship with Tibet was laid down in the treaty signed by the two countries in 1684.[5] Among other clauses, the treaty provided for the triennial *lo phyag* trade/tribute mission between Leh and Lhasa; the annual *cha pa* mission in the reverse direction; and the sale of wool from Western Tibet to Kashmir via Ladakh. The treaty formally separated Ladakh from Western Tibet *(mnga' ris skor gsum)*, and in doing so established what is roughly Ladakh's present frontier with Tibet although the precise demarcation of this boundary remains open to dispute to this day.

In Western Tibet the Lhasa government was represented by the two governors known as Garpons (*sgar dpon*), and these were responsible for most ordinary Tibetan government communications with Ladakh. The Garpons were appointed for fixed terms of three to six years[6] and their seat of government was at Gartok, some 18 days' march east of Leh. A hierarchy of more junior officials served under the Garpons. As far as Ladakh was concerned, the most important of these was the Dzongpen (*rdzong dpon* - also frequently transliterated as "Jongpen") at Rudok, some two days' journey east of the Ladakhi frontier.

Few Lhasa officials welcomed a posting to Gartok which was distant, isolated and uncomfortable: the main advantages of the position were financial. There were annual trade fairs at Gartok, Purang, Karko and Gyanima,[7] and the Garpons were well-placed to profit from trade and taxes - or a combination of the two. Under the the *pujjar* system their subjects were required to buy quantities of tea and other goods at prices which exceeded the market rate.

National University Press, 1973). Lamb does not refer to the Kashmir Residency records, which are particularly helpful on the background and consequences of the Lhagyal affair.

5. See: Luciano Petech, "The Tibetan-Ladakhi-Moghul War of 1681-1683." *India Historical Quarterly* 23 (1947), pp. 169-199; *The Kingdom of Ladakh* (Rome: Istituto Italiano per il Medio ed Estremo Oriente, 1977); Zahiruddin Ahmad, "New Light on the Tibet-Ladakh-Mughal War of 1679-1684." *East and West* 18 (1968), pp. 340-361.

6. Charles A. Sherring, *Western Tibet and the Indian Borderland*. (London: Edward Arnold, 1906; reprint ed.: New Delhi: Cosmo Publications, 1974), p. 309.

7. F.M. Bailey, *Report on the Trade and Trade Routes Between India and Nari Khorsum*. (Simla: Government Central Printing Office, 1905).

The Rudok district depended on Ladakh for its grain supplies. Muslim traders from Leh enjoyed special privileges and were traditionally exempt from local taxes.[8] The goods they brought to the region included flour, rice, carpets, sugar and cups of Yarkand stone. Ladakhi Buddhist farmers brought grain and dried apricots to exchange for salt, wool and small quantities of gold. Mules, ponies and donkeys were used for the journey from Ladakh to Rudok: sheep and goats bought in Tibet were drafted in as additional pack animals on the return journey.

Official Tibetan traders regularly visited Leh. The most important of the Tibetan trade missions was the *cha-pa* which carried some 200 animal-loads of brick tea from Lhasa once a year. Under the terms of the 1684 treaty, the *cha-pa* was entitled to free carriage in Ladakh (the system whereby villagers along the main routes provided free transport was known in Tibet as *'u lag* and in Kashmir as *kar begar).* Several other Tibetan representatives also were entitled to free transport. For example, the representatives of the Garpons were entitled to the provision of 30 pack animals and two riding ponies on their annual journeys to and from Ladakh.[9] Similarly, the representatives of Tashi Lhunpo monastery in Tibet were entitled to the use of 60 baggage animals and seven riding ponies on their visits, which took place at intervals of ten to fifteen years.

In 1834 Raja Gulab Singh of Jammu sent an army to conquer Ladakh, and the subsequent war interrupted the region's traditional relationship with Western Tibet. However, under the terms of the 1842 treaty between Tibet and Jammu, the Tibetan government recognised Raja Gulab Singh's title to Ladakh, and guaranteed the continuation of existing trade arrangements between the two countries - including the all-important wool trade which supplied Kashmir's shawl and carpet industries. Gulab Singh assumed the King of Ladakh's political and commercial responsibilities towards Tibet, including the sponsoring of the *lo-phyag* mission.[10]

When he conquered Ladakh, Gulab Singh was a feudatory of the Sikh empire in Lahore. However, in 1846, the British ceded Kashmir to him as a reward for his support in the First Sikh War. Gulab Singh thus became the first Maharaja of Jammu and Kashmir

---

8. IOLR. L/P&S/12/4163, p. 146.
9. Copy of a note dated 30th May 1900 by R.L. Kennion. IOLR L/P&S/7/125.
10. Although the King now held no formal political authority, he went on living in Ladakh and remained at the apex of the Ladakhi social hierarchy. Until the 1880s he continued to issue the *lam-yig* (passports) which the *lo-phyag* mission required to obtain free transport under the *'u-lag* system in Tibet. See Bray, 'The Lapchak Mission...", p. 86 ff.

under British paramountcy. The Kashmir Durbar (court) was responsible for the state's internal administration, but the British supervised its external relations including its links with Tibet - at least in theory. In practice, Gulab Singh tried to conduct a secret foreign policy of his own.[11]

In 1853 Basti Ram, who was Gulab Singh's Thanedar (governor) in Ladakh, signed a trade agreement with the representatives of the two Garpons.[12] The agreement was intended to settle a dispute which had arisen the previous year when Kelzang Gyurme, a Tibetan government trader, had complained that the Ladakhis failed to supply him with the prescribed number of pack animals. He had therefore been unable to bring his full quota of tea into Ladakh. Among other provisions the agreement stated that:

> It was agreed that the Ladakhis would supply horses to the Tibetan trade agencies according to the limit previously agreed upon.
>
> Salt and wool carried from Rudok [Western Tibet] to Ladakh should not be turned back. Similarly, tsamba and grain taken from Ladakh to Rudok should not be restricted. The prices of commodities and customs duties must not be raised by traders on either side; they must be maintained at the previous level.
>
> Tibetan traders carrying a permit from the Gartok governor and Ladakhi traders carrying a similar permit from the Thanedar are exempted from customs duties and need only make a token offering to the authorities. Traders without permits will have to pay a two per cent custom duty.
>
> Both parties agree that the local inhabitants of the two countries will provide free transport and accomodation to special agents travelling in emergencies. These agents will carry letters of authority.

Later official correspondence suggests that the British were unaware of the 1853 agreement, presumably because they were not consulted at the time. In practice, the British initially were handicapped by ignorance of Ladakh's historical links with Tibet - for example they did not learn the details of the 1684 treaty until the late 1880s - and by the fact that no British officials were stationed in Ladakh until the appointment of the first British Joint Commissioner from 1867 onwards. Even after 1867 the British Joint Commissioner

---

11. See: K.S. Warikoo, *Central Asia and Kashmir*. New Delhi: Gian Publishing House, 1989.

12. An English translation of the 1852 treaty is cited in: W.D. Shakabpa, *Tibet: a Political History* .' (New York: Potala Publications, 1984), pp. 328-329.

only spent the summer months in Leh, whereas much of the trade with Western Tibet took place in the winter.

The Government of India acquired new resources in Western Tibet after 1904. Under the terms of the 1904 Lhasa Convention British Trade Agents spent the summer months in Gartok and sent regular reports back to the Political Agent for the Punjab Hill States in Simla. However, the Trade Agents in Western Tibet were Indian rather than European officials, and Gartok never assumed great importance as a centre either for trade or for intelligence gathering. In spite of the presence of the Trade Agents in Gartok, Western Tibetan custom and reasoning frequently remained obscure to British officials in the Government of India External Affairs Department.

The Rudok grain dispute (1897-1899)

One of the purposes of the 1853 trade agreement was to ensure that essential grain supplies to Rudok would not be disrupted. However, in 1897 the Kashmir authorities banned the export of grain from Ladakh because of a local shortage, and this led to frictions between Ladakhis and Tibetans in Rudok.[13]

The Tibetans argued that the export ban constituted a breach of treaty and custom: the following year they expressed their anger by pulling down houses owned by Ladakhi traders in Rudok on the excuse that the traders had refused to pay rent. In late 1898 the authorities in Leh sent a Ladakhi Muslim called Ramzan Ali to Rudok to enquire into the causes of the dispute. He was able to negotiate an agreement according to which the Ladakhi traders would receive compensation for the damage to their houses, but would agree to pay rent in future. Meanwhile, the Garpons wrote to the authorities in Leh complaining of the prohibition on grain imports.

In August 1899 Captain R.L. Kennion, the British Joint Commissioner, was in Hanle district (eastern Ladakh) when he heard that fresh trouble was brewing in Rudok. He also heard that the people of the Ladakhi village of Shashol (Chushal?) were complaining that they were forced to pay grazing fees to the Tibetans in a disputed area near the Panggong lake. Kennion therefore rode to Rudok and held two days of talks with the Dzongpen. He was able to assure the Dzongpen that the ban on grain exports had been lifted because of that year's excellent harvest, and that the Kardar of Tankse in eastern Ladakh would cease making exactions from Rudok salt carriers. In

---

13. Captain R.L. Kennion to the Resident in Kashmir, 8 November 1899. Reproduced in Amar Singh Chohan, *Historical Study of Society and Culture in Dardistan and Ladakh*. (New Delhi: Atlantic Publishers, 1983), pp. 253-257.

return, the Dzongpen promised that Ladakhi traders would be well-treated in Rudok. He also said that the people of Shashol need not pay grazing fees until the boundary in the Panggong lake area was properly delimited although, as Kennion pointed out in his report, they had to some extent put themselves out of court by paying the fees on previous occasions.

In this case Kennion was able to settle disputes with Tibet amicably enough although tensions over grain exports and the boundary near the Panggong lake were to recur in subsequent years.

The Lhagyal affair (1917-1924)

The next major controversy concerned the Tibetans' kidnapping in 1917 of a Ladakhi called Lhagyal at Dokpo Karpo north of the Panggong Lake.[14] As a young man Lhagyal had gone to Tibet where he had married a Tibetan woman, worked hard and accumulated a fortune consisting of 30 yaks, two ponies and a large flock of sheep and goats. Having become rich by local standards, he returned home to Ladakh with his wife and his flocks - until he was abducted and carried off to Rudok. His brother, who visited him in Tibet, claimed that he was kept under surveillance to prevent him escaping.

The Government of India duly took up the Lhagyal abduction case with the Tibetan administration. It took some time to obtain an answer, but in December 1919 Lonchen Sholkhang, the "Chief Minister" in Lhasa, explained that Lhagyal had come under the authority of the Tibetan government while living with his wife, who was a subject of Ding-med near Rudok.[15] He had failed to pay taxes in Ding-med, and the local villagers had therefore submitted a petition to the effect that he might be taken to Rudok and made a regular tax-payer there. Dokpo Karpo was inside Tibetan territory, and the Tibetans were acting within their rights when they seized him.

In October 1920 the Tibetan authorities at last responded to British pressure by handing Lhagyal over to the British Trade Agent in Gartok. Before his release, Lhagyal agreed to pay an annual sum of Rs 75 in lieu of taxes due from his wife. At the time this was a considerable sum, and the Trade Agent commented that Lhagyal was not a clever man: he might not have been very clear-minded when he gave this undertaking.[16]

---

14. IOLR. R/2 (1066/57A).

15. *Ibid.*, British Trade Agent Gartok to Superintendent Hill States, Simla. 12 October 1920.

16. *Ibid.*, British Trade Agent Gartok to Superintendent Hill States, Simla. 12 October 1920.

Lhagyal's release solved his personal problems but the controversy over his abduction had raised several other issues. The first was the question whether Dokpo Karpo was in Kashmiri or Tibetan territory. Initially the Government of India had no doubt about the matter. Major D.G. Oliver, the British Joint Commissioner in 1918, claimed to have visited Dokpo Karpo and was certain that it lay well within the boundaries of Kashmir.[17] However, in 1921 the Ladakhi leader of the *lo-phyag* mission to Lhasa confided to C.A. Bell that he thought Dokpo Karpo was actually in Tibet.[18] The British Trade Agent from Gartok visited Dokpo Karpo on his own initiative and came to a similar conclusion.

The second issue was the status of Tibetan citizens in Ladakh. The Tibetan government clearly felt that it had made a significant concession in releasing Lhagyal and suggested that Kashmir should reciprocate by extraditing 12 Tibetan families living in Ladakh. This was as much an economic as a political question. As F.M. Bailey (then Political Officer in Sikkim) explained:

> The Tibetan Government regard their subjects settled on the land as revenue-producing serfs. They are not allowed to leave their land under any circumstances. Were they to do so, no revenue could be paid and, still more important from some points of view, no one would be able to travel as it is the duty of these same serfs to supply all transport and supplies required by officials travelling.[19]

---

17. *Ibid.*, p. 40. Major D.G. Oliver to Major C.H. Gabriel. 25 July 1918.

18. *Ibid.*, p. 125. C.A. Bell to Secretary, Government of India Foreign and Political Department.

19. *Ibid.*, p. 206. Letter from F. M. Bailey. 24 October 1920. The status of the Tibetan peasant has been the subject of a protracted debate in the pages of *The Tibet Journal*: Melvyn C. Goldstein, "Re-examining Choice, Dependency and Command in the Tibetan Social System: 'Tax Appendages' and Other Landless Serfs." *TJ* 11 [1986], No. 4, pp. 79-112; Beatrice D. Miller, "A Response to Goldstein's 'Re-examining Choice, Dependency and Command in the Tibetan Social System.'" *TJ* 12 [1987], No. 2, pp. 65-67; Melvyn C. Goldstein, "On the Nature of the Tibetan Peasantry: a Rejoinder." *TJ*. 13 [1988], No. 1, pp. 61-65; Beatrice D. Miller, "Last Rejoinder to Goldstein on Tibetan Social System." *TJ* 13, No. 3, pp. 64-66. The debate focused on the question whether the Tibetan word *mi ser* should be translated as "serf" or as "subject" or "commoner". Miller objected to Goldstein's use of the term "serf" because it implied an inappropriate comparison between the Tibetan system and Western feudalism. One of the main issues in the debate was the degree to which the *mi ser* exercised freedom of choice. The India Office records report that Western Tibetan peasants frequently chose to leave their estates, but that the penalties for doing so could be severe. For example, in 1931 the British Trade Agent in Gartok reported that two youths from Dongbo had been caught while trying to

The third issue echoed the 1897 grain dispute. In December 1919 the Garpons and the Rudok Dzongpen sent their representatives to Ladakh to purchase grain supplies as usual. However, they failed to receive the usual preferential treatment. As the British Trade Agent reported:

> They went to the Ladakhi officer concerned to ask for free Begar and a permit for export of provisions to Tibetan territory according to the treaty rights, but they were refused both concessions totally for the first time. After waiting for four months in Ladakh in the hope that they would succeed in securing free Begar and export permit, they reached Gartok, empty handed, in March 1920.[20]

The Trade Agent thought that the Ladakhi grain embargo might have been instrumental in persuading the Tibetans to release Lhagyal, but at the same time it raised new problems because the Garpons threatened to introduce a retaliatory ban on exports of wool, salt and borax to Ladakh. The Garpons' reference to their "treaty rights" raised a further question: what exactly were the Tibetans' entitlements?

It was in this context that Government of India officials first became aware of the 1853 trade agreement between Kashmir and Tibet. Their initial response was to suggest that the Garpons may indeed have been entitled to certain rights under the 1853 treaty, but that it had been superseded by the 1904 Lhasa convention.[21] Nevertheless, they eventually decided that the best way of resolving all these issues was to hold a face-to-face meeting on the Tibetan border.

The Dokpo Karpo meeting of 1924 and its consequences

The meeting duly took place at Dokpo Karpo itself in the summer of 1924. The Wazir represented Kashmir and the senior of the two Garpons represented Tibet. Major Robson, the British Joint Commissioner, also attended on the ground that the disputes involved Kashmir's foreign relations and any decisions would therefore require ratification by the Government of India.

---

flee to India. The estate-owner had responded counter-productively from an economic point of view - by having the youths flogged so heavily that they died (Diary of the BTA Gartok. IOLR. L/P&S/12/4163, p. 379). When using such terms as "serf", Bailey and his colleagues did not apply the analytical rigour required of modern anthropologists. Nevertheless, one suspects that they would have sided with Goldstein rather than Miller.

20. IOLR. R2 (1066/57A). British Trade Agent to Superintendent Hill States, Simla.
21. *Ibid.*, pp. 103-132.

Dr A. Reeve Heber, a Moravian missionary based in Leh, accompanied Robson and wrote a colourful account of the meeting.[22] He described Dokpo Karpo as a "large grassy plain surrounded by snow mountains". The Joint Commissioner and the Wazir pitched their tents at the far end, with the British and Kashmiri flags flying outside, and a carpeted square tent with a table and chairs served as the conference room. The Garpon was preceded not by a flag but by an "Umbrella-of-State-Bearer" and, with an eye to the picturesque, Heber commented on the wide variety of hats worn by the Tibetans. The actual discussions were amicable, but largely inconclusive.

Neither Kashmir nor Tibet were prepared to give ground on the boundary issue either at the Dokpo Karpo meeting or subsequently. In 1929 the Surveyor General of India conducted a detailed analysis of the evidence.[23] He concluded that Tibet's claim was by far the better, and recommended to the Kashmir Durbar that it concede gracefully. The Durbar rejected this advice, and the Government of India therefore decided to let the matter drop, on the ground that it had "no real practical importance". The dispute was therefore left unresolved, although it never flared up into a major controversy until after independence.

The status of Tibetan citizens in Ladakh also was left unresolved. The Tibetans argued that their economy would collapse if serfs were allowed to leave the country. On the other hand, the British said that the Tibetans in Ladakh had committed no offence, and could not be forced to return to their own country against their will. This response did not satisfy the Tibetans. In subsequent years the people of Rudok organised a series of armed raids into the Ladakhi territory of Rupshu to capture recalcitrant Tibetan tax-payers.[24]

The British and Kashmiri representatives were able to make one favourable gesture in that they explained that the 1919 embargo on grain exports to Rudok had been a temporary measure in reponse to a local shortage and had now been lifted. However, they proposed that the system whereby certain privileged traders - such as the Garpons -

---

22. A. Reeve Heber, *In Himalayan Tibet.* (First published 1926; reprint ed. *In Himalayan Tibet and Ladakh*. New Delhi: Ess Ess Publications, 1977), pp. 100-108.

23. H.E. Richardson. *Tibetan Precis.* (Calcutta, 1945; IOLR. L/P&S/20/D222), pp. 122-123. This is the best available account of the Dokpo Karpo meeting and its consequences, but it is only a summary. The Kashmir Residency records cited above give a detailed account of the run-up to the Dokpo Karpo meeting, but the file dealing with the meeting itself is not in the IOLR index.

24. *Ibid.* There is another reference to Tibetan raids into Kashmir in the correspondence on the Champa Skaldan murder case: IOLR. L/P&S/4204. Statement by Lala Ramesh Chandra. 1 September 1939.

were exempt from taxes should be abolished. Instead, both Kashmir and Tibet should impose a uniform two per cent tax on all imports into their respective territories .

This proposal merely added to the existing confusion. The Kashmir government immediately imposed the tax without waiting for it to be ratified by the Government of India.[25] On the other hand, the Lhasa government announced that it preferred the previous system and refused to ratify the Dokpo Karpo proposals. Confusion over the issue dragged on for years. In 1932 the Rudok Dzongpen was found to be levying the tax on Ladakhi traders, but the Garpons were not doing so. Letters from the Tibetan government in 1924, 1927, 1931 and 1937 treated the tax question and the whole of the Dokpo Karpo proceedings as still under discussion.

In 1945 Hugh Richardson summed up the then state of play:

> The position is unsatisfactory and the two per cent duty appears to have been taken out of its proper place as part of the proceedings at Dokpo Karpo which do not appear to have been ratified by the Government of India or the Tibetan Government. In spite of this, the Kashmir government has been levying the duty, and the Government of India has informed the Garpons, but not the Tibetan Government, that the two per cent duty may be levied. The Rudok Dzongpen appears to be levying the duty, but there is no sign that the Tibetan government are aware of this.[26]

Thus, the Dokpo Karpo meeting failed to make significant progress in any of the issues under discussion.

The Champa Skaldan murder case (1935-1940)

In 1937 there was a further meeting between British, Kashmiri and Tibetan representatives on the Tibetan frontier. It appears that the main issues discussed were the imposition of taxes on goods passing to and from Ladakh and Tibet, and the extradition of Tibetan subjects from Ladakh. The file concerned with the 1937 meeting is not available in the India Office, but it appears that the talks were inconclusive.[27] The next major dispute on which we have detailed information concerned the murder of a Tibetan villager called Champa Skaldan in Rupshu in 1935.[28] Controversy over the murder lasted at least until 1940.

---

25. *Ibid.*
26. *Ibid.*
27. The missing file is R/2 1068/113.
28. IOLR. L/P&S/12/4204. Indo-Tibetan Frontier. Disputes between Kashmir and Tibet.

As with Lhagyal's abduction in 1917, disagreements over grazing rights and the payment of local taxes lay at the heart of the murder case. The three Tibetan villages of Kharak, Barquog and Phuncok Rabtan shared an area of winter grazing land with the people of Rupshu in Ladakh. According to the Tibetans, the then *go-ba* (headman) of Rupshu had seized control of the grazing area 40 years previously, although they claimed to have ancient documents showing that they were entitled to the land themselves. Since then, the three Tibetan villages had paid an annual grazing fee of six rupees to the *go-ba* in Rupshu.

The trouble started when Chhewang, the present *go-ba*, decided to raise the grazing fee to fifteen rupees. The Tibetan villagers selected a representative to negotiate with him. The man they chose was Champa Skaldan, a former monk who had left his monastery after having an affair with a village woman, but was respected for his shrewdness. Champa Skaldan set out to meet Chhewang in January 1935, but never returned. In the spring, when the snows began to melt, his disfigured body was found floating in a stream not far from Chhewang's tent.

The principal Tibetan witness to Champa Skaldan's last hours was Champa Rigzin (also spelt "Jhemba" Rigzin), who had accompanied him to Rupshu. In his subsequent testimony, he stated that he and his companion had been invited into Chhewang's tent. However, after some time Champa Skaldan was taken outside and bludgeoned to death with a wooden stick six inches thick. Champa Rigzin had not seen the alleged murder, but he had been forced to help carry the corpse to the stream where it was thrown into a hole in the ice. Chhewang's family then gave Champa Rigzin seven rupees, and told him to tell no one what he had seen and heard. Champa Rigzin was so intimidated that he told no one of his experiences until some time after Champa Skaldan's body had been found the following spring.

The Kashmir government undertook a police investigation into Champa Skaldan's death, but concluded that there was no case to answer. The Tibetans may have brought up the murder at the 1937 border meeting. If so, the outcome was inconclusive. The representatives of the British, Kashmiri and Tibetan governments therefore held a further joint meeting at Demchog on the Ladakhi/Tibetan border between 21 July and 3 August 1939. The representatives were Rai Bahadur Dr Kanshi Ram (the British Trade Agent), Lala Ramesh Chandra (the Kashmiri Wazir of Ladakh), the junior Garpon of Gartok, the "Nerpa" (agent) of the senior Garpon, and other senior Tibetan officials. The stream at Demchog constituted a "natural boundary", and the enquiry was held on the Kashmiri and Tibetan banks on alternate days.[29]

There were several sources of friction between the three representatives. First, the Tibetans wanted to try Chhewang according to their customary procedures, and this meant allowing the Tibetan witnesses to give their testimony as a group rather than individually. One Tibetan official explained that "according to Tibetan law the statement of an accused person could not be recorded without first giving him lashes to find out the truth".[30] Kanshi Ram had to explain that these procedures were contrary to normal British legal practice. Secondly, acccording to Kanshi Ram, who seems to have been sympathetic to the Tibetan point of view, the Wazir was consistently discourteous to the Garpons. Thirdly, the Garpons confused the issue by raising other questions - such as the extradition of Tibetan subjects in Ladakhi territory - which had nothing to do with the case. Finally, and most crucially, several key witnesses failed to attend the meeting. In the Garpons' view the most important was Chhewang's father Kunzang who was seven days' journey away in Lahul.

The absence of these witnesses meant that the case could not be brought to a satisfactory conclusion. The Wazir proposed that the Tibetans should continue to pay grazing fees until the affair was finally settled, though he conceded that they might be handed to a Kashmiri official, who would hold them in trust, rather than to Chhewang. The Garpons refused to accept this proposal. On 3 August they left Demchog in anger, having threatened to cut off the salt trade with Ladakh until justice was seen to be done.

The day after the Garpons and the British Trade Agent had left Demchog, Kunzang arrived from Lahul. The Wazir sent a message to the Garpons asking them to return to continue the enquiry. In their letter of reply, the Garpons claimed that the Wazir had come "as an agent (mukhtar) on behalf of the alleged murderer" and not as a dispassionate judge. They refused to return unless the enquiry were conducted according to their own procedures.[31]

The Wazir and the British Trade Agent differed widely in their subsequent reports on the meeting.[32] Kanshi Ram stated that Ramesh Chandra had been consistently rude in his dealings with the Garpons,

---

29. *Ibid.* Dr Kanshi Ram to Political Agent, Punjab Hill States, Simla. 14 August 1939. Indian maps now place Demchog well to the west of the boundary line. See Lamb, *Tibet, China and India*, p. 360.

30. *Ibid.*

31. *Ibid.* Letter from the Garpons. Tashigang. 20th day of the 6th month.

32. *Ibid.* Report of the Wazir-i-Wazarat. 1 September 1939.

and complained that his conduct had jeopardised future Ladakhi relations with Western Tibet. He feared that the Garpons would take their revenge by discriminating against Ladakhi traders. By contrast Ramesh Chandra gave a detailed account of the inconsistencies in the evidence presented by the Tibetans. He concluded that there was no *prima facie* case against Chhewang, and recommended that the case be dismissed. He supported Chhewang's own claim that the Garpons were anxious to discredit him because they found him an obstacle in "their armed raids in bringing back the Tibetan settlers of Rupshu".

Reports on the meeting were submitted to the Goverment of India External Affairs Department in Simla. However, on 17 April 1940 E.W. Fletcher, the Additional Deputy Secretary, wrote:

> The Government of India desire as far as possible to avoid being drawn into the border disputes between Kashmir and Tibet and, owing to the distance of the scene from Lhasa, and the negligible control exercised by the Lhasa government over officials on the border, they doubt whether the appointment of a commission to settle the issues would serve any purpose.[33]

The Government of India's decision not to pursue the murder enquiry and related issues means that no further references to the Champa Skaldan case appear in the India Office Political and Secret records: after the outbreak of the Second World War the authorities in New Delhi, Simla and London had much more pressing concerns. Meanwhile, the Kashmir government selected Tsetan Phuntsog, a Ladakhi aristocrat from Sabu (near Leh), to continue negotiations with the Tibetan authorities. According to his wife Sungkil Phuntsog, he held talks with the Tibetans lasting over a month in the summer of 1940, and came to an amicable settlement. The murder charge was eventually dropped for lack of firm evidence.[34]

This was not quite the end of the story. Chhewang was able to elude Kashmiri, British and Tibetan justice, and - over half a century later - it is impossible to be sure whether he was guilty or not. Nevertheless, many ordinary Ladakhis believed that he really had murdered Champa Skaldan. Subsequently, he and his family encountered a series of misfortunes: they were struck by lightning; wolves entered their tent (a sign of bad luck); and soon afterwards Chhewang and one of his sons died of dysentery. Local people

---

33. *Ibid.* E.W. Fletcher to Political Officer in Sikkim. 17 April 1940.
34. Sungkil Phuntsog, "My Husband Kaga Thsetan Phuntsog." In *Yarked* (25th anniversary souvenir of the Moravian Institute, Rajpur. Published privately in Dehra Dun, 1988), pp. 66-71.

attributed their deaths to black magic from Chhewang's enemies in Tibet.[35]

Epilogue

In 1940 the unresolved controversies on the Ladakhi/Tibetan frontier were much as they had been since the 1920s and even the 1890s. In summary, they were:

-disputes over the precise location of the boundary north and south of the Panggong lake;

-disputes over the grazing rights of pastoralists on either side of this boundary;

-Tibet's demand for the extradition of its subjects who had migrated to Ladakh and therefore were unable to fulfil their tax and corvée labour obligations at home;

-and disagreements on the level of taxes either side was allowed to impose on goods passing between Kashmiri and Tibetan territory.

Lhagyal's abduction and Champa Skaldan's alleged murder dramatised these controversies, but did not start them: the two cases were symptoms and not causes of the differences between the British, Kashmiri and Tibetan governments. As far as can be ascertained from the Indian Office records, the three governments had made no significant progress towards a lasting settlement by the time the British left India in 1947.

In retrospect, it seems remarkable that the disputes were allowed to drag on for so long. Several factors contributed to the three governments' failure to find a solution. First, transport and communications were slow. Even in the 1930s and 1940s, it took several weeks for letters - or individuals - to travel between Gartok and Lhasa. Secondly, cultural differences meant that the representatives of the three governments had different expectations from the conduct of diplomacy. The squabbles over court procedure in Demchog in 1939 are symptomatic of these differing perspectives. Thirdly, the Ladakh frontier was peripheral to all three governments - both geographically and politically.

The Government of India almost certainly would have been able to press for a settlement with Tibet if it had considered Ladakh border issues sufficiently important. However, as noted above, in 1929 it was able to dismiss the Dokpo Karpo dispute as being "of no practical importance". Similarly, the Tibetan government in Lhasa seems to have lacked proper information on tax procedures in either

35. Personal reminiscences of Mrs Sungkil Phuntsog. May 1992.

Gartok or Rudok. The Kashmir government cared for its prestige on the frontier, but apparently was little concerned with the daily lives of the Rupshu nomads who were most affected by the disputes.

In Alistair Lamb's analysis, Britain's principal objective in the Himalayas was to sustain Tibet's role as a buffer state without raising too many awkward questions about the niceties of China's political status in Lhasa.[36] The British were therefore reluctant to focus on Indo-Tibetan border issues too closely, at least in the western sector, because this might have invited unwelcome attention from China.

During the British period, the Government of India did not have to reckon with a Chinese military presence in Western Tibet, and its relaxed attitude to Ladakhi border issues may therefore have appeared justified. All this changed after the Chinese occupation of Tibet in 1950, and especially after the construction of a Chinese road across the Aksai Chin. Since the Sino-Indian war of 1962, the dispute over the demarcation of the border in Ladakh has become much more than an academic question. It still has not been resolved.

---

36. *Tibet, China and India*, p. 351.

DEVELOPMENT AND CHANGE IN ZANGSKAR, 1977-1989

James Crowden *

When I first visited Zangskar in 1976 my first concern and the main reason that I spent a winter there, was to find out an answer to a simple question. How on earth do these people survive? It is a simple question and yet the answers are complex and I ended up studying everything from agriculture to monastic painting. There was also a sense of urgency about the study for I knew that the road was soon to be completed and that it was of vital importance to get an understanding of the valley before the road crossed the Pensi La. Also I was aware that here was a classic opportunity to study the effect of a road on a fairly large community. As a civil engineer I was aware that very few long term studies if any had been carried out by engineers on the effects of their projects, and in the third world these projects, though small by western standards have a vast effect on everybody. Also I was aware that anthropologists had done little work. There seemed therefore scope for study and so I returned in 1989 after a gap of 12 years and this paper is the result of that study. It is brief and yet I believe that the main trends can be outlined.

My original study had focussed on agriculture and so the first comparison was diet. This has changed significantly. and as a direct consequence of the road. Such factors as Government rations, religious unrest, accidents, new buildings, electricity, dress, travel, education are all affected. More than anything I am aware of the briefness of this report and would hope it could be used as a guide for further study.

Most of the information was gathered in Padum from both Buddhists and Muslims. My main informants were Puntsok Dawa and his brother-in-law Sonam Wangchuk from Karsha, and Mohammed Khan also of Padum.

In 1977 Zangskar would have appeared little different from what Csoma de Kôrös saw in the 1820's, although the King's palace at Padum would then have been standing and the bridge over the river to Karsha would have been intact. No doubt other fortifications would

---

* Forge House, Fore St., Winsham, Chard, Dorset TA20 4DY, UK.

have been standing and manned. Apart from that, little I suspect had changed: that is until the road came.

Diet - grains

Annual consumption for one family in Padum

(1977 = 4 adults + 4 children: effectively 6 people. 1989 = 2 adults + 8 children: effectively 6 people)

	1977 (kg)	1989 (kg)	% Change
Barley (food)	500	450	-10%
" (Chang)	150	300	+100%*
Peas	300	180	-40%
Wheat (local)	500	420	} +14%
" (imptd)		150	
Rice	300	700	+130%
Total	**1750**	**2050**	

*150 kg barley made into chang in 1989 was given to harvest labourers.

As can be seen, consumption of grains is slightly up between 1977 and 1989, but a significant change has occurred in the diet. Less barley is consumed, and slightly more wheat, the main bulk of the latter now being imported and probably of inferior nutritional value though more finely ground, i.e. *atta*. Less peas are consumed, but more than double the quantity of rice. In fact the diet has changed dramatically in this one household. In some Muslim houses all the barley is sold to the Buddhists to make more chang.

The use of imported harvest labour is also significant, the labourers coming from Machel in Pardar and some from Nepal. The figures would also indicate either a reduction in cultivable area or a drop in yields. In this particular household the owner was a teacher and had less time to work in the fields, i.e. he was able to buy extra rice with his salary. The rice and *atta* are obviously subsidised and the full cost of transporting it by lorry would make it only a luxury. In 1977 all Government rations had to be carried in by horseback, each horse carrying 80kg. One truck carries 60 quintals i.e. 6,000 kg or the same as 75 horses which was one caravan. From Kargil a truck takes 12-14 hrs. A caravan could take anything from 6-8 days from Panikar to Padum. The tariff from Srinigar to Padum is 160 Rs /quintal; i.e. a truckload costs 9600 Rs. In practice a bit more can be squeezed on and the going rate is 10,000 Rs /truckload. In 1976 a horse was 40 Rs/day: Government rate 20 Rs /horse /day.

Diet - other foodstuffs

	1977	1989	
Ghee	5	5	kg
Mustard oil	10	15	kg
Dalda (Veg. fat)	-	23	kg
Rapeseed		4	kg
Dal	30	30	kg
Butter	36	33	kg
Churpe (Cheese)	25	15	kg
Potatoes	35	80	kg
Cabbage	-	10	kg
Veg Local	6	6	kg
Meat Yak	70	120	(=186 on bone)
Sheep/goat	20	20	kg
Onions	5	21	kg
Milk	1500	1000	litres
Chang	4-600	500	litres
Salt	20	20	kg
Sugar	12	20	kg
Tea Namkin	20	15	kg
" Lipton	1.5	5	kg
Dried Apricots	5	10	kg

Some changes are evident: i) Greater use of imported cooking oils; ii) Great increase in potatoes, mainly imported although some are grown in small gardens: iii) Cabbage and fruit like bananas are totally new; iv) More meat is consumed, but less milk; v) Chang is about the same; vi) Salt and tea are the same but sugar is up significantly, possibly due to the large number of visitors. Also available now are aubergines, coconuts, apples, tomatoes, a wider selection of biscuits, honey, Amul butter, chocolate, lemon squash, even Nescafe. Half a yak costs 725 Rs for approx 90 kg; a whole yak alive costs 1450 Rs. The sugar ration is 400 gms/head/month + 1.5 kg extra/month per family if stocks are sufficient. The diet is therefore healthier in terms of vegetables and fruit; less so in terms of rice.

Government rations

	1977	1989	Price 1989
Atta	1,000 kg	25,000 kg	2Rs 36p /kg
Rice	1,000 kg	23,000 kg	2Rs 63p /kg
Sugar	1,000 kg	5,000 kg	5 Rs /kg
Salt	3,000 kg	5,000 kg	3 Rs /kg
Kerosene	30,000 ltrs.	120,000 ltrs.	12Rs /5ltrs.

(These rations were for the Padum plain only.)

In 1977 the government rations of atta and rice were almost exclusively for government officials and a few select families in the plain of Padum. Sugar, salt and kerosene were the main ration items then, kerosene obviously helping out with the use of dried dung and firewood. Salt is still brought down from the Karnak region by the Changpa in their caravans of up to 1000 sheep at a time. The wool is still needed and anyway the salt is better than the government salt and has a market value of nearly double - as, interestingly enough, does the local butter in Leh when compared to the government Amul butter.

The main reason for government rations is to avert famine, which can easily occur either with an early fall of snow or hail preventing a good harvest, or a heavy snowfall in the spring which prevents early ploughing and also prevents early access with transport. In 1988 they ran out of kerosene and it had to be airlifted in for government. officials. The rice ration is 8 kg /head /month (= 96kg /head /year); the atta ration 6kg /head /month (=72 kg /head /year). Zangskar is of course cut off from the rest of Ladakh for half the year from November to May. In the winter of 1987-88 many Bihari roadworkers were caught out in late Sept. Nobody knows how many died - somewhere between twenty and fifty. On 8th March 1988 massive avalanches killed fifty-five in Shagar Yogma - nearly the whole village - and another nine in Uberag. Fatal accidents are not uncommon for other reasons. The road has killed many in truck accidents. In 1982 eleven were killed on the Pensi La and in 1984 another nine, besides those killed during construction.

The government rations prevent famine and keep people in the valley who would otherwise leave. Many still find jobs either in Ladakh in the army or SSB or JKBP or go south to Manali. Many students also go down to the plains or even South India to study. The road has made this easier but the Zangskaris have always travelled far: either to Lhasa or Kashgar. Many Zangskari horses were used on the old trade routes and they were second only to Yarkandi horses for carrying loads at high altitude. This trade has obviously decreased but the cattle trade has increased as cattle can now go to Kargil in a truck and arrive in better condition. Cattle are even driven over Pangi and sold in Padum. The change in trade routes has been marked and to research all its subtleties would take a long time.

The reason why Zangskar is so fascinating is that unlike Ladakh it did not have a tradition of ancient and lucrative trade routes, and neither did it have the vast infrastructure of the government and military or indeed the wars which have occured since 1947. In 1976-77 it was still functioning much as it must have done for the last five hundred years, i.e. on a non-cash or barter system and very complex this was too, reaching over long distances. Zangskar, far from being remote, was the centre of a large trade in grain and even supported quite large populations outside the valley as well as in its higher reaches.

The road has of course upset this balance but if anything it has, by bringing in money and government rations, not only reduced the likelihood of famine but increased the surplus grain for trading or as some prefer, making chang. Also the road has with the tourists provided an income within the valley and a significant number of younger people who would have left to find employment can now make enough in the summer to keep them there. In a sense although things have changed considerably, they have the best of both worlds. During the winter there is still plenty of time for storytelling, chang-drinking sessions and monastic festivals.

Curiously enough, whilst Leh has experienced a considerable amount of religious and political unrest in the last few years, tensions have been low in Zangskar after the initial riot in 1976, although Padum has both Buddhist and Muslim permanent inhabitants.

Their solution is not just to have a headman but also two Buddhists chosen by the Muslims and two Muslims chosen by the Buddhists.

The road from Kargil to Padum

The road was started from Kargil in 1962 at the time of the war with China but because it was to no strategic purpose the road construction was slow and the physical problems of keeping the road stable enormous: avalanches, floods, mudslides and rockfalls, to say nothing of low temperatures and the fact that the road is closed for half the year. That it was ever built at all is an extraordinary tribute to the Indian Engineers. The construction of the road is all the more remarkable because of the lack of materials and equipment. Nearly all the work was done by pick and shovel with the odd use of compressors, drills and plastic explosive. So unimpressed were the Zangskaris with earning money when they should have been trading or in the fields that considerable labour had to be drafted in from Nepal and Bihar, and even Backerwals and Gujars worked for a month or two. The rates of pay were 15 Rs a day for the men and 12 for the women. Masons got 30Rs./day. The headmen of each village were responsible for the section through their village and they acted as subcontractors. Bridges were of course specialised constructions and engineers from the Punjab were called in to help with the larger girder bridges.

The main problems were traversing the foot of Nunkun between Panikar and Parkachik, and crossing the Pensi La. The chronicle of progress is as follows:

Kargil 1962	0
Sanku 1965	↓
Panikar 1967	
Parkachik 1970	
Ringdom 1974	
Pense La 1976	
Tungri 1978	↓
Padum 1980	234 km

Unoffcially the first vehicles actually arived in Padum in late Nov 1976. Two J&K police jeeps arrived to undertake investigations into the disturbances of 6th November and arrested 6 Muslims, who were taken to Kargil and Leh. The jeeps were able to make the journey because the streams were frozen and the snow had not yet come. The sound of their engines as they crossed the irrigation ditches was eerie to say the least. It is ironic however that the first vehicles should have been those belonging to the State Police.

Attitudes to the road before it arrived were varied.Generally speaking the older people were suspicious and the younger people who had been down to Kashmir and India welcomed it. Even monks in Karsha monastery who were artists painted pictures in their cells of buses going to monastery up a winding road, rather like at Macleod Ganj. And this long before the road had arrived. Even whilst they were painting a whole new temple in Padum, they included amongst the scenery and all the buddhas and bodhisattvas, a man in shorts representing the trekkers.

One older man was more sceptical. "We cannot stop the road. We may become richer but we will lose our peace of mind," and walked off with his mani wheel.

So far there are four tipper trucks in Zangskar: two owned by Muslims, one by a Buddhist and one jointly owned by a Muslim and a Buddhist. There are plans to extend the road not only beyond Zangla to meet the road to Chiling but to extend it past Bardan Gompa and over the Shingo La down to Darcha. A formidable undertaking, and one that is likely to take many years.

In 1976 there were only three shops in Padum; now there are thirty, as well as eight hotels. Over half are owned by Muslims and some rented out to people from Manali. One in Padum is owned by Karsha Gompa. Land, which was formerly never bought or sold, is now changing hands for up to 30,000 Rs /kanal. Land bought by compulsory purchase by the Government is only 13,000 Rs/kanal. Also there is now piped water in Padum from the mountain, but in winter they still have to go down to the river with jerrycans. Electricity is supplied from diesel generators, the cost to the consumer being 8-9 Rs per bulb per month.

As an example of modern economics, one man got a 50,000 Rs subsidy to build a hotel, which cost 230,000 Rs. He borrowed from friends, and at the same time bought a tipper truck which cost 390,000 Rs. The money derived from Government work with the tipper helped to pay for the hotel, which he now rents out. Big new ventures are financed by family and friends, in much the same way as trading expeditions must have been in the past.

New buildings are much in evidence. Public Works compounds, the tehsildar's office, the police, the tourist bungalows, the hospital, the schools: - the whole infrastructure that was 12 years ago left to about half a dozen officials. Concrete and reinforcing rods are now used where mud and straw bricks and timber were used. The village of Chiling has become almost denuded of trees. Timber is therefore a major import to Zangskar and a major expense in any construction.

In terms of new houses in the village, the most significant change has been in the khangchung, which traditionally was the small house for the parents. Now the khangchung is built on new ground in the fields, near the road, and is often much larger than the khangchen and more spacious and uses a lot more glass, and looks more like houses in Ladakh.

In short, Padum has become a town and no longer a village. But then in the old days when the King of Zangskar lived there he had a palace of seven stories, not dissimilar to the old palace in Leh though only about half the size.

My own feeling is that because the road took so long to reach

Padum, this was an extraordinary benefit, as the people were able to prepare themselves for the changes. The interesting thing psychologically is that the political/religious unrest took place before the road actually arrived. One of the main problems leading up to it was shortage of land for the Muslim families. Now they can survive on trade and other work, the tensions have reduced somewhat. It is interesting to note here that there are close biological ties between Buddhists and Muslims.

Even dress has changed. The women wear plastic gloves at harvest to avoid their hands becoming cut and chafed and they wear the headscarf instead of the perag in the fields. The men will only wear their gonche's in winter or for special occasions, preferring western dress. For the Buddhists there has been one very significant development: the building of Photang Gompa. This is on its own in the plain of Padum and is where the Dalai Lama originally spoke to the people of Zangskar on his visit in 1980. It is sponsored both by the gelugpa monasteries and by the kargyu, and the head of the monastery changes every two years. It is really only used for special occasions, like the visit of Taglom Rimpoche on 15th Sept. 1989. As an incarnation of Vajrapani he gave teachings on Tsongkhapa, which at least 1500 people attended. Taglom Rimpoche travelled by horseback and was also supposed to be the incarnation of the monk who shot Lang Darma. Photang Gompa is a visible focus for Zangskar and in a sense its construction has resolved some of the differences between the two types of monasteries.

Also there is the Buddhist Lamdon school at Pipiting which had just started in May 1989, but was short of funds. Zangskar with its road now looks more to Kargil than to Leh for its economic links, and has always considered itself independent from Central Ladakh. Indeed they even talk about going to Ladakh and even in 1976 regarded Leh as decadent like Srinagar. The interesting thing is that with the increased wealth they are keen to turn the wealth back either into the monasteries or into education. I suspect however that the number of monks going into the monasteries has dropped. Even in 1976 I knew of one or two monks who had run away to join the Ladakh Scouts. Whilst the road is effectively a cul-de sac development will be controlled to a certain extent. What happens say in ten or twenty years time when the road to Lahoul is completed is anyone's guess. I only hope that the road is not being constructed for mineral and mining purposes.

The fieldwork was conducted from July 1976-Aug 1977 and the return visit to Zangskar was in Aug/Sept 1989. However as harvest was in full swing interviews could only be conducted during breakfast and supper. There is of course scope for a far larger study but I hope that some of the more significant changes have been highlighted. Tourist levels are about 1000 a year though during the troubles in 1989 in Leh these figures tripled as tours diverted their clientele from the main Indus Valley. Winter however in Zangskar with snowfalls of six to eight feet remains the same and will I am sure be their greatest ally. I wonder what Csoma de Kôrös would make of all this.

THE TIBETANISATION OF LADAKH: THE LINGUISTIC EVIDENCE

Philip Denwood [1]

The nature of the Ladakhi language

In an article published in 1980[2] I expressed the opinion that the modern spoken dialects of Ladakhi are, in both their vocabulary and their grammar, overwhelmingly variants of Tibetan. As far as I know this view has not been challenged since - not surprisingly, as it is far from controversial. At the same time, documents written in Ladakh (mostly religious or historical) have until very recent times been virtually indistinguishable from their counterparts in classical Tibetan, a form of the language which serves, in Ladakh as elsewhere (for Buddhists at least), as a standard literary medium largely lacking the differentiating features of the local spoken dialects. Thus Alexander Csoma de Kôrös could as well study classical Tibetan in Ladakh or Zangskar as anywhere else, though he also picked up many local words from the spoken dialects when he came to write his dictionary.

In speaking of the Ladakhi dialect it is useful to note some remarks made by R.A.Miller[3] namely "the remarkable closeness of Ladakhi to Purik and Balti, and the ease of comparison of these three with Central Tibetan, makes the application of the comparative method to this area attractive and rewarding", Certainly Ladakhi, Purik and Balti dialects form a linguistic continuum which it would be arbitrary to split up, and there is a clear dialectal break between Ladakh and western Tibet.

It is worth adding here that as well as spoken and written forms of the language, in Ladakh as elsewhere there exists a form intermediate between the spoken and the written, acting as a kind of bridge between the two. This is the language of, for example, folksong and epic, mostly oral in delivery but sometimes found in written form also. Its texts often bear close resemblance to variants found elsewhere in the Tibetan-speaking area, but with a generous

---

1. SOAS, Thornhaugh St., Russell Square, London WC1H 0XG, UK.

2. Denwood, 1980.

3. Miller, 1956.

admixture of Ladakhi vocabulary, and in performance delivered with a Ladakhi pronunciation. The whole ensemble of linguistic forms - spoken, written and intermediate - hangs together as an organic unity in Ladakh exactly as it does in other parts of the Tibetan-speaking world.

"Tibetans" and "pre-Tibetans"

The question I am concerned with today is: When did this state of affairs come into being? Snellgrove and Skorupski, in volume 1 of their *Cultural Heritage of Ladakh,* following A.H.Francke, do not probe back beyond the 10th century in their discussion of Tibetan culture in Ladakh. Petech, in his *Kingdom of Ladakh,* assumes that the Tibetanisation of Ladakh took place after 1000 AD.

One problem with such a dating is that it becomes very tempting to try and fill the supposed void - to assume that before the tenth century and the advent of the Tibetan speakers, there was someone else in Ladakh - a mysterious aboriginal population crying out for a name and identity. From the works of A.H.Francke we are familiar with stories culled from oral Ladakhi traditions of the Mon, alleged predecessors of the Ladakhis as we know them today, a remnant of whom may survive in the social stratum of the same name. Other groups of so-called Mon are well known in other parts of the Tibetan borderlands, though generally as neighbours rather than as predecessors of the Tibetans. The present-day Mon of Ladakh, like their congeners the Bheda, seem to speak exactly the same Ladakhi as everyone else, and no evidence has been adduced as to the language of their alleged ancestors.

Western scholars since Francke have often cast the so-called Dards in the role of the aborigines, a question fully discussed by Graham Clarke.[4] A Dardic language group, intermediate between Indic and Iranian, has at least some claim to scientific status, though of course it is a bold step from that to populating pre-Tibetan Ladakh with Dardic-speaking aborigines. Another rather enigmatic enitity is the kingdom and language of Zhang zhung, conquered by the Tibetans in the mid-7th century. I shall leave aside all these shadowy peoples and their languages with the suggestion that the need to fill a historical gap may have played a part in the stories about them.

The notion that this historical gap ends in the 10th century AD stems essentially from Tibetan written sources, mostly of the literary genre of the *rGyal-rabs* or "royal chronicle" type. These

4. See Clarke 1977.

relate various conflicting accounts of how descendants of the old Tibetan royal family established themselves in the different provinces of the old empire, including the west. The primary function of all these works in their original form, of which the *La-dvags rgyal-rabs* published by A.H.Francke is a typical but by no means the fullest example, is to legitimise the claims to rulership of the families which had them written, by genealogical means. Their authors are not interested in the language or ethnicity of the populations in the areas concerned.

Thus the statement that certain descendants of the last Tibetan emperor Lang Darma migrated to the west in the 10th century, if true, can be interpreted in various ways. The western areas may already have been Tibetan in culture, making the acceptance of a new ruler of Tibetan stock quite natural. Alternatively, the new ruler, presumably helped by a significant fighting force of Tibetans, could have taken over an essentially non-Tibetan area, which was only later thoroughly Tibetanised. Then again, the events referred to could have actually been massive folk movements of Tibetans, led by the rulers named, settling largely empty territories or swamping some pre-existing population. Scholars working on the Anglo-Saxon takeover in the British Isles, with vastly more evidence at their disposal, still hotly dispute similar questions.

Inscriptional evidence

The evidence for the early use of Tibetan in Ladakh is of two very different kinds: the first is early inscriptions in Ladakh itself; the second is data on the pronunciation of Tibetan, taken from a wide range of modern spoken dialects and from the Tibetan spelling system, aimed at reconstructing the sounds of early Tibetan. I shall begin with the inscriptions.

In volume 2 of Snellgrove & Skorupski (118-160) I published a series of rock inscriptions scratched onto boulders by the bridge over the Indus near Alchi, of a type similar to others at many sites in Ladakh. I argued that in language, orthography and content they bear close similarities with documents emanating from the Tibetan army of occupation in East Turkestan in the period 760-840 AD. A study of some very similar inscriptions at other places along the Indus in Ladakh published by G.Orofino reaches essentially the same conclusion.

In an article written with Neil Howard[5] I reexamined

5. Denwood & Howard.

A.H.Francke's edition and translation of the rock inscription at Balukhar, which is no mere graffito like the above inscriptions, but the connected text, in verse, of a eulogy of a nearby fortress. Although I differ greatly with Francke over the text and translation of this inscription, I have no quarrel with his view that it and others like it show close linguistic and orthographic similarities with Tibetan documents from East Turkestan, particularly the Tibetan-occupied Khotan area. Indeed, an inscription at Char Zampa consists of the name, written in Tibetan, of an individual who is not Tibetan but Khotanese.

Tibetan military control of Ladakh may date back to the early 8th or even late 7th century, though the likeliest date for the inscriptions so far studied seems to be the late 8th-early 9th. Whatever their precise dating, we must envisage troop concentrations encamped on the river terraces at many points along the Indus, and probably in a number of fortresses as well. Perhaps they came under the Khotan command, and included Khotanese personnel, though most of the personal names seem to be Tibetan enough. Where they were recruited we do not know.

All this still tells us nothing about the language spoken by the local population of Ladakh. They may already have been speakers of Tibetan dialects, and some of the army may even have been recruited from among them. On the other hand, the presence of Tibetan inscriptions need not imply a predominantly Tibetan-speaking population in Ladakh, any more than it did in Khotan. Possibly the military occupation was the actual beginning of the Tibetanisation of an aboriginal population, Mon, Dard or whatever. Again, possibly the Tibetan troops all left Ladakh after the collapse of the Tibetan empire in the mid-9th century, and the real Tibetanisation did not start till the mid-10th.

Dialect evidence

Turning now to the reconstruction of the early Tibetan language, one may notice two different approaches which have been adopted. The first, used by scholars such as Shafer and Benedict, regards the spellings of written Tibetan, with their multifarious consonant clusters particularly in syllable-initial position, as representing essentially the early or original Tibetan from which the modern dialects have evolved, largely by simplification of consonant clusters and even the elimination of consonants in some cases. Modern dialects are classified according to the degree of intensity of this simplification,e.g. by A.Róna-Tas into "archaic" dialects, such as Balti, Purik and Ladakhi, as well as Golok and others in northeast

Tibet; and "non-archaic" dialects such as those of central Tibet. Thus written Tibetan is a reflection of the "original" situation, Ladakhi of the "archaic" situation and Lhasa Tibetan of the "non-archaic" (presumably "modern") situation.

At the terminological level this classification has its absurd side, since if written Tibetan, Ladakhi and Lhasa Tibetan all go back to the same point, and if all are in use today, then all three must necessarily be of the same age. Even if we replace the term "archaic" by "conservative", things are not always as straightforward as they seem. It is not difficult to find cases like Ladakhi *miduk* or *miruk*, versus Lhasa *mindu*, where the supposedly non-archaic or non-conservative Lhasa dialect has preserved a consonant cluster (*-nd-*) lost from the archaic or conservative Ladakhi and Balti.

More fundamental criticisms of this whole approach have been made by both R.A.Miller and R.K.Sprigg.

Firstly, it concentrates on vocabulary and phonology, largely ignoring both grammar and actual usage as encountered in texts.

Secondly, the western-compiled dictionaries which provide the material for the method do not in fact sample the language at any one time in history; nor are they confined to the written language, for they include entries from many nineteenth-century spoken dialects. They are rather compendia of all the items known to their authors from written texts of many genres and periods, along with colloquial material, and certainly do not depict a single *état de langue*.

Thirdly, the oldest known stratum of the language, sometimes called "pre-classical", is of known early date (the 8th-10th centuries) and has a distinctly archaic character. Although it must surely be the starting point for any research into the origins of the language, it is hardly represented in these dictionaries at all, as its texts were not known to their compilers.

Fourthly, classical Tibetan (and for that matter pre-classical) seems to be an essentially written dialect with a pronounced literary and "artificial" character, whereas one would expect the ancestor language which is being sought to be a "natural" and essentially spoken one.

Fifthly, the status of many of the spellings of the dictionaries is uncertain, as their authors would freely admit. Often alternative spellings are given for the same lexical item, and even where a single spelling is given, this may sometimes reflect the judgement of the author rather than being derived from incontrovertible evidence. In some cases one may suspect that native grammarians have invented spellings in order to rationalise the language according to some linguistic theory.

The preferred approach of Miller and Sprigg to the problem of reconstruction is almost the opposite one. In the former's words: "Only with the eventual reconstruction of the origins of all the major regions of spoken Tibetan and this on the basis of the present-day dialects of these areas, and the subsequent reconstruction, on the basis of these preliminary reconstructions, of proto-Tibetan, can the exact historical value of the script be fully and accurately assessed."

R.K.Sprigg's attempts at proto-Tibetan reconstruction along such lines yield some interesting results. His genealogical trees for consonant clusters written in Tibetan as *zl-* and *bsl-,* if correct, suggest that the Balti forms are more "archaic" than the written Tibetan forms, not less. In other words, by the time the written Tibetan spelling system was reasonably standardised, i.e. by the mid-eighth or possibly even the mid seventh century, the ancestor of what is now Balti (and presumably Ladakhi) was already distinct from whatever dialect (perhaps a central one) was the basis of the script. Thus the ancestors of the Ladakhis and Baltis, identifiable by their distinctive speech, would have already occupied a distinct area, presumably somewhere in the west. Of ourse they may not have been in Ladakh and Baltistan - they could have been somewhere in western Tibet, ready for further westward migrations - though if so, they seem to have left no linguistic traces behind them.

I am the first to admit that the conclusions that can be drawn from the above linguistic considerations are pretty vague. Nevertheless I would say that they do rule out some scenarios. Tibetan and Ladakhi histories would have us believe that certain scions of the old Tibetan royal line migrated to western Tibet and eventually Ladakh from the 10th century. They may well be right. But the dialects spoken nowadays in Baltistan, Purig and Ladakh could never have descended from anything brought in by these people or their followers from central Tibet. The ancestor dialects of Ladakh etc. were already distinct in the eighth or ninth centuries, while from Chinese evidence we know that central Tibetan had by the mid ninth century become still less conservative than written Tibetan. The simplest alternative hypothesis is that the ancestors of the Ladakhis etc. were already where they are today. When we see the evidence of the 8th-9th century inscriptions before our very eyes along the banks of the Indus, it is hard to avoid the proposition that the incorporation of Ladakh into the old Tibetan empire was either a cause or an effect of the Tibetanisation of the local population - perhaps a bit of both. I can see no reason why the process could not have started in the 7th century or even earlier

Bibliography

CLARKE, Graham, 1977. "Who were the Dards? A review of the ethnographic literature of the north-western Himalayas." *Kailash* V/4.

DENWOOD, P.T., 1980. "Linguistic studies in Ladakh." *Tibetan Sudies in Honour of Hugh Richardson: Proceedings of the International Seminar on Tibetan Studies, Oxford*. edited by M.V. Aris & Aung San Suu Kyi , Warminster: Aris & Phillips,93-6. [Reprinted Atlantic Highlands, NJ: Humanities Press 1981.]

DENWOOD, P.T.& N.HOWARD, 1990. "Inscriptions at Balukhar and Char Zampa and archaeological observations on the fort of Balukhar and its environs." *Indo-Tibetan Studies. Papers in honour and appreciation of Professor David L.Snellgrove's contribution to Indo-Tibetan studies* (= *Buddhica Britannica* vol.2) ed. by T.Skorupski. Tring: The Institute of Buddhist Studies, 81-88.

MILLER, Roy Andrew. 1956. "Segmental Diachronic Phonology of a Ladakh (Tibetan) Dialect." *Zeitschrift der Deutschen Morgenlandischen Gesellschaft* 106. 345-362.

OROFINO, G., 1990. *East & West* 40.

RONA-TAS, Andras, 1966. *Tibeto-Mongolica. The Tibetan Loanwords of Monguor and the Development of the Archaic Tibetan Dialects* (=*Indo-Iranian Monographs* VII.) The Hague: Mouton.

SNELLGROVE, D.L. & T.SKORUPSKI, 1977-80. *The Cultural Heritage of Ladakh.* Warminster: Aris & Phillips.

SPRIGG, Richard Keith. 1972b. "A Polysystemic Approach in Proto-Tibetan Reconstruction to Tone and Syllable-initial Consonant Clusters." *Bulletin of the School of Oriental & African Studies* 35. 546-587.

ETHNOHISTOIRE DES MUSULMANS DU LADAKH CENTRAL[1]

Pascale Dollfus [2]

Pays de hautes terres, situé à l'extrémité occidentale du vaste plateau tibétain, le Ladakh, royaume indépendant jusqu'à son annexion définitive en 1846 à l'état indien du Cachemire, s'il ne fut jamais soumis à la loi du Dalaï-lama, a "la seconde propagation de la doctrine", soutenue par les rois et l'aristocratie y connut un rapide essor. Aujourd'hui encore, l'Eglise lamaïque y est fermement établie avec de nombreux monastères et une population monastique importante. La pensée religieuse, profondément dominée par le bouddhisme tibétain, investit tous les actes de la vie matérielle et interfère à tous les niveaux de l'édifice social. Toutefois, si la communauté bouddhiste est largement majoritaire, elle n'est pas la seule composante de la société ladakhi, qui compte, outre une faible minorité de chrétiens convertis à la charnière des XIXème et XXème siècles par les missionnaires protestants de l'Eglise morave, une forte minorité musulmane, résultats d'apports extérieurs anciens et de conversions, essentiellement féminines.

Etablis à Leh, la capitale de l'ancien royaume, et dans ses environs immédiats, les musulmans sont désignés par les bouddhistes sous le nom de *phyi-pa*, "étrangers", "gens de l'extérieur", par opposition aux *nang-pa*, "les gens de l'intérieur", ceux qui suivent le *dharma*, la loi bouddhique. Les sunnites et leurs lieux-saints sont connus sous l'appellation *kha-che*, c'est-à-dire cachemiri, les shî'ites sous celle de *sbal-ti* ou originaires du Baltistan, quelle qu'en soit leur réelle origine géographique.

Pour comprendre comment ces populations immigrées ou converties se sont adaptées à une société dont la cohésion repose sur le partage de pratiques portant l'empreinte du bouddhisme, il apparait utile de retracer leur histoire et d'élucider les raisons qui les ont amenées à s'établir au Ladakh ou à embrasser une religion autre que la leur, tel est l'objet de cet article.

---

1. English abstract at end.
2. CNRS, UPR299, 1 Place Aristide Briand, 92195 Meudon, France.

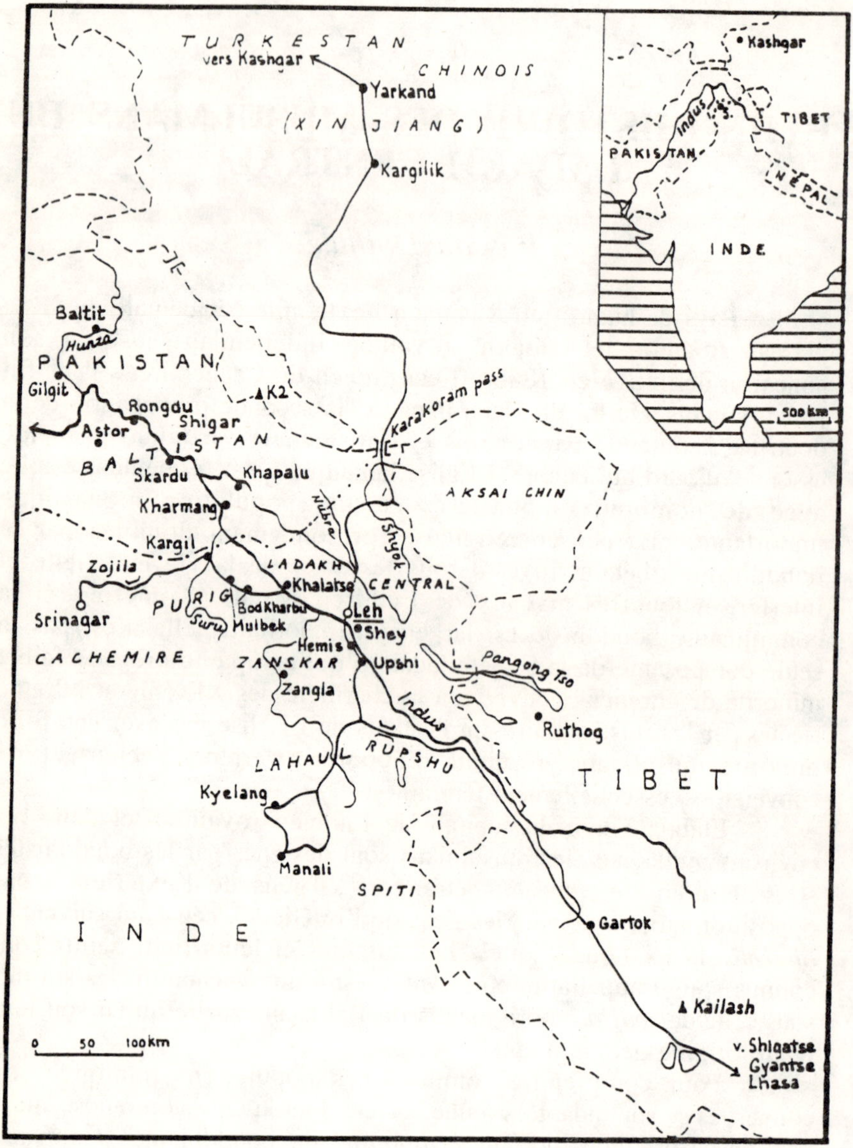

P.Dollfus: Carte.

1. Origine de l'Islam au Ladakh

Les premiers contacts entre le Ladakh et le monde islamique remontent au VIIIème siècle, époque à laquelle les armées arabes affrontent les Tibétains sur les marches-frontières de l'ouest (Gilgit) et du nord-ouest (Turkestan). Dès lors, dans la littérature musulmane, le Ladakh confondu avec le Tibet central est désigné sous le nom de "Grand Tibet", par opposition au Baltistan, petite principauté de l'ouest appelé "Petit Tibet".[3]

Au XIVème siècle, après le Punjab et la plaine du Gange, les musulmans conquirent le Cachemire, avec lequel le Ladakh entretenait des liens économiques étroits. Dans les siècles qui suivirent, le royaume du Ladakh, déjà affaibli par des querelles intestines, dût faire face à des invasions répétées perpétrées sous couvert de "guerre sainte" (*jihad*). Or, ironie de l'histoire, c'est Rincana Bhotta, le fils d'un chef ladakhi (?)[4] réfugié au Cachemire et converti à l'islam, qui, en 1320, sous le nom de Sadr-ud-din, fondait le premier sultanat du Cachemire et établissait la première mosquée de Srinagar sur l'emplacement d'un temple bouddhiste.

En 1405, sous le règne du sultan Sikandar (1394-1416),[5] l'islam fit irruption aux portes du royaume. Conduite par Rai Madari, la première armée musulmane franchît le Zoji-la, col ouvrant l'accès au Baltistan, au Purig et au Ladakh. Seul le Baltistan fut occupé, mais la menace était là. Quelques années plus tard, Zain-ul-Abidin (1420-70), à peine monté sur le trône, conduisit ses hommes à la conquête du Tibet. Le royaume du Ladakh, alors divisé entre deux frères, fut envahi, de nombreux monastères pillés, des statues et des objets rituels pris comme butin. En 1483, Hasan Shah (1472-1484) envoya Sayid Hasa et Jahangir Magre conquérir une nouvelle fois le Baltistan et le Ladakh, qui profitant de la situation troublée régnant au Cachemire après la mort de Zain-ul-Abidin avaient recouvré leur indépendance. Si le premier revint victorieux à Srinagar ayant converti de force le Baltistan,[6] le second fut vaincu par les armées ladakhi d'un royaume

---

3. Au XIXème siècle, les voyageurs occidentaux dénommeront le Ladakh, "Petit Tibet", opérant un glissement de sens, source de nombreuses confusions.

4. L'origine de ce prince "tibétain", qui selon le Rajatarangini (vv.157-254) aurait fui après avoir vengé dans le sang le meurtre de son père, fait l'objet de nombreuses spéculations. Venait-il du Ladakh? du Gugé ? ou du Baltistan ? (cf. L. Petech, 1977, p.21; P.N.K. Bamzai, p.309, Ataullah Siddiqi, p. 73).

5. Nous suivons les dates et les faits établis par L.Petech, qui diffèrent parfois de ceux donnés par les historiens indiens P.N.K. Bamzai et S.S. Charak.

6. Selon la tradition musulmane, l'islam aurait été introduit pacifiquement dans les chefferies balti de Skardu, Shigar et Khapulu au Baltistan ainsi qu'au Purig par Sayed Mohamed Nur Baksh ("Don de lumière"), disciple de Hazrat Sayed Ali

récemment unifié. L'accalmie fut cependant de courte durée.

En effet, à l'automne 1532, le royaume était à nouveau envahi. Cette fois l'envahisseur n'était plus un sultan cachemiri, mais le grand aventurier Mirza Haidar Dughlat à la tête d'une armée mongole. Parti de Kashgar, il pénètra au Ladakh par la vallée de Nubra, au nord-ouest, décimant ceux qui tentaient de l'arrêter. "Bur Kapa" - écrit-il dans le récit de ses campagnes faisant référence au gouverneur de Nubra[7] - "fût tué avec ses hommes; leurs têtes formèrent un noble minaret et la vapeur des cerveaux des infidèles de ce pays montèrent vers les cieux." Son but, conquérir Ur-sang, c'est à dire les provinces de U (*dBus*) et de Tsang (*gTsang*) au Tibet central; mais, l'hiver extrêmement rigoureux, l'altitude, les difficultés du terrain et les problèmes de ravitaillement lui firent rebrousser chemin à huit jours de marche de Lhasa. De retour au Ladakh, il se retirait avec ses hommes dans la forteresse orientale de Shey qu'il occupait jusqu'à son départ en 1536 pour le Badakshan.

En 1540, devenu maître du Cachemire, Mirza Haidar, n'oubliait pas ses premières conquêtes. Plus que la propagation de l'islam, c'étaient les intérêts commerciaux qui l'attiraient vers le plateau tibétain. En 1548, il s'empara et assujettit le Baltistan et le Ladakh pour assurer la sécurité des routes et développer le commerce en Asie centrale. A la tête des deux pays, il nommait des gouverneurs choisis parmi ses fidèles. Seuls sa mort en 1551 et l'avènement au Ladakh d'un souverain énergique et ambitieux permirent au royaume de recouvrer sa gloire passée et d'être pour une seconde fois la principale puissance de l'Himâlaya occidental.

En 1562, ce dernier, bKra-shis rnam-rgyal (c.1555-75), qui venait d'annexer le Purig à l'ouest du pays, ne parvint toutefois pas à vaincre l'armée du roi cachemiri Ghazi Chak placée sous le commandement de son fils, Ahmad Khan, et de Fath Chak, mais il en obtint le retrait contre la promesse d'un tribut. Quelques années plus tard, il repoussait brillamment une attaque des *Hor* (probablement des Turks de Yarkand ou de Kashgar). Les corps des envahisseurs - narre la Chronique des rois du Ladakh (*la-dvags gi rgyal-rabs*) - furent déposés dans le *mGon-khang* du palais royal de Leh au pied des divinités protectrices du royaume

Sous le règne de son neveu, Tshe-dbang (c. 1575-1595), l'un des rois les plus efficaces de la dynastie rnam-rgyal, le Cachemire sur lequel régnaient les Chak (1561-1586), musulmans d'origine turque,

Hamadani, au XVe siècle.

7. *Tarikh-i-Rashidi* par Mirza Muhammad Haidar Dughlat, traduction de E. Denison Ross, Patna, 1973, p. 418.

fut conquis par les Moghols. Perdant son identité, la vallée devint une des provinces de leur vaste empire. Sous leur domination (1586-1707), les premiers commerçants musulmans vinrent s'installer au Ladakh qui, situé au carrefour des grandes pistes caravanières d'Asie centrale, était déjà un entrepôt important où transitait toute sorte de denrées.

Au début du XVIIème siècle, 'Jam-dbyangs rnam-rgyal (c. 1595-1616), désireux d'asseoir sa renommée, partait à la reconquête du Purig annexé quelques années auparavant par des chefs balti. Profitant de son absence, Ali Mir (ou Ali Sher Khan), fils de Ghazi Mir, roitelet de Skardu, marchait sur le Ladakh, pillant les monastères et les villages se trouvant sur sa route. Revenu en hâte reprendre le commandement de son armée en déroute, le roi du Ladakh était alors fait prisonnier. Pour recouvrer sa liberté, il acceptait de donner sa fille en mariage au vainqueur, de revoir le tracé des frontières séparant le Ladakh du Baltistan et de payer un tribut annuel en échange des territoires de Bodkharbu et de Mulbeck au Purig.

Pour affermir encore leur nouvelle alliance, Ghazi Mir offrait au roi vaincu la main de sa fille, à la condition expresse que celui-ci se convertisse à l'islam et surtout que l'enfant né de cette seconde union du roi ladakhi fut l'unique héritier du trône du Ladakh. Selon une tradition locale, pour célébrer ce mariage et accompagner la princesse rGyal Khatun, le roitelet de Skardu envoya à Leh une cohorte de serviteurs et de servantes, ainsi que des musiciens balti, qui devinrent les musiciens du palais (*mkhar-mon*). A la cour, 'Jam-dbyangs fit également venir sept marchands cachemiri réputés pour leur habilité commerciale, qu'il nomma "marchands du palais" (*mkhar-phyog-pa*) et dota de terres. La reine fit construire pour elle et son intendance des mosquées shî'ites dans les capitales orientales de Leh et de Shey.[8] A la mort de son mari, elle se retira au Baltistan, où elle érigea pour le repos de l'âme du défunt deux mausolées. De l'union du roi ladakhi et de Rgyal-Khatun, reconnue comme une incarnation de la déesse bouddhique sGrol-ma (Tara blanche), naquit celui qui, pour les Ladakhi, restera le plus grand roi de leur histoire: Seng-ge rnam-rgyal (1616-1642).

En 1638, ce dernier alors au pouvoir, les troupes mogholes de l'empereur Shah Jahan (1627-1658) entrèrent au Baltistan et firent

8. Cette tradition est rapportée par Abdul Ghani Sheikh, "A brief history of muslims in Ladakh", (manuscrit de 4 p.) et dans un livret publié par les musulmans des districts de Leh et de Kargil pour asseoir leur légitimité après les émeutes violentes de 1989 opposant bouddhistes et musulmans dans le district de Leh.

une incursion dans l'ouest du Ladakh. En représailles, le roi ladakhi décida d'interdire le passage et la présence de marchands cachemiri sur son territoire. Cette mesure, visant à affaiblir le commerce du Cachemire, ruina en fait l'économie du Ladakh qui tirait sa principale richesse de ces échanges et amorça le déclin de ce royaume enclavé.

En 1663, lors de l'unique visite d'Aurangzeb (1658-1707) au Cachemire, le roi ladakhi bDe-ldan rnam-rgyal craignant une nouvelle invasion fit spontanément acte d'allégeance.[9] Outre le paiement d'un tribut, il promit l'édification d'une mosquée sunnite à Leh, la récitation de la *khuṭba,*[10] la diffusion de l'islam à travers le royaume et la frappe de monnaies à l'effigie de l'Empereur. François Bernier, médecin présent à cette époque à la cour du Grand Moghol, en témoigne en ces termes:

> "Maintenant que le roi de ce grand Thibet a su qu'Aureng-Zebe est à Cachemire et qu'il le menace de guerre, il lui a envoyé un ambassadeur avec des présens du pays, du cristal, de ces chères queues blanches de certaines vaches particulières de ce pays là qu'on attache par ornement aux oreilles des éléphans, de quantité de musc, et d'une pierre de jachen qui est de grand prix parce qu'elle est d'une grandeur extraordinaire ... on en fait des tasses et autres vases ..."
> (F. Bernier, 1830, p.290)

En 1077 de l'Hégire (1666-67), Shaik Muhi ud-din érigeait la grande mosquée de Leh, *Jamia Masjid.* Ce fut toutefois douze ans plus tard que des événements déterminants pour l'avenir du royaume et l'implantation des musulmans au Ladakh intervinrent.

En 1679, une puissante armée tibéto-mongole envoyée par le Vème Dalaï-lama - *dGe-lugs-pa*[11] - pour conquérir le Tibet occidental et montrer son ressentiment contre le soutien apporté par les Ladakhi au souverain *'brug-pa* [12] du Bhoutan, envahissait le royaume. Le roi bDe-legs rnam-rgyal, alors au pouvoir, n'arrivant seul à la repousser se vit contraint de demander l'aide d'Ibrahim Khan, gouverneur

9. Une source cachemiri donne de cet évènement la version suivante: "The rebel chief of Ladakh was brought to chains in Srinagar, forced to embrace islam, and then despatched to Delhi" R.K. Parmu, p.234.

10. *khutba* : "Prône". Allocution polititique précédant la prière du vendredi et affirmant la hiérarchie légitime des gouvernants.

11. *dGe-lugs-pa* : "les Vertueux", école réformée du bouddhisme tibétain fondée par Tsong-kha-pa (1357-1419) et cherchant à renouer avec la tradition d'Atisha.

12. *'Brug-pa* : "les gens de *'Brug* ", branche de l'école des *bKa'-gdams-pa,* "les Fidèles de la transmission de l'instruction" qui se rattache au siddha indien Naropa et à son élève Marpa.

moghol du Cachemire (1683). Les *sog-po* ("mongols") furent mis en déroute, mais le prix à payer fut lourd.

A l'issue des traités de paix signés en 1682 avec le Cachemire et en 1684 avec le Tibet, de nouvelles frontières furent établies privant le royaume du Ladakh de la moitié de son territoire. A l'ouest, le Baltistan et le Purig redevenaient des principautés indépendantes; au sud, le Lahaul supérieur était donné au roi de Kulu; à l'est, le Tibet annexait le Guge, le Ruthog et le Purang.

Une nouvelle fois, le roi du Ladakh était contraint de se convertir à l'islam. Son fils cadet envoyé en otage au Cachemire, il prit le nom de 'Aqibat Mahmud Khan, promit de payer un tribut annuel élevé, de réparer la mosquée de Leh et de frapper monnaie au nom de l'Empereur.

Le commerce de la laine et du poil de chèvre, qui représentait alors près de 50% de la totalité du trafic, devint désormais le monopole exclusif des marchands cachemiri.

Parallèlement, au terme du traité avec le Tibet, il fut convenu que chaque année une caravane *ja-ba* ("porteurs de thé") de deux cents animaux chargés de thé se rendrait de Lhasa à Leh et que, réciproquement une caravane *lo-phyag* serait envoyée à Lhasa tous les trois ans par le roi du Ladakh, apportant de nombreux présents en marque d'allégeance au Dalai-lama, ainsi que de l'or, de l'encens et des étoffes brodées pour le trésor du *Lha-brang* de Lhasa.

Le blocus commercial imposé en 1638 par Seng-ge rnam-rgyal levé, la suzeraineté des Grands Moghols réaffirmée, des musulmans cachemiri, encouragés par l'empereur Aurangzeb, vinrent s'établir définitivement à Leh et dans les localités voisines de Spituk, Phyang, Shey et Thiksey. Bien que l'on compta parmi eux quelques hommes religieux soucieux de propager pacifiquement leur foi,[13] la plupart quittèrent les vallées riantes du Cachemire pour les terres austères du Ladakh désireux de s'enrichir dans le négoce à grande distance entre l'Inde, le Tibet et l'Asie centrale.

A la même époque, ils établirent des colonies de plusieurs milliers d'individus à Lhasa, à Tsethang, à Gyantse, à Shigatse, à Gartok et au Tibet occidental, où ils étaient connus sous le nom de

---

13. Leurs noms sont mentionnés sur une inscription persane de la mosquée sunnite de Leh.

kha-che [14] "cachemiri "

Le 20 juin 1715, deux jésuites, un jeune théologien italien, Ippolito Desideri, et un père portugais, depuis longtemps à Goa, Manoel Freyre, en route vers Lhasa, arrivaient à Leh. Dans sa relation de voyage, le premier signale la présence d'un certain nombre de marchands cachemiri établis dans le royaume et la présence occasionnelle de caravaniers venus du Royaume de Khotan et du "Troisième Tibet" (Tibet central).

Plus que la conversion du roi, ce furent les clauses commerciales des traités ladakhi-tibéto-moghols qui s'avérèrent décisives pour l'établissement de la communauté musulmane dans le royaume bouddhiste du Ladakh. L'islam n'arriva ni par la conquête, ni par le prosélytisme de missionnaires zélés, mais avec les marchands caravaniers circulant entre le Cachemire et le Turkestan oriental.

2. Les rois ladakhi face à l'islam

En 1683, bDe-legs rnam-rgyal n'était ni le premier, ni le dernier des rois de la dynastie à se convertir à l'islam ou à épouser à des fins politiques une princesse musulmane. Déjà, nous l'avons vu, à l'aube du XVIIème siècle, 'Jam-dbyangs rnam-rgyal défait par Ali mir, allié au roitelet de Skardu, avait été contraint d'adopter la foi musulmane et de prendre pour épouse la princesse balti rGyal Khatun. Un siècle plus tard, Nyi-ma rnam-rgyal (1694-1720) pour garantir les frontières occidentales du royaume convolait en justes noces avec Zizi Khatun, petite-fille du chef balti de Khapalu. Après lui, c'était au tour de Tshe-dpal-don-grub (1802-1837 & 1839-40) de se marier avec la veuve de son frère aîné, une femme de Paskyum; puis à celui de son fils, Tshe-dbang rab-brtan rnam-rgyal (mort en 1839), plus connu dans l'histoire ladakhi comme le prince *mchog sprul*, de s'unir dans la même année à une femme du Purig et à une musulmane appelée Zora Khatun.

---

14. Ce terme tibétain signifie "cachemiri", mais désigne par assimilation au Ladakh - comme au Tibet - l'ensemble des musulmans sunnites.

S.C. Das, *A Tibetan-English Dictionary* (Calcutta, 1902), p.126 : "A native of Kashmir, a Mahomedan; a person that has command over much ..."

Et W.W. Rockhill, *The Land of the Lamas* (New-York, 1891), p 111, n.2 : "Tibetans and Ts'aidan Mongols use the word *kha-che*, originally applied to Kashmiris, to designate all and any people of Mohammadan type or wearing turbans, just as the Chinese use Ch'an tou".

Sur les Cachemiri au Tibet, voir M. Gaborieau, 1973; Abdul Ghani Sheik, 1991; Ataullah Siddiqi, 1991. En 1959, ils étaient encore environ 3000 au Tibet Central (cf. Dawa Norbu, 1990).

Tous cependant continuèrent à régner en accord avec les usages du pays, à respecter les préceptes bouddhiques et à soutenir l'Eglise lamaïque, faisant ériger de nombreux temples et statues et envoyant des dons considérables aux fondations religieuses du Tibet qui achevèrent d'ailleurs de ruiner le royaume.

Seule exception notable, le roi Tshe-dbang rnam-rgyal qui régna à la fin du XVIIIème siècle (1753-1782). Souverain inefficace et influençable, il s'entoura de favoris musulmans dont l'un lui donna la passion des chevaux: il en posséda plus de cinq cents, chacun doté d'un lad. Marié à une princesse bouddhiste du Zanskar, il s'éprit d'une musulmane de basse extraction connue sous le nom de Bibi qu'il épousa en seconde noces et sous l'influence de laquelle il se livra à maintes exactions. Après la mort tragique de cette dernière, clouée sur la porte du Bazar puis lynchée par une foule déchaînée, il prit pour femme Be-kim (Begum) dbang-mo originaire du Purig et également musulmane. Peu à peu, il délaissa le bouddhisme au profit de l'islam shî'ite refusant d'entretenir les temples de la capitale, d'alimenter en beurre les lampes rituelles et dépensant les sommes ainsi économisées pour soigner ses chers chevaux.

Excessif, tyrannique, détesté de ses sujets, on comprend que ce roi, qui ruina le royaume pour satisfaire ses propres plaisirs, n'encouragea pas - bien au contraire - la propagation de l'islam dans le royaume.

Conséquence de la tolérance bouddhiste,[15] de la suzeraineté du Cachemire sur ce petit royaume, ou plus prosaïquement, par peur de représailles, le roi et le gouvernement ladakhi manifestèrent toujours une grande tolérance à l'égard des musulmans établis sur leurs terres, qui comme le précisait I.Desideri (p.79) en 1715 "sont autorisés à avoir des mosquées et à pratiquer ouvertement leur religion."

Témoignage de cette entente, la direction et l'organisation matérielle de la caravane officielle *lo-phyag* fut confiée à des musulmans. En tant que représentants de celle-ci, ils participaient à la grande cérémonie du *smon-lam* organisée au Potala après la fête du Nouvel An, à l'occasion de laquelle ils remettaient, de la part des bouddhistes ladakhi et du roi, le tribut et les présents destinés à sa sainteté le Dalai-lama, "qui, selon l'usage traditionnel, se composaient d'une petite quantité d'or, de safran, de châles du Cachemire, de divers textiles du Sinkiang ainsi que d'un produit typique de leur pays, des abricots secs." (A.W. Radhu, p.134).

---

15. La *jihad*, obligation de propager l'islam et de le défendre n'a pas d'équivalent dans le monde du Bouddhisme.

Par ailleurs, malgré les pressions de la hiérarchie religieuse, les rois n'essayèrent jamais - à notre connaissance - d'enrayer par la force les nombreuses conversions féminines, pas plus qu'ils ne s'opposèrent à l'ouverture de lieux de culte ou à celle d'écoles coraniques.

Une anecdote rapportée par L. Petech (1977, pp.133-34) à propos d'un des derniers souverains de la dynastie rNam-rgyal illustre bien les liens complexes qui unissaient ceux-ci à la communauté musulmane.

En 1828, Abdul Sattar, prince de Khokand, fuyant les Chinois, gagnait le Ladakh avec 300 hommes et 250 chevaux. A Leh, il était reçu par le roi avec tous les égards dûs à un dignitaire étranger et installé avec ses hommes dans la résidence de l'abbé du monastère d'Hémis (*He-mis bla-brang*). Cependant, alertés, les ambans (envoyés de l'Empereur de Chine à Lhasa) demandaient leur extradition et envoyaient un messager pour les arrêter. Emmenés au Tibet, "les rebelles" étaient tués avant même que le Dalaï-lama n'en prenne connaissance. Les Chinois pour récompenser le souverain ladakhi de son aide le gratifiait d'une décoration, mais cette histoire le laissait mal-à l'aise, malaise aggravé par les menaces de mort proférées à son encontre et à celle de son fils par les réfugiés du Khokand lors de leur arrestation. Aussi, afin de contrer ces présages funestes, le souverain décidait de faire l'aumône aux musulmans pauvres de son royaume le 15 et le 30 de chaque mois, et finançait généreusement la lecture de prières protectrices par le Dalaï-lama.

3. Musulmans au Ladakh, musulmans ladakhi

Les informations que nous possédons sur les musulmans établis au Ladakh, du XVIIIème siècle aux événements qui secouèrent l'Inde, le Tibet et la Chine au cours de la première moitié du XXème siècle, sont fragmentaires. Elles permettent toutefois de brosser un premier portrait des différents groupes en présence: les Cachemiri, les caravaniers d'Asie centrale, les Balti et les *'ar-gon*, nés de père musulman et de mère ladakhi bouddhiste convertie à l'islam.

Venus de Srinagar au XVIIème siècle par le col du Zoji-la, les Cachemiri (*kha-che*) furent parmi les premiers musulmans à s'établir dans ce petit royaume bouddhiste. Commerçants pour la plupart, accompagnés parfois de spécialistes religieux qui diffusaient la culture et la spiritualité, ils prenaient part aux échanges entre le Ladakh, le Tibet, le Turkestan oriental et leur contrée d'origine

Du Cachemire et d'Inde, ils apportaient des épices, du

safran,[16] des cotonnades imprimées, des tissus brodés, des perles et du sucre de canne qui était transformé à Yarkand en sucre candi et réimporté. Du Ladakh, ils exportaient principalement des laines de haute qualité, *pashminah* [17] et *shahtush* (800 charges par an d'un poids de 28 "tereks"). Provenant de l'Est du royaume et du Tibet occidental, elles étaient destinées à être tissées au Cachemire afin de confectionner les châles réputés pour leur extrême légèreté, leur douceur et leur chaleur.

En 1715, le père jésuite Ippolito Desideri relate un incident montrant combien les marchands cachemiri étaient alors soucieux de conserver leurs privilèges et le monopole de leur commerce.

Jaloux de l'attention que le roi ladakhi Nyi-ma rnam-rgyal leur portait, ces derniers dans l'intention de leur nuire firent courir la rumeur qu'ils n'étaient pas les "Docteurs de la Loi" qu'ils prétendaient être, mais de riches marchands venus de l'étranger avec des perles, des pierres précieuses et beaucoup d'autres denrées rares et valeureuses. Le roi envoyait des messagers auprès des missionnaires afin de contrôler ces assertions. Puis, vérifications faites, la vérité rétablie, le souverain, n'ayant découvert que des bréviaires et quelques images pieuses, présentait ses excuses aux missionnaires et punissait les Cachemiri de leurs mensonges, leur défendant désormais l'accès au palais et à la cour. (I. Desideri, p.80.)

Il est intéressant de noter qu'un siècle plus tard, W. Moorcroft et G. Trebeck furent victimes de la même mésaventure.[18]

A cette époque, la communauté cachemiri connaissait un essor démographique considérable avec l'arrivée d'immigrés fuyant la domination dure et oppressive de Ranjit Singh, souverain sikh du Punjab, qui avait conquis le Cachemire en 1819.[19] Appauvris par un

---

16. Spécialité du Cachemire, le safran est appelé *kha-che skyes*, c'est-à-dire "né au Cachemire".

17. Le mot persan *pashminah* (Platts, p. 264) signifie étoffe de laine. En Inde, il désigne généralement les châles et le tissu fin du Cachemire faits d'une laine très fine prélevée sur le ventre de chèvres vivant en haute altitude. Quant au *shahtush* ou *tusi* considéré comme le sommet qu'aucune laine ne peut égaler par sa légèreté et sa chaleur, il provient de chèvres sauvages (*Asali Tus*) qui ne vivent que dans les hauts plateaux désertiques du Ru-thog et du Chang-thang à la frontière du Ladakh et du Tibet occidental. Voir sur ce sujet, Moorcroft, pp.348-349 et p.410.

18. "He confessed that the Kashmiris have endeavoured to prejudice him against us and prevail on him to prevent our coming to Lé." W. Moorcroft et G. Trebeck, vol.1, p. 252.

19. Au siècle précédent, sous la domination afghane, l'émigration toucha essentiellement les shî'ites persécutés par les gouverneurs afghans, mais ces derniers émigrèrent essentiellement au Baltistan et au Purig, contrées acquises à

système d'imposition extrêmement lourd, persécutés par des fonctionnaires arbitraires et un gouvernement qui déclara les mosquées propriétés d'état et ferma à la prière publique la plus importante d'entre elles, la population musulmane s'exila massivement vers les contrées voisines au régime plus clément. C'est ainsi que W. Moorcroft rencontra à Shey Khaja Shah Nyas, un descendant du prince timuride Baber qui, ses terres lui ayant été confisquées par le nouveau gouvernement et se sentant corporellement menacé, s'était réfugié à l'âge de soixante ans au Ladakh en dépit de l'offre de Mohammed Yar Khan de l'accueillir à Kaboul et de le doter d'un important *jagir* [20]

> "short and stout, with a pleasing expression of countenance although his features were Uzbek. He had a large turban on his head, and was dressed in a wrapper of brown cloth lined with chintz"
> (W. Moorcroft, Part 2, ch.1, pp.242-243)

Aucune donnée ne permet de chiffrer cette population, mais en 1820, W. Moorcroft note dans son carnet de voyage qu'un "nombre très considérable" de Cachemiri réside dans la capitale. Le portrait qu'il brosse de ceux qu'il qualifie de "peuple peut-être le plus corrompu au monde" ("the most profligate race, perhaps in the world") est sévère. "Ici, comme ailleurs - écrit-il - les Cachemiri sont renommés pour toutes les sortes de débauche, et là où ils abondent, les gens du pays sont atteints des mêmes vices", à savoir "la malhonnêteté, le mensonge et des moeurs dissolues".[21] En 1888, leurs négoces, au

l'islam shî'ite.

20. *jagir* : "taking *gir* a place *ja* , a tenure common under the Mohammadan Governement in which the public revenues of a given tract of land were made over to a servant of the state, together with the powers requisite to enable him to collect and appropriate such revenue, and administer the general governement of the district.

"The term is also in use, although with some license, to designate temporary grants, allowances or stipends from the government to individuals." (H.H. Wilson, p.224).

21. W. Moorcroft et G. Trebeck, vol I, p.346 ; vol.2, p.43-44. "The Ladakhis are, in general, a mild and timid people, frank, honest, and moral when not corrupted by communication with the dissolute Kashmiris, but they are indolent, exceedingly dirty, and too apt to be addicted to intoxication. The Kashmirians here, as well as everywhere else, are notorious for every kind of profligacy, and where they abound the people of the country are tainted by similar vices." (id.I, p.321). Cette image des Ladakhi braves et souriants et des Cachemiri rapaces et corrompus, souvent utilisée pour opposer bouddhistes et musulmans, est

nombre de 130, sont tous installés dans le Bazaar, vaste avenue rectiligne construite par les Dogras, dont les maisons blanchies et alignées au cordeau tranchent avec le dédale des ruelles de l'ancienne ville.

A Leh, les marchands indiens rencontraient ceux arrivant du Tibet chargés de thé conditionné en briquettes et de soieries chinoises et les caravaniers d'Asie centrale venant vendre des poneys, des ballots de feutres, des harnachements et des bottes, des tapis, des tasses de jade, des pièces d'argent, du tabac, des herbes médicinales et diverses denrées comestibles.

Qu'ils fussent natifs de Khotan, de Yarkand, de Kashgar, de Peshawar ou même de Perse, ces derniers étaient tous dénommés *hor*.[22] Les Ladakhi bouddhistes s'adressaient à eux en les appellant *Hajji* ("celui qui a fait le pèlerinage *hajj* à la mecque") ou encore *khaja, kwaja* [23], terme cachemiri désignant les enseignants religieux de l'islam. Enfin, les plus riches d'entre eux étaient connus sous le nom de *bias* (?), mot yarkandi signifiant "millionnaire". Par leurs dons généreux, ils entretenaient la mosquée de Leh pour laquelle ils apportaient d'épais tapis de laine de leur contrée d'origine.

Les caravanes étaient constituées de 30 à 40 chevaux placés sous la direction d'un chef caravanier, *bashi*, et escortés par cinq à huit serviteurs. La charge de chaque animal était fixée à 92 kg. Selon Mir Izzah Ullah (p.290), un "jud" (1/24 de roupie) devait être payé à l'*imam* de la mosquée de Leh pour chaque charge.

A l'encontre des Cachemiri, peu de marchands turks élurent domicile à Leh, la plupart repartant en octobre, la saison des caravanes achevée. La prostitution étant interdite par l'islam, ils se mariaient temporairement avec des femmes ladakhi, qui, le temps de cette union, renoncaient à leur religion pour embrasser la foi islamique.[24] Il suffit en effet de prononcer en arabe la profession de foi en Allâh, la *shâhâda* [25] "Il n'y a Dieu que Dieu et Muhammed est l'envoyé de

---

présente dans l'ensemble de la littérature occidentale et ce, jusqu'à nos jours. Cf. à ce sujet, la contribution de N. Grist dans le même volume.

22. H.A. Jäschke, p.58. "*Hor* : in Western Tibet, the Turks".

23. *kwaja(h)* : "un monsieur, un homme respectable", titre honorifique.

24. "The male parents are traders who come to Leh to exchange or dispose of their merchandise, and while they marry there they induce Tibetan women to adopt islam and get married to them. These marriages under the sanction of islam are dissolved with the departure of the merchants; but so great is the liberty of Tibetan women that nothing wrong is supposed to have been done by either of the parties when contracting these temporary alliances." Ahmed Shah, p.45.

25. La *shâhâda* est l'un des "six piliers de l'islam" avec la prière rituelle, le pèlerinage à la Mecque, le jeûne, l'aumône légale et la guerre sainte.

Dieu" pour être musulman.

Dans les caravansérails, où ils logeaient le temps de mener à bien leur négoce, ils rencontraient des pèlerins en route vers la Mecque, accompagnés parfois de femmes et d'enfants. Chacun portait son viatique et quelques pièces ou lingots d'or ou d'argent qu'il échangeait au fur et à mesure de son voyage pour couvrir ses dépenses.

> "A man rides alone, his grey robe is short, and on his feet he wears high leather boots; at his back, his possessions are fastened to his saddle, and above them is a monkey in cage. A pilgrim returning from Mecca, he has bought a monkey in India to sell, perhaps to some Chinese official in Turkestan;" (G.E. Hutchinson, 1936, p.49).

Quand le calendrier s'y prêtait, pèlerins et marchands faisaient route ensemble. Mais en hiver, les *hajji* turks étaient les seuls à tenter de passer de Yarkand à Leh par le col élevé du Karakoram. Certains mouraient en cours de route, victimes du froid ou d'avalanches.[26]

> "Voyageurs insouciants, ils sont souvent arrêtés par le mauvais temps, ce qui leur coûte des doigts ou des orteils gelés amputés ensuite par quelque médecin local. Méprisant les avis qui leur conseillent d'attendre, ils se remettent en route, possédés par le seul désir d'atteindre le but sacré, et assurés de la couronne du martyre s'ils tombent en route."
> (Marco Pallis, p. 200.)

Venus seuls s'établir au Ladakh, nombreux furent les Cachemiri, qui épousèrent des femmes ladakhi. Dès les premières générations, les enfants de ces immigrés se considérèrent comme des autochtones et tinrent à se se démarquer des commerçants cachemiri ne séjournant dans la capitale que de façon temporaire. Appelés avec dédain par les Cachemiri *naami musulman*, "musulmans par leur seul nom", ils sont connus dans la littérature sous l'appellation d''*ar-gon* . Ce terme, orthographié "argon", "arghon", "arghand", ou "arghaun" par les auteurs occidentaux et traduit en anglais par "half-caste", "half-blood" ou "hybrid", regroupe l'ensemble des personnes nées au

26. Le calendrier musulman est lunaire. Il prend donc dix jours environ d'avance sur notre calendrier solaire chaque année. Aussi le mois *Zu-l-Hijja* pendant lequel on fait le pèlerinage à la Mecque peut-il se trouver en été comme au plein cœur de l'hiver.

Ladakh d'une mère ladakhi convertie à l'islam et d'un père musulman, quelle qu'en soit l'origine ethnique (cachemiri, punjabi, yarkandi, balti, etc.),et tous leurs descendants.[27]

H. Ramsay (1890, p.56-57), qui leur consacre un article de plusieurs colonnes dans son dictionnaire ethnologique anglais-tibétain sous le terme "half caste", écrit :

> "This is the general and only term for hybrid, and by no means always signifies a half caste. Arghons are all Mahomedans, most of them are Sunnis, but some also Shiahs. The former are the result of connections formed by the Mahomedan traders, who yearly visit Leh in large numbers, and the women of the country, while the latter are the result, generally speaking, of connections formed between men of Baltistan and women of Ladakh. ... The offspring of these connections are, in the first instance, half caste Tibetan Mahomedans called "arghons", and these again frequently marry pure Tibetan women (converted to Mahomedanism), but their children too are "arghons", thus it may happen that a man is practically a pure Tibetan, nevertheless if he traces his descent from a connection formed between a Mahomedan and a Ladaki woman, he is termed an 'arghon'."

Installés dans la capitale ou dans ses environs immédiats, les *'ar-gon*, descendants de Cachemiri, continuèrent d'entretenir des relations étroites avec les membres des branches aînées ou cadettes restées au Cachemire ou établies au Tibet, voire au-delà du Karakoram, dans le Turkestan chinois. Leurs liens personnels avec les contrées voisines et la notoriété acquise sur les pistes de l'Asie centrale leur conférèrent rapidement d'autres rôles. Ils étaient - nous l'avons vu - chargés d'organiser la caravane *lo-phyag* qui, tous les trois ans, apportait l'hommage des bouddhistes ladakhi et de leur roi au Dalai-lama. En chemin, ils en profitaient pour négocier pour leur propre compte, ce que leur autorisait le traité de 1684. A Leh comme à Lhasa, ils tenaient des petites boutiques au centre de la ville. Leur activité commerciale leur donna un peu la fonction d'intermédiaires avec le monde extérieur. Leur connaissance du terrain et leur sens des

---

27. H. A. Jäschke, p. 606, "*'ar-gon* : an offspring of parents not having the same rank, not the same religion, and not belonging to the same nation".

"In Baltistan the children of a person (male or female) belonging to one of the families of the local Rajas, and of a person belonging to a family of cultivators are called Argon", Biasutti-Dainelli, 140 cité par L. Petech, 1977, p.128 n.4.

affaire reconnus par tous firent très tôt d'eux les interprètes et les guides privilégiés des premiers voyageurs occidentaux, missionnaires, explorateurs puis administrateurs, désireux de se rendre au Tibet ou dans les oasis d'Asie centrale. Au Ladakh comme au Tibet, "ils acquirent progressivement une influence sans commune mesure avec leur nombre du fait de leur puissance commerciale et de leur instruction." (M. Gaborieau, 1973, p.22.)

A cet égard, l'histoire de la famille Radhu contée par Abdul Wahid Radhu dans son livre "Caravane tibétaine" est exemplaire.

Descendant de brahmanes hindous appartenant à une sous-caste de "pandits cachemiri" dénommée Trakru, les Radhu se convertirent à l'islam à une époque difficile à préciser. Le premier à s'établir au Ladakh fut un homme religieux, le cheik Asad, qui quitta ses frères pour venir au milieu du XVIIIème siècle prêcher l'islam aux infidèles de ces hautes vallées. Son fils Faruq devint marchand caravanier. Entretenant d'étroites relations avec les rois ladakhi, il reçut une terre au village de Stok, près du palais royal. Ses fils aînés s'établirent à Leh, tandis que le cadet se mariait avec une Chinoise musulmane du Turkestan avant de gagner Lhasa pour y ouvrir un commerce. Rapidement, la famille occupa une position éminente et enviée. Riches, les Radhu possèdaient de belles propriétés et d'importants entrepôts où transitaient d'abondantes marchandises.

Au XIXème siècle, plusieurs membres de la lignée occupaient des situations sociales élevées. Ghulam Muhammad, qui était dans les meilleurs termes aussi bien avec la cour du Maharaja qu'avec le résident britannique à Srinagar,[28] fut autorisé à ajouter à son nom le titre de Khan Sahib. Il était également introduit dans les milieux dirigeants du Tibet où l'agent politique anglais aurait voulu faire de son fils, malheureusement mort prématurément, une sorte de chef de la communauté musulmane de Lhasa,[29] (A.W.Radhu, p.39). Le grand oncle d'Abdul Wahid, Ghulam Rassul "avait reçu de Lord Minto, vice-roi des Indes, le titre de Khan Bahadur en reconnaissance des services rendus à l'explorateur suédois Sven Hedin" (id.) Son grand-père, Muhammad Siddiq, demeuré à Leh, détenait le privilège de diriger la caravane *lo-phyag*. Enfin, un autre de ses oncles, Abdullah Shah, avait été nommé *aksakal*.[30]

---

28. En 1849, l'Inde est entièrement contrôlée par les anglais, soit directement, Inde britannique, soit indirectement, Etats princiers (comme le Cachemire). En 1857, l'Inde devient colonie directe de la couronne.

29. Le *kha-che go-ba* ,"chef des Cachemiri", jouait un rôle considérable au sein de la communauté musulmane de Lhasa. Voir à ce sujet, M. Gaborieau (1973), p. 25.

30. A propos de cette famille, E. Joldan (p.61) écrit: "the two Muslim aristocrat families - Haider Shah and Nasar Shah - were well known beyond Ladakh. While

Recrutés par l'administration britannique, essentiellement parmi la communauté musulmane, les *aksakal* ("barbe blanche" en turkmène) étaient chargés de surveiller l'activité des caravaniers d'Asie centrale qui empruntaient la "Route du Traité", et particulièrement le trafic du haschich, dont le Turkestan chinois cultivait de grandes quantités qu'on écoulait en Inde. "Le traité en question était celui que le gouvernement de l'Inde avait signé à la suite de la campagne militaire menée en 1811 par Lord Durand dans les régions les plus septentrionales de l'Etat du Cachemire afin d'assurer la liberté et la sécurité du commerce le long des pistes menant en territoire chinois." (Ibid. p.62).

Commerçants, citadins pour la plupart, les *'ar-gon* n'entraient pas en compétition avec les bouddhistes pour la possession de la terre comme les paysans balti. Nés de père cachemiri ou turk, le négoce était souvent leur seul moyen de subsistance.

> "The Arghons, as a rule, have no land, and they therefore have to keep their wits about them to earn their bread. They are far better traders than the Buddhists, they are quite ready to work for money, and they generally speak two languages, viz. Tibetan and Turki, or Tibetan and kashmiri."
> (H. Ramsay, p.57).

Heureux en affaires, qualité appréciée dans le monde tibétain, occupant souvent des postes élevés dans l'administration, leur statut et leur richesse égalaient ceux de la noblesse locale avec laquelle ils entretenaient d'excellentes relations n'excluant pas le mariage. Considérés par la strate des "gens ordinaires" (*dmangs-rigs*) comme des "corps nobles", ils jouissaient des privilèges réservés à l'aristocratie et aux religieux bouddhistes de haut rang comme celui de porter des habits de brocart de soie ou d'assister aux danses masquées du monastère d'Hémis depuis les fenêtres des appartements privés de l'abbé.

Tous cependant n'étaient pas engagés dans le commerce transhimalayen. Outre les prêcheurs, *akhon* [31] qui occupaient la

---

the former turned their attention towards Sinkiang, the latter traded with Lhasa in a big way.

"Abdul Hamid Khan who served for many years as British Aksakal in Yarkand and may be in Kargalik was conferred the title of Khan Bahadur, which was second only to Knighthood in the British Indian Empire of those days.

"Gulam Rasul of the Nasar Shah family also received the same title, mainly for rendering assistance to the well known explorer Sven Hedin."

31. *akhon, akhon-pa* : expression d'Asie centrale désignant à l'origine les *mollah, molla,* mot persan d'origine arabe (*mawla* : maître), docteurs de la loi coranique.

fonction de *muezzin*[32] de la mosquée et plus tard, celle de maître dans les écoles coraniques traditionnelles, on comptait parmi la communauté musulmane originaire du Cachemire des artisans spécialisés dans le travail du bois ou la confection de tapis, des tailleurs et des orfèvres-bijoutiers. Certains de leurs ancêtres étaient venus à la demande des rois ladakhi de la dynastie rnam-rgyal pour effectuer à la cour des tâches précises: traduire et écrire en persan la correspondance royale avec les gouverneurs moghols du Cachemire, dessiner et frapper la monnaie, ou encore mettre en oeuvre leurs talents de menuisiers et d'ébénistes.

Dans le concert unanime des voyageurs louant l'aptitude au commerce, l'honnêteté et le dynamisme des *'ar-gon*, en particulier des descendants de Cachemiri, une seule voix détonne, celle de F. Drew, qui sillonna le Ladakh de 1869 à 1871 au service du Maharaja du Cachemire, et qui considère tous ces "métisses" comme des êtres sans foi, ni loi, car sans racines.

> "The result of the crossing of breeds, in each of these cases, cannot be said to be good. The half-castes are for the most part thoroughly untrustworthy, and in other respects they are of worse character than either of the races they spring from. This is probably due (...) to the want of family ties and of the training in social habits of which children of almost every race get something in the ordinary course of things, but which is broken through when unusual connections are made."
> (F. Drew, pp. 244-245)

Seules trouvent grâce à ses yeux quelques "respectables" familles issues de l'union ancienne de marchands du Cachemire et de femmes ladakhi, mais cette exception corrobore, à ses dires, sa thèse :

> "insomuch that these have for some generations formed a community of settled habits and have again acquired a standard of morals which the miscellaneous half-castes seem quite to avoid" (id.).

Bien que minoritaires, certaines de ces familles musulmanes possédaient des terres près de Leh, données par le roi en échange de services rendus à l'époque de la dynastie rnam-rgyal ou achetées à des nobles bouddhistes grâce aux bénéfices réalisés avec le commerce

32. *muezzin* (en arabe), celui qui récite l'*adhan*, c'est-à-dire, l'appel à la cérémonie cultuelle du vendredi et aux cinq prières rituelles.

transhimâlayen. Le plus souvent, les musulmans ne les cultivaient pas eux-mêmes, et les donnaient en fermage à des métayers bouddhistes. En bons commerçants, les chefs de famille prêtaient du grain aux fermiers en difficulté à des taux d'intérêt élevé, ce qui leur assurait un revenu supplémentaire non négligeable.

Les *'ar-gon*, nés de l'union temporaire d'une femme ladakhi avec un marchand de passage, souvent plus pauvres, se spécialisaient dans le ramassage et le commerce du *pashminah* et du *shahtush*. Ils pratiquaient avec les marchands cachemiri de Srinagar une sorte de troc, recevant des textiles divers et des ustensiles de cuisine en cuivre ou en fer blanc en échange de la précieuse laine. Ils écoulaient ensuite ces marchandises parmi les nomades du Chang-thang qui leur procuraient la matière première. Mais selon A.W.Radhu (p. 276), "ils ne s'enrichissaient guère à ce trafic, car ils avaient l'habitude de dépenser à peu près tout ce qu'ils gagnaient à bien manger et à s'acheter de beaux vêtements qui leur donnaient fière allure." A l'encontre de leurs alter-ego bouddhistes, natifs du Bas-Ladakh, qui, économes, "avaient l'habitude de charger leurs ballots sur des ânes qui ne cheminaient que de nuit, se reposaient de jour et ne coûtaient pratiquement rien à leurs propriétaires", ils tenaient à monter des chevaux, ou du moins des mules.

A ces musulmans, descendants de marchands caravaniers traditionnellement engagés dans le commerce et pour la plupart de confession sunnite de droit hanafite,[33] s'opposaient les immigrants venus les mains vides des contrées de l'ouest, du Purig et du Baltistan, à la recherche d'un travail.

La majorité d'entre eux était établie à Chushot, un village de deux cents maisonnées situé dans la plaine alluviale de l'Indus, à une dizaine de kilomètres au sud de Leh, et décrit en 1871 par F. Drew (p.270) en ces termes :

> "Chushot has not the picturesqueness of the villages which we have looked at lower down the valley; here fruit trees do not grow, on account of the severity of the wind that blows along the length of the flat; still we see some poplars and small willows and it is probable that plantations arranged in belts - one protecting the other - would flourish."

33. L'école hanafite (hanifite) du nom d' Abou Hanifa (mort en 767) est le rite le moins contraignant. Elle fait une large place au jugement personnel, à la recherche du mieux et à l'effort de recherche personnelle. Elle détient les faveurs des non-arabophones (Turcs, Afghans, Pakistanais, Indiens et Chinois).

On connait peu leur histoire. Certains seraient les descendants des musiciens et des serviteurs de la princesse. Rgyal-Khatun, l'épouse balti imposée au roi ladakhi à l'aube du XVIème siècle. D'autres, originaires de la même région ou de la contrée voisine du Purig seraient venus dès les XVII-XVIIIèmes siècles, leurs terres ne suffisant pas à les nourrir. D'autres enfin, natifs du Cachemire, auraient fui la domination afghane particulièrement répressive à l'égard des musulmans shî'ites et, après s'être réfugiés au Baltistan, se seraient installés au Ladakh.

De langue tibétaine et de confession shî'ite, le plus souvent nurbakshi, les Balti sont méprisés tant par les bouddhistes que par les sunnites de droit hanafite, pour lesquels le persan est langue de culture et de religion, et qui ne reconnaissent pas dans ces hérétiques de "vrais musulmans". Pauvres, illettrés, rejetés, les Balti (*sbal-ti*) étaient employés par les musulmans cachemiri de Leh ou les riches *'ar-gon* pour effectuer les tâches subalternes: entretien des caravansérails et des entrepôts, portage de l'eau, du combustible, aide au chargement et déchargement des caravanes. Les femmes louaient également leurs bras et, à la saison des récoltes, se proposaient pour vanner, cribler le grain ou glaner les épis restés sur les champs moissonnés. Avec les plus démunis,[34] ils partageaient le travail ingrat du traitement des laines *pashminah* et *shahtush.* En effet, avant d'être exportées au Cachemire, ces dernières devaient être nettoyées des nombreux poils qu'elles renfermaient, puis lavées et triées en fonction de la longueur des fils de laine et de la présence des poils de chèvre restant. Ces poils, qui représentaient entre un cinquième et sept-huitièmes du poids global leur étaient donnés comme salaire pour être transformés en cordes ou tissés en sacs de bâts. Les Balti exerçaient également les fonctions d'équarisseurs, de tanneurs, de bouchers, de cordonniers, tâches que les bouddhistes évitent car, contraires à leur religion, elles nuisent à leur *karma.* Selon A. Cunningham, dans les années 1841/42, certains d'entre eux furent condamnés à mort et pendus à Leh pour avoir tué et mangé de la vache, le Ladakh étant alors sous le contrôle de Gulab Singh, homme décrit par ses biographes comme un hindou dévôt.[35]

---

34. Après la conquête dogra et l'annexion du royaume du Ladakh en 1842 par Gulab Singh, les "ghulamzada", "nés-esclaves", enfants naturels nés de l'union des femmes ladakhi avec des soldats dogra furent également affectés à cette tâche. F.Drew, p.244.

35. "In 1841 and 1842 ... single individuals were put to death and their bodies exposed on gibbets by Jhandu, the thanadar of Leh for killing and eating kine. All these were musulmans from Balti... The skeleton of the man gibbeted at Leh in 1841 was still nearly perfect in october 1847 when I saw it." (A.Cunningham,

Bien sûr, on compte des exceptions. Tous les Balti n'étaient pas pauvres, et certains, Sayed, descendants du prophète, se réclamant de lignées venues d'Arabie, hommes riches et puissants, se livraient également avec succès au commerce transhimâlayen et possédaient de nombreux biens. Aujourd'hui encore, le fils de l'un d'eux, établi à Leh, parle avec nostalgie des nombreux chevaux et des diverses propriétés que sa famille détenait sur les routes menant du Turkestan chinois au Cachemire en passant par le Ladakh et le Purig. Enfin, parmi ceux que la naissance ne prédestinait pas à de telles aventures, certains réussissaient à établir leur renommée sur les pistes d'Asie centrale en accompagnant d'abord comme muletier, puis comme guide et chef de caravane de nombreux voyageurs occidentaux. Le cas le plus célèbre étant celui de Ghulam Rassul Galwan, qui nous a laissé son autobiographie et dont de nombreux voyageurs du siècle dernier - parmi les plus illustres - vantent les qualités.[36]

Marchands caravaniers, guides, muletiers ou cuisiniers au service de voyageurs occidentaux, artisans qualifiés ou main d'oeuvre pour les plus pauvres, on comptait également parmi la communauté musulmane alors établie à Leh des musiciens mendiants itinérants *bhe-da*, des barbiers, des boulangers qui cuisaient le pain dans des fours en terre ronds et verticaux, des bouchers et des restaurateurs chez lesquels on dégustait des petits morceaux de mouton grillés et une cuisine où se mêlaient saveurs indiennes et traditions d'Asie centrale.

4. La situation en Asie centrale et au Tibet et ses répercussions sur l'ancien royaume du Ladakh (1947-1989)

La conquête du royaume du Ladakh et son annexion par Gulab Singh, devenu Maharaja du Jammu et Cachemire sous protectorat britannique en 1846, affectèrent peu les musulmans établis au Ladakh et le commerce transhimâlayen. En revanche, l'amélioration notable du réseau de communications indien dans la première moitié du XXème siècle les condamna à brève échéance. Très vite, les caravaniers délaissèrent les pistes transhimâlayennes, leur préférant la route passant par le Sikkim et Gyantse, plus rapide, plus

p. 268).

36. Sur Ghulam Rassul Galwan, né en 1860 et qui commença à voyager en accompagnant son prestigieux homonyme Ghulam Rassul, grand oncle d'Abdul Wahid Raddhu, on peut lire l'autobiographie et les descriptions que font de lui Sven Hedin, Lord Dunmore, Cdt Younghusband, etc.

sûre et plus rentable. Leh, jadis entrepôt prospère où convergeaient les caravanes d'Asie centrale, s'endormit. Evalué à 93 lakhs de roupies en 1920, le commerce transhimâlayen tomba en vingt ans à 78,000 roupies. Les marchands musulmans établis au Ladakh, déménagèrent leurs biens et leurs négoces à Lhasa et à Kalimpong, tentant leur chance dans les échanges directs entre l'Inde et le Tibet.

En 1947, au moment de la partition, le Maharaja de Jammu, hindou, mais régnant sur une population musulmane, décida d'adhérer à l'Inde et non au Pakistan, provoquant le premier conflit indo-pakistanais. En février 1948, les habitants du Baltistan rejetèrent sa suzeraineté, demandant au gouvernement pakistanais d'assurer l'administration de leur région.

Au cours du mois d'octobre 1950, les premières troupes chinoises de l'armée rouge dite de "libération" envahirent l'est du Tibet. Les autorités indiennes minimisèrent les événements et réagirent à peine à cette invasion militaire.

En 1959, après la grande révolte de Lhasa qui provoqua l'exil du Dalai-lama et la fuite de milliers de Tibétains, la Chine annonça la fermeture de ses frontières avec l'Inde. Quelques mois plus tard, les Chinois pénétraient en Aksai-Chin, désert montagneux couvrant le Nord-Est du Ladakh, pour y construire une route leur permettant d'assurer une communication avec le Turkestan oriental rebaptisé depuis 1950 Xinjiang ou "Nouvelle Province". Ceci sans que le gouvernement de Delhi ne s'en inquiète. Cependant deux ans plus tard, devant l'ampleur des territoires occupés par la Chine, l'Inde réagissait et envoyait ses armées combattre le long de la frontière. De nombreux camps militaires furent alors établis à Leh et en différents lieux stratégiques et une route reliant la capitale du Cachemire à celle du Ladakh construite en 1962-63 pour en faciliter le ravitaillement.

Cette rupture sino-indienne ruina l'économie de l'ex-royaume du Ladakh, déjà amputé du Baltistan (sous contrôle pakistanais depuis 1949), le vouant à un irrémédiable déclin. Le commerce de la laine, qui, malgré les aléas politiques, s'était jusqu'alors maintenu, s'en trouva condamné. Les Chinois achetaient eux-mêmes la production de laine brute aux nomades du Chang-thang pour l'écouler sur leur propre marché. Les marchands cachemiri regagnèrent le Cachemire. Ceux de Yarkand et de Kashgar que la guerre avait coupé de leur patrie et qui craignaient de retourner au Xinjiang, théâtre de conflits meurtriers, s'installèrent à Srinagar, où ils se spécialisèrent dans la confection de bonnets brodés, de feutre ainsi que dans le traitement et le commerce de peaux et de fourrures. Ne pouvant obtenir la nationalité indienne et désireux de quitter un pays troublé par les hostilités indo-pakistanaises, nombreux furent ceux qui acceptèrent l'offre du gouvernement turc et émigrèrent vers la Turquie.

Les camions, empruntant la route conduisant de Srinagar à Leh, remplacèrent peu à peu les dernières caravanes qui survivaient grâce au commerce de fruits secs, de produits manufacturés indiens et de cosmétiques. Ladakhi, Turks, Tibétains furent remplacés par des camionneurs indiens, punjabi ou cachemiri autorisés à circuler dans toute la Zone Nord (North Zone), c'est-à-dire le Jammu & Kashmir, le Punjab, l'Haryana et Delhi.

Dans les années 60, Leh n'est plus la bourgade pittoresque, animée l'été par le va-et-vient des caravanes venant d'Asie centrale, d'Inde et du Tibet. Ce n'est plus cet immense caravansérail cosmopolite décrit par l'ensemble des voyageurs depuis le XVIIIème siècle, où - pour reprendre les termes du peintre Lafugie (c.1940) - se croisent de grands Cachemiri maigres au nez crochu et en vilains haillons euro-indiens, des Balti trapus vêtus d'épais lainages gris-brun, la tête serrée dans un bonnet; des marchands du Turkestan, aux robes capitonnées, coiffés de calots de peau de mouton et chaussés de hautes bottes cosaques; leurs femmes chastement voilées et habillées de belles robes brodées oranges ou roses; leurs soeurs du Ladakh aux lourdes robes sales, aux immenses coiffures ornées de turquoises, portant sur le dos la hotte remplie de fourrages destinés aux chevaux.[37]

Les Cachemiri présents, délégués à Leh par le gouvernement de l'Etat de Jammu & Kashmir, dont le Ladakh constitue désormais un des districts (le plus grand et le moins peuplé de l'Union indienne), occupent les postes les plus élevés dans l'administration et la fonction publique (police, école, hopital, banque). Face à cette discrimination, les vieux stéréotypes se réveillent. L'image du Cachemiri malhonnête et profiteur perdure. Le mépris et la méfiance sont réciproques. Le Cachemiri vit mal son exil chez "ces gens frustes et qui ne mangent même pas de riz" et le Ladakhi exprime clairement son manque de confiance à l'égard de ce peuple "roublard et sans parole". "Confier un secret à un Cachemiri, c'est comme verser de l'eau dans une passoire" dit un proverbe ladakhi.

Avec l'ouverture partielle du Ladakh aux touristes étrangers en 1974, ils reviennent l'été vendre sur le Bazaar de l'artisanat cachemiri et, surtout, des "antiquités" ladakhi rachetées pour quelques roupies à des paysans bouddhistes et revendues avec un large bénéfice aux occidentaux de passage; commerce fructueux, dont ils partagent

---

37. Pour des descriptions de Leh, ville cosmopolite et plaque tournante du commerce caravanier transhimalayen, lire: I. Desideri, p. 39; W. Moorcroft, p. 296; M. Pallis, p. 252; Lafugie, p. 69.

le monopole avec une poignée de marchands montés de Manali et des Tibétains réfugiés au Ladakh depuis l'invasion de leur pays par l'armée chinoise.

L'esprit d'entreprise reconnu aux *'ar-gon*, héritiers de l'islam marchand, n'a pas faibli. Comme le note P. Kaplanian (1987, pp.101-102), "leur capacité à saisir toutes les opportunités et un certain respect pour l'éducation (la tradition de la lecture du Coran dispensée en ourdou, langue de communication de tout le J & K, et à l'écriture près, de toute l'Inde du Nord) leur ont permis de contrôler une bonne partie des nouveaux secteurs économiques, plus que le pourcentage dans la population du tehsil de Leh l'aurait laissé penser." En 1974, ils sont les premiers à aménager leurs maisons pour accueillir les touristes et offrir leurs services en tant que guide ("tour leader"), chauffeur, ou cuisinier. Ceux qui ont appris des rudiments d'anglais au Collège Tyndale Biscoe de Srinagar (fondé par le missionnaire protestant du même nom) mettent à profit leur connaissance. Leur maîtrise de l'ourdou, et souvent de la langue cachemiri, fait d'eux les intermédiaires privilégiés auprès du gouvernement en place,[38] et bon nombre d'entre eux obtiennent des emplois salariés. Ce sont également vers eux que les agences de voyage de Srinagar, qui ont dans les années 80 le quasi-monopole du tourisme dans la région, se tournent quand elles acceptent de collaborer avec des Ladakhi. Ils sont musulmans et de surcroît sunnites

Maîtres d'un commerce florissant, avec des boutiques bien achalandées, où ils vendent des denrées comestibles (thé, sel, riz, farine, épices), du kérosène, des textiles (cotonnades, velours) et des produits manufacturés indiens (cosmétiques, savons, allumettes, vaisselle de fer blanc), leurs échoppes sont établies sur l'artère principale de la capitale (Main Bazaar), celle des bouddhistes, plus petites, occupant les ruelles adjacentes.

Propriétaires des premiers hôtels bâtis dans la capitale, puis des premiers camions et voitures particulières, ils éveillent la convoitise de leurs homologues bouddhistes, qui accusent le gouvernement cachemiri de les favoriser.

La situation des Balti et de leurs descendants, auxquels se sont mélés des Purig-pa également shî'ites[39] ne s'est pas améliorée. Parias

---

38. Depuis 1948, les "chief-ministers" gouvernant le J & K ont tous été musulmans: Shaik Mohammad Abdullah, Bakshi Ghulam Mohammad, Shamass-u-din-Ghulam Mohammad Sadia, Syed Mir Qasim, puis de nouveau Shaikh Abdullah, et après lui son fils Farooq Abdullah.

39. J'utilise le terme Balti (*sbal-ti*) pour désigner les habitants du Baltistan, aujourd'hui pakistanais, qui englobait autrefois les chefferies de Skardu, Shigar,

de la société, ils sont engagés aux côtés d'Indiens venus du Sud pour gagner quelques roupies dans les travaux publics. Balayeurs, cantonniers, manoeuvres, ils construisent les routes, les goudronnent, percent les canalisations, épurent les égouts, tâches pénibles et dévalorisantes que refusent d'effectuer les Ladakhi. Signe révélateur du mépris dans lequel ils sont tenus, les enfants nés des rares mariages entre Balti et Ladakhi ne sont pas considérés comme des *'ar-gon*, mais comme des Balti.

Estimée dans les années 80 à plus de 3,000 individus pour le canton de Leh, soit 12% de la population, majoritaire dans la région de Kargil et au Cachemire, la communauté musulmane est une minorité dynamique. Sa croissance démographique supérieure à celle de la population bouddhiste, ne cesse d'inquièter les dirigeants des mouvements bouddhistes, qui y voit une menace pour l'identité de leur communauté.

5. 1989: crise passagère ou rupture dans les relations entre musulmans et bouddhistes?

Eté 1989, manifestations, campagne de désobéissance civile, et actes de violences contre ceux qui représentent le pouvoir et ceux qu'elle accuse de lui être inféodés, se succèdent dans la capitale et ses proches environs à l'appel de l'Association Bouddhiste Ladakhi (LBA).[40] La promesse faite par le gouvernement de Delhi lors des précédentes émeutes d'accorder aux Ladakhi un statut spécifique n'ayant pas été tenue et la peur éprouvée par les bouddhistes d'assister impuissants à "l'islamisation de leur pays" les ont conduits de nouveau dans la rue pour réclamer une fois encore le statut de territoire de l'Union (Union Territory Status). Ce statut, dont bénéficient en Inde des villes et des régions posant des problèmes particuliers (comme Delhi, Chandigarh ou les Iles Andaman et Nicobar) placerait le Ladakh sous l'autorité directe de New-Delhi, le

---

Rongdu, Khapalu, et Kharmang, et celui de Purig-pa (*bod-rigs-pa ?*) pour ceux du Purig, contrée qui occupe aujourd'hui l'ouest du district du Ladakh.

Pour les locuteurs bouddhistes ladakhi, *kha-che* ("cachemiri") désigne l'ensemble des musulmans sunnites, *sbal-ti* ("du Baltistan"), l'ensemble des shî'ites.

40. Ladakhi Buddhist Association, association fondée en 1934 sous l'égide d'un Cachemiri bouddhiste Shri dhar Kaul et soutenue par la hiérarchie religieuse et l'aristocratie ladakhi. Parmi ses actions: la publication de livres en ladakhi pour les enfants et l'obtention d'un enseignement du ladakhi à l'école, l'obtention d'une terre dans le centre de Leh pour l'érection du nouveau Jo-khang, la construction d'une école de philosophie bouddhiste pour l'éducation des novices ne pouvant plus se rendre dans les monastères du Tibet.

dégageant ainsi de la tutelle cachemiri, cause - selon les Ladakhi bouddhistes - de tous leurs maux.[41]

Comme vingt ans auparavant, c'est - semble-t-il - une dispute privée entre musulman et bouddhiste qui a mis le feu aux poudres. Aujourd'hui comme hier, les griefs dont les deux partis s'accusent mutuellement sont les mêmes : conversions forcées, favoritisme au niveau de l'emploi et de l'allocation de terres, violences et voies de fait contre des personnes ou des lieux saints appartenant à l'une ou l'autre communauté religieuse.[42] De même, les circonstances dans lesquelles ces violences prennent place sont similaires: manifestations contre la domination cachemiri et en faveur d'un Ladakh libre, répression policière et arrestation de figures charismatiques (le "head-lama" du monastère de Phyang en 1969, Thubstan Tsewang, membre respecté de la famille royale en 1989) engendrant une aggravation des troubles, cessation de l'agitation à la libération des dits "meneurs" et devant la promesse du gouvernement indien d'accorder aux Ladakhi le statut de "tribus répertoriées" (Scheduled Tribes Status) leur permettant de bénéficier de quotas dans l'administration et les universités et les mettant de fait à l'abri de la concurrence cachemiri

"L'histoire se répète" titre l'association des musulmans des districts de Leh et de Kargil...

Certes... Mais aujourd'hui, aux revendications essentiellement économiques des années passées sont venues se greffer des revendications culturelles et religieuses. Faisant du bouddhisme le fer de lance de leur mouvement, la LBA, soutenue par le clergé et la noblesse, lutte non seulement pour la réhabilitation sociale, politique et économique des bouddhistes du Ladakh, mais aussi pour la propagation de la foi bouddhique et contre "l'aliénation culturelle" qui les guettent. Ses membres combattent les "envahisseurs" (Cachemiri, musulmans d'origine cachemiri, *'a-rgon*), qui selon le porte-parole de l'association détiennent 40% des emplois gouvernementaux bien que ne représentant que 12% de la population du district, et renient tous ceux qui refusent de s'allier à eux, comme les Tibétains réfugiés des camps de Choklamsar et d'Agling près de Leh, qui accueillis par l'Inde après l'invasion de leur pays par l'armée chinoise, ne désirent pas se mêler à un combat qu'ils ne jugent pas le leur.

Outre le problème de l'éducation et de l'emploi, l'hégémonie

---

41. "Kashmir Govt.: the root cause of all feuds and problems in Leh. The source of all the evils" peut-on lire dans les manifestes et placards apposés dans le Bazaar.

42. Cf. *Ladakh People's movement for Union Territory Status.* et *History repeated in Ladakh- The Muslim viewpoint of the Ladakh Agitation of 1989.*

de l'ourdu et de l'alphabet arabe qui menace l'existence de la langue ladakhi et de l'écriture tibétaine, la conversion des femmes bouddhistes à l'islam (et dans une moindre mesure au christianisme) est, depuis de nombreuses années, l'un des chevaux de bataille des associations bouddhistes.[43] En effet, tous les recensements le montrent, la population musulmane en vertu de son système matrimonial et de ses règles d'héritage, de l'apport continu d'immigrants musulmans venant des régions de l'ouest et de conversions - essentiellement féminines - augmente plus rapidement que la population bouddhiste. La polyandrie et la règle de primogéniture qui, jadis ont permis aux habitants du Royaume du Ladakh de vivre dans un environnement contraignant sans connaître de grandes famines ou d'exodes et sans mettre en péril les ressources naturelles en maintenant une croissance démographique modérée et en évitant le morcellement des terres arables, contribuent aujourd'hui à l'expansion démographique de la communauté musulmane. Les femmes bouddhistes "en surplus" préfèrent se marier à un homme fût-il musulman ou chrétien et se convertir que de rester dans la maison familiale en tant que co-épouse, vivre avec leurs parents dans la "petite maison", ou devenir nonnes. Pour beaucoup d'entre elles, l'islam représenté par les *'ar-gon* représente la modernité, l'accès au monde occidental.

De plus, si autrefois la conversion à l'islam n'était - semble-t-il - qu'une procédure à respecter pour que le contrat de mariage (*nika*) soit conclu entre les époux et avait peu d'incidences sur les pratiques quotidiennes de la femme, aujourd'hui sous l'influence grandissante des gardiens de la loi islamique, la situation change. La femme convertie doit désormais se conformer aux règles de l'islam et les enfants qui, jadis, embrassaient la religion de leur père (pour les garçons) ou de leur mère (pour les filles), naissent tous musulmans et reçoivent des noms témoignant de cette appartenance.

Pour les associations bouddhistes, le recours au religieux sert à rétablir une identité que l'imposition d'une modernité étrangère - dûe à l'essor touristique et à l'implantation massive de militaires indiens dans la région - et la sujétion économique cachemiri ont mis à mal.

---

43. Depuis 1969, date de la création de la Lamdon Social Welfare, les leaders bouddhistes tentent d'éradiquer la polyandrie, qui favorise - par un surplus de femmes - l'accroissement de la population musulmane et nuit à l'image de leur communauté. Une de leurs principales campagnes contre la polyandrie - abolie théoriquement en 1941 mais toujours pratiquée dans les villages du Bas-Ladakh et du Zanskar - fut montée à l'aide de saynètes mettant en scène avec humour le désagrément que procure à ceux qui y sont engagés un mariage polyandre. Dans un même registre, cette association lutte contre l'abus de bière d'orge.

Moyen de défense contre ce qui aliène et opprime, le bouddhisme fonctionne comme un fort ciment identitaire et apparait indissociable d'une dynamique "nationaliste". Symbole de ce "nationalisme bouddhiste", le drapeau aux couleurs du bouddhisme qui flotte sur le nouveau temple de Leh, sur l'école privée bouddhiste (Lamdon Model School) et sur certaines habitations, ou qu'arborent en badge, souligné de la phrase "I love buddhism" - un coeur rouge remplaçant le mot "love" - de nombreux Ladakhi. Autre signe de ce combat contre "l'invasion musulmane", les enseignes des échoppes du Bazaar de Leh et des environs sont désormais écrites avec l'alphabet tibétain, le nom du propriétaire qu'il soit hindou ou sikh et le titre de de son commerce étant phonétiquement transcrit, ce qui donne parfois lieu à des formules incongrues.

Depuis 1989, les bouddhistes suivant les directives de leurs leaders se livrent à un boycott social et économique, qui ne se limite plus aux seuls Cachemiri, mais englobe l'ensemble de la communauté musulmane. Ce boycott, très suivi, appuyé par les moines qui refusent parfois l'entrée de leur monastère aux touristes venus à bord d'un taxi musulman, commence à poser de sérieux problèmes financiers aux nombreux musulmans de Leh, dont le commerce constitue traditionnellement la principale source de revenus. Ne s'approvisionnant plus que dans des magasins bouddhistes ou hindous[44] et engageant les visiteurs occidentaux à les imiter, les bouddhistes en sont venus à se faire boulangers, voire même bouchers (un "intouchable" (?) abattant la bête, l'écorchant et la livrant au boucher, qui se charge de la découper et de la vendre). Pour renforcer leur boycott et profiter de la manne touristique qui leur a longtemps échappée, la communauté bouddhiste a récemment construit de nombreux hôtels dans la capitale, acheté des voitures particulières servant de taxis et des minibus, qui assurent des liaisons quotidiennes entre Leh et les villages de la vallée de l'Indus, procurant à leurs propriétaires un revenu non négligeable et rendant les villageois indépendants des transports gouvernementaux. Taxis, bus, hôtels et commerces bouddhistes sont aisément reconnaissables par les portaits du Dalaï Lama ou d'autres dignitaires bouddhistes qui les ornent, et par les autocollants, apposés en évidence sur vitres et pare-brises, célébrant "la victoire des dieux sur les démons", librement traduit en anglais par "Truth will prevail", ou réclamant un "Ladakh

44. Fuyant la répression dont ils sont victimes à Srinagar et dans la Vallée heureuse depuis la montée des mouvements fondamentalistes et indépendantistes qui agitent le Cachemire, beaucoup d'hindous ont trouvé refuge au Ladakh, où leurs échoppes remplacent peu à peu celle des Cachemiri musulmans.

libre du Cachemire" ("Free Ladakh from Kashmir") sous la calligraphie du célèbre *mantra* "Om mani padme hum".

Symbolique également de ce combat pour le pouvoir et l'appropriation de l'espace, la lutte - par hauts-parleurs interposés - auxquels se sont livrés la grande mosquée et le nouveau *Jo-khang* de Leh pour dominer l'espace sonore au cours du mois de mars 1992, où les musulmans célèbraient le ramadam (*ramzân*) et les bouddhistes le "Mane Tung chur" (*ma-ni dung phyur*). Diffusant l'un l'appel à la prière et les oraisons spéciales de ce mois de jeûne, l'autre le *mantra* d'Avalokiteshvara répété des milliers de fois par les bouddhistes présents dans le temple, les deux lieux-saints rivalisèrent en décibels pour couvrir le brouhaha de la ville.

La tension, née des événements de 1989 et entretenue par le boycott, est particulièrement sensible à Leh où, musulmans et bouddhistes ne s'invitent plus comme autrefois à l'occasion des fêtes calendaires (Nouvel an ladakhi, *lo-gsar*, fête de la rupture de jeûne *'Id-ul-fitr* ou fête du sacrifice *Bagra 'id*), ou de toute autre festivité (don du nom, mariage, ou funérailles). Elle se manifeste également dans les crises familiales, villageoises ou "nationales", que génèrent la plupart des mariages mixtes, dont la célébration, de plus en plus rare, a lieu dans une grande discrétion.

La décision du Ministre de l'Intérieur, Buta Singh, de n'attribuer le "Scheduled Tribes Status" qu'à certaines "catégories" de Ladakhi, excluant des pourparlers les *'ar-gon* et tous ceux qui, bien que vivant depuis des décennies au Ladakh, comptaient parmi leurs ancêtres un Cachemiri, un Punjabi ou tout autre indien non qualifié selon les critères de la commission de "tribal", a contribué à envenimer les relations entre les bouddhistes et les autres membres de la société ladakhi. Cette mesure, jugée discriminatoire par tous ceux qui en étaient exclus, a servi de surcroît d'argument à certains leaders bouddhistes pour refuser à ces derniers le droit de se proclamer "Ladakhi" et de combattre à leurs côtés. *Phyi-pa,* "gens de l'extérieur", les musulmans ladakhi sont présentés comme des étrangers, des immigrants auxquels toute "ladakhéité" est déniée.

Parallèlement à ce durcissement des relations entre les deux communautés manipulées par certaines de leurs élites en quête de pouvoir, on assiste à une revitalisation des pratiques orthodoxes bouddhiques et du sentiment religieux (ou tout au moins de son expression visible). Outre l'apparition de drapeaux, d'affiches, d'autocollants, de badges aux couleurs du bouddhisme déjà mentionnée, on note une recrudescence de la participation des citadins, et particulièrement des jeunes gens, aux célébrations bouddhistes comme le *Mani dung phyur* célébré dans la capitale ou le jeûne du premier mois lunaire effectué dans le monastère voisin de Sankar. Si des pratiques apotropaïques, comme celle consistant à orner une maison nouvellement construite de dessins à la peinture rouge et d'éléments de protection divers (pénis en bois, *sa-sgo-gnam-sgo*) pour en éloigner les démons, tendent à disparaître dans la région de Leh, un renouveau de pratiques "oubliées" ces dernières années, comme celle de la prosternation complète *mgo phyag*, où l'exécutant accomplit la circumambulation de lieux saints en se prosternant de tout son corps, renaissent.[45]

Dans les villages, l'argent gagné par la communauté villageoise auprès des touristes par la location d'emplacements de camping l'été ou la visite du monastère du village, est géré par des associations de jeunes (Youth Associations), qui l'utilisent pour améliorer l'habitat du moine-prêtre de village, agrandir le hall d'assemblée du *dgon-pa*, payer la fabrication d'un grand moulin à prière ou l'exécution d'un grand rituel nécessitant la présence de nombreux moines.

Comme dans d'autres régions du monde, on assiste au Ladakh à l'influence grandissante du religieux dans les enjeux politiques, sociaux, et idéologiques. Comme dans le reste de l'Inde, clivages religieux et politiques se recoupent. La jeune génération, beaucoup plus politisée que celle de ses parents, radicalise ses positions, accentuant ses divergences avec l'"Autre" pour fonder sa légitimité.

Aujourd'hui où, en Orient comme en Occident, on constate une montée des "nationalismes religieux", et où l'Inde est le théâtre de conflits violents entre communautés religieuses, la crise que traverse la société ladakhi est-elle simplement conjoncturelle et passagère, ou marque-t-elle une rupture dans l'histoire des musulmans et des bouddhistes de l'ancien Royaume du Ladakh? Et, dans ces conditions, dans quelle mesure le compromis adopté pour concilier les règles coutumières fondées sur le bouddhisme tibétain aux injonctions de l'Islam peut-il rester stable?

---

45. De nombreux jeunes gens firent ainsi le tour du monastère de Sankar le jour de jeûne, et d'autres, jeunes et moins jeunes, la circum-ambulation de Leh et de l'ancien temple, qui aux abords du palais royal domine la ville. Par ailleurs, la distance parcourue chaque jour par un homme du village de Sakti, parti pour accomplir le pélerinage des lieux-saints et monastères du Ladakh en prosternation complète, était au début de l'année 1992 l'une des nouvelles quotidiennes données par la radio locale.

Bibliographie

AMIN PANDIT. "Mosques and Imambaras." *Cultural Heritage of Ladakh,* ed. by P.N. Chopra, Ministry of Education and Welfare, Delhi.

ANON, 1989. *Ladakh People's Movement for Union Territory Status.* Leh.

ANON, 1989. *History repeated in Ladakh: The Muslim viewpoint of the Ladakh agitation of 1989.* Muslims of Leh & Kargil Districts.

BAMZAI, Prithivi Nath Kaul, 1962. *A History of Kashmir.* Metropolitan Book, Delhi.

BERNIER, François, 1830. *Voyages de François Bernier.* 2 vols. Paris

BIRDWOOD, Lord, 1952. "The Asian Frontiers of Kashmir." *Journal of the Royal Central Asian Society* 39, 241-245.

CHARAK, S. Singh, 1980. *History and Culture of Himalayan States.* Vol.5. Jammu Kingdom. Light & Life Publishers, New-Delhi.

CUNNINGHAM, Alexander, 1854. *Ladak, Physical, Statistical and Historical with notices of the surrounding countries.* W.H. Allen, London (rééd. 1970, New-Delhi).

DEVADAS, David, 1988. "Voices of Protest." *Indian Today,* 15 Juillet 1988, pp. 62-65.

DESIDERI, Ipolito, 1932. *An Account of Tibet. The Travels of Ippolito Desideri of Pistoia, S.J. 1712-1727.* Préface de Filippo de Filippi, introduction de C. Wessels,.London (rééd. Taipei, 1971).

DREW, Frederic, 1875. *The Jummoo and Kashmir territories, a geographical account.* Edward Stanford, London.

Encyclopédie de l'Islam, 2ème édition, articles "Baltistan", "Kashmir", "Ladakh", "Tibet".

FRANCKE, A. H., 1907. *A History of Ladakh.* Calcutta. (Rééd. en 1977 with critical introduction et annotations par S.S. Gergan et F. M. Hassnain. New-Delhi, S. Chand & Co).

----------- 1926.*Antiquities of Indian Tibet, Part. 2: The Chronicles of Ladakh and Minor Chronicles.* Archeological Survey of India, New Imperial Series, 50, Calcutta.

------------1929. "Islam among the Tibetans." *The Moslem World,* 19, 134-140.

GABORIEAU, Marc, 1973. *Récit d'un voyageur musulman au Tibet.* Klincksieck, Paris.

GALWAN, Ghulam Rassul, 1923. *Servant of Sahibs.* W.Heffer & Sons, Cambridge.

GRIST, Nicky, 1985. "Ladakh, a trading State." *Acta Biologica Montana* 1985 (5), 91-102.

HEDIN, Sven, 1909. *Transhimalaya.* Macmillan, Londres (3 vol.)

JOLDAN, E. 1985. *Harvest Festival of Buddhist Dards of Ladakh and other essays.* Kapoor Brothers, Srinagar.

KAK, B. L., 1978. *Chasing Shadows in Ladakh..* Light and Life Publishers, New-Delhi-Jammu.

KAPLANIAN, Patrick, 1982. "Le Ladakh: évolution politique récente." *L'Afrique et l'Asie modernes,* 4e trim. 1982, n°135, 12-22.

KHAN, Hasmatullah, 1987. *History of Baltistan.* Trad. anglaise de Adam Nayyar, Lok Virsa , Islamabad, (édition originale en ourdou 1939).

KHAN, Muhammad Ishaq, 1985. "Islam in Kashmir: Historical Analysis of its Features." in *Islam in India*. ed. by C.W. Troll; vol. 2. Religion and Religious Education, Vikas Publishing House, New-Delhi.

KULBUSHAN Warikoo, 1985. "Ladakh, an Entrepot of Indo-Central Asian Trade during the Dogra rule." *South Asian Studies* 20, n°2.

LAFUGIE, C., s.d. c. 1950. *Au Tibet*. J. Susse, Paris.

MIRZA HAIDAR DUGHLAT, 1973. *The Tarikh-i-Rashidi*.. Traduction de E. Denison Ross. Academica Asiatica, Patna.

MOORCROFT, William & TREBECK, George, 1837. *Travels in the Himalayan Provinces of Hindustan and the Panjab, in Ladakh and Kashmir, in Peshawar, Kabul, Kunduz and Bokhara*. 2 vols. John Murray, London.

OSMASTON, Henry, 1990. "The Kashmir Problem." *Geographical Magazine* 62 (6),.1 & 17-21.

PAREJA, F. M., 1963. *Islamologie*. Beyrouth.

PARMU, R.K. 1969. *A History of muslim rule in Kashmir 1320-1819*. People's Publishing House, Delhi.

PETECH, Luciano, 1947. "The Tibetan-Ladakhi-Moghul War of 1681-83." *Indian Historical Quarterly* 23, 169-199.

PETECH, Luciano, 1977. *The Kingdom of Ladakh, c. 950-1842 A.D.* Serie Orientale Roma LI, Rome.

PETER of GREECE and DENMARK, Prince, 1952 "The Moslems of Central Tibet." *Journal of the Royal Central Asian Society* 39, 233-240.

PHUNTSOG STOBDAN, 1989. "Ladakh: Folly in the Frontier. *Link* 17, sept. 1989, 5-10, New-Delhi.

RADHU, Abdul Wahid, 1981. *Caravane tibétaine*. Fayard, Paris.

RAHUL, Ram, 1961. "Kashmiri Muslims in Tibet." *International Studies* III, n°2, 181-182.

RAMSAY, H. 1890. *Western Tibet : a Practical Dictionary of the Language and Customs of the Districts Included in the Ladakh Wazarat*. W. Ball, Lahore.

RIZVI, B.R., 1986. "Religion and Peasantry in Kargil (J&K)." in *Ecology, Economy and Religion of Himalayas*, ed. by L.P. Vidyarthi and Makhan Jha,. Orient Publications, New-Delhi, 217-229.

RIZVI, Janet, 1985. "Peasant Traders of Ladakh: a Study in Oral History." *India International Centre Quarterly* 12, n°1,13-27, New-Delhi.

ROVILLE, Gérard, 1990. "Contribution à l'étude de l'Islam au Baltistan et au Ladakh." *Wissenschaftsgeschichte und gegenwärtige Förschungen in Nordwest-Indien*, Staatliches Museum für Völkerkunde, Dresden, .113-124.

SIDDIQI, Ataullah, 1991. "Muslims of Tibet." *The Tibet Journal* XVI, n°4, 71-85.

SHEIK, Abdul Ghani, 1991. "Tibetan Muslims." *The Tibet Journal* XVI, n°4, 86-89.

ULLAH, Mir Izzet, 1843, "Travels beyond the Himalayas." *Journal of the Royal Asiatic Society* 7, 283-342.

WAHID, Siddiq, 1989, "Riots in Ladakh and the Genesis of a Tragedy." *Himal* sept-oct. 1989, 24-25.

ETHNOHISTORY OF MUSLIMS IN CENTRAL LADAKH (abstract)

Pascale Dollfus

In the 14th century Muslims conquered Kashmir, with which Ladakh has close economic ties. In the period that followed, the Ladakhi kingdom, already weakened by internal conflicts, faced repeated invasions made in the name of a holy war or *jihad*.

At the beginning of the 16th century the Ladakhi king, Jamyang Namgyal was defeated by the Muslim rulers of Baltistan, which obliged him to marry the Balti princess Rgyal Khatun. According to a Balti tradition, the first mosque of Ladakh was built in Shey for her .

In 1666/7, the great sunni mosque of Leh was built as a symbol of the suzerainty of Aurangzeb the Moghul emperor. The decisive events concerning the Muslim presence only occured some years later.

In 1679, King Deldan Namgyal, unable to repulse the powerful Tibetan-Mongol army sent by the 5th Dalai Lama, was obliged to ask for help from the Moghul Governor of Kashmir. The Mongols were ousted, but there was a heavy price to pay.

Ladakh signed a peace treaty with Kashmir (1682) and then with Tibet (1684). When new boundaries were drawn, Ladakh was deprived of half of its land. Once again the Ladakhi king was obliged to convert to Islam. He promised to pay tribute; to keep the Leh mosque in good repair; and to strike coins in the Emperor's name. Meanwhile, trade in wool and goathair, 50% of Ladakh's total trade, became the monopoly of Kashmiri merchants.

In accordance with the Tibetan treaty, it was agreed that every year a caravan of tea would be sent from Lhasa to Leh, and that in return every 3 years a *lo-phyag* of numerous gifts would be sent from Leh to Lhasa as a sign of allegiance to the Dalai Lama.

After the disastrous trade blockade imposed in 1638 had been lifted, and the suzerainty of the Grand Moghuls reaffirmed, Kashmiri Muslims came to settle permanently in Leh and the nearby villages of Spituk, Phyang, Shey and Thiksey.

Islam came to Ladakh neither by conquest, nor with zealous missionaries, but with the caravans that traded between Kashmir, Tibet and Central Asia.

The Kashmiris who came from Srinagar in the 17th century were among the first Muslims to settle in the small Buddhist kingdom.

Most were traders, but occasionally they were accompanied by men of religion.

During the 19th century, the Kashmiri population grew considerably with the arrival of immigrants fleeing from the harsh rule of Ranjit Singh, the Sikh ruler of the Punjab who had conquered Kashmir in 1819.

In Leh, they met the traders from Central Asia. Unlike the Kashmiris, few of them lived there. Most would leave Leh when the caravan season was over.

Many of the Kashmiris who settled in Leh married Ladakhi women. In the first generations, the children of these immigrants born in Ladakh were seens as locals, and they tried to distinguish themselves from the Kashmiri merchants who maintained a temporary presence in the capital. Those who were born in Ladakh of a Ladakhi mother converted to Islam, and a Muslim father, whatever his origins, were known as Argons.

In the capital or nearby, the Argons continued to maintain close ties with their relatives in Kashmir, Tibet, or even Chinese Turkestan. Their close personal links with neighbouring countries, and the fame they acquired on the trade routes of Central Asia, gave rise to new roles. They were made responsible for organising the *lo-phyag* (the triennial caravan to Lhasa). On the whole they were traders and townspeople, who, unlike the Baltis, did not compete with the Buddhists for agricultural land. Their status and wealth equalled that of the local nobility with whom they maintained excellent relations.

However not all were engaged in the transhimalayan trade. They were also preachers, specialist craftsmen: carpenters, carpet-makers, tailors, goldsmiths and jewellers. They were mostly sunni, and adhered to Hanafi law.

Unlike the latter, the poorer immigrants from Purig and Baltistan came to Ladakh in search of work. Little is known of their history. Some were descendants of the musicians and servants who had accompanied the Balti princess to Ladakh. Others, facing poverty and hardship in their own lands, came to Ladakh between the 17th-18th centuries.

The Baltis who were Shia, mainly Nurbakshi, spoke a Tibetan dialect. They were held in contempt not only by the Buddhists but also the Sunnis, for whom Persian was the language of culture and religion, and who did not recognise them as "real" Muslims. Poor, illiterate and rejected, the Baltis were employed by the Kashmiri Muslims of Leh, or by rich Argons, in lowly tasks. They worked also as butchers, leatherworkers and shoemakers. The women worked, especially during the harvest. The poorest among them were employed in the thankless work of sorting, carding and washing *pashminah* and *shahtush*. The goathair which they separated from the wool was given to them in payment.

Not all Baltis were poor however. A few Sayed, or descendants of the prophet, were wealthy, powerful and became successful merchants.

The conquest of the Ladakhi kingdom in 1846 had little effect on the transhimalayan trade. But the dramatic improvement of communications in the first half of the 20th century was to change things. Very rapidly the Ladakhi trade routes were abandoned for routes through Sikkim and Gyantse, which were faster, safer and more economical. The Muslim merchants previously settled in Leh, now took their goods and business to Lhasa and Kalimpong.

In 1962, the Sino-Indian conflict destroyed the wool trade of the former Ladakh kingdom. Leh which had been a prosperous entrepot for trade, went into decline.

The Kashmiris present in Ladakh today have been posted there by the governement of Jammu & Kashmir of which Ladakh is now a district. They occupy important positions in administration. This has contributed to the rising tension between the communities.

The opening of Ladakh to tourism in 1974 also led to an influx of Kashmiris. Some came in the summer months to sell Kashmiri handicrafts and Ladakhi antiques.

The enterprising spirit of the Argons has not declined. They control many new businesses. They were the first to turn their homes into guest houses and hotels for the tourists, and to work for travel agencies as tour-leaders, drivers, and cooks. They became the owners of the first hotels, taxis and main shops in the Bazaar. The Buddhists became increasingly envious of them, and accused the Kashmiri government of favouritism.

The situation of the Baltis and their descendants, however, has still not improved. They can be seen working alongside South Indians in road construction and building projects.

In the summer of 1989, the Ladakhi Buddhist Association called for demonstrations, a campaign of civil disobedience aimed at those in power. The government in Delhi had not granted Ladakhis the special status they had been demanding during previous riots. Because of this, and because the Buddhists felt powerless in the face of what they saw as increasing Islamisation, they took to the streets again, demanding Union Territory Status.

"History repeated in Ladakh" reads the title of one of the publications of Muslim Association of Leh and Kargil. Perhaps. But now, religious and cultural demands have been added on to the economic demands of previous years. Buddhism has been placed at the forefront of the Ladakh Buddhist Association movement. Its members have been critical of the Muslims who according to the Association, occupy 40% of government employment even though they account for only 12% of the population of the Leh district. Groups such as the Tibetan refugees at Choglamsar and Agling near Leh who have not joined with them in their struggle, have been ostracised.

Besides the problem of education, of employment, of Urdu and the Arabic script which threaten the Ladakhi language and its Tibetan script, there is also the issue of the conversion of Buddhist women to Islam. The censuses show the Muslim population is increasing more rapidly than the Buddhist. This is because of the Muslim system of marriage and inheritance, the continuing immigration of Muslims from the western area of Purig, but also because of the conversion of previously non-Muslim women. Polyandry which is practised by the Buddhists, has also contributed to the demographic expansion of the Muslim community. Nowadays, some Buddhist women prefer to convert and marry into the Muslim community rather than to be part of a polygamous marriage; to remain in their natal homes with their parents; or to become nuns. For many, Islam represents modernity.

For the Budddhist Association, religion serves to reaffirm an identity that has been threatened by the rise of tourism, the establishment of a large Indian military presence in the region, and the Kashmiri control of the economy. Buddhism has provided a strong notion of identity, inseparable from a "nationalist" movement which is symbolised by a Buddhist flag. Now shopkeepers, even Hindu or Sikh, write their shopsigns and names in Tibetan script.

Since 1989, the Buddhists, following their leaders, have established a social and economic boycott, which has affected the whole Muslim community, not just the Kashmiris. Sometimes monks refuse admission to those tourists who have come to the monasteries in Muslims' taxis. The boycott has begun to pose serious economic problems to many Leh Muslims, for whom business has traditionally provided the main income. The Buddhists make their purchases from Buddhist or Hindu shops only, and they encourage western visitors to do the same. Buddhists have become bakers and butchers! Members of the Buddhist community have built many hotels and guest houses in the capital, bought cars and minibuses, thereby securing a substantial income and making the villages independent of government transport. Pictures of the Dalai Lama, as well as stickers proclaiming "the victory of gods over demons" (translated into English as "truth will prevail") or "Free Ladakh from Kashmir", make Buddhist taxis, buses, hotels and shops easy to identify.

The tension arising out of the events of 1989 and maintained during the boycott, is particularly evident in Leh, where Muslims and Buddhists no longer exchange visits as before.

The Indian Minister of Home Affairs, Buta Singh, decided to grant Scheduled Tribes Status only to certain categories of Ladakhi. Argons and all those whose ancestors were Kashmiri, Punjabi, or "non-tribal" Indians, were excluded from the negotiations. The relations between Buddhists and others became more difficult. All those who were excluded considered the measure to be discriminatory. It has also reinforced the view held by some Buddhist leaders of Ladakhi Muslims as "outsiders" and immigrants, to whom Ladakhi identity is denied.

Alongside the hardening of relations between the two communities, or some of their powerful elites, there is also evidence of a revival of orthodox Buddhism.

As in other parts of the world, the influence of religion in the world of politics and ideology, is growing. Political and religious cleavages cross-cut each other. In order to establish its own identity, the younger generation, has become far more politicised than ever before.

In a context where religious nationalism is spreading rapidly throughout the world. and India has become a stage for violent conflicts between religious communities, is the crisis of Ladakhi society a temporary one, or does it mark a real break in the history of Buddhist-Muslim relations there ?

[Note: "The Ladakh Autonomous Hill Development Council Act" was signed on 9 May 1995 and published in the Official Gazette of the Government of India. This authorised the establishment of such Councils for the Districts of Leh and Kargil. Ed.]

MOORCROFT'S CONTRIBUTION TO LADAKH STUDIES

Nicky Grist *

The subject of my talk is William Moorcroft's writings on Ladakh. Other writers in this volume will give us an account of the friendship between Moorcroft and Alexander Csoma de Kôrös and of Moorcroft's support of the latter's studies in Ladakh. For those of you who are not familiar with him, Moorcroft's actual job was that he worked for the Royal Stud of the East India Company. On his death a friend of his wrote: "He was, in his way, eminently gifted. Physician, artizan, horse-doctor, he knew a little of everything and most of what was most useful." [quoted by Alder p.371]. When he came to Ladakh in 1821, with a large party which included George Trebeck and Mir Izzat Ullah, he was ostensibly on a mission to get to Yarkand in Central Asia in order to obtain horses for the stud. As he was a total enthusiast for many things, despite the fact that he never managed to reach Yarkand, he took full advantage of the two years he spent in Ladakh, to try to open up the area and its neighbours to British trade and to study Ladakhi agricultural production with a view to using similar techniques and crops in Britain and elsewhere. Garry Alder, in his life of Moorcroft "Beyond Bokhara", says that Moorcroft's interest in Csoma de Kôrös' work was that he saw a future commercial benefit in the mastery of Tibetan.

Moorcroft was an indefatigable journal and letter writer; however, the sources that I am going to use are not his (and to some extent Trebeck's) own journals and letters, but rather Wilson's edited version of those, published in 1837 as "Travels in the Himalayan Provinces of Hindustan and the Panjab, in Ladakh and Kashmir, Peshawar, Kabul, Kunduz and Bokhara". I make no apology for this, despite the fact that Alder says that even Wilson himself "as good as admitted, in his introduction, that the book was uninteresting and many of the reviewers thought so too" [Alder p.369]; and that those familiar with the originals attest to the fact that it does not fairly represent them. The reason being that Wilson's book is the form in

---

* 12, Hopton House, Loughborough Estate, Loughborough Rd., London SW9 7SP, UK.

which most readers, including Ladakh scholars, come across his work; and so rightly or wrongly it has been very influential. I wish to address not just the informational content of the published works but also some issues to do with the style of the writing, and in particular their legacy as the first major English language work on Ladakh.

My original intention was simply to eulogise Moorcroft's work vis-a-vis Ladakh, as I have never found it in the least bit boring; but on closer and more critical re-reading of the Wilson book I found that interspersed with the wonderfully descriptive accounts of farming, negotiations and encounters on the road, there is the odd passage of contemptuous stereotyping of the Ladakhis and their neighbours which I had hoped not to find there.

I had previously noticed a tendency in many foreign popular writings on Ladakh, both from this century and the last to objectify its peoples by making very broad generalisations about their character and behaviour which have little basis in reality. In terms of the popular published writings, they are made more insidious by the fact that they are read by future generations of visitors to Ladakh and so the myths are perpetuated and often enhanced.

The stereotyping has two major forms, the first is more obvious and just involves making extremely derogatory comments about people such as that they are dishonest, dirty etc. all or which imply that they are in some way dangerous; the second is more subtle, but in my opinion just objectifying, which are the descriptions which believe they are sympathetic or even adulatory but which are actually patronizing and suggest that the people so described are weak. Frequently these two sets of generalisations will be used in a single sentence. I think that their juxtaposition is no accident as they are in fact two sides of the same coin, which is that the people are presented as either being good but weak or even child-like and therefore in need of being ruled for their own good or bad and unruly and therefore in the same need of being ruled for everyone else's good. Therefore I would argue there is a significant link between such views and the desire of Britain to subject the people of India at that time.

First I will use some examples from the "Travels" to illustrate the attitudes that I refer to. Soon after Moorcroft's party enters Ladakh, they arrive in Leh. As they enter the town: "The streets were crowded with people to sce the entrance of the Firingis, and in the groups were mingled the good-humoured faces of the Ladakhis, and the sullen designing countenances of the Kashmiris..." [Vol I p.246]. We see here already what is one of the central themes I wish to bring out, which is that the Ladakhis especially the Buddhist Ladakhis are described as being happy smiling people, whereas the Kashmiris and often Ladakhi or Balti muslims are described as unhappy and frequently by much more derogatory terms.

In another quote we can see the Ladakhis being described in both good and bad terms and compared with Kashmiris: "The Ladakhis are, in general, a mild and timid people, honest, and moral when not corrupted by communication with the dissolute Kashmiris, but they are indolent, exceedingly dirty, and too apt to be addicted to intoxication. The Kashmirians, here, as well as everywhere else, are notorious for every kind of profligacy, and where they abound the people of the country are tainted by similar vices." [Vol I p.32 1].

Trebeck's description of Spiti has two further examples of characterisation of the Ladakhis as weak and child-like. The first is that when they are raided by Kulu, they hide with their possessions in the hills and he says that this is: "amusingly characteristic" behaviour [Vol II p.641.] The second is where at the beginning of a very contemptuous description of a coucil of village representatives we have: "... when they meet, these delegates of the Piti commons display more vehemence than wisdom: they seldom proceed to business before their faculties are whetted by copious draughts of chang and the cup circulates freely during the debate." [Vol II p.69]. We have already been told of the people of Spiti that: "The men are much less industrious than those about Le, and are of worse character, being quarrelsome, dishonest, and still more addicted to chang, being rarely quite sober." [Vol II p.68].

Moorcroft's comment on the effect of the conversion to Islam on those in Western Ladakh is: "One good effect is its promotion of temperance by the prohibition of chang and fermented drinks, but on the other hand it has introduced much more dissoluteness, dishonesty, and disregard for truth, than prevails in those places where lamaism still predominates." [Vol I p.345].

Unfortunately, it may well be these kind of views, which have been the more important legacy of Moorcroft and Trebeck's writings to popular views of Ladakh; rather than their excellent detailed descriptions.

Wilson's book came out in 1837 and later on in the 19th century several writers expressed similar views. In a book published in 1854 called "Ladak, Physical, Statistical and Historical with notices of the surrounding countries", which was researched after the Dogra conquest of Ladakh, Alexander Cunningham claims that the Ladakhis are better off after the Dogra conquest because: "In my opinion, the measures which the maharaja has taken for the maintenance of his power in Ladak are judicious and effective. Many people grumble; but the dissatisfaction is principally confined to the upper classes; who have lost all their power; and to the Kashmiri Mohammedans, a despicable race, who are ever wishing for change, and who, if they were under the British tomorrow, would long for the Chinese on the next day." [p.282]. He praises the Dogras for the imposition of more even taxes, law and order and better roads. He says: "Such are some of the advantages which have resulted from the conquest of the country by an energetic people." [p.282]. This view is strongly contradicted by other writers at the time, including Vigne, who visited Ladakh, just after, and Baltistan just before, they were each conquered by the Dogras. He says that the people of Nubra, in northern Ladakh, are much poorer since they were taken over [Vigne Vol. II p.360].

Cunningham says that longevity is rare in Baltistan and his explanation for this is: "The differences between this and the average of the Ladakhis can only be accounted for by the general dissoluteness of all Musalmans, and the consequent spread of loathsome and fatal diseases." [p 301].

By the turn of the century views had become more polarised, in that Ladakhis were then usually depicted as rather quaint but harmless characters and Kashmiris, when mentioned, are usually described in negative terms, as are sometimes Baltis and Ladakhi Muslims. Knight in "Where Three Empires Meet" published in 1891 says: "All the men of Shergol wore queues in the Chinese fashion, and had features of the pure Tibetan type, there being little, if any, admixture of Aryan blood here. I soon realised that I had reached a very strange land, a country of topsy-turveydom, where polyandry prevails instead of polygamy; where praying is all conducted by machinery, and where, in short, the traveller fresh from beyond the mountains is bewildered by the quaint sights, the strange beliefs superstitions and customs he comes across every day." [p.45]. He goes on to say: "One comes to like these amiable Ladakhi Buddhists, they are highly spoken of by all who have travelled in their country, as being truthful, honest, hospitable and straightforward. They are a harmless, simple race, with no bigotry or prejudice." [p.46].

Later on he says: "Cheerfulness is the chief characteristic of the long-suffering Balti. He is always ready to laugh. He is the most easily amused person in the world... You only have to look in a good temper yourself, and your Balti followers will be contented and amiable under the most depressing circumstances." [p.76].

The Hebers in 1903 say, after Knight: "We are not exactly in Looking-glass Land, but we are certainly in some sort of Wonderland, where many things are upside down; topsy-turvey or just the reverse of our notions of correctness, and where the strangest incongruities prevail." [p.17]. They observe a Ladakhi woman thus: "A dear old grandmother with her white uncovered locks blowing round her cheery wrinkled old face, ..." [p.66]. They say of some Buddhists that they meet that they are: "Dirty and ragged, but delightfully cheery enjoying us as we did them, all looked ready to pop into a fairy tale"; but of a Balti: "Here was a living representative of Absalom, a Balti wearing a little round cap with rolled up edges, dark, curling locks falling onto each shoulder, big black eyes, and unlike our Buddhist Ladakhis, an expression of utter gloom." [p.68]. When they stop off in Kargil, the only mention they make of their visit is about bed bugs.

I would like to be able to say that in the latter part of this century we have become more enlightened, but unfortunately some of the more recent books carry on in this tradition. For instance, Harvey's book "A Journey in Ladakh", published in 1983, takes what in my view, is a very idealised view of Ladakhi Buddhists whilst representing Kashmiris as reprehensible, for example in this description of a bus journey: "We had been told that the bus for Tak-Tak would leave at eight. Nothing happened until nine when a young Kashmiri driver got into his seat at the front, yawning, rubbing the sleep from his eyes, and smiling around at everyone, satisfied, evidently, that he had caused the most discomfort possible." [p.83]. The only solution to this is "you just have to give in, to accept everything without hope or reserve." [p.84].

It is easy for us to sneer at some of the views expressed by the early writers; however I do think that the more contemporary versions of these do have great currency among foreign visitors to Ladakh today and even show up in some current views on development. I have ancecdotal experience, as I am sure that many of you do, of talking to other foreigners who may or may not have been there who will say what a marvellous place Ladakh is; but, and there very often is a but, that the place is being destroyed by the Kashmiris or the Ladakhi Muslims, the Baltis now being out of the picture.

Having discussed what I see as the negative side of Moorcroft's published work, I will now describe what I think is good about it in terms of the description of Ladakh, at that time. Firstly, as an observer, despite being a person of his time, as we all are, Moorcroft was very open to new ideas. The continuation of the quote from his friend at the beginning of the article is: "Moreover, he was liberal, frank, open and courageous, just the man, in short, for the tribes amongst whom he travelled, and better suited than probably one individual in a thousand to raise our character for general intelligence and fellow feeling." [Alder p.372]. He also came fairly early on in Britain's domination of the area when colonial values were not so fully formed and prevalent as they were shortly to be.

Secondly, the main bulk of the original writing is in the form of journals and letters which are highly descriptive and not overburdened with generalisations as text written specifically for publication would have been. Moorcroft, if nothing else, showed a great attention to detail which was, again unusual for his time. Some of the most interesting descriptions of people and events are due to his recording everyone he met and what they said. For instance, he introduces us to several of the main Ladakhi characters in the Dogra wars. He can also be forgiven a lot for referring to most of his friends and acquaintances by their names. For instance in Nubra he says: "... we stopped at the house of an old lady, named Amma Bunzun, who had consulted me at Le for a liver complaint, and to whom my advice had been an advantage. Her gratitude was extreme, and she insisted on our dining with her." [Vol I p .402].

Thirdly, Moorcroft offers us the only detailed account of Ladakh before the Dogra conquest, which occurred about fifteen years after his visit. This is very valuable as we can get a much clearer picture of how the state worked at that time. This is aided by the fact that Moorcroft's writing in the most part is not objectifying and has real historical and political depth.

The view we get from him of the Ladakhi state at that time is "The government of Ladakh is a simple despotism, but it is curiously modified by the circumstances of the people and the influence of the hierarchy, so that unless a person of more than common talent and energy, the Raja is an individual of little real power, and may be deposed or elevated at pleasure; his successor in the former case being a member of the reigning family." [Vol I p.332]. He then goes on to describe in detail a very Machiavellian plan by the Leh Lonpo to get the current king deposed in favour of his son. Later in his stay seditious posters were put up which implicated Moorcroft himself, but were obviously not an uncommon way of expressing dissent.

The other major figure in the state was the Kalon or chief minister, who Moorcroft believed actually did most of the governing. He certainly seems to have carried out a wide range of duties, as he appears to have been chief diplomat, leader of the troops and a major trader. He carries out most of the negotiations over Moorcroft's visit, both with him, and with foreign authorities on his behalf. Early on in Moorcroft's stay he returns to Leh to find that: "The Khalun and Khaga Tan-zin were absent having gone with some troops to retaliate upon the territory of Balti an inroad committed by the Raja of that country upon Ladakh." [Vol I p.412]. On a visit to the Tibetan border areas he reports: " At Chibra we were joined by five men and a boy, servants of the Khalun, with one hundred and fifty six sheep loads of shawl-wool, and three or four of coarse wool; each load being about thirty pounds, and the value of each pack eight or nine rupees. They had been eleven months absent from Le." [Vol I p 444].

As well as the Khalun Moorcroft mentions ministers such as the (Leh) Lonpo, the Chagdzot and the Bangka.. The Lonpo was a noble of considerable influence as he was trying to depose the king in favour of his son. The Chagdzot took responsibility for the organisation and smooth running of the trade with Ladakh's neighbours. The Bangka seems to have been the leader of the cavalry. On visiting his house new Chemray, Moorcroft says: "The Banka, who to his office of master of the horse adds the government of this district..." [Vol I p.425]. He (or his son) played a major part in the Dogra war.

In addition to these officials there were a great number of appointed or hereditary governors of areas. Thus, for instance, Spiti is assigned to an appointed governor who at that time was called Khaga Khan; but places like Giah and Pashkyum have hereditary rulers. The Raja of Pashkyum is a recent convert to Islam and his wife is a daughter of the Nono Kalon [Vol II p.22]. Other parts, such as the area around Hemis gonpa are subject to the officials of the gonpa; and we are told that the Chagdzot of Hemis's brother is the governor of part of Suru-Kartse. These local officials appear to have had a fairly free hand in exacting taxes; and Moorcroft records that many of them were very rapacious to the households in their area. In addition to these officials there were various other people of influence such as Kwaja Shah Nias who was a refugee from Central Asia resident in Ladakh, who was very helpful to Moorcroft and obviously had influence with the Kalon; and, of course, the Kashmiri merchants, who under previous treaties, held a special place in the pashmina trade.

A typical chance meeting on the road gives us a view of one of the district governors: "Between Minji and Lang Kartse we met the son of the Nuna Khalun (Nono Kalon), with three or four females of his family, on horseback, the women riding astride; they were dressed in brocade with mantles of broad-cloth, and seal-skin boots. As I was in advance of our party, and without an interpreter, our greeting was brief. The Khalun was preceded by a large flock of sheep, goats, cows, and horses, too probably the produce of exaction or compulsory gifts. This young man imitates his father's example, and although scarcely twenty is detested for his rapacity." [Vol II p.86]. Although the source of the animals is debatable, we had previously met the Nono Kalon himself making heavy exactions for the building of a fort from the people of the Dras area. We are offered a much more sympathetic view of the wife of the Nono Kalon: "At Molbi

(Mulbekh) I was appealed to by the wife of the Nuna Kalon, who was absent at Zangskar, on account of the refusal of my carriers to pay certain fees customary at this place. Going to her to discuss the subject, she received me with much graciousness, taking my offered hand between both hers and carrying it to her forehead. A seat was given me, and at my request, she sat down beside me and entered, with great fluency and animation, upon the subject in dispute. The Cho-Cho, as she was called, was rather good-looking, and of juvenile appearance, although the mother of twelve children. She was a complete woman of business, and commanded great influence in the district." [Vol I p.85].

The family of governors about whom we hear the most, is that of Khaga Stanzin the Nanso of Nubra. He was clearly a very important at the time of Moorcroft's visit and he was shortly to become the virtual commander of the arrny; however Petech tells us that he never became a minister [p. 129]. Moorcroft encounters his family several times, particularly at their numerous residences in Nubra. This is the best account of such a meeting: "During the 3rd the daughter-in-law of the Khaga Tanzin came down the pass, on her road to Le. She was about twenty, a tall well-looking brunette, with an oval face, red cheeks and fine teeth. Her head was covered with a rich brocade cap, and her neck loaded with gold and silver ornaments, turquoises, and coral beads. She rode a yak, and had a fine ruddy boy, about three years old, on her lap. She was accompanied by her brother, and about fifty attendants, with as many yaks, and the appearance of the whole party denoted considerable affluence." [Vol I p 397].

It is clear from this and the previous quote, that, despite Moorcroft's rather popular-press descriptions of them, women were very active participants in administration and trade. He also reports that ordinary women do the majority of the farm work, although this is put to us along with a rather unlikely theory: "The women of Ladakh, in consequence of their great proportionate number, find it difficult to obtain subsistence, and besides domestic occupations and wool-picking, in which they are very expert, they are the principle labourers in the fields." [Vol I p.322]. Similarly when Trebeck is in Spiti and the Kalon has put most of the men on standby for military service, he is offered women as his carriers to Ladakh [Vol II p.60].

In the course of the account we are given a glimpse of more than fifty villages in Ladakh, and frequently we are told how many houses there are and the general appearance of the village. This is his description of Digar in Nubra: "The place contains about 16 houses. It lies very high and lofty, and considerably above Le. The only grains cultivated are barley and buckwheat. The people, who are very poor, subsist partly by keeping yaks for the hire of travellers." [Vol I p.400]. Where there is something notable, as in the following account of Kharbu, Moorcroft has usually tried to find from the people the reasons for things: "The village of Kherbu ... seemed to be in a state of decay, many of the houses were in ruins, and the people declared they were unable to furnish us with supplies. The poverty and dilapidation of the place were ascribed partly to a snow-slip, which had destroyed many dwellings, and partly to the great havoc made by the late epidemic amongst the sheep. A third and more mischievous cause, was the rapacity of the chief man, or Garpun." [Vol. IIp.16].

In the time that Moorcroft was in Ladakh there were several raids or disputes with Ladakh's neighbours. On the one previously mentioned with Baltistan he says: "The quarrel was not likely to lead to any serious results, for the people on both sides took little interest in the dispute, and their propensities were at no time of a very warlike disposition." [Vol I p.412]. We know from the histories quoted by Hashmatullah Khan and Petech, that there were frequent minor wars with Baltistan and its satellites. A trade dispute with Kulu resulted in a raid on Spiti, also mentioned previously; and on that occasion the Khalun ordered each house in Spiti to produce their obligatory armed man. The third was an attack on Dras by raiders from Hasora which caused the people of Dras to send a large delegation to Leh to demand that the king do something about it. The picture that we get of external relations is a very dynamic one, but also one where conflicts with major neighbours such as Kulu and Baltistan are tempered by diplomacy and negotiation.

To conclude, I think there are real problems with the writings of Moorcroft and Trebeck as published by Wilson; but what I do like about Moorcroft's description of Ladakh is that it presents it as a dynamic truly historical state, and he has very often managed to record the Ladakhis own view on circumstances and events with an openness which is very rare for any 19th century writer.

Bibliography

CUNNINGHAM, A. 1854. *Ladak, Physical, Statistical and Historical with notices of the surrounding countries*. London: W. H. Allen.

HARVEY, A. 1983. *A Journey in Ladakh*. London: Cape.

HEBER A.R. & K. M. 1926. *In Himalayan Tibet*.. London: Routledge.

KHAN, Hashmatullah. 1939. *Tarikh Jammun, Kashmir, Laddakh aur Baltistan*. Lucknow: Noor Ahmad Malik and Mohammed Tegh Bahadur.

KNIGHT, E.F. 1893. *Where Three Empires Meet: a Narrative of Recent Travel in Kashmir, Western Tibet, Gilgit and the Adjoining Countries.* London: Longman.

MOORCROFT W. & G.Trebeck, 1837. *Travels in the Himalayan Provinces of Hindustan and the Panjab, in Ládakh and Kashmir, in Peshawar, Kabul, Kunduz and Bokhara..* Ed. H. H. Wilson. 2 Vols. London: John Murray.

PETECH, L. 1977. *The Kingdom of Ladakh (c.950 -1842 A.D.)* . Roma: Instituto Italiano Per Il Medio Ed Estremo Oriente.

VIGNE, G. T. 1842. *Travels in Kashmir, Ladak, Iskardo.* 2 Vols. London: Henry Colburn.

KINSHIP IN ZANGSKAR: IDIOM AND PRACTICE[1]

Kim Gutschow [2]

Kinship may be divided into two reinforcing domains: practice and idiom. Idiom, the symbolic or semiotic realm, and practice, the realm of observable behavior, reinforce but do not always reflect each other. This distinction admits of separate causal mechanisms in the two realms. The production of meaning in society is not always congruent with the production of individual practice. The lived practice of kinship cannot be reduced to a symbolic system.

In Zangskar, the realm of idiom is concerned primarily with descent, while the realm of practice centers on residence. The Zangskari idioms of descent can be read as clues to the larger Tibetan cultural context where these idioms may have originated in the first place. The contextualization of Zangskari kinship in the larger Tibetan framework tells us little about how kinship works in the present day, but suggests how it may have worked in the past. My primary emphasis will be a close reading of the lived practice of kinship in Zangksar. It is important to study Zangskari kinship in the present before it is fully encompassed by the inevitable socioeconomic changes that are taking place throughout India.

Rus and *sha:* the idioms of descent in Zangskar

In a Tibetan context, the terms *rus* and *sha*, bone and flesh, symbolize the father's and mother's patriline, respectively.[3] Children of both sexes receive an identity known as *rus* or bone from their

---

1. This essay is dedicated to the Karsha blon po, bSod rnams Dbang phyug, a scholar, priest, and extraordinary man without whom this paper would not have been possible. I would like to thank N.Allen, M.Aris, E.Dargyay, N.Levine, and N.Yalman, all of whom commented on this paper in its earlier stages. I am grateful to P.Dollfus and M.Phylactou (whose most recent works are not available in America) for their comments in London, and K.Getchell for her generous assistance in translation.

2. Dept. of Anthropology, Harvard University, Cambridge MA 02138, USA.

3. The following discussion of *rus* and *sha* was gathered in conversation with a Ladakhi-Tibetan informant who was born in the Tibetan refugee settlement of Choglamsar, Ladakh.

father, and an identity known as *sha* or flesh from their mother. While children carry these dual identities through their lifetime, they will only pass on *rus* but not *sha,* to their children. Their mother's *sha* is lost after one generation. How is this possible? Sons pass on their father's *rus* to their own sons. However, the *rus* that a daughter inherits from her father is transformed to *sha,* which she then passes on to her children. Strictly speaking, Tibetans and Zangskaris do not define descent bilaterally, for they trace descent only through their FA's and MO's patrilines.[4] While descent is neither strictly patrilineal nor fully bilateral, exogamy is calculated more bilaterally. The Zangskari consider as exogamous all blood kin on both MO's and FA's sides, ideally to a depth of five generations.[5]

Authors who have written about Ladakh have either misinterpreted *rus* as a patrilineal descent group, or conflated it with *pha spun,* the association of households which worships a common

---

4. Zangskaris conceptualize *rus* as a link to their past ancestors and *sha* in a more limited genealogical sense as a link to their matrilateral affines. For comparison, Levine (1988: 37-61) notes that for the Nyinba, *rus* signifies descent (through males) while *khrag* (i.e. flesh, the Nyinba equivalent of the Zangskari *sha*) represents matrilateral affiliation. Levine states that *rus* represents a core kinship identity, or a principal substance, while *khrag* is a secondary substance. Levine's comment (1988: 38) that "descent is conceptualized as a line of *males* over time (my emphasis)", suggests a patrilineal bias in Nyinba descent, which one also finds in Zangskar. Following Levine, I would note that both *rus* and *sha* are terms for which there are no proper western equivalents, and thus one cannot jump to the conclusion that Zangskari descent is strictly patrilineal. I would also refer the reader to Levine's summaries of how the conceptual idioms of bone and flesh have been characterized in other Tibetan societies (1981: 64ff and 1988: 38, f.1).
5. Since descent is traced through patrilines, it is not clear if the reckoning of exogamy is completely bilateral and would include the MMS's blood descendants for example. N.Allen, who has written extensively on Bodic kinship terminology (1975,1976,1978a, 1978b) notes (in correspondence, 1992) that Tibetan kinship was historically patrilineal but has shifted to a more bilateral form of reckoning. Aziz (1978: 122) notes that that among the D'ing ri Tibetans exogamy is reckoned bilaterally and includes all blood kin on both MO's and FA's sides. In Zangskar, I found that older villagers could cite full family genealogies to a depth of five generations, and that the rules of exogamy were still roughly adhered to as many individuals looked for marital partners in neighbouring villages.

ancestor deity *(pha lha)*.[6] The late S.S. Gergan of Ladakh noted that *rus* is inherited from the father and *sha* from the mother, but we do not know what else he said on this topic.[7] The lexicographers Das and Jaeschke define *rus* as: (1) lineage, family; and (2) bone.[8] One of the earliest references in western literature to *rus* and *sha*, from the 18th century Italian missionary Desideri, is more accurate than most.[9] Following Desideri's lead, I would characterize *rus* as a "patrilineal affiliation" and *sha* as a "matrilateral affiliation". Both *rus* and *sha* are conceptual idioms that denote kinship identities in Ladakhi society more than membership in a corporate group *per se*.

In Zangskar, by contrast, there has been no complete kinship study. Dargyay has given the most detailed account of how Zangskaris conceptualize *rus* and *sha*. Dargyay defines *rus* as a lineage descended from a common ancestor and *sha* as a Tibetan medical term which signifies the kinship identity that a child receives from its mother.[10] Her primary emphasis has been to delineate the cult of the ancestor deity or *pha lha*, which is associated with a *rus*. Although Dargyay denotes *rus* as a lineage or clan, who can trace their ancestry back to a common progenitor, this does not always appear to be the case in the present. Zangskari families I interviewed did not always know the full genealogical relationship between themselves and the other members of their *rus*. I would suggest that *rus* is a descent concept but does not refer to a corporate descent

---

6. Prince Peter (1963: 327-8) and Brauen (1980b: 54, 55; 1980a: 23) referred to *rus* as a patrilineal descent group while Carrasco (1959: 39) conflated *rus* wilh *pha spun*. Earlier misreadings of *pha spun* include: "exogamous, patrilineal clans" (Carrasco, 1959: 38); *Vater-bruderschaften* or father-brotherhoods (Francke, 1904: 364-5; 1914: 478), *Sippe* or clan (Ribbach, 1940: 237), and "brotherhoods" or "menbrethren" (Heber, 1903:132).

7. Erdmann (1983: 141) cites the late S.S. Gergan.

8. See Das, 1969: 1188; Jaeschke, 1975: 532.

9. Desideri understood *rus* and *sha* as follows: "The Thibetans recognize two classes of kinship. The first are called relations of the Rupa-cik, or of the same bone; the second, relations of the Scia-cik, or of the same blood. They recognize, as relations of Rupa-cik, or of the same bone, those who descend from a common ancestor, however remote, even when they have been divided into different branches during many generations. Relations of the Scia-cik, or the same blood, are those created by legitimate marriages...". See Filippi, 1932: 192.

10. Dargyay noted: "Gemeinsame abstammung von einem ahnherren wird in Zanskar mit dem Wort *Rus pa* (Knochen) bezeichnet..." (1980: 93); and "the term *rus pa* identifies a number of families which are related by male kinship. In other words, only families that can trace back their origin to a common male ancestor belong to the same *rus pa*" (1988: 127).

group or clan as commonly defined in anthropological literature. The members of a single *rus* do not gather for collective worship (although they individually worship the same guardian deity in their houses), and they do not have hereditary leaders or joint property.[11] *Rus pa* must be distinguished from *pha spun* and *bcu tshog*, which do function as corporate groups in Ladakh and Zangskar.[12]

Kinship terminology

Zangskari kinship terminology is symmetrical; the terms used to differentiate kin on the matrilateral and patrilateral side are of equal number. The terms are roughly similar to those described by Aziz for central Tibet.[13] Consanguine kin are termed *gnyen* or *spun*, divided into matrilateral kin (*a ma'i spun)* and patrilateral kin *(pha pa'i spun)*. While close kin *(spun nye po)* and distant kin *(spun ma nye)* are identified, the system is classificatory with reference to ascending generations on both sides. It is an ego-centered system in which the kinship term employed for a person depends on the speaker. As do Tibetans, Zangskaris use a unique kinship terminology to identify status within the household.[14] With the same kinship terms used more generally, members of a house are identified as "uncle", "father", or "brother" rather than by their proper names or actual blood relation to ego. These names represent the differential status and roles accorded to each member of the household.

---

11. Levine notes that *rus* has political and jural salience in Nyinba society, but does not generate corporate groups, as understood by Fortes (1988: 44). The multiple connotations of *rus*, lineage, clan, and hereditary social strata, form the basis for social identity and status, instead of placing individuals into groups with definite socio-economic functions.

12. *Pha spun* denotes an association of households engaged in mutual assistance and collective rituals at times of birth, death and weddings in Ladakhi and Zangskari society. *Bcu tshog* ("group of ten") denotes a Ladakhi neighborhood organization, whose male members gather to read religious texts on auspicious days of the month and to offer juniper *(bsangs gyi mchod pa)* at the shrine *(lha tho) of* their tutelary deity, who is secondary to the tutelary deity of the village *(yul lha)*. See Dollfus, 1989 and Brauen, 1980a, 1980b.

13. Prince Peter (1963: 335-394) and Dollfus (1989) have given the most complete descriptions of Ladakhi kinship terminology. For Tibetan kinship terminology, see Aziz, 1978: 266; 1974: 30-31 and Levine, 1988: 51-3.

14. For a Tibetan example of the secondary, household kinship terminology, see Aziz, 1974: 32; 1978: 130-133. For example, terms are used to distinguish the different "fathers" in a polyandrous marriage: eldest FA is a *pha chen po*, the middle is a *pha chung tse*, and the youngest is *a gu*. Similarly the older wife is *ma chen*, the younger one(s) are *ma chung*. See Prince Peter, 1963: 327.

Rus in kinship practice

Idiom and practice of kinship intersect in the Zangskari effort to maintain a continuous *rus* in the household. Ordinarily, *rus* is passed on from a father to the son who becomes the next household head. Although rules of exogamy require that this son's wife should have a different *rus*, their children will receive the same *rus* that he once received from his father. Hence, household *rus* remains continuous. *Rus* is an inalienable kinship identity that cannot be abandoned by either sons or daughters. However, it is not always possible to maintain the household *rus* when a family has no sons. In the absence of sons, a daughter becomes household head and a matrilocal marriage is contracted with a husband known as a *mag pa*. Ideally, exogamy is purposefully disregarded so that the husband is of the same *rus* as the woman he marries. In this case, his children will inherit the *rus* which has characterized the house in the past. However, in practice, it may not be possible to find a suitable husband of the same *rus* who is a more distant relative. If the incoming husband is of a different *rus* than his wife, he will pass on this new *rus* to his children. This change in household *rus* demands a corresponding change in the guardian deity *(pha lha)* associated with *rus* and house.[15] In a special ceremony, the new husband and village monks install the husband's guardian deity in the household shrine and ritually expel the former deity who resided there.

In the more common virilocal marriage, *rus* is "automatically" continuous as it passes from father to children. In this instance, the wife will not share her husband's *rus* (for she cannot abandon her inalienable *rus)* but she will shift her allegiance from her old house deity *(pha lha)* to the house deity of her new husband's home. A woman is formally initiated into her marital household when she takes leave of her natal house deity and first "greets" her new guardian deity in the household shrine *(lha tho)* of her husband's house. On the day when she first arrives in her husband's home, the wife is officially introduced to her new household deity *(pha lha)* in the presence of several monks and her husband's family. Thereafter, her allegiance to her natal home is symbolically severed and her primary obligations

---

15. *Rus* and *pha lha* are interconnected. A given *rus* is always connected with a certain *pha lha*, a deity that is worshipped as the guardian deity of the household. Dargyay (1980: 924) notes that *rus* enotes common descent from an ancestor in the distant and untraceable past, while the *pha spun* (named after the *rus* in Zangskar) denotes a present-day, mutual assistance group of households. For a complete discussion of the symbolic and ritual aspects of the house in Ladakhi society, see Dollfus, 1989.

are to her marital home.[16] In this manner, Zangskari adults become associated with and defined by their household residence.

The primacy of residence in Zangskari kinship and society

The Zangskari household is the principal nexus around which the economic relations of labor, production, and subsistence are arranged. The household serves as one of the primary corporate groups of society.[17] An individual's rights of inheritance and communal obligations stem first from the natal (and later, the marital) household. The most critical obligation an individual owes to society is labor, the limiting resource in Zangskar as in other Tibetan societies.[18] Labor exchanges are conceptualized as relations between households rather than individuals. In a metonymic substitution which binds together village households, each individual involved in a reciprocal labor exchange serves as a part which stands in for the whole (house). Individuals owe their primary allegiance to the household where they reside, rather than to kin residing in a distant (or not so distant) village. Nuns or monks owe labor obligations to their natal household, regardless of whether it is in the village where their monastery is located or not. Zangksari nuns would walk several hours or days to work on their family fields in times of acute labor shortage such as the fall harvest. In this instance, allegiance to the household took precedence over presence at nunnery rituals and other

---

16. For mention of the marital ceremony in which the wife greets her husband's guardian deity see Reis, 1983: 225 and Dargyay, 1988: 127.

17. For a description of the other corporate groups in Ladkahi society, including *pha spun* and *bcu tshog,* see Dollfus, 1989 and Brauen, 1980a, 1980b. Due to smaller village size, some Zangskari villages do not have subsections called *bcu tshog,* which Dollfus identified in Hemis shug pa can. When present, Zangskari village subsections, known as *yul,* are spatially and ritually unified. Each subsection has a member who reports to the village headman for joint village matters. Subsection members co-operate on joint labor projects within their territory such as cleaning out the irrigation channels each spring and caring for village paths and chortens. They may also join together on ritual days of the month to read religious texts and drink chang in celebration of the particular Buddhist saint they are honoring on that day. Among the Nyinba, these subsections are known as *rus tsho,* after the patrilineal ancestor who allegedly founded the village section (Levine, 1988: 45-49). In Zangskar, there is no evident correlation between *pha spun* and village sections.

18. Aziz confirms: "It is labour and not limited natural resources that seem to be the critical factor in economic growth...Every economic transaction, from household organization to taxation, seems to reflect the constraints of labour shortage in the area." (1978: 102).

duties (labor, collecting donations, etc.) commonly owed to the nunnery.

The house posits an authority structure that socializes Zangskari individuals. It is oriented towards the past and the future: it maintains inherited traditions and nurtures individuals who are responsible for social continuity in the future. The set of household roles which each individual passes through in their life cycle determines the individual's role in many ritual or social contexts.[19] The head of household attends village meetings, and will be called upon to speak for the household in a dispute or in any marital negotiations, even though he/she may not be the most senior member of the household. In contrast, the aged parents are relegated to an adjunct household (known as *khang chung)* after they have passed on authority to the next generation. They have little or no voice in household decisions once they have ceased to be fully productive members of the household. The parents are given some livestock and fields, known as *lto zhing* ("food fields"), which are sufficient for their subsistence and will be subsumed under the main household *(khang chen)* upon their demise. In Zangskari society there is no formal ceremony to mark the succession of household head from one generation to the next. In general, there are few initiation (or other life cycle) rites which distinguish or isolate the individual from other members of the household. This lack of ceremony indicates that ideals of household continuity and corporateness are more important than individuality and personal autonomy.

Zangskaris themselves stress the importance of household continuity. For example, they justify fraternal polyandry by noting its ability to maintain a continual labor supply in the household.[20] Polyandry assures that not just one but two or three adult males will contribute to the welfare of a single household. This allows for diversification of tasks as different brothers will be involved in trading,

---

19. For comparison, Levine (1988:111) suggests that the Nyinba household fulfils the critical features of corporate groups as defined by Fortes: (1) universal succession of rules and other prerogatives, (2) continuity in the sense that while individual members die, the corporation lives on, and (3) it can be treated as a single "juristic person" in the context of village affairs.

20. Zangskaris view polyandry as a means of maintaining household labor resources, despite family conflicts and its attendant psychological distress. In Zangskar, I witnessed a case in which the younger of two brothers engaged in a polyandrous marriage wished to leave the union and become a monk, but to no avail. When his wife and older brother firmly rejected his wishes, he became temporarily insane. After a visit from a famous reincarnate Tibetan priest who performed an exorcism on his behalf, he eventually regained his "health" and was persuaded to rejoin the family union.

farming, or herding, all of which are necessary to maintain the household as a self-sufficient production unit. Until recently, when other opportunities for employment became available (i.e. government service, teaching, tourism), polyandry was partly a case of making a virtue out of necessity: households could only sustain themselves by concentrating and diversifying their adult labor resources.

Polyandry demands a certain subordination of individual desires to the household good. Younger brothers must submit to the authority of their older brother who is household head. Further, these younger men may have to accept his choice as their joint wife. Ultimately, marriage is conceptualized as a relation that occurs between households, rather than individuals. Marital transactions are decided by household heads, and the individuals concerned often have little say in the matter, even though recent socio-economic changes and increased vocational options have given young adults some degree of autonomy from their parents. For instance, women still are married off at a later age or are destined for lifelong spinsterhood in their natal home (and given the symbolic title of "nun") instead of joining a nunnery, so that their labor power may be more fully exploited by their families.[21]

In Zangskar, the principal marker of individual identity is the household (or *grong)* rather than a clan or lineage. A child traditionally receives its name from a *bla ma* or its parents, but this name is not sufficient outside the village context. In public contexts, a person is referred to by their house name, *grong ming*, which defines a person's status in the village. Outside the village, a person is referred to by their village name suffixed with their house or personal name. An individual acquires a housename by virtue of the household he/she is born, married, or adopted into. If a man or woman marries outside of their natal residence, and thus transfers households, they will take on a new house name. The housename may be suffixed with a kinship term, to indicate "daughter of..." or "wife of..." a given household. All children, including illegitimate ones, take the name of their natal residence, regardless of whether this is the same as their father's or mother's natal housename.[22]

---

21. Reis (1983: 218) and Aziz (1978: 106) confirm the tendency of Tibetan households to keep celibate women at home rather than allowing them to join a nunnery. This topic needs far more systematic research, for it may partly explain why there have historically been fewer and less populated nunneries in Tibetan societies.

22. See Reis, 1983: 217-229; Prince Peter, 1963: 352-355; Dollfus, 1989: 150ff.

Kinship practice: inheritance

The primacy of residence also is reflected in the assignment of inheritance rights. When a household has no male heirs, the eldest daughter contracts a matrilocal marriage and effectively becomes household head, inheriting the house, its property, and livestock. Residence serves as the basis for inheritance in the case of illegitimate or adopted children, regardless of their reputed paternity and maternity. If an illegitimate child is raised along with other natural-born siblings, he/she will have the same rights to inheritance that the other siblings will. In other words, an adopted boy has the option of joining the brothers in a polyandrous marriage and an adopted daughter will be married out with a small dowry. Traditionally in Zangskar, all brothers are entitled to a share of the family estate, as long as they join their eldest brother in a polyandrous marriage. If childless, polyandrously wed brothers may bring in a second and even a third wife, usually related to the first wife.[23] Ultimately, a childless couple will adopt a son or daughter who will become the next household head.[24] Thus, household residence shapes the dynamics of inheritance, as well as individual identity and obligation.

Conclusion

Research confirms that the household is the crucible in which individual identity is formed, alliance and inheritance arrangements are sealed, and polyandrous marriages are anchored. Nevertheless, much research remains to be done, particularily on land records and other sources which reveal kinship and residence arrangements. One might look at the resilience of polyandry in light of recent laws (the Hindu Succession Act of 1956) declaring it illegal and a changing normative and socio-economic ethic which devalues fraternal solidarity. Because Zangskar has experienced less direct social engineering and socio-economic change than Tibet proper, it is an ideal place to study kinship. Lying at a far remove from the outside world to which there is no paved road, Zangskar is closed off for eight

23. In the case of such secondary marriages, there is often no official ceremony, merely an offering of beer to relatives *(khri chang)* and the laying of scarves on the bride's head *(mgo ras)*. See Prince Peter, 1963: 347.

24. In Zangskar, I witnessed a case in which a man was childless after marrying twice and thus resorted to a publicly sanctioned form of adultery in order to produce children. A liaison with one woman in a distant village resulted in the birth of a retarded daughter, who was unsuited to be household head because she was retarded, not because she was female. Another liaison with a different woman in a new village resulted in the birth of a son who was raised as the family heir.

months of the year due to snow on the high passes. The impact of Indian government officials and army is negligible and in the harsh winter months almost non-existent.[25] In Ladakh by comparison, the Indian army nearly outnumbers the local population, while foreign tourists (roughly 15,000 per annum, equivalent to one tenth of Ladakh's population) have had a tremendous impact in the last three decades.

If anthropology is driven by the desire to find a new insight into reality, one must allow for the incomprehensible, rather than merely recording what one had expected to find. Hence, while one may look for patrilineal descent in Zangskar, it is is more fruitful to examine the idiom of *rus* and *sha* which do not fit into preconceived categories of kinship. Similarily, Zangskari kinship suggests that the house, and not (as expected) the individual, is the primary unit of analysis. In kinship, as elsewhere, the human mind seeks patterns rather than chaos. We find meaning in the process of making order out of randomness; however, let us beware that the order is not merely a reflection of our own minds. If we are to see beyond the borders of our own cultural norms, we must venture into new landscapes where we may learn something about the uniqueness of human experience.

Bibliography

ALLEN, Nicholas. 1975. "Byansi Kinship Terminology: A Study in Symmetry." *Man* n.s. 10: 80-94. 1976. "Sherpa Kinship Terminology in Diachronic Perspective." *Man* 11: 569-87.

---------- 1978a. "Fourfold Classification of Society in the Himalayas." In J. Fischer, ed., *Himalayan Anthropology: The Indo-Tibetan Interface*. The Hague: Mouton.

---------- 1978b. "Quadripartition of Society in Early Tibetan Sources." *Journal Asiatique* 266: 569-87.

AZIZ, Barbara. 1974. "Some Notions About Descent and Residence in Tibetan Society." In C. von Furer-Haimendorf, ed., *Contributions to the Anthropology of Nepal*. Warminster: Aris & Phillips.

---------- 1978. *Tibetan Frontier Families*. New Delhi: Vikas.

BRAUEN, Martin. 1980a. *Feste in Ladakh*. Graz: Akademische Druck und Verlagsanstalt.

---------- 1980b. "The *Pha Spun* of Ladakh." In M. Aris and Aung San Suu Kyi, eds., *Tibetan Studies in Honour of Hugh Richardson*. Warminster: Aris & Phillips.

CARRASCO, Pedro. 1959. *Land and Polity in Tibet*. Seattle: University of Washington Press.

25. The estimated non-local administrative personnel in Zangskar (pop. 12,000) during the winter months is not more than 10 persons.

CROOK, John and Shakya, T. 1983. "Six Families of Leh." in R. Sander and D. Kantowsky, eds., *Recent Research on Ladakh*. London: Weltforum Verlag.

DARGYAY, Eva and Lobsang. 1980. "Vorlaufiger Bericht Uber Zwei Forschungreisen Nach Zangskar (West-Tibet)." *Zentralasiatische Studien*. 14(2): 85-114.

----------- 1988. "Buddhism in Adaptation: Ancestor Gods and Their Tantric Counterparts in the Religious Life of Zanskar." *History of Religions* 28(2): 123-134.

----------- 1989. "The House as Sacred Space in the Folk-Religion of Zanskar (West Himalyas)." in S. MacEachern, et. al. *Households and Communities*. University of Calgary: Chacmool.

DAS, Sarat Chandra. 1969. *Tibetan-English Dictionary*. Kyoto: Rinsen Book Company.

DOLLFUSS, P. 1989. *Lieu de Neige et de genévriers: Organisation Sociale et Religieuse des Communautés Bouddhistes du Ladakh*. Paris: C.N.R.S..

ERDMANN, Ferry. 1983. "Social Stratification in Ladakh: Upper Estates and Low Castes." In Sander and Kantowsky, eds., *Recent Research on Ladakh*. London: Weltforum Verlag.

FILIPPO, Filippo de. 1932. *An Account of Tibet, The Travels of Ippolito Desideri of Pistoia, S J. 1712-1727*. London: George Routledge and Sons.

FRANCKE, A. H. 1904. "A Language Map of Western Tibet With Notes." *Journal of the Asiatic Society of Bengal*. 73(4): 223-33.

----------- 1914. *Antiquities of Indian Tibet. vol. 1*. Calcutta: Archeological Survey of India.

HEBER, Reeve and Kathleen. 1903. *Himalayan Tibet and Ladakh*. New Delhi: Ess Ess.

JAESCHKE, H.A. 1975. *A Tibetan-English Dictionary*. Delhi: Motilal Banarsidass.

LEVINE, Nancy. 1980. "Nyinba Polyandry and the Allocation of Paternity." *Journal of Comparative Family Studies* 11: 283-98.

----------- 1981. "The Theory of Ru: Kinship Descent, and Status in a Tibetan Society." In C. von Furer-Haimendorf, ed., *Asian Highland Societies*. New Delhi: Sterling.

----------- 1988. *The Dynamics of Polyandry*. Chicago: University of Chicago Press.

PETER, Prince of Greece and Denmark. 1956. "The *Pha Spun* of Leh Tehsil in Ladakh, Eastern Kashmir, India." *East and West* 7: 138-146.

---------- 1963. A *Study of Polyandry*. The Hague: Mouton & Co.

---------- 1980. "Comments on the Social and Cultural Implications of Variant Systems of Polyandrous Alliances." *Journal of Comparative Family Studies* 11: 371-5.

REIS, R. 1983. "Reproduction or Retreat: The Position of Buddhist Women in Ladakh." in Sander and Kantowsky, eds. *Recent Research on Ladakh*. London: Weltforum Verlag.

RIBBACH, S.H. 1940. *Drogpa Namgyal, Ein Tibeterleben*. München: Otto Wilhelm Barth Verlag.

MILITARY ASPECTS OF THE DOGRA CONQUEST OF LADAKH, 1834-1839

N.F.Howard [1]

This paper grew out of an originally simple project to combine the three accounts of the Dogra conquest of Ladakh which Francke published in the second volume of his *Antiquities of Indian Tibet* into a single synthetic document which would describe the military events of that conquest fully and coherently. These accounts are: the conquest as included in the section containing the Chronicle (*La-dvags-rgyal-rabs*), the reminiscences of the old soldier from Khalsi, Tshe-brtan, and Cunningham's edition of Basti Ram's recollections (which had already been published in Cunningham's *Ladakh*).[2]

In cutting and pasting these accounts together, my basic assumption has been that each is true, until any part of it has been proved otherwise, but that no account contains the whole truth. Furthermore, I must fit every part of each account into my synthetic account in the order in which it occurs in the original - again, unless good evidence comes to hand to show that some other sequence is preferable. No final judgement on this latter point is available yet.

The work continues. Meanwhile further source material has come to light which must be incorporated into this exercise and which will be referred to as it is used. However one document reqires a short separate introduction. This is the report from Col. H.T.Tapp, Political Agent at Sabathu on a number of conversations which he had with the Vakeel of the young king of Ladakh - the *mC'og-sprul* - after he had fled into exile. Compiled between 10 and 22 November 1836, this is our only truly

---

1. 27 Clarendon Road, Edgbaston, Birmingham B16 9SD, UK.

2. Francke, The Rev. A H, *Antiquities of Indian Tibet*, Vol. 1. 1914, Vol. 2. 1926, Calcutta; reprint: S Chand, New Delhi, 1982. Cunningham, A, *Ladakh, Physical, Statistical, and Historical*, London 1854 (of course, we do not know to what extent Cunningham reports Basti Ram's own words and to what extent Cunningham edited them; for the purposes of this paper, I shall assume they are Basti Ram's).

contemporary source of information on the conquest.[3] Datta published this document in his biography of Zorawar Singh, based on documents in the Punjab State Archives, and another version of it exists in the India Office Records in London (which Datta seems also to have known). This latter is the one I am using here. Tapp's conversations took place "through the medium of an interpreter" - presumably translating from Ladakhi into Hindustani - then Tapp compiled his report in Persian, which was translated into English by T.T.Metcalf, and finally the translation was copied into the Political Consultation book in two hands, one of which is semi-illegible. There are a number of differences between Datta's Punjab Archives and the London versions. The Tapp report and certain other sources will receive further exploration at a later date.

However it is already possible to present a summary of the evidence available, and for the first time to propose a reasonably secure chronology for the events of 1834-39. As we shall see, the war of conquest is more interesting than has been previously realised; the Dogras did not have things all their own way all the time, and it is neccessary to challenge a few previously-held beliefs - including the apparent belief of most commentators that Basti Ram's account is the most comprehensively reliable and that the others are too muddled to be worth paying much attention to.[4]

Initial Dogra successes in Suru, July-September 1834

The Dogras advanced on Ladakh through Kishtwar, up the Wurdwun river valley: *Man-ldra-bahi* of the Chronicle, explained by Francke as Mandre and Waran, "Wure Mundi of the Ladakis" on Vigne's map of 1846.[5] They crossed the Bhot Khol Pass (not

---

3. Political Consultation No. 24, entry for 9 January 1837 (India Office Library & Records, London).

4. The standard work on the Dogra conquest of Ladakh is contained within: Datta, C L, *Ladakh and Western Himalayan Politics 1819-1848*, New Delhi 1972; additional material is to be found in the same historian's *General Zorawar Singh; His Life and Achievements in Ladakh, Baltistan and Tibet*, New Delhi 1984 (it seems that perhaps Datta followed Basti Ram too closely when considering the purely military events of the campaigns of conquest; at any rate, a close examination of the chief sources, and the advantages of a personal aquaintance with the geography of much of the terrain over which the Dogras fought, suggests a number of different interpretations of the events of the war and the timing of their occurrence).

5. *Map of Kashmir, Ladakh and Little Tibet, etc*, "from the surveys of G Vigne,

Mayum/Maryum La as in Datta) and assembled at Donara in the Chalong Nala. The first engagement took place in the Chalong Nala on 16 August 1834 (Basti Ram). The Dogras attacked up a hill; the 200 Ladakhi advance guard were led by Bkra-shis-dban-phyug and his son, governors of Suru-Kartse, who were killed (Chronicle). Basti Ram confuses matters by naming the Ladakhi leader Mangal, presumably rDo-rje-rnam-rgyal, the "Minister of Tog" but the Chronicle says that he was the general in charge of the army raised in reply to the warning sent by Bkra-shis-dban-phyug.

The Dogras then camped on the north side of the hill - to prevent its being reoccupied - before advancing to Suru. Neve is almost the only commentator who has shown this first engagement to be separate from later ones, presumably on the basis of oral evidence he gained when passing that way himself;[6] but he must be right since this is the only battle site from which one can advance northwards to Suru. The site of the engagement is a rocky shoulder of the mountainside on the left bank, roughly half way between the mouth of the Chalong Nala and the broad open confluence of the valley's headwaters at Donara; a number of loopholed breastworks are to be seen on the rock, facing up the valley.

By the 19th the Dogras were in Suru, making a settlement with the zemindars. Eight days later they began to build a fort which they occupied for one month (Basti Ram).

Advance to Sanku and Pashkyum, October-November 1834

Allowing three days for a leisurely advance to the Sanku/Langkartse district, the Dogras would have occupied the Khri-sultan's fort of Sag-mkhar (Basti Ram), probably at Langkartse, on about the first of October. The next few days would have been spent making the "summary settlement" here, which Basti Ram tells us of.

Immediately after that, the Dogras left small garrisons "over the bridge" (on the Suru river, presumably) and in the Khri-sultan's fort and advanced to Pashkyum bridge, via Mainji (Basti

---

Esq.", etc, by John Walker for the East India Company, London 1846.

6. Neve, A, *Thirty Years in Kashmir*, London 1913, pp 245-246 (unfortunately, after such a promising start, Neve also follows Basti Ram too closely).

Ram). This is the left bank route shown on all maps from Vigne's onwards and appears to have been the main route. But the fact that Basti Ram specifically mentions this route may indicate that there was another on the east bank - and one is shown on later maps - and that it was occupied by the Ladakhi army under it leader, rDo-rje-rnam-rgyal of sTog. The Dogras thus attempted to outflank the Ladakhis and cut their communications, which they did after a hard fight at Pashkyum bridge (Basti Ram).

Pashkyum bridge is strategically important for two reasons: firstly because the road from Ladakh through Purig to the west crosses from the north bank of the Wakha river to the south bank here, and secondly because the army which holds that bridge holds all the Pashkyum/Sod/Kargil area with its agricultural resources and its communications to the four points of the compass. All the maps show that the bridge was then just below the west side of Pashkyum castle (properly *Men-tog-mkhar*), probably where the present motor road bridge to Pashkyum village leaves the main road. The Ladakhis failed to prevent the Dogras crossing, who then sacked Pashkyum castle, took Sod castle (as graphically described by Basti Ram) and captured its Kiladar Salam Khan (Vakeel).

Meanwhile, both the Chronicle and Tshe-brtan tell us, there was fighting in the Sanku/Langkartse district as the Ladakhis, led by the "Minister of Tog" (Chronicle) in their turn tried to cut the Dogras communications - "great battles", the Chronicle calls them. The Dogra forces here must have been greater than Basti Ram tells us and they presumably held their river bridge for in the end the Ladakhi armies were beaten and retired eastwards across the Rusi La to Shergol, which seems, from the various references, to have been the Ladakhis' advance command post. "Then during one or two days snow fell more or less" the Chronicle says - winter had begun, bringing an end to the campaigning season, perhaps around the first of November. The reason why Basti Ram does not mention this fighting in Sanku/Langkartse is probably that he was not there. He may, of course, have not thought the battles as significant as did Tsh-brtan and the Chronicle writer; or he may have forgotten them, having already credited the Ladakhis with 5000 men under "Mangal" in the first battle in Chalong Nala. But the Chronicle is quite clear that there were two separate engagements with the Dogras before the snow fell, the Ladakhis being led first by Bkra-shis-dban-phyug and later by rDo-rje-rnam-rgyal of sTog.

Negotiations at Pashkyum and the Dogras' retreat, November 1834

After their military successes, the Dogras found a new obstacle in the way of victory; Basti Ram tells us: "A whole month was then wasted in fruitless negotiations with the zamindars of the district (ie. Pashkyum/Sod), who would not agree to the terms of settlement proposed by the Vazir (Zorawar Singh)". In other words, they called the Dogras' bluff. That month must equate to the period between late October and late November. Winter was setting in and the pass to Kishtwar would soon be closed, if not closed already; neither retreat nor supply was possible in the south. The Ladakhis were mobilised and pressing from the east and Ahmad Khan of Skardo was free to join an alliance against the Dogras if he decided to do so. The zamindars no doubt felt that time was on their side and starvation might rid them of the invader.

This must be why Zorawar Singh decided to try negotiations with the Ladakhis - from weakness, not from strength as Basti Ram seeks to imply. The Dogras sent a Kishtwari as messenger to the Ladakhis and proposed to retreat in return for a small tribute of 1000 Rs (Chronicle), the Dogras' honour thus assuaged. rDo-rje-rnam-rgyal of sTog advised acceptance but he was over-ruled by the Queen and her party (not surprisingly, since Zorawar Singh had destroyed her family's property in Pashkyum) and he was replaced in his command by Dngos-grub-bstan-'dzin and the "Minister of Ldumra" (Chronicle). During the negotiations the Ladakhis tried the effects of treachery, apparently killing the small party of Dogra emissaries (Basti Ram). And finally the Ban-kha bka'-blon mounted a daring raid "by a circuitous route" (Basti Ram), across the pass from the Indus to the Sod area (Chronicle, probably out-of-order), recaptured the treasure the Dogras had looted from Pashkyum and which was on its way to Kishtawar, and killed the 100-strong Dogra escort by drowning them "in sight of their comrades" who could do nothing (Basti Ram). This happened at Bhatura (Chronicle), which has not been identified, but may be in the Sanku area (if the Vakeel's account is to be so interpreted).

The Vakeel and Basti Ram are in agreement that at this point in the campaign, the Dogras, "seeing the danger" of their situation (Basti Ram) retreated "three stages" (Vakeel) "with some difficulty to Langkarchu (Lan-mkhar-rtse)" (Basti Ram). There they remained "unmolested for four months, procuring a precarious subsistance by plunder alone" (Basti Ram) - in other words, from late November 1834 until some time in February 1835.

The Ladakhi counter-attack and defeat, February 1835

Tshe-brtan tells us that "on the first of the twelfth month" (ie. 29 January 1835[7]) the Ladakhi army felt strong enough to take advantage of the Dogras' weakness and the winter conditions to mount a strong attack with the hope of expelling the invaders. Shortly afterwards (presumably) the Ladakhi forces arrived at Skyid-mar-rtse, or as Basti Ram says, one kos from Lan-mkhar-rtse. Here, as they were preparing their evening meal, they were surprised by a Dogra advance party and defeated. The events of the battle are difficult to unravel: according to the Chronicle, the battle lasted two days, and the Vakeel seems to be saying that at some stage unexpected darkness confused the Ladakhis. Further information may yet come to light. But the outcome was total defeat for the Ladakhis, the death of rDo-rje-rnam-rgyal of sTog and the capture of one of the Ladakhi generals, Dngos-grub-bstan-'dzin, along with other notables, although the minister of Ldumra and some of the army escaped over the pass north of Sod. The Dogras lost three important officers, which is an indication of the severity of the fight.

Ladakhi collapse and Dogra occupation of Leh, February-July 1835

Using their prisoners as porters (Basti Ram), the Dogras immediately followed up with an advance to Mulbhe (Mulbek), the district centre of administration, where they halted for 15 days (Basti Ram) and plundered the fort (Vakeel). Tshe-brtan graphically describes how all resistance had crumpled and one village after another sent pathetic emissaries of their submission to the advancing Dogras. At Lamayuru, Zorawar Singh received a message from the King of Ladakh lamenting that "eight months ... had now elapsed in the vain struggle for independence" and

7. Tshe-brtan's dates have been converted using the tables in: Schuh, D, *Untersuchungen zur Geschichte der Tibetische Kalenderrechnung*, Wiesbaden 1973, assuming that Tshe-brtan used the classic post-17th. century calendar (but bearing in mind that Tshe-brtan's dates may contain an element of spurious *post facto* accuracy).

offering personally to meet Zorawar Singh and negotiate peace terms, in return for guarantees of his personal safety (Basti Ram).

It was now, we may calculate, about the middle of March; the meeting took place at Bazgo and was followed by the King and Zorawar Singh removing to Leh, which they reached on the first of the second month, Tshe-brtan tells us (ie. 30 March 1835). This chronology appears to receive approximate confirmation from two British documents. The opening statement of the Vakeel's account in Tapp's words says that the Dogras invaded Ladakh - Leh and district, in the English usage of the time - in the month of Chyt in Sambhat 1892 (ie. March/April 1835). A letter which Charles Kennedy sent from Subathu to T T Metcalf on the 18 May 1835, contained a translation of a letter addressed to Dr James Gerard, which had been passed to him that day because Gerard was now dead. This letter was written by "Lama Junkar who instructed Mr Alexander Csoma de Koros in the Tibetan language a few years ago". The Lama writes: "In the present days the Sikh troops have advanced to Leh, and have fought a battle with the Ladawkees. Four thousand of the latter with several great officers have been placed *hors de combat*. The Sikhs demand 50,000 Rs. per annum Nuzzaranah from Ladawkee (sic)". We do not know the date the letter was written, but perhaps no more that 4 weeks earlier.[8]

Rebellion in Sod and Suru, July-August 1835

There are uncertainties about both the amount of tribute finally agreed and the length of the Dogras' stay in Leh: four months according to Basti Ram or from the second to the fourth months according to Tshe-brtan. In either case, they may have arrived at Lamayuru, on their way to Jummu, by early July. Here they heard that the the chief of Sod had reoccupied his fort (Basti Ram). By forced marches they reached Sod, only to find the chief had fled again. After spending thirteen days imposing their authority on the local people, the Dogras marched to Suru in two days (Basti Ram). An unknown number of days was spent suppressing the Suru people, but it cannot have been less than 10. The work may, perhaps, have been completed by 10 August and it was discovered that the rebels had received aid and encouragement from the Sikh governor of Kashmir. Then:

8. Board's Collections, Vol. 1642, Collection No. 65,650, India Office Records (perhaps Junkar = Jankar = Zanskar? or Junkar = Dzonkhul = Kun-dga'- chos-legs?)

"Leaving Suru, the Vazir (Zorawar Singh) marched in ten days to Jasku (Zanskar)" says Basti Ram.

The Vakeel states that this rebellion was started by Sher Ali Khan, the "Raja's vazeer". We learn no more of him, but a person with that name was *dmag-dpon* of Parkuda at that time.[9] If this is the person referred to we have a possible hint of the stirrings of a general rebellion in the Muslim districts bordering on Skardo territory and an explanation of a Dogra raid on Chorbat (next door to Parkuda) reported by Vigne (and nobody else). This took place in 1835 and involved "a few hundred Sikhs from the garrison at Ladakh, which had lately been taken by Zorawar Singh".[10]

The implication of the Chronicle's narrative seems to be that the Ban-kha-bka'-blon and Bsod-nams-dbang-phyug, the King's current chief councillors, advised the king to take advantage of these uprisings in order to reassert his independence (Chronicle). Perhaps they were encouraged by the idea of using Dr John Henderson as a bargaining counter. He must have arrived in Leh at about this precise moment since Charles Kennedy wrote to T.T. Metcalf on the 8 August 1835 to say that he had heard that day from Basahr a report from Ladakh that Henderson was on his way to Leh.[11] We know little other than that Henderson had no desire to get involved in Ladakhi affairs and eventually he arrived in Srinagar, via Skardo, on 18 November 1835[12] and died a few weeks later.

Dogras in Zanskar, August 1835

Meanwhile Zorawar Singh received a warning of the plot from a party opposed to the king while he was at Rangdum (Chronicle and Vazeer), on his way to consolidate his rule in Zanskar. It would appear that he received little opposition in

9. Francke *Antiquities*, Vol. 2, p 191.

10. Vigne, G T, *Travels in Kashmir, Ladak, Iskardo*, 2 Vols., London 1842, vol. 2, p 321.

11. Board's Collections, Vol. 1643, Collection No. 65,660 (other commentators have deduced that Henderson arrived on the scene earlier, eg. Alastair Lamb in *Britain and Chinese Central Asia, The Road to Lhasa* states that he was in Ladakh in 1834 - presumably a slip; Datta, in *Ladakh and Western Himalayan Politics* places his visit after the sack of Pashkyum and L. Petech, in *The Kingdom of Ladakh, c.950-1842* follows him).

12. Hugel, Baron C, *Travels in Kashmir and the Panjab*, trans. T.B.Jervis, London 1845, pp 101-102, 144. Vigne, *op. cit.*, vol. 2, pp. 104-6.

Zanskar. Oral tradition and Hashmatullah Khan's history[13] suggest that from the outset the rgyal-po of Zangla and the chief of sTe-sta welcomed the Dogras and only the king of Padum sought to oppose him for a time. The sources published by Francke do not mention these details; but Basti Ram does tell us that eventually one Midphi Sata offered to guide the Dogras to Leh. I suspect that this name is a corruption of *mi-dpon* of sTe-sta, whom Hashmatullah Khan names Singge Puntsok. Basti Ram tells us how well he was rewarded, the Karsha Lonpo that the king of Padum lost much land in consequence of his opposition, and Hashmatullah Khan that in his day the descendent of Singge Puntsok was the zeldar of Zanskar.

For the moment, I am of the opinion that the route Zorawar Singh took to Ladakh, with the sTe-sta chief's guidance, ran from Dran-rtse over the Phirtse La, to the upper Tsarap River, to join Cunningham's Southern Road (coming from Darcha on the Bhaga River) and so to Gya and Chimre.[14] This route is shown on all the earliest maps from Vigne's onwards, and was a major shawl-wool route; it was therefore practicable for the Dogra army but Zorawar Singh would not have known how to join it from Zanskar. Cunningham himself supports this choice[15] and his, or Basti Ram's, estimate of ten days for the journey of about 200 miles is reasonable (roughly double daily stages) although daily marches of 45 to 60 miles, as they state, are unnecessary for a journey of 10 days; nor are they possible on this route.

If indeed Zorawar Singh heard of the insurrection in Leh when he was at Rangdum, then he may have had two reasons for counter-attacking through Zanskar. Suru and Purig may not yet have been as quiet and safe for him as our sources suggest he had recently left them, until the King in Leh had been brought to heel. But one wonders why he did not counter-attack by way of the Lingshet-Lamayuru route or the Zangla-Chachar La-Markha route. However, by passing through eastern Zanskar - the last direction from which he would be expected - he completely out-

---

13. I am very grateful indeed to my colleagues Ms Nicky Grist, for allowing me to see records of her unpublished conversations with the Karsha Lonpo, and Dr Rohit Vohra, for allowing me to consult the translation of Hashmatullah Khan's history which they are both working on.

14. Cunningham, *op.cit.* pp 153-157.

15. Cunningham, *op. cit.* p 153 (he calls it the Winter Route, although he does not appear to realise that much of it is identical to his Southern Road but with different stages named).

flanked the Ladakhis.

The deposition of the King in Leh and the Dogras' return to Jummu, September-October 1835

The result was that the King was deposed, Dnos-grub-bstan-'dzin installed as regent and the young king, the *mC'og-sprul*, fled to Spiti (Chronicle, Tshe-brtan and Vakeel) where he tried to solicit British help and ultimately died in exile in Kotgarh in 1839.

A fort was built at Leh, from which to control the Ladakhis; and Zorawar Singh set off once again for Jummu - following the suggested chronology, probably in the second half of September, after a couple of weeks to settle matters in Leh (but any time before late October would probably have been feasible for the journey). On the way - and I think Tshe-brtan's timing is right here - they sacked Temisgam, perhaps because Zorawar Singh still thought the tribute inadequate even after all the goods which had been offered in lieu of cash (Basti Ram).

Consolidation of Dogra control in Zanskar and annexation of Padar, September-October 1835

At the same time, September and October 1835, Zorawar Singh sent Basti Ram and Lakpat Rai to procede with 1500 men, through Zanskar, against Padar, on the south side of the Umasi La - a territory belonging to Chamba. They took over the fort of Chatargarh, left a garrison there and passed on to Jummu (Basti Ram). The purpose of this piece of realpolitik was to provide the Dogras with an alternative route to Ladakh, should the Suru/Purig route ever be blocked in future.

And there matters rested, militarily, until 1839 as far as we know, with the possible exception of some skirmishing on the borders of Basahr in an attempt to capture the young King.

It appears that in the early spring of 1839[16] a general

16. Petech *op. cit.* p 143. There is some uncertainty about the date of this rebellion and Zorawar Singh's return to Zanskar and Ladakh. At present, the balance of probabilities is that it must have been in the summer of 1839 because that was followed by the winter conquest of Skardo (Basti Ram), folowed by the old King's death in the spring (Basti Ram/Cunningham, Tshe-brtan, Chronicle) which was followed by a winter in Ladakh (Tshe-

rebellion broke out in greater Ladakh. We are not told what caused it but Petech makes the interesting suggestion that it may have begun in Zanskar. Basti Ram says that "the new king had revolted and killed the thanadar of Balde (Padar)", which seems a very odd thing for Dngos-grub-bstan-'dzin, ruling in Leh, to do. But Hasmatullah Khan, in his very confused account of the Dogra conquest of Zanskar, seems to be saying that, during the first Dogra conquest, the ruler of Padum was first deposed but later reinstated; Basti Ram (or Cunningham) may be referring to the reinstated ruler of Padum. Later, Hashmatullah Khan says, the thanadar of Zanskar, Lar Singh, was killed at Marling while leading an attack on "Karja", and that that caused Zorawar Singh's second attack on Zanskar, but he gives us no clues to the wider circumstances of the thanadar's death. On the other hand, if "Karja" is Kartse in Suru, Lar Singh may have been marching west to halt the spread of a rebellion which began in Dras,[17] see below.

The Dogra recapture of Padar, April-July (?) 1839

This campaign of Zorawar Singh's is well told by Basti Ram, our main source. Two months after hearing in Jummu of the revolt, he had travelled up the Chandra-bhaga River as far as Chatargarh where he could not cross because the Padar people had removed the only bridge and the river was too high to be forded. After a further two months, "with the help of some villagers (he managed to pass) a *jhula* across the river a few miles lower down ... and thus, advancing under the cover of night, effected an entrance into Chatargarh by the bridge over the Bhutna Nala, which had been left intact".[18]

Savage retribution quickly brought submission from the Padar people and leaving a garrison, the Dogras pushed on to Zanskar, by way of the Umasi La (Basti Ram). Presumably, it was

---

brtan) during which Zorawar Singh plotted an expedition against Yarkand (Chronicle) which was given up in favour of an invasion of Tibet which took place during the summer and winter of 1841-1842 (Petech and Datta support this chronology - the latter with a wealth of references to British Indian sources).

17. No Lar Singh is to be found in our primary sources; if "Karja" is Kartse by Suru, then the Marling of his death cannot be the Marling in south-east Zanskar - it is hoped that further exploration of other sources will illuminate these matters.

18. *Punjab States' Gazetteer, Chamba State*, 1910, p 105.

after the whole rebellion was supressed that the Dogra fort of Gulabgarh was built in a new position, say late 1839.

We may guess that it was now August. The Umasi La - approximately 17,400 feet above sea level - consists of a knife-edge pass approached on each side across two glaciers. During the crossing 25 men died of cold and ten suffered severe frost-bite (Baṣti Ram) - presumably in a monsoon storm.

The Dogra recovery of Zanskar, August-September 1839

As he descended to Dzongkul monastery, Zorawar Singh received the submission of the abbot and confirmed him in his lands (Karsha Lonpo/N.Grist). The population of Zanskar had fled in fear, according to Basti Ram, but during their two months stay in Zanskar "everything was arranged satisfactorily" (Basti Ram). It appears from Hashmatullah Khan that the various rulers of Zanskar quickly re-offered their submission to Zorawar Singh and that the ruler of Zangla was particularly helpful. The Chronicle recounts how the deposed old King came to meet them at Pi-pi-ti "and the Wazir showed him great kindness". A general desire to deny any involvement in whatever had happened even extended to Dnos-grub-bstan-'dzin and his followers who arrived the day after the king; but their overtures were rejected.

At this time the Dogras built the fort at Ubti, Hasmatullah Khan tells us.[19]

The Dogra advance on Leh, September 1839

Bearing in mind that the Dogras had spent 2 months in Zanskar, it must by now have been late September (but hardly any later, since the attack on Skardo began before the winter snows filled the valleys). Everybody proceded towards Leh - in two separate parties, according to Hashmatullah Khan. He says one party went "through the stream of Rangdum", which probably means over the Pensi La to Suru and Purig in order to combat the rebellion there (see below) but might mean that for unknown reasons they took a short cut from Rangdum over the Kanji La to Henaskut in upper Purig. Perhaps this group was comprised of the 1000 men under Rai Singh and "Mia Tota", mentioned by

19. For a description of this and the other Dogra forts mentioned, see: Howard, N.F. 1992, "The Dogra Forts of Greater Ladakh, North-west India", in *Fort* vol. 20, pp. 71-86, pub. Fortress Study Group.

Basti Ram.

The other group went by a more easterly route. Hasmatullah Khan says via the Zangla route (and seems to confuse Karnak with Kurna Sumdo). This is Cunningham's Direct Route from Zanskar, over the Charcha La, through Markha to Leh.[20] One might have expected the Dogras to follow the well-known Southern Road, as in 1835. We do not know whether Hasmatullah Khan had historical authority for his statement or guessed on the basis of his knowledge of Cunningham's routes and the fact that the ruler of Zangla supported Zorawar Singh. But his statement may be supported by Tshe-brtan's that "Zorawar arrived at Slel (Leh), coming by the Zans-dkar road".

At any rate, probably on this journey, Dnos-grub-bstan-'dzin realised his game was up and tried to escape, being caught at Tabo in Spiti - which may explain why the chief of Gya was fined in the general retribution (Chronicle): his lands span the Southern Road and are easily reached from the Markha Valley and he may have helped the escape.

The rebellion in Purig, 1839

The one act of rebellion at this time which we do know something about is that raised by Sukamir of Dras, as recounted by Tshe-brtan. Sukamir stirred up all Purig and led his followers towards Leh; but when they met the Dogra troops their courage failed them and they claimed they had come merely to present a loyal petition. After he had dismissed their followers, Zorawar Singh questioned the leaders and soon discovered Sukamir's involvement. His tongue was cut out and his amputated hand displayed on Khalsi bridge - which is how Tshe-brtan came to know this story.

Plates

N.Howard Pl 1: The Ladakhi position in the Chalong Nala, seen from the up-stream, the Dogras', side: stone breastworks on the top of the hill-shoulder; the river is out of sight below the flat land on the right.

N.Howard Pl.2: Inside one of the Ladakhis' breastworks in the Chalong Nala: three typical triangular loopholes (the stick is one meter long).

N.Howard Pl.3: The entrance to Basti Ram's Haveli in Leh

20. Cunningham, *op. cit.* p 153.

HISTORICAL BACKGROUND OF CSOMA DE KôRöS' SOJOURN IN LADAKH (ZANSKAR) between 1822 and 1826

Bernard Le Calloc'h [1]

Whoever reads any of the numerous biographies of the Hungarian scholar Alexander Csoma de Kôrös, must be greatly surprised that his life is narrated without any reference to the historical events which marked the different countries where he travelled during several years.

These books ignore totally the background of his activities and do not allude to it, as if there would have happened nothing worth of notice, nothing which would have had any influence upon himself or upon his own studies. They give the strange impression that in those remote Himalayan kingdoms and principalities, politics, wars, inroads, military operations, dynastic rivalries, do not exist, or that they have no consequence on Csoma's life.

Of course, it is the contrary which is true. Ladakh's days do not glide by in untroubled ease. Beset with dangers and foes, it enjoys a more and more uncomfortable situation, it has to face more and more difficulties.

In short, even in those hidden parts of the world, there is no escaping history.

Across Purig

Alexander Csoma de Kôrös leaves Srinagar on the 19th of May, 1822, together with four Kashmiri merchants. He crosses the Great Himalayan Range at the Zoji-La (3529 meters) just when it is re-opened to traffic after winter season. The footpath is hardly practicable; it creeps along vertiginous abysses between snowdrifts and heaps of rocks. There is no real road, but only a narrow track, as "difficult and rocky" as in the time when Mir Izzet Ullah travelled "beyond the Himalaya" in 1812, so that goods can be carried only by men. After the Zoji-La Csoma finds himself in another world, with

1. 110, rue de Montreuil, 75011 Paris, France.

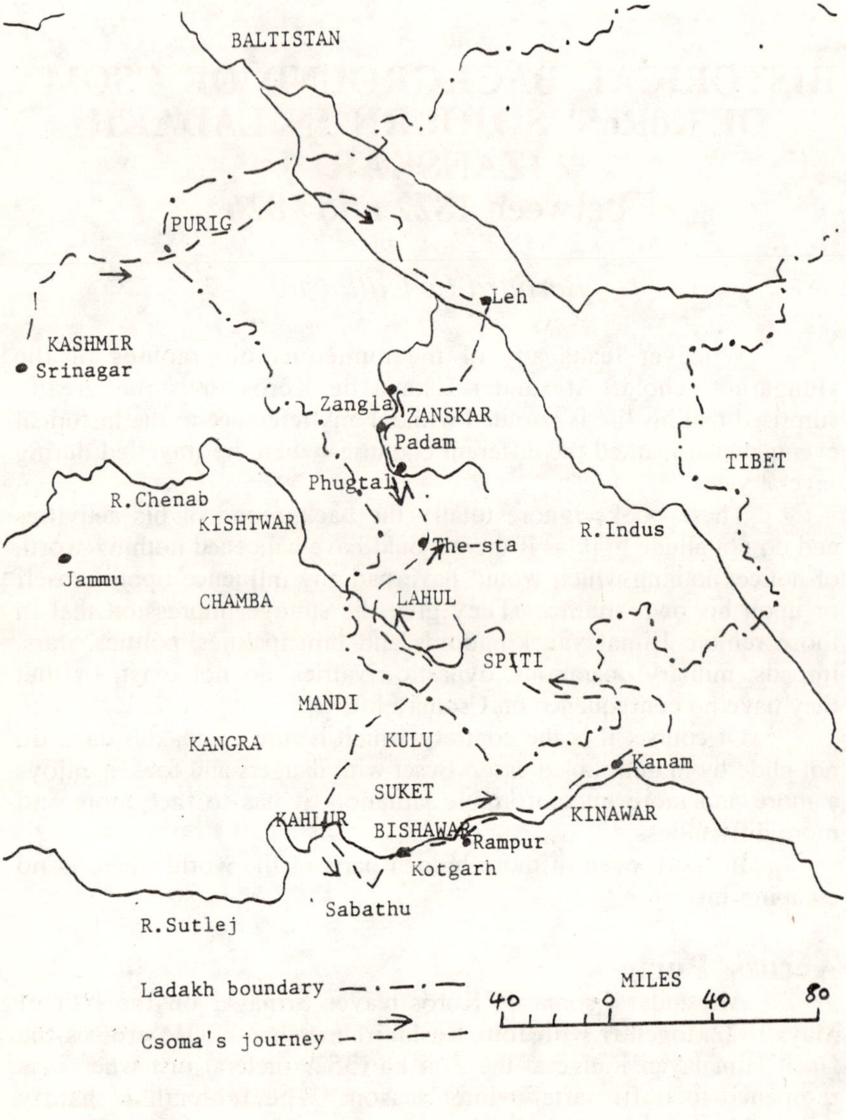

B.Le Calloc'h: map

very high mountains, rough climate, and inhabited by Tibetans. From now onwards he is in the kingdom of Ladakh.

The high valley of the river Dras (Him-babs) which follows the pass is called Purig. It has been annexed to Ladakh in 1758. Till this year it had its own sovereign, but after the death of the last king, bKra-shis rNam-rgyal, in the absence of any heir apparent, the little country has been occupied by Ladakhi troops. The late king's widow became a nun and her brother, dBang-rgyal, has been appointed governor of the sole fortress of the valley, the small stronghold of Dras. To seal the new union with Ladakh, the young king Tshe-brtan rNam-rgyal - born in 1782 - marries in 1794, when he comes of age, a princess of the Purig royal family, born at Pa-skyum, and called either dPal-mdzes dBang-mo or Tshe-dbang Rig-'dzin sGrol-ma. Unfortunately, she is left a widow at twenty-one, the king dying of smallpox in 1802.

Purig is like a long narrow corridor, cold and windy, constituted by the upper course of the river Dras, which often flows through deep gorges. It streches from the Zoji-La till Pa-skyum, that is till beyond its junction with the river Suru. It is a Tibetan country, though its inhabitants have been converted to mohammedanism more than two centuries ago.

On the 16th of October 1822, William Moorcroft and his fellow-traveller George Guthrie are again at Dras. The little village has just been plundered on the preceding night by a party of eight hundred men leaded by the Raja of Hazara. "All the cattle and everything of value", writes Moorcroft, have been carried off by the invaders who retired immediately.[2] Some time before, another foray coming from Hazara had already stolen several horses from Matayan, a village of Purig near the Zoji-La. This was the opportunity for the Ladakhi government to remind the Sikh governor of Kashmir - to whom heavy tribute must be paid every year - of his obligation to assist Ladakh in case of foreign unprovoked aggression against any part of the kingdom, but the Kashmiris are more impatient to levy taxes than to help their tributary.

As the greatest part of Ladakh's national income derives from the caravans crossing the country between Tibet or Turkestan and Srinagar through the Zoji-La, possession of Purig is of great economic and strategic importance. Moreover the route across Purig is also the main way of entry into Kashmir and the Indian provinces, as Ladakh is almost completely enclosed within gigantic, impassable mountain ranges.

---

2. Moorcroft, *Travels* II, p.88.

In Ladakh Proper

Beyond Mulbeck, Alexander Csoma de Kôrös crosses the Manika-La (3718 m.) and enters Ladakh proper. Immediately after this first pass he crosses another one, the Fatu-La (4080 m.), the highest of the whole route, and he arrives at Leh, the capital, on the 9th of June, with the purpose of continuing his journey to Yarkand as soon as possible, i.e. as soon as he can find a caravan proceeding to Eastern Turkestan. After twenty five days of vain waiting, realising that the plan he had formed cannot be carried out, he turns back to Kashmir, intending to join in Lahore two French officers with whom he came from Afghanistan between January and March.

The king who is reigning over Ladakh in 1822 belongs to the rNam-rgyal dynasty and is called Tshe-dpal Mi-'gyur Don-grub (and not Tsimma Panchik, as Moorcroft writes). He has been invested with royal power in 1802 on his brother's death, giving up the frock of a monk to ascend the throne, but he is in reality "hardly more than a cypher".[3] This was also the opinion of Mir Izzet Ullah in 1812 who declared that "the Raja takes no part in the affairs of the State".[4] All the powers are in the hands of the Prime minister Tshe-dbang Don-grub (and not Tsiva Tandu, as Moorcroft writes) who, having married the king's half sister, is also his brother in law.[5] It is obvious that the government of Ladakh "is a simple despotism".[6] The kingdom's real master is "the Kalon" (bka-blon), as he is called by Csoma de Kôrös in his letter to Captain Kennedy dated 28 January 1825, the main historical figure of those times. Not only is he the chief of the executive, he has also the entire control of the kingdom's economical and financial life. He is in all matters "the supreme authority", as it is pointed out by Mir Izzet Ullah.[7]

In spite of its natural isolation, Ladakh's situation has considerably deteriorated since the beginning of the XIXth century. The emergence of the Sikh empire in the Punjab between 1799 and 1819, the conquest of Kashmir against the Afghans, and the extension of the British colonial rule in India after the Anglo-Nepalese war of 1814-1816, have effected deep changes in the traditional balance of power in North-Western Himalaya. Furthermore, Ladakh has an old and tenacious enemy in Baltistan, a Tibetan kingdom whose

---

3. Moorcroft, *Travels* I, p 334.
4. Mir Izzet Ullah, *Travels beyond the Himalaya*, p.288.
5. B. Le Calloc'h "A Ladakhi statesman, Tsewang Dhondup", *The Tibet Journal* XIV N°4 (winter 1989).
6. Moorcroft, *Travels* I, p.332.
7. Mir Izzet Ullah, *Travels*, p.288.

inhabitants have been converted to shiia mohammedanism. Balti armed parties, year after year, attack its northern border along the course of the river Indus. This aggressive neighbour is often the main cause of trouble for the government of Leh, whose policy is only defensive. In 1820, the king of Skardo, Ahmad Shah, takes hold of Kapulu. In June 1821, the Ladakhi forces must again bar the way to a Balti raid.

On the South-western border of Ladakh, the new Raja of Jammu, Gulab Singh, does not conceal his ambition to expand his power as far as possible in the Himalayan countries to the prejudice of his neighbours. Becoming Ranjit Singh's first vassal and ally, he has been authorised to raise his own army under the high command of the fearless Zorawar Singh Kahluria. He has already subdued several small principalities such as Riasi, Sambha, Dalpatpur and Akhnur. In 1820, on Ranjit Singh's special order, he invaded Kishtwar and conquered it within two months, thus reaching Ladakh's immediate border. In 1822, in the very moment when Csoma de Kôrös is staying at Leh, waiting for a caravan, he takes hold of two other Himalayan states, Behandrate and Chaneni, rounding off once again his land in the name of the Sikh Maharaja.

The presence of the British East India Company's rule in the upper valley of the Sutlej (Kinawar and Bishawar) is also very disquieting for the Ladakhi authorities. This is the reason why in September 1820, when Moorcroft arrives near Leh at the head of a rather numerous expedition, he is thought to be the advance party of a British invading army. Mir Izzet Ullah, Khoja Shah Nyas, Abdul Latif have the greatest difficulty in persuading the Kalon that Moorcroft is simply a veterinary surgeon in search of Turkish horses. It is clear that from Ladakh's standpoint the fact that the English are now extending their frontiers to those of the kingdom is a serious cause of apprehension. The official position of the Calcutta government is that the Sutlej is the extreme limit of their extension, but one can know from experience that such an official statement is liable to rapid change.

From the economic point of view Ladakh enjoys a very important privilege. Since the treaty signed in 1684 with Tibet and the Moghol empire, at the end of a four year war, it has the monopoly of all the pashmina shawl wool produced in the so called Byang-thang of mNa-ris skor-ǧsum, Western Tibet. The exportation of this very fine under-coat of a special tan-coloured breed of goats is reserved to Ladakh, provided that it will be dispatched only to Kashmir. It goes without saying that this monopoly means for both countries a lucrative and regular source of income. Therefore Moorcroft's arrival at Leh is regarded by all the Kashmiri merchants and by the Ladakhi authorities as a threat against the financial standing of Kashmir and Ladakh. It is an open secret that already in 1812 when he travelled to Lake Manasarowar and stayed at Gartok, Moorcroft tried to divert the shawl wool trade for the East India Company's benefit. He is suspected of trying again, though he asserts he has no ill intent at all. Owing to Khoja Shah Nyas and Mir Izzet Ullah's clever intercession, the English explorer becomes rapidly the Kalon's friend and confidant, but he remains the enemy of the merchants. This explains that an attempt is made on George Trebeck, Moorcroft's principal assistant, in the night of 27th June 1821. Obviously, it is Moorcroft who was aimed at, but the attempt failed and the sly traveller continues to win over the Kalon to the cause of an alliance with India. At the beginning, Tshe-dbang Don-grub was hesitating. He did not know what direction to take, but he had the presentiment of an unexpected possibility: to escape from Sikh suzerainty if he succeeds in being on friendly terms with the English. He thinks that Ladakh can reap advantage from the competition between its two neighbours inasmuch as the Honorable Company's power can easily counterbalance the Sikh dominion. English influence must be used to refuse the tribute, which is so heavy and unpopular for his poor nation. Though Moorcroft is not on official duty, he signs with the Kalon a draft of engagement in July 1821 and informs immediately the Governor General of India. Instead of congratulations, he meets with a slashing refusal. He receives the order not to mind public affairs and to keep out of political questions. Sadly disappointed, the Ladakhi Prime Minister hopes that the little Himalayan state will not be placed at Ranjit Singh's mercy and probably cannot imagine that it will be annexed to the Sikh empire within fourteen years, the Company's government coldly looking at the annexation.

Indeed Ladakh is falling into decay. From every side great dangers are hanging over it. The King has no authority and does not take care of politics. He is unable to help his subjects when they are the victims of foreign inroads. In 1822, just when Csoma de Kôrös is in Ladakh, parties coming from Kulu sacked Zanskar and Spiti. The Prime Minister is now an old man (he will die probably in 1825) whose authority is impaired. The general situation is worsening.

Furthermore, other forces come into play. Russia is just in Csoma's time playing a diplomatic game in this part of the world. Through a secret agent named Aga Mehdi Rafaïl, she tries to establish trade and political relations with Ladakh and Punjab, the only independent states with Nepal of the Indian sub-continent. Csoma de Kôrös does not meet with the Aga, as he died while crossing the

Karakorum pass, coming from Yarkand, in the first days of April 1821, but he has to translate into Latin a letter, written in Russian by the minister for foreign affairs of Russia, Count Robert von Nesselrode, sent through Aga Mehdi Rafail to Ranjit Singh and Tshe-dpal Mi-'gyur Don-grub. Though he is desiring to hold aloof from any kind of political activity, the Hungarian traveller is kept abreast of political events of considerable importance. It is not probable that the aim of Czar Alexander was to invade India, as it is often said. But he certainly had the ambition to play a part, and perhaps a prominent part, in Indian affairs. The Calcutta government was aware of their Russian ally's secret desire. This was the reason why they did not want to cause Ranjit Singh dissatisfaction with Ladakh's tender of allegiance. For the Lord Governor the alliance with Punjab was much more significant than with the small and poor kingdom of Ladakh.

Csoma de Kôrös was still involved in another quarrel due to Moorcroft's presence at Leh. It happened that in 1821 and 1822 the supply of shawl-wool sent to Kashmir from Tibet through Ladakh diminished considerably. Immediately the Kashmiri merchants accused Moorcroft and the English of smuggling great quantities of this precious good into India under British control, in order to bring ruin upon Kashmir and Ladakh. Moorcroft was suspected of being the real cause of this sudden decrease which threatened both the traders and the weavers. The veterinary explained that an epidemic broke out in Byang-thang, killing thousands of pashmina goats, and that this was the sole reason of so unexpected an event. He repeated on this occasion that he was in the Himalaya to buy horses and not shawl-wool. Anyhow the Kashmiri merchants wish evil to this European whom they are afraid of. They tried to kill him; now they cast discredit on him and make attempts to compromise him with the Ladakhi government. A seditious placard is affixed on one of the gates of Leh during a night. The placard says that "according to a resolution already adopted", the King will be deposed if he does not alter his conduct, and "the most respectable of his subjects" will request "the principal European now at Le to assume the government". Fortunately the news does not gain credence, and Moorcroft can write in his diary: "No change occurred in my familiar and confidential intercourse with the ministers".[8]

After two years's stay in Ladakh, Moorcroft leaves it on the 20th of September 1822, no longer hoping to cross Turkestan to Bukhara. Trebeck remains with Csoma de Kôrös for a month and a half, the latter beginning to learn colloquial Tibetan from Abdul Latif,

---

8. Moorcroft, *Travels* I, p.458.

who can explain him in Persian the rudiments of Tibetan grammar. About December 15th, they arrive at Srinagar with the rest of the expedition.

On the lst of June 1823, the Hungarian is again in the Ladakhi capital. He pays a visit to Anwar Baba, the imam of the mosque, who is Moorcroft's friend since the Englishman has been recommended to him both by Mir Izzet Ullah and by Khoja Shah Nyas. He calls also on Mohin Ali, a Kashmiri merchant who became Moorcroft's mercantile broker and contact man in spite of the hostility of his fellow-countrymen. Then he is introduced to the Kalon who receives with great pleasure Moorcroft and Mir Izzet Ullah's presents. In return Tshe dbang Don-grub gives him six pounds of Tibetan tea and a letter for "the lama of Zangla". Furthermore the minister puts at his disposal a guide to cross the totally uninhabited mountains which extend between the valleys of the Indus and the Zanskar rivers. On the 26th of June, he is in Zangla after a very quick journey of only nine days.

In Zanskar

Zanskar (Zangs-dkar) is one of the most remote places on the earth. The huge mountain ranges which surround it on every side are impassable during seven months at least, so that this part of the kingdom is unapproachable during more than half the year. Indeed it is situated "at the back of beyond". The average altitude of this very high and landlocked valley is of 3500 metres (11,500 feet). The climate is particularly severe and the cold intense. One can say without any exaggeration, that till Csoma de Kôrös it was a country totally unknown to Europeans. Csoma de Kôrös is the first European to stay in this out-of-the-way place, and surely the only such visitor for more than 150 years.

However Zanskar is an old kingdom, probably founded in the Xth century, which maintained its independence until 1562. In this year it made its submission to the Ladakhi King bKra-shis rNam-rgyal (1555-1575) together with Nubra, Suru, Rudok and Spiti. During 'Jam-dbyangs rNam-rgyal's reign it recovered its freedom (1595-1616), but in 1640 it is again annexed to Ladakh by Seng-ge rNam-rgyal (1616-1642) the greatest Ladakhi sovereign. After the latter's death, Zanskar is devolved in 1647 to the late king's second son bDe-mchog rNam-rgyal. The queen mother bsKal-bzang sGrol-ma takes her residence in Zanskar, where she dies in 1650. In 1680, when bDe-ldan rNam-rgyal (1642-1694) is expelled from Gu-Ge and Ru-dok (Ru-thog) by the Tibetan army, Zanskar rises in rebellion against the Ladakhi power, but in vain. It is definitely a dependency of Leh, though there is still a king (rgyal-po) in Padam (dPal-ldum) and another one in Zangla (bZang-la).

In 1788 a foray coming from Kulu destroys several monasteries, among which the famous monastery of Phuktal (P'ug-dal). Tshe-brtan rNam-rgyal does not retaliate on the plunderers. His successor's attitude is the same in 1822 when Zanskar is again attacked by parties of from Mandi and Kulu through Spiti. In fact, the Ladakhi authorities are unable to help the poor Zanskaris in such circumstances. They are forsaken by all, except the tax collectors.

In Lahul

Csoma de Kôrös's first sojourn in Zanskar lastes sixteen months, from June 1823 to October 1824. During the never-ending winter he suffered so much from cold and lack of the most elementary comfort, from dirtiness and total isolation, that he induces his master Sangye Phuntsog (Sangs-rgyas Phun-tshogs) to move out to Kulu, like some of the rich families of Ladakh, on the southern side of the Great Himalaya, where the climate is rather moderate and the poor man's lot not so awful. The lama agrees to the plan, but just as the Hungarian is on the point of starting, under the pretext of having to do some urgent business, he remains in Zangla. However he assures his pupil of his joining him as soon as possible in Sultanpur, the town of Kulu where they have decided to winter.

Therefore Alexander Csoma de Kôrös starts alone on the 22nd of October, trusting in his master's promise, and sure that they will meet within a few days, before snowfalls close the passes. He brings in his luggage the matter for his Tibetan dictionary, intending to work on it with the lama. He knows that he cannot do anything without the latter's permanent help, as he is the first European to undertake such a compilation.

He goes along the valley of the Zanskar river upstream, through Padam and sTe-sta, till the last Zanskari village of dKar-rgya, crossing the Zanskar range at the Shingo-La (5,096 m.), after which he enters Lahul in the first days of November.

Lahul is a very small state along the upper valley of the Chenab river which from Tandi upwards is called Chandra, and the river Bhaga, its main affluent coming down from the Baralacha-La (4,685 m.). It is caught between the two huge ranges of the Great Himalaya in the north (maximum altitude 6,700 m.) and the Pir Panjal range on the south (maximum altitude 6,200 m.).

From the European point of view Lahul enters History in 1631, when two Portuguese Jesuits, Francisco de Azevedo and Joao de Oliveira, cross it in November,on their return journey from Leh, where they have been received by king Seng-ge rNam-rgyal and queen bsKal-bzang and permitted to preach the gospel in the Himalayan provinces. In 1649 it is annexed to Ladakh by the same king, who gives estates and privileges to the 'Brug-pa order wherever he is the master. But in 1682, Lahul is invaded by Bidhi Singh, Raja of Kulu (1672-1688). During two centuries it is an apple of discord between Ladakh and Kulu.

Contrary to their neighbours of Zanskar and Spiti, the inhabitants of Lahul are all more or less involved in transit trade, which is for them of paramount importance. Everybody traffics in something, as transportation and commerce are the main business. They are also inclined to plunder their peaceful neighbours when they can take advantage of some opportunity. Two or three years before Moorcroft crosses the principality in 1820, under the reign of Pritam Singh, a Lahuli party makes a foray in the main valley of Zanskar and reaches Padam without being harassed by their victims.[9]

When journeying in Lahul, Moorcroft is surprised by the fact that, though Lahul pays tribute to the Raja of Kulu, four villages of the Chandra valley between Tandi and Gramphu pay also tribute to the King of Ladakh, not because of old feudal vassalage but as an insurance for their trading activity. Moorcroft meets in Kyelang with Dharma Singh, the richest landowner of the country and its real master. The Raja resides either in Tandi or in Kyelang and like his subjects, is eagerly interested in transit trade because of the duties he imposes both on imports and exports.

Csoma de Kôrös quickly goes through Lahul. He is impatient to reach the last great pass of Rohtang (3,955 m.) before it is blocked by snow, and in the same time he is afraid that Sangye Phuntsog will not be able to join him in due time.

After the Rohtang pass he enters Kulu.

In Kulu

Kulu is already mentioned in the *La-dvags rgyal-rabs*, the Ladakhi Chronicle, in the XIth century, but it is only pointed out that it pays tribute to Ladakh. Nothing else is known of its history till the XVIth century, when an inscription alludes to a victory of bKra-shis rNam-rgyal (1555-1575) over the king of Kulu. From this time onward the Raja's usual place of residence is Sultanpur, but he has also another residence at Nagar, in the upper valley of the Bias river.

In 1682, Bidhi Singh, King of Kulu, annexes Lahul, becoming

9. Francke, *Antiquities of Western Tibet*, pp. 22-24.

an immediate neighbour of Ladakh and competing with it for the rule over the Himalayan kingdoms, but it is the time of bDe-ldan rNam-rgyal (1642-1694), successor of the great Seng-ge rNam-rgyal, and Kulu must quickly lower its ambitions.

One century later, in 1782, troops coming from Kulu invade Zanskar and destroy several religious buildings. However Kulu's star is on the wane. In the Punjab the increasing power of the Sikhs, under Ranjit Singh, is a new danger. In Kangra, Sansar Chand, who comes to the throne in 1775, does not conceal his intention to conquer all his neighbours and thinks he can prosecute his ambitious designs not against the Sikhs but with their help. But at the same time he comes up against an unexpected difficulty: the ambitions of the Nepalese Gurkhas, extending their power beyond the course of the upper Sutlej. In this diplomatic and military imbroglio Kulu loses its independence. It must pay tribute to Ranjit Singh and acknowledge the Sikh sovereign as its suzerain. This is the reason why in 1820, when Moorcroft and his party arrive in Kulu from Mandi, they must show due permission from the Maharaja to cross the country. The present King is Ajit Singh, a child born in 1812 who, on Bikrana Singh's death in 1816, has been put on the throne, the kingdom's true master being the Regent, Vazir Sobha Ram. The English explorer witnesses the bad relations existing between Kulu and its northern neighbours. Some traders of Kulu having been detected in an illicit trade in shawl-wool - a Ladakhi monopoly, as we know - and their goods seized on the border, Sobha Ram sent a troop into Ladakhi territory, i.e. into Zanskar with the order to carry off as many horses and cattle as possible. Moreover the invaders destroyed several temples or monasteries. According to Moorcroft, "the object of the Kulu Vazir, whatever might be pretended, was no doubt to raise means for paying the exactions of Ranjit Singh".[10]

In November 1824, when Alexander Csoma de Kôrös is at Sultanpur, waiting for his master, the situation is again in its normal state. He could easily remain in the country to work on his dictionary if Sangye Phuntsog would join him rapidly. During ten days he waits for the lama, but in vain. There is no longer hope of seeing the lama, for the passes are now closed for half a year by snowfalls. Suddenly, he realises that he has been deceived and that he is alone in this little foreign town, unable to undertake the task for which he came. He remembers that Moorcroft has given him letters of introduction to the British authorities of India in case he might need their help. Therefore he decides to proceed on his way to the Indian border. He

---

10. Moorcroft, *Travels* I, p.457.

leaves Sultanpur and after Bajura enters the principality of Mandi.

In Mandi

Mandi means "market" in Hindi, the language of its people. It is famous among the Buddhists as the country where Padmasambhava is said to be born. In Csoma de Kôrös's time, the capital of this little Himalayan state, which is also called Mandi, is on the left side of the river Bias, whereas it was on the right side previously. This change of situation is due to a change in the course of the river.

During more than a century it had been subdued by the Moghols. In 1752, with the help of Ahmad Shah Durani, it was freed from the heavy Moghol rule, and became theoretically the vassal of the Afghans. As the new masters were far from here their suzerainty was reduced to the payment of an annual tribute.

After 1775, Kangra's new Raja, Sansar Chand, claims to be the lord paramount of all the hill states. He demands that Mandi acknowledge itself Kangra's vassal. Upon its refusal, Mandi is subdued and the capital sacked. The young sovereign, Ishwari Sen, is taken prisoner and exiled at Nadaum, where he remains twelve years. Among the three districts which are seized by Sansar Chand, one is given to Suket for its allegiance. Till the last years of the XVIIIth century the Kangra Raja is the undisputed lord of the Himalaya, North of the Sutlej. However in the meantime the Nepalese Gurkhas reach the left side of the river, their unconcealed design being to establish a large Himalayan empire stretching from Katmandu to Srinagar. Against Sansar Chand's conquering policy, Mandi and the other vassal territories of the right side of the Sutlej form a coalition and do not hesitate to invite Amar Singh Thappa, the Gurkha commander, to cross the river in order to punish the common enemy. Sansar Chand is defeated, but as usual the new conquering army is not willing to withdraw. This is the opportunity that Ranjit Singh seizes immediately to force back the Gurkhas beyond the Sutlej and, of course, to impose his own dominion upon the newly freed states. Thus Mandi became the vassal of the Sikh Maharaja, falling from Scylla into Charybdis.

This is the reason why, when he arrives in Mandi in March 1820, Moorcroft is requested to mind Ranjit Singh's permission to cross the country. The Raja, Ishwari Sen, who has been freed in the meantime from his prison in Kangra, dares not permit the English expedition to proceed on its way without his suzerain's explicit order. This compels Moorcroft to leave George Trebeck in Mandi with the rest of the expedition and to go to Lahore together with Mir Izzet Ullah. The unexpected complication delays considerably the travellers who can start again only on the 11th of July.

In November 1824 Alexander Csoma de Kôrös crosses the country between Bajura and Suket in two or three days without incident. The mendicant-looking Hungarian pilgrim passes unnoticed, contrary to Moorcroft and his companions who are accompanied by a great many men, horses and beasts of burden.[11]

In Suket

Suket is a very small princedom, it has no more than 50,000 inhabitants. In its major events, its history is the same as Mandi's. As it has been said in the preceding section, it acknowledged itself vassal of Kangra immediately after Mandi has been invaded and destroyed by Sansar Chand's army, annexing on this occasion a district of its northern neighbour. However, it is compelled to give it back to Mandi in 1809, when both principalities become Ranjit Singh's tributaries. The Sikhs demand an annual tribute of 22,000 rupees, which is at last reduced to half. This is still a very heavy burden for such a tiny state.

Since 1791 the Raja is Bikrama Sen. He has left Suket for a new capital in Banerd, ten kilometers south of Suket, in a much more practical and protected place, which he christens Purananagar (now Sundarnagar). In 1805, he has joined the general coalition of the hill states against Kangra and called on Amar Singh Thappa to invade the common enemy.

It is funny to note that, when Moorcroft makes his appearance near Purananagar, the population is thrown into a panic by the approach of an unknown foreign "army". The explorer's expedition is so important in number and in impedimenta, that the Suketis imagine they are invaded by a hostile army coming from the south. Probably it is the first time that they see Europeans.

As soon as he arrives in the capital, Moorcroft asks to visit the Raja, who has the reputation of being an energetic sovereign and very scrupulous in the performance of his duties. He does not allow abuses, corruption, robbery and slavery, which is in those times a very unusual behaviour on the part of an Indian Raja.

Crossing the Sutlej near Dehar, Alexander Csoma de Kôrös enters the principality of Kahlur about the 10th or the 11th of November 1824.

11. It is interesting to note here that Mandi will be conquered in 1840 by the French general Jean Baptiste Ventura at the head of maharaja Ranjit Singh' s army. He will be made "Earl of Mandi".

In Kahlur

The first European to visit this Himalayan state is the English traveller George Forster who crossed it in 1783 disguised as a Moslem merchant. Theoretically, the Raja is already Mahan Chand, but he is only eleven years old, being born in 1772. The regency is in the hands of the queen-mother, widow of Devi Chand. She reigns but it is the vazir Raman who governs. After he comes of age, the Raja proves not interested at all in public affairs. It is the new vazir, successor of Raman (died in 1785) whose name is Zorawar Chand, who rules the country uncontrolled.

In 1795, Sansar Chand of Kangra claims to be the undisputed master of all the hill states and demands oaths of allegiance. With the help of a rebellion of the local nobles against the Raja, whom they accuse of keeping them out of the public life, he invades Kahlur, seizes Bilaspur, sacks and destroys the town. In 1804 he annexes the portion of the principality lying on the right bank of the Sutlej. Fearing for his possessions, Mahan Chand joins the coalition and presses the Gurkhas to cross the river. But in the meantime a new empire is born in the Punjab, under Maharaja Ranjit Singh. The Sikhs become another conquering power, audacious and invincible. In a first time (1805), the Gurkhas free Bilaspur, restore the Raja to his throne, and take hold of Sujanpur, Sansar Chand's capital. For a second time (1809), the Sikh army drives back the Nepalese and takes possession of the main strategic points in the mountain, so that in 1812 Mahan Chand has no other solution than to acknowledge himself vassal of the Punjabi king and to do homage to him. As a matter of fact, the Raja of Jammu, Gulab Singh, is taking the place of the Raja of Kangra. In these Himalayan provinces the Sikh power is now represented by the Hindu family of the Dogras. Gulab Singh is helped by his brother Dhyan Singh, member of the Lahore government, and by his other brother Suchet Singh. Moreover, Gulab Singh's army is trained and directed by Zorawar Singh, born in Kahlur, who will later be Ladakh's conqueror.

In 1814, Mahan Chand seizes the opportunity of the Anglo-Nepalese war to beg for English military intervention against the Gurkhas, who still hold the city of Bilaspur. In 1815, after the Gurkhas' withdrawal, an agreement is concluded, according to which the Raja of Kahlur is officially recognized as sovereign of the portion of his princedom which is on the left bank of the Sutlej. As regards the other portion, on the right bank, he must pay homage to Ranjit Singh, who demands a heavy tribute. In 1819, to compel Mahan Chand to fulfil his obligations towards his suzerain, the Sikh general Desa Singh Majithia, governor of the mountains of Kangra, lays hands on several strongholds of Kahlur and reaches the course of the Sutlej. He crosses it, but retires rapidly because of the arrival of a British division.

In February 1820, Moorcroft is in Bilaspur. He describes the city as strongly ruined. The only beautiful building is the newly built palace of the Raja. People look very poor and the government is a simple tyranny.

In November 1824, when Alexander Csoma de Kôrös travels in Bilaspur, Mahan Chand is dead and his successor is his son, born in 1813, Kharak Chand. All the power is in the hands of his vazir, the same as previously, Zorawar Chand.

After Bilaspur, he crosses the Sutlej in south-eastern direction, and by Ratanpur, Malown and Sallaghat, proceeds to the Indian border. A few kilometers before Sabathu, he crosses once again the course of a little affluent of the Sutlej coming down from Simla, and enters the territory of the East India Company.

At Sabathu

Alexander Csoma de Kôrös arrives at Sabathu on the 20th of November 1824, intending to introduce himself to the English of India. He has been given a letter of recommendation by William Moorcroft in April 1823, whereas another one has been sent to George Swinton, Secretary to the government of Calcutta. Hence he imagines that his Tibetan studies in Ladakh are well known and that he will be received with open arms. He does not intend to stay in this remote checking station near the border. His desire is to go to Calcutta and to be permitted to reside on Indian territory. When he will be in the Indian capital he will visit the Asiatic Society and request the books which Moorcroft requested in vain for him.

On his arrival, Captain Charles Pratt Kennedy, the head of the border garrison, is away. Csoma is welcomed by the surgeon, Dr James Gilbert Gerard, who turns out to be very friendly. The latter inquires after his visitor, his travels, his studies; he gives him a Bible, but he cannot decide anything.

It is a matter of fact that, instead of being welcome, the poor Hungarian pilgrim is detained at Sabathu in rather bad conditions until instructions are received from the Governor General. He is suspected to be a Russian spy because he has neither passport nor any kind of official document proving his assertion according to which he is a "Siculo-Hungarian of Transylvania", subject of the Austrian Emperor.

After six weeks, he is requested to give a complete account of himself and of his plans. This account is dated 28th January 1825. It is one of the most important documents we have on him. In the 17th paragraph of this long letter, he confesses how much he was disappointed at not being cordially received. "At my first entrance to the British Indian territory," he says, "I was fully persuaded that I should be received as a friend... because I supposed that my name, my purpose, and my engagement for searching after Tibetan literature, were well known in consequence of Mr. Moorcroft's introduction".[12]

Csoma de Kôrös is obliged to wait for the Governor's answer till the month of May, but he has the pleasure to hear that he is granted a monthly allowance of fifty rupees which set him free from money worries. He can henceforth prosecute his Tibetan studies without being anxious for the future.

Through the tiny princedom of Keonthal, he starts on his second journey to Ladakh in June 1825. He leaves Sabathu, which is at an altitude of 1280 meters,and climbs to Simla (2200 m.), where he puts up at Captain Kennedy's bungalow, the first house of the new-born hill station. Then he goes down into the valley of the Sutlej and stays at Kotgarh. This little town is placed on the border between the principality of Suket, on the right bank of the river, and the Sikh principality of Baghal, on the left bank, but it belongs now to neither. When Bishawar, the largest hill state of the left bank, came under British protectorate in 1815, the East India Company retained possession of this town for economic and strategic considerations. The first reason, the economic, was that the English intended to make Kotgarh a trade center for shawl-wool of Western Tibet and established here a weaving factory. The second reason, the strategic, was that Kotgarh was already under Gurkha occupation an important military position and that it can prevent troubles or invasion in a country which is inhabited by restless Sikh tribes.

After Kotgarh, Alexander Csoma de Kôrös has to choose between two routes. He can go back to Zanskar with the same route he has come from, through Suket, Mandi, Kulu and Lahul. He can aternatively go the Sutlej upstream to a small Tibetan village called Kanam, where there is apparently in the library of the local monastery the complete collection of the Buddhist canonical scriptures, indispensable for prosecuting his philological researches. At the crossroads, he decides to go to Kanam.

In Bishawar

Five kilometers beyond Kotgarh, he enters Bishawar, a Rajput

12. Theodore Duka, Life of Alexander Csoma de Kôrös, p. 30.

princedom as the other Himalayan states between Nepal and Kashmir, one of the nineteen states that are now gathered under Captain Kennedy's wing. The British officer, in spite of his low place in the military ranking, is the true viceroy of a region as large (30000 km^2) as half the Transylvania of those times (58900 km^2).

The most celebrated Bishawari Raja is Kehari Singh. In 1679, he grants military help to the armies of the fifth Dalai Lama[13] waging war against Ladakh in order to recover the western provinces of his realm. Owing to the reinforcing troops dispatched by Kehari Singh, the Tibetan general dGa'-ldan Tshe-dbang re-occupies mNga-ris and Gu-ge, overthrows the Ladakhis, and reaches their capital, Leh, which he occupies, compelling king bDe-ldan rNam-rgyal to make overtures for peace. In consequence of the agreement signed in 1685, the Tibetan Regent Sangs-rgyas rGya-mtsho gives Kinawar to his ally, i.e. the upper valley of the Sutlej this side of the Shipki-La, though it is inhabited by Tibetan Buddhists. This means the total dismemberment of Seng-ge rNam-rgyal's great empire and the return of the Dalai Lama's state to the traditional frontier.

The second great historical event in Bishawari history is the advance of the Nepalese till the course of the Sutlej as soon as 1804. Then the annexation to their growing empire, their crossing the Sutlej at the request of a coalition of several rajas of the right bank, and their victory over Kangra's Raja Sansar Chand. The annexation is accompanied by atrocities and many exactions, but it lasts only a few years. In 1809 the Gurkhas are checked in their westward expansion by Ranjit Singh,and in 1814 the Anglo-Nepalese war puts an end to the dream of a Great Nepal extending from Sikkim to Kashmir. In 1815 Ochterlony's column drives back Amar Singh's army. Bishawar is totally reconquered on 6th November,and peace is signed at Sigauli in March 1816. The Raja is restored on his throne, paying a small tribute of 3950 rupees to the English as a token of allegiance. All the territories lying between the rivers Kali and Sutlej are ceded to the East India Company, so that the latter becomes contiguous to the Kingdom of Ladakh.

After 1815, hence during the years that precede Alexander Csoma de Kôrös's journey the English make a lot of alterations in Bishawar's life. They decide that shawl-wool trade will be developed, as Bishawar is a direct route from Western Tibet to the plains of India. Many Kashmiri weavers take their abode in Rampur, the capital, and in Kotgarh, where they establish a factory. This change is not due to

13. The most celebrated Dalai Lama, Ngag-dbang blo-bzang rgya-mts'o (1617-1682), known in Tibetan history as "The Great Fifth"

Moorcroft's activity, but the natural consequence of a change in the economy of the Himalayan countries. The aim is to divert the wool trade from Kashmir into territories under British control. To insure a convenient transit traffic it is not enough to induce the Tibetan traders to smuggle their goods into Bishawar, it is also necessary to improve the roads. "Tracks which in 1818 could hardly be used by the travellers," says Alexander Gerard, "and were almost impassable, were repaired and within two years the people of Kinnaur started bringing sheep, laden with wool, to Rampur."[14]

About June 15th, Csoma de Kôrös is in Rampur, waiting for the help of the vazir, Tikum Dass, to whom Dr.Gerard has written a letter. The Bishawari capital[15] looks very romantic and pleasant. All the travellers remark upon its curious architecture, which is half Chinese and half Hindu, with slated roofs. The Raja's palace is on a hill, overlooking the town, the houses of which huddle together on the river's bank.

In possession of a letter to the vazir of Kanam, Basant Ram,[16] the Hungarian goes on, proceeding to Kinawar, the upper part of Bishawar, slowly, from a village to another, on the river's right bank, with a sole porter given by Tikum Dass.

All along the narrow path which leads to Tibet, he follows in several British geographers' tracks, such as Captain Herbert or the three Gerard brothers, who in the preceding years have systematically surveyed valleys and mountains, drawn maps, and described this new Anglo-Indian province, which remained unknown till the recent conquest.[17]

When he reaches Kanam, he hopes to stop here. He imagines that among the inhabitants of the monastery, he can find a learned man who will be able to work with him, to explain him Tibetan language and culture, in short to take Sangye Phuntsog's place. But in vain. He can see that none of the monks, even the prior, speak good Tibetan. They are illiterate. They cannot and probably are not willing to help him in his difficult researches.

Therefore he leaves Kanam rapidly, having certainly no idea

14. Alexander Gerard, Account of Koonawur, pp. 115-116.

15. Contrary to what is said by J.Terjek (*Kôrösi Csoma dokumentumok az akadémiai Kônyvtár gyüjteményeiben*, p.179), Kanam is not the capital of Bishawar.

16. Basant Ram is the name of the vazir of Kanam, in Csoma's time. Csoma makes a mistake when he writes to Kennedy (letter from sTe-sta, dated 16th october 1825) "the basuntram of Kanam". Basant Ram is a name, not a title or a function.

17. The three Gerard brothers were officers in the armies of the Bengal establishment, one of them, James Gilbert, being military surgeon of the garrison at Sabathu. He was the first geologist of the Western Himalaya.

that within two years he will be back and settle in the little Kinawari village for three and a half years, till October 1830.

Instead of going due North to Spiti through Songnam and the pass of Manerang, he proceeds to Nako (he writes Naho), the highest village of Kinawar (3658 m.) because he has a letter for the local vazir. He arrives there on the 26th of June to be informed by the vazir that he cannot give him the porters he needs for his luggage and books, but he puts at his disposal an old man from Hangrang called Padma who immediately proves willing to help and a good companion. Then he continues his journey, going slowly on an arduous winding mule track, among gigantic mountains (almost 6000 m.), in a more and more denuded landscape. At last, in the first days of July, he arrives at the border between Kinawar and Spiti.

In Spiti

Spiti is a large uninhabited country, almost a desert. According to Moorcroft[18] there are only 2,000 men in the country, all living in the valley of the river Spiti.

Spiti became the vassal of Ladakh after it has been conquered in 1562 by bKra-shis rNam-rgyal. Under his successor, Tshe-dbang rNam-rgyal (1575-1595) it was kept under strict control and became a province of the kingdom. However, during 'Jam-dbyangs rNam-rgyal's reign, it recovered its independence. Not for a long time as Seng-ge rNam-rgyal takes again possession of it in 1628.

In 1647, after Seng-ge rNam-rgyal's death, Spiti is given with Zanskar to the second son of the deceased king, bDe-mchog rNam-rgyal, the Ladakhi empire being divided into three parts. In 1685, Spiti is annexed to Tibet, but ten years later it returns under Ladakhi suzerainty. In 1774 a Bishawari army lays siege to the fortress of Dankhar, the main stronghold of Spiti, and takes it after two years.

After the Anglo-Nepalese war, British geographers surveying Kinawar try to venture into this unknown province, in spite of the official prohibition, but no one can reach Dankhar. They are driven back as soon as they are reported.

In 1819 Spiti is invaded by an armed party sent from Kulu by vazir Sobha Ram, as it has already been said in a preceding chapter. In 1821, to make peace with Kulu and Bishawar, Spiti agrees to pay tribute to them. Acknowledging itself vassal of all its neighbours, it hopes to live in peace and quietness. However in 1822 new inroads from Kulu ravage the country as a result of a long dispute. The

18. Moorcroft, *Travels* II, p.68.

people claim for retaliation, but the Ladakhi government must confess that they are unable to do it. In the same year, Trebeck and Ghulam Hyder Khan, members of Moorcroft's expedition, make an excursion into Spiti from 8th June to 29th August. At the end of the excursion, Ghulam Hyder Khan starts to Sabathu and Trebeck returns alone to Leh, where he makes acquaintance with Alexander Csoma de Kôrös, who arrived from Purig with Moorcroft and Guthrie on the 26-th. Accompanied by the old Padma of Hangrang, Csoma de Kôrös crosses Spiti along the river's bank, stopping at Dankhar and Losar. Then he climbs the pass of Kunzom and enters Lahul in the upper valley of the river Chandra (Chenab). He goes through Tandi and Kyelang, crosses the pass of Shingo and arrives at last on the border of Zanskar. On the 12th of August, after a 68 day journey, he reaches sTe-sta, Sangye Phuntsog's village. This is the end of a long and hazardous peregrination, during which he has lost plenty of time - nine months. On the other hand, he receives now a monthly allowance from the British authorities. He is secure from want and can work quietly. Though he was compelled to go back to where he started from, he hopes he will rapidly resume his lexicographic researches.

Let us note as a final point that at the very moment when the Hungarian arrives afresh in Zanskar, William Moorcroft dies near Andkhoy, in the emirate of Bukhara, and after him all the members of the expedition except Ghulam Hyder Khan. The Kalon also dies probably in 1825.

Bibliography

BARNES, G.C. *Settlement report of the Kangra district*. Lahore, 1889.

CUNNINGHAM, J.D. *History of the Sikhs*, ed. by H.L.O. Garrett. Oxford, 1918.

DREW, F. *The Jammu and Kashmir territories*. London, 1875.

FORSTER, G. *Travels*. London, 1798.

FRANCKE, A.H. *A history of Western Tibet*.. London, 1907.

---------- *Antiquities of Indian Tibet*. Calcutta, 1914 and 1926.

HARCOURT, A.F.D. *The Himalayan districts of Kooloo, Lahoul and Spiti*. London, 1871.

HUTCHISON, J. and J. Ph. Vogel *History of the Panjab hill states*. Lahore, 1933.

SAYID MUHAMMED LATIF *History of the Punjab* . Calcutta, 1891.

MOORCROFT, W. and G. Trebeck, *Travels in the Himalayan Provinces* ... London, 1841.

PRINSEP, H.T. *The origin of the Sikh power in the Punjab* . Calcutta, 1834.

UJFALVY, K.E. von *Aus dem Westlichen Himalaja*.. Leipzig, 1884.

VIGNE, G.T. *Travels in Kashmir and Ladakh*. London, 1842.

BODHISATTVA CSOMA DE KôRöS: MYTH OR REALITY?

P.J. Marczell [1]

In Hungary in 1948, the art historian Lajos Fulep (1885 - 1970) received a letter from Rome stating: "The One Hungarian who has won universal significance since the beginning of the 19th Century, Alexander Csoma de Koeroes, the founder of Buddhist Studies and of Tibetology in the Western World, who has been canonized as a Buddhist Saint in Japan in February 1933, in my presence and at my initiative, is almost forgotten by the new generation of Hungary, while in India thousands of Scholars, Christians and Buddhists, Hindus and Chinese, Japanese and others go on pilgrimage to Csoma's tomb, 20,000 feet high in the Himalayas, above Darjeeling, where Csoma died of malaria in 1842. His tomb is a National Monument cared for by the Government of India."[2]

The event mentioned in this passage has been described in different terms in Hungary and Japan, its meaning construed in different, sometimes extravagant, ways, while its timing, the protagonists and the motivations behind it have been paid little attention. Under its impact, Csoma's veneration became a worship at least by one community enjoying serious official status. The alleged eastern sainthood has impressed and intrigued the biographers and the public alike but still awaits impartial appraisal. As it is believed to stand mainly on merits accumulated in Zanskar-Upper Bishawar,[3] I take the opportunity to submit the case to this Conference. In doing this, I am trying to act as a substitute for someone much more competent than me in the field, Dr. Bulcsu Siklos, who finally declined to discuss the matter last March at the Csoma de Kôrös Symposium in Paris, partly for lack of access to the literature on the subject. I have taken advantage of his bibliographical researches, and added to them of my own. The alleged "canonization" seems to have

---

1. 24/b, rue Lamartine, CH-1203 Geneve, Switzerland.
2. The Hungarian Academy of Sciences, Department of MSS: Ms. 4590/174.
3. At Zangla (3 May 1823 - 6 November 1824), at Phuktal (6June 1825 - end of November 1826), at Kanam (early June 1827 - November 1830). Cf. e.g., le Calloc'h, Bernard: "Sur un point d'histoire concernant Alexandre Csoma de Kôrös." *La Nouvelle Revue Tibétaine*. 1986. N° 13. 82-91.

been induced by a present. This is suggested by the official invitation which runs as follows:

> "TAISHO UNIVERSITY, TOKYO. COMMEMORATION for ALEXANDER CSOMA de KÔROS (1784-1842) / Hungarian Pioneer of Oriental Learning. Author of the first Tibetan-Sanskrit-English Dictionary (1834) and the first Sanskrit Vocabulary of Buddhism, one of the most heroic figures in the History of Knowledge, whose memory is honoured all over the world on the occasion of the arrival of his Statue in Japan, offered by the 'Hungarian Oriental Society' of Budapest as a gift to the Japanese people and as a manifestation of Hungarian friendship in appreciation of the great services of Japanese Scholarship to Oriental Research and International Co-operation, to be held on February 23, 1933, Wednesday Afternoon 3 o'clock in the Auditorium of Taisho University, Nishi Sugamo-machi, Tokyo."

The statue involved (see Plate) was 29.1 cm (9.57 inches) high, made of bronze by Géza Csorba[4] and represented an idealized Csoma sitting like an Amitabha Buddha.[5] "Inscribed on the figure are the words: KÔRÖSI CSOMA SANDOR / THE BODDHISATTWA OF THE WESTERN WORLD. CSORBA".[6]

The Hungarian and the Japanese reports concurred on the importance of the ceremony attended by several hundred people, including high-ranking government officials, diplomats and distinguished scholars. After the greeting by Dr. Shiio Benkyo, Dr. Felix Vályi, the representative of the Hungarian Oriental Society delivered his commemorative address [7] This was followed by a ritual carried out by the President of Taisho University. The program continued with three lectures. (According to Vályi, it ended by singing sutras in front of Csoma's statue surrounded by burning candles.)[8]

---

4. Cf. Ichisima, Masao: "Körösi Csoma Sándor." *Annals of the Institute for Comprehensive Studies of Buddhism, Taisho University*. 1981. N° 3. 47-58, p.58.

5. Remark by Dr. Ernest Hetényi to the author, 9 May 1992.

6. *Op. cit.* [4], p.54.

7. Vályi, Felix: "Kôrösi Csoma Sándor (1784-1842)." *Journal of the Taisho University*. 1933. Vol. XV. June. 1-6.

8. *Op. cit.* [3], p.35.

If we trust Vályi,[9] the contents of the three lectures can be summed up as follows:

> Junjiro Takakusu, sanscritologist, editor of the *Encyclopedia Buddhica*: Japan should learn from the example of Csoma, imitate his self-sacrifice in order to preserve its lead in Buddhist studies which have been taken over by Western universities, as under the impact of materialism, Japan has neglected its own spiritual values. Csoma risked his life for establishing the scientific foundations of Buddhist studies and deserved the great thankfulness of the Japanese spiritual world as the *first Western hero of Buddhism*. Buddhism is not a sectarian movement, it is not restricted by racial limits and therefore is glad to include Csoma among the historical heroes of Buddhism, among the canonized "bodhisattvas".
>
> Forty-one years earlier than the ceremony, Professor Ekai Kawaguchi, the famous tibetologist, who visited Central Asia four times, had decided to continue Csoma's work. It was the study of Csoma's life which induced him to go to Tibet. In 1896 he made a pilgrimage to Csoma's tomb in Darjeeling and tried to penetrate into Tibet in secret through Nepal. He obtained his visa into that country only when the Nepalese consul noticed that he was studying Csoma's dictionary. Csoma was venerated everywhere Kawaguchi went in Nepal and Tibet. He was considered as a bodhisattva a long time before it was realised that his tomb attracted many Buddhist pilgrims who copied and cherished its inscriptions. He is one of the greatest saints of Buddhism. As the Hungarian Bosatsu, Csoma will live for ever in the hearts of Japanese Buddhists.
>
> The historian Kurakiçhi Shiratory, who had spent half a year in Hungary studying historical research there, dwelled on the contribution of Hungarian Oriental researches to world history and stressed that the Japanese people had special reasons for treating the Hungarians as brothers.

Vályi's address itself was published in English in the Journal of the Taisho University, Tokyo, Vol. XV, June 1933, pp. 1-6. It described Csoma as "one of the greatest Orientalists of the Western World", who discovered for the Western mind the Three Treasures of Buddhism so long hidden before the Christian world, "one of our Holy Men in the West". After meeting Moorcroft in 1822,

9. Instead of taking his words in *op. cit.* [3] with a big pinch of salt. Cf. e.g., my doubts on Kawaguchi's testimony.

"Twenty years of untiring devotion and sacrifice followed in Korosi Csoma's life, devotion to a field of study of which the world then was entirely ignorant and which became the starting point of Western Research on Budhism. The years passed under privations such as have been seldom endured, and his patient labours in the cause of science, have given the most powerful stimulus to Oriental Research.

"Kôrösi Csoma's life and Work symbolises in the face of the sceptical Western mind *the great miracle of Will Power*. Japan, herself a miracle of Will Power in face of a sceptical world, will certainly appreciate the symbolism" of Csorba's statue presented by the Hungarian Oriental Society. "Legend took hold of the solitary Hungarian. The Lamas visiting his tomb ... take their visitors to the grave for a moment of silent prayer. They accepted Kôrösi Csoma as a Holy Man, as one of *their own* boddhisattvas, who came from Magyaristan to open the heart of the Western world to the study of Buddhism."

Unlike Vályi, the Japanese account also provides details on the commemorative exhibition staged before and after the ceremony in the Sanskrit Seminar Office, where "works of Csoma and related materials were shown publicly with the cooperation of the Taisho University Library and the Tokyo University Library. Along with this were the personal belongings of Ikegami, Ikeda, and Arimatsu. Csoma's *Tibetan-English Dictionary, Tibetan Grammar, Tibetan studies,* and *Tibetan Mahavyutpatti,* along with the bronze image, were exceptionally interesting exhibitions. Rev. Tokan Tada was kind enough to send, via Prof. Jiko Hazama, a picture of Csoma's tombstone from far distant Tibet."[10]

Vályi, however, added that on March 7th, prior to meeting Secretary of State Oaya, he had been to a reception by the Minister of the Imperial House, the President of the Imperial Museum and the Head of the Department of Fine Arts. It was after these preliminaries that Csorba's statue was solemnly accepted - against a caligraphic receipt - by the Museum of the Imperial House. The hosts reciprocated with two albums reproducing in colour the silk collection at the *Sosho-in*, Nara.[11]

At this point, one may question Vályi's report on what the Journal of the Taisho University called simply "presentation ceremony of the bronze image from Dr. Vályi to President Fukuda of Taisho

---

10. *Op. cit.* [4], p.53.
11. *Op. cit.* [3], p.34.

Univ." Here is the translation of Dr. Vályi's version on what happened:

> "In accordance with the third point of the program, the Rector of Taisho University, Abbot Fukuda took solemnly thereafter from the hands of the Hungarian speaker the statue of Csoma, he placed it on the lotus-throne of the Buddha-altar, then, in complete silence, he *embarked on the 10--minute sanctification* which, in Tendai rite, is made effective through the symbolical gestures of Buddhism. These are wonderful motions of the hands. In old Sanskrit such mystical gestures of the fingers are called *mudras*, ... (garbled)
>
> "The artists in the public commented with wonder for days the manual magic of this prestidigitation. These symbols stem from a tradition of two thousand five hundred years, they stand for the deepest mysteries of the Asian soul. In this case they signified that the head priest of the Tendai Monastery made Alexander Csoma de Kôrös a saint, a saint of Buddhism, whose Sanskrit name is *Boddhisattva* (the Buddha to come), while in Japanese the Sanskrit word became *Bosatsu*. Only the canonizing rite of the Roman Church can be compared to the extraordinarily impressive Buddhist ceremony, which tremendously surprised all the European and American guests who were present. It was only then that they realized that Japanese Buddhism bestowed one of the highest honours in world history on the Hungarian ascetic buried at Darjeeling one hundred years earlier, who had opened the soul of the Western world to the values of Buddhism, and gained such a tremendous importance for Hungary."

Would the Japanese protagonists have endorsed this rendering?

The Dean of Academy, Taisho University, Masao Ichishima, recalled the 1933 commemoration in March 1981, apparently as a supplement or background information to the presentation of a new theory on Csoma's birth. He relayed Prof. Lászlo Kádár's claim on Csoma having been born five years later than held by the consensus.

He headed his contribution by the title "Kôrösi Csoma Sándor - Further information concerning the birth date of the first Western Bodhisattva and his bronze image", recounted how he took on Nov. 9th, 1973 the son of Prof. Kádár, Dr. Imre Kádár, to the image and paid their respects to the great Hungarian hero" and concluded: "He was recognized as the first Western Bodhisattva in a ceremony at Taisho University on 22 February, 1933." In this wording he used no quotation marks. However, he accompanied his conclusion by a footnote referring to L. Kádár.

The subtleties of bodhisattvahood are not less easy to grasp. In this regard, let me ask three questions: "What is a Bodhisattva? Could Csoma qualify for being one? Could the Japanese involved have taken him for one?

I shall answer the first question on the bacis of Dr. N. Bakshi's study on the *Iconography of the Bodhisattva (Bosatsu) images in Japan and India.*[12]

In a simplified Mahayanist view, the Bodhisattva (*Bodhi:* Enlightenment; *sattva:* essence) had acquired great spiritual merit, and was capable of attaining Enlightenment, i.e. Buddhahood.[13] He was, however, foregoing this since he had taken the vow of helping all beings to reach the same ideal state and until this was achieved, he would not become a Buddha. As a personification of boundless compassion and refusal of *Nirvana*, he is an ideal. He is supportive, able and willing to lead the faithful to the paths of Enlightenment, to confer unbound benefits and provide reliefs from afflictions. The Theravadins or the Hinayanists, however, would hardly subscribe to such a doctrine, as in their belief *Bodhi* could be achieved only by the great *Arhat* (worthy), like the Sakyamuni, while Arhathood itself lies beyond the reach of others except disciples or monks *(Bhiksu)*. The followers of their system *(Sravakas)* seek only their own liberation through their own individual practices.[14] Other schools of religious thought appreciate the status of the Bodhisattva still otherwise. While the Saila school regards the Bodhisattvas as average beings, who "may be born in the lower states of existence",[15] the spiritual successors of the Mahasanghikas in the early period of Mahayanist Buddhist history hold that "the Bodhisattvas, like the Buddhas, are supramundane and they do not pass through the embryonic stages in the mothers' wombs like the ordinary beings".[16] In the *Sambhogakaya* (Body of Enjoyment) concept derived from the *Trikaya* (three bodies) doctrine,[17] "all the Bodhisattvas assuming various names are but the spiritually glorified transcendental Personages, possessing wisdom and compassion, beyond all historicity." With the Buddhas and various lesser divinities, they

12. Calcutta: The Centre of Japanese Studies. 1991
13. *Op. cit.* [12], p.10.
14. *Op. cit.* [12], p.12.
15. *Op. cit.* [12], p.16.
16. *Op. cit.* [12], p.14.
17. *Op .cit.* [12], p.17.'

belong to a specific category of the Buddha-nature.[18] In *Tantrik* belief, all these deities are the "bright affluences of the 'bright essence uncreate' of the Absolute." [19] Through the combined concentration and meditation of esoteric *yoga*, one can visualize their forms.[20] In the Buddhist pantheon of Vajrayanists, the five central Dhyani (meditative) Buddhas (also considered as *Jina* (conqueror) "split themselves up in the form of Bodhisattvas and their female principles who are responsible for creating everything found in existence."[21] They are the progenitors of almost all the Bodhisattvas. Their spiritual families serve "as the *upaya* or means or something material or perceptible for devotion in the process of realisation of higher truth." [22] They "lead to the 'formless' existing beyond discriminative knowledge".[23] This is how their material representations, the icons, are integrated into the process of one's efforts to realise the Ultimate Truth.

Biographical data on Csoma do not allow an easy fitting of him into any of the classical spans of these interpretations. There is no evidence on his being a Buddhist and even less on taking the vow to cultivate the perfections of different magnitudes and various forms of ascetic practices, progressing thus through the various stages of sanctification, the *dasabhumi* or ten fields, analysed in the *dasa-bhumika-sutra* with their respective *paramitas*.[24]

Apparently, he did not engage in strict religious practices. However, he was a religious specialist who acquired his theological knowledge of Buddhism by conscious, painstaking work, despite inhumane hardship. He showed abnegation and other moral qualities and made Buddhism accessible to Westerners. In the light of texts like the *Upayakausalya-parivarta,* he might have approached Buddhahood through these virtues.[25]

One may wonder if the fate of Csorba's statue in Japan can

---

18. *Op .cit.* [12], p.21
19. *Op. cit.* [12], p.22.
20. *Op. cit.* [12], p.23.
21. *Op. cit.* [12], p.26.
22. *Op. cit.* [12], p.28.
23. *Op. cit.* [12], p.29.
24. *Op. cit.* [12], pp.18, 115-17.
25. On the importance of religious specialists who did not take the full set of precepts *(upasampada)* in the development of Mahayana (which "itself should be properly called Bodhisattvayana" - as claimed by B.N. Bakshi in op. cit. [12], p.11.), cf. Hirakawa, Akira; "Stupa worship." *The Encyclopedia of Religion.* New York: Macmillan. 1987. Vol. 14 pp.92-96.

give a clue to the stand of the Taisho University monks on the issue.

The Tokyo National Museum registered the Hungarian donation on March 23rd, 1933 as "Name - Csoma image ... Csoma, Hlungarian, Tibetan Buddhist Scholar". - "The image of Kôrösi Csoma Sándor (1784-1842), a pioneer Buddhist Scholar in Europe". In 1972 the statue was located by Dr. Dénes Balázs, a prominent Hungarian geographer visiting Japan. He found it in an air-conditioned storage room of the National Museum at Ueno Park. It was carefully wrapped in a cloth and kept in a glass showcase. After the second world war, it has been exhibited to the general public only once, when a Buddhist Conference was held in Tokyo.[26]

Clearly, it was not used as a vehicle for invocations in search of Enlightenment, for removing distress or for enlightening the souls of the departed ones in the next world - the three possibilities that come to mind regarding Boddhisattvas. It seems that the image did not conform to Japanese Bosatsu iconography. According to D.N. Bakshi, the Bosatsu icons generally feature Prince Siddhartha before he became Buddha. They are, therefore, ornate with princely crowns, earrings, necklaces, a thin scarf and other stately paraphernalia. Maitreya Bodhisattva (Miroku) figures, however, may portray an ascetic "dressed in the fashion of the Buddhas" (which they will become).[27] Typically, they are then represented on a seat put on a lotus pedestal and covered with cloth, with the right foot bent horizontally and placed over or near the knee of the left foot which remain pendant. The fingers of the right hand slightly touch the cheek, while the image is in a contemplative mood.[28]

Csorba's portrayal of Csoma as a Buddha appeared probably not less incongruous to Japanese Buddhists than would to European Christians a Japanese Catholic martyr crucified by Hideyoshi, depicted on a Japanese painting as God Almighty in, say, Michelangelo's style. If so, Abbot Fukuda's presentation ceremony might have been propitiatory of Hungarian nonsense rather than canonizing.[29]

The inscription "KÔRÖSI CSOMA SANDOR - THE

---

26. Balàzs, Dénes: "Megvan Körösi Csoma Sándor japàni szobra." *Magyar Nemzet* 23 February 1981. p. 9. (Dissemination through the press of a finding communicated to the Alexandre Csoma de Kôrös Society by Dr. Balàzs on 17 June 1972. The text of this communication is deposited at the Magyar Földrajzi Múzeum, 2030 ERD, Budai útt 4.)

27. Cf. *op. cit.* [12], p.33.

28. Cf. *op. cit.* [12], p.37.

29. In fact, it is hard to see why such a ceremony was needed if the statue was given to the Museum of the Imperial House (as Vályi informed the Hungarian public) or offered to the Japan Orientalist Society (as Dr. Balàzs was told in 1972).

BODDHISATTWA OF THE WESTERN WORLD" was perhaps easier to put up with. It could be taken at its face value, letting the Hungarian donors take the responsibility for its tenets. Csoma's bodhisattvahood would then be a Western status *sui generis* .[30] I suspect that Csoma was accepted by a group of Japanese Buddhists - but not as *one of their own* bodhisattvas, a difference crucial to Vályi. Kôrösi's uncritical worshippers felt free to project into it their notions of Catholic saintliness. As Catholic sainthood is validated officially by the Pope, Christians expected something similar to be done for Csoma de Kôrös by a Buddhist hierarchy.

An approach of such a nature seems to underly a French article of 35 pages by Bernard Le Calloc'h on the "Hungarian bodhisattva".[31] In another context, this author pointed out that sometime before 1975, a stupa had been erected to the memory of Kôrösi in Vietnam presumably by a Japanese bonze.[32] In his Presses Universitaires de France contribution, he described in detail the building and inauguration in Budapest of another stupa in Tibetan style, consecrating Csoma's proclamation as bodhisattva by the Japanese buddhists 50 years after that event.[33]

The ambiguity under this head became a well of fertile inspiration. It could even secure legal status, political recognition, advantages in kind and a source of pecuniary income. In fact, five years after the jubilee inauguration, yet another stupa honouring Csoma was set up at Szilvásvárad, Hungary, by the same community. This samgha enjoyed considerable renown through its seminar, the Kôrösi Csoma Institute for Buddhology, established jointly by the Hungarian Buddhist Mission and the Budapest Centre of the Arya Maitreya Mandala (founded by Lama Anagarika Govinda). It benefited from government approval as an institution of higher education.

More recently, further stupas have been constructed in Hungary by other Buddhist groups, whose movement seems to gain momentum.

Csoma's popularity, however, spreads far beyond Buddhist

---

30. It reminds one of Father Gabet and Father Huc introducing themselves in Mongolia and Tibet as "Lamas of the West". That happened around 1844-46. (Cf. Thevenet, Jacqueline: *Le Lama d'Occident*. Paris:Seghers, 1989.).

31. "Alexandre Csoma de Kôrös le Bodhisattva Hongrois." *Revue de l'Histoire des Religions*. 1987. CCIV. 4. (Oct.-Dec.) 353-88.

32. Correspondence with Dénes Balàzs and Erno Hetényi, reported by the former in "Kôrösi Csoma sztupaja Vietnamban." *Foldrajzi Mùzeumi Tanulmanyok*. 1991. 10. 68-69.

33. *Op. cit.* [31], pp.354-58.

circles. It is not only nationwide but international. This is attested to by a treasury of articles, poems, novels, works of visual arts and the number of educational, cultural and other institutions glorifying his name.[34]

Contests among schools, youth rallies, conferences and exhibitions perpetuate his memory[35] - as does our meeting here.

We live in a complex world, where opinions and behaviours are easy to manipulate and sincerity may be corrupted by incompetence. This is no reason for getting discouraged. In pursuing my attempt to clarify somewhat the true meaning of the celebration organised jointly by a club of Hungarians and a congregation of Japanese scholars, I shall try to determine the interests of the main protagonists on three levels: individual, institutional and governmental.

These motivations had to be strong, as the commemoration under review did not mark any particular event in Csoma's life. In other words it was probably not easy to justify. On the Japanese side, Le Calloc'h perceived the 30th anniversary of Kawaguchi's return to Japan. From this observation he jumped to the following conclusion which he did not substantiate: "This is why ... on hearing that the Hungarian orientalists intended to present to his country a statue of their illustrious compatriot, he, who was full of admiration for this brave pioneer of Buddhistic studies, decided that one had to do something spectacular in his favour to strike the imagination. It was at that moment that he took the initiative to organise the ceremony during which the Hungarian scholar had to be proclaimed bodhisattva." [36] The French biographer could have also established, that the Taisho University had been founded 30 years before Vályi's visit was negotiated and that it was opened to the Amidist Jodo current (as well as to the esoteric Shingon creed) five years prior to the presentation of Csorba's statue (which represented precisely an Amitabha Buddha).

On the Hungarian side, there were probably personal and institutional ambitions at play. In 1932, Vályi set out to realise his old dream of a trip to the Far East, stopping over in India (for one month), Ceylon, China and Japan and possibly staying in historical

34. Cf. Estéli, Jòzsef, - Hetenyi, Ernö. *Körösi Csoma Sàndor dokumentàciò* Budapest; Buddhist Mission. 1984. It is being brought up to date.

35. Cf. e.g., the provisional program in Hungarian and French on the events to mark the 150th anniversary of the death of Csoma de Kôrös, produced in March, 1992 by the Committee for the Commemoration.

36. *Op. cit.* [34], p. 363.

monasteries at Buddhist centres.[37] He was a cosmopolitan journalist and writer who liked to take personal initiatives to recommend and sponsor colleagues, organise lectures, launch periodicals, open schools and promote philosophic ideas.[38] It was most probably he who masterminded the deputation to Japanese Buddhist circles, bringing with him a small statue as a gift. He placed high hopes in such a mission, pointing out: "In the history of Japan, the arrival of Buddhist

---

37. Cf. his letters to L. Fülep, respectively of April 9th 1932 from the Hotel Bristol, Budapest and of October 21st, 1932 from the "Conte Verde" liner of Lloyd Triestino at Colombo. (The Hungarian Academy of Sciences, Department of MSS: Ms. 4590/170.

38. Conclusions reached on the basis of the correspondence kept by the Hungarian Academy of Sciences. Apparently, he had no scruples in improving on facts for the sake of a good story. Thus, he introduced Csorba as a Székely like Csoma, whereas the sculptor was born in the Lipto district, northern Hungary, where his family had a documented past for generations. (Finding based on researches at the Database of the Hungarian National Gallery.) One should also put in doubt his report of Kawaguchi's words on Csoma's influence on his trip to Tibet. (See p.385 of this paper.) Kawaguchi published a detailed journal of this venture without any mention of Kôrösi. (*Three Years in Tibet*. Benares & London: Theosophical Publishing Society. 1909.)

There he tells us how reading in Chinese the Aphorisms of the *White Lotus of the Wonderful or True Law (the Saddharma Pundarika)* "determined" him at Kyoto "to undertake a visit to Tibet", and compare the Chinese texts with Tibetan translations as well as with the original Sanskrit texts contained in Mahayana Buddhism. To this purpose he decided to attempt to study the Tibetan language and Tibetan Buddhism, and try to discover Sanskrit manuscripts in Tibet, if any were there available. (Preface: pp.V-VI.) Before setting out in earnest, he spent 17 months at Darjeeling, studying Tibetan with the assistance of Rai Bahadur Sarat Chandra Das.

This highly educated Bengali "posing as a pious Buddhist scholar, although actually on the British payroll and a Hindu,... twice visited Tibet, first in 1879 and again in 1881". [Hopkirk, Peter: *Trespassers on the Roof of the World*. Oxford, etc.: Oxford University Press. 1987 reprint, p.55.] Kawaguchi was quite aware of his background. He learned vernacular Tibetan language from Lama Shabdung and his household and had regular schooling in the same language at the local Government School. (Tutor: Prof. Tumi Onden, Head Teacher of the language department of Tibetan in that School. [pp.12-13]. He entered Tibet from Nepal where he had been admitted with a pass obtained at the border at Beeganj in no time under the identity of a Chinaman living in Tibet. [p.31.] This formality was certainly facilitated by a companion of his, the Lama of the Great Tower of Mahabodha in Nepal, to whom he had been recommended "by Mr. Jibbahadur, an official of the Nepalese Government, then residing in Calcutta." [p.29] Two and a half years later, Kawaguchi had returned from Tibet through Darjeeling, where he worked three months on a grammar of the Tibetan language to append to the Tibetan-English dictionary of his old friend and host, Sarat Chandra Das. [p.676] In this endavour, they tried to improve on what Csoma had produced 67-79 years before them.

statues from abroad gave often rise to lasting spiritual movements. It was with the help of works of art that the Chinese emperors gained the friendship of Japan 1,200 years ago. The beginning of Japanese Buddhism itself can be traced back to the present of a statue which arrived from Korea 522 A.C."

In his adventurous plan, he obtained the support of a banker and former prime minister, Sándor Simonyi Samedam (1864-1946), who was the co-president of the Hungarian Nippon Society founded in 1924.[39] This public figure had good contacts in Japan, as it was he who prepared the exhibition of Japanese painting in 1932 in the National Exhibition Hall (Nemzeti Szalon), Budapest. Actually, thanks to its Japanese relations, the Hungarian Nippon Society would have been a more obvious donor to Japan than the Hungarian Oriental Society. The latter came into existence only in 1932, at the time of Vályi's first trip to the Far East.and did not compete with the Nippon Society, whose scope was much more limited.[40] The celebration staged in Tokyo in honour of Csoma de Kôrös was an ingenious means (gimmick) to publicize its birth to the general public.[41]

Broad-based, the Hungarian Oriental Society could cover all the Near, Middle and Far East, including India, which also lay outside

---

39. Cf. *A Magyar-Nippon Tàrsasàg Magyar-Japan Emlékkiàllitàsasa*. Budapest. 1936. p.17 (in English).

40. As it had been set up to cultivate the memory of "the Hungarian prisoners-of-war being redeemed from the Bolshevik captivity" by the Japanese interventionist forces, it devoted itself to "Bushido" ("the code of behaviour attributed to the warriors of feudal Japan"), and tried to popularize the poet Sàndor Petôfi (1823-1849) and the pianist-composer Ferenc Liszt (1811-1886) in Japan. Cf. the quarterly *Tàvol Kelet,* February 1936.

41. Personal communication by Mrs. Marianne Mészàros, daughter of the Orientalist Dr. Zoltàn Felvinczi Takàcs (1880-1964).

The Hungarian-Nippon Society, however, also seemed to tamper with history. In the catalogue of its 1936 exhibition, for instance, it described item 28 as follows: "The statue of Alexandre Csoma de Kôrös. Copy by Géza Csorba of his own work, which had been sent to the University of Tokyo by the Hungarian Oriental Society and is standing, at present, in a Buddha-temple". (*Op. cit.* [39], p.14.) The Taisho University was probably not identical to the Tokyo University. More to the point: Csorba's statue could hardly stand in a Buddha temple, as it belonged to the National Museum. Information on such details could not be lacking from Tokyo because contacts with the Taisho University were good. Otherwise Dr. Metzger could not have lectured in the same year at that institution on "The Hungarian spirit and Petôfi's works". (Reported in the *Young East,* 1936, winter.) Actually, there seems to be a policy based on parallel reciprocity at work - as earlier. (In 1932-33, the Hungarians organised an exhibition of Japanese painting in Budapest, while the Japanese staged a commemoration of Csoma de Kôrös in Tokyo. As simple as that.)

the purview of yet another oriental association, the Turan Society (founded around 1911 but penetrated by the "Casino-spirit" of the era and turned unscientific).

Higher political considerations could also militate in favour of the type of celebration which Vályi provoked in Tokyo. Japan had to fight against its isolation brought about by the so-called "Stimson doctrine" and the moral condemnation by the League of Nations in reaction to its invasion of Manchuria in 1931-32, the creation of the Manchukuo satellite state, its political recognition and the claim of the right to occupy it. Increasing international hostility to Japanese dumping also prompted the search for foreign sympathy. Hungary did not recognize Manchukuo until 1939. However, as a nation fighting for the revision of the Treaty which deprived it of historical possession of territories in the wake of the first world war, it could understand Japan's grievances against millions of Chinese immigrants submerging and provoking its citizens and threatening its communication lines in southern Manchuria.[42] Hungarian ambassador Pelényi reported reaching reciprocal sympathy along such lines in Geneva with Japan's ambassador Sugimura on 19 January 1933.[43]

Diplomatic ties, however, remained loose until 1939, when the two countries stationed consuls and ambassadors in each other's capital for the first time. By then the Hungarian orientalists had withdrawn from Far East - West lobbying, leaving the responsibility of managing Hungarian-Japanese relations to the government.

To sum up: Csoma was used to promote East-West understanding by an intellectual adventurer and nationalistic lobbies six years before these were superseded by professional diplomats. His credit has been drawn upon, sometimes in a similar fashion, ever since[44] without lasting damage to its rating. The specialists, who

---

42. "Stimson doctrine": Condemnation and non-recognition of conquest expressed by the U.S. in the note addressed simultaneously on January 7th, 1932 to China and Japan. It referred expressedly to American rights in China and to the Briand-Kellogg Agreement of 1928 trying to outlaw war. The League of Nations had sent the "Lytton Commission" to enquire on the spot, which suggested to declare Manchuria autonomous under Chinese sovereignty. On February 24th, 1933, the League followed suit, stressed that the Manchukuo had to be deprived of recognition but did not qualify Japan "aggressor". (Duroselle, Jean-Baptiste: *De Wilson á Roosevelt*. Paris: Armand Colin. 1960, pp. 225-231.)

43. Records kept at the National Archives, Budapest: K 63 KUM 15/7

44. Let me refer to two breaches of journalistic ethics under this head, respectively in *Lobogò* and *Ùj ember*. the first published an article by Gy(ula) N(agy) (*Tòkiòi randevù*. 18 August 1965, p. 11.), pretending that Csoma's two main tutors in Tibetan lore acted on high instruction to enable their pupil to prepare the descent

respect Kôrösi's achievements, should see to it that his memory is protected against partisan politics combined with charlatanism and the practice of make-believe.

Plate

Marczell Pl.1: Statue of Alexander Csoma de Kôrös as Bodhisattva by Géza Csorba, from Elemér Ecsery's monograph on the sculptor.

---

to earth of Maitreya Bodhisattva, the Buddha of the future, bringing to humanity peace and love. They supplied to their superiors regular reports on his advance in learning, on his character and on his spiritual progress and taught him how to generate heat from his own body so as not to be handicapped in his studies by the temperature of his ice-cold room. The role assigned to Kôrösi was to produce the Tibetan dictionary and grammar helping Westerners to understand Buddhism through original texts. Zen Buddhists consecrated the Hungarian scholar Bodhisattva to express the high esteem in which they held him. Statues of Csoma can be found not only in the temple of the Buddhist University in Tokyo but also in many other temples of Zen Buddhism (left unspecified). This message was put into the mouth of a·professor Imaoka (otherwise not identified) to whom two pretty local girls had introduced two young Hungarian tourists (who had known Csoma much less than their charming Japanese guides). Prior to the meeting with the professor, they dated in front of Csoma's Bodhisattva statue in the temple of the University! The article ended by concluding: "how interesting that, beside his world famous scientific work, the great Hungarian scholar also helps in such a way the establishment and development of present relations between the two nations."

The second example of unchecked reporting I want to quote goes back to 25 August 1968 ("Kôrösi Csoma Sàndor mint Buddhisatva." *Új Ember* XXIV, 34, p. 3.) According to the core information from the Rumanian periodical *Magazin Istoric* author: Istvàn Korda) on which it enlarged, the Japanese erected in a temple in Tokyo a gilt statue to exalt the bodhisattvahood of Csoma de Kôrös on the 125th anniversary of his death (location unspecified). "The Japanese Buddhists presented on that occasion Csoma de Kôrös as Bodhisattva to their faithful, as we present in our churches the pictures and statues of our saints as examples to the faithful". No wonder. For Csoma realised and proved the religious depths of Asian Asceticism through his own life.

A.H. FRANCKE - A "BROTHER IN SPIRIT" TO ALEXANDER CSOMA DE KôRöS

Gudrun Meier [1]

August Hermann Francke (1870-1930) served as a missionary of the Moravian Church (Herrnhuter Br. der-Mission) in the Himalayas from 1896-1909.

In succession to Heinrich August Jaeschke, Francke worked intensively on the problems of Tibetan language and the translation of Tibetan texts. In addition he had extensive historical interests. He was not searching for the original homeland of his people, as Alexander Csoma de Kôrös had done a few decades earlier, but - like Csoma - he made penetrating studies of classical Tibetan and the history of Ladakh and Tibet.

Csoma was the first European to make a systematic study of the Tibetan language *in situ*, in the monasteries of Zanskar and Kinnaur. The British government in India commissioned him to translate part of the Kanjur into English, and it was through him that knowledge of the Tibetan Buddhist scriptures first reached Europe.[2] His index of the Kanjur served as the basis of all later work on the same subject. Another copy of the Kanjur, which like Csoma's consisted of only 100 volumes, reached St Petersburg, and a few years later the Moravian scholar Isaak Jakob Schmidt made an index of this edition with the help of a Mongolian lama from the Buriat district.[3]

It took many years before the great number of Tibetan Buddhist texts became accessible to researchers in Europe. While Csoma was studying the Tibetan language in the monasteries of

---

1. Staatliches Museum für Völkerkunde, Japanesisches Palais, Karl-Marx-Platz, 8060 Dresden, Germany.

2. Csoma de Kôrös, Alexander: "Analysis of the Dulva, a Portion of the Tibetan Work entitled the Kah-Gyur." *Asiatic Researches*, Calcutta, Vol. XX, Part I (1836), pp.41-93. *Collected Works*, Vol. 4. pp.175-227. "Analysis of the Sher-chin p'hal-ch'hen dkon-séks do-dé nyáng-dás and Gyut; being the 2nd, 3rd, 4th, 5th, 6th, and 7th divisions of the Tibetan Work, entitled the Kah-Gyur: and Abstract of the Contents of the Bstan-Hgyur." *Asiatic Researches*, Calcutta, Vol. XX, Part II (1839) pp.393-585., *Collected Works* Vol. 4. pp.265-457.

3. Francke, August Hermann: "Geistesleben in Tibet." *Allgemeine Missionsstudien*, 2.(1925) Gütersloh. p.17.

Zanskar, he heard of ancient historical works which were said to be available in Leh, the capital of Ladakh. However, his attempts to find them proved fruitless. The same applied to the Englishman Alexander Cunningham who came to Ladakh some years later. In response to his enquiries, he was told that all Tibetan chronicles had been destroyed during the wars with Baltistan.[4]

Only in 1856 did the Schlagintweit brothers succeed in buying a copy of the old Ladakh chronicles from the former King of Ladakh, and they brought this to Europe the following year. However, the translation prepared by Emil von Schlagintweit was of little use.[5] His knowledge of the Tibetan language was too limited, and he found it difficult to identify names, geographical expressions and technical terms.

Dr. Karl Marx, who came to Leh as a medical missionary in 1886, knew of Schlagintweit's work, and took a copy of it with him to Ladakh. He was able to acquire further, more detailed manuscripts of the Ladakh Chronicle. He found Schlagintweit's version very unreliable when he compared it with the other texts, and begin work on an improved translation.[6] Unfortunately he died when only a third of his work had been printed. His manuscripts and the drafts of his translations of the second and third parts were sent to his brother in Germany.

Some 20 years later Francke - who, like Csoma, was working under commission for the British government - began a new translation of the Chronicle, and he eventually published the entire text.[7]

In addition to translating historical texts, Francke worked on folk literature. He collected, translated and published various versions of the Kesar epic, songs of spring and marriage songs which are narrated and sung on festive occasions in Ladakh to this day. He made his collection available to the wider academic world in monographs for *Mémoirs de la société Finno-ougrienne*[8] and the

4. Cunningham, Alexander: *Ladak. Physical, Statistical and Historical, with Notes of the Surrounding Countries*. London, 1854.
5. Francke, August Hermann: *Tibetische Geschichtsforschung und was man dabei erleben kann*. Vortrag, Missionsbuchhandlung Herrnhut, 1911.
6. Marx, Karl: "Three documents relating to the History of Ladakh." *Journal of the Asiatic Society of Bengal*. Calcutta.
7. Francke, August Hermann: *A History of Western Tibet*. London, 1907.
8. Francke, August Hermann: "Der Frühlings- und Wintermythos der Kesarsage: Beiträge zur Kenntnis der vorbuddhistischen Religion Tibets und Ladakhs." *Mémoirs de la societé Finno-ougrienne*. Vol. 15. Helsingfors, 1902.

Bibliotheca Indica series.[9] He often referred to this folk literature in his lectures on the mission in Ladakh, and pointed out comparisons with German sagas and folk songs. He summed up the results of his researches in his book, *Geistesleben in Tibet*, which appeared in 1925.[10]

Francke and his colleague Samuel Ribbach, who later worked at the Hamburg Völkerkundemuseum, also translated folk stories about "the cunning fox", and these too have parallels in Europe.[11] It possible to make direct comparisons with Goethe's "Reinecke Fuchs". Erika Taube from Leipzig discussed this theme in a paper delivered at the conference on Ladakh in Herrnhut in 1987.[12]

Certain names, dates and places kept cropping up in this folk literature, and Francke was very interested in their historical background. Through archaeological excavations and the study of rock carvings, inscriptions and ruins Francke was able to make considerable advances in our knowledge of Ladakhi history, and he was able to show that some stories had their basis in historical fact.[13]

In 1909 the Archaeological Survey of India commissioned Francke to undertake an expedition to research historical inscriptions and documents. Much earlier on, the missionaries had come across rock carvings of different age, appearance and workmanship during their travels through Ladakh. Hunting scenes were particularly common, but there were also the outlines of stupas and signs which resembled some form of writing and were perhaps the work of foreign travellers or soldiers. In 1901 Bishop Benjamin La Trobe, the director of the Moravian Church's foreign missions, visited Khalatse in the course of an official visitation, and noticed a number of rock inscriptions near the bridge over the Indus. He asked Francke

---

9. Francke, August Hermann: *The story of the 18 Heroes (preface to the Kesar-saga)*. Pub. for Bibliotheca Indica by the Asiatic Society of Bengal, Calcutta, 1905.

10. Francke, August Hermann: *Tibetische Hochzeitslieder: Übersetzt nach Handschriften von Tag-Ma-Cig, mit einer Einleitung über die Mythologie der tibetischen Sagenwelt und Bildern, meist nach den Aufnahmen des Verfassers.* Darmstadt, 1923; "Geistesleben in Tibet." *Allgemeine Missionsstudien*, 2 (1925) Gütersloh.

11. *Fuchsgeschichten, erzählt von rGya-mtsho-pa dkon-mchog-bkra-sis aus Khalatse*. Leh, 1903.

12. Taube, Erika: "A.H.Franckes Fuchsgeschichten aus Ladakh im Kontext der zentralasiatischen Folklore." *Wissenschaftsgeschichte und gegenwärtige Forschungen in Nordwest-Indien*. Dresden, 1990 (Dresdner Tagungsberichte, 2).

13. Francke, August Hermann: "Notes on Rock Carvings from Lower Ladakh." *Indian Antiquary*. vol XXX (1901) pp.329-344; vol. XXXI (1902) pp.147-157.

to record them. In the course of this work Francke noticed short inscriptions next to the drawings. He translated these and made them available to academic specialists.[14] His publications on this subject led to an invitation to help evaluate the Tibetan finds which Aurel Stein had brought back from his excavations in Turkestan.

Francke found other interesting inscriptions in, among other places, a ruin known as Balukhar. This must once have been the residence of an official whose role was to supervise the trade passing through this area from Central Asia to India. The forms of the letters and the style of orthography were related to those in the texts which Francke evaluated for Aurel Stein.

Today, Francke's archaeological finds are to be found in Herrnhut, in the Völkerkundemuseum of Leipzig and the Völkerkundemuseum in Munich. In addition there are unpublished typescripts of Francke's in the India Office archives here in London. I discussed these collections at the conference in Zurich in 1990.[15]

The 1909 expedition took Francke right up to the Tibetan border and, in one case, beyond. He recorded rock carvings and inscriptions and collected historical documents. In Tabo monastery in Spiti, which also had been visited by missionaries from time to time, he found numerous inscriptions and frescoes. Laboriously he read and copied the inscriptions in the dim light, and, where possible, had them photographed. Among many other inscriptions Francke found details of the building of the monastery and was able to establish that it had been founded in 1025 AD. The reader can readily understand the difficulties of such researches from reading Francke's lively accounts of his work in such publications as "Tibetische Geschichtsforschung und was man dabei erleben kann", which appeared in 1911.[16] He published his academic findings in the second volume of *The Antiquities of Indian Tibet,* which came out in 1926.[17]

For several years a whole team of scholars from the Academy

---

14. Francke, August Hermann: "Kleine archäologische Erträge einer Missionsreise nach Zanskar in West-Tibet." *Zeitschr. d. Deutschen Morgenländischen Gesellschaft. Leipzig* 60 (1906), pp.645 - 661.

15. Meier, Gudrun: "Sammlungen der Missionare der Herrnhuter Brüdermission aus Ladakh - Inhalte und Standorte." Beitrag zur Internat. Konferenz "Anthropology of Tibet and the Himalayas." Zürich 1990. i. p.

16. Francke, August Hermann: *Tibetische Geschichtsforschung und was man dabei erleben kann.* (Vortrag) 1911.

17. Francke, August Hermann: *The Antiquities of Indian Tibet, part II: The Chronicles of Ladakh and minor chronicles.* Archaeological Survey of India. Calcutta, 1926.

of Sciences in Heidelberg and from Pakistan has been working on the discovery, preservation and interpretation of rock carvings and inscriptions in the wider region surrounding Francke's own research area. The latest dating techniques make it possible to establish the exact age of the carvings. Today the rock carvings are like an open history book. In 1990 the Völkerkunde Museum in Dresden organised an exhibition of the rock inscriptions along the Karakorum Highway in Pakistan and we can complete it with the finds and publications of Francke. The publications of the scholars who worked on this project and the exhibition catalogue, which was compiled by Karl Jettmar, report on the progress which has been made in the study of these rock carvings and inscriptions.[18] Again and again they refer to the work of A.H. Francke in the early years of this century.

Francke much admired Csoma. In the course of his own journeys he visited places that Csoma had known, and saw his grave in Darjeeling. In 1924, by which time Francke had long since returned to Germany, he received a letter from H.Lee Shuttleworth, a British official who had visited Dzongkhul monastery in Zanskar with some members of the Moravian congregation in Kyelang (Lahul). There they had found a document which referred to Csoma. Francke initially doubted its authenticity, but wanted to know more and requested Yoseb Gergan, the Ladakhi pastor in Kyelang, to make further enquiries. In 1925 Gergan visited the monastery again, and reported to Francke that he had found a manuscript entitled *The Questions of Csoma,* and the life history of an abbot of the monastery which described his work with Csoma. Later a copy of *The Questions of Skandher Beg* came into Francke's hands, and he was able to gain an insight into Csoma's studies in Zanskar.[19]

Csoma and his researches on the Tibetan language were the beginning of Tibetan studies in Hungary. In 1925 A. H. Francke, the Moravian missionary and passionate historian, became the first Professor of Tibetan in Germany. The motives for the two scholars' journeys from Europe to Central Asia were quite different, but both men greatly expanded our knowledge and understanding of Tibetan language and history.

---

18. *Antiquities of Northern Pakistan. Reports and Studies* ed. by Karl Jettmar. Vol 1, 2: *Rock Inscriptions in the Indus Valley.* Mainz, 1989.

19. Francke, August Hermann: "Neues über Csoma de Kôrös." *Ungarische Jahrbücher.* 6 (1927), pp.330-332. "Die Fragen des Alexander." *Ungarische Jahrbücher* 8 (1928),. pp.375-377.

Biodata: August Herrmann Francke (and Anna Theodora née Weiz)

1870 Nov.5: Born at Gnadenfrei. Parents: Aug.Herm.Francke (Clothdyer), † 14.8.1898, & Charlotte Susanne née Beyer, † 1890.
-1886: Attended boys' school at Gnadenfrei.

1886 **-1891**: 5 years at teacher training college, Niesky.

1891 Easter: Final examination in Niesky.
Appointed teacher at boys' school at Kleinwelka.

1893 Spring: Passed examination at teacher training college, Bautzen, giving him the right to vote. Took up the study of Wendish.

1895 Easter-Christmas: Prepared for missionary service at Fairfield College; studied Greek and Hebrew.
Nov.: Called to a mission in British India.

1896 March 22: Ordained as Deacon in Gnadenfrei.
April: Departure from Germany.
June 8: Arrival in Leh.

1897 March 30: Married Anna Theodora Weiz at the Church Mision Society Church, Amritsar.

1899 April: Transferred from Leh to Khalatse.
July 1: Occupied official post at Khalatse (till 1904).

1904-5 Travelled home to Kleinwelka owing to illness of wife.

1905 June: Returned to Khalatse (remained till 1906).

1906-7 In Kyelang, Lahul.

1908-9 Travelled home to Kleinwelka owing to illness of wife.

1909-10 Took part in journey of exploration along the western border of Tibet (with archaeologist, Sir John Marshall, commissioned by the British Indian Government).

1910 Returned to Europe.

1911 Sept.: Called for Tibetan Bible translation work while resident at Niesky. Awarded Doctorate of Philosophy by University of Breslau.

1914 Sent to India by the Bible Society.
Sept.: Arrived in Leh. Interned by the British.

1916 Returned to Germany in exchange of prisoners. Employed as ambulance worker and translator

1916-18 Military service in France, Romania and Serbia. Taken prisoner in Serbia.

1919 July: Released from prison. Appointed travelling missionary and Bible translator.

1922 Appointed lecturer in Department of Philosophy, University of Berlin.

1925 Appointed professor in Berlin. Continued Tibetan Bible translation.

1930 Feb: died in Berlin aged 60. Buried in Moravian cemetery, Berlin.

Bibliography

Biography in *Silberbraun,* May 1930.

Personal files of the Moravian Mission.

Mitteilungen 1930, 4, p.118ff (Obituary only).

BECHLER, "Theodor, August Herman Francke: Obituary." Missionsblatt der Brüdergemeine 1930,4.

------------ Die evangelischen Missionen. 1931,5.

----------- Namhafte Missionsmänner der Brüdergemeine aus dem letzten Halbjahrhundert. Herrnhut 1932, p.43ff.

HAHN, Michael, "August Hermann Francke." *Maschinenschrift,* 1965.

JANNASCH, Hans Windekilde, "Bildnis eines Erziehers." *Die Sammlung* 1956,3.

Plate

Meier Pl.1: Portrait of August Hermann Francke.

A SOURCE USED BY ALEXANDER CSOMA DE KôRöS FOR HIS TIBETAN STUDIES
(Giorgi, *Alphabetum Tibetanum*)

ElizabethTóth [1]

On 16th July, 1822, the village of Dras in Ladakh near the Kashmiri frontier was the scene of an important event: the meeting of Alexander Csoma de Kôrös with William Moorcroft. The following spring, in April, 1823, Csoma was ready to start his scientific work in the "terra incognita" of Tibetan culture. In his letter written to Captain Kennedy he recollects his decision as follows:

"...considering what I had read and learned on the Tibetan language, I became desirous to apply myself, if assisted to it, to learn it grammatically, so as to penetrate into the contents of those numerous and highly interesting volumes which are to be found in every large monastery..."[2]

As Csoma's decision can be considered as a starting point not only of his personal scientific career but also of a new branch of science: Tibetan studies, it seems to be worth getting acquainted with those sources which enabled him to acquire some elementary information concerning this unknown world.

From the meeting with William Moorcroft in the summer of 1822 until leaving Leh for Zangla monastery on 2nd May, 1823, Csoma had two principal sources: on the one hand the help of - as Csoma puts it in his letter mentioned above - "an intelligent person, who was well acquainted with the Tibetan and Persian languages".[3] Under the assistance of this person Csoma could have the opportunity to learn the colloquial language. This skill proved to be very useful later during the cooperation with his Lama, Sangye Puntsog. A few years ago, thanks to the tireless efforts of M.Bernard Le Calloc'h, the name of this person became known: he was called Abdul Latif.

---

1. Magyar Tudományos Akadémia Könyvtára, H-1361 Budapest, V.Arany János u. 1, Hungary.

2. Letter to Captain C.P. Kennedy, Sabathu, 28th January 1825. In: Theodore Duka, *Life and Works of Alexander Csoma de Kôrös*, London 1885 [Duka], p.29.

3. Ibid. p.28.

On the other hand Csoma's basic fund of information on the nature of Tibetan culture was Giorgi's *Alphabetum Tibetanum*, which was given to him by William Moorcroft in September, 1822. Regarding this book three points will be mentioned here: the character of the author, the structure of his work and finally the main questions: what knowledge could Csoma obtain from this book? How could he make use of this volume?

Antonio Agostino Giorgi, an Augustinian friar was born in 1711 in the Papal State near Rimini. He knew perfectly 11 languages. He was a classical scholar with wide education covering the learning of the classical Greek and Roman scholars and ancient Christian theologians, as well as the scholarly activity of scientists and theologians of his own age. He became a professor of the Holy Scripture in Rome. From 1764 until his death in 1797 he occupied high dignity in the Order of the Hermit Friars of Saint Augustine. Describing his character the biographer[4] emphasizes that Giorgi was a fighter against any reforms that were not in accordance with the Augustinian ideas, especially against Protestantism.[5]

He wrote his most significant work, *Alphabetum Tibetanum*, at the age of 51, in 1762. This voluminous book begins with a long Introduction, then comes the table of contents, or rather the summary of the paragraphs and chapters. The main body of the work, which counts 820 pages falls into two parts; the first part is divided into paragraphs and lacks any structure or sequence of topics and is much longer than the second one, which reveals the characteristics of the Tibetan language and writing. In the three appendices there are specimens of the Tibetan language: translations of essential Christian prayers, and after that a Tibetan text with interpretation in Latin, notes and explanation. The book ends in an index of proper names and subjects.

Now let us turn our attention to the main questions: what could Csoma find in this book, which was edited 60 years earlier? How could it arouse his interest? Csoma studied theology in Göttingen: he and Giorgi both had a similar basis of education, so most of the topics discussed in the book were familiar to Csoma also. He too, was fond of learning languages, and liked history and

---

4. *Dictionnaire d'Histoire et de Géographie Ecclésiastiques sous la direction de R. Aubert.* Paris. 1984.; T. 20, p.1450.

5. Giorgi's work was re-published in 1987 in Cologne with an excellent introduction by Professor Rudolf Kaschewsky providing more detailed information concerning the author and his activity. *Giorgi, Antonio Agostino, Alphabetum Tibetanum. Editiones Una Voce,* Köln, 1987.

geography. He himself speaks of this as follows: "Among other liberal disciplines, my favourite studies were philology, geography, and history. Although my ecclesiastical studies had prepared me for an honourable employment in my native country, yet my inclinations for the studies mentioned above, induced me to seek for a wider field for their further cultivation".[6]

What aroused his interest was that the names of the Uigurs, Buharia, and Turkestan, where Csoma hoped to find the early homeland and the brethren of the Hungarians, are frequently mentioned in the *Alphabetum Tibetanum* in connection with the neighbouring Tibetans. In this way the task proposed by William Moorcroft coincided with his own plans. Csoma thought that there might be some information on the ancestors of the Hungarians in the Tibetan historical sources. And besides all this it was an incomparable challenge: an opportunity to test his talent in a perfectly unknown field, which he could be the very first scholar to enter. It was evident for Csoma that Giorgi's book would not be sufficient for his scientific purposes. That was quite clear from its full title which is as follows:

Alphabetum Tibetanum missionum apostolicarum commodo editum: praemissa est disquisitio qua de vario litterarum ac regionis nomine, gentis origine moribus, superstitione, ac Manichaeismo fuse disseritur; Beausobrii calumniae in sanctum Augustinum aliosque ecclesiae patres refutantur studio et labore Augustini Antonii Georgii.

The title emphasises three points about the work:

1st: that it was edited for the use of the apostolic missions;

2nd: that it provides a study on several aspects of Tibet;

3rd: that the author wishes to fight against Protestantism.

Thus Giorgi's main purpose was to help the missionaries to convert the Tibetan people to (Catholic) Christianity, which he regarded as the only true faith. Csoma's purpose was of different character, he intended to get acquainted with that unknown world, to investigate its specific features as unbiassed as possible, without being influenced by prejudice. His way of thinking can be illustrated with his own words:

"I am not merely a linguist -- I have learnt several languages to learn polite literature, to enter into the cabinet of curiosity of remote ages, to acquire useful knowledge, and to live in every age and with every celebrated nation..."[7]

---

6. Letter to Captain C.P. Kennedy, Sabathu, 28th January 1825. In: Duka p.25.
7. Letter to Captain C.P. Kennedy, Subathu, 5th May 1825. In: Duka p.52.

Csoma's task was difficult, he had to try to pick out the pieces of correct information from among the material Giorgi compiled on the basis of the letters and reports of former missionaries. The most significant sources of information for Giorgi were the Capuchin friars who maintained a mission in Lhasa between 1708-45, among them Francesco Orazio della Penna and Cassiano da Macerata; and two Jesuit missionaries, Ippolito Desideri and Emmanuel Freyre, whose activity was also focused on Lhasa between 1715-21.

As an elementary source-book, the *Alphabetum Tibetanum* was a rich fund of information for Csoma on various aspects of the Tibetan culture. He got acquainted with its geography, history, language, religion, church, literature, etc. To look at these basic topics one after the other:

1. Giorgi gives a detailed description on the regions of Tibet, which was certainly very useful and very important for Csoma - he himself wrote an article under the title: "Geographical Notice of Tibet", and published it in 1832.[8]

2. Orazio della Penna's account on history provided Giorgi with the material for his chronological tables, which give a short summary of the history of Tibet, the list of the most famous kings and other outstanding persons, the important events. He gives the dates too, calculated according to the Christian calendar with a consistent error of 20 years. Csoma also prepared a similar study, with the difference that he used a Tibetan source, Sangye Gyatso's famous work on astrology *The White Lapis-lazuli.*[9] Csoma's chronological table was published as an appendix to his Tibetan grammar in 1834.[10]

3. He got to know the primary characteristics of the Tibetan language, too, as well as the peculiar system of Tibetan writing. Giorgi's description only covers the pronunciation and writing of syllables, he does not deal with morphology and syntax. Nevertheless this part of the book can be considered as the most systematic and Csoma was able to make use of it for his Tibetan grammar.

4. It is quite natural that the most obscure field in Giorgi's book is religion. Yet Csoma was able to find a lot of useful information concerning Buddha's life, the Three Jewels, the

---

8. Published in J.A.S.B. Vol. I. (1832) pp.121-127. New edition: *Collected Works of Alexander Csoma de Kôrös,* ed. by J. Terjék. Budapest, 1984. Vol. 4. Tibetan Studies pp.1-7.

9 Sde-srid Sangs-rgyas Rgya-mtsho, *Baid.uurya dkar-po.*

10. Alexander Csoma de Kôrös, *A Grammar of the Tibetan Language*, Calcutta, 1834., *Collected Works of Alexander Csoma de Kôrös,* ed.by J. Terjék, Budapest, 1984. Vol. 2, pp. 181-198.

transmigration system, and Buddhist cosmology.

5. Giorgi's work gives long, valuable descriptions about the main Tibetan monasteries like Sera, Drepung, Gandan, and other sacred places, about the Dalai Lamas, about Lhasa, about the hierarchy of Tibetan Buddhist monks.

It is no surprise that it is on the subject of religion that Giorgi is the most erratic. Sometimes he provides a perfect, precise definition of a Buddhist term even in Tibetan, at other times he uses totally distorted, unintelligible phrases.

6. Regarding the domain of literature it was from the *Alphabetum Tibetanum* that Csoma first read about the collection of Kagyur, as well as many other works on various branches of learning: e.g. medicine, astrology, history. Later he also read through the other collection, the Tengyur, and wrote detailed analyses of both.[11]

To sum up: Csoma had to treat Giorgi's book critically, yet it helped him to acquire a general picture, to make the first steps in an unknown world.

William Moorcroft and Csoma both valued highly Giorgi's work. Moorcroft kept it with him until he gave it to Csoma, and Csoma in turn took it with him everywhere as if it were a relic, from1822 until his death, even if he far surpassed the knowledge it represented after a few months spent with his Lama, Sangye Puntsog.

---

11. "Analysis of the Dulva, a Portion of the Tibetan Work entitled the Kah-Gyur." *Asiatic Researches*, Calcutta, Vol. XX, Part I (1836), pp.41-93. *Collected Works*, Vol. 4. pp.175-227. "Analysis of the Sher-chin p'hal-ch'hen dkon-séks do-dé nyáng-dás and Gyut; being the 2nd, 3rd, 4th, 5th, 6th, and 7th divisions of the Tibetan Work, entitled the Kah-Gyur; and Abstract of the Contents of the Bstan-Hgyur." *Asiatic Researches*, Calcutta, Vol. XX, Part II (1839) pp.393-585., *Collected Works* Vol. 4. pp.265-457.

THE POLITICS OF LADAKHI SONG:

Three versions of a praise song attributed to Morup Stanzin, c.1825

A. Mark Trewin *

The composition of songs of social or political comment in Ladakh is not entirely a modern phenomenon, for even during dynastic times certain types of song had important political functions - as in Tibet. The Tunhuang Documents, for example, mention two types of song which seem to have played a role in the political functioning of the early Tibetan kingdom: praise songs *(mgur)*, sung in celebration of another's deeds, renewed oaths of loyalty, while songs of provocation *(mchid)*, sung during public song contests, tested the fitness and skill of those aspiring to gain political influence (Ellingson 1979: 67-70). In Ladakh, both these categories of song exist, but praise songs *(gzhung glu)* extolling the virtues of kings and religious leaders are particularly widespread, for although many of them were composed by known - or at least named - individuals, they have survived to the present day because they have become absorbed into the unwritten living tradition of the Ladakhi people.

In oral traditions, song clearly has an important role in maintaining cultural continuity because it serves as a vehicle for transmitting verbal expressions of values considered essential for the survival of a community. However, broadly speaking, we find that the tunes of songs undergo greater change than their texts. Individual singers may, accidentally or deliberately, alter the tune of an existing song, or may invent or borrow another one; but whether such changes survive depends upon whether it is ultimately accepted or rejected by the wider community. Since this is neither a conscious nor concerted action, it is not unusual to find the same song sung to more than one melody, or to variants of a single melody, at any given point in time.

Although individuals inevitably vary their songs, musical variation does not exceed the boundaries set by the community. In Ladakh, these limits are relatively narrow: in general, only small

* School of Scottish Studies, University of Edinburgh, 27 George Square, Edinburgh EH8 9LD, UK.

variations are acceptable and substantial changes tend to be rejected. A singer is only regarded as "good" if the text is complete and the tune is correct; he or she is therefore expected to have a good memory as well as a good voice. Accidental errors due to loss of memory or voice control are descibed as *khyor ces* ("staggering" or "stumbling", especially when due to drunkeness), whereas deliberate deviations from the "correct" version are more often than not dismissed as *bcos ma* ("artless" or "mocking"). Musical correctness is therefore not only a matter of aesthetic taste, but also - as in dance - an expression of moral propriety and socio-political conformity.

Although Ladakhi scholars claim that every song has a unique tune (Shakspo 1985), this only reflects the ideal situation; in practice, one comes across different tunes for a given song. Such is the case with the Ladakhi song *bkra shis phun sum tshogs pa,* a *gzhung glu* said to have been composed by the Leh *bka' blon* (minister), Morup Stanzin *(dngos grub bstan 'dzin),* in praise of the last independent king, Tshepal Tondup Namgyal *(tshes dpal don grub rnam rgyal)* (ruled 1802-40), before the Dogra invasion (1834-5). In the last few years of visiting Ladakh, I have collected three different musical versions of the song, each of which appears, from the style used, to date from different points in the recent past (example 1). The nature of oral transmission being what it is, this is not a remarkable observation; however, given the particular type of song it is and the historical setting in which it was allegedly composed, it is worth considering whether any political meanings are assigned to musical changes which have evidently occurred since the end of the Ladakhi monarchy in 1842.

From the point of view of performance practice, the adaptation of a single text to different musical schemes is facilitated by the use of non-lexical filler syllables *(tshig lhad)* and, in some instances - so long as the meaning of the text is not unduly obfuscated - by dropping some lexical syllables. In principle, such practices allow poetic stresses to coincide meaningfully with musical accents, without having to resort to unwieldy articulations in the melodic pattern; indeed, as a Ladakhi saying shows, the judicial use of these extemporary habits is considered idiomatic in performance: *la la li li med na glu med; ta ra ru ru med na dbyangs med:* "Without 'la la li li' there is no song; Without 'ta ra ru ru' there is no tune."

Thus, some degree of individual musical variation is allowable, but the particular use of these techniques to adapt texts to different tunes, as demonstrated here, is normally frowned upon. Disputes concerning the validity of a tune may in fact form the basis of song contests *(glu ston)* between singers at festive gatherings.

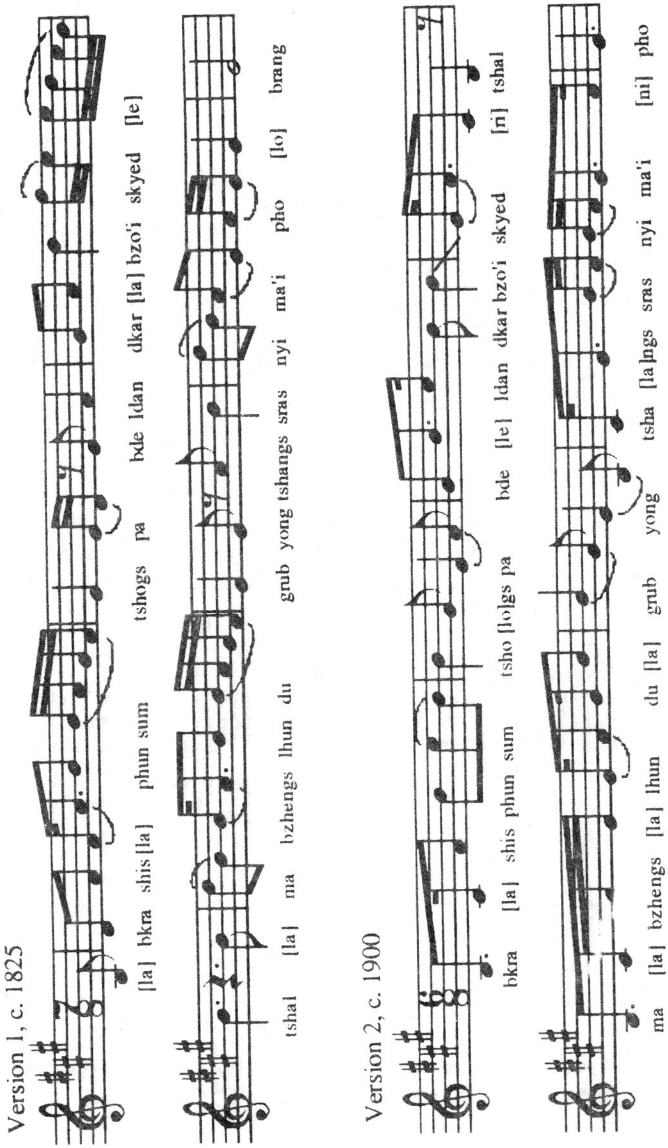

M.Trewin: Examples 1a (upper), 1b (lower).

The composition of completely new songs - texts together with tunes - as distinct from the interchanging of pre-existing words and melodies has, nevertheless, always been an important aspect of the Ladakhi living tradition. In the past, as today, song composition was closely associated with state patronage: in particular, praise songs were sung in honour of the king at royal feasts, and played a part in the legitimation of his authority. Very often these songs were simply traditional ones with the name of the current ruler inserted, thus constituting a transferable type of charisma which, in Weberian terms, was of the "routinized" sort. In other cases, as in this instance, songs were newly composed in honour of the king at the time, and their identity is preserved. It is not unusual, in fact, to sing songs in praise of past kings, and the memory - as preserved in this song - of the one who turned out to be the last independent king of Ladakh seems to have lingered longer than it might otherwise have done. Francke, who collected the original version of the song at the turn of the century (example 2; cf. example 1a), noted that "all the virtue of his predecessors were believed to have been united in him" (Francke 1907: 134) and remarked: "If at the present time the power of the ex-king is praised in a song it sounds like irony, but as the Ladakhis are still very loyal to their old royal family. they would never think of composing ironical songs regarding it." (Francke 1902:83).

Why then, given the understanding that the singing of traditional songs to new tunes is indeed often regarded as "mocking", do we find different versions of this particular song? Firstly, it seems that the song, after the Dogra conquest, assumed a special poignancy as an expression of national sentiment. After all, it not only refers to the first and (now) last Ladakhi kings, but also glorifies the divine foundation of the royal garden which had now become the grounds of the British Joint Commissioner's residence. Secondly, tastes and values were at the same time changing, and the Ladakhi people were susceptible to new musical styles with which historical circumstances had brought them into contact.

Unlike many parts of the colonial world, Western music was, at least until recently, mainly rejected in Ladakh. For example, Francke's harmonized version of the tune (example 3) which he apparently used as a setting for hymns in the Moravian Church in Leh - a striking example of how he used the fruits of his studies in his missionary work (Trewin 1992) - is unlikely to have ever had any lasting impact on the development of Ladakhi music; if any Ladakhis ever did in fact hear it on the church harmonium, they would no doubt have described it as *bcos ma,* or mocking. Instead, the main modernizing influence was Balti music, Baltistan having been brought under joint state

M.Trewin: Examples 1c (upper), 2 (lower).

administration with Ladakh. The second version of the praise song (example 1b), a musical variant of tne first, appears to have been influenced by the Balti-type *ghazal* (Ladakhi *ga zal*), an Urdu romantic song form sung to Persio-Arabic melodies. The tune, like those of *ghazal*, has a more flowing, even contour than traditional Ladakhi melodies and is sung in a quicker, simpler metre characteristic of the *ghazal*. In some cases, Balti *ghazals*, or Ladakhi imitations of them, were adapted to the quick rhythmic pattern of the Ladakhi male dance *(pho rtses)*, enabling them to be performed as a medleys of tunes - still highly popular today - in conjunction with social dance. Thus this version of the song, combining the traditional Ladakhi elements of the first version with new Balti ones, gives the Ladakhi text a nostalgic feeling by setting it in a more sentimental, modern-sounding idiom that has now become widely accepted.

The final version (example 1c) - recorded from a young man in Stok village - is anomalous, and is a clear example of *bcos-ma*. The text is retained intact (except for one missing verse), but the tune has been "borrowed" from a Hindi film song. When I returned to the Cultural Academy in Leh to have my recordings checked, this song was received with outbursts of laughter, for the limits of acceptable musical change had been breached. Although probably a joke directed at me, the very possibility of its occurence underlines a deeper irony. Indian film music (Hindi *filmi gıt*, Ladakhi *phi lim glu)*, consisting mainly of a stereotyped popular form of the Urdu *ghazal* has, since the 1960s, been used by Ladakhi composers as a model for a new generation of songs *(glu so ma, di ring gi glu)* whose verbal message is unambiguously moralistic and instructional. Most of these composers, although patronized by Indian state radio rather than the Ladakhi monarchy, see themselves as occupying traditional Ladakhi roles, and yet little of the musical idiom is Ladakhi; their music is not, therefore, widely accepted by all social groups.

In conclusion, I would say that the survival of Morup Stanzin's song shows a wish to preserve the cultural values it expresses. Yet the changes in the music through which the song is interpreted demonstrates more fundamental changes in emotional meanings attached to those values. Moreover, the co-existence of different musical versions of the song - contrary to traditional Ladakhi practice - indicates that these emotional meanings are in a state of conflict. Music in Ladakh therefore remains firmly in the political arena, for it is partly through music that the Ladakhis have sought to find ways of retainlng their traditional values whilst at the same time gaining a sense of belonging in the modern world.

M.Trewin: Example 3.

Bibliography

ELLINGSON, Ter 1979. *The Mandala of Sound: Concepts and Sound Structures in Tibetan ritual music.* PhD tesis, University of Wisconsin-Madison.

FRANCKE August Hermann 1902. "Ladakhi Songs." *Indian Antiquary* 31, 87-106; 304-311.

----------- 1905. "Musikalische Studien in West-tibet." *Zeitschrift der deutschen morgenländischen Gesellschaft* 59, 91-102.

----------- 1907. *History of Western Tibet.* London.

----------- 1922. "La musique au Thibet." *Encyclopédie de la musique et dictionnaire du conservatoire*, ed. by Lavignac, Paris, 3084-8093.

RABGIAS Tashi 1985. *La dwags kyi yul glu [Folk songs of Ladakh].* 2nd ed, Srinagar, Jammu & Kashmir Academy of Art, Culture & Languages.

SHAKSPO, Nawang Tsering 1985. "Ladakhi Folk Songs." *Soundings in Tibetan Civilization,* ed. by B.Aziz & M.Kapstein, New Delhi, 97-106.

TREWIN, A.Mark 1992. "Musical Studies in Western Tibet (Ladakh): some historical and comparative aspects of the pioneering work of August Hermann Francke." *European Studies in Ethnomusicology: Historical Developments and Recent Trends. [Intercultural Music Studies Vol. 4],* ed. by M.P.Baumann, A.Simon & U.Wegner, Wilhelmshaven.

ARABIC INSCRIPTIONS OF THE LATE FIRST MILLENNIUM A.D. FROM TANGTSE IN LADAKH

Rohit Vohra [1]

Introduction

The boulders engraved with inscriptions, petroglyphs, Tamgas and other symbols are located at Trangtse at the junction of the roads leading south to Chushul and east to Pangong Tso. The site has been known since the beginning of this century when the long Sogdian inscription mentioning Caitra the Samarkandian and the monk Nos-farn's visit to the Tibetan Qaghan in 841-2 (latest translation by Sims-Williams 1992: 3) was reported by the Moravian missionaries. Since then other travellers have mentioned the existence of inscriptions and rock-carvings about which I had written in detail in another paper delivered at Zürich University (Vohra 1990: 1-4). In 1932 Evelyn Hutchinson discovered a Thokarian inscription on the west face of the same boulder as the Sogdian inscription when visiting the area during the Yale North India Expedition. Almost a decade ago I documented from the same site several Arabic, Sogdian, Tibetan and Sharada inscriptions (Field trip summer-autumn 1983). There are a total of five boulders engraved with inscriptions, Swastikas, Christian crosses (Maltese crosses) and other petroglyphs. Their authors were travellers, traders, monks and missionaries and here under the shelter of these huge boulders they rested before continuing their journeys covering great distances.

The eight Arabic inscriptions which are the subject of the present paper are principally characterised by their documenting the names of the authors. In certain cases they also indicate the authors' religious inclination or reveal the nature and purpose of their journey.

Central Asiatic context of the inscriptions

These inscriptions can be understood in the context of the disintegration of the Turkish empire in Central Asia and the vacuum being contested for during the 7th and 8th centuries.

---

1. 75 Grande Rue, L-9051 Ettelbruck, Grand Duchy of Luxembourg.

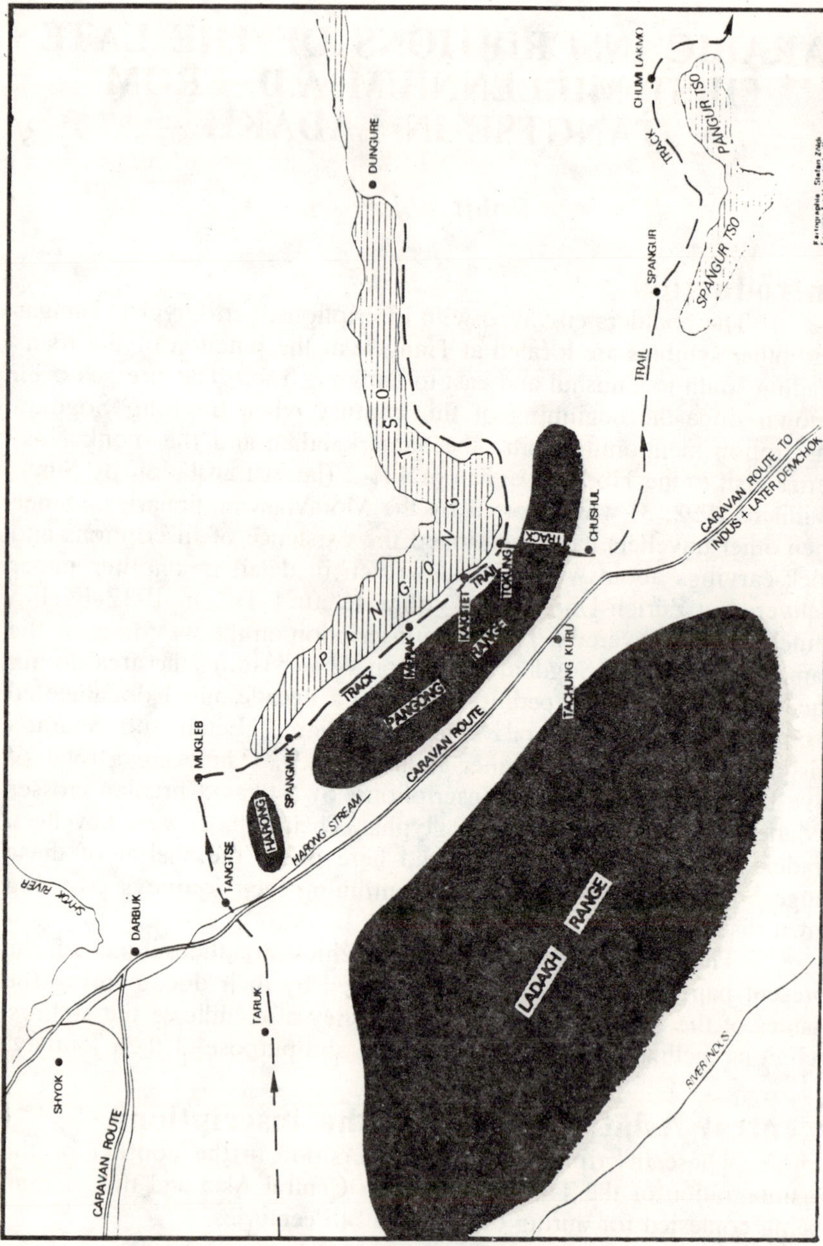

R.Vohra Map 1: showing location of Tangtse.

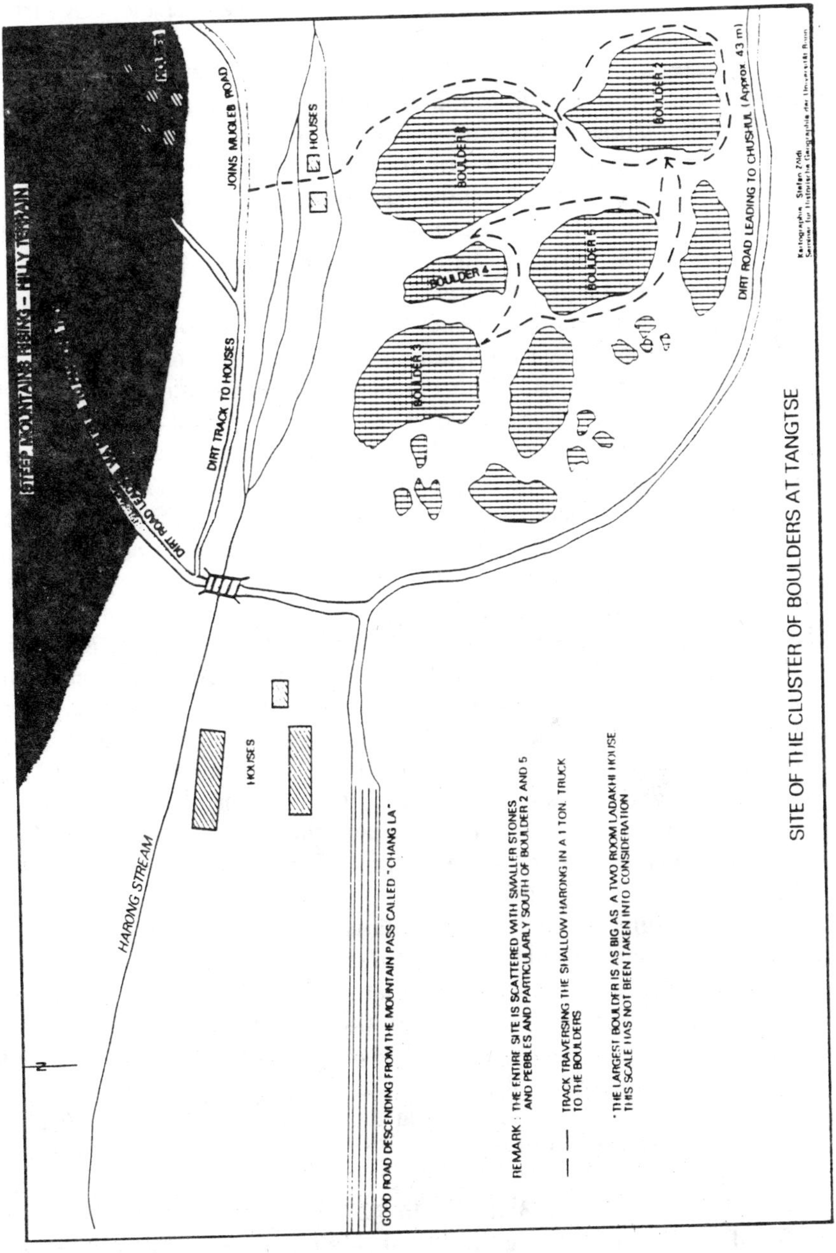

R.Vohra Map 2: The boulders at Tangtse.

The Chinese effected their military victory over the Ten Tribes of the Turks between 657-659 AD, and maintained their suzerainty over the region until 665. However hostility with the Tibetans engaged their full attention and hence they rarely intervened in the affairs of the lands between the Indus and the Jaxartes.

Tibet, after having conquered Kukunor in 663, occupied Kashgar between 670-692, cutting off the routes across the Pamirs for the Chinese. Chinese sources inform us about the alliance between the Tibetans and the Turks in their expeditions in the Tarim Basin and Dru-gu-yul, i.e., Ferghana (Uray 1979: 281).

These events had beneficial effects for the Arabs. The Chinese had established their administration in the area but were not in effective control and as the Persians had held control of the Turk heritage, at least up to the Jaxartes, so now the Arabs took over this position. It however took the Arabs one century to consolidate the regions of Transoxania and Tokharistan.

The first direct relations of the Tibetans with the Arabs are to be witnessed, according to the Chinese and Tibetan sources, at the end of the 7th century. This is when a Western Turk Prince A-shih-na T'ui-tzu (identified with Ton Ya-bgo Qaghan of the Tibetan Annals; Petech 1988a: 289-290; Uray 1979: 281) first paid homage to the Tibetan king in 699 and in 700 (DTH: 39) led a Tibetan army to Ferghana. Tibetan soldiers from this army possibly helped the Arabs by attacking the rebel Musa in Tirmidh (Beckwith 1979: 33). Following this event we find increased cooperation between the Tibetans and the Arabs in undermining Chinese influence in the area. In 715, according to Chinese historians, the Arabs and the Tibetans nominated a certain A-leao-ta as king of Ferghana (Chavannes 1903: 148 n. 3).

The support that the Tibetans gave to the Arabs on the Jaxartes was reciprocated by the Arabs in their help at Kashgar. Thus we find in 717 the Chinese protector at Kucha announcing in a report to the Emperor that the Arabs and the Tibetans had captured the towns of Yara-aryk and Aksu and had attacked the Four Garrisons (Chavannes 1903: 284 n. 2). In the same year the emperor conferred the title of King to the ruler of Great P'o-lu (Great Bolor of the Arabic sources = Baltistan; Vohra 1988: 538-543), in order to gain his support and thus prevent the Tibetans from passing through his territory (Chavannes 1903: 165). In 720 the Emperor sent emissaries to confer brevets on the kings of Uddyana, Khottal and Yasin compensating them for having resisted the Arabs (Chavannes 1903: 165). All these were allies of the Chinese not only against the Arabs but also the Tibetans.

The Chinese, in order to preserve relations with Kashmir, Uddiyana, Kapisa and Zaboulistan, had to maintain the route open which traversed Wakhan and the valley of Gilgit. This route was menaced by the Tibetans for whom this was the most natural passage to Kashgar. For this reason they maintained an active policy of relations with the petty rulers of the region and off and on even demonstrated their military might. However in Little P'o-lu (Gilgit) after the death of Ma-hao-lai his successor in 740 was given a Tibetan wife, Khri-ma-lod, and in this way the Tibetans brought him under their dominance (Chavannes 1903: 151; DTH: 51). As a result of this diplomatic success more than twenty kingdoms situated on the north-west of Little P'o-lu declared their suzerainty to the Tibetans and no more paid tribute to the Chinese Emperor.

It was important for the Chinese to regain this lost influence and in 747 General Kao Sien-tche (by origin a Korean in the service of the Chinese) crossed the Pamirs over the Baroghil and Darkot Passes right up to Gilgit (Chavannes 1903: 152, n. 1). This however did not avert the Tibetan threat as we find the Ya-bgo of Tokharestan appealing to the Imperial Court for assistance against the petty mountain chief of Kie-che (= Chitral = Chieh-shi; Jettmar 1977: 415-6; Enoki in Tucci 1977: 86-91; Vohra 1988: 539-542) who had made alliance with the Tibetans and intercepted the communications between Kashmir and Gilgit. In 750 General Kao Sien-tche responded to this appeal and captured the king of Kie-tche, Poi-t'o-mo, and placed on the throne his more complacent brother Sou-kia (Chavannes 1903: 158; 214-216).

General Kao Sien-tche, who had brilliantly directed the successes of the Chinese army, was in fact a disloyal and covetous person and his defects brought him his ruin. In 750 he intervened in the affairs of Tashkend. The ruler paid his submission but was taken prisoner and then beheaded and the General plundered the riches of the country. The son of the king escaped and made propaganda out of the shameless behaviour of the Chinese and asked for the help of the Arabs. The emissary of the Abbasids in Khorasan, Abu Muslim, did not miss this opportunity to increase the influence of the Caliph at the expense of the Chinese Emperor and immediately dispatched an army under Ziyad ibn Salih. Kao Sien-tche reunited his troops and along with the king of Ferghana marched against the enemy. However the Qarlugs revolted against him and he being attacked from the front and then from the rear was defeated in the grand battle which took place at Athlach, close to the River Tharaz (Talas) in July 751 by Ziyad b. Salih (Chavannes 1903: 142, n. 2; Barthold 1968: 195-6). This battle put an end to the Chinese suzerainty in the region.

This in turn left Tibetan hegemony over the entire expanse of the Tarim and West Turkestan uncontested and even resulted in the capture of Ch'ang-an.

In Transoxiana the Turks continued to interfere in the disorders. The defeat of the Chinese was followed by the formation of two kingdoms, Semiryechye, eastern Syr-Darya provinces and Suyab (former Turgesh capital), and the lower reaches of Syr-Darya the Oghuz. While in Eastern Turkestan there were the Toquz-Oghuz who assisted the native rulers and the Arab rebels. The Arab rulers constructed defensive walls (for Rasht, Bukhara and Shash) to protect themselves against the Turk raids. According to al-Ya'qubi, shortly after 777 Caliph Mahdi sent ambassadors to Sogdiana, Farghana, Quarluqs, Toguz-Oghuz, China and Tibet to demand tokens of submission. However we know that during his residence at Khurasan, Ma'mūn (809-818), in order to acquire external peace, was forced to recognise the existing territories of the rulers of the Qarluqs, Kabul and Tibet, who had not shown subordination, and guarantee them assistance.

Arabic inscriptions[2]

Boulder 1.

Boulder 1 has been taken as the orientation point and is located at the easternmost end of the cluster of boulders at the site. This is the boulder from which the long Sogdian inscription was reported as well as the Tokharian inscription on its west face.

Inscription No. 1. Photograph No. 3 - on top of boulder 1 approximately behind the Sogdian inscription No. 3 but visible only from the top of the boulder,

The first word is unclear but could be eventually read as 'We remembered'.

We remembered ... Ziyād, client of Ḥāmid al-Baṣrī
(or: al-Naṣrī)

2. All numbering of the inscriptions other than the Arabic corresponds to the numbering in the manuscript of the book being prepared in collaboration with Prof. Klimkeit. The numbering of the Arabic inscriptions, here 1-8, corresponds to 10-18 of the manuscript.
I would like to thank Prof. Klimkeit of the University of Bonn, Prof. Sundermann of the University of Berlin and Prof. Diem of the University of Cologne for assisting in the translation of the inscriptions. All translations are by Prof. Diem except where specifically indicated.

Boulder 2. Located southeast of Boulder 1.

Inscription No. 2. Photograph No. 4 - West face of the boulder The brittle brown patina of the west face is peeling away and will lead increasingly to the disappearance of the inscriptions.

Inscription No. 3. Photograph No. 5 - Located on the uppermost edge of the west face of the boulder and can be distantly seen on Photograph No. 13.

Naṣr ibn Ṣālih
Abu Manṣūr
I recollected (or 'dakarna' = we recollected)
Muslim[3]

Inscription No. 4,. Photograph 6 - Sloping north face of the boulder. The inscription is located on the bottom right hand corner of the photograph. Prof. Diem is unable to interpret the text.

Inscription No. 5. Photograph 7 - On top of the boulder

Top line:

bi-smi llāhi ("in the name of God")

Text below:

Ḥāmid/ḥāmid (?)
Allāh

Inscription No. 6. Photograph 8 - On top of the boulder. Inscription on the bottom of the photograph with a swastika turning anti-clockwise. However the fourth arm of the swastika is turned in the opposite direction.

Abū Layṭ

Inscription No. 7. Photograph 9 - On top of the boulder. Upper word:

Šabr/Šibr

Lower word:

that

Boulder 5. Located approximately 40 metres southwest of the west face of boulder 1.

Inscription No. 8. Photograph 10 - Located on the slope of

---

3. Reading by Prof. Sundermann:
nṣr bn(?) ṣ'lh
'bw mnṣwr y
ykwb
mslm

Translation:
Naṣr ibn Ṣālih
Abū Manṣūr
Ya'qub (??)
Muslim

the boulder. Om symbol can be seen carved which due to the level of patination proves to be of a more recent origin.

Zakarīya
ibn Qāsim

or better

we remembered ibn Qasim
(ḍakarnā bna Qāsim)

Preliminary remarks on the Arabic inscriptions

In inscription 1 the first word is uncertain but could eventually be "we remembered" and then follows "Ziyād, client of Ḥāmid". The next line has the name "al-Baṣrī (or -Naṣrī)". Here we find the use of the first name which shows a personal relationship and the word "client" indicates some sort of commercial connection between the two. In inscription 5 we have above "Bismillāhi" and below the same name "Ḥāmid" and then "Allāh". Inscription 2 is a long one but is engraved very shallow and cannot be read. The patina of the rock is also peeling off so that much of the inscription does not exist any more. However Prof. Diem, upon identification of a particular word in the first line, is of the opinion that it is Arabic.

Inscription 3 is one of the most informative inscriptions:

Nasr ibn Ṣālih
Abū Manṣūr
I recollected (or 'dakarna' = we recollected)
Muslim

Prof. Diem remarks that the paleography shows an angular script form which is archaic but could be a result of the hard rock surface. On the orthography he says that the "ā" in Ṣāliḥ in the first line points to the fact that it could not be earlier than the third quarter of the 9th century and possibly later. From this period the name Mansur among the Arabs in Central Asia is well documented. One Ziyād ibn Ṣāliḥ was a powerful commander under Abu Muslim and suppressed a revolt in Bukhara. In fact it was this Ziyād ibn Ṣālih who defeated Kao Sien-tche leading the Chinese army in 751 AD at the battle of Talas. Another Nasr b. Ṣāliḥ is known as the leader of a rebellious party with the Kharijites in Sijistan. In fact in Samarkand a street in the Ghatfar quarter was known under the name Salih. (Barthold 1968: 90, 194-195, 216).

Inscription 6 mentions Abbu Layt and just below it is an anti-clockwise turning Swastika one arm of which is engraved in the wrong direction. The engraving of the inscription and the Swastika are to be attributed to the same author. This observation is based upon my own examining of pecking or incisions on the rock and the level of repatination. Layt (Layth) as a family name is similarly known from leading families in Arab Central Asia and also from a street named as 'Bu-Layth. The Layths are known as the founders of the Saffarid dynasty who put an end to the Tahirids and attained supremacy in Persia and later extended their rule over Transoxania (Barthold 1968: 90, 111, 215-216). Closer to our inscription would come the reference to Rafi 'b. Layth who conducted a rebellion in 806 and succeeded in killing the governor of Samarkand (Barthold 1968: 200) and who later in 809 was assisted by Tibetan troops in his rebellion against the 'Abbasid government (Beckwith 1979: 35).

In inscription 7 we possibly have a name Sabr/Sibr. In inscription 8 we again have a memento of ibn Qasim. Zakariya ibn Qasim as a name is similarly known from Arab Central Asia.

Prof. Petech in his paper "Il Tibet nella Geografia Musulmana" (Petech 1988: 18) examined the Arab geographical traditions categorised under three sections: al-Ma'mun, Gaihani and the various tales of muslim travellers in India and in the Chinese towns of Kansu and the region of Lop-nor. He comes to the following conclusion on the Arab knowledge of Tibet:

- During the 9th and 10th centuries Arabs regarded Turkestan, with which they had direct contacts, as the centre of the Tibetan state.
- Khotan at that time was the most important town in Tibetan Turkestan (post 790 AD) and was recognised as the capital of Tibet. The real Tibet was ignored as an unimportant part of the land.
- It was only by the year 1000 AD, as Islam spread to Turkestan and Khotan that the real Tibet was recognised.

However according to al-Ya'qubi, the Tibetans had sent an embassy to the Arab governor of Khurasan requesting for a teacher of Islam (Beckwith 1979: 33).

The military might of the Tibetans must have led to increased exchange of religious and trading relations. However the export of Tibetan musk is well known from reports of Arab writers. There were other items like sheep's wool and dyed cloth which were traded through Jewish and possibly Sogdian merchants (Utas 1968: 130-131; Róna-Tas 1984: 324-330).

Concluding comment

Tibetan military engagement and rule in the Tarim basin possibly continued until the end of the Uighur invasion (860-873) when the region lost all political unity. Therefore despite the fact that after 842 the Tibetan state structure collapsed and the centre of power was contested by old aristocratic cliques there must have been a semblance of order within the expansive military bureaucratic organisation. Under these circumstances we can envisage contacts with the Arabs at least until the third quarter of the 9th century. We know that Tibetan cultural influence survived well into the 10th-11th centuries in at least the region of Khotan (Emmerick 1967; Vohra 1988).

Bibliography

BACOT, J., Ch. Toussaint & F.W.Thomas, 1940-46, *Documents de Touen-Houang relatifs à l'Histoire du Tibet*, Paris.

BARTHOLD, W. 1968 (3rd ed.), *Turkestan down to the Mongol Invasion, Southern Materials Center, Inc.,* Taipei.

BECKWITH, C.I., 1979, "The Tibetan Empire in the West", in *Tibetan Studies in Honour of Hugh Richardson*, ed. by M.Aris & Aung San Suu Kyi,

CHAVANNES, E., 1903, *Documents sur les Tou-kieu (Turcs) Occidentaux, recueillis et commentés*, Librairie d'Amérique et d'Orient, Paris.

---------- 1904, "Notes additionelles sur les Tou-kieu (Turcs) Occidentaux", T'oung Pao Série II, vol. II.

DTH, see Bacot, J. 1940-46.

EMMERICK, R.E., 1967, *Tibetan Texts Concerning Khotan*, London.

JETTMAR, K. 1977, "Bolor - a Contribution to the Political and Ethnic Geography of North Pakistan", Zentralasiatische Studien 11, 411-448.

PETECH, L., 1988, "Il Tibet nella Geografia Musulmana", in *Selected Papers on Asian History (Serie Orientale Roma LX)*, ISMEO, Rome, 1-18.

---------- 1988a, Glosse Agli Annali di Tun-Huan, in *Selected Papers on Asian History (Serie Orientale Roma LX)*, ISMEO, Rome, 261-299.

RONA-TAS, A., 1984, "Tibet"; in *Documenta Barbarorum: Festschrift für Walter Heissig zum 70 Geburtstag*, ed. by Klaus Sagaster & Michael Weiers, Wiesbaden.

SIMS-WILLIAMS, N., 1992, *The Sogdian Inscriptions of Ladakh* (to appear in book edited by K.Jettmar).

TUCCI, G., 1977, "On Swat, the Dards and Connected Problems", *East & West* New Series 27, 1-2.

URAY, G., 1979, "The Old Tibetan Sources of the History of Central Asia up to 751 AD", in *Prolegomena to the Sources on the History of Pre-Islamic Central Asia*, ed. by J.Harmatta, Budapest, 41-60.

UTAS, B., 1968, "The Jewish-Persian Fragment from Dandan-Uilig", *Orientalia Suecana* XVII, 123-136.

VOHRA, R., 1988, "Ethno-Historicity of the Dards in Ladakh-Baltistan: Observations and Analysis", in *Tibetan Studies (Proceedings of the 4th Seminar of the International Association for Tibetan Studies)*, ed. by H.Uebach & Jampa L. Panglung, Band II.

---------- 1990, "Antiquities on the Southern Arteries of the Silk Route: Ethnic

Movements and new Discoveries." Paper presented at the Conference on the Anthropology of the Himalayas and Tibet September 1990, Völkerkunde Museum der Universität Zürich.

Plates

R.Vohra Pl.1: General view of Boulder 1.
R.Vohra Pl.2: Boulder 1: closeup of Tibetan inscription and petroglyphs.
R.Vohra Pl.3: Inscription 1.
R.Vohra Pl.4: Inscription 2.
R.Vohra Pl.5: Inscription 3.
R.Vohra Pl.6: Inscription 4.
R.Vohra Pl.7: Entire Inscription 5.
R.Vohra Pl.8: Upper line of Inscription 5, and to the left possible Sogdian inscription.
R.Vohra Pl.9: Lower line of Inscription 5.
R.Vohra Pl.10: Inscription 6.
R.Vohra Pl.11: Inscription 7.
R.Vohra Pl.12: Inscription 8.
R.Vohra Pl.13: Inscription 9.

N.Howard Pl.1: The Ladakhi position in the Chalong Nala, seen from the up-stream, the Dogras' side: stone breastworks on the top of the hill-shoulder; the river is out of sight below the flat land on the right.

N.Howard Pl.2: Inside one of the Ladakhis' breastworks in the Chalong Nala: three typical triangular loopholes (the stick is one meter long).

N.Howard Pl.3: The entrance to Basti Ram's Haveli in Leh, the seat of his governorship.

Marczell Pl.1: Statue of Alexander Csoma de Kôrös as Bodhisattva by Géza Csorba, from Elemér Ecsery's monograph on the sculptor.

Meier Pl.1: Portrait of August Hermann Francke.

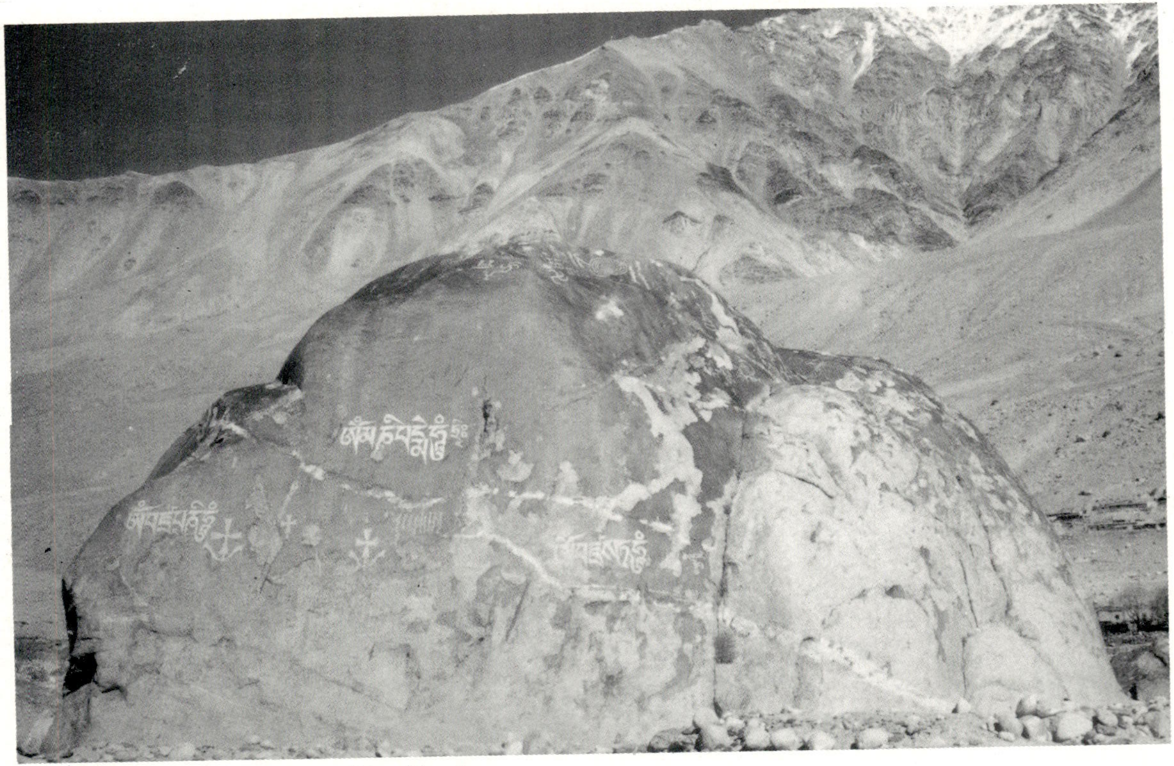

R.Vohra Pl.1: General view of Boulder 1.

R.Vohra Pl.2: Boulder 1: closeup of Tibetan inscription and petroglyphs.

R.Vohra Pl.3: Inscription 1.

R.Vohra Pl.4: Inscription 2.

R.Vohra Pl.5: Inscription 3.

R.Vohra Pl.6: Inscription 4.

R.Vohra Pl.7: Entire Inscription 5.

R.Vohra Pl.8: Upper line of Inscription 5, and to the left possible Sogdian inscription.

R.Vohra Pl.9: Lower linc of Inscription 5.

R.Vohra Pl.10: Inscription 6.

R.Vohra Pl.11: Inscription 7.

R.Vohra Pl.12: Inscription 8.

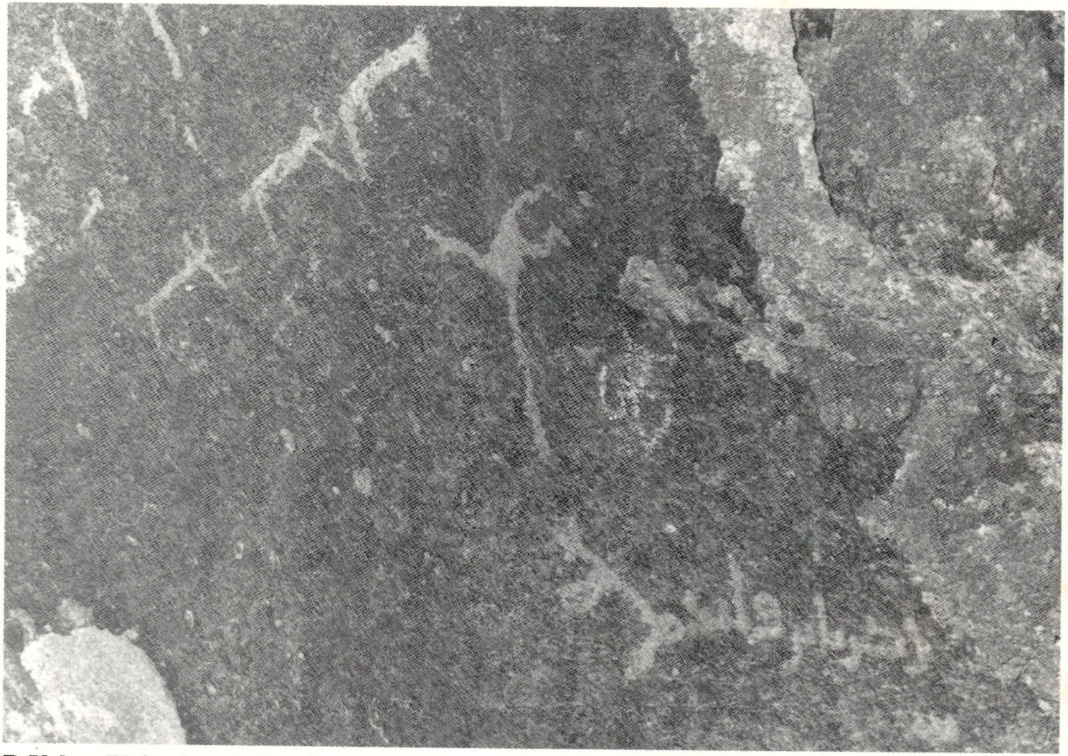

R.Vohra Pl.13: Inscription 9.